T0326617

# Slavery in the Circuit of Sugar

FERNAND BRAUDEL CENTER
STUDIES IN HISTORICAL SOCIAL SCIENCE

*Series Editor: Richard E. Lee*

*The Fernand Braudel Center Studies in Historical Social Science will publish works that address theoretical and empirical questions produced by scholars in or through the Fernand Braudel Center or who share its approach and concerns. It specifically seeks to promote works that contribute to the development of the world-systems perspective engaging a holistic and relational vision of the world—the modern world-system—implicit in historical social science, which at once takes into consideration structures (long-term regularities) and change (history). With the intellectual boundaries within the sciences/social sciences/humanities structure collapsing in the work scholars actually do, this series will offer a venue for a wide range of research that confronts the dilemmas of producing relevant accounts of historical processes in the context of the rapidly changing structures of both the social and academic world. The series will include monographs, colloquia, and collections of essays organized around specific themes.*

VOLUMES IN THIS SERIES:

Questioning Nineteenth-Century Assumptions about Knowledge I: Determinism
*Richard E. Lee, editor*
Questioning Nineteenth-Century Assumptions about Knowledge II: Reductionism
*Richard E. Lee, editor*
Questioning Nineteenth-Century Assumptions about Knowledge III: Dualism
*Richard E. Lee, editor*
The *Longue Durée* and World-Systems Analysis
*Richard E. Lee, editor*
New Frontiers of Slavery
*Dale W. Tomich, editor*
Slavery in the Circuit of Sugar, Second Edition: Martinique and the World
Economy, 1830–1848
*Dale W. Tomich*

# Slavery in the Circuit of Sugar

## Martinique and the World-Economy, 1830–1848

### SECOND EDITION

Dale W. Tomich

FERNAND BRAUDEL CENTER
STUDIES IN HISTORICAL SOCIAL SCIENCE

Published by State University of New York Press, Albany

For information, contact State University of New York Press, Albany, NY
www.sunypress.edu

Production, Ryan Morris
Marketing, Kate R. Seburyamo

**Library of Congress Cataloging-in-Publication Data**

Tomich, Dale W., 1946–
    Slavery in the circuit of sugar : Martinique and the world economy, 1830–1848 / Dale W. Tomich. — Second edition.
        pages cm. — (SUNY series, Fernand Braudel Center studies in historical social science)
    Includes bibliographical references and index.
    ISBN 978-1-4384-5917-2 (hardcover : alk. paper)
    ISBN 978-1-4384-5918-9 (e-book)
    1. Slavery—Martinique—History—19th century.  2. Slave labor—Martinique—History—19th century.  3. Sugarcane industry—Martinique—History—19th century. 4. Sugar trade—Martinique—History—19th century.  5. Sugar trade—History—19th century.  6. Martinique—Economic conditions.  I. Title.

    HT1108.M3166 2016
    306.3'62097298209034—dc23                                    2015005370

10 9 8 7 6 5 4 3 2 1

*For my parents,*
*John and Dorothy Tomich*

# CONTENTS

# TABLES

# ILLUSTRATIONS

# FOREWORD

The Fernand Braudel Center for the Study of Economies, Historical Systems, and Civilizations is pleased to present this revised edition of *Slavery in the Circuit of Sugar: Martinique and the World-Economy, 1830–1848*, by Dale Tomich, part of its series Studies in Historical Social Science produced in collaboration with the State University of New York Press. Its original 1990 imprint has long been unavailable; its reissue with a new introduction and conclusion responds to a contemporary renewal of interest in analyses of capitalism and the world-economy that relate local trajectories to what now have become global processes. The book won the Political Economy of the World-System Section of the American Sociological Association Book Award in 1991. It develops and extends the world-systems perspective to treat the formation of local spaces and their specific social relations as instances of the long-term, large-scale processes of historical capitalism, whatever their forms of labor force control.

In this distinctive analysis, the circuit of sugar links the histories of planta-tion production based on slave labor to wage labor regions. Thus, what we have is a distinctive and original contribution that is at once about Martinique *and* the world as a symbiotic, mutually determinative relationship. This treatment of the sugar-slavery complex in Martinique in terms of sugar production and its technol-ogy, slave provision grounds, and the labor process—and resistance—has long been regarded as outstanding in the field.

The reissue of this classic text will be much appreciated by a wide range of scholars, the more so as this revised edition of *Slavery in the Circuit of Sugar* also includes a new introduction in which the author offers an explicit discussion of the methodological and theoretical issues entailed in developing and extending the world-systems perspective and clarifies the importance of the approach for the study of particular histories.

—Richard E. Lee

# PREFACE TO THE SECOND EDITION

It is twenty-five years since the initial publication by the Johns Hopkins University Press of *Slavery in the Circuit of Sugar*, and a number of colleagues and friends have encouraged me to make it available again. It is rewarding to find that the book continues to be a reference for scholars in a number of disciplines, both for its substantive historical account of sugar and slavery in Martinique within the formation of the nineteenth-century world-economy, and for its distinctive analytical approach to social historical change. It is, of course, possible to incorporate new data into the study, and some arguments I would now make differently. However, such changes would not substantively alter the analysis presented in the book. For this reason, I have not changed the body of the text, with the exception of the conclusion. I have always found endings to be difficult, and I have used the occasion of this new edition to attempt a more satisfactory conclusion than the original. In addition, I have written an introduction to this new edition that presents the influences that shaped the writing of *Slavery in the Circuit of Sugar*. My intention is that this new introduction will give readers, especially younger scholars, a better understanding of how and why the book was written. In particular, this introduction addresses problems of theory and method more explicitly than does the book. It analyzes the limitations of both Marxist and world-systems approaches to the conceptualization of the relation of slavery and capitalism, and above all, explicates the theoretical approach to the reinterpretation of slavery and the reconstruction of specific local histories within a world-systems perspective that I developed in the course of writing the book.

≈

I would like to thank Amy Keough and Kelly Pueschel of the Fernand Braudel Center and Ina Brownridge and the staff of the Binghamton University Multimedia

Information Technology Services for their assistance in preparing the manuscript for publication.

Since the original publication of *Slavery in the Circuit of Sugar* I have enjoyed the intellectual and personal support of a community of friends and coworkers: Rafael Marquese, Cathérine Coquery-Vidrovitch, the late Chris Schmidt-Nowara, José Antonio Piqueras, Michael Zeuske, Juan Giusti Cordero, Yann Moulier Boutang, Richard Lee, Ricardo Salles, Tony Kaye, Reinaldo Funes Monzote, Carlos Venegas, Olivia Maria Gomes da Cunha, Phil McMichael, Chris DeCorse, Flávio dos Santos Gomes, Enrico dal Lago, Robin Blackburn, Ed Baptist, John Higginson, Stanley Stein, Michaeline Crichlow, Richard Steven Street, Antoní Furio, Pedro Ruiz Torres, Fouad Makki, Sidney Mintz, Maria Sylvia de Carvalho Franco, Joan Scott, Immanuel Wallerstein, Richard Yidana, Wazir Mohammed, Luiz Felipe de Alencastro, Luis Miguel Garcia Mora, Jason Moore, Dan Rood, the late Barbara Solow, Mark Selden, and the members of the Second Slavery Research Network. They have made the journey a rich and rewarding one and I am grateful to be sharing it with them. Luiza Moreira and Laura Tomich are also part of this community, but more importantly they make everything possible every day.

I would like to dedicate this revised edition to the memory of Harvey Goldberg, who showed me the power of history as a way of understanding the world, and to Immanuel Wallerstein, who provided the intellectual and institutional space in which I could develop my thinking.

# ACKNOWLEDGMENTS

A great many people have contributed to the making of this book. The late Harvey Goldberg first stimulated my interest in history and in the Caribbean and taught me invaluable lessons about the historian's craft and intellectual commitment. Years of friendship and continuing discussion about history and theory with James O'Connor shaped the project and have been a great source of both pleasure and support. Sidney Mintz has been generous in his encouragement and in sharing his enormous understanding of sugar, slavery, and the Caribbean. Philip McMichael, Jane Collins, and Michael Painter provided invaluable support, reading and rereading various drafts at short notice, and providing both critical perspective and moral support. The manuscript also benefitted from the knowledge and critical insight of Catherine Coquery-Vidrovitch, Maria Sylvia de Carvalho Franco, Antônio Barros de Castro, Rebecca Scott, Robert Bach, Juan Giusti, Terence K. Hopkins, Joan Smith, and Alain Buffon. Many of the ideas in the book owe much to discussions over the years with students and colleagues in courses, seminars, and informal encounters at the State University of New York at Binghamton, the Universidade Estadual de Campinas, the Universidade Federal de Parana, the Universidade Federal de Fluminense, and the Universidade Federal de Bahia. The opportunity to live and teach in Brazil formed my thoughts about sugar and slavery in many ways. A Fulbright Lectureship made it possible for me to first go there, and Edgar De Decca, Italo Tronca, Maria Stella Bresciani, Malu Gitahy, Bob Slenes, João Reis, and the late Peter Eisenberg helped to make it a rich and rewarding experience. Eric Perkins has been a marvelous friend whose enthusiasm, support, and wide knowledge have kept me on course ever since I first became interested in the themes of this book. Luiza Franco Moriera has provided tireless encouragement and a critical eye, but what she has given goes far beyond the writing of a book.

The research for this book was carried out at the Archives Nationales, Section d'Outre-Mer, and the Bibliothèque Nationale in Paris as well as the Archives

Départmentales de la Martinique and the Bibliothèque Schoelcher in Fort-de-France. I would like to thank the staffs of these institutions for their kindness. I am particularly grateful to Madame Liliane Chauleau of the Archives Départmentales de la Martinique for her gracious assistance and kind hospitality during my stay in Martinique. I also made extensive use of interlibrary loan services at the State University of New York at Binghamton and would especially like to thank Rachelle Moore without whose extraordinary efforts searching for materials the research could not have been done.

A National Endowment for the Humanities Summer Stipend enabled me to do archival research in Martinique. A National Endowment for the Humanities Fellowship for Independent Study and Research provided the opportunity and incentive to explore the history of sugar and sugar making. This research was also assisted by a Postdoctoral Grant for International Research from the Joint Committee on Latin American Studies of the American Council of Learned Societies and the Social Science Research Council. I would like to express my gratitude to these institutions for their generous support.

# Introduction to the First Edition

## Sugar, Slavery, and Capitalism

The history of Martinique and the other islands of the Caribbean has been molded by two fundamental factors, the sugar plantation and Negro slavery. The cultivation of sugar cane was introduced into Martinique during the 1640s by Dutch refugees from Pernambuco, and the intimate connection between the making of sugar and the labor of African slaves was quickly established. By 1696, Jean-François Robert, the Intendant des îles de l'Amérique, wrote:

> The wealth of the island is the sugar that it produces. Sugar is so much the heart and soul of the island that if it failed the colony would unquestionably fail and come to nothing. . . . The richest of the planters are those who have the most Negroes, because the more of them they have, the more sugar they can make, and it is only by making sugar that one becomes rich in this country. Thus a handsome and rich plantation is one furnished with land worked by a considerable number of Negroes and with a large refinery and all its outbuildings.

The fateful combination of sugar and African slavery appeared to contemporaries as an almost natural and inevitable association. Together, they formed the matrix of the subsequent historical development of Martinique and imposed a new pattern of social and economic organization on the colony. Other crops were displaced;

other forms of labor were supplanted. Plantation monoculture secured a dominant position in Martinique and wove it tightly into the international division of labor.[1]

Such changes were neither fortuitous nor natural. Rather, they were the product of the historical evolution of the network of commodity production and exchange established on a world scale by European capital and marked a further stage in its development. Sugar and slavery formed two of the strands that wove together the separate histories of Europe, Africa, and the Americas, creating at once a new unity and a profound and unprecedented divergence in the paths of historical development of these regions and their peoples. They brought Europeans and Africans together on the plantations of the New World and shaped their encounter under the unequal conditions of bondage and colonialism.

From the end of the fifteenth century to the middle of the nineteenth, sugar played a preeminent role in the expansion of the European world-economy. After gold, it was the most sought-after commodity in the New World. In those tropical and subtropical regions of the Americas without vast deposits of gold and silver, sugar became the surrogate for precious metals. Even when the extractive industries declined, it continued as the source of colonial wealth and focal point of imperial rivalries, naval wars, and mercantilist politics. The decline of the Spanish and Portuguese empires, and the ascendance of and competition between Holland, Britain, and France cannot be fully comprehended without reference to sugar. Within the shifting patterns of trade and political power, the epicenter of world sugar production shifted from São Tomé and the Atlantic islands, to Brazil, and then to the Caribbean. By the eighteenth century, sugar was far and away the main crop cultivated in the Caribbean colonies. The "sugar islands," as they came to be known, dominated world production for more than two hundred years and were at the center of competition among European colonial powers. In the course of this long historical process, sugar production was continually reorganized, the scale of operations increased, and techniques improved. Of all the exotic spices that stimulated European overseas expansion, sugar was the most thoroughly transformed from a luxury item to an article of mass consumption through the systematic organization of production and exploitation of labor. Both because of its precocious social and technical organization and because of its role in incorporating new regions of the globe and their populations into the growing European world-economy, the sugar plantation was a pioneer institution of capitalist development.[2]

Throughout this entire period, sugar production was virtually synonymous with slavery—more specifically African slavery. The cultivation and manufacture of sugar and slave labor were closely linked at least as early as the eleventh century in the Levant. The two marched in tandem slowly westward across the Mediterranean and pushed out into the Atlantic. With the foundation of the sugar industry in São Tomé in the early sixteenth century, a new dimension was added to this scheme. Sub-Saharan Africa became virtually the exclusive source for the recruitment of slave labor for the expanding European economy. As sugar migrated to Brazil and the Caribbean, the relations of slavery not only transformed Africans into commodities to be bought and sold, but provided the means through which they were forcibly concentrated as the mass of cheap, coerced labor required for the large-scale commercial production of sugar in the New World. While not by any means universal, nowhere was the identification of slave labor with the sugar plantation so nearly exclusive as in the Caribbean colonies of France and Britain from the seventeenth to the early nineteenth centuries. According to Curtin's estimate, of the nine-and-one-half-million Africans transported to the Americas during the entire history of the slave trade, more than three million were destined for the French and British Caribbean during this period, and of these, the great majority were destined for the sugar estates. (Richard Sheridan estimates that 84 percent of the slave population of Jamaica during the 1770s was directly or indirectly engaged in the production of sugar.) The sugar plantation worked by African slaves and their descendants created the wealth and prosperity of the West Indies, yet left an enduring legacy of poverty, exploitation, inequality, and dependence. The contours of Caribbean economic life, class structure, race relations, cultural patterns, and political organization were shaped within the matrix of sugar and slavery.[3]

During the nineteenth century, the relation between the sugar plantation and slave labor underwent a complex transformation. While the relative importance of sugar in the world-economy declined, world production and demand increased absolutely. New and fast-growing production centers emerged in the Americas, the Indian Ocean, the South Pacific, Asia, and Africa that outstripped the older sugar regions, while beet sugar production in Europe and North America became a significant factor. The spatial relocation of sugar cultivation and the transformation of its production processes dissolved the close bond between sugar and slave labor. In some places slavery was abolished. In others, it was intensified. Nearly everywhere planters experimented with new sources of labor and new forms of labor organization, at times in combination with slave labor but increasingly as a substitute for it. These changes were part of broader political and economic processes that were to result in the abolition of African slavery throughout the Western Hemisphere by the end of the century.[4]

This book is an attempt to reconstruct the historical development of slave labor and plantation agriculture in Martinique during the period preceding slave emancipation in 1848 within these world economic processes. By means of a historically grounded account of the specific relations and processes through which sugar production and slave labor in Martinique were constituted and reconstituted in the development of world-economy, it seeks to establish, theoretically and historically, the specific conditions and limits of slave commodity production and exchange.[5] Thus, the central concern of this study is the question of how relations of production and exchange are socially constructed in history. The emphasis here is less on the profitability or unprofitability of slavery in the narrow accounting sense than on the historical conditions under which the social relations of slavery are reproduced.

The book focuses on how the changing social-historical conditions of sugar production transformed the character of slave labor in Martinique, and conversely, on how the social relations of slave production shaped and constrained the development of the sugar industry there. However, here the relations of slave production can be understood only with further reference to the wider economic and political networks of which they form constituent parts. The world market and division of labor are not just the background for slavery in the Americas but the historical conditions of the existence of this particular form of production. The development of colonial slavery in the New World was predicated on European expansion and the formation of the modern world-economy beginning in the sixteenth century. The world market, the world-scale integration and divisioning of labor, and the level of development of global productive forces are constitutive of slave relations and shape their social-historical content. At every point in their historical evolution, the social relations of slavery and the slave labor process structurally presuppose these broader relations and forces and are conditioned and constrained by them. Conversely, as a form of commodity production, slavery finds its extension and completion in exchange relations. The establishment and development of slave labor in the Americas created conditions of commodity production and exchange that augmented and elaborated the division of labor, expanded the world market, and permitted the emergence of new forms of labor.

Thus, neither the world market nor the relations of production can be treated as isolated phenomena. Rather, these relations and processes of commodity production and exchange should be understood as simultaneous and mutually formative. They are not only interconnected, but their interaction with one another forms a unified, structured, contradictorily evolving whole. In this perspective, capitalism *as a concrete historical phenomenon* is not identified simply with production for the market, nor is it confined to the wage form of labor. Although the market and wage labor may be regarded as essential in their different ways to determining the capitalist character of the world-economy, when viewed in isolation from historical process both categories remain abstract, static, and unchanging. Thus, while it may be argued that wage labor emerged as the decisive organizing force in the nineteenth-century world-economy, this was not the only form of social relation in which capital organized labor. The world-economy encompassed a variety of other forms of social production, including not only slavery but also, among others, serfdom, debt peonage, sharecropping, and petty commodity production. Even though each of these forms retains its specificity and imposes its own conditions on social production and reproduction, the question is not which relations seen in isolation are capitalist and which are not. Instead, each form must be seen in relation to the others as a constituent part of the historically developing totality of social relations of capital. The world-economy thus appears as a heterogeneous, interdependent, antagonistic, contradictory whole—that is, the unity of the diverse.[6]

Here the focus of historical analysis is on the interrelation and mutual conditioning of the various relations and processes of commodity production and exchange constituting the world-economy. However, the interrelations among forms of social labor, kinds of production processes, and the various forms of class struggles are themselves historical processes in which various forms of social labor and forms of struggle of social producers influence, interpenetrate, and transform one another. These relations are continually recomposed, and the meaning of each form within the changing totality is never static. They are created and continually reconstituted—sometimes slowly, sometimes very rapidly—through the global reorganization, reproduction, and recomposition of labor. Thus, in accordance with the development of this whole, the categories of analysis move with respect to one another. They represent real social processes whose interrelationships and significance vary over time and are relational and historically specific rather than universally valid. Instead of having a single, fixed meaning, each illuminates the other, and their specific contents and meanings derive from the totality of relations of world-economy. It is the specificity of the changing relations among the various complexes of production and exchange within this totality that enables us to grasp both the qualitative and the quantitative recomposition and transformation of the world-economy and therefore to understand the historically developing nature of capital itself.

Within this theoretical-historical framework, the full complexity of the relation of Caribbean slavery to the development of the capitalist world-economy as a definite *historical* social economy can be posed. This approach may be contrasted to studies that privilege one or another partial aspect of the ensemble of relations shaping plantation slavery in the Americas—exchange relations, production relations, or the plantation itself—and that subordinate the analysis of the whole to the selected part. Slavery may then be variously constructed as capitalist or precapitalist, and the plantation system as archaic or modern, depending on the criteria chosen. In contrast, slavery and capitalism are here seen neither as mutually exclusive categories nor as directly coincident. Slave labor is not regarded as capitalist simply because it entails production for the market, or as noncapitalist because it is not the wage form of labor. Rather, slave labor is conceived as part of the organization of social labor on a world scale. Slave relations are not treated as existing separate from or prior to the world market and division of labor. Instead, they constitute a specific form of commodity production that is related to other such forms through the world market and world-scale processes of integration and division of social labor. Conversely, the world market is viewed neither as a transhistorical universal nor as a mere secondary and external factor abstracted from production relations. Rather, it is seen as a substantive social and political relationship, at once formed by and formative of specific social relations. It is the product of the variety of forms of social production encompassed within the world division of labor, and it links and structures the relations among those forms. The market both expresses and mediates the ensemble of these relations of production in the reproduction of the world-economy and therefore remains the ongoing condition of the reproduction of social relations of production, in this instance the condition of the reproduction of slavery. The capitalist character of slavery and the slave character of capitalism therefore derive from the real historical relations among the various forms of production and exchange within this evolving totality.[7]

Thus, the concern of this study is not simply to examine the interaction of distinct global and local "levels." Rather, it attempts to go beyond the fact of the extroversion of the colonial economy and its domination by European capital in order to *unite* the local history of plantation slavery in colonial Martinique with the history of world capitalism. Instead of approaching world, national, and local dimensions as discrete empirical entities, it treats them as mutually formative parts of a larger whole. Such a focus on the global ensemble of exchange relations, material and social relations of production, and the political mediations between them as a unified, structured, continually evolving totality permits the historical specification of each of the relations and processes constituting colonial slavery in Martinique and the examination of their interrelation and mutual conditioning. In this way, the inner connections between the world market, French colonialism, and the system of plantation slavery in Martinique may be established. It is thus possible to grasp both the particular local form of world historical processes and the world historical character of local events. The history of Martinique can thereby be understood not merely as "local particularism" but as part of the global processes of capitalist development. This approach reveals the world historical character of local processes while giving specific historical content to the concept of world-economy through the concrete analysis of particular phenomena. Thus, from this perspective, the examination of slavery in Martinique opens the way for a reinterpretation of slavery throughout the Americas and contributes to an understanding of the unity of complex, uneven, and asymmetrical relations and processes of the historical development of the capitalist world-economy itself.[8]

This emphasis on the unity and interdependence of the world-economy leads to an unconventional organization of the material. Monographs normally observe events within a specifically delimited chronological and spatial framework. The implicit if not explicit bias of this approach is that the empirical existence of the subject matter is taken to be identical with the intellectual conditions of inquiry. Such an approach too often presumes without examination that the object of historical inquiry, in this instance Martinique, is given as a discrete unit and, further, that it is comprehensible through processes either "internal" or "external" to it. Geographical boundaries are thus regarded as coincident with the social processes forming relations and organizing space. In this way the inner unity of slavery, the world market, and capitalist development is theoretically fragmented, and both the world economic origins of slavery and the slave origins of the world-economy are obscured. Slavery is isolated from the totality of relations that constitute the world-economy. The historical development of the various specific forms of social labor and the relationships among them are eliminated as subject matter. The world-economy is treated as merely the sum of its parts, any one of which can be removed and treated in isolation from the others.

In contrast, the line of inquiry pursued here both requires and permits the reconstruction of the world historical processes forming relations in Martinique, as well as the role of sugar and slavery in Martinique in the formation of the world-economy. Consequently, although the object of inquiry of this account is slave production in Martinique between 1830 and 1848, the unit of analysis is not Martinique itself. Rather, attention is paid to processes of commodity production and exchange beyond these boundaries to reconstruct the temporal and spatial frameworks that are constitutive of relations of slave production and exchange in Martinique in the historical process of development of the world-economy. Thus, the world market and French colonial system are not treated as an "external" context or background for processes and relations in Martinique, but are taken to be formative of them. Conversely, Martinique represents a particular concatenation of diverse world processes. Each such process is revealed in the others, but none is reducible to any other.

To call attention to the unity of world market forces, the French colonial system, and slave labor in Martinique, the chapters are organized and presented according to the theoretical movement from the world to the local level. If the world, national, and local phenomena are separated here for analytical purposes, no hierarchy of causality is implied. These dimensions exist simultaneously and condition one another. It is the task of this study to examine their interrelation as they shape Martinique in this historical conjuncture. Like a set of Russian dolls, the chapters are contained within one another. The movement from one chapter to the next, and thus the movement of the analysis, does not represent a shift from one discrete empirical level to another, but rather a movement from one methodological level of specificity to another. Through the course of the text, the chapters successively become more specific and therefore more concrete. Each chapter logically precedes those following it, and the subsequent chapters further develop the preceding ones. The establishment of the boundaries of these networks of commodity production and exchange, the means by which they were organized, and the processes of their transformation delineate the architecture of the world-economy as a unified and unifying totality within which the diverse processes of historical transformation can be seen as parts of an interrelated whole. It reveals the international origins and consequences of the historical transformation of slave relations of production while defining the specific and constantly evolving content of slave relations in Martinique.

Chapter 1 examines the political and economic transformation of the world sugar market inaugurated by the Haitian Revolution, the destruction of the French colonial empire, and the emergence of British hegemony over the world-economy. Between 1815 and the middle of the nineteenth century the world sugar market was quantitatively and qualitatively restructured around the dominance of British capital. World consumption and production grew steadily. New producing regions emerged, and new production techniques were developed. A greater volume of cheaper sugar was available to consumers than ever before. Further, the reintegration of the world market under the hegemony of British capital changed the character and role of both colonialism and slavery in the development of the capitalist world-economy, and put greater emphasis on productive efficiency and market competition for colonial planters. Thus, the conditions of sugar production and slave labor in the world-economy changed dramatically, and different producing regions responded in different ways to this global process of capitalist development.

Chapter 2 locates the evolution of the French sugar market and French colonial policy within the larger processes of the transformation of the world market. French policy and practice were shaped in response to British political and economic superiority after 1815. As France was relegated to the position of a second-rank economic power, its foreign trade depended in large measure on trade with its remaining colonies. This, in turn, required the revitalization of the colonial sugar industry. France attempted to reconstruct its empire and colonial trade through a system of protectionism intended to stimulate colonial production, to build up both commercial shipping and naval power, and to contribute to metropolitan economic development. A tariff policy evolved that protected the French colonies from cheaper foreign sugar and gave them a virtual monopoly of the French market. As part of this effort, France acceded only slowly and reluctantly to British pressure to abolish its slave trade. In the wake of these protectionist measures, sugar production in the colonies underwent an unprecedented period of expansion. Nevertheless, the consequences of this policy were quite different from what had been intended. Despite its rapid development, the colonial sugar industry was unable either to become competitive with other producers or to supply metropolitan demand. The tariff system, rather than serving the interests of metropolitan France, was seen by the colonists as the guarantee of a market to which they felt entitled. The relation of metropolis and colony was thereby reversed. Colonial monopoly restricted the development of the French domestic market and of French foreign trade. However, the exclusion of foreign sugar from France opened the door for the revival of the beet sugar industry in the metropolis. Colonial producers, unable to transform their own production processes and unable to renew their labor supply after the suppression of the French slave trade, faced a potentially powerful new rival. For the first time, slave labor and free labor competed in the same product in the same market. As the two sugar industries battled over tariff policy, the superior productive capacity of the beet manufacturers put mounting pressure on colonial producers to increase the quantity and quality of their product as well as the productivity of their operations and provoked a crisis of colonial sugar production.

The concerns of chapter 3 are twofold: on the one hand, to understand how the global restructuring of the sugar market altered the conditions of sugar production in Martinique, on the other, to account for the way in which local conditions circumscribed and shaped the growth of sugar production initiated at the world and French levels. Encouraged by favorable tariff policies, more land and labor were shifted to sugar cultivation in Martinique. Sugar displaced virtually all other commercial crops, and production was sustained at all-time high levels. The link between sugar monoculture and slave labor was strengthened. But this expansion was checked by geographical and historical factors. The island offered limited opportunities to open new lands, while the existing estates were unable to transcend the scale and level of technical organization on which they had been historically established. The concentration of property was further inhibited by local laws that effectively prevented the seizure of sugar estates for debt. The rationalization of the plantation system was thus blocked. Increased production took place through the multiplication of small and inefficient units that replicated traditional constraints. The sugar boom thus reinforced a structure of plantation production that was becoming increasingly archaic in comparison with new producing areas. At the same time, the expenses entailed in the restoration of the sugar industry burdened the planters with chronic debt that impeded innovation and made them more vulnerable to declining market conditions after 1830. As the position of the planters deteriorated, metropolitan credit was withdrawn from the colony and was replaced by short-term loans against the crop offered by local merchants. The structural blockage of the plantation system in Martinique was further aggravated. Productive capital was insulated from market forces while merchants and planters struggled over the appropriation of the produce of plantation agriculture.

Taken together, these first three chapters reconstitute the specific historical economic and political conjuncture of the world-economy that shaped the crisis of plantation agriculture in Martinique between 1830 and 1848. This transformation of the world market pushed the slave plantation system in Martinique to its physical, technical, and social limits and provoked a crisis throughout the circuit of sugar production and exchange in France and its colonies. The remaining chapters examine the roots of this crisis in the structure of the slave plantation of Martinique itself. They are concerned with the relation between the technical conditions of sugar production and the social process of slave labor and discuss the capacity of local producers to adapt to the changing conditions of international sugar production.

Chapter 4 sets the theoretical framework for the argument presented in the subsequent four chapters. However, the purpose of this chapter is not to develop a general theory of either slavery or capitalism in which Martinique represents a particular "case." Rather, slavery is seen here as a specific form of social labor that is both formed by and formative of the historical development of the world-economy. By differentiating between the material-social conditions of commercial sugar production and the social relations of slave commodity production, the chapter constructs the slave labor process as a complex of interrelated and historically evolving relations and processes. This approach allows slavery to be distinguished from other forms of social labor, and the labor of sugar production from other types of slave labor. The variety of material and social factors determining the character of plantation slavery in Martinique can then be related to one another in a systematic way, and their interrelation and coherence examined as parts of a larger whole. Within this framework, this chapter seeks to conceptualize the relations and processes through which sugar and slavery shaped each other and constituted the plantation as a distinctive form of socio-economic organization, in order to permit their historical reconstruction in subsequent chapters.

The technical imperatives of sugar production developed the collective social force of slave labor and subjected it to industrial discipline in a manner different from that of other slave-produced staples, while slave relations of production shaped the social-economic conditions of commercial sugar production and give it its specific social-historical form. The material requirements of the mass production of sugar required a developed division of labor, coordination among a large number of workers, supervision, quantification, and economy of time. At the time, social relations of slavery imposed their own conditions on the entrepreneurial activity of the planter class, technological development, and the activities of the laborers, and distinguished slave labor from other forms of commodity production in the world-economy. This form of social labor inhibited the rationalization of labor and thus limited the possibilities of technical change. The activity of labor (i.e., labor-power, in Marx's sense of the term) is not a social relation of slavery. Instead, the slave owner controls labor through the direct appropriation and domination of the person of the laborer. Thus, for the slave work process to be organized, a given number of workers must be adapted to a predetermined number of jobs. Furthermore, the costs of reproducing the slave labor force constitute a fixed sum that remained independent of the performance of work and is in no way altered by increased output. Thus, within the social relations of slavery, the adoption of new production techniques neither saves labor nor reduces the costs of slave maintenance. Rather, the reorganization of the labor process simultaneously intensifies work and creates redundant laborers without affecting the productivity of labor. The technical division of labor and the social organization of the labor force thus confront one another as given external presuppositions; there is no necessary inner connection between them. The expansion of sugar production reinforced the existing technical and social divisions of labor. The organization of production on the plantation became more and more elaborate at the same time that it became more and more rigid and unable to adapt to changing conditions.

From this perspective, the specific relations and processes through which sugar production, slave labor, and the plantation system in Martinique were constituted and reconstituted in the historical development of the world-economy may be reconstructed. The remaining four chapters examine in detail the historical development of these social relations and material conditions of production and the changing relations among them in order to establish the changing character and conditions of sugar production and slave labor and thus the specificity of plantation agriculture in Martinique.

Chapter 5 describes the organization of sugar production in Martinique from the point of view of its technical requirements and their evolution. The *habitation sucrière* integrated agricultural and manufacturing operations necessary for sugar production within a single productive unit. The interdependence of the various sectors of the production process required that a strict equilibrium be maintained among them. Labor and productive resources could only be distributed within definite proportions. This close technical integration imparted internal solidity to the plantation and set the parameters of the organization and possible transformation of the labor process. However, the course of development of the sugar plantation in Martinique cannot be reduced to technological determinism. A wide variety of techniques, all with a significant effect on the outcome, were practiced in every phase of the process, and their selection and combination depended on a variety of factors. Nonetheless, prevailing technology was imprecise and inefficient, and the understanding of the scientific principles involved in sugar making was rudimentary. Production remained particularistic, empirical, and artisanal. Colonial sugar was inferior to beet sugar in both quantity and quality, and the inability of colonial producers to ameliorate their production methods made them dependent on protective legislation to maintain their position in the national market.

Chapter 6 is concerned with attempts to apply scientific principles to colonial sugar manufacture and to adopt the technical innovations in sugar refining developed in the beet sugar industry. Although great strides were made in both technique and knowledge during this period, their effective application was suppressed by the structure of the plantation itself. Historically, the interdependence of agriculture and manufacturing operations and the appropriation of the labor force as slaves set firm limits to the scale of production and established a rigid division of labor on the sugar plantation. Technological innovation was thereby inhibited, and its effects on the labor process were restricted. The pressures engendered in this historical conjuncture pushed the *habitation sucrière* to the limit of its potential. The form of plantation organization itself was called into question, and a new model of plantation organization, the *usine centrale*, emerged for the first time in the French Antilles. The *usine centrale*, which separated manufacturing operations from agriculture to take advantage of the most advanced technology available, revolutionized the nineteenth-century sugar industry. In Martinique, however, its impact was limited by the preexisting organization of land and labor. Only after emancipation did it develop fully.

Chapter 7 examines the organization of work on the plantation as a social process. The planters were under great pressure to effectively utilize the time and labor that they did have at their disposal, particularly as market conditions declined. However, their efforts were limited by the slave relation. They could only increase surplus production by adapting the activity of a fixed body of laborers to the technically predetermined division of labor for a period of given duration. Surplus production thus rested on effective labor discipline and the integration of the labor force to the routines of sugar production. However, the very processes that integrated the slaves into the plantation system allowed them to struggle within the day-to-day relations and processes of slavery rather than simply against the slave form itself. Within the plantation routine, the slaves were able to form practices, values, and interests of their own; to appropriate and redefine material and social resources for their own purposes; and to make claims to rights and entitlements that the master was compelled to recognize to ensure the successful operation of the estate. These initiatives allowed the slaves to establish a degree of control over their lives and labor while still enslaved. Such actions formed customary routines that restricted surplus production, constrained master's authority and ability to exploit their labor, and at times broke out into open conflict.

Chapter 8 continues the examination of the social processes of plantation production but focuses on the development of provision-ground cultivation and independent marketing by the slaves. These activities indicate the complexity of the slave relation. They were promoted by the planters since the foundation of the colony to reduce their costs. But here too, the assertion of autonomy by the slave population enabled them to appropriate aspects of these activities and assert their needs and identity within and against the slave form. Through their own initiatives, the slaves were able to establish customary rights to free time, property, and disposition over their own activities, and to form extensive social and economic networks outside the plantation. The development of these practices transformed the nature of the slave relation and widened the struggle between master and slave over the conditions of labor and of social and material life within slavery. As these confrontations between master and slave dissolved the slave relation from within, seeds of a new organization of social life emerged, which anticipated emancipation.

Thus, the expansion of sugar production engendered by the transformation of the world-economy simultaneously developed the *habitation sucrière* and slave labor in Martinique to their fullest extent and undermined them as forms of social-economic organization. In this process, the elements for the transition to a new form of social production emerged. Yet alternative modes of organization were suppressed by the persistence of the preexisting forms of labor and property. The failure to transform colonial production blocked the further expansion of the French national market, allowed the restoration of the French beet sugar industry, and undermined the protected market for colonial sugar. A crisis was generated throughout the entire circuit of French sugar production and exchange that was only resolved with the abolition of slavery.

# Introduction to the Second Edition

## The Capitalist World-Economy as a Small Island

*Slavery in the Circuit of Sugar* examines the slave/sugar complex in Martinique during the first half of the nineteenth century. It offers a distinct approach to the study of specific histories—local, national, regional—as parts of the capitalist world-economy.[1] It also established the trajectory of my subsequent work. On the occasion of this new edition I would like to reflect on how it came to be written and what I think is valuable about its contribution. What became *Slavery in the Circuit of Sugar* is not a book that I set out to write. Rather, it is the product of the combination of two quite different but in the end complementary trajectories: my experiences as a history student at the University of Wisconsin and my involvement with the Fernand Braudel Center and the Program in World Historical Change established by Immanuel Wallerstein at Binghamton University.

I did both my undergraduate and graduate work at the University of Wisconsin between 1964 and 1976. These years spanned the cycle of the radical movements of the 1960s, and Madison was a major center of student activism. But it is also important to note that Wisconsin also had a tradition of radical intellectual dissent that preceded the 1960s, whose most prominent expression was the group around the journal *Studies on the Left*. When I first arrived in Madison I had no particular intellectual or political orientation, but I had the good fortune to work with four remarkable teachers and scholars who shaped my intellectual and personal development.

At the end of my first year I met Harvey Goldberg. A professor of European history, Goldberg was an iconoclast, a radical intellectual with a broad humanist and political culture, a passion for history, and an uncommon devotion to teaching. He was engaged with what was emerging as the new social history and invited me to take the upper-division course on modern European social history that he was preparing to teach the next fall. With audacity that was uniquely Goldberg's, the course was a tour de force of European history around the themes of property, power, social thought, and popular movements. It began with the Essenes in 2000 BC and was moving toward its conclusion with a class on comparative contemporary societies when I completed my doctoral work twelve years later. Both Goldberg and the course became icons of Madison in the 1960s. For me, the course provided a broad, critical foundation for understanding historical change. But more importantly, Harvey Goldberg became my friend and mentor, and I continued to work with him through my doctoral studies. Goldberg pushed me toward developing a broad intellectual formation. Through him I came to see history not simply as the study of the past, but as a way of thinking and of understanding the world.

Goldberg encouraged me to participate in an undergraduate exchange program for history students with the University of Warwick (England) and to study with E. P. Thompson. The semester at Warwick had a profound effect on me. Thompson's energy, commitment, passion for history, and generous support made me want to master the craft of being a historian. His *Making of the English Working Class* had just been published, and I had the opportunity to see firsthand what went into a work like that. His course on industrialization combined a broad conception of economic and social history together with his approach to working-class history and a close reading of primary sources. It both challenged me and opened new perspectives. (It was in Thompson's course that I first read Eric Williams's *Capitalism and Slavery*. I should note too that my partner in the tutorial with Thompson was Anna Davin, who was later to become a distinguished feminist historian in her own right and a founding member of the *History Workshop Journal*. My interest in African and Latin American history was first stirred by a chance meeting with her then-father-in-law Thomas Hodgkin at a luncheon she organized.)

When I returned to Madison I continued studying comparative European social and labor history with Harvey Goldberg and also took some courses in Latin American and African history. In addition, I began to systematically study social theory and political economy. Unlike the majority of my fellow students of those years, who were drawn to Herbert Marcuse and the Frankfurt school, I was attracted to Marx, Georg Lukács, and Karl Korsch, and I saw theory as a way of critically deepening my understanding of history, and particularly labor history. I also had the good fortune to get to know and study with Hans Gerth, former assistant to Karl Mannheim and translator of Max Weber into English. Gerth possessed tremendous culture and learning and, for me, he remains an example of the remarkable intellectual life of Germany and Central Europe before the 1930s. It was from Gerth that I received a firm grounding in classical sociology, especially the work of Max Weber.

In my senior year, Harvey Goldberg went on leave to Paris and was replaced by Georges Haupt, a close collaborator of Goldberg. A historian of socialism teaching in Paris, Haupt's experience bridged eastern and western Europe. Born in Romania, his life was shaped by world war, fascism, and the hopes and failure of the international socialist movement. Cosmopolitan, ironic, unassuming, he remained committed to a vision of socialism and to history and close documentary analysis as a means of freeing the international working-class movement from the distortions of ideology.

I remained at Wisconsin for graduate school and studied European social history with Harvey Goldberg as well as with Georges Haupt, whose visits to Madison to substitute for Goldberg became more regular. I also helped Paul Buhle edit the journal *Radical America*. While working with Buhle I published a critique of the structuralist Marxism of Louis Althusser that was important for the subsequent development of my perspective. I also spent several days with C. L. R. James preparing a special issue of James's work. My contact with James crystallized my decision to write a dissertation on the Caribbean. What was rapidly becoming institutionalized as labor history was anchored in a view of labor as wage labor, while the histories of slavery at the time emphasized race. Under the influence of both Thompson and James, I wanted to write a social-cultural history that focused on Caribbean slaves as laborers. Fortunately Goldberg gave me considerable leeway in my work and was interested in French colonialism. We eventually settled on Martinique as the site of my research, and, at Goldberg's suggestion I wrote a master's thesis on Aimé Césaire. This was my introduction to the remarkable history of Martinique and of Caribbean peoples and a new way of looking at the history of the modern world that was the point of departure for all my subsequent work.

My field of study remained European social history, however. The week after I completed my qualifying examinations in European history I found myself in the French colonial archives in Paris, where I spent a year researching my dissertation. Through Haupt I developed a lasting friendship with Michael Löwy, nourished by our common interest in Lukács and surrealism. I learned Caribbean history through studying the primary sources in the old Archives nationales d'outre-mer in the rue Oudinot. My ambition of writing a social-cultural history of the enslaved laborers of Martinique under the inspiration of Thompson could not be supported by the available documentation. Instead, the material I was able to work with led me to write a dissertation that examined slavery and labor in Martinique through the lens of the plantation system and colonialism.

My experiences at Wisconsin had taught me to think about capitalism and about social history broadly and provided a theoretical perspective to organize my thinking. The point of departure for the dissertation was C. L. R. James's understanding of the modernity of the Caribbean. I rejected any conception of the Caribbean as "backward" and instead sought to develop James's emphasis on the collective, industrial character of plantation slavery by examining the conditions and limits of slave labor in Martinique within processes of capitalist development. The dissertation examined the relation between French colonial policy, the French sugar market, and the development of slave sugar plantations in Martinique during the period preceding the abolition of slavery in 1848. The analytical core of the dissertation was the slave labor regime and slave resistance to labor. It sought to specify slave labor and colonial dependency within the development of capitalism as a historical whole, and in this way it problematized understandings of slavery, wage labor, colonialism, and capitalism itself.

I came to Binghamton in 1976 with a broad formation in social and labor history and an interest in the problem of capitalism and slavery that engaged both Europe and the Caribbean. In addition, I had a strong background in classical sociological theory, especially Max Weber, which complemented my engagement with a version of Hegelian Marxism as a means to critique Marxist orthodoxies and to analyze historical change. This theoretical framework informed my effort to formulate a critical political economic approach to capitalism and slavery in order to provide a conceptual foundation for my historical work. Here I benefitted greatly from the close association I had formed with economist Jim O'Connor beginning in my last years in graduate school. Yet *Slavery in the Circuit of Sugar* would not have been what it became if I had not had the experience of working in Binghamton.

When I first joined the Binghamton Sociology Department as an assistant professor, many people were perplexed by what I was working on. Why, they asked, if the program was supposed to be about world-scale change, was I studying an island that was some 400 square miles in size. My response was straightforward. The first volume of *The Modern World-System* had been published two years before. What was the point of trying to repeat what Wallerstein had done? Would it not be more interesting and more productive to look at the problem he was looking at from a different angle, in this instance from the perspective of a small island that most would consider of marginal importance to the system, and see what issues emerged?

If my initial response was instinctive, it nonetheless entailed the task of rethinking the entire conceptual framework within which I had organized my research on Martinique. My introduction to the world-systems perspective at Binghamton soon made it clear to me that this approach disrupted conventional narratives of the history of capitalism and dependency. It offered a totalizing framework that provided a more coherent and systematic approach to understanding the historical development of capitalism than did the other approaches that were available. First, it was an alternative to Marxist approaches that treat slavery and other peripheral formations as enclosed enclaves and view their "backwardness" as the result of precapitalist or noncapitalist relations and present a fragmented view of capitalism as a whole. Second, the world-systems approach allowed analysis to incorporate polyvalent and multilateral relations forming Martinique within a complex spatial-temporal whole. It thus contrasted to the emphasis on bilateral relations between metropolis and colony (most often understood as externally conjoined with one another through trade and imperial politics and resulting in hybrid categories such as dependent capitalism) that characterized theories of dependency. Finally, it allowed me to take advantage of the insights of the work of scholars who emphasized the plantation as the key analytical category by radically historicizing the concept of the plantation and stressing its interdependence with slave relations and world division of labor.[2] Consequently, the world-systems perspective allowed me to pull together my various concerns and interests in a new way. I set about reworking my research from the perspective of the capitalist world-economy through writing *Slavery in the Circuit of Sugar* and began what has become a long-term effort to reinterpret modern slavery and the capitalist world-economy.

I was in the ideal environment for such an undertaking. The Binghamton sociology department and the Fernand Braudel Center brought together a remarkable group of international scholars and graduate students and established itself as an exceptional center for work on large-scale historical change. Over the years and particularly during the early period, Immanuel Wallerstein, Catherine Coquery Vidrovitch, Giovanni Arrighi, Mark Selden, Joan Smith, Phil McMichael, Juan Giusti, and Ravi Sundaram were important for the support, friendship, and intellectual exchange that they provided. I cotaught the seminar on the modern world-system with Immanuel Wallerstein for many years. It was through working with Wallerstein that I came to appreciate the work of Fernand Braudel and long-term perspectives on historical change, and much else. I also taught a graduate seminar on Smith, Marx, and Weber, which allowed me to rethink social theory in relation to the understanding of historical capitalism as world-system that was developing in the department. Importantly, these seminars were also occasions for rich and productive dialogue with a remarkable group of international graduate students.

Above all, I benefitted immeasurably from the generous support and encouragement of my friend and colleague, the late Terence Hopkins. I could have hoped for no better interlocutor than Terry. Through many long conversations, including intense discussion of various drafts of what became the book, he emphasized the world-systems approach not as a theory, and still less as the study of a specific and given object of inquiry. Rather, he treated it as a perspective for thinking that entails a distinct methodological and conceptual approach to understanding modern historical change.

The discussions with Hopkins resonated with the emphasis on the importance of method in my own reading of Marx. From this vantage point, my project was not a question of fitting Martinique into an already-provided theory of the modern world-system. Rather it entailed rethinking the historical formation of the capitalist world-economy from the perspective of Martinique. My concern was to use the world-systems perspective to go beyond general categories of capitalism and slavery to grasp their specific and concrete historical expression in Martinique. To this end, I continued my efforts to formulate a critical political economy and to establish the relation between Marx's theory of capital and Wallerstein's conception of world-economy. As I shall explain below, I have come to emphasize the difference between the two projects. In *Slavery in the Circuit of Sugar* I used Marx's method to extend Wallerstein's analysis in ways that facilitated the integration of historical particulars into the world-systems perspective and enabled me to treat the capitalist world-economy from the vantage point of Martinique. This reworking of the world-systems perspective entailed its own distinct problems of method, theorization, and presentation, and disclosed problems and aspects of the world-systems perspective that are not evident in *The Modern World-System*.

Two further developments were decisive for the development of *Slavery in the Circuit of Sugar*. First, I met Sidney Mintz when he came to give a seminar at the Fernand Braudel Center. I had read everything of his that I could get my hands on, and I had sent him a copy of my dissertation during the summer before I came to Binghamton. When I met him, I was impressed by his generosity and supportiveness as well as the humility and seriousness with which he approached his work. It was the beginning of what has become a lifelong friendship. I have been greatly influenced by his historical approach to anthropology, and through him I came to understand the Caribbean, sugar, the plantation, and rural producers. Though I was never formally his student, he remains my teacher.

Mintz recommended me for a Fulbright Fellowship to Brazil for the 1982–1983 academic year. It was a year like no other. It was the ending of the military dictatorship and the beginning of free elections in Brazil. It was a year of political, social, and cultural explosion as pent-up energies found expression. Outside the classroom I followed the labor movement and the beginning of the Workers Party in São Paulo, and learned *futebol* and much about social movements by becoming a supporter of Sócrates and the remarkable *Democracia Corinthiana* movement. I was exceptionally fortunate not only in that I was able to experience the profound transformation occurring in Brazil, but because my primary posting was to the State University of Campinas, which had managed to sustain itself as perhaps the only center of critical discussion in Brazil during the years of the dictatorship. I found myself in the midst of a dynamic group of scholars who were pushing the boundaries of historical and social scientific inquiry. The Fulbright Fellowship also allowed me to travel and meet Brazilian students and intellectuals throughout the country. I gave month-long seminars in Salvador, Bahia, where I got to know historian João Reis, and in Curitiba. I also spent much of the spring 1983 term in Rio de Janeiro, where I was affiliated with the Federal University of Fluminense.

The year in Brazil allowed me to intensely read Brazilian historiography, especially the work on slavery, as well as social science work on dependency and development, and to discuss my readings with Brazilian colleagues. This was especially important because *Slavery in the Circuit of Sugar* was actually written in Brazil and in dialogue with Brazilian scholarship. (I should add that Cuban historian Manuel Moreno Fraginals's monumental *El Ingenio* as well as other works by Cuban scholars were also major influences on me.) Most important for me were discussions with Antônio Barros de Castro and Maria Sylvia de Carvalho Franco. Both had written on slavery and capitalism in Brazil and were deeply critical of the dualism of dependency and mode-of-production approaches. They also stressed the importance of specific products and the material processes of their production for understanding the historical development of peripheral formations such as Brazil or Martinique. My discussions with them not only reinforced my understanding of the capitalist character of slavery, but more importantly, led me to give priority to the history of sugar rather than the history of slavery as the organizing axis of the book and to interpret the history of slavery in Martinique through the history of the sugar industry. This decision transformed not only the character of the book, but my understanding of slavery and historical processes of capitalist development.

~

Immanuel Wallerstein's *The Modern World-System* has been subject to two related criticisms. The first dismisses it because it supposedly identifies capitalism with production for the market and is insufficiently specific to grasp "real" capitalism, which is generally identified with wage labor and understood as a property of national economies. The second response criticizes his conception of the capitalist world-economy for being an abstract functionalist system. In my view, this first criticism misses the mark. Wallerstein indeed rejects wage labor as the defining characteristic of capitalism. However, he does not identify capitalism simply with production for the market. Rather, he posits the capitalist world-economy as a unified yet spatially and temporally complex historical relation of production and exchange constituted by a world division of labor organized through the interstate system and world market. Since the origins of the system in the sixteenth century, the single world division of labor is formed through the relation and mutual for-mation of core, semiperipheral, and peripheral zones. Each zone is characterized by a distinct mode of labor control: wage labor and self-employment in the core, tenancy and sharecropping in the semiperiphery, and coerced cash crop production in the periphery. Each mode of labor control is necessary for the others and for the functioning of the system as a whole. The coexistence and interdependence of these multiple forms of labor control define the unified division of labor. In Wallerstein's view, this historically singular world structure promotes the constant accumulation of capital and permits the maximization of surplus production over time and space.

The formalization of this conception of world-economy leads to the second criticism. The world-system is presented in terms of abstract and unchanging general categories whose functional requirements constitute the system. The system thereby appears as an overarching whole that takes priority and predominates over its constituent elements. Here particular historical relations or facts are treated as individual instances of the fixed general categories that define the system, while the functional relations between these categories account for the lawfulness and historical reality of the system. Such a conception implies that the modern world-system represents a reality separate from and superior to that of particular historical relations and facts. Its categories of analysis can account for any particularity because all of them can be absorbed into the general framework while none are constitutive of it. New or particular phenomena are reduced to a priori general conditions and prerequisites of the system that are outside of themselves. They are thus treated as if they are accidental and contingent instances of already given conditions rather than constitutive of world-historical relations. Consequently, there appears a kind of "reduction to the whole" where any part is treated simply as a functional aspect of the whole. Such separation of the whole from its parts allows continual rearrangement of changing relations within an invariant overall structure that remains determinant. The new is reduced to repetition of the same. Qualitative historical change within the system is referred back to abstract and general structures and is thereby displaced by already-known general determinations. Here theory and history are collapsed into one another and we are left with a historical structure without historical change.[3]

From such a perspective the study of the slave/sugar complex in Martinique or of any historical particular does not appear to be very important, or at best it has illustrative value. Indeed, much of the criticism of the world-systems perspective is directed at the abstract and functionalist character of this formulation and is motivated by the desire to more adequately comprehend local particularity and historical agency. The majority of critics have rejected Wallerstein's conception of capitalism as an integrated world-economic whole. They have instead either confined themselves to the analysis of national or local units or they have treated the world-economy as a separate and distinct level of reality over and above that of states.[4] Paradoxically, however, approaches that emphasize the particularity of such local relations or agencies because their empirical subject matter appears to be more proximate to a presumed "reality" (including comparative sociological or Marxist mode-of-production approaches) invariably treat local or national societies as internally integrated, externally bounded entities that possess their own properties, internal laws, and historical reality. The relation of such units to others is necessarily external and contingent. Here, what the world-systems perspective treats as parts are either regarded as themselves wholes or are constructed as independent from and superior to the whole. The world appears as the sum of its parts or as a distinct level outside that of the parts rather than as mutually constitutive relations between the whole and its parts. Such formulations appear to grasp historical complexity and specificity more adequately than does that of Wallerstein, but in fact they offer dualist conceptions that fragment the object of theoretical inquiry and eliminate from consideration the very processes and relations that form and order historical capitalism as a world-economy.[5]

~

Whatever its apparent limitations, Wallerstein's initial construction of world-economy posits a problematic that goes beyond the particular criticisms of his work. These criticisms are shortsighted insofar as they fail to recognize the broad challenge that Wallerstein's world-systems perspective poses to our received models for understanding modern social change. *The Modern World-System* is a remarkable pioneering work that defines a new and distinctive object of inquiry and implies new methodological directives for its study. In general terms, Wallerstein has laid out a model of historical capitalism as a world-system whose conceptual status is quite different from the treatment of capitalism in Marx or, for that matter, Weber. His operating assumption is that the modern world-system constitutes a singular, comprehensive, structured, and unified historical totality in which national or local societies are conceived as parts of a larger whole. Because this perspective treats capitalism as a single unified historical system of accumulation, the analytical task is to explain the formation and development of the system. Wallerstein's project requires that he construct a comprehensive and integrated historical account of world capitalism that both identifies consequential world-systemic processes and relations that have not received attention and reinterprets conventional sequences from the perspective of the world-system.

The world-systems perspective is not a given "theory" but rather is a set of assumptions that guide a process of cognition. It has set a new agenda for rethinking social historical studies and must be evaluated and developed on its own terms. This approach entails its own theoretical assumptions, logic of inquiry, and methodological procedures that are distinct from those of approaches grounded in national or local conceptions. Here, national or local societies are treated, not as independent entities, but rather as parts of the larger whole, and their comprehension contributes to our understanding of that whole. The purpose of conceiving of the capitalist world-economy as a unified whole—that is, as a totality—is not to account for all possible facts and relations but rather to posit the relatedness of historical phenomena and the processes through which they develop. Both cognition and history are regarded here as ongoing, open-ended processes. Cognition is neither absolute (*wie es eigentlich gewesen ist*) nor simply heuristic (as in abstract model building), but continually appropriates historical reality through successively more concrete approximations.[6]

Wallerstein's comprehensive formulation of the capitalist world-economy provides the point of departure for the further development of this approach. To further develop the concept of world-economy, it is necessary to critically reexamine the relations between parts and the whole, that is, to at once recognize the unity of the whole and the specific lawfulness and reality of historical particulars *as parts of the whole*. Without investigation of such particulars, it is difficult to recognize difference, qualitative change, and what is new within the totality of relations. This reexamination entails not a movement from one empirical level (global) to another (national-local), but the theoretical appropriation and historical reconstruction of the relation of the various parts of the world-economy to one another and to the world-economic whole. This cognitive process is similar to Marx's method of moving from the abstract to the concrete and his understanding of the concrete as "the concentration of many determinations."[7]

This conception implies a complex and dialectical relation between the whole and its parts. Here, the world-economy is not regarded as the sum of its relations, processes, and facts, but as a structured relation that is continually formed and reformed *through* the relation of historical particulars with one another and with the whole. Here every relevant particular relation or fact is treated as *a part of the whole*, not as an independent or autonomous entity. Each particular relation or complex of relations is at once formed through and is formative of the spatial-temporal whole. Each occupies its own distinctive position relative to the others. Because the world-economy is continually formed and reformed through the process of the accumulation of capital, this totality of relations is not fixed and static. Rather, it produces its own temporal rhythms, and its spatial boundaries are continually changing, as is the relation of particular parts to one another and to the whole. Thus, from the perspective of the world-system, no "case" can be regarded as independent of the others because each is related to the others through the whole. Further, no two cases can be commensurate with one another even if they share similar morphological features, because each case, or more precisely each "instance," is singular in space and time.[8]

Seen in this way, the world-systems perspective offers advantages that have been too little appreciated. In contrast to conventional sociological approaches that presume the independence and commensurability of cases as the condition of comparative analysis, the world-historical approach presumes the social, historical, and geographical heterogeneity of particular phenomena. This approach seeks to account for specificity rather than to "explain" variation. It embodies a different logic of inquiry where the focus is on relations and their historical formation and reformation rather than the properties of things; that is, it offers a science of historical change and transformation. Here, the focus is on spatially and temporally singular "instances." The object of analysis is not the attributes of the case, but the relations and processes forming and reforming particular instances within the totality of relations. Thus, this approach is able to disclose the ways in which apparently similar relations, such as slavery or indentured labor, are constituted differently within the processes forming the system as a whole. Instead of the elaboration of invariant structures, general laws, or the accumulation of facts, inquiry is directed toward the historically formed interconnection and interdependence between facts and their generalization.[9] In this way the world-systems perspective turns conventional comparative approaches to social historical inquiry inside out. Its goal is to comprehend difference and specificity within a unified and unifying historical framework.

Here it is useful to distinguish between the concept of world-economy as analytical framework (the conceptual assumptions and presuppositions guiding analysis) and historical world-economy as object of analysis (that is, the concrete *outcome* of theoretical-historical reconstruction). As a unit of analysis, the concept of world-economy is the operating assumption that forms the conceptual starting point for further analysis. It provides a comprehensive general framework that enables us to examine and order particular relations and facts and to theoretically and historically reconstruct part-whole relations. It necessarily frames the analysis and remains the reference throughout, even as it is continually reworked and modified in the course of theoretical appropriation of particular historical materials. This starting point of theoretical inquiry is necessarily abstract and partial precisely because the relations under investigation have not yet been established. The purpose of analysis is to move beyond abstraction by specifying and concretizing those relations, thereby constructing the world-economy as the *outcome* of analysis.

In accordance with this procedure, particular units of observation (which may include the world-economy itself) are selected in order to construct the object of inquiry. Here, particular objects are theoretically and historically reconstructed by critically selecting, interpreting, and evaluating the appropriate factual material, analyzing in detail the forms of their development, and tracing the relations through which they are connected to the world-economy.[10] The whole is understood as being formed and reformed by the changing interactions among its constituent elements. Each particular element derives its analytical significance through its relation to the totality. It is at once a partial outcome of complex causes and a partial cause of complex outcomes. Each contains, encompasses, and expresses the totality of world-economy while the totality expresses, unifies, and gives order to the relations among the particulars.[11] Analysis moves continually back and forth from concepts to historical facts and from historical facts to concepts, from whole to parts and from parts to whole. Through successive approximations of historical particulars, it seeks to disclose the changing relations and processes through which historical particulars are formed within the world-economy, not the properties of the particular viewed in isolation or the sum of isolated facts.

This procedure enables us to incorporate new material, to establish appropriate levels of analysis, and to specify and order the selected relations within the unified whole in a way that is not possible without the theoretical-historical appropriation of particular phenomena. By thus situating particular phenomena in their historical relations, we may reconstruct particular phases, forms, and aspects of world-economic development and modify and elaborate our understanding of the complex whole. Individual elements, including particular events and contingent actions, are formed and acquire meaning as part of the totality, that is, through multiple, complex, and historically mediated relations forming the world-economy. The world-economy thus establishes a structure of meanings that forms its specific internal content.[12]

Through this movement of theoretical-historical appropriation, the concept of world-economy progressively moves from being the abstract presupposition of historical analysis to being its elaborated product. It allows us to account for difference, specificity, and the new within the unifying framework of the world-economy. Specification of particular parts at the same time specifies and discloses the structure of the world-economic whole. Through successive reconstructions, the analysis returns to the beginning, but now as the developed, elaborated, rich complex of historically formed relations. It establishes a more fully developed conception of the world-economy as a comprehensive, structured, and internally unified totality of diverse historical relations, as a contradictory unity, not an integrated duality.[13]

From this perspective, the world-economy is not understood as either an overriding structure with a reality of its own or as the sum of its parts. Rather it is the historically changing interrelation and interaction between the world-economic whole and its constituent elements. This interrelation and interaction is at once structured and structuring. Understood in this way, the importance of studying historical particulars (such as the slave/sugar complex in Martinique) is clear. Analysis of particular phenomena elucidates the relation between the general and the particular, the whole and its parts, the global and the local. It discloses how unified world processes produce diverse local outcomes. It contributes to an understanding of the historically complex and mediated relations and processes that form the world-system as a historically comprehensive and structured totality.

∼

Viewing the world-systems perspective in this way, it becomes possible to go beyond abstract and formal conceptions of world-economy as well as general categories such as "periphery," "coerced cash crop production," or "the plantation" and the antinomies of "market-production" and "internal-external" that have characterized debates over the transition from feudalism to capitalism and over dependency. Each of the major approaches gives priority to a single abstract aspect of complexly interdependent social economic relations and thereby produces a one-sided account of historical change. Dependency theory privileges exchange relations and the world market at the expense of production relations; Marxist mode of production approaches emphasize the specificity of particular relations of production at the expense of commodity exchange and the world market; plantation studies focus on the plantation as a sui generis general institutional form of social economic organization independently of particular production or exchange relations.[14]

To go beyond the limitations of these partial formulations I have come to draw a distinction between what I term "historical theory" and "theoretical history."[15]

In my view, the purpose of Marx's *Capital* is not to provide an account of the *history* of capital. Rather, in *Capital*, Marx abstracts from that history to establish a conceptual framework that enables us to analyze and explain capital as a historically specific relation.[16] Marx's concept of capital posits definite social-historical forms of development as its presupposition. For example, commodities, money, and markets existed long before capital and form its historical presuppositions, "the point of departure in reality." However, Marx does not trace the historical movement from these relations to capital. Rather, he abstracts from the historical movement and interprets these preconditions as simpler forms of the complex and fully developed capital relation.[17] He thereby treats them as *logical* conditions of the more complex totality of relations comprising capital. It is in this developed totality that the simple relations find their fullest expression.[18] Thus the theoretical presentation of capital is not identical to its historical development. By this means, Marx seeks to demonstrate the inner unity and historical specificity of the complex totality of relations comprising capital, "stripped of its historical form and disturbing accidents."[19] He is thus able to distinguish the antecedents of capital—for example, commodities, money, market, and so on—from the role and meaning the same relations assume within the developed totality of relations of capital. In contrast, Wallerstein constructs a theoretically informed account of the capitalist world-economy as a *historical* system. Here there is an identity between theory and history. The general categories constituting the concept of the world-system directly organize and interpret an account of its historical development. The explication of the history of the world-system is its theory. The object and logical status of each approach is quite distinct. From this perspective, Marx's concepts provide the conceptual ground needed to reconstruct the world-economy as a concrete totality, that is, a specific historical unity of parts and whole.[20]

Marx's approach is grounded in the historicity of theory. However, the logical development of the concepts in *Capital* is not identical with the historical development of the relations of capital. The theoretical presentation in *Capital* appears as if it were, in Rosdolsky's phrase, "a dialectic of concepts."[21] Real history—that is, the historically formed activity of social individuals—remains both the empirically given presupposition and the object of theoretical inquiry. Yet the categories of analysis are neither directly identifiable with the given "facts" of history, nor do they express "laws of history" that remain external to empirical history yet determine its development. Rather, the method of Marx's critique of political economy allows us to theoretically reconstruct the part-whole relations historically forming the capitalist world-economy.[22] By stressing method, we may open up Marx's categories of analysis and distinguish his way of thinking and formulating historically specific concepts from particular interpretations of his theory of capital, especially those that regard *Capital* as disclosing "laws of motion" of capital.[23] The logical (dialectical) exposition of the concept of capital proceeds from the commodity as the elementary cell-form of capital through ever more complex determinations to the developed concept of capital. The categories themselves change in relation to one another as Marx develops the concept of capital. The inner logic of these categories constructs the concept of capital as an open-ended yet unified, structured, and contradictory totality of relations.[24] The logical structure of these categories provides the key to reworking our understanding of the world-economy and comprehending the historical development of capital.

To develop an adequate conceptual ground for constructing a theoretical history of the capitalist world-economy, it is necessary to critically reevaluate conventional Marxist conceptions of "historical materialism," above all the concept of "mode of production." Such conceptions conflate "historical theory" with "theoretical history" and consequently produce historical accounts driven by the logical relation of its categories. The concept of mode of production disaggregates the historical whole and, taking the part for the whole, creates its own abstract totality, or what Karel Kosík refers to as the "pseudo-concrete."[25] It abstracts social relations of production from relations of exchange, and both from their historical contexts. Social relations of production are formalized as a "mode of production" and treated as an enclosed, self-contained, a priori general concept with laws of their own. Such conventional Marxist approaches identify capitalism as a mode of production exclusively with the wage labor–capital relation and regard the world market and division of labor as secondary and derivative. By these criteria, modes of production are either capitalist or noncapitalist. The theoretically derived "laws of motion" of each mode of production are already known independently of the historical phenomena under consideration.

The wage form of labor, or the commodification of labor power, is indeed the *differentia specifica* of Marx's exposition of value relations, the condition of the full development of the capital relation, through which he constructs his conception of capital.[26] However, the centrality of the category "wage labor" in the theoretical construction of the concept of capital is not identical with its role in the history of capital. To claim that the wage labor–capital relation alone defines the capitalist mode of production, as does conventional Marxism, freezes the history of capital in a static and abstract formula.[27] Such an interpretation isolates the wage labor form both from its own processes and from its historical interdependence and interrelation with other forms of labor. The conception of the capital-wage labor relation that characterizes this perspective invariably refers back to its formal characteristics as presented in the sixth and seventh chapters of *Capital* ("The Sale and Purchase of Labor-Power" and "The Labor Process and the Valorization Process"). Consequently, Marx's categories of dialectical historical analysis are treated in practice as if they are classificatory categories. Historical phenomena are simply sorted and placed in the appropriate box.[28] Ironically, from this conventional Marxist perspective, once the capital-wage labor relation is established, capital itself is deprived of historical content. The abstract, general categories of "wage labor" and "capital" are taken as the determinants of capitalist development, and the approach is subject to the same criticisms as the functional categories of Wallerstein's modern world-system discussed above.

The confusion between the logical structure of Marx's *Capital* and the real historical movement of capital in conventional Marxism is evident in the treatment of Marx's presentation as if it were a direct explanatory account of the "laws of motion" of capital. The conventional Marxist insistence that capital only exists in a mode of production based on wage labor and capital seems to ignore Marx's insistence that *capital as historical social relation cannot begin in production, but must begin with the circulation of commodities, however produced, on an adequate scale*: "The circulation of commodities is the starting point of capital. The production of commodities and their circulation in its developed form, namely trade, form the historic presuppositions under which capital arises. World trade and the world market date from the sixteenth century, and from then on the modern history of capital starts to unfold."[29] In contrast to conventional Marxism, capital appears in this formulation not as a fixed universal but as a historical process. The world market itself appears here as a definite historical relation, and therefore a complex and changing relation between the world market, the division of labor, and diverse forms of social production. At the same time, the passage cited here indicates the complex relation between the history of capital and Marx's exposition of the concept of capital and suggests the utility of distinguishing between "historical theory" and "theoretical history." Here the world market appears as the starting point and presupposition of the historical development of the capital relation (but not yet part of its developed structure). At the same time, trade, or the circulation of commodities, is the presupposition of Marx's theoretical exposition of the concept of capital. However, in the presentation of *Capital*, Marx subordinates the history of capital to the logical development of its concept. He presents this passage within the logical sequence of "commodities–money–capital," whereas his treatment of the world market as the historical presupposition of capitalist production is in the section on "original accumulation," which comes at the end of the volume after the elaboration of the concept of capital has been completed.[30]

Historically, wage labor has never been the exclusive form in which capital organizes labor. The cognitive framework of Marx's *Capital* allows us to extend its categories and procedures in order to theoretically appropriate diverse historical relations and processes forming and reforming the capitalist world-economy. This framework enables us to differentiate between the historically diverse yet theoretically distinct relations between waged and unwaged forms of labor: on the one hand, the role of forms of unwaged labor in the process of original accumulation where the predominance of wage labor is the outcome of the historical process; on the other hand, the interdependence and interrelation of forms of waged and unwaged labor in the historical reproduction of the capitalist world-economy that is the outcome of the wage labor–capital relation. By this means we may theoretically comprehend the changing relations among diverse forms of social production and reconstruct the capitalist world-economy as a complex, differentiated, and contradictory historical totality.

By emphasizing the methodological and conceptual character of *Capital* and the nonidentity of theory and history, the perspective developed here stands in contrast to conventional historical materialist approaches. It does not treat the theoretical presentation in *Capital* as either directly identifiable with the given "facts" of the history of capital or as the expression of its "laws of motion." Rather, the logical totality of concepts presented in *Capital* serves as the abstract theoretical point of departure for the reconstruction of capitalism as a historical world-economy as the concrete outcome. The commodity form—that is, the elementary form of the capital relation in Marx's exposition—provides a very powerful and flexible tool for the reconstruction of historical relations within the framework of the world-economy perspective. In contrast to the developed concept of capital (the capital–wage labor relation), the commodity relation is common to all forms of social labor within the world-economy and provides a means of disclosing their historical interrelation. By establishing the contradictory unity of use-value and exchange-value and of production and product, Marx's account of commodity fetishism reveals the social-historical processes forming the "objective," thinglike character of the commodity relation. It thereby allows material processes and social relations, production and exchange, to be treated within a unified yet differentiated and structured analytical framework, and allows their intersection, interrelation, and mutual formation as world-economic processes to be established.

Interpreted in this way, the theoretical exposition in *Capital* provides a complex of open, relational, and specific concepts that allow historical relations and processes to be examined, ordered, and reconstructed. This conceptual core serves as point of departure for theoretically appropriating historical materials and reconstructing the world-economy. However, once we deal with even a single real commodity—and there is perhaps no better commodity to choose than sugar—the relation of theory and history is inverted. We move from the logical conditions of capital to its historical conditions. Here the entire totality of relations—production, distribution, exchange, and consumption—is already historically given for any particular relation that we wish to examine and affects its development.

The totality of concepts allows us to organize our inquiry, but real development can only be comprehended though empirically grounded historical inquiry. The process of cognition moves outward from the abstract categories of this theoretical core toward concrete historical determinations of the world-economy by incorporating new and diverse phenomena into the totality of relations. This procedure critically exposes, interprets, and evaluates empirical historical materials and discloses their content and meaning within the conceptual totality of capitalist relations. It historicizes, specifies, and concretizes both particular relations and the concept of world-economy by establishing part-whole relations. Here the purpose of theory is not to elaborate a more comprehensive theory, but to critically explicate and reconstruct the formation of the capitalist world-economy through conceptually grounded *historical* inquiry.[31]

This approach outlined here has enabled me to go beyond the limitations of prevailing conceptual frameworks for interpreting dependent socioeconomic formations such as Martinique (and perhaps accounts for the continued interest in *Slavery in the Circuit of Sugar*). The commodity form provides a unified conceptual field in which to examine the interdependence and mutual formation of the world sugar market, slave relations of production, and the material conditions of sugar production. Nonetheless, I needed to find an analytical focus that would enable me to organize empirical inquiry into each of these aspects of the study and establish their historical interrelation. Here the choice of sugar rather than slavery as the organizing thread of the book was decisive. In contrast to most books on slavery, I interrogated slave relations through the material and social conditions of sugar production and exchange. This approach enabled me to examine the complex historical interconnections between slave labor, the material conditions of sugar production in Martinique, and the world market. I could thus analyze the substantive ways that sugar and slavery shaped one another and reconstruct Martinique as a specific historical geographical complex within the world-economic division of labor.[32]

This approach overcomes the antimonies between production and exchange, internal and external, that have characterized the debates over the transition from feudalism to capitalism and over dependency. It specifies the general categories of slavery or coerced cash-crop production and provides a framework in which to historicize and concretize relations. It results in a more theoretically and historically grounded interpretation of the slave relation within a historical process of world capital accumulation. It not only demonstrates the capitalist character of slavery and the slave character of capitalism, but also explains how slave relations in Martinique were reconstituted in the political and economic conjuncture under consideration.

～

This strategy led to the unconventional structure of the book. My goal was not to study general categories—plantation, slavery, or sugar in a conceptually given place. Rather, it was to establish the specificity of the processes forming the slave/sugar plantation complex in Martinique, hence forming the space of Martinique. Instead of "horizontal" comparison of Martinique with presumably equivalent relations elsewhere, I focused on the "vertical" articulation of processes forming the slave/sugar complex in Martinique as part of the world-economy.[33] Here the idea was not to write the "sugar and slavery in Martinique" book, but to trace the linkages making the slave/sugar complex in Martinique within the world-economy and disclosing processes and relations that produce it as a specific outcome. Instead of construing Martinique as a fixed entity with clearly delineated internal and external boundaries, the structure of the book emphasizes the relational character of these processes and seeks to reconstruct global and local processes as necessarily related and mutually formative.

While the object of inquiry is ultimately the slave/sugar complex in Martinique, the unit of analysis is the capitalist world-economy. The chapters do not represent different empirical levels. Rather, they represent distinct objects of analysis and levels of specificity. They move in logical progression from the world sugar market, through the French sugar market, the reorganization of the sugar and slave plantation zone in Martinique, the sugar plantation and the material-technical organization of sugar production, to the social organization of slave labor. As a means of exposition I adopted the metaphor of Russian dolls. Metaphorically, each chapter fits inside of the preceding one. Taken together, they move from whole to part, from general and comprehensive to specific and concrete, from global to local. Each chapter successively moves out from the preceding ones to examine a particular aspect of the slave/sugar complex, itself partial and abstract, and incorporates it into the analysis by examining its interrelation, interdependence, and interaction with other relations and processes forming the world economic whole.

Conceptualization of each analytical level allows historical reconstruction of particular processes and relations. Each individual chapter provides the theoretical presuppositions and historical conditions for the subsequent chapters in a movement from world sugar market to the production relations of plantation slavery, from world-economy to Martinique. Each subsequent chapter expresses and further develops the preceding ones by extending, specifying, and concretizing the analysis from a new perspective. In this way our reconstruction of the relation between world-economic processes and local conditions becomes progressively more dense, mediated, and concrete and enables us to more adequately interpret the possibilities and constraints of historical social action.[34]

This relational logic moves both forward and backward. The more specific and concrete subsequent chapters are regarded as partial causes of the broader and more general relations of the chapters that precede them and find their extension and completion in them. This back-and-forth movement through analytical levels progressively specifies plantation slavery in Martinique by spatially and temporally ordering it within the world-economic totality and continuously disclosing the mediations between global and local relations. Our understanding of the whole is reworked with the incorporation of each new part into the analysis. At the same time, this analytical movement concretizes the slave/sugar complex by disclosing the multiplicity of relations that determine its development. The historical-geographical complex in Martinique is reconstructed as a singular instance of slave plantation production formed by the confluence of diverse processes and relations of varying duration and spatial scope. From this perspective, the issue is not whether slavery was profitable or unprofitable, but how relations of production and exchange are constructed in history and the concrete social and material conditions under which the social relations of slavery and sugar production in Martinique are formed and reproduced.

The book begins by specifying a particular economic and political cycle within the process of world-economic accumulation of capital through the empirical reconstruction of the spatial-temporal conjuncture of the world sugar market from the 1790s to the 1850s.[35] The conception of the world market used here includes not only the circulation of commodities, but also their physical movement and the division of labor underpinning and expressed through commodity exchange. The world sugar market is treated as part of the world-economy, and its development serves to indicate world-economic trends. The key processes restructuring the world-economy during this conjuncture include the emergence of industrial capital and wage labor as the pivot of the world division of labor, U.S. independence, the Haitian Revolution, the decline of France as a world power, and Britain's economic and political hegemony over the world-economy.

In methodological terms the world sugar market is used to define the totality of relations through which the book is organized and serves to order the analysis. It allows us to trace the cyclical movement of the levels of price and production, of exchange and consumption of sugar in order to delineate their overall rhythms of expansion and contraction. The duration and rhythm of these cycles provides the temporal ground around which the conjuncture of world sugar production and exchange is reconstructed. These temporal rhythms are related to the changing spatial distribution of world sugar production and the demand for slave labor throughout the various zones of sugar production.

The political and economic conjuncture forms a spatially and temporally complex, multilateral matrix that allows us to examine the interconnections of politics, economy, and the material and social conditions of sugar and slavery within a unified conceptual field. By this means, it is possible to contextualize and specify the changing relations between politics within and between colonial empires, the expansion and restructuring of the sugar market, the shifting conditions of the slave trade, and specific historical geographies of accumulation and rule through which specific slave/sugar complexes were constituted.

Thus, this approach calls attention to the way in which the world-economic conjuncture shaped the distinctive character of French colonialism, sugar market, and demand for slave labor. It at once illuminates the complex interplay of politics and economy in determining French policy toward sugar and slavery and specifies the historical conditions for the development of the French West Indian sugar colonies. The second chapter examines the French colonial empire and sugar market during the period 1814–1848, not as independent entities to be compared with equivalent independent entities such as the British or Spanish Empires, but in relation to the political economic conjuncture as a whole. Emphasis is given to their specific historical configurations and relative weakness in relation to France's rivals. This perspective allows us to pose the question of capitalism and slavery, not at the level of abstract general categories, but rather to inquire into how specific combinations of historical relations are produced and reproduced within world-economic processes and to establish their conditions and limits. It at once specifies the French colonial empire and concretizes our understanding of the historical restructuring of the modern world-economy.

The remainder of the book attempts to disclose what I have termed "the local face of global process" by examining the transformation of the sugar industry in Martinique as part of the world-economic conjuncture. By shifting the unit of observation to Martinique, these chapters seek to disentangle the diverse material conditions and social relations (at once global and local) that constitute the historical-geographical complex of slavery and sugar in Martinique and to establish its specific characteristics. They seek to disclose the response of a variety of local and national actors to changing world and national conditions, as well as to identify the material, historical, and social constraints on the development of the sugar industry in the colony. These chapters demonstrate the analytical and explanatory advantages of the perspective employed here. Conventional approaches would regard Martinique as a given, stable, internally integrated social whole and treat it as the unit of analysis. Although it may be influenced by external forces, the primary explanatory factors are situated within this bounded whole and its peculiar features are emphasized. In contrast, by treating Martinique as a part of the world-economic totality, the strategy pursued here seeks to explain the formation of the slave/sugar complex itself. Taken together these chapters examine how the interaction and mutual formation of world-market, material conditions of sugar production and slave labor within the economic and political conjuncture remade the historical-geographical complex of Martinique and shaped the crisis of the system of plantation slavery.

From the world-systems perspective, time and space are regarded as substantive aspects of social relations. From this point of view, relations develop *through* time and space, not *over* time and space.[36] Rather than an autonomous mode of production with only external linkages to capital, Martinique is treated as part and parcel of a world-economy where industrial capital and wage labor were emerging as the strategic pivot of accumulation, but were far from the only forms of organizing labor. The acceleration of accumulation, expansion of world demand, intensification of competition, and enhanced command over labor increasingly synchronized production and necessary labor time across different forms of labor organization throughout the world-economy, unifying conditions of production.[37] However, world-economic time is at the same time spatialized, and particular historical-geographical configurations produce their own temporalities in relation to world-time. The slave/sugar complex in Martinique produced its own distinct spatial-temporal cycle as part of world-economic conjuncture.

The pressure of the world market influenced the material organization of sugar production and slave labor in Martinique and shaped the course of their development. At issue was not just the amount of surplus product, but the rate of production itself. However, planters in Martinique had reached the limits of physical expansion, and abolition of the slave trade prevented them from expanding the labor force. At the same time, the material and technical organization of the sugar plantation and the social relations of slavery blocked the transformation and restructuring of land and labor. The confluence of the world market and social and material conditions of production in Martinique intensified the exploitation of slave labor and shaped the cycle of expansion of sugar production.

Chapter 3 continues to specify the slave/sugar complex by examining the confluence of world-economic forces and local conditions in Martinique. This chapter incorporates environment, physical and social geography, and material conditions as integral and formative aspects of the slave/sugar complex. After1815 the economic and political conjuncture promoted a speculative sugar boom that remade the social and economic space of Martinique. Sugar monoculture expanded at the expense of other crops and strengthened the bond between sugar and slavery despite the abolition of the slave trade to the island. However, local conditions limited the expansion of sugar production. Opportunities to open new lands to sugar cultivation were limited. For reasons that are treated in greater detail in subsequent chapters, the extension of production took place through the multiplication of small and inefficient units that inhibited fundamental reorganization of production and simply reproduced existing technical and social constraints. The inability to restructure production aggravated the financial situation of planters and put more pressure on slave labor. The conjuncture of 1815–1848 pushed the plantation system in Martinique to the fullest extent of its possibilities and stimulated a crisis throughout the circuit of French sugar production and exchange. This chapter serves to frame the analysis of the sugar plantation that I pursue in the remainder of the book.

Chapters 4 through 8 further narrow the analytical focus by shifting from the re-formation of the sugar zone as a whole to the organization of production on the plantation and the slave labor process. Chapter 4 builds on Marx's analysis of social forms in order to specify the characteristics of slavery as a specific form of commodity production.[38] It thus emphasizes the difference between slavery and wage labor as well as other forms of coerced cash crop production such as serfdom or indenture.[39] Under the slave form, production is organized through the appropriation of the person of the laborer as property rather than through the sale and purchase of labor-power. Paradoxically, the activity of labor, because it is not a commodity, is not a social relation, and production is organized through relations of domination and coercion of the person of the laborer. However, rather than treating slavery as an independent and autonomous "mode of production" as in Marxist accounts, or as "embedded" in the world market as in Polanyian accounts, my purpose in this chapter is to specify slavery as a form of commodity production within the world-economic division of labor. Here, the world market and division of labor are not regarded as external and secondary to relations of production. Rather, by emphasizing slavery as a form of commodity product I call attention to the way in which slave relations are historically and substantively constituted through their specific relation to the world market and to the material processes of sugar production.[40] In this formulation slavery is not regarded as capitalist because it produces commodities for the world market, nor is it regarded as noncapitalist because it is not the waged form of labor. Rather, the capitalist character of slave commodity production derives from its historically changing relation to other forms of social labor through the world division of labor and world market.

These chapters further specify and concretize the preceding analysis by examining the interrelation of slave labor and the material conditions of sugar production. Here the unit of observation is the plantation itself. The plantation as productive unit does not directly express world-economic trends but represents a distinct configuration of commodity production whose organization is mediated through specific material-social conditions. In these chapters the insights of political economy, labor history, and Sidney Mintz's historical anthropology are combined in order to reconstruct and specify the material and social organization of the labor process on the plantation. This approach discloses the interplay of diverse factors that limited innovation and eroded master-slave relations by intensifying struggles over the working day and slave provision-ground cultivation.

The slave labor process is understood not simply as a process of surplus production and appropriation. Rather, it is a practical activity of physically producing sugar as a commodity. The material conditions of sugar production impose their own conditions on social labor. The commercial production of sugar is necessarily an industrial process. The need to combine agricultural and manufacturing operations in a fixed period of time requires cooperation, division of labor, and economy of time and space. To adapt to these material conditions of the crop, slave labor requires industrial organization and discipline. This coincidence of the social relations—slavery and the material processes of sugar production—shapes the sugar plantation as the cell unit of colonial economy and society. The interaction and mutual formation of material processes and social relations under the historical conditions prevailing in Martinique determined the scale and organization of the plantation as a productive and social unit.

Chapter 5 gives historical substance to the analysis of the slave form made in chapter 4 by reconstructing the material and technical organization of sugar production in Martinique during the period under consideration. Through the extensive use of primary sources, it analyzes each sector of production—agriculture, the mill, the refinery, the purging house—and the prevailing practices of sugar cultivation and manufacture. Efficient production required that proportional relations be maintained between all sectors. The interrelation between sectors fixed the spatial organization, scale of production, and size of the labor force around the technologies prevailing in the eighteenth century and made the sugar plantation a stable unit that inhibited innovation and technical transformation even as the world market exerted pressure for higher rates of production. At the same time, this chapter emphasizes the nonlinear character of technological change and the ways that local material and historical conditions shape and constrain the choice of technologies. This chapter reframes the question of technology and slave labor in ways that go beyond the debates over the slavery and the "transition to wage labor" and suggest broader questions about technological innovation, labor forms, and agricultural production.

Chapter 6 continues the discussion of the material processes of production by examining attempts at technological innovation in Martinique and the obstacles to them. The position of colonial producers on the metropolitan market was under constant pressure by the French beet-sugar industry and foreign competition. By the 1830s the beet-sugar industry pioneered the application of science and technology to sugar production, dramatically increasing the quantity and quality of production. Planters in Martinique were able to ameliorate piecemeal the technical efficiency of their operations, but the need to maintain proportional relations between agriculture and industry blocked restructuring of the plantation as a productive unit. Further, the physical appropriation of the labor force as slaves meant that innovation was not labor saving. (As Weber argued, the appropriation of the labor force as slaves means that it cannot easily be adjusted to technological innovation or market fluctuations.) The most radical proposal for restructuring the world cane sugar industry, the central factory, was first conceptualized and attempted in Martinique. However, it was rejected both because of the scale of production and the amount of capital that were required and because it threatened the social status of the planters. The analysis of technology and the material conditions of sugar production in these two chapters takes us beyond commonplace assertions about the inevitability of technological innovation and incapacity of the slave labor force to adapt to technological change. It allows deeper insight into the conditions and limits under which sugar plantations in Martinique operated and permits more adequate understanding of the historical specificity of slave labor itself.[41]

The following chapter revisits the production process on the sugar plantation in Martinique, but now as a social rather than a material process. It examines the ways in which the social relations of slave production and the slave labor process were historically formed by the requirements of the world market and the material conditions of sugar production. In this way it seeks to concretize the slave relation and establish the historical contexts and conditions of social action rather than treating slavery in Martinique as the expression of abstract and a priori "laws of motion" of a slave mode of production. This chapter focuses on the contradiction between the physical appropriation of the laborers as property and their development as a collective and cooperative productive force.

Because the labor force was permanently appropriated as property, the plantation had to coordinate its social reproduction and its productive activities. Consequently, the slave plantation could not operate simply as an economic enterprise. Slave owners had to adapt a fixed body of laborers to the requirements of sugar production. It was difficult to adjust the available workers to the necessary tasks, and changes in technology and organization did not save labor. The chapter examines the conditions under which slave owners compelled slave laborers to cooperate with one another. It analyzes the relations among the scale of operation, division of labor, structure of authority, management strategies and labor discipline, variation of routines over the productive cycle, and the acquisition of skills by workers. Because land, labor supply, and technology were relatively stable, and because slave relations did not permit labor saving and increasing the productivity of labor, increases in output were achieved by more closely integrated economies of time, time discipline, and intensification of work. Through quantification and calculation, planter strategies sought to increase the amount of sugar produced by the slave labor force in a given amount of time. Further, planters attempted to reduce the costs of maintaining the labor force and provide incentives to work by allowing slaves free time and marginal lands to provide at least part of their own subsistence needs.

Within these relations enslaved workers asserted their own needs and purposes. By attending to the material and social conditions of production, this approach is able to contextualize slave agency and identify the conditions, sources, and consequences of individual and collective forms of resistance.[42] Thus, the labor process is understood not as determined by economic or technological necessity or by unilateral planter power, but as a sphere of contention and negotiation between masters and slaves. It is the site of social and cultural contestation over the purposes and meanings of work and its place in social life that finds its expression in the struggle over the working day. This chapter and the following one extend Sidney Mintz's concept of "proto-peasantry"[43] by examining slave provision-ground practices in relation to labor routines in sugar production. It discloses how enslaved workers in Martinique used the tensions developing within the slave plantation regime to combine struggles over provision grounds with struggles over the labor discipline and the organization of labor. Slave strategies of resistance were simultaneously elaborated inside and outside of sugar production, within the social conventions of the slave relation and pushing beyond it. Enslaved workers simultaneously sought to establish customary rights to free time, provision grounds, and access to internal markets and to resist labor discipline and the organization of the working day, particularly night work in the sugar mills. Struggles in one sphere reinforced struggles in the other. On the one hand, slaves reduced the disposable labor time available to planters. On the other hand, they were able to extend the sphere of their own material, social, and cultural reproduction in ways that undermined slavery and the plantation. These struggles created a crisis of labor and of slavery as a social relation and shaped the transition to a post-slavery regime in Martinique. World market forces drove the slave relation to its limit. On the one hand, pressures to achieve higher levels of productivity were blocked by the social and material organization of production. On the other hand, the social relations of slave production could no longer contain the initiatives of the laboring population either in terms of the conditions of production or of social struggle. Postemancipation society and economy were confronted with the problems of the restructuring production and reestablishing labor and social discipline over a population that had successfully asserted itself against the plantation regime.[44]

∾

*Slavery in the Circuit of Sugar* demonstrates that the world-systems perspective is not opposed to richly textured local histories but rather requires them and allows us to more adequately explain them. This perspective not only provides a more theoretically coherent account of specific local histories than conventional approaches, it allows us to understand how unified world processes *produce* local difference.[45] Here the global and the local are two sides of the same coin. The historical formation of the world-economy is at once unified and unifying and differentiated and differentiating. Through a cumulative and relational explanatory account, this approach incorporates plural temporal and spatial relations to specify the slave/sugar complex in Martinique. It thus calls attention to the temporal and spatial variability of slavery within the historical formation of the capitalist world-economy and generates new perspectives and new interpretive insights. At the same time, because the particular local histories are construed as mutually formative parts of the world-economic whole, once this totality of relations is established we can move up and down the temporal-spatial scale and back and forth between parts and parts, and parts and the whole. Such a multidimensional approach that incorporates specific local histories gives more adequate insight into the spatially and temporally complex and mediated structure of the capitalist world-economy itself.

# Chapter 1

# Sugar and Slavery in an
# Age of Global Transformation, 1791–1848

Sugar was the foundation of the golden age of West Indian prosperity during the eighteenth century. Probably the most sought-after commodity of the period, it was the largest single English import and the most valuable item in the French overseas trade. Its consumption increased steadily throughout the century as its use and that of its complements, coffee, tea, and cocoa, were incorporated into the diet of ever-broader strata of the European population. The movement toward sugar monoculture grew on an unprecedented scale in the Caribbean as sugar consumption expanded in Europe. The "sugar islands," as the West Indies came to be known, were by far the most important suppliers of this product to Europe and dominated world production. They nourished the trade in slaves from Africa and gave impetus to European manufactures and commerce. Accordingly, the Caribbean colonies were of central importance for economic development during the eighteenth century and became a focal point of international political conflict as the colonizing powers vied with one another for domination over the region and control of its sugar industry.

The eighteenth-century world sugar market was constituted by means of competing colonial empires. Each metropolitan power maintained an exclusive sphere of production in its colonies. The division of labor between metropolis and colony and the nature and direction of commodity flows were defined through politically enforced monopolies, privileges, and restrictions determined in the metropolis, while slavery and the slave trade forcibly concentrated laborers and forced them to engage in commodity production. Each metropolis reserved for itself the produce of its own colonies, monopolized colonial shipping, and used the colonies as a sheltered market for its industry. By means of these mercantilist policies, rival nation-states forcibly expanded their markets, stimulated production, and promoted the accumulation of national wealth. This system, known as the *exclusif* in France and the mercantile system in Britain, expressed not only the limits of commodity production and exchange but also the weak integration of the world market during this period. As a result of this form of market organization, world sugar production grew slowly but steadily within a more-or-less stable structure, and colonial producers were relatively insulated from direct competition with one another by their reliance on the political conditions of their monopoly of their respective metropolitan markets.

The Haitian Revolution, together with the ascendance of British capital between 1792 and 1815, signaled the beginning of a structural transformation of this form of organization of the world sugar market. These changes in the international sugar economy were part of broader processes restructuring the world-economy as a whole. The unparalleled expansion of world sugar production and consumption during the first half of the nineteenth century provoked the development of new producing areas and hastened the decline of old ones. (See Table 1.1.) There were shifts in the centers of production within the Caribbean, together with the appearance of substantial amounts of sugar from areas outside the Caribbean. This transformation of the world sugar market included not only the spatial redistribution and quantitative increase of international sugar production but also the qualitative restructuring of the social and political relations and processes organizing the market. The world market was no longer constituted through direct political domination over the sources of colonial production. Rather, the key to power under the emerging conditions of world-economy was, as David Brion Davis has emphasized, economic control over the flow of commodities: "Even before Britain had won full naval supremacy . . . it was clear that the economic struggle would center not on the control of colonial production but on the control of colonial commerce to European markets. By 1804, Britain had no need to fear a rival slave

Table 1.1. International Sugar Production, 1791–1842

| Location | 1791 Metric tons | (%) | 1815–19 (avg.) Metric tons | (%) | 1838–42 (avg.) Metric tons | (%) |
|---|---|---|---|---|---|---|
| British Colonies | 100,015 | (37.9) | 173,822 | (47.4) | 160,046 | (24.8) |
| French Colonies | 102,891 | (39.0) | 39,279 | (10.7) | 84,414 | (13.1) |
| Cuba | 16,731 | (06.3) | 44,734 | (12.2) | 150,603 | (23.4) |
| Brazil | 21,000* | (08.0) | 75,000* | (20.4) | 82,000 | (12.7) |
| Dutch Colonies | 13,550 | (05.1) | 8,140 | (02.2) | 64,256 | (10.0) |
| Danish Colonies | 9,429 | (03.6) | 26,000 | (07.1) | 9,000 | (01.4) |
| U.S.A. (Louisiana) | — | | — | | 51,712 | (08.0) |
| France** | — | | — | | 30,536 | (04.8) |
| Germany** | — | | — | | 11,688 | (01.8) |
| Total | 263,616 | | 336,975 | | 644,255 | |

*Source*: Manuel Moreno Fraginals, *El ingenio. Complejo económico social cubano del azúcar* (Havana, 1978), I, pp. 40–42; II, p. 173.

*Estimate.

**Beet sugar.

trade augmenting the production of her competitors. The crucial problem was not the supply of labor but how to control the flow of commerce to Europe."[1]

The nexus of colonial control was broken, and the relation of sugar producers to the growing markets no longer corresponded to the old lines of imperial domination. Increasingly the market became the mediation between producers and consumers, and supply, demand, and price appeared as the determinants of the division of labor and of the flow of commodities within the international circuit of sugar. The character, meaning, and function of formal colonial domination was transformed in a variety of ways as peripheral sugar producers and metropolitan elites contended between and among one another in the new and changing circumstances of the world-economy. The new pattern of markets and the emergence of new forms of social labor fundamentally altered the conditions of slave labor in the world-economy and challenged its hold on world sugar production. The previous identity of sugar, slavery, and colonialism that had characterized the Caribbean during the eighteenth century was dissolved. Within the processes of development of the capitalist world-economy, each of these elements was dissociated from the others, and the relations between them were recast under new conditions as part of an emerging global mosaic of capital and labor.

## The Destruction of a Sugar Empire

Saint Domingue was at the vortex of the international economic and political currents of the eighteenth century. It occupied a position of strategic importance in the century-long struggle between England and France for domination of the world-economy. The international rivalry between these two competing empires as well as the stresses and contradictions within France and Saint Domingue generated the conditions for the Haitian Revolution. The revolution in Saint Domingue developed as a part of the French Revolution and was inseparable from it. The two revolutions developed in tandem, conditioning, influencing, and reinforcing one another. C. L. R. James, in his classic study of the Haitian Revolution, writes: "Men make their own history, and the black Jacobins of San Domingo were to make history which would alter the fate of millions of men and shift the economic currents of three continents. But if they could seize the opportunity they could not create it."[2]

The Haitian slaves were dependent on the French Revolution to create the political conjuncture that made their struggle possible. However, once the revolutionary movement developed among the slaves, it both strengthened the revolutionary process in France and went beyond it. Although constrained by the course of events both in France and internationally, the struggle of the Haitian slaves to secure their own emancipation added new dimensions, ideologically and practically, to the struggle to overthrow the ancien régime, and was a decisive blow to the French colonial empire. It precipitated the dramatic transformation of the world sugar market between 1792 and 1815, had a significant impact on the outcome of the Anglo-French rivalry, and altered the character and conditions of slavery throughout the hemisphere for the remainder of its history.

Saint Domingue had been the world's foremost sugar producer and the most valuable of Europe's overseas colonies since the mid-1740s. It provided France with a large and expanding sugar frontier, and the costs of production there were lower than in the older and more settled British Caribbean colonies. Between 1760 and 1791, sugar production in Saint Domingue increased by almost 40 percent, from 56,646 to 78,696 metric tons. Even though world production rose significantly during this period, Saint Domingue's share of the total increased slightly, and in 1791 it accounted for nearly 30 percent of the world's commercial supply. Sugar was supplemented by rum and molasses exports as well as by substantial amounts of coffee, cotton, and indigo. In 1791 the colony's slave population numbered 480,000, the majority concentrated on the sugar estates of the fabled North Plain; an estimated 25,000 new slaves, more than to any other colony in the Caribbean, were imported in that year alone.[3]

Saint Domingue was the fulcrum of the French colonial system. Even though sugar production in the British West Indies increased more rapidly than it did in the French colonies as a whole between 1760 and 1791, the growth of Saint Domingue enabled France to maintain its supremacy in the world sugar market and to attain nearly the same total output as its rival. French colonial sugar production increased from 80,646 to 102,891 metric tons while that of the British West Indies rose from 70,593 to 100,015 metric tons during this period. The British gain was due to the acquisition of the ceded islands of Grenada and the Grenadines, Dominica, and Saint Vincent—all formerly French—as a result of the Seven Years' War, and to the remarkable growth of the Jamaican sugar industry, whose production increased by 53 percent during these years. Nevertheless, Jamaica lagged well behind its French rival. In 1791, it exported 60,900 metric tons of sugar and had a slave population of 250,000 compared to the nearly 79,000 metric tons and 500,000 slaves for Saint Domingue. The expansion of the British West Indian sugar industry, swift and impressive though it was, was not sufficient to displace Saint Domingue from its preeminent position, and the British colonies remained unable to compete with the cheaper French product in the continental European market.[4]

The productive advantage provided by Saint Domingue, aided by a commercial policy favoring sugar reexports, allowed France to dominate the world sugar market and to control the entrepôt trade in colonial produce to Europe. French domestic consumption of sugar was extremely limited, particularly outside the urban centers, and, although Mathiez reports that an increase in the price of sugar touched off a riot in Orléans in 1792, sugar does not appear to have been a regular item in the diet of the mass of the French population. France only consumed about one-fifth of its sugar imports on the eve of the revolution and reexported the rest. In 1791, France reexported nearly 80,000 metric tons of sugar, which accounted for 65 percent of the world free market in sugar. Saint Domingue alone supplied 50 percent of this free market. In contrast, British sugar reexports averaged only 16,186 metric tons per year during the period 1788–92, barely 13 percent of the world free market. Sugar production in the British Caribbean was dependent on the British metropolitan market. Britain was the largest consumer of sugar in Europe both in absolute terms and per capita. Sugar was woven into the pattern of British industrial life from the beginning. Either by itself or in combination with tea, sugar supplanted traditional foods and drinks. It was considered a basic part of the diet of even the very poor in Britain by the end of the eighteenth century and linked them to the market in consumer goods. It was estimated that sugar and tea accounted for between 8 and 11 percent of the budget of working class households. British sugar consumption rose from six to eight pounds per person in the 1750s to twenty-five pounds per person in the 1850s. (By 1900, British annual per capita sugar consumption would reach seventy-eight pounds. Small wonder that T. S. Ashton in his study of the standard of living of the English working class during the Industrial Revolution comments that his index seems to have been drawn from the diet of a diabetic.) Nonetheless, despite growing domestic consumption, the potential expansion of British commerce and of sugar production in the British Caribbean was constrained by French superiority in the continental market.[5]

The trade with the colonies and the reexport of colonial produce stood behind the rapid growth of French overseas commerce during the eighteenth century and enabled France to challenge Britain in international commerce and politics. Led by West Indian sugar, the colonial trade was the most dynamic sector of the French economy. It increased tenfold between 1716 and 1787 and was in large measure responsible for propelling French foreign trade to a level comparable with that of England by the end of the century. The importance of the Antilles for France increased throughout this period. In 1730, the French West Indian colonies accounted for one-sixth of the commerce of France. The value of this trade was 30 million livres, of which 20 million were imports into France and 10 million were exports. By 1789, French imports from the colonies were worth 185 million livres, and France's exports to them were worth 78 million livres. About two-thirds of French maritime exports went to its West Indian colonies. But even more significantly, the value of colonial products, principally sugar, reexported from France rose from 15 million livres in 1715 to 152 million livres in 1789. The reexports of colonial produce made up one-third of total French exports, and they alone allowed France to maintain a favorable balance of trade. In the 1780s, Saint Domingue alone was responsible for three-quarters of the total French trade with the colonies and supplied most of the reexports.[6]

The trade with the West Indian colonies enabled France to offset the growing commercial and productive superiority of Britain's more diversified economy between the end of the Seven Years' War and the outbreak of the French Revolution and to achieve a rate of economic and industrial growth surprisingly similar to that of England during this period. The centers of French industry were located on the Atlantic seaboard and oriented toward seaborne trade and colonial markets. The traffic in sugar and slaves was the basis of the wealth of Nantes, Bordeaux, Le Havre, La Rochelle, Saint Malo, and Marseille. Through a system of monopolies and privileges, the merchants of these cities, backed by the power of the French state, controlled the transport, processing, and marketing of colonial produce as well as imports into the colonies. The colonial trade stimulated a wide variety of industrial and commercial activities that were concentrated in these cities and their hinterlands. These included shipping, shipbuilding, sail and rope making, sugar refineries, distilleries, textile manufactures, metallurgical industries, the manufacture of trade goods, glassworks, wheat and wine production, and coal, iron, and lead mining. The West Indian colonies promoted the development of large-scale, specialized production, increased the volume of trade, encouraged the centralization of markets, and made possible the concentration of wealth and power in the hands of the merchant class. As a result of their domination of colonial production and trade, these maritime cities were the most dynamic centers of industry and commerce in France. In their drive to accumulate wealth and augment their power, the bourgeoisie of these port cities aggravated the conflicts within French society and deepened the divisions of race and class in the colonies. In so doing, they unleashed social forces beyond their control.[7]

The bonds of colonial domination that made the West Indies one of the crucial pivots of the world-economy during the eighteenth century also brought the slaves of Saint Domingue into contact with the most advanced political ideas and developments of the epoch and made possible the emergence of a slave revolution there. In 1794, the National Convention in Paris, struggling to preserve the revolution from its enemies at home and abroad, and under the radical influence of the Parisian *sans-culottes* and the blacks and mulattoes of Saint Domingue who had declared their allegiance to the Republic, proclaimed slavery abolished in all French colonies and decreed that "all men, without distinction of color, domiciled in the colonies, are French citizens, and enjoy all the rights assured by the Constitution." This act, all too often overlooked in the rich and complex history of the revolution, had profound and far-reaching consequences for the subsequent development of slavery and the sugar industry in the Caribbean and their place in the international economy.[8]

The doctrines of *liberté*, *égalité*, and *fraternité* became powerful weapons in the hands of the slaves of Saint Domingue who had revolted. However, neither the ideology nor the practice of the Haitian Revolution was simply a French export to the colonies. Rather, both were appropriated and interpreted by the slaves in accordance with their own needs and experiences. For the slaves, the revolutionary principles of the French Republic were inseparable from the abolition of slavery. They waged an uncompromising struggle against the enemies of the revolution and gave practical significance to the decrees of the Convention. Under the leadership of Toussaint L'Ouverture, they found both ideology and allies and transformed their revolt into a revolutionary movement. Even after the course of the revolution had been altered by the counterrevolution in France, the exslaves of Saint Domingue continued to defend its principles. Only when Napoleon's threat to restore slavery made compromise impossible did they throw off the chains of European domination and establish the independent republic of Haiti. They defeated both the French and British forces sent to reconquer them and to reimpose slavery. With their victory, Saint Domingue, the most lucrative colony in the world during the eighteenth century and the keystone of colonial slavery in the Caribbean, disappeared from the European imperium.[9]

The turmoil of war and revolution touched the other major French colonies as well and further weakened the condition of the French Empire. In Guadeloupe, slavery was abolished in 1794. A revolutionary army of exslaves led by Victor Hugues defeated the English expeditionary force sent to occupy the colony and attempted to spread the revolution to neighboring islands until they were defeated and slavery reimposed by Napoleon in 1802. In Martinique, the proudly aristocratic planters, hostile to the revolutionary government in France and threatened by events in Saint Domingue and Guadeloupe, preferred to desert the nation and turn the island over to the British to preserve their property and guarantee the maintenance of chattel slavery. British occupation from 1793 to 1801 spared Martinique the upheavals visited on Saint Domingue and Guadeloupe, but it was a period of political chaos, civil conflict, and economic uncertainty that seriously prejudiced the island's sugar industry.[10]

Both Martinique and Guadeloupe were occupied a second time by the British from 1809 to 1814. The consequences of this second occupation were almost fatal for the sugar industry in the two colonies. French West Indian sugar was effectively excluded from the European market during this period. Britain, concerned to protect its own colonies from competition, prohibited sugar from the occupied French colonies from entering its domestic market. It was classified as foreign sugar and could only be sold in Britain for reexport abroad. At the same time, the Continental blockade was in full force and cut off nearly all cane sugar imports to the Continent. Prices fell so sharply because of the restricted market that planter revenues were unable to cover the costs of production. Sugar cane was almost abandoned during this period, and most planters concentrated on cultivating provision crops. This difficult condition was aggravated by the hurricane that devastated Martinique in 1813.[11]

The Haitian Revolution and the collapse of the French colonial sugar industry between 1792 and 1814 precipitated the dramatic transformation of the world sugar market. The destruction of the world's largest and most efficient producer and the withdrawal of Haitian sugar from the market opened the way for rival producers. Sugar cultivation was intensified in existing areas and expanded into new ones as planters rushed to fill the void left by the exit of Saint Domingue. Aided by population increase and stimulated by an expanding consumer market in Europe, world sugar output grew rapidly, despite the loss of Haiti.

At the same time, the decline of France as a colonial power in conjunction with Britain's triumph in the revolutionary wars and the Napoleonic Wars broke down the previously existing structure of the market. War and political rivalry between France and Britain played a vital role in this reorganization of the world sugar market. British naval superiority accelerated the destruction of France as a maritime and colonial power and allowed Britain to control colonial trade. During the wars between Britain and France from 1793 to 1814, the French navy and merchant marine were decimated by superior British sea power. Britain severed the lines of communication and trade between metropolis and colonies and ruined French maritime commerce, while British control of the sea lanes and occupation of the colonies of its enemies in the East and West Indies gave it a virtual monopoly of colonial produce. Britain was also able to assert its control over the continental European market despite being excluded from the sphere of French political and economic domination. The resale of colonial products, especially sugar, allowed Britain to expand its foreign trade. Control of European overseas trade augmented

Britain's commerce and stimulated its industry. It proved to be a decisive advantage in its war with France for domination of the world-economy. By 1815, France was definitively defeated, and the main obstacles to British expansion were eliminated. Britain moved into the vacuum left by France, and the process of reintegrating the world market began under the aegis of British capital.[12]

## The Emergence of British Hegemony and the Reintegration of the World Sugar Market, 1815–1848

With the collapse of the French colonial empire, there was no power that could rival Britain in the international arena, and a process of reintegration of the world market began under the hegemony of British capital. Britain's position during the first half of the nineteenth century was not due simply to technological superiority. Rather, British commercial, financial, and maritime supremacy sustained its industrial development, and in turn, as Britain's productive advantage over its rivals widened, its control over the market strengthened. British economic expansion depended on international trade for raw materials, foodstuffs, and, to a lesser extent, as an outlet for manufactured goods. Britain's commercial and technical advantages enabled it to establish trade with the periphery on the basis of complementarity—peripheral raw materials and agricultural products for British manufactures (and other services such as capital, shipping, banking, and insurance).[13]

The establishment of this division of labor between core and periphery was organized by the City of London, whose position as center of world trade was both instrument and expression of British hegemony. The extension of commodity production in the periphery and the expansion not only of British trade with the periphery but also that of its rivals relied on the financial power of London banks. As McMichael has argued, British loan capital extended the scope of the world market for all states. A system of multilateral trading emerged that depended on sterling balances and the credit of London banks as well as the City's ability to settle trade balances among states indirectly. Bills of exchange drawn on London banks replaced the transfer of precious metals in organizing international exchanges, and sterling balances were used to adjust the status of national currencies in world trade. The centralization of banking enabled Britain to maintain and extend world exchange and to achieve financial supremacy beyond its commercial and industrial supremacy. The creation of these global exchange relations centered on Britain established a world division of labor dependent on and responsive to an integrated world market. Within this new configuration the conditions of sugar production and trade, colonialism, and slavery in the world-economy were altered.[14]

The advance of industrialization resulted in a diversification of the pattern of demand in the world-economy. New raw materials were required on an unprecedented scope and scale, and an international network of supply was established that went beyond the limits of the old imperial boundaries. Britain extended its commercial penetration of Africa and Asia and attempted to break Spain's hold on Latin America (here and there, as in Argentina and Uruguay, successfully). Over the course of this period, industrial raw materials, fibers, minerals, grain, timber, fruit, and meat came to replace sugar, tobacco, furs, and naval stores as the key commodities in world trade. The amount of raw cotton consumed by British industry was unparalleled, and by 1831, it supplanted sugar as Britain's leading import. The cotton crop of the U.S. South multiplied sixty-fold from 1790 to 1810 and by 1860 accounted for two-thirds of U.S. exports. Egypt, India, and Latin America also developed into major centers of cotton production during this period.[15]

While its relative significance in world trade may have declined, in absolute terms sugar consumption and production, underpinned by demographic growth, urbanization, and industrialization, rose steadily and rapidly throughout the nineteenth century. The development of mass middle and working classes in Europe was associated with new patterns of consumption of food and drink. Sugar increasingly entered the diet of all sectors of the European population as a sweetener in coffee, tea, and cocoa, in jams and preserves, and as a confection, while the expansion of world output, improved production techniques, and reduced duties resulted in a marked decline in prices. Britain emerged as the keystone of the international sugar trade. It was not only the world's largest consumer of sugar, but it also commanded the reexport market and was the only purchaser that could absorb increased New World sugar production. On the other side of the coin, it was the only country that could supply the credit, machinery, and manufactured goods to support this expansion. British commercial and industrial superiority enabled it to penetrate the markets of the other colonizing powers. World sugar production and consumption were progressively shaped around the conditions imposed by the requirements of British capital accumulation and integrated into its rhythms and cycles.[16]

The immediate beneficiaries of the destruction of the sugar industry in Saint Domingue and Britain's rise to hegemony were the British West Indies. Between 1791 and 1815 sugar production in the British Caribbean rose more rapidly than at any other time in its history. The old colonies increased their output and new sugar territories were added to the empire. By 1815–19, the British colonies accounted for nearly half of the world's supply, which had risen by 38 percent in spite of the collapse of Saint Domingue. However, the impact of the transformation of the sugar market was felt differently among the various British colonies (See Table 1.2). The small islands of the Lesser Antilles, intensively exploited since the seventeenth century, expanded rapidly during these years. Between 1792 and 1816, sugar production rose from 9,025 tons to 14,431 tons in Barbados and from 3,676 tons to 9,634 in Antigua, while St. Kitts went from 6,958 tons in 1792 to 9,685 tons in 1807 (but fell back to 6,237 tons in 1816). Sugar cultivation was increased in the islands conquered during the Seven Years' War as well. Although production in Dominica actually declined during this period, sugar production in St. Vincent went from about 6,000 tons in 1792 to over 13,000 tons in 1816, and Grenada and the Grenadines expanded rapidly and in 1816 had one of their largest harvests ever: 13,302 tons. However, despite such increases, these islands rapidly reached the physical limits of expansion as well as the technical limits of the slave plantation. The capacity of planters in these islands to respond to the new market opportunities was severely restricted, and increases in the amount of sugar produced were marginal at best. After 1814–18, sugar production ceased to expand in the British Lesser Antilles, and they accounted for a progressively smaller share of the output of the British Empire.[17]

Table 1.2. British Colonial Sugar Production, 1792–1843 (long tons)

| Years | British Lesser Antilles[a] | Jamaica | Trinidad | British Guiana | Mauritius | Total |
|---|---|---|---|---|---|---|
| 1792 | 45,527 | 54,644 | | | | |
| Index | 66 | 70 | | | | |
| 1800 | 47,486 | 70,100 | 3,300 | | | |
| Index | 69 | 90 | 47 | | | |
| 1807 | 52,971 | 89,800 | 9,400 | | | |
| Index | 77 | 115 | 135 | | | |
| 1814–1818[b] | 68,591 | 78,094 | 6,955 | 17,416 | 2,538 | 173,594 |
| Index (base) | 100 | 100 | 100 | 100 | 100 | 100 |
| % total | 39.5 | 45.0 | 4.0 | 10.0 | 1.5 | 100.0 |
| 1819–1823[b] | 64,696 | 78,943 | 8,302 | 29,058 | 8,905 | 189,904 |
| Index | 94 | 101 | 119 | 167 | 351 | 109 |
| % total | 34.1 | 41.6 | 4.4 | 15.3 | 4.7 | 100.0 |
| 1824–1828[b] | 66,221 | 67,432 | 10,409 | 46,173 | 17,117 | 207,352 |
| Index | 97 | 86 | 150 | 265 | 674 | 119 |
| % total | 31.9 | 32.5 | 5.0 | 22.3 | 8.3 | 100.0 |
| 1829–1833[b] | 65,256 | 69,502 | 14,234 | 57,197 | 33,158 | 239,347 |
| Index | 95 | 89 | 205 | 328 | 1306 | 138 |
| % total | 27.3 | 29.0 | 5.9 | 23.9 | 13.9 | 100.0 |
| 1834–1838[b] | 61,525 | 54,165 | 15,287 | 51,276 | 32,750 | 215,003 |
| Index | 90 | 69 | 220 | 294 | 1290 | 124 |
| % total | 28.7 | 29.0 | 7.1 | 23.8 | 15.2 | 100.0 |
| 1839–1843[b] | 49,822 | 33,403 | 14,054 | 32,636 | 33,713 | 163,628 |
| Index | 73 | 43 | 202 | 187 | 1328 | 94 |
| % total | 30.4 | 20.4 | 8.6 | 19.9 | 20.6 | 100.0 |

*Source*: Noel Deerr, *The History of Sugar* (London, 1945), I, pp. 193–201.

[a]British Lesser Antilles: Barbados, Nevis, Antigua, Montserrat, Saint Kitts, British Virgin Islands, Grenada and the Grenadines, Saint Vincent, Saint Lucia, Dominica, and Tobago.

[b]Average.

There was still room for new investment and territorial expansion in Jamaica at the time of the Haitian Revolution. Sugar output there nearly doubled between 1792 and 1805. In the latter year, Jamaica exported 110,158 metric tons of sugar, more than Saint Domingue on the eve of the French Revolution. By means of this enormous increase, Jamaica regained the position it had enjoyed at the beginning of the eighteenth century as the Caribbean's premier sugar producer. However, Jamaica never again attained this level of production using slave labor. Much of this new wave of expansion was into the fertile inland valleys, and the high cost of overland transport raised the cost of the Jamaican product in relation to other new sugar areas. Erratic wartime markets, fluctuating prices, changing sugar duties, and the abolition of the slave trade all had their effect on Jamaican production, while debt and falling profit margins took their toll on the planters. After the downturn of the sugar market in 1806, a quarter of Jamaica's new plantations were abandoned. Nonetheless, even though sugar production stagnated, Jamaica continued to produce substantial amounts of sugar until the plantation system was undercut by slave emancipation in the 1830s. In 1820, Jamaica still produced 97,832 metric tons of sugar. Production gradually declined thereafter, and Jamaica was replaced by Cuba as the world's largest single supplier during the decade of the 1820s. Despite the gains made in the international market between 1792 and 1815, the expansion and intensification of sugar production during this period pushed the old British Caribbean colonies to their limits, and they were surpassed by newer sugar-producing areas in an expanding market.[18]

Wartime conquests also augmented the supply of sugar under British control. The incorporation of a new and fertile frontier for colonial products into the empire offset the stagnation of the older West Indian colonies and enabled Britain to continue to dominate world production until the 1820s. Britain temporarily occupied several foreign sugar colonies at various times between 1807 and 1814. These included not only the French colonies of Martinique, Guadeloupe, and Cayenne (French Guiana), but also the Danish colonies of Saint Thomas and Saint John, and the Dutch colonies of Surinam, Berbice, Demerara, and Essequibo. Britain was able to use this opportunity either to encourage or to disrupt the development of sugar production in these areas, depending on what it saw as its own advantage at any given moment. But more important than these temporary occupations were the new territories permanently acquired after the peace in 1815. Berbice, Demerara, and Essequibo had been continuously occupied by Britain from 1803 onward and were united as the colony of British Guiana in 1829. Led by Demerara, the Guianese colonies were the most important acquisition of the British Empire during this period. They provided Britain with seemingly vast tracts of virgin land and excellent soil and climatic conditions for sugar and cotton production. Although sugar monoculture distorted the overall promise of the colony and confined its development to the coastal strip, British Guiana grew rapidly and became a valuable addition to the empire. Guianese production rose from 3,000 metric tons under the Dutch in 1791 to 16,521 metric tons in 1816 under the English. Its annual average production for the period 1829–33 was more than three times that of 1814–18; after this, British slave emancipation (1834–1838) limited its further development. In contrast, the progress of the sugar industry in the Crown colony of Trinidad, captured from Spain in 1797 and ceded to Britain in the Treaty of Amiens in 1802, was retarded by the struggle over land and labor policies between pro- and antislavery forces in Parliament. Sugar production in Trinidad went from 2,700 tons in 1799 to 9,500 tons in 1805. By 1834, it had reached almost 17,000 tons, a substantial increase but far below its potential. Of the colonies gained from France in the Peace of Paris, the output of Tobago reached 6,958 tons of sugar in 1816 and remained relatively stable for a decade before declining, while production in Mauritius in the Indian Ocean jumped from 4,000 tons in 1816 to 38,483 tons in 1832. However, while Trinidad, Mauritius, and above all British Guiana compensated for the stagnation of Jamaica and the Lesser Antilles, the British Caribbean could not keep pace with world production and demand.[19]

The changes in the world sugar market initiated by the Haitian Revolution thus brought the British West Indian colonies to the apogee of their development. Their rapid expansion both resulted from the emergence of British hegemony over the world-economy and contributed to the consolidation of British supremacy. But these changes were part and parcel of broader processes quantitatively and qualitatively reshaping the world-economy as a whole around the dominance of British capital. Within these processes, sugar, slavery, and colonialism were being redefined, and the place of West Indian colonies themselves was shifting both in the politics and economics of the British Empire and in the world-economy as a whole.

Britain's position in the world-economy put it on the path toward a policy of free trade. To the extent that it came to control commerce outside the bounds of its own empire, Britain became relatively indifferent to formal colonialism as the means of defining the nature and direction of commodity flows and the division of labor between core and periphery. The control of international finance by London and the establishment of the pound sterling as the international money of account, prefiguring the international gold standard, represented new levels of integration of the world-economy and new channels for economic domination. Britain's industrial development accentuated the differential between industrial and agricultural prices in the world-economy, while the transformation of class relations reinforced the tendency toward free trade. With the formation of a wage-earning proletariat there was systemic pressure to lower the value composition of the wage bill. In Britain this could be most readily accomplished by free trade and lay behind the campaign for "the cheap breakfast table" and the abolition of duties on grain during the 1840s.[20]

The effect of these developments was not to destroy archaic forms of social organization and establish the general mobility of capital and labor in a universal free market. Rather, previously existing social relations were recast within the new constellation of political and economic forces. The former interdependence of sugar, colonialism, and slavery was dissolved, and the conditions of the existence, the function, and the significance of each were modified. Colonial policy and economic protectionism had now become the means for altering politically the economic processes that integrated peripheral producers into the world-economy and defined the world market and the international division of labor. They no longer constituted them. Colonialism, protected markets, and slave labor did not disappear; they assumed new and diverse relations to the processes reconstituting the world market. They now existed as a part of new and different relations and processes of the world-economy and helped to shape the mode and limits of its integration. The world sugar market formed the axis along which these new and varied relations of colonialism and slavery developed.

Rather than the generalization of free trade, the very success of Britain in establishing its hold on the world market provoked a protectionist response on the part of its rivals. C. E. Labrousse calls this process "a second continental blockade," as the second-rank European powers sought to protect their "national economies" from British economic power and world market competition through high duties or outright prohibition. The world sugar market was especially notorious for the tariff barriers, export subsidies, rebates, and other measures that shaped its development throughout the nineteenth century. State protectionism was responsible for the growth of the European beet sugar industry as continental nations sought an alternative to the onslaught of cheap New World sugar and dependence on British commerce. The transformation of the world sugar market created new conditions for colonial domination and sugar production, as well as for the relations between the two. New poles of attraction and repulsion were created between core and periphery that did not coincide with old imperial boundaries. As British economic power undermined old colonial empires, rival powers were forced into greater reliance on their colonies and tried to strengthen their control over them. At the same time, colonial producers were increasingly brought into competition with one another in an expanding market. Those in a strong competitive position were compelled to struggle against the limitations of the colonial policies of their own metropolitan centers and against protectionism in general. Under the conditions of the new market, they were often able to gain some advantages for their sugar industries. In contrast, the demand of producers in a weak position was that colonial policy and market preferences be used to protect them from world competition.[21]

In like manner, the transformation of the world-economy created new conditions for slave labor internationally. As Britain extended its domination over the world-economy—and, in this instance, the world sugar market—the particular form of social labor became largely a matter of indifference. The British interest was in cheap sugar, and therefore in cheap labor. To the degree that Britain was able to exercise influence over world production through its control of the market, it moved toward the emergence of a whole gamut of forms of labor, ranging from slaves, to tenants, sharecroppers, and peasants, and from indentured laborers to free wage laborers. This proliferation developed slowly but steadily during the first half of the nineteenth century, and the availability of such diverse forms and sources of labor allowed Britain more flexibility in developing a global economic and political strategy.[22]

These structural shifts in the world-economy contributed cumulatively to the effectiveness of the antislavery movement in Britain. However, this movement was not simply a function of economic factors, but added another dimension to those processes leading to the destruction of slavery, and imposed different paths of development on British and non-British colonies. The abolition of the slave trade not only cut off the labor supply to the British slave colonies, but, as Paula Beiguelman has emphasized, destroyed the commodity market most intimately linked to the slave form—the market in slaves. Meanwhile, British slave emancipation disrupted the sugar industry in both the declining and the vital British slave colonies alike.[23]

The interplay of market forces and the antislavery movement pushed Britain toward free trade and undercut the competitive position of the British West Indian colonies. The high price of British West Indian sugar and the protective tariffs it required risked the dampening of British domestic consumption and seriously weakened Britain's position in the reexport market. By 1815, British territorial expansion in the Caribbean had come to an end. The abolition of the slave trade limited the labor supply to the British colonies, and, with the exception of Trinidad and Guiana, British Caribbean sugar production had reached its saturation point. British West Indian planters were faced with rising costs and the inability to expand production. As cheaper Latin American and Caribbean sugar invaded European markets, reexports of British West Indian sugar had to be subsidized by the government by means of drawbacks and export bounties to make them competitive with sugar from countries that were often substantial customers for

British manufactures. British West Indian reexports dropped from about 100,000 tons in 1802 to 27,000 tons in 1827.[24]

As their competitive position in foreign markets was weakened, the British Caribbean colonies were compelled to place ever greater reliance on the British domestic market and preferential duties. But the high cost of British West Indian sugar and the demand of Caribbean planters for protection from both foreign and East Indian sugar restricted the growth of per capita British consumption, prejudiced the development of the British refining industry, and hindered the development of the British East Indian colonies. Nonetheless, by the 1820s, the East Indian sugar industry appeared to many observers to be a powerful and viable competitor to West Indian sugar within the empire. With the support of the antislavery forces, who were enthusiastic about the "free" labor of India, a campaign was waged to extend privileges to East Indian sugar and encourage its development. In 1825, sugar from Mauritius was admitted into Britain under the same conditions as West Indian sugar.[25]

At the same time, British domestic consumption was growing rapidly despite the obstacles it faced. It nearly doubled between 1815 and 1840, going from about 100,000 tons per year to nearly 200,000 tons. By the 1830s, the British West Indies were unable to supply British domestic consumption. They had lost their stranglehold on the metropolitan market. Emancipation gave the fatal blow to the social organization of the West Indian sugar industry and was quickly followed by the equalization of duties between the East and West Indies. But preferential treatment for British colonial sugar still inhibited the full development of the British sugar trade. With its former antislavery foes as allies, "free" British West Indian sugar now received protection from foreign "slave-grown" sugar in the British market. This restriction on foreign sugar resulted in the massive growth of "spot markets" as British merchants carried Latin American and Caribbean sugar directly to European markets instead of reexporting it from Britain. Finally, in 1846, the preferential duties for British colonial sugar were removed and a policy of free trade in sugar was established.[26]

In contrast to Britain, rival producers were made more dependent on slave labor by the expansion of demand, the competitive nature of the market, and the lack of alternative sources of labor. The same historical processes of the development of the world-economy that led to the abolition of slavery within the British Empire resulted in its expansion and intensification outside of the empire. Slavery developed on a massive scale in Cuba, Brazil, and the United States during the course of the nineteenth century as part of the new international division of labor. The rapid development of new zones of exploitation, where broad expanses of fresh land could be brought under cultivation, often with the stimulus of British capital but in any case without the political liabilities faced by producers in Britain's slave colonies, eroded the dominant position of the British Caribbean and changed the economic and political conditions of slave labor globally. Production in the new areas was premised on a competitive and expanding market and an industrializing world-economy. By midcentury, slavery increasingly coexisted and was combined with other forms of labor at the level of the world-economy. But locally as well, as in the case of Cuba, the slaveholders, in their drive to increase efficiency, developed slave production to its highest peak and began to experiment with both new sources and new forms of labor. Seen from this perspective, the apparent continuity of the history of slavery and slave emancipation and their singular relationship to capitalist development masks the diversity and complexity of the relations and processes constituting slavery in the nineteenth-century capitalist world-economy.

The crisis of the world sugar market rejuvenated the Brazilian sugar industry. Initially, Portuguese neutrality spared Brazilian producers the wartime disruption suffered by their rivals and improved the competitive position of Brazilian sugar. Their position improved still further when the Portuguese court fled to Rio de Janeiro in 1808 to escape Napoleon's armies. On the one hand, Brazil was fortuitously freed from the parasitic restrictions of the Portuguese monopoly of trade. On the other hand, favorable commercial policies opened the way for the penetration of British capital and stimulated Brazilian sugar production. The old centers of the sugar industry in Bahia and Pernambuco regained their vitality, and sugar became increasingly important in the state of Rio de Janeiro and to a lesser extent in the state of São Paulo, although it remained below the level of the Northeast. In 1791, Brazil produced only 21,000 metric tons of sugar. By 1815–19, this figure reached an estimated 75,000 metric tons per year, and, by 1822, climbed to over 100,000 metric tons. However, the technical bases of Brazilian sugar manufacture did not change significantly from what they had been in the seventeenth century, and the lack of an adequate transportation network limited geographical expansion. Further, the relatively poor quality of Brazilian sugar hampered its competitiveness on the international market. Although Brazilian sugar production was increasing in absolute terms, its share of the world market was declining sharply, and by midcentury, its total output had begun to stagnate as well.[27]

In Havana, the news of the revolution in Saint Domingue had been greeted with rejoicing by the Cuban planter class. The destruction of their greatest competitor encouraged their ambitions, and the aggressive creole sugarocracy was prepared to take maximum advantage of the opportunity offered to them. Over the long term, Cuba was the greatest gainer from the crisis of world sugar production provoked by the Haitian Revolution. Although Cuban sugar production had been growing steadily since the English occupation in the 1760s, it catapulted forward beginning in the 1790s, aided by refugees from Saint Domingue who provided technical expertise and at times even capital for the growth of the Cuban sugar industry. In 1791, Cuba exported 16,731 metric tons of sugar. This increased to 32,586 metric tons in 1799 and reached 45,396 metric tons by 1815. New and ever-larger plantations were established at a frenetic pace, and old ones increased their capacity. In the diocese of Havana alone, the number of sugar mills jumped from 237 in 1792 to 416 in 1806. The average output per mill more than doubled during this period, and the first generation of giant Cuban mills appeared. San José de los Dolores, belonging to the Marquis de Arcos; Bonificio Duarte's San Miguel; José Ignacio Echegoyen's La Asunción; Francisco Arango y Parreño's La Ninfa; and San Cristóbal de Baracoa, the property of the Reverend Bethlehemite Fathers—each produced over 300 metric tons of sugar and had over 300 slaves. Cuba's slave population went from 85,900 in 1792 to 199,100 in 1817, and in the latter year over 32,000 slaves were imported. The feverish activity of the sugar boom left no aspect of Cuban life untouched as the planter class pushed relentlessly toward what Manuel Moreno Fraginals describes as *"la primera danza de los milliones."*[28]

Cuban sugar production increased rapidly and continuously in the years after the Napoleonic Wars. In 1827, Cuban output reached 76,669 metric tons and surpassed Jamaica's peak year. By 1830, Cuba emerged as the world's largest producer with an output of 104,971 metric tons. World demand continued to grow at an accelerating rate, and Cuban production more than kept pace with it. In 1838, Cuba produced 136,185 metric tons, a little more than 19 percent of world sugar production. By 1848, the 260,463 metric tons produced accounted for nearly one-quarter of the world's supply. According to estimates from the census, the slave population of Cuba reached 286,900 in 1827 and stood at 436,500 by 1841. These developments aggravated the Cuban oligarchy's relations with Spain, which could not provide adequate markets for Cuban sugar. Cuba profited from the growing world demand for sugar and especially from the shortage of supply following slave emancipation in the British colonies, exporting its products not only to Spain but to the United States, Britain, Germany, France, Russia, and the Low Countries. Important commercial relations developed with Great Britain and, above all, with the United States, but Cuba's ability to place its sugar in a variety of markets enabled it to avoid becoming dependent on either of these powers. However, without a preferential market of its own, Cuba was forced to compete against protected sugar both in Europe and North America. It was compelled to protest against protectionist policies and to increase the efficiency of its own production. The Cuban sugar mill developed on a giant scale, and the technology of sugar production there attained the most advanced level known under slavery, while the search for greater productivity led the Cuban planter class to experiment with new forms of labor organization and new sources of labor. The stage was set for Cuba's domination of world sugar production during the second half of the century.[29]

Thus, the world market and the economic and political processes structuring it changed dramatically during the first half of the nineteenth century. The reintegration of the world-economy under the economic and political domination of Britain completely altered the parameters and conditions of world sugar production. A new cycle of expanded and intensified sugar production opened, one that was organized around the predominance of British capital. The geography of world sugar was transformed as old production centers declined and new ones emerged. Beyond the regions already discussed, Java, India, Mauritius, Bourbon (Réunion), and Louisiana could be listed among the world's significant sugar-producing areas by midcentury, to be followed later by Natal, Australia, Hawaii, and the Philippines as well as the beet sugar producers in Europe and North America. Prices fell and world demand grew while changing market patterns and processes brought peripheral producers into competition with one another.

This transformation of the world sugar market redefined the nature, role, and significance of both colonialism and slavery in new and complex ways throughout the world-economy. For some planters, colonialism and economic protectionism provided a means of self-protection in an increasingly integrated and competitive market; for others, they were an obstacle to their ability to take advantage of the new conditions. But for all of them, the underlying processes of market integration, expansion, and competition put the premium, directly or indirectly, on productive efficiency. Thus, new varieties of cane were developed, the technology of sugar grinding and refining underwent almost constant innovation, and, most importantly, labor was reorganized. The impact of these changes on slavery was very uneven. While slave labor was abolished within the British Empire, it expanded substantially in regions outside it. At the same time, new forms of labor organization were introduced into the world sugar industry, either in combination with slave labor or as a substitute for it. Paradoxically, the consequence of the transformation of world-economy was that there was more and cheaper slave-produced sugar on the market than ever before. However, the character and conditions of slave labor in the Caribbean and elsewhere were altered as slavery had to both coexist and compete with a variety of forms of social production in an expanding and competitive market.

The restoration of the French colonial empire after 1815 developed as a counterpoint to the forces and relations reorganizing the world-economy. Sugar and slavery assumed renewed importance in the French colonies even as the global supports for them were being dissolved. However, French colonial policy in the

Caribbean did not simply represent the persistence of old forms or a return to the status quo ante. Rather, it was a highly contradictory attempt to create an enclave of protected economic activity in response to profoundly altered conditions. Although merchants, shippers, refiners, and planters in France and its colonies as well as the French state played an active role in colonial reconstruction, in the revival of the sugar trade, and in the restoration of slave labor, the impetus for these changes was not so much within the ambit of the French colonial system as within the processes restructuring the world-economy. The unprecedented development of sugar production and slave labor in the colonies remaining to France would have been unthinkable without the transformation of the world-economy as a whole. These global forces shaped and constrained the particular trajectory of the French sugar colonies. The capacity of the sugar industry and of slavery as a form of organization of social production to respond to these new conditions to a great extent shaped the experience of the French colonies and underlay the process of emancipation there.

# Chapter 2

# The Contradictions of Protectionism

## Colonial Policy and the
## French Sugar Market, 1814–1848

France reestablished control over its colonies under new historical circumstances. The character and conditions of both sugar production and slavery within the world-economy were being rapidly, albeit unevenly, transformed after 1814. The development of the French colonies both contributed to and was shaped by this unevenness. The reorganization of the French colonial system during this period was conditioned by overwhelming British economic and political domination of the world-economy, on the one hand, and by both the relative weakness of France and the decline of its Atlantic-maritime sector on the other.

With its empire virtually destroyed and its overseas trade and great port cities debilitated, France was unable to gain access to other markets and sources of supply or to control its domestic market in the face of cheap foreign competition. The economic recovery, not only of the French colonies but of the whole circuit of French colonial commerce, rested on the restoration of metropolitan privilege in the colonies and the creation of a protected market for colonial products in France. The colonial policies of the French state established the interdependent yet unequal relationship between colonial planters and metropolitan merchants, shippers, and manufacturers, and mediated their relation to both national and international markets. State intervention created an enclave of protected economic activity that permitted the renewal of sugar production and slave labor in the colonies and the recovery of overseas trade. The French sugar market was reorganized behind protective barriers, while sugar production and slave labor in Martinique and the other French colonies were developed with unprecedented intensity to compensate for the loss of Haiti and the decline of maritime commerce. Sugar thus assumed a privileged position in French colonial trade, and the reliance of France on its remaining colonies was reinforced.

Yet French colonial policy was not, and could not have been, a simple return to the old mercantilism of the seventeenth and eighteenth centuries. The French colonial system was rehabilitated as part of a broader protectionist response to British commercial and industrial supremacy. Its protective barriers were now defined against and continually undermined by the forces restructuring the world-economy both quantitatively and qualitatively. The reestablishment of the French colonial system contributed to the creation of uneven tempos of change within these complex, differentiated, but unitary global processes. It allowed the rapid development of the colonies even as the entire colonial complex was outpaced by the accelerated expansion and transformation of the world-economy as a whole. Under the umbrella of protective policies, the exploitation of the French colonies was maximized by reinforcing and elaborating existing structures. These were made archaic even as they attained new levels of development by the still more rapid advance of world-scale forces. The French colonies were increasingly marginalized even as the forms of production and exchange prevailing in them were developed to their fullest extent and became infused with a new content. As development accentuated unevenness, growth and progress coincided with stagnation.

The rapid expansion of sugar and slavery in the French West Indies was constrained by its own technical and social organization, including the political organization of markets, on the one hand, and the rapid expansion and transformation of the world-economy as a whole on the other. The unevenness of world economic development compounded the contradictory and fragile character of the French colonial system. The very growth of the colonial sugar industry deepened the colonies' reliance on protective legislation and the French national market even as it undermined the conditions that sustained and justified the protected market. The expansion of colonial sugar production resulted in relatively higher costs and a limited output. The colonies came to rely more and more on preferential tariffs to maintain their place in the French national market at the same time that their small size both as producers and consumers inhibited the growth of metropolitan commerce, shipping, and industry. Conversely, the restricted development of metropolitan overseas commerce limited its ability to compete in alternative markets and made it even more reliant on the colonial trade and state protection. Thus, from the perspective of both metropolitan and colonial interests, protection begot the need for more protection, and the entire colonial trading complex became increasingly dependent on state intervention to secure its markets. Paradoxically, colonial commerce came to require such high tariff barriers to maintain its position in the national market that the way was opened for the revitalization of the French beet sugar industry. Colonial producers were then confronted with a powerful competitor in their own market. Their demand for protection had created the very conditions within the national market that they were unable to contest in the world market.

These contradictions within the French colonial system were exacerbated by its position in the world-economy. The French program of colonial reconstruction evolved against constant British pressure. British economic and political superiority excluded France from alternative markets and turned the path of French development inward with increasing reliance on economic protectionism, while the eventual success of British demands for the abolition of the French slave trade altered the character of colonial exploitation. Fragmented both in its goals and the means of its execution, French colonial policy developed piecemeal and with contradictory results. It became both the arena and the object of intensive conflict between various interest groups that contended with one another over the political conditions for the maximum exploitation of the limited opportunities remaining to them.

## Reconstruction of the French Colonial Empire

The decades of revolution, war, and blockade between 1789 and 1814 had disastrous consequences for the colonial and maritime interests of France. Defeat by Britain left France a second-rank power no longer able to vie for economic and political supremacy in the international arena. The French colonial empire contracted and declined. The loss of Saint Domingue to the revolutionary struggles of the slaves was a crushing blow to France's colonial position in the Americas. It crippled French imperial ambitions and led to the sale of Louisiana to the United States. Moreover, according to the terms of the Treaty of Paris, France lost Saint Lucia and Tobago in the Caribbean and the Île-de-France (Mauritius) in the Indian Ocean to the British. The colonies remaining to France after 1814 had been of only secondary importance in comparison with Saint Domingue during the ancien régime. Of these, Martinique and Guadeloupe suffered from the consequences of revolution and British occupation. French Guiana remained commercially unremunerative, and Bourbon (Réunion) was as yet undeveloped. The remainder of France's colonial holdings included trading stations in India and Senegal as well as the tiny islands of Saint Pierre and Miquelon. The four plantation colonies (Martinique, Guadeloupe, Guiana, and Bourbon) were considered to be the only overseas colonies of value and were at the center of the French effort to reconstruct their colonial empire.[1]

The effects of war, revolution, and blockade were devastating for the great port cities of France as well. French foreign trade fell to nearly half of its prewar level. The combined population of Bordeaux and Marseilles fell from 120,000 inhabitants in 1789 to 75,000 at the end of the First Empire. The loss of colonial and overseas markets, and to a lesser extent, the shortage of raw materials led to the collapse of industry in the port cities and their hinterlands. Large portions of the Garonne Valley, Brittany, and Normandy suffered deindustrialization. The center of gravity of French economic activity shifted to the north and east and developed within the framework of continental European markets, while the maritime centers of the west and south declined.[2]

The great Atlantic port cities of the ancien régime based on the colonial trade no longer represented the hubs of French commercial and industrial development. They ceased being entrepôts for international trade and declined to the status of regional ports. Nantes and Bordeaux, the centers of French maritime activity in the eighteenth century, fell from prominence even among French port cities. Nantes underwent a commercial and industrial decline and only began to recover under the July Monarchy. Unlike Le Havre and Marseilles, which began to be transformed into outlets for industrial goods, it lacked an industrial hinterland and remained dependent on its traditional commercial and maritime activities. Bordeaux tried unsuccessfully to extend the scope of its trade internationally but was constrained by the protectionist policies of the government, which forced it into dependence on colonial trade. The colonial trade, particularly with Martinique and Guadeloupe, was crucial for the recovery of Bordeaux. Although below eighteenth-century levels, sugar remained the basis of this trade. (According to Tudesq, it represented 74 percent of the return cargoes of ships from Bordeaux sent to Martinique and Guadeloupe in 1818.) Bordeaux retained close commercial ties with the West Indian colonies and played an important role in their development. However, after 1817, it experienced increased competition from Le Havre and Nantes and a perceptible decline in its commerce. By 1826, Bordeaux was relegated to fourth place among French ports behind Marseilles, Le Havre, and Dunkerque. By 1829, Le Havre, benefitting from the presence of Paris in its commercial hinterland, came to dominate colonial trade.[3]

Throughout the Restoration, the merchants of the French port cities were anxious to build up their shipping and overseas commerce. However, attempts to extend overseas trade outside the traditional colonial sphere were inhibited by political divisions, lack of an infrastructure, government policy, inadequate markets, and especially British economic and political predominance. Bordeaux and Marseilles particularly were active in the trade with Senegal. This commerce was further linked with the Antilles, India, Bourbon, and Mauritius. However, treaty agreements with Britain prohibited the slave trade in Senegal, and in the absence of a substitute for it, trade remained light. Similarly, the attempts of Bordeaux merchants to develop trade with Cochin China were frustrated by the failure of the government to establish a trading station there and reduce duties on return cargoes. French merchants were also enthusiastic about the possibilities of trade with the newly independent republics of Latin America as a substitute for the lost colonial trade. But their ability to penetrate these markets was limited by Britain's presence and the Restoration government's antipathy towards these rebels against

Bourbon Spain. No commercial treaties were possible until France recognized the new regimes in Chile, Peru, Colombia, and Buenos Aires in 1827. France did profit from the opening of Cuba to foreign commerce, while trade with Brazil developed slowly because of British preeminence there. French trade with the United States also increased, but was dominated by American shipping.[4]

In the absence of adequate foreign markets, the colonies, and particularly the colonial sugar industry, were of strategic importance for the economic recovery of France's Atlantic port cities. Throughout the Restoration, the foreign trade of France remained essentially trade with its colonies. Because France lacked the broad field of action enjoyed by Britain as well as the capacity to exploit that field, it promoted the intensive development of its remaining colonies. Although Martinique and Guadeloupe, the focal points of French colonial enterprise, were geographically, socially, and economically similar to the British Lesser Antilles, Britain could allow slave production in her colonies to decline, while Martinique and Guadeloupe as well as Bourbon underwent a large infusion of capital and slaves and a renewed emphasis on sugar production. If, in Britain, the elaboration of a vision of global empire and capitalist development can be seen, in France the reconstruction of colonial empire was a patchwork process catering to a variety of particular interest groups—colonial planters, metropolitan shippers and merchants, sugar refiners and beet sugar producers, in addition to the French state—whose overall development was constrained by British domination of the world market.

France reestablished control over its colonies between 1814 and 1817 and, under the guidance of Baron Portal, the Minister of the Marine, began to reorganize its colonial empire. A *bordelais*, Portal developed a colonial policy in the interests of the metropolitan merchants, notably those of Bordeaux, who were exempted from various duties in order to build up trade and shipping. At the time of their repossession, the French colonies remained open to foreign trade. Due to the general economic crisis and the disruption of overseas trade that France suffered, it was unable to provide its colonies with either adequate markets for their produce or sufficient provisions. Nonetheless, the commercial interests of the metropolitan port cities called for the rigorous suppression of foreign commerce and a return to the policy of strict exclusion in force during the eighteenth century. Over the opposition of intransigent colonists and liberal anticolonial ideologues alike, Portal initiated a program of naval reconstruction, active prosecution of the slave trade, and the systematic exploitation of the colonies in the interest of the metropolitan merchants that determined in broad outline the framework of Restoration colonial policy.[5]

Consistent with its ultraprotectionist economic policies and the demands of the maritime bourgeoisie, the Restoration government reestablished the relation between France and its colonies on the basis of the *exclusif*. The *exclusif* had originated during the seventeenth century in Colbert's efforts, directed especially against the Dutch, to reassert French domination over its Caribbean colonies and secure the monopoly of their trade for the benefit of France. Its principles continued to govern French policy toward its Caribbean colonies until 1861. The premise of the *exclusif* was that the colonies were the sole property of the metropolis and existed only for its benefit. Colonial production and trade were to be organized for the profit of the mother country. In principle, the colonies were prohibited from selling their produce anywhere else but in France and from transporting it in anything but French ships, while the colonial market was strictly reserved for French imports. No foreign merchandise could be imported into the colonies by either French or foreign ships under penalty of confiscation of ship and cargo. Further, the colonies were forbidden to engage in any activity that would conflict with metropolitan interests or reduce the trade between France and the colonies. The colonies could not raise or manufacture anything that would compete with metropolitan goods, and even semirefined sugar was taxed heavily on entry into France. In compensation, the colonies received certain concessions and subsidies for their products, which assured them a privileged position on the French market. Through this edifice of restriction and monopoly, France secured markets for its goods protected from foreign competition, guaranteed a supply of valuable tropical products independent of foreign sources without exporting specie, and stimulated its marine and subsidiary industries. The *exclusif* thus established an unequal relationship between metropolis and colonies. It allowed France to secure a surplus in trade and expand its commerce and manufactures, while the colonies were forced to subordinate their production to the metropolis and become dependent on it.[6]

Although the doctrine of the *exclusif* remained intact and continued to guide French colonial policy for nearly 200 years, in practice it was hampered by the chronic inability of France to insure an adequate supply of slaves, food, and other necessities as the colonies grew in wealth and population. Throughout the seventeenth and eighteenth centuries, this problem was periodically accentuated by bad harvests, insufficient shipping, and wars that disrupted navigation and cut the colonies off from France. But even in times of prosperity the colonial planters could buy cod, timber, and whatever else they needed from the English, Americans, and Spanish at half what their countrymen charged for the same materials. The legislation governing the application of the *exclusif* attempted to reconcile its principles with the practical realities of West Indian life and the shifting currents of the world-economy by recognizing certain "exceptions" to the complete control of colonial commerce by France. The first significant alteration of the *exclusif* came in 1763. The loss of Canada and Louisiana in the Seven Years' War deprived the French Caribbean colonies of an important source of lumber and foodstuffs. Through a series of edicts the colonies were granted permission to import wood, cattle and other livestock, leather, fur, resin, and tar from foreign sources. These goods could be exchanged for colonial rum and syrup, which were excluded from France to keep them from competing with domestic brandy, or for goods imported to the colonies from Europe. Selected colonial ports were opened duty-free to foreign ships abiding by these conditions. Britain was also allowed to supply slaves to the French islands, although there was a special duty on them to appease the French slave traders. Britain and America were quick to take advantage of these opportunities as each nation sent sizeable fleets to the French Antilles. The pattern of commerce changed, and alongside the legal trade there grew another trade that went beyond authorized merchandise. The French merchants complained bitterly and tried to reassert their old control, but the economic pressures were too great for them to change the situation.[7]

The relaxation of the *exclusif* begun in 1763 was further augmented by the decree of August 30, 1784. This legislation, known as the mitigated exclusive (*exclusif mitigé*), increased the number of designated open ports and extended the list of merchandise that could be imported from foreign countries to include charcoal, salt beef (but not pork), codfish, salt fish, rice, maize, and beans. The greater relative freedom permitted by the mitigated exclusive stimulated the growth of colonial commerce during the last five years of the ancien régime. Nonetheless, from the point of view of the colonists even these ameliorations were less than satisfactory. Foreign trade remained encumbered with restrictions, and France was still unable to provide sufficient provisions, especially for the Windward Islands. Although on a smaller scale than before, illegal trade continued, and local exceptions to the regulations were tolerated by the colonial governors. Finally, these prohibitions were effectively abandoned between 1789 and 1815 as recurrent economic and political crises compelled local authorities to open the colonies to foreign trade virtually without restriction, simply to insure their survival. This brought the classic period of the *exclusif* to an end.[8]

In 1817, France reasserted control over the colonial trade by reinstating the decree of August 30, 1784, supplemented by the Navigation Act of September 21, 1793. This latter act encouraged the French marine by reserving navigation between France and the colonies for it and by suppressing the indirect trade. Authorized foreign goods could only be imported to the colonies by French ships or by those of the country of origin, though the latter were subject to a prohibitive duty. However, the transformation of the world-economy made the strict implementation of this legislation untenable. Its burden fell most heavily on Martinique and Guadeloupe. The colonists complained constantly about the insufficient supply of French goods, their high cost, and their poor quality. Adequate food imports were difficult to obtain, and the industrial development of these colonies was inhibited. The restrictions seemed all the more onerous with the availability of cheap British goods and increased U.S. trade with the Caribbean. The colonists demanded more freedom of trade, but the interests of the metropolitan merchants remained decisive. Commercial policy was much more liberal in the case of Bourbon because of both its isolation in the Indian Ocean and the difficulties in breaking its traditional economic ties with its sister island of Mauritius, which had been recently ceded to Britain. Chronically poor and neglected French Guiana, the other "major" colony, was open to foreign merchandise and shipping, though under conditions less favorable than those of trade with France.[9]

The commercial relations between France and its colonies underwent gradual modification throughout the decade of the 1820s. The royal ordinance of February 5, 1826, formalized the list of exceptions and the conditions of the mitigated exclusive and relieved the colonial commercial regime of some of its harsher features. Although this ordinance reaffirmed the principle that no merchandise coming from foreign countries could be imported into the colonies by either French or foreign ships under penalty of confiscation of ship and cargo, it allowed limited and controlled trade with foreign countries at designated entrepôts. Certain enumerated articles of foreign origin could be brought by either French or foreign shipping into the ports of Saint Pierre, Fort Royal, and Trinité in Martinique and Basse-Terre and Pointe-à-Pitre in Guadeloupe. Later the list of designated ports was extended to include Marin in Martinique and Moule, Grand-Bourg, and Port-Louis in Guadeloupe.[10]

This legislation sought to allow the colonies a greater measure of flexibility in securing necessary imports while still maintaining metropolitan domination of colonial production, commerce, and shipping. The authorized foreign imports were restricted to items that France could not supply easily or cheaply. These included live animals, salt beef, dried vegetables, maize, rice, codfish, salt, tobacco, lumber, charcoal, leather, fodder, and fruits. The import duties on these articles varied according to the nature of the merchandise when imported by foreign ships. If imported from France in French ships, these items were subject to a uniform and very light duty. All other goods imported from France were subject to a moderate 1 percent duty. Other foreign imports were only to be tolerated in situations of extreme emergency. While imported French or foreign merchandise could be reexported abroad duty-free under any flag from the open ports, colonial products could only be exported to France in French ships. Syrups and tafia (*eau-de-vie*) were exempted from this latter prohibition and could be sold abroad and carried in foreign ships. Colonial governors were expressly forbidden to modify the established duty rates, and despite France's chronic inability to furnish adequate grain supplies to the colonies, special measures were taken to prevent colonial governors from abusing their right to authorize special imports of American wheat in times of famine. It was feared, not without justification, that such authorizations were merely the pretext for illegal trade.[11]

This system of exclusion remained in force throughout the July Monarchy, even though it came under increasing economic and political pressure, particularly after the rise of the French beet sugar industry. The detail and means of administration of the 1826 legislation were modified in 1832, 1835, 1836, and again in 1839. The most significant changes were the introduction of foreign grain imports on a permanent basis and, in response to the crisis of 1838–39, authorization to export excess sugar abroad in times of emergency when France was unable to provide a remunerative market. All these ordinances were systematized by the law of April 29, 1845, which included a list of seventy-eight items whose importation from foreign sources was authorized. However, these items were still subject to relatively high duties, while the import duty on merchandise of French origin was abolished. When it appeared in the West Indian market, French merchandise retained its advantage. Although the export duty on colonial products shipped to France was suppressed, there was no change in the prohibition against exporting them to foreign countries or against using foreign carriers.[12]

Although the gradual modification of the *exclusif* increased the colonies' access to key foreign goods, by 1826–28 the high price of their sugar made them unattractive customers for foreign merchants. The French colonists had a more difficult time selling their sugar abroad, and instead of using sugar to pay for foreign goods, they had to use hard currency, which was increasingly rare in the colonies. The planters of Martinique and Guadeloupe had actively engaged in contraband trade with the neighboring English, Swedish, and Danish islands to obtain cheap foreign manufactures, foodstuffs, and raw materials. But by 1826–28, this clandestine trade became unprofitable and virtually ceased on a significant scale, although as late as 1842 Victor Schoelcher wrote that the West Indian colonists preferred smuggled English manufactures, even at high prices, to French ones of inferior quality. Instead, what contraband there was consisted of foreign sugar smuggled into France to take advantage of high protective duties. Neither French commerce nor the authorized foreign imports were sufficient to meet the needs of the colonies, and the irregularity and high price of imports contributed to the high cost of colonial production.[13]

This system of protection established during the Restoration provided the framework for the reorganization of colonial production and the recovery of French maritime commerce. Under its umbrella, colonial sugar production grew from almost nothing in 1814 to the 71,500 metric tons reported by the parliamentary commission of inquiry into the sugar industry in 1829 (see Table 2.1). This activity stimulated French shipping, refining, and manufacturing, and gave France needed overseas markets during a period made difficult by British commercial preeminence. In 1816, French exports to the colonies were worth only 18,600,000 francs. By 1829, they reached 50,800,000 francs. French imports from the colonies grew from 28 million to 55 million francs over the same period. The number of ships

Table 2.1. French Colonial Sugar Production, 1818–1829 (metric tons)

|      | Martinique | Guadeloupe | Guiana | Bourbon | Total |
|------|-----------|-----------|--------|---------|-------|
| 1818 | 16,068 | 21,126 | 706 | — | 37,900 |
| 1819 | 18,160 | 18,737 | 105 | — | 37,002 |
| 1820 | 21,447 | 22,300 | 526 | 4,500 | 48,773 |
| 1821 | 22,078 | 23,019 | 263 | — | 45,360 |
| 1822 | 20,173 | 23,477 | 439 | — | 44,089 |
| 1823 | 20,587 | 24,324 | 258 | — | 45,169 |
| 1824 | 20,294 | 30,645 | 444 | — | 51,383 |
| 1825 | 26,477 | 24,015 | 484 | 7,607 | 58,583 |
| 1826 | 28,425 | 34,330 | — | 10,000 | 72,755 |
| 1827 | 24,476 | 28,266 | — | — | 52,742 |
| 1828 | 33,339 | 35,812 | 574 | — | 69,725 |
| 1829 | 29,083 | 22,698 | 679 | 12,506 | 64,996 |

*Source*: Deerr, *History of Sugar*.

engaged in the colonial trade and their tonnage doubled as well. Most of this increased trade was due to colonial sugar, and it accounted for the bulk of French overseas commerce. Yet the very growth of colonial trade altered the economic and political relations between France and the colonies. The character and function of the *exclusif* itself was modified in this process. Its content was transformed, and it no longer served the purpose for which it was intended. The focal point for these changes was the French sugar market.[14]

## From *Exclusif Mitigé* to *Pacte Colonial*, 1814–1826

Between 1814 and 1826 a system of protective tariffs developed in France that virtually excluded foreign sugar from the metropolitan market and secured a predominant position for French colonial sugar. These tariffs developed within the framework of a broader system of protection promoted by the large manufacturers and above all by the great landed proprietors of France. They were justified by the deplorable condition of the French colonies and the maritime interests of France after the fall of the empire. The costs of sugar production in the French West Indian colonies were higher than elsewhere, and without protection they would have been unable to compete with foreign sugar, even in the French metropolitan market. Protection was the condition for the rapid recovery and intensive development of the French colonial sugar industry.

During the empire, sugar consumption was limited in France, and the price of sugar was high. In 1813, France, a nation of 45 million, consumed only 7,000 tons of sugar, and sugar cost six francs per livre. The public still purchased sugar from the pharmacist, not the grocer. With peace and the end of wartime shortages, French sugar consumption grew rapidly, and until the late 1820s when it was constricted by high prices, it exceeded colonial production. With the Restoration, the Bourbon government attempted to alleviate temporarily the problems caused by the shortage of sugar in the immediate postwar period, and set uniform duties on French colonial and foreign sugar. This measure allowed the British to flood the French market with sugar that had been stockpiled during the war years. The deluge of cheap foreign sugar caused serious difficulties for the French colonial sugar industry and resulted in the decline of the French beet sugar industry, which was pushed to a marginal position on the French market for nearly fifteen years. French refiners as well were unable to compete with the influx of cheap foreign sugar.[15]

This brief but intensive influx of foreign imports evoked the demand for protection from French sugar producers. Under pressure from both French agricultural and colonial interests, the government was increasingly forced to forsake its commitment to moderate tariffs, and, by means of a series of "provisional" measures, a de facto system of protection gradually evolved. In December 1814, the duties on raw sugar of foreign origin were raised, and colonial privilege was reestablished. At the same time, the duties on semirefined sugars, both colonial and foreign, were set at excessively high rates to exclude them from the market in the interests of French shippers and refiners. Further, even though French refiners were unable to meet the demand of the French market, the importation of refined sugar of whatever origin was prohibited. Encouraged by these protective duties, colonial production increased rapidly. By 1816, more than 17,600 metric tons of colonial sugar were consumed in France. However, French consumption grew even more rapidly than colonial production and had climbed to 24,600 metric tons by 1816. The difference still had to be supplied by foreign producers.[16]

These conditions led to the modification of the sugar duties in 1816. It was felt that because of growing consumption sugar could support a higher tax, and the duty on colonial raw sugar was raised. However, the principle of protection was not abandoned, and the gap between colonial and foreign sugar was widened. Foreign sugar was now taxed not only according to its quality, but also according to its place of origin. At the same time, an export bounty (*prime d'exportation*), which subsidized all reexported sugar at a fixed rate, was established to offset the duty on colonial sugar and to encourage French refining interests. In 1818, differential duties according to place of origin were applied to French colonial sugar as well. The tax on all sugar from the island of Bourbon was reduced to compensate for its distance from the market and make its product competitive with that of Martinique and Guadeloupe. The following year, the export bounty on refined sugar was increased, and it was stipulated that it should apply only to cane sugar. French beet sugar was excluded from receiving the export bounties on the grounds that it was not subject to an import duty and had no need of compensation. The bounties were not enough to offset the high duties on foreign sugar, but were much higher than the duties paid on colonial sugar. (According to Boizard and Tardieu, the protection accorded to colonial sugar had resulted in exaggerated bounties. In assuring colonial sugar a preponderant place on the metropolitan market, the legislation secured a surplus for it. For the metropolitan refiner to be able to export the sugar, he had to be compensated not only for the duty taken by the treasury but also for the surplus created by law.) Finally, in 1820, the provisions of the 1818 sugar legislation were modified. The duty on raw sugar from Bourbon was lowered once again, while that on clayed sugar of the same origin was raised. The duties on raw sugar from foreign sources in the Americas were also increased.[17]

These preferential duties, while they did not exclude foreign sugar, allowed French colonial sugar to carve out a predominant position in the metropolitan market (see table 2.2). With this encouragement, sugar production in the French colonies increased rapidly, and French consumption of colonial sugar nearly doubled between 1816 and 1817, going from 17,667 metric tons to 31,419 metric tons. Yet demand kept ahead of supply. During the same two years, total French consumption climbed from 24,590 metric tons to 36,536 metric tons of sugar. By 1820, France consumed more than 48,000 metric tons, of which the colonies supplied nearly 41,000 metric tons. Although France still needed to import foreign sugar, prices were high and remained stable with an expanding market. However, world sugar prices began to fall sharply between 1820 and 1822. In London, the price of sugar fell from 60 francs to 36 francs per 50 kilograms. The falling price of foreign sugar brought down the price of French colonial sugar despite the protective duties. In France, the average sale price of sugar fell from 90 francs to 74 francs 50 centimes in 1820, while the real sale price in the French West Indian colonies (after shipping costs and duties were deducted) fell to only 31 francs 75

Table 2.2. The French Sugar Market, 1816–1848 (metric tons)

| Year | General Commerce[a] | | Special Commerce[b] | | Estimated beet sugar production | Estimated consumption[c] |
| | Colonial | Foreign | Colonial | Foreign | | |
|---|---|---|---|---|---|---|
| 1816 | | | 17,667 | 6,913 | | 24,580 |
| 1817 | | | 31,419 | 5,118 | | 36,537 |
| 1818 | | | 29,875 | 6,145 | | 36,020 |
| 1819 | | | 34,361 | 5,401 | | 39,762 |
| 1820 | | | 40,752 | 7,865 | 50 | 48,667 |
| 1821 | | | 43,372 | 3,067 | 100 | 46,539 |
| 1822 | | | 52,034 | 3,177 | 300 | 55,511 |
| 1823 | | | 38,545 | 2,998 | 500 | 42,043 |
| 1824 | | | 56,882 | 3,149 | 800 | 60,831 |
| 1825 | | | 53,188 | 2,893 | 1,000 | 57,081 |
| 1826 | 73,266 | 9,668 | 69,316 | 2,148 | 1,500 | 72,964 |
| 1827 | 65,828 | 12,128 | 59,373 | 944 | 2,000 | 62,317 |
| 1828 | 78,475 | 8,715 | 70,923 | 680 | 2,700 | 74,303 |
| 1829 | 80,997 | 11,695 | 74,010 | 529 | 4,400 | 78,939 |
| 1830 | 78,676 | 10,602 | 68,885 | 777 | 5,500 | 75,162 |
| 1831 | 87,872 | 9,585 | 81,290 | 446 | 7,000 | 88,736 |
| 1832 | 77,308 | 3,440 | 82,248 | 347 | 9,000 | 91,595 |
| 1833 | 75,597 | 6,108 | 69,919 | 1,588 | 12,000 | 83,507 |
| 1834 | 83,049 | 12,080 | 66,475 | 4,367 | 20,000 | 90,842 |
| 1835 | 84,250 | 10,434 | 69,340 | 3,292 | 30,000 | 102,632 |
| 1836 | 79,326 | 9,462 | 66,189 | 1,013 | 40 | 107,202 |
| 1837 | 66,536 | 10,618 | 66,490 | 3,343 | 49,000 | 118,833 |
| 1838 | 86,993 | 12,390 | 68,147 | 3,309 | 49,200 | 120,656 |
| 1839 | 87,662 | 6,397 | 71,613 | 655 | 35,000 | 107,268 |
| 1840 | 75,544 | 17,355 | 78,445 | 6,666 | 28,100 | 113,211 |
| 1841 | 85,851 | 21,512 | 74,514 | 12,042 | 27,200 | 113,756 |
| 1842 | 89,484 | 17,394 | 77,443 | 8,210 | 35,100 | 120,753 |
| 1843 | 83,104 | 19,909 | 79,455 | 9,605 | 29,200 | 118,260 |
| 1844 | 89,257 | 11,829 | 87,382 | 10,269 | 32,100 | 129,751 |
| 1845 | 102,363 | 19,584 | 90,958 | 11,542 | 35,100 | 137,600 |

| Year | General Commerce[a] | | Special Commerce[b] | | Estimated beet sugar production | Estimated consumption[c] |
|------|---------|---------|---------|---------|------------|------------|
|      | Colonial | Foreign | Colonial | Foreign | | |
| 1846 | 78,575 | 27,854 | 78,632 | 15,185 | 46,800 | 140,617 |
| 1847 | 99,555 | 19,627 | 87,826 | 9,626 | 52,400 | 149,852 |
| 1848 | 63,960 | 26,433 | 48,371 | 9,540 | 48,100 | 106,011 |

Sources: Ministère de la Marine et des Colonies, *Commission formée avec l'approbation du Roi . . . pour l'examen de certaines questions de législation commerciale. Enquête sur les sucres* (Paris, 1829), p. 9; Louis Napoleon Bonaparte, *Analyse de la question des sucres* (Paris, 1843), p. 115; *Tableau décennal du Commerce de la France. 1836 à 1856*, Vol. I, pp. 60, 152; France Archives Nationales, F 12 2546 (1816 à 1830). Chambre des Députés, Séance du 21 avril 1886 (Annexes), Documents statistiques publiés par l'Administration des Douanes. Annuaire Statistique de la France (1951), p. 260, cited in Jacques Fierain, *Les raffineries du sucre des ports en France. XIXe–début du XXe siècles* (New York, 1977), pp. 116–19.

[a]General commerce includes all goods arriving from abroad, the colonies, and the fisheries without regard to their country of origin or their ultimate destination, whether it be consumption, entrepôt trade, goods in transit, or temporary admissions.

[b]Special commerce only includes goods that enter into the internal consumption of the country.

[c]Estimated consumption is the sum of special commerce and estimated beet production.


centimes as compared with 50 francs in 1818. The French colonists complained about competition from foreign countries, and from French territory in India. (Ample opportunity for contraband made it difficult to distinguish between sugar from French India and sugar from British India.) The planters' complaints resulted in increased duties on both foreign and Indian sugar. But falling prices continued to put pressure on the colonial sugar industry despite these tariffs. By 1822, the average sale price fell to 63 francs 87 centimes, which left the sale price in the colonies at only 21 francs 12 centimes—and only 18 francs according to some calculations. This was well below the planters' production costs. At the same time, French consumption reached 55,000 metric tons in 1822 and the colonial sugar industry provided 52,000 metric tons to the French market, while the consumption of foreign sugar fell from 8,000 to 3,000 tons and no longer provided much competition for colonial sugar. But these conditions still were not sufficient to maintain the position of the French colonial sugar industry. As the price of sugar continued to decline, the colonists demanded more protection.[18]

In response to the colonists, the law of July 27, 1822, further raised the duty on foreign raw sugar from the Americas and on sugars from India. With this new tariff, the price differential between colonial and foreign sugar was so great that the colonists believed themselves to be the masters of the French market. Their response to this situation was a speculative boom in sugar. They developed sugar at the expense of other crops, often extending its cultivation to marginal lands that were not well suited to it, and they borrowed heavily to undertake this expansion (see chapter 3). However, while the new import duties strengthened the position of colonial sugar producers against foreign competition in the national market, changes in the method of subsidizing sugar exports from France restricted colonial access to the reexport market. The ordinance of July 15, 1823, replaced the fixed-rate export bounties by a system of drawbacks or rebates set at rates proportional to the respective duties paid by the various grades of sugar of foreign and colonial origin. This provision aided French refiners, who could avoid the effects of the high price of sugar in France, but it provoked protests from the colonial planters who lost their advantage over foreign sugar in the reexport market. Further, the rates set by the ordinance were based on an imprecise appreciation of the refining process. A portion of the byproducts and lower-grade products of the refining process of foreign origin were thereby exempted from duties and gained access to the metropolitan market, to the detriment of colonial sugar. The ordinance also opened the door for fraud by refiners who could buy sugar with a lower duty and, on obtaining false documentation, be reimbursed at the highest rate. As a result of this ordinance, both the amount of sugar reexported and the amount paid out in drawbacks increased rapidly (see table 2.3). Foreign sugar appears to have substituted for colonial sugar in the reexport trade from 1822 to 1826, and a great deal of it entered directly into French consumption as well.[19]

The legislation of 1822 and of 1823 both made the French market very inflexible and put colonial planters in a difficult position. The cost of colonial sugar remained extremely high, and despite increased output, the colonies were unable

Table 2.3. Exports of Refined Sugar from France Receiving Bounty, 1820–1827

| Year | Quantity (kilograms) | Bounty (francs) |
|------|---------------------|-----------------|
| 1820 | 364,178 | 270,136 |
| 1821 | 1,654,741 | 1,534,479 |
| 1822 | 1,961,207 | 2,128,966 |
| 1823 | 512,501 | 687,326 |
| 1824 | 1,502,744 | 2,622,403 |
| 1825 | 3,067,157 | 4,002,746 |
| 1826 | 3,320,785 | 4,738,886 |
| 1827 | 3,789,498 | 5,487,296 |

*Source*: Ministère de la Marine et des Colonies, *Enquête sur les sucres*, p. 25.

to supply the metropolitan market. With no other source available, the effective demand for sugar in France expanded and contracted sharply as international sugar prices fluctuated between 1823 and 1826. The French sugar market alternated between years of low prices and high volume and high prices and low volume. This irregular market pattern threatened the profit margin of colonial planters when prices were low and prevented them from selling their sugar when prices were high. They needed protection in the metropolitan market, but had no other outlet when it was unable to absorb their sugar. The solution to their dilemma lay in the reexport market, where cheap foreign sugar still predominated.[20]

In 1826, the system of protection was consolidated, and colonial sugar effectively secured complete domination over foreign sugar in the French market. The colonial sugar interests succeeded in gaining recognition of the principle that it was the duty of the state not only to protect colonial sugar in the metropolitan market, but to secure its position in the reexport market. The system of drawbacks was eliminated, and uniform export bounties were established for all sugars, regardless of origin and despite the wide variation of import duties. Thus, preferential import duties widened the differential between French colonial and foreign sugars to the overwhelming advantage of the former, while the imposition of a fixed export bounty guaranteed that colonial sugar would monopolize the supply to metropolitan refiners. By 1827, foreign imports to France fell below 1,000 tons, an insignificant amount in the French market. Colonial sugar now enjoyed excessive advantages. The bounty was calculated in such a way as to not only guarantee the exporter reimbursement for the import duties, but also a bonus equivalent to the normal difference between the sale price of foreign sugar and colonial sugar. The government export subsidy allowed French sugar manufacturers to sell refined sugar in foreign markets below its real value and still realize a considerable profit. With such an advantage, no other nation could compete with French sugar in the foreign market, and the reexport trade provided an outlet for the colonial sugar that the metropolitan market could not absorb.[21]

However, the effect of the 1826 legislation was to invert the economic relation between metropolis and colonies and block the development of the French sugar trade. With the aid of the protective tariff and the virtual monopoly of the French market, the colonies exported 78,500 metric tons of sugar to France by 1828. For the first time since the beginning of the Bourbon Restoration, colonial supply was sufficient to meet metropolitan demand. But the colonies were fast approaching the limit of their productive capacity and seldom surpassed this level of production during the remainder of the slavery period. The principal sugar colonies, Martinique and Guadeloupe, had no more opportunity for physical expansion. There was still room for development in Bourbon and Guiana, but neither was able to attain the level of the two older and more established colonies. The colonies could neither lower production costs nor expand their output, while the protective tariffs maintained the price level of sugar and tried to preserve the planters' margin for profit. The growth of the French sugar market was frozen. Between 1829 and 1836, colonial production and metropolitan consumption maintained a state of equilibrium. The relation between them only varied with the size of the harvest and modifications of the export bounty, while prices remained stable at an average of 67 francs 80 centimes per 50 kilograms.[22]

The triumph of colonial preference fundamentally altered the relation of the colonial sugar industry to the *exclusif* and brought it into conflict with the interests that had fostered its development. By committing itself to a system of politically administered price supports that attempted to guarantee the level of profitability of colonial sugar, France was paradoxically confronted with the problem of simultaneous colonial overproduction and the restriction of growth of metropolitan consumption. On the one hand, the expulsion of foreign sugar was not sufficient to resolve the problems of the colonial sugar industry. The need to underwrite the high cost of colonial production required that the colonies be protected not only from foreign competition, but from their own overproduction, which was driving the price of sugar down below the cost of production. Planters complained of falling selling prices because the metropolitan market could not absorb all their sugar. The oscillations in the French market continued even after the 1826 tariff. In 1827, consumption fell by about 10,000 metric tons as the average price rose to 78 francs 50 centimes. The following year, the price fell by one franc 20 centimes, and consumption rose by 2,500 metric tons. After 1826, the alternative outlet was the highly subsidized reexport market, which might offer immediate relief, but the export bounty placed a heavy burden on the state treasury and did not resolve the problem.[23]

On the other hand, the tariff barriers and high sugar prices constrained the growth of French consumption. Only a limited portion of the population could afford sugar, and the market fluctuated greatly with even small changes in price. The government commission examining the French sugar industry in 1829 estimated that, leaving aside the duties, the colonial sugar consumed in France cost French consumers 20,219,800 francs, or 41 percent more than if it had been sold at the same market price as foreign sugar. This surcharge became a bonus of 13,000 to 14,000 francs for each colonial sugar plantation, thus subsidizing their existence despite high production costs. The metropolitan consumer was sacrificed to colonial interests. "In the existing system, it is not the colonies that belong to the nation, it is the nation that appears to be a dependency of the colonies," stated one commentator cited in the *Enquête sur les sucres*.[24]

Under these conditions, the *exclusif*, instead of providing France with a supply of cheap tropical products, became a means of guaranteeing remunerative conditions for French colonial sugar in the only market available to it. High prices and not simply juridical constraint defined the relation of colonial sugar to the French market.

Ironically, as their sugar became less and less competitive on the world market, the colonies became increasingly tied to both protective duties and sugar monoculture. In this context, as Christian Schnakenbourg has shown, the colonial planters radically reinterpreted the *exclusif* and elaborated the concept of the *pacte colonial* or colonial compact. Unlike the *exclusif*, which expressed the unilateral subordination of the colonies to the metropolis, this new doctrine emphasized the obligations of the metropolis toward the colonies. If the colonies were compelled to specialize in sugar production, then it was the duty of the metropolis to provide a market for their products. Thus, the colonists attempted to transform the *exclusif* into a defense of colonial interests. From 1826 onward, the colonists used the concept of the colonial compact to demand protection for their sugar, though at the same time they also protested the French monopoly of the colonial market, arguing that more foreign imports would help them to lower production costs. Meanwhile, in the metropolis, sugar remained expensive and the market restricted while the tariff system created difficulties for consumers, refiners, the treasury, shippers, and merchants.[25]

Opposition to the sugar legislation of 1822 and 1826 developed among metropolitan merchants and refiners. While they agreed that protective legislation was necessary for the French colonies, they felt that the existing measures were excessive and demanded the reduction of duties on foreign sugar to guarantee an adequate supply of sugar to the metropolitan refineries. The differential between the duties on colonial and foreign sugars was so great that the cost of the latter became prohibitive, and it was effectively excluded from the French market. As a result, French consumption remained stationary. The merchants and refiners hoped that a reduction of duties on foreign sugar would enable it to complement colonial sugar while allowing the latter to maintain a predominant position on the French market. Most representatives of the metropolitan sugar industry were cautious about the effects of such a reduction on domestic consumption as long as the duties on colonial sugar remained high. If, however, the duties on both foreign and colonial sugar were to be lowered, the price of sugar in France would go down, and the supply would be greater and more regular. France could buy more sugar for the same amount of money. Those who already consumed sugar would buy more, and new strata of the population would begin to buy more sugar as well. French consumption would thereby increase considerably. The spokesman of the metropolitan sugar interests hoped to continue to provide protection for colonial sugar but gradually reduce the duties over a ten- or twelve-year period. As the rate of the duties on colonial and foreign sugar were equalized, the colonies would be allowed to purchase the goods they needed from sources other than France. These measures would enable the colonists to increase the efficiency of their production and liquidate their debts. In their eyes, the amelioration of colonial production was of paramount importance and the sole justification of continued protection. They envisaged that the French colonies would eventually be able to compete with their rivals without such extensive protection.[26]

In the absence of such a major overhaul of the tariff system and colonial policy, a reduction of duties on foreign sugar that left the relative position of colonial sugar intact would not by itself transform the French sugar market, but simply make it more flexible. Nonetheless, the metropolitan merchants and refiners pressed for an immediate reduction in the duties on foreign sugar to resolve the difficulties the tariffs created for them in the reexport market and exploit a significant opportunity to expand their exports to Switzerland, southern Germany, Italy, and the Levant.[27]

The export bounty established in 1826 could provide a lucrative return to refiners under certain conditions. But when the price of colonial sugar went too high, the export bounty was not sufficient to offset the disadvantages to the refiner, and French exports of refined sugar were curtailed. Further, the supply of colonial sugar available for reexport was limited, and the high import duty made the reexportation of foreign sugar refined in France prohibitive. One merchant actively involved in trading with Havana told the sugar commission that because the tariffs precluded the possibility of finding a market for Cuban sugar in France, he shipped it directly to Antwerp and Hamburg. He estimated that it would cost him 25 to 30 percent more if he brought Cuban sugar to a French port and reexported it. The metropolitan sugar interests felt that lowering the duty on foreign sugar was a better solution to the problem than trying to compensate them by adjusting the export bounty. The bulk of the projected increase of foreign sugar imports would be destined for reexport, and merchants and refiners would be able to increase their activities in that sphere. The supply of sugar would be more stable, and the price of colonial sugar could be maintained at an acceptable level.[28]

However, for France, there were barriers to the expansion of the reexport trade within and without the national market. On the one hand, it was feared that if the demand for foreign sugar became too great, the price of colonial sugar would be driven up. It would impossible to reexport the latter profitably, and perhaps national consumption would contract as well. Any increase in the reexport of foreign sugar had to be coordinated to maintain the position of colonial sugar and the composition of the French market. On the other hand, French merchants and refiners were constrained by British predominance in world commerce. Unlike France, Britain, because it controlled such a great volume of trade, could exclude foreign sugar from its national market while still importing large amounts for reexport. British commercial and industrial superiority meant that costs were lower, profits were higher, and British reexports could undersell the French in foreign markets. Because of the higher production costs of French manufactures and agricultural goods, French merchants did not enjoy as great a margin of profit on the goods exchanged as did the British. Britain had the advantage of formal treaty relations with various Latin American countries that France lacked. British shipping was superior, and freight rates were lower. The volume, diversity, and regularity of British overseas trade meant that British ships had full cargoes on both outbound and inbound voyage, while French ships could not always be certain of a full load for the whole voyage. Consequently, French merchants often had to engage in more costly and complex trading patterns utilizing American, Dutch, and German ships. Britain could also profit from multilateral trade linkages in another way. Britain paid for Cuban and Puerto Rican sugar with Latin American currency obtained in exchange for British manufactured goods rather than with pounds sterling. The advantage provided by the exchange rate contributed to the lower cost of British sugar reexports in European markets. Because of these conditions, French merchants estimated that they were at a 10 to 12 percent disadvantage with the sugar they exported to foreign markets.[29]

The system of protective duties for colonial sugar put the metropolitan maritime and commercial interests in a contradictory position. On the one hand, it created the conditions for their recovery after 1815, but on the other hand it blocked their potential economic expansion and provoked crisis. The colonies did not provide sufficient markets for French manufactures. Merchants and shippers could buy French West Indian sugar but were unable to sell French goods. Testimony before the 1829 sugar commission complained that the balance of trade was unfavorable to the metropolis and that French goods seldom sold in the colonies at a price commensurate with their cost. French ships often went out with empty holds to return with a cargo of sugar. However, for lack of alternative outlets, the French shipping interests concentrated their efforts in the colonies, and because of the number of ships involved in the colonial trade, many were unable to get full cargoes in the colonies. These either had to return in ballast or go to the United States to try to pick up a cargo. The intense competition drove freight charges down more than 60 percent between 1821 and 1828. Until 1825, the balance-of-payments problem and shortage of money provoked monetary crises in the French maritime centers, while the tariffs of 1822 and 1826 which raised the import duties on sugar and iron aggravated their condition. These were the main items exchanged for Bordeaux wines, and Bordeaux especially suffered declining shipping, business failures, liquidations for debt, and bankruptcies between 1821 and 1826. In 1822, its exports fell by one-third and were only one-half of their 1789 level.[30]

The metropolitan merchants looked to foreign trade as the solution to their problems, and here, too, they came into conflict with protection for colonial sugar. By tying their activities to the colonial preference, the protective system prevented metropolitan merchants and shippers from expanding their activities overseas. Metropolitan merchants all agreed that if France were to buy more foreign sugar, they would be able to sell more French manufactured goods abroad, and French ships could return home with full cargoes. Because of higher production costs, France, with few exceptions, could not undersell German and, above all, British goods in foreign markets. Nonetheless, there was a market for French quality and luxury goods. Furthermore, several merchants expressed the feeling that in a few years' time the need to expand trade, the lure of new habits and practices, and the development of greater efficiency in French industry would compensate for present disadvantages. Brazil, Cuba, and Puerto Rico were all seen to be excellent potential markets, as were the independent republics of Latin America. However, the absence of a market for foreign sugar in France made it less attractive to French merchants, and because of the duty, they lost more on their sugar than they made on the sale of their other merchandise abroad. Conversely, the inability of foreign producers to sell their sugar in France limited their capacity to buy French manufactures.[31]

Antiprotectionist sentiment grew rapidly in France's maritime cities beginning in the 1820s. Spokesmen for various commercial groups saw increased trade with Latin America as the way out of commercial stagnation. Although their ability to penetrate the Latin American market, except in particular areas, was restricted to traditional and prestige merchandise, this trade did not suffer from competition with mechanized production and could be lucrative. Thus, French merchants and manufacturers wanted to lower the duties on foreign sugar and establish reciprocal trade agreements with various Latin American countries in order to expand French overseas trade. This plan was opposed by those interests most closely tied to the colonial sugar industry. They feared that the admission of cheap foreign sugar would flood the French market. Prices would fall to the detriment of refiners, shippers, and colonial planters, and result in commercial crisis.[32]

Thus, the colonial monopoly of the French sugar market inhibited the general development of French overseas commerce. It was injurious to key groups of merchants, manufacturers, and refiners and was costly to the state treasury. The *exclusif* locked metropolis and colonies into an antagonistic relation that was the inverse of that of the eighteenth century. An important body of metropolitan opinion that had previously supported colonial privilege fell away from the protective system and began to articulate its interests in terms of free trade doctrines that it was never able to sustain in practice. For their part, the colonies became increasingly dependent on the protective duties as their productive position weakened. Between 1830 and 1848, the colonial sugar industry entered a period of prolonged political and economic crisis. The July Monarchy effectively suppressed the slave trade to the colonies, passed reforms ameliorating the conditions of slave life and labor, and committed itself in principle to the abolition of slavery. Further colonial expansion, the growth of domestic consumption, and the development of French manufactures reduced the relative importance of the West Indian colonies as a market for French goods, while the very success of the colonial sugar industry in securing a monopoly of the French market from foreign producers opened the door for a new competitor—metropolitan beet sugar. The colonies, already in a precarious position, began a new struggle over protective duties, but this time the opponent was in France itself.[33]

## The Abolition of the Slave Trade

Before discussing the impact on colonial sugar producers of the evolution of the French sugar market and the rise of the beet sugar industry in France after 1826, it is necessary to examine the French policy toward the slave trade. The slave trade was seen as a key element in the reconstruction of France's colonial empire after 1814. It was regarded as an important means of rebuilding the prosperity of the French port cities and maritime commerce, as well as of providing the colonies with an adequate labor force and reanimating their production. However, the international context was unfavorable for France's attempt to restore this trade. By 1807 Denmark, the United States, and Great Britain had abolished their national slave trades, and Great Britain, in particular, sought to secure the international suppression of the trade. Britain pursued this policy aggressively and consistently, and, through a combination of diplomacy and force, attempted to impose it on its rivals. Especially important for this effort was Britain's attempt to establish by treaty the reciprocal right to inspect vessels suspected of carrying slaves by warships of the powers party to the agreement. The British argued that this was the only efficacious way of suppressing the trade. However, even without such treaties, a British squadron was active on the African coast by 1813. Suspected slave ships, whether subject to reciprocal inspection treaties or not, were searched, seized, and brought before international commissions for judgment. In violation of international maritime law, the superiority of the Royal Navy was used arbitrarily to end the slave trading activities of Britain's rivals.[34]

The campaign for the international suppression of the slave trade was caught up in the international political rivalries of the first half of the nineteenth century. Britain presented the case for the abolition of the slave trade as a moral obligation, but the response to this claim was conditioned by considerations of diplomacy and international politics and economics. Portugal, Spain, Holland, Sweden, and Brazil were economically, politically, or diplomatically dependent on Britain and agreed to reciprocal search rights. On the other hand, France, like the United States, agreed that the reciprocal right of search was the most practical means of stopping the slave trade, but regarded such an agreement as an infringement on its national sovereignty. Both nations saw Britain's proposal as a strategy to undermine their commerce and to surrender their shipping to the hands of the Royal Navy. Rather than subordinate national honor and interests, they refused to sign international treaties and instead acted within the framework of their own national laws. The development of national slave trade policies was subject to the interference of the British suppression squadron and continuous British diplomatic pressure. Within this framework, France acted slowly, ineffectively, and grudgingly to suppress its own slave trade, while consistently making concessions to British demands.[35]

The restoration of the Bourbons was greeted with enthusiasm in all of the port cities of France. In these cities, former centers of republicanism, support for the restored monarchy was not only political, but also represented hopes for economic recovery after twenty-five years of chaos. In the eyes of French merchants and shippers, the prosperity of the ports, the colonies, and the merchant marine were closely tied to the slave trade, and they counted on the support, if not the active encouragement, of the government for its revival. They were, however, wary of British support for the Bourbon Restoration and saw Britain's demand for the immediate abolition of the slave trade as a strategy that, by depriving the colonies of their indispensable labor supply, would at one stroke destroy the recovery of the colonies, the marine, and the ports. For its part, while the Bourbon Restoration government regarded the maritime bourgeoisie as an important base of support for the regime and encouraged their aspirations, it was not in a position openly to challenge British policy. In 1814, Louis XVIII promised Britain to "discourage" the slave trade. In negotiating the Treaty of Paris, Talleyrand agreed in principle to abolish it, but gained a five-year period of grace during which French ships would have a monopoly of the slave trade to the French colonies. Malouet, the Minister of the Marine and a partisan of the slave trade, intended to use this period for the intensive importation of slaves into the colonies, and shippers from Marseilles, Le Havre, and Nantes began requesting clearance for slaving expeditions to the African coast.[36]

The terms of this agreement were harshly criticized by British abolitionists and shippers alike, and Britain demanded that France take stronger measures against the slave trade. Britain wanted France to completely forbid the slave trade north of the equator and west of 25 degrees longitude (i.e., west of the Cape Verde and the Canary Islands and Madeira), to agree to the reciprocal right of search of suspected slavers by warships of the two countries, and to pass a law restricting the number of slaves imported into the French colonies to that strictly necessary for immediate needs. The French response was equivocal. It did not concede the right of inspection, nor were slave imports to the colonies restricted. As a concession, France did prohibit its slave trade north of the mouth of the Niger River. But the Ministry of the Marine, caught between the interests of the colonists and the shippers, which it tried to defend, and the requirements of foreign policy, took this step by means of administrative order rather than law, and there were no penalties or provisions for enforcement. The government itself was divided over this measure. Talleyrand demanded a more formal enactment, while Ferrand, Malouet's successor as Minister of the Marine, resisted. Amid the various conflicts and maneuvers, the government flirted with the possibility of abolishing the trade in exchange for the return of Senegal from Britain. The colonists were advised of the possibility of the future abolition of the trade while the Ministry of Marine studied the problem and formulated a complete set of laws to enforce the abolition of the traffic. But these proposals were never put into effect.[37]

The return of Napoleon from exile in Elba dramatically cut short the evolution of the first Restoration government's slave trade policy. To try to gain Britain's favor, one of Bonaparte's first acts during the Hundred Days was to decree the immediate abolition of the French slave trade. This precipitous act left French maritime and colonial interests dismayed. They presented their claims for the restoration of the trade and demanded that this act be annulled along with the rest of the legislation of the "Usurper." But Britain regarded Napoleon's decree as definitive, and Castlereagh intervened to demand that the law be maintained. Louis XVIII declared the law null and void, but was compelled to give formal assurances that the slave trade was to be prohibited in France. Finally, in August 1815, ships engaged in the slave trade were forbidden to leave French ports. The French slave trade was abolished. But this was done without public statement. There were no official ordinances or decrees. The Ministry of the Marine simply advised the directors of the ports not to authorize such sailings and to privately inform shippers that this measure was "a concession to higher interests."[38]

As a result of this action, French diplomacy was able to win a great success at the international conference on the slave trade. France, protecting its national sovereignty, refused to agree to reciprocal search rights with Britain, and British policy was attacked for being based on self-interest rather than philanthropy. Britain's demands for an international agreement to suppress the slave trade were thwarted. But, faced with continued British pressure abroad and liberal opposition to the slave trade at home, the French government was compelled to consolidate its position by giving the force of law to its policies for the abolition of the slave trade. In 1817–18, a series of laws prohibited the arrival of slaves in the French colonies, although they did not prevent the sale of slaves already in the colonies, nor were preparations for engaging in the slave trade outlawed. In addition, penalties were enacted against slave traders violating the law. These measures included (1) confiscation of the ship, (2) the removal of the captain from all command, (3) confiscation of the entire cargo, (4) making slaves the property of the state and employing them in public works. To the consternation of the maritime and colonial interests, France had officially abolished the slave trade and instituted the means to suppress it. Despite its diplomatic defeat, Britain had again gained a concession.[39]

The history of the suppression of the slave trade by France from 1818 to 1831 has been described by French historian Serge Daget as "the phase of pretense and strategy against a background of opportunism." The repression of the illegal slave trade was ineffective. The trade was officially prohibited, but the clandestine traffic continued virtually unabated. Enforcement of the new law depended on officials who by and large viewed their charge as counter to the interests of the ports, the colonies, and France itself. In the Council of Ministers, only Richelieu favored suppressing the trade. The others saw it as either a philosophical pipe dream or English Machiavellism. Portal, and his successor, the Comte de Villèle, a former colonist with family ties to Bourbon, were seen to be lenient in prosecuting slave traders if not tacitly encouraging the illicit slave trade. Such attitudes filtered down to the lower levels of the bureaucracy. The officials charged with enforcing the law in the field in large measure favored the slave trade and, according to some abolitionist accounts, were at times actively involved in it. Port authorities conformed to the letter of the law but turned a blind eye to the activities going on around them. They deplored the inadequacies of the 1818 law, but at the same time rejected legislation providing for more vigorous inspection, which, they warned, would be prejudicial to commerce. Similarly, the French squadron established on the African coast in 1818 to suppress the trade did little to stop it, taking action against French slavers only when there was no way to avoid it.[40]

The ineffectiveness of French policy and the dilatory tactics of the French government stirred British criticism. The British government demanded more active enforcement of the French law, while both official and private sources exposed French involvement in the slave trade. During the entire period of the Bourbon Restoration, the Royal Navy actively seized and prosecuted French slave traders despite Admiralty reprimands about the illegality of such action. The French fleet was driven by British pressure to take more aggressive action against French nationals to preserve national honor and respect for French law. At the same time, the abolitionist movement reemerged among the elite in France. Purged of its association with Jacobinism, the liberal opposition used it as a means of attacking the government and the Bourbon monarchy. The slave trade came under public attack by such prominent and able figures as J. B. Say and Madame de Staël. The *Société de la morale chretienne* was formed and actively fought the slave trade. The appeal for the suppression of the slave trade and the amelioration of slave conditions in the colonies was made by Benjamin Constant in the Chamber of Deputies and the Duc de Broglie in the Chamber of Peers. The actions of these committed spokesmen were given added urgency by the slave revolt in Martinique in 1822 and the suppression of appeals for civil rights for the freedmen of color there. This combination of internal and external pressure had some effect on the government. In 1823, it ordered the general mobilization of the French navy against slave ships and instituted a bounty to be paid by the colonies of 100 francs for each slave taken. Under the command of Villaret de Joyeuse and Massieu de Clairval, the French squadron undertook more active repression, although it was never mounted on the same scale as the illicit slave trade. The courts in France and the colonies followed suit, but without enthusiasm.[41]

With the accession of Charles X to the throne in 1824, Britain renewed its campaign against the clandestine French slave trade, and a law was passed in England classifying the slave trade as an act of piracy. In France, the abolitionists inaugurated a new campaign against the slave trade. These initiatives culminated in the law of April 25, 1827, which increased the penalties for those engaged in the slave trade and extended the liability to not just the ship and the captain but to all those involved either directly or indirectly, from the merchants and shippers down to the crew. This was the last major piece of legislation concerning the slave trade under the Restoration. But once again, penalties were insufficient and enforcement was inadequate. Abolition of the slave trade ran against the grain of this reactionary period. Restoration policy catered to the narrow interests of the few and beyond this was determined by political and diplomatic considerations. The government neither provided the means nor had the will to enforce its own legislation. Whether through "benign neglect" or tacit complicity, the flow of African laborers to the French sugar colonies continued without interruption.[42]

The Revolution of 1830 brought a decisive change in the attitude of the French government toward the slave trade and slavery. On the one hand, the fall of the Bourbons brought the liberal opposition, including the abolitionists, to power. On the other hand, the July Monarchy was eager for détente with Britain, and treated the suppression of the illegal slave trade not simply as a question of French colonial policy but rather as a part of its foreign policy. Humanitarianism combined with political opportunism, and in March 1831 the new regime passed still more severe legislation against the clandestine trade with stiff criminal penalties and took vigorous steps to bring it to an end. However, this action failed to satisfy the British, who continued to press for the right to inspect French vessels in search of contraband slaves. In November 1831, the first mutual search agreement was signed between the two nations, followed by an improved version in March 1833. The right to search raised a storm of protest in France, particularly among maritime and colonial interests, who attacked it as a threat to French maritime commerce and freedom of the seas. This opposition, rallying anti-British sentiment behind it, led to the failure to ratify the Treaty of London of 1841, which attempted to replace the bilateral convention between Britain and France with a multilateral treaty including Britain, France, Austria, Prussia, and Russia. However, despite the defeat of this treaty and the continuing controversy over the right to search, the measures taken by the July Monarchy signalled a dramatic shift in French policy. They effectively sealed the fate of the illegal trade, which thereafter dried up to an insignificant trickle, while the government turned its attention to the institution of slavery itself.[43]

Although a full discussion of the processes resulting in slave emancipation lies beyond the scope of this study, the slave regime of the French West Indies was the object of mounting governmental and popular pressure throughout the period from 1830 to 1848. The July Monarchy not only abolished the slave trade but prepared the way for general emancipation as well. Influenced by the abolition of slavery in the British colonies, the government of Louis-Philippe favored the emancipation of the slaves in the French colonies but was undecided about how such a change should be carried out. While the government supported abolition in principle, it was concerned to find a means of accomplishing that end that would preserve public order, maintain economic stability, and prepare the slaves for freedom. Thus, the debate over the modalities and conditions of emancipation raged for the duration of the regime and was the principal battleground of proslavery and antislavery forces in the legislative chambers. In anticipation of the eventual abolition of slavery, the government passed several laws ameliorating the conditions of slave life. In 1832, the tax on manumissions was abolished, and the procedures were simplified. The next year, the branding and mutilation of slaves was declared illegal and a census of the slave population was made obligatory. Also in 1833, full civil rights were granted to free men of color, and, in 1836, the old custom was revived whereby slaves became free on arrival in metropolitan France. These measures were symptomatic of the growth of antislavery sentiment in France and the shifting political conditions of slavery in its West Indian colonies during the July Monarchy.[44]

The abolition movement was also growing in numbers and gaining influence during this period. In 1834 the *Société pour l'abolition de l'esclavage* was founded in Paris. The Duc de Broglie was its president, and Odilon Barrot and the economist Hyppolite Passy were its vice presidents. Its members included many politically and intellectually prominent figures, among whom were Alphonse de Lamartine and Alexis de Tocqueville. The society's purpose was to publicize the lot of the slaves and to study the best means for abolishing slavery. Although the members of the society tended to favor the gradual abolition of slavery, there was no general agreement among them on what measures were necessary to bring about emancipation. In the Chamber of Deputies in 1836 and again in 1837, Isambart, de Tracy, and Lamartine, all members of the society, demanded that the government present a proposal for the immediate abolition of slavery. On each occasion the colonial spokesmen, led by Maugin and Charles Dupin, successfully countered the challenge by arguing that the questions involved great difficulties that required caution and full discussion before action could be taken. The issue of emancipation received more serious consideration after 1838 when Passy proposed that all children born of slave mothers after that date be declared free and all slaves should have the right to buy their freedom at prices fixed by the metropolitan government. The debates over this proposal demonstrated that a majority of the deputies were sympathetic toward abolition. But the plan itself aroused the opposition not only of the colonialists but of abolitionists such as Lamartine who felt that partial and progressive abolition could well inspire insubordination and perhaps even revolt on the part of the slaves. He felt that if conflict and agitation between masters and slaves were to be avoided and property in the colonies preserved, total emancipation would have to be realized in a single step, the colonists indemnified, and steps taken to guarantee the labor force necessary for the plantations. Passy's proposal was unsuccessful, and another proposal for gradual emancipation over ten years by de Tocqueville and de Tracy was not even considered by the chamber.[45]

In 1840, the government moved a step closer to abolition by attempting to ameliorate various aspects of slave life. Ordinances were enacted to provide at least rudimentary religious and elementary education for the slaves, to promote marriages among the slaves, and to regulate slave discipline. The following year, the post of Magistrat de Parquet was established in the colonies. These magistrates were charged with protecting the slaves and were directed to inspect the plantations periodically to be sure that all regulations regarding the slaves were enforced. The practical consequences of these measures were extremely limited, both because they failed to challenge the legal authority of the slave owners directly and because of the intransigent opposition of the colonists to them. In the same year, a commission headed by the Duc de Broglie was appointed to study the question of emancipation and the economic and administrative reforms that would have to accompany it. After three years of work the commission advanced two proposals for abolition; one called for general and simultaneous emancipation after ten years with indemnity for the proprietors, the other for partial and progressive emancipation. This inconclusive report reflected the dissension and timidity that prevailed among the members of the commission and satisfied no one.[46]

During this period, the leadership of the antislavery movement passed into the hands of Victor Schoelcher. Schoelcher had begun as an advocate of gradual emancipation, but after wide travels in the French Antilles, Cuba, the United States, Mexico, and Senegal he became an intransigent and uncompromising champion of the cause of the slaves and dedicated his immense energy and skill as a propagandist and political leader to the immediate and general abolition of slavery in the French colonies. Antislavery propaganda increased, and popular agitation against slavery grew. In 1844, the workers of Paris sent three petitions with more than 3,000 signatures to the Chamber of Deputies demanding immediate emancipation. In 1847, the de Broglie Commission received a petition with 11,000 signatures including 3 bishops, 19 vicars general, 858 priests, 86 presidents of consistories and pastors of the reformed church, 7 members of the Institute, 151 elected councilors, 213 magistrates and members of the bar, and more than 9,000 electors, businessmen, proprietors, and workers, which decried transitory and preparatory measures and demanded emancipation without delay.

Despite this growing pressure for immediate emancipation, the government committed itself to a policy of partial and progressive abolition. As a step in this direction a law was passed in 1845 under the direction of Baron de Mackau, the Minister of the Marine and Colonies and former governor of Martinique. It provided for compulsory manumission and it limited corporal punishment, recognized the legal personality of the slave, and made elementary and religious education mandatory for the slaves. This law was supplemented by ordinances that regulated the discipline of the slaves, their diet, and their moral and religious status, and limited the duration of the working day. The content of these measures was limited and inadequate, and they had few practical consequences for the slaves. At best, they simply gave legal sanction to existing practices; at worst, they were illusory. These changes were not simply and crudely a response to the abolition of the slave trade and lack of supply of slaves, but also represent an attempt to eliminate the worst abuses of the slave system, regulate punishment, and find more rational and efficacious means of enforcing discipline. Yet if some of the more brutal aspects of the slave regime were legally removed, it remained a harsh system. Delays in enacting the legislation, legal ambiguity, the intransigent resistance of local whites, including the Colonial Councils and the colonial judiciary, and inadequate enforcement prevented them from having much effect in the colonies. Nevertheless, debate over the passage of these measures became an indicator of the strength of antislavery sentiment in both the legislature and public opinion. The abolitionists, instead of accepting the Mackau Law as a step forward in an orderly and gradual march toward emancipation, stressed its inadequacies and increased their agitation for immediate abolition after its passage. For their part, the colonists became aware for the first time that general emancipation was imminent.[47]

The debates on emancipation in the legislative chambers during the July Monarchy revealed that a majority of members, even including some colonial slaveholders, favored abolition, while public opinion in France was increasingly hostile to slavery. But emancipation was not achieved under the July Monarchy. The government, feeling that the support of the planters was necessary to make any plan work, equivocated over the means to bring it about. The government's uncertainty was exploited by the adversaries of the abolition movement, who only rarely defended slavery as an institution and instead emphasized the difficulties involved in emancipation and the need for careful preparation. They stressed both the amelioration of slave conditions that had already taken place in the colonies and the difficulties in guaranteeing a free labor force after emancipation, without which there would be economic ruin for black and white alike. (Until such a transition could be secured, it was, of course, essential that reforms not be allowed to undermine the necessary authority of the master.) The proslavery forces skilfully used the press and the tribune to plead their case and shrewdly tied slavery to a number of economic and political issues to forge alliances with other groups. These tactics allowed them to effectively blunt the abolitionist offensive. The impasse between these forces was broken by revolution. Only with the fall of the July Monarchy in 1848 was the institution of slavery abolished in the French colonies.[48]

## Beet Sugar Versus Cane Sugar, 1826–1848

The nascent French beet sugar industry, which had flourished briefly with the encouragement and protection of the Napoleonic state, all but disappeared as a significant factor in the economic life of the nation after 1814. Deprived of state protection, beet sugar producers had to confront the massive influx into France of cheap foreign and colonial sugar. Sugar prices dropped drastically, and the beet sugar industry virtually disappeared from the French market. The number of beet sugar refineries fell from 334 producing 7,700 metric tons in 1813 to 100 producing 2,000 metric tons in 1825. The gradual restoration of protective tariffs aided the recovery of the beet sugar industry by reducing the amount of foreign sugar on the French market and raising the price of colonial sugar while the beet sugar industry remained exempt from all duties. But recovery was a long and difficult process, and the surviving factories were compelled to develop more efficient means of producing to compete with more abundant and cheaper cane sugar.[49]

The resurgence of the beet sugar industry in France received a great impetus from the 1826 tariff, which virtually eliminated foreign sugar imports from the French market, placed a duty on colonial sugar, and kept sugar prices high. Further, the high bounty given to encourage the exportation of refined colonial sugar between 1826 and 1833 gave the metropolitan beet sugar producers a larger share of the national market. Although designed to offset the import duty on colonial sugar, the export bounty on refined sugar proved to be of even greater benefit to metropolitan producers. Unlike colonial planters, who were subject to heavy duties if they produced refined sugar, metropolitan beet sugar producers were able to produce refined sugar without restriction, and the export bounty allowed them to dump it on the foreign market even below the costs of production.[50]

Sheltered by the high tariff barriers, yet exempt from paying any duties itself, the beet sugar industry developed rapidly. In 1827 only 2,700 metric tons of beet sugar were produced, but by 1828, its influence began to be felt. In the latter year, fifty-eight beet sugar factories were in operation and thirty-one were under construction. Output per factory increased, and sugar beets were cultivated on 3,130 hectares. Production rose to over 4,000 metric tons. To the close observer, the potential for the development of the beet sugar industry seemed almost unlimited. In 1828, Crespel-Delisse, a pioneer of the beet sugar industry who played a key role in its survival after the Napoleonic Wars, predicted that in ten years' time the French beet sugar industry would be able to produce 57,000 metric tons of sugar at an average price of 45 francs per 50 kilograms. Metropolitan producers would then be able to withstand the competition of colonial sugar and supply all the needs of France. His prediction was not far from the mark. With its position on the home market assured and its exports subsidized, beet sugar production in France rose spectacularly in the ten years after 1828. Production went from 7,000 metric tons in 1830 to 20,000 metric tons in 1833 and doubled to 40,000 metric tons in 1835. By 1836, 361 factories were in operation, and 105 more under construction in thirty-six departments of France. Sugar beet cultivation covered 16,700 hectares, and production had risen to 45,000 metric tons. The following year, there were 543 factories in operation and 39 more under construction. Production approached 50,000 metric tons, and the beet sugar industry supplied one-third of French domestic consumption. The prediction of Crespel-Delisse had been realized. In ten years' time the beet sugar industry in France had undergone a remarkable development, and the colonists were faced with a fundamental challenge.[51]

Colonial producers were at a serious disadvantage in the face of the potential of their rival. The development of the beet sugar industry was concentrated in the departments of the Nord, Pas-de-Calais, Somme, and Aisne, where, in 1836, there were 261 factories producing 20,333 metric tons of sugar. These were some of the most advanced agricultural regions of France. Wages were low, and there was a stable labor force accustomed to an industrial work routine. Land was available for expansion, fuel was plentiful and cheap, and the region was linked to markets by a network of rivers, roads, canals, and railroads that was being improved each year. Behind its dramatic advance was the power of modern science and technology as well as large-scale capital investment. Efficient and scientific production methods offset the natural superiority of sugar cane, which had nearly twice the sucrose content of the sugar beet. Production techniques were constantly improved, the average output per factory increased, and the costs of production fell steadily.[52]

In contrast to the rapid and steady expansion of beet sugar, colonial sugar production fluctuated between about 70,000 and 80,000 metric tons for most of the period after 1826. The colonies were plagued by limited land resources, soil exhaustion, outmoded refining technology, shortage of credit, commercial disruption and decline, and an uncertain labor force. The restriction on producing anything but unrefined sugar retarded the incentives for technological innovation in the colonies. The sugar colonies were far from markets, and high charges for long-distance transport, made even more costly by the French monopoly of all shipping, raised the cost of the final product. Unlike his metropolitan competitor, the French West Indian planter had to bear the expense of import duties, insurance, the deterioration of unrefined sugar during shipment, and the charges of commercial middlemen, even before his product got to market. The French colonial sugar industry was thus in an unprecedented situation. During the first half of the nineteenth century, beet sugar never accounted for more than 10 percent of world production and was usually a good deal less. Yet by an ironic quirk of historical development, French colonial producers found themselves in a head-to-head struggle with an increasingly dynamic and formidable opponent for their own metropolitan market, the only market available to them.[53]

The rapid rise of the French beet sugar industry during the two decades between 1827 and 1847 undermined colonial domination of the metropolitan market and was in large measure responsible for declining sugar prices beginning in the 1830s (see table 2.4). Yet the colonies were initially rather indifferent toward their metropolitan competitor. The rapid recovery of the colonial sugar industry and the growth of French consumption, along with the general prosperity between 1815 and 1830, tended to obscure the gravity of the potential threat to the colonies. While the technical possibilities for the expansion of the beet sugar industry in France seemed almost unlimited, its position was precarious, at least until the early 1830s. The level of beet sugar production was relatively low in comparison with cane sugar, and beet sugar producers allied with the colonists in demanding protection from foreign sugar. Like their colonial rivals, protective duties were the condition of their advance. However, the development of the beet sugar industry could only upset the uneasy equilibrium between production, consumption, and price established for colonial sugar by the tariff system. Charles Forbin Janson, the owner of the largest beet sugar factory in Europe as well as the largest refinery in Marseille, and thereby a man linked to both the beet and cane sugar industries, observed that the rapid advance of beet sugar would not only increase sugar production beyond the current level of French consumption, but would also augment the amount of sugar exported. The price levels could not be maintained. As

Table 2.4. Colonial and Metropolitan Beet Sugar Prices, 1820–1848
(average price per 100 kilograms in Paris in francs)

| | Colonial sugar | | | Beet sugar[a] | | |
|---|---|---|---|---|---|---|
| Year | Nominal price | Real price[b] | Real cost at entrepôt | Nominal price | Real price[b] | Real cost price for manufacturer[c] |
| 1820 | 162.41 | 146.58 | 88.6 | | | |
| 1821 | 151.65 | 136.87 | 84.37 | | | |
| 1822 | 139.19 | 125.61 | 73.11 | | | |
| 1823 | 187.15 | 168.91 | 116.41 | | | |
| 1824 | 159.64 | 144.11 | 91.61 | | | |
| 1825 | 181.7 | 164 | 111.5 | | | |
| 1826 | 161.32 | 145.59 | 93.09 | | | |
| 1827 | 172.13 | 155.35 | 102.85 | | | |
| 1828 | 168.5 | 152.07 | 99.57 | | | |
| 1829 | 159.54 | 144.01 | 91.51 | | | |
| 1830 | 155.03 | 139.9 | 87.4 | 147.7 | 133.32 | 130.32 |
| 1831 | 142.6 | 128.72 | 76.22 | 132.08 | 119.2 | 116.2 |
| 1832 | 149.1 | 134.57 | 82.07 | 132.22 | 119.35 | 116.35 |
| 1833 | 144.97 | 130.89 | 78.39 | 142 | 128.22 | 125.22 |
| 1834 | 144.97 | 130.89 | 78.39 | 138.2 | 124.72 | 121.72 |
| 1835 | 139.01 | 125.49 | 72.99 | 128.2 | 115.73 | 112.73 |
| 1836 | 141.7 | 129.82 | 77.32 | 130.74 | 118.01 | 115.01 |
| 1837 | 130.8 | 118.09 | 65.59 | | | |
| 1838 | 126.25 | 113.97 | 61.47 | 121.75 | 109.93 | 101.93 |
| 1839 | 119 | 107.18 | 61.28 | 120.25 | 109.53 | 93.28 |
| 1840 | 138.75 | 125.27 | 79.37 | 141.25 | 127.47 | 102.97 |
| 1841 | 129.75 | 117.13 | 64.63 | 130.25 | 116.48 | 86.48 |
| 1842 | 124.75 | 112.63 | 60.13 | 124.25 | 112.23 | 82.03 |
| 1843 | 122.75 | 110.03 | 57.53 | 123 | 111.08 | 81.08 |
| 1844 | 124.25 | 112.13 | 59.63 | 130 | 118.18 | 85.43 |
| 1845 | 128.5 | 115.98 | 63.48 | 131.75 | 118.92 | 80.67 |
| 1846 | 129.25 | 115.68 | 63.18 | 130.5 | 117.82 | 74.07 |
| 1847 | 124.8 | 112.68 | 60.18 | 120.75 | 109.03 | 60.78 |
| 1848 | 116.3 | 104.98 | 52.48 | 112.25 | 101.33 | 49.33 |

*Source*: Augustin Cochin, *L'Abolition de l'esclavage* (Paris, 1861), I, 476–77.

[a] The price of beet sugar only began to be quoted at the Bourse in 1830.

[b] Real price is calculated by deducting depreciation and interest charges from the nominal price.

[c] The real cost price is calculated by deducting the average duty and transportation costs from the nominal price.

the beet sugar industry progressed, a confrontation over the tariff system and the structure of the French sugar market appeared inevitable. The beet sugar industry could not continue without paying duties, and although the attempt failed, as early as 1828 the treasury saw beet sugar as a valuable source of revenue and wanted to tax it. For their part, once they felt threatened, the colonies responded with cries of distress and claimed protection from the state. By 1836, metropolitan and colonial sugar producers were engaged in a serious conflict that exerted continuous pressure on the colonial sugar industry.[54]

Yet even before French beet sugar production developed sufficiently to threaten the colonial sugar industry, fiscal reform of the tariff system deprived the colonies of their hold on the French reexport market and made them even more vulnerable. The law of April 26, 1833, was a temporary measure intended to redress several of the most pressing problems arising from the bounties for the reexport of refined sugar established in 1826 without yet directly confronting the problem of beet sugar. These bounties were costly for the treasury and alarmed government officials. The rapid growth in state subsidies was not offset by the proportional growth of revenues from imports (see table 2.5). The net revenue of the treasury progressively diminished, and some critics claimed that the treasury itself was threatened. In the face of growing criticism, the fixed export bounty was once again replaced by the drawback in 1833. In presenting the project for the law, Humann, the Minister of Finance, declared that beyond assuring the colonial producers their monopoly over the French market, the state owed them nothing. The drawback should simply offset the import duty. For the first time, colonial sugar was placed on an equal footing with foreign sugar for exportation after refining. Further, in accordance with the demands of the metropolitan refiners, the import duties on foreign sugar were lowered while the duty on one of the higher grades of colonial sugar, *brut blanc*, was raised. Although these measures were supported by metropolitan refiners, merchants, and shippers, over the long run they could only deepen the crisis of colonial sugar. While the return to the drawback was initially successful in reducing payments by the treasury, it totally disrupted the reexport market. In 1834, the first full year the law was in operation, the treasury paid

Table 2.5. Import Duty Collected and Export Bounty Paid on Sugar, 1817–1836

| Year | Import duty collected (francs) | Export bounty paid (francs) | Net for treasury (francs) |
|------|-------------------------------|----------------------------|---------------------------|
| 1817 | 22,726,734 | 57,588 | 22,669,146 |
| 1818 | 21,491,775 | 74,700 | 21,417,075 |
| 1819 | 22,133,540 | 96,392 | 22,037,154 |
| 1820 | 27,513,904 | 512,745 | 27,001,159 |
| 1821 | 23,869,977 | 1,985,023 | 21,884,954 |
| 1822 | 28,899,356 | 2,627,371 | 26,271,985 |
| 1823 | 22,901,776 | 956,813 | 21,944,963 |
| 1824 | 32,256,512 | 3,012,704 | 29,245,808 |
| 1825 | 29,592,228 | 4,571,317 | 25,020,911 |
| 1826 | 36,545,055 | 5,271,611 | 31,273,444 |
| 1827 | 30,160,116 | 6,123,657 | 24,036,453 |
| 1828 | 35,090,120 | 6,315,502 | 28,774,618 |
| 1829 | 36,354,744 | 8,696,755 | 27,565,989 |
| 1830 | 33,535,174 | 10,889,667 | 22,645,507 |
| 1831 | 39,264,743 | 12,133,255 | 27,131,488 |
| 1832 | 39,596,177 | 19,110,557 | 20,485,620 |
| 1833 | 34,538,667 | 12,907,115 | 21,631,552 |
| 1834 | 35,620,503 | 3,890,753 | 31,729,750 |
| 1835 | 35,974,248 | 4,978,500 | 30,995,748 |
| 1836 | 32,321,642 | 5,706,931 | 26,614,711 |

Source: Chambre des Députés, *Session 1837. Rapport fait au nom de la Commission chargée d'examiner le projet de loi sur les sucres par M. Dumon*, Séance de 8 mai 1837 (no. 200), Tableau H.

only 3,890,753 francs via the drawback. However, exports of refined sugar from France dropped to a mere 2,745 metric tons, compared to 16,878 metric tons in 1832. This was a serious blow to the colonies, which after 1826 produced between 3,500 and 4,000 metric tons of sugar above French consumption annually. To cut off the export bounty and substitute the drawback was to deprive this high-priced colonial sugar of access to foreign markets, even as the amount of foreign sugar reexported by France increased.[55]

With their position on the reexport market weakened, the colonies now faced a serious challenge in the metropolis as well. In 1836, the confrontation between colonial cane sugar and metropolitan beet sugar broke into the open. By that year, beet sugar was no longer limited to a marginal position in the French market, but competed directly with colonial sugar and restricted the market for the latter product. Consequently, the colonies could only place 57,000 out of a total of 80,000 metric tons of sugar in France. The only outlet for the remainder was the reexport market. This crisis touched off the biggest battle over tariff policy in nineteenth-century France and generated an enormous number of pamphlets and tracts. The terrain of this struggle remained within the parameters of the protective system. Despite its promise for the future, the beet sugar industry was as dependent on the tariff system as the cane sugar industry. It still needed the protection offered by the duty on colonial sugar, and a tax on beet sugar would threaten its yet-fragile foundation. The two industries represented quite distinct possibilities and conditions for sugar production and economic development. Further, political, fiscal, and strategic considerations influenced the course of legislation. Beet and cane sugar engaged in a struggle as much political as economic over protective duties and tariffs that touched on the very nature of sugar production, the colonial system, slavery, and the course of French economic development.[56]

Even though the development of the beet sugar industry in France had not yet progressed to the point of threatening colonial sugar production, the government had unsuccessfully attempted to tax beet sugar production for fiscal reasons in 1829, 1832, 1834, and 1835. The government wanted to impose the tax to secure an additional source of revenue. It was estimated that the treasury would gain 17 million francs annually if beet sugar were taxed. The government felt that this could be done without threatening the gains beet sugar had made or the progress that was possible for it within the existing structure of the market. However, when metropolitan beet sugar began to displace colonial cane sugar from the French market in 1836, the entire situation was transformed. Government revenues fell when beet sugar, which paid no duties, was substituted for foreign and colonial sugar, which did. In 1836, the net income to the treasury from customs duties on sugar dropped from 31 to 26 million francs. But this was not simply a problem of state revenues. Rather, it was a question of precluding the dislocation of the colonial sugar industry and preventing the colonists from losing the only outlet for their product. In 1832 and 1835, the colonists had supported the government's attempts to tax beet sugar. By 1836, the question assumed greater urgency. Beet sugar upset the fragile equilibrium of the metropolitan market. By implication, the colonial system itself was threatened. If France could not supply a sufficient market for colonial sugar, the colonies would have to be granted the freedom to buy and sell elsewhere. Not only was colonial production threatened, but there would be losses for French shipping and for the merchants of the port cities who were creditors of the colonies. The strategic and military value of the colonies to France might also be jeopardized.[57]

In January 1837, the first of a series of measures designed to address the problems created by the rise of the beet sugar industry was proposed to the legislature. The legislative history of these measures is rather complex and included two ministerial changes. The debates turned on whether the best solution was to reduce the tax on colonial sugar, to tax beet sugar, or some combination of the two. The way in which the tax on beet sugar was to be assessed was also an important issue and was used by the beet sugar forces to forestall imposing a tax on their production. After a variety of proposals and studies and much debate, a law taxing beet sugar was passed by a small majority on July 18, 1837. The measure was a concession to the colonies and to the fiscal interests of the state. A tax was imposed on beet sugar of 10 francs per 100 kilograms for 1838–39 and 15 francs thereafter.[58]

The tax levied on beet sugar was not sufficient to stop its progress. In 1837–38, beet sugar production reached 50,000 metric tons. The producers rushed to sell it before the new tax went into effect on July 1, 1838. By chance, the 1838 colonial harvest reached 87,000 metric tons, the largest ever, and 20,000 tons more than the previous year. The market was glutted, and sugar prices fell sharply. *Bonne quatrième*, the standard grade of sugar in relation to which the price of all other grades was calculated, sold for 65 francs per 50 kilograms at the beginning of 1837. At the beginning of 1837 it fell to 61 francs; in 1838, to nearly 52 francs.

In the colonies, the selling price of sugar fell from 30 francs in 1836 to 20 francs in 1839. In the latter year, prices fell so low in the colonies that the governors of Martinique and Guadeloupe authorized the export of sugar to foreign countries and opened their ports to ships of all nations. There were shortages of everything, and barrels of sugar piled up in warehouses and on the wharves without buyers until foreign ships appeared in the harbors. Fortunately for the colonists, this move coincided with an exceptional period of short supply and high prices in other producing areas, and French West Indian sugar found access to other markets. Local prices rose briefly until the government in France moved quickly to abrogate the colonial decrees and reestablish the metropolitan monopoly of buying and selling in the colonies. The government attempted to alleviate the situation of the colonies by the ordinance of August 31, 1839, which reduced the duty on colonial sugar. However, this measure was regarded as only temporary and merely postponed a more fundamental discussion over the relation between metropolitan beet and colonial cane sugar.[59]

The crisis of 1838–39 revealed the fragility of the position of the colonies and heightened the antagonism between the two sugar industries. The colonists saw the beet sugar industry as a parasite dependent on excessive protection whose production, if unchecked, would lead to the ruin of the colonies. The colonial planters demanded that both sugar industries be subject to the same duties. For their part, the beet sugar producers stressed the salutary effects of their industry on French agriculture and rural life. Their demand was that the colonies be set free from the *pacte colonial* and be allowed to trade elsewhere. These slogans masked the depths of the struggle. The colonies would not have been able to survive their "freedom," nor could beet sugar producers endure equal duties. Each was, in fact, calling for the destruction of the other. The issue went beyond sugar and touched important commercial, political, and military considerations. If the *pacte colonial* were to be dissolved, the French merchant marine would not be able to compete with foreign carriers. The failure of the merchant marine would in turn weaken the navy. Thus, the colonial sugar industry drew support for political and military as well as economic motives. Opposition to the beet sugar industry crystallized around colonial planters, and metropolitan refiners, merchants, and shippers who held it responsible for the crisis and viewed it as a threat to the maritime and colonial interests of France.[60]

Though generally blamed for causing the crisis of 1838–39, the beet sugar industry did not escape its consequences unscathed. In 1837–38, forty-eight beet sugar manufacturers, seeing that they would not be able to withstand the new tax, closed their doors. In 1838–39, the reduction of the duty on colonial sugar coincided with the planned increment in the tax on beet sugar. The resultant fall in prices and increase in costs caused numerous failures among beet sugar producers. Of 547 factories, only 418 were able to withstand the shock. Production was wiped out in twelve departments, and the total output of the industry fell to about 22,000 metric tons. The failures were most common in the departments where agricultural conditions were least favorable to beet sugar cultivation and among small producers. (Paradoxically, Mathieu de Dombasle, one of the pioneers of scientific sugar production, urged the promotion of precisely these sectors of the beet sugar industry because of their positive effect on agriculture and employment.) The cause of this sharp decline was not simply the increase of the tax and the reduction of the duty on colonial sugar, but the excessive protection enjoyed by beet sugar, which encouraged the establishment of marginal producers. These were able to develop under the shelter of the tariff, but over the long run could not have survived the competition of the larger, more efficient beet sugar producers of the north, who not only shared the protection but had a real advantage in production. The crisis resulted in the concentration of beet sugar both at the level of the firm and regionally. Despite the possible long-term benefits of such concentration, the condition of the industry in 1839 discouraged beet sugar producers. Aside from the losses they had already suffered, they were faced with the prospect of competition with colonial and foreign sugar that was subject to reduced duties. Not even the strongest of them would be able to survive such conditions. The only solution that appeared to be open to them was to try at least to protect their personal interests as much as possible. Therefore they took the radical step of demanding the liquidation of their industry with an indemnity.[61]

At the same time that they prepared to face the possible dissolution of their industry, the propagandists for beet sugar launched a vigorous assault on their rival. They emphasized the capacity of the metropolitan sugar producers to improve their technology and the importance of the beet sugar industry in modernizing French agriculture and stimulating economic development. The beet sugar industry, they claimed, employed more workers, paid higher taxes, encouraged more subsidiary industries, and utilized more capital than its colonial rival. In 1839, Lestiboudois, a spokesman for the beet sugar interests, asserted that in a single arrondissement in Lille or Valenciennes, "there would be more people affected by the ruin of sugar production than there are whites in our four sugar colonies." The publicists for indigenous sugar charged that the colonies had reached the height of their prosperity and could only decline. They argued that the government had to pay for the maintenance of the colonies and that colonial sugar production was backward and incapable of innovation. In their view, debt, soil exhaustion, and competition inhibited colonial production. The abolition of the slave trade, manumissions, amelioration of slave conditions, and desertion reduced the colonial work force. General emancipation was inevitable, and free laborers would never work in the tropical cane fields. The colonies would be faced with ruin. The two rival interests, Lestiboudois concluded, would have to be reconciled, but the beet sugar industry brought greater prosperity to the metropolis, and its interests ought to be favored over those of the colonies. The beet sugar industry thus presented a clear set of alternatives. Its development was in the best interests of the nation, but if the government could not or would not guarantee the conditions of its survival, it merited an indemnity.[62]

The claims of the beet sugar propagandists were often exaggerated. Lestiboudois, for example, systematically maximized the importance of the beet sugar industry and the number of people dependent on it while minimizing the influence of colonial sugar. Yet their arguments had an undeniable force behind them. In comparison, the counterarguments of the colonies—the duty of France to fulfill its obligations under the *pacte colonial*; the importance of colonial taxes for the treasury; the importance of the colonies as markets for metropolitan manufactures and agriculture; and their role in stimulating commerce, the merchant marine, and indirectly French naval power—seem weak, timeworn, and vitiated by self-interest and special pleading.[63]

The government's response to the situation was to try to balance the interests of the two sugar industries by establishing conditions of equal taxation. After 1839, prices rose to the benefit of the colonial and maritime interests, and treasury revenue from sugar duties fell. The government's fear was that the high prices would stimulate the beet sugar industry and result in another drop in prices that would damage the benefits the colonies had gained from the reduction in duties. To avoid a new crisis, it proposed that the tax on colonial sugar be restored to what it had been before 1839 and that an equal tax be levied on beet sugar. An indemnity of 40 million francs was to be set aside to compensate those beet sugar manufacturers already in operation who would fail as a result of the proposed law. In addition, a change in the calculation of the drawback was proposed to encourage exports. This proposal was attacked by the beet sugar interests in a special commission named by the Chamber of Deputies. Bugeaud argued forcefully that the equalization of duties meant the effective destruction of the beet sugar industry. The abolition of that industry was a more just solution. After a long, intense, and many-sided debate, the commission rejected the demand for the liquidation of the beet sugar industry and decided that the two industries could coexist not on the basis of absolute equality, but of relative equality. Equal conditions were to be established on the basis of the production costs of each industry.[64]

This solution was far from ideal. The production cost was impossible to calculate, and every advance in one or the other industry disrupted the equilibrium. Nonetheless, although it was not seen as a definitive measure, the law of July 3, 1840, was an attempt to redress, at least temporarily, the balance between the two sugar producers. The old tariff of 1816 was reestablished for colonial sugar at the rate of 45 francs per 100 kilograms, and the method of calculating the drawback was modified to encourage exports. Beet sugar was taxed on a sliding scale from 25 francs to 36 francs 10 centimes per 100 kilograms, depending on its quality. Despite the increased sugar duties, the 1840 law improved the relative position of metropolitan beet sugar. The duty on colonial cane sugar increased by 13 francs 20 centimes over the tariff of 1837, while that on beet sugar went up only by 11 francs 20 centimes. Beyond the differential in its favor on the duty, every attempt to establish conditions of equality between the two sugars was upset by the constant amelioration of beet sugar production.[65]

The law of 1840 created the conditions for another crisis in the sugar industry. The concentration and expansion of beet sugar production continued as a result of the 1840 legislation, and the malaise of the colonial sugar industry deepened. In 1840–41, the number of beet sugar factories fell from 418 to 388, but output rose from 23,000 to 27,000 metric tons. Officially, the 1842–43 beet sugar harvest was 31,000 metric tons, but Boizard and Tardieu estimate that because of fraud and attempts to evade taxation it was really 50,000 tons. In that same year, the colonies sent 80,000 tons to the French market. In addition, encouraged by the reduction of the surtax and change in the calculation of the drawback, foreign sugar imports rose from 6,200 metric tons in 1840 to 12,000 metric tons in 1842. Meanwhile, French consumption remained between 115,000 and 120,000 metric tons. Sugar stocks grew in entrepôt, and, aside from a brief rise in early 1840, prices fell steadily. The market was glutted, and pressure continued to mount on colonial producers. West Indian planters charged that sugar selling for 56 francs per 50 kilograms left them with only 17 francs while their production costs were 17 francs 50 centimes. By 1842, the price of *bonne quatrième* at Le Havre dropped to 52 francs. After deducting transportation costs and various local and commercial charges, only 31 francs remained to be divided between the treasury and the planter. The duty accounted for 25 francs, leaving the planter with six francs. The situation was ruinous for the colonies. The protected market that was necessary to sustain the less efficient production of the West Indian slave plantation could no longer be maintained against the superior productive capacity of its rival and falling sugar prices.[66]

"The privilege accorded to beet sugar," wrote Adolphe Gueroult in 1842, "has broken the *pacte colonial* in two, letting all the burdens weigh on the colonies while depriving them of all the advantages stipulated in their favor. France still reserves the colonial market for itself; it no longer reserves the monopoly of its market for the colonies." Baron Charles Dupin, a prominent colonial spokesman, elaborated the inequities the colonies suffered under the *exclusif*:

> The colonies remain subject to the onerous clauses of the contract. The transport of their product is exclusively reserved to metropolitan navigation. They are compelled to deliver those products unrefined in order to stimulate metropolitan employment. They can only buy from metropolitan industry. They can only sell to metropolitan commerce. The market in the metropolis is the only one that is open to them, and they are forced to dispose of all their products there. The restrictions to which colonial industry submits for the profit of the navigation, commerce, and manufactures of the metropolis are mercilessly enforced, and the privilege on the domestic market, which is only equitable compensation, has been transferred to the metropolitan competition which legislation has raised up against the colonial producers. The latter bear the charges, the former receive the advantages of the colonial system.

The colonies now had access to the metropolitan market only under unfavorable conditions. Their right to protection was recognized in principle but denied in fact. France, which had been the main market for colonial sugar, now became an important producer in its own right, but with limited exceptions, the colonies were still compelled to buy only French goods and sell their produce only in the metropolis. The shortage of capital and the disruption of commerce caused by the unequal relationship between metropolis and colonies brought debt and ruin to many West Indian planters, impaired their capacity to produce efficiently, and reduced the importance of the colonies as a market for French goods. Yet the colonies remained dependent on the protection offered under the *exclusif* and were unable to transcend the system of which they were a part. The impossibility of finding a solution to the conflict between the two sugars called into question the entire organization of the French sugar trade.[67]

In the face of their dilemma, the West Indian planters had two potential options. The first was free trade. Failing to obtain adherence to what they interpreted as the colonial compact, the colonist demanded equal tariffs and the end of restrictions on the quality of sugar produced in the colonies, the right to trade with all nations limited only by the same tariffs as the metropolis, and the end of monopoly shipping. However, the French government, influenced by various interest groups tied to the colonial trade, would not relinquish its privileged colonial markets or reserved shipping. Furthermore, as the leading planters clearly understood, the French colonies would be even less able to withstand the competition and the tariffs on the world market than they could the contention for control of the metropolitan market. The colonies were indissolubly tied to the *exclusif*, and sought to resolve their situation within its framework. Their second option was strict adherence to its terms and a protected position on the French market, even if this meant the suppression of the beet sugar industry.[68]

The 1840 sugar duties and the rapid growth of beet sugar production aggravated the tensions between the various interest groups concerned with the French sugar market and once again raised the prospect of the abolition of the metropolitan beet sugar industry. To alleviate the continuing plight of the colonies, the members of the Council of Delegates of the Colonies, supported by the chambers of commerce of the port cities, no longer petitioned for equal duties for the two sugars, but claimed their legal right to a privileged position on the metropolitan market. The colonies demanded their "right to life." The *pacte colonial* raised colonial production costs if they had to buy only from France; in compensation, they should receive a privileged position on the French market. In their view, equal duties were inadequate to resolve the problem. Reciprocity should govern the relationship between metropolis and colony, and if necessary the beet sugar industry should be abolished with an indemnity. The demand for the abolition of the beet sugar industry resonated through other sectors of the French sugar industry as well. A majority of beet sugar producers declared that they preferred to abolish their industry with an indemnity rather than increase their duties. Many were already producing at a loss and continued operations only to have a claim if expropriated. They often increased their production simply to have an increased claim. The government was also fearful of lost tax revenue if beet sugar replaced cane and proposed the abolition of beet sugar with an indemnity just when all the encouragement given to beet sugar production had begun to pay off.[69]

In January of 1843, the government, alarmed by the decline of maritime commerce and the fall of tax revenues, joined with the colonies to demand the suppression of the beet sugar industry. The project was thwarted in the Chamber of Deputies in large part due to the maneuvering of Thiers. The commission formed to examine the problem felt that it was not in the national interest to abolish beet sugar: it was too important to the development of agriculture, trade, and employment. The committee supported the coexistence of the two sugars and proposed an elaborate plan to modify the tariffs, which was abandoned when it was presented to the legislative chambers. In the legislature, the call for the abolition of beet sugar was revived and subject to a lively debate. However, it became evident that even at their maximum output, the colonies could not meet the demands of metropolitan consumption by themselves, nor could they provide the potential development of which the market was capable. To grant the colonies the monopoly of the French market would make France increasingly dependent on foreign sugar over the long run. Rather than eliminating the beet sugar industry, the legislature adopted the principal of equal duties on metropolitan and colonial sugar. This solution was to be realized, not by decreasing the duty on colonial sugar, but by gradually increasing the duty on beet sugar. The law of July 7, 1843, progressively increased the tax on beet sugar by five francs a year for four years, beginning in August, 1844, and continuing until it reached parity with the duty on colonial cane sugar. The law also simplified the classification of both cane and beet sugar to facilitate the application of the new duties. This law was the last major piece of legislation on sugar passed under the July Monarchy, and, in the opinion of the government, it definitively resolved the question of the sugar tariff.[70]

The equalization of duties did not impede the progress of the metropolitan sugar industry. Beet sugar production suffered a slight and temporary setback as a result of the law, but the primary effect of the legislation was to accelerate the concentration of beet sugar production and the rapid increase of its output. The 1843 law marked the definitive end of the small, isolated beet sugar factory that had only continued operations in the hope of being expropriated with an indemnity. The equal duties drove beet sugar producers to develop more efficient means of production. In the first year of its operation, the number of factories fell from 384 to 325, and the number of departments producing sugar dropped from thirty-four to twenty-two. By 1847–48, there were only 298 beet sugar factories in eighteen departments. These were overwhelmingly concentrated in the departments of the Nord, Pas-de-Calais, l'Aisne, Somme, and Oise, which collectively had 277 factories. Beet sugar production dropped slightly to 29,000 metric tons in 1843–44 under the impact of the new tax. Over the next three years, however, it rose steadily and dramatically despite the annual increment in the duties. In 1844–45, 36,000 metric tons were produced. The following year, the total climbed to 41,000 metric tons, and in 1846–1847, it reached 54,000 metric tons. With the benefit of a stable duty, more than 64,000 metric tons were produced in 1847–48.[71]

The viability of the beet sugar industry in France was finally established. Its development transformed the division of labor between metropolis and colony and the relations of the *exclusif* on which rested the colonial sugar industry and plantation slavery. The colonies had lost their privileged position in the metropolitan market at the same time that their economic fate was tied more closely than ever to sugar monoculture. Colonial production continued to expand and in 1845 reached 105,000 metric tons. Growing colonial and metropolitan production and falling prices pushed up French sugar consumption, which reached 132,000 metric tons in 1847. But the colonial sugar industry's relative share of the growing market stagnated and declined. While beet sugar continually drove the price of sugar down, the colonies could no longer secure the conditions necessary for their prosperity. The colonial demand for more protection was no longer adequate. The dynamic character of the beet sugar industry, its potential for expansion and technological rationalization, threatened to shatter any tenuous equilibrium established between the two sugars and gave a note of futility to any legislation that attempted to strike such a balance.[72]

The development of a protected market in France permitted the revitalization of sugar production and slave labor in the colonies, but the very growth of the colonial sugar industry undermined the conditions that sustained it and eroded the purposes of the protective system. The absolute increase in colonial production coincided with higher relative costs, including the social, political, and economic costs of slavery and the colonial system. The limited capacity of colonial producers to expand their output and lower their production costs made them dependent on preferential tariffs to guarantee an outlet for their sugar and to keep prices high enough to maintain a margin of profit. The political influence of the colonial interests was used to offset problems in the sphere of production, and the policy of protection laid the groundwork for a crisis that touched every aspect of the French sugar industry. The effect of the tariff was to subsidize the increasingly archaic organization of colonial production and promote the growth of sugar monoculture in the colonies on the one hand, and to restrict the development of the French national market and foreign trade on the other. The traditional relation between metropolis and colony was inverted. Instead of the colony existing for the benefit of the metropolis, the metropolis was bound to colonial production. The colonies required more protection but offered less to the metropolis. At the same time, the growth of the French beet sugar industry put constant pressure on colonial planters to increase the productive efficiency of their operations even as they sought legislative remedies for their deteriorating position. In this process, the slave plantation in Martinique was pushed to its fullest development as the existing social and technical organization of production was reinforced and exploited more intensively. The amelioration of production processes made the structure of the plantation more rigid and incapable of adapting to the new conditions, while the burden of labor weighed more heavily on the enslaved. A structural crisis gripped the slave plantation as a productive enterprise and as a form of social organization of labor that exacerbated the precarious condition of the entire circuit of French colonial sugar. Only when slave emancipation brought about its ruin were the conditions created for restructuring of the French sugar market and rebuilding the colonial sugar industry in a new political and economic context.

# Chapter 3

# The Local Face of World Process

Sugar manufacture had dominated the economy of Martinique since at least 1710, and until the end of the 1780s, only Saint Domingue, Jamaica, and Brazil produced more sugar. Nevertheless, monoculture in the colony was pushed to unprecedented proportions. The exploitation of slave labor intensified by a speculative boom in sugar touched off by the transformation of the world-economy and the development of a protected market in France after 1815. The number of sugar estates multiplied, and more land and labor were devoted to sugar cultivation at the expense of other crops. However, this expansion was circumscribed by the physical and social environment. The amount of suitable land available was limited not only by the geography of the island, but by the spatial organization of plantation agriculture that had been established over the course of the preceding two centuries. The existing estate system froze the framework for organizing land, labor, and the technology of sugar manufacture. It was difficult for already existing plantations to increase the scale of their operations or to modify their technical and social organization. New techniques were either adapted to given conditions or they were abandoned. Prevailing patterns of activity were reinforced and became more rigid. At the same time, the presence of these older estates limited the quantity and quality of land available for the formation of new estates. Indeed, a great many of the new sugar plantations founded in Martinique during this period were small, inefficient units located on marginal lands. The reorganization of production was thus inhibited, and existing constraints of production were reproduced and strengthened. Although the increased number of plantations resulted in an absolute increase in the amount of sugar produced, this went hand in hand with declining efficiency per unit.

Further, the growth of sugar production in Martinique cemented the bond between sugar monoculture and slavery. Only slavery could provide the hands necessary to increase sugar production, and only sugar could pay the costs of maintaining the slave labor force. Yet the very progress of the slave system generated the seeds of its own destruction. The planter could only respond to the market by increasing the exploitation of slave labor. This could take the form of either expanding production to marginal lands or intensifying production on the better lands. In either case, the labor component of the product could not be reduced. The planter was continuously burdened with the enormous fixed costs of slave maintenance. These costs were independent of sugar prices and had to be paid whether the slave worked or not. They thus compelled the planter to keep producing no matter what. As market conditions declined, the slave owner could not reduce his labor force. Instead, the need to cover the costs of slave maintenance created pressure to increase production. His situation obliged him to produce more sugar to generate more absolute income, although the average rate of return to labor was diminishing, since all labor expended in commodity production, even if it was wasteful in relative terms, was remunerative as long as it did not interfere with the reproduction of the laborer. Thus, the response to a declining market was to increase output rather than reduce costs. Increasing the total product under these conditions reduced the average yield. In this way, the social relations of slave production deepened the economic crisis of the sugar industry in Martinique and gave it its particular form. The very processes that brought the sugar industry in Martinique to the height of its development sealed the fate of the island as a backward and inefficient producer in the rapidly expanding nineteenth-century economy. Under these conditions, colonial planters were forced into an ever-greater dependence on protection to maintain their position in the French market.

The archaic character of the agrarian structure in Martinique was reinforced by commercial and financial relations and the legal constitution of property in the colony. The expansion of sugar production after 1815 depended on the extension of metropolitan credit. New debt was added to the outstanding debt and accumulated interest from the period of wars and revolution. Indebtedness became a constant burden for the planters, and their condition was aggravated after 1830 when declining prices coincided with rising costs. Faced with fixed costs and falling property values, the planters had to continue to produce to secure any revenue, and they had to continue to borrow to continue to produce. Local law afforded the planters protection from their creditors by effectively precluding the seizure of sugar plantations and slaves for debt. While such measures may have offered short-term relief for individual planters, their long-term consequences deepened the crisis of the colonial sugar industry. They occasioned fraud and led to withdrawal of metropolitan credit by removing guarantees to the creditor. Especially after 1830, in place of long-term mortgage credit from metropolitan lenders, local merchant capitalists offered planters short-term credit against their crop. As a result, commercial speculation, high interest rates, and chronic debt increasingly plagued the colonial sugar industry. Local merchant and planter, creditor and debtor, became locked together in a perpetual cycle of mutual dependence and antagonism. The struggle between them over the appropriation of the product consolidated and reinforced existing production units and impeded innovation and reorganization.

## Land, Labor, and Sugar: The Expansion of Monoculture

Data are lacking on the rural economy of Martinique before 1831, in part because all official documents before 1815 were destroyed by the English during the occupation, while the accuracy of official statistics after 1831 is disputed. According to P. Lavollée, who had been sent to inspect colonial agriculture in 1839, agricultural statistics could only be regarded as approximate, even though procedures had improved in the years just prior to his report. There was no cadastre or land tax, the boundaries of estates were inexact, and large plantations left large tracts of land uncultivated. Often the planters themselves did not have precise knowledge of the extent of their holdings and how much the land yielded. The data were gathered by the commandants of each *quartier*, who required each planter to appear before them and declare what crops were cultivated, how much land was planted in each crop, the number of slaves employed in agriculture, and so forth. There were no controls over the declarations, and nothing assured their sincerity or accuracy. Many planters failed to appear before this official but instead sent a neighbor with the information. There is also a difference between production and export figures too great to be accounted for by internal consumption. Lavollée attributes most of this difference to the fact that the barrels were not weighed on departure. Instead, they were simply assessed at 500 kilograms each when actually they often weighed 650–700 kilograms each. In this way the colonists avoided paying up to one-third of the duty on their sugar. Despite these difficulties, no less an authority than Moreau de Jonnes, a pioneer of statistical research and founder of the French national census, vouched for the accuracy of the statistics gathered after 1831. He commented: "As for the official figures for the French colonies given by the central administration since 1831, all the tests to which we have submitted them have convinced us that they are almost all exact and much better than is commonly thought." Moreau's remarks seem to apply especially to slave population data. These figures served as the base for a possible indemnity after manumission, and thus provided a more powerful incentive to independently guarantee the accuracy of the masters' declarations.[1]

Sugar production increased extensively and intensively, and exports to France climbed dramatically in response to the favorable tariffs and high prices during the period between 1815 and 1830 (see table 3.1). The extent and rhythm of the expansion of sugar cultivation in Martinique after 1815 can be appreciated more clearly against the background of the preceding decades. During the years before the outbreak of the French Revolution, sugar production in Martinique increased sharply and attained its highest levels of the eighteenth century. In 1778, 13,507 hectares of land were planted in sugar cane on 257 plantations, and 11,300 metric tons of sugar produced. By 1789, the number of sugar plantations increased to 324, and the area planted in cane reached 19,108 hectares. About 18,500 metric tons were produced. Sugar exports reached 13,315 metric tons in 1790 before falling off to 7,223 in 1791 as the effects of the revolution in France began to be felt in the colonies. There is little information available for the period from 1789

Table 3.1. Martinique: Sugar Production and Exports of Sugar, Molasses, Rum, and Tafia, 1818–1847

| Year | Sugar production (metric tons) | Sugar exports (metric tons) | Value of sugar exports (francs) | Molasses exports (liters) | Rum and tafia exports (liters) | Value of all sugar products exported (francs) | Value of total exports (francs) | Sugar products as % of total exports |
|---|---|---|---|---|---|---|---|---|
| 1818 | 13,507 | 11,612,824 | 4,917,063 | 1,542,807 | 15,235,782 | 25,193,060 | | 60.48 |
| 1819 | 15,390 | 10,328,766 | 6,347,827 | 376,917 | 12,805,447 | 21,746,250 | | 58.88 |
| 1820 | 18,483 | 9,983,654 | 7,337,637 | 213,149 | 12,145,792 | 20,767,232 | | 58.59 |
| 1821 | 19,566 | 8,901,003 | 6,926,645 | 1,055,237 | 11,079,995 | 20,351,768 | | 54.44 |
| 1822 | 16,337 | 6,118,532 | 8,526,765 | 666,216 | 8,330,805 | 16,908,041 | | 49.27 |
| 1823 | 17,845 | 8,590,540 | 6,563,201 | 95,734 | 10,116,436 | 16,840,615 | | 60.07 |
| 1824 | 20,015 | 11,322,867 | 5,151,282 | 218,739 | 12,499,817 | 18,152,853 | | 68.86 |
| 1825 | 26,143 | 15,504,673 | 6,438,258 | 253,685 | 17,112,179 | 22,418,913 | | 76.33 |
| 1826 | 28,168 | 18,393,398 | 5,927,561 | 623,124 | 19,966,992 | 26,577,635 | | 75.13 |
| 1827 | 24,394 | 17,234,659 | 4,650,965 | 284,757 | 18,596,727 | 25,726,196 | | 72.79 |
| 1828 | 33,064 | 19,663,662 | 5,401,637 | 215,004 | 20,873,308 | 26,171,288 | | 79.76 |
| 1829 | 28,890 | 1,5664,244 | 4,059,376 | 256,039 | 16,248,625 | 17,714,847 | | 91.72 |
| 1830 | 28,150 | 14,097,508 | 4,643,564 | 244,620 | 14,594,442 | 17,547,862 | | 83.17 |
| 1832 | 29,568 | 22,454 | 10,568,385 | 3,597,484 | 76,967 | 11,203,173 | 13,946,941 | 80.33 |
| 1833 | 28,755 | 20,054 | 10,800,290 | 3,289,582 | 251,764 | 11,483,944 | 14,176,044 | 81.01 |
| 1834 | 28,692 | 26,258 | 12,660,069 | 3,372,962 | 730,227 | 13,540,447 | 16,189,565 | 83.64 |
| 1835 | 30,505 | 24,374 | 11,841,747 | 3,561,408 | 509,473 | 12,536,222 | 14,857,254 | 84.38 |
| 1836 | 34,160 | 22,444 | 12,179,525 | 2,483,614 | 241,237 | 12,763,263 | 15,986,324 | 79.84 |
| 1837 | 30,090 | 20,455 | 10,355,853 | 2,512,892 | 250,099 | 10,941,983 | 13,942,169 | 78.48 |
| 1838 | 32,538 | 26,159 | 9,789,080 | 4,634,976 | 574,358 | 10,670,609 | 13,790,319 | 77.38 |
| 1839 | 25,186 | 23,719 | 8,781,848 | 4,723,408 | 692,179 | 9,839,644 | 13,517,546 | 72.79 |

continued on next page

Table 3.1. Continued.

| Year | Sugar production (metric tons) | Sugar exports (metric tons) | Value of sugar exports (francs) | Molassis exports (liters) | Rum and tafia exports (liters) | Value of all sugar products exported (francs) | Value of total exports (francs) | Sugar products as % of total exports |
|---|---|---|---|---|---|---|---|---|
| 1840 | 28,254 | 21,677 | 10,571,327 | 2,241,492 | 498,090 | 11,249,948 | 14,445,615 | 77.88 |
| 1841 | 28,150 | 24,944 | 11,480,590 | 2,725,796 | 957,550 | 12,258,649 | 15,501,545 | 79.08 |
| 1842 | 32,116 | 27,987 | 9,759,395 | 1,851,796 | 1,363,468 | 10,239,589 | 13,580,977 | 75.4 |
| 1843 | 29,920 | 25,477 | 10,751,300 | 1,961,181 | 863,366 | 11,150,223 | 15,054,021 | 74.07 |
| 1844 | 37,968 | 33,109 | 15,132,719 | 2,249,473 | 951,633 | 15,709,403 | 19,588,527 | 80.2 |
| 1845 | 35,057 | 30,030 | 14,474,549 | 2,664,815 | 1,293,482 | 15,197,711 | 18,127,978 | 83.84 |
| 1846 | 34,230 | 25,580 | 12,588,551 | 329,468 | 1,417,407 | 13,137,137 | 16,185,432 | 81.17 |
| 1847 | 29,318 | 31,337 | 14,118,198 | 853,714 | 1,726,748 | 14,764,959 | 18,323,921 | 80.58 |

Source: A.N.S.O.M., Martinique. État de Culture; l'Annuaire de la Martinique (1884), in Liliane Chauleau, Histoire Antillaise: la Martinique et la Guadeloupe du XVII<sup>e</sup> siècle à la fin du XIX<sup>e</sup> siècle, pp. 306–7.

to 1815. According to Lavollée, production rose to 22,000 metric tons in 1802. This increase was undoubtedly stimulated by the return of the colony to France and the destruction of Saint Domingue. However, this high level of production could not be sustained. In 1805, 17,600 metric tons of cane were produced on 345 plantations cultivating 15,600 hectares, and by 1807 land in sugar was extended to 16,105 hectares. Lavollée estimates average annual exports between 1802 and 1807 at a bit more than 16,000 metric tons. Production cannot be followed with any precision for the years of the second British occupation between 1807 and 1814. However the combination of British exclusion of the sugar of the occupied colonies from its domestic market and the Continental blockade were especially damaging to the sugar industry in Martinique, and by 1815, the first year after the occupation, only 7,277 metric tons were exported to France.[2]

The coming of the peace and the revitalization of the sugar market in France signaled the recovery and beginning of a new period of growth of sugar production in Martinique. By 1816 there were 15,684 hectares devoted to sugar cane cultivation. Production remained relatively stable until 1820, when there were 16,469 hectares of land planted in cane on 351 sugar plantations, while export statistics show a steady increase from 13,507 to 20,015 metric tons between 1818 and 1824. However, sugar production jumped sharply to unprecedented levels during the boom years of the mid-1820s as colonial sugar interests secured the legislation that consolidated their hold on the metropolitan market. The protective tariffs touched off a wave of speculative expansion in Martinique that put all possible land under sugar cultivation. According to the testimony of Delavigne, a planter from Martinique in 1829: "When we saw ourselves assured of the protection of the metropolis, we sought the greatest possible extension of sugar cane cultivation. We cleared forests and drained marshes. The increase of production must be attributed to this expansion of plantings and to the amelioration of agricultural techniques, that is, the use of the plow where it is practical and the employment of a greater quantity of fertilizer."[3]

Planters responded to the incentive of the tariff subsidies and their domination of the French market by pushing sugar cultivation to the maximum between 1825 and 1836. Sugar exports to France climbed to 26,143 metric tons in 1825 and reached 33,064 in 1828. Although the export statistics show a relative decline after 1831, the amount of land cultivated in sugar, the number of sugar plantations, and the amount of sugar produced continued to increase. According to de Lavigne, much of the initial expansion of sugar production during this period was restricted to lands contiguous to existing cane fields and of comparable quality. However, as the boom continued, the number of plantations multiplied, new lands were cleared, and lands already planted in other crops were converted to sugar cane. In 1826, there were still only 17,620 hectares planted in sugar, although the number of plantations increased to 405. In 1829, it was estimated that there still remained in the island 6,000 hectares in woods or in uncultivated lands that could be planted in cane. Their exploitation would augment production by 15,000 to 18,000 metric tons. By 1832 sugar covered 20,186 hectares and was grown on 466 plantations. Production reached 29,568 metric tons. This development reached its high point in 1836, when 515 sugar estates planted 23,777 hectares in cane and produced 34,160 metric tons of sugar.[4]

By 1836, the year that beet sugar began to displace colonial sugar in the French market, the sugar industry in Martinique had reached the physical limits of its expansion. The rapid growth of the previous decade effectively precluded further expansion onto virgin land, although some possibility still existed for expansion within the boundaries of individual estates. The number of sugar plantations fluctuated erratically after 1836, ranging from 473 in 1844 to 498 in 1847. The amount of land planted in cane declined slowly each year from a high of 20,339 hectares in 1837 to a low of 17,451 hectares in 1843. Annual production remained relatively stable at about 30,000 metric tons, with a range from 25,186 metric tons in 1839 to 32,538 metric tons in 1838. Export figures varied a bit more, but even the low years between 1832 and 1841 were higher than any time before 1825. In contrast, the amount of land planted in sugar increased perceptibly during the last four years before emancipation, with a high of 20,332 hectares in 1846. Sugar production and exports increased even more rapidly during these years, and in 1844 production reached the highest level recorded during slavery,

37,968 metric tons, while the 33,109 metric tons exported matched the record level attained in 1828.[5]

Thus, after 1825, Martinique sustained sugar production at an unprecedented level. Even after the peak years of high prices between 1825 and 1830, sugar accounted for an increasingly large share of the value of total exports. It remained the surest source of revenue for the colonies and the cornerstone of the colonial trade. But as prices fell, increased production was necessary to maintain the total value of exports. The grip of sugar monoculture on the colony tightened, and the planters were having to run faster and faster just to stay in the same place.

This expansion of sugar production depended on securing an adequate labor force. The size of the harvest was dependent on the area of land that was cultivated, and this in turn was determined by the number of slaves available. The size of the slave labor force was thus the crucial factor in limiting the extent of cultivation. Possibly as many as 33,000 to 52,000 Africans were imported to Martinique between 1814 and 1830 (see Appendix 1). With the end of the slave trade, however, the planters were faced with a diminishing slave population. More importantly in the short run, they were unable to control the size and composition of their labor force through the purchase of imported Africans. The labor supply became more inelastic, and planters had to depend on natural increase and the internal redistribution of the slave population to secure the labor necessary for the sugar estates. Thus forced to draw from a fixed population, the structure of which they could no longer manipulate, the masters found it more difficult to respond to the changing demand for labor.[6]

The abolition of the slave trade prevented the planters from replacing or expanding their labor force. After 1832, the total slave population declined slowly until emancipation in 1847 (see table 3.2). What is most striking about the evolution of the slave population, however, is its overall stability. It does not exhibit the drastic mortality frequently attributed to West Indian sugar colonies. Despite the disproportionate number of adults and aged in the slave population, births exceeded deaths for most years, and manumissions, which were facilitated by laws passed in 1832 and 1845, are necessary to account for the overall diminution.

Table 3.2. Slave Births, Deaths, and Manumissions, 1832–1847

| Year | Total slave population | Births | Deaths | Manumissions |
|------|------------------------|--------|--------|--------------|
| 1832 | 82,873 | * | * | 8,976 |
| 1833 | 79,767 | * | * | 2,129 |
| 1834 | 78,233 | 2,232 | 2,092 | 2,283 |
| 1835 | 78,076 | 2,485 | 2,261 | 975 |
| 1836 | 77,459 | 2,340 | 2,230 | 1,178 |
| 1837 | 76,012 | 2,305 | 2,592 | 899 |
| 1838 | 76,517 | 2,376 | 2,454 | 901 |
| 1839 | 74,333 | 2,390 | 2,324 | 447 |
| 1840 | 76,403 | 2,594 | 2,114 | 380 |
| 1841 | 75,225 | 2,622 | 2,418 | * |
| 1842 | 76,172 | 2,533 | 2,541 | * |
| 1843 | 75,736 | 2,595 | 2,015 | 828 |
| 1844 | 76,117 | 2,661 | 1,921 | 591 |
| 1845 | 76,042 | 2,349 | 2,396 | 616 |
| 1846 | 75,339 | 2,468 | 2,267 | 1,010 |
| 1847 | 72,859 | 2,352 | 2,251 | 755 |

Source: A.N.S.O.M., Martinique, État de Population; Victor Schoelcher, Des colonies françaises. Abolition immédiate de l'esclavage, pp. 435–36.
*No data.

The decline of the total slave population thus reflected the distortion of the demographic structure because of the slave trade, and slavery was not jeopardized in any immediate sense by the end of the traffic in slaves. Rather, the immediate decline in the number of available laborers was gradual, and there was a possibility for establishing a new equilibrium over the long run between the slave population and the demand for labor.

The reproduction of the slave labor force through natural increase rather than through imports would compel the slave system to support more women and children. Yet to a large extent this transition was already in progress in Martinique. Large numbers of women had been imported to the colony, and the slave trade had been complemented by natural increase for some time. Throughout the post-trade period the ratio between men and women remained fairly stable, with women outnumbering men (see table 3.3). Births and deaths in the sugar sector cannot be isolated with the available data. In 1829, while the slave trade was still in progress, de Lavigne testified before the parliamentary commission on the sugar industry that on his plantation, births almost compensated for deaths and sometimes surpassed them except at times of exceptional mortality such as epidemics. In his opinion, this was the case on every well-ordered plantation. On the other hand, Sainte Croix estimated the annual loss of slaves on a well-administered sugar estate at 5 percent, but the commission dismissed this figure as exaggerated. Nevertheless, the general slave population remained stationary after the end of the slave trade. Despite the apparent slight decline in absolute numbers, the structure of the slave population was remarkably stable. Most importantly, that portion of the rural slave population under fourteen years of age remained intact and may have even increased slightly. The persistence of this young creole slave population provided a continuing source of potential labor for the colonial planters.[7]

Table 3.3. Age and Gender Distribution of Rural Slave Population, 1832–1847

|  | 1832 (%) | 1837 (%) | 1842 (%) | 1847 (%) |
|---|---|---|---|---|
| Male 0–14 | 9,875 (14.7) | 9,818 (14.4) | 10,245 (15.2) | 10,143 (15.7) |
| Female 0–14 | 10,363 (15.4) | 9,471 (14.8) | 10,416 (15.5) | 10,656 (16.5) |
| Total 0–14 | 20,238 (30.2) | 18,669 (29.2) | 20,661 (30.7) | 20,779 (32.2) |
| Male 14–60 | 20,726 (30.9) | 20,037 (31.4) | 19,541 (29.0) | 19,606 (30.4) |
| Female 14–60 | 21,271 (31.7) | 21,490 (33.6) | 22,884 (34.0) | 20,192 (31.2) |
| Total 14–60 | 41,997 (62.6) | 41,527 (65.0) | 42,425 (63.0) | 39,798 (61.6) |
| Male over 60 | 2,207 (03.3) | 1,338 (02.1) | 1,534 (02.3) | 1,383 (02.1) |
| Female over 60 | 2,659 (04.0) | 2,345 (03.7) | 2,768 (04.1) | 2,669 (04.1) |
| Total over 60 | 4,866 (07.3) | 3,683 (05.8) | 4,302 (06.4) | 4,052 (06.2) |
| Total Male | 32,808 (48.9) | 30,573 (47.9) | 31,320 (46.5) | 31,132 (48.2) |
| Total Female | 34,293 (51.1) | 33,306 (52.1) | 36,068 (53.5) | 33,517 (51.8) |
| Total | 67,101 | 63,879 | 67,388 | 64,649 |

Source: A.N.S.O.M., Martinique. État de population.

Even under the best of circumstances, however, natural reproduction of the slave population would provide an extremely inflexible labor supply and would impose extreme conditions on the economic rationality of the plantation in an expanding and increasingly competitive market situation. This problem would be particularly acute during the transition to full self-reproduction, because the aging and mortality among the disproportionate number of active workers provided by the slave trade would not be immediately compensated for by births. Slaves were normally considered ready for field work at age fourteen. Therefore, a slave born in 1832 would only be ready to enter the labor force in 1846. Thus, even though births were greater than deaths after the end of the trade, the number of active adult workers and the aging of that portion of the labor force increasingly became a consideration for planters.

Although the possibility may have existed for the slave population in Martinique to reproduce itself after the abolition of the slave trade, its structure did not coincide with the demand for labor. While the general slave population declined slowly between 1832 and 1847, the number of slaves employed in agriculture increased by more than 10 percent, and the number of slaves employed in sugar production increased by over 23 percent (see table 3.4). The consequence of the lack of congruence between the movement of the general slave population and the demand for slave labor was a labor shortage and the restructuring of the labor force as slaves were shifted from other activities to sugar. The biggest rates of decrease were among urban slaves and rural slaves in nonagricultural occupations, but slaves in these categories were the most probable candidates for manumission and less likely recruits for the cane fields. On the other hand, there was also a sharp decline in the number of slaves engaged in the production of coffee, cacao, cotton, and other secondary crops. Only the labor force engaged in provision cultivation went up at a rapid rate, though the absolute numbers involved in it were relatively small. Thus, the increase in the sugar labor force was at the expense of secondary crop cultivation as slaves employed in their production were shifted to sugar.

Sugar planters were able to sustain the expansion of the sugar industry in Martinique by obtaining labor from secondary crop producers. To this end, they bought

Table 3.4. Composition of the Slave Agricultural Labor Force, 1832–1847

| Year | Total slave population | Urban | Rural | Rural adults | Slaves employed in sugar | Slaves employed in minor crops | Slaves employed in provisions | Rural slaves employed in agriculture | Rural slaves not employed in agriculture |
|---|---|---|---|---|---|---|---|---|---|
| 1832 | 82,873 | 15,772 | 67,101 | 41,997 | 32,719 | 13,844 | 6,250 | 52,813 | 14,288 |
| 1833 | 79,767 | 13,722 | 66,045 | 41,814 | 32,900 | 13,193 | 5,686 | 51,779 | 14,266 |
| 1834 | 78,233 | 13,146 | 64,817 | 41,132 | 34,011 | 13,019 | 5,756 | 52,786 | 12,301 |
| 1835 | 78,076 | 20,282 | 57,794 | 36,626 | 35,735 | 13,258 | 7,293 | 56,556 | 1,238 |
| 1836 | 77,459 | 10,338 | 67,121 | 42,842 | 34,240 | 12,856 | 7,677 | 54,773 | 12,348 |
| 1837 | 76,012 | 12,133 | 63,879 | 41,257 | 32,043 | 9,635 | 6,720 | 48,398 | 15,481 |
| 1838 | 76,517 | 11,375 | 65,142 | 41,911 | 31,514 | 10,225 | 7,779 | 49,518 | 15,624 |
| 1839 | 74,333 | 10,327 | 64,006 | 40,269 | 33,426 | 9,956 | 6,643 | †50,025 | 13,971 |
| 1840 | 76,403 | 8,163 | 68,240 | 43,435 | 35,308 | 9,845 | 9,236 | 54,389 | 13,851 |
| 1841 | 75,225 | 6,911 | 68,314 | 42,847 | 33,857 | 9,654 | 9,488 | †52,999 | 15,215 |
| 1842 | 76,172 | 8,784 | 67,388 | 42,425 | 37,067 | 9,796 | 7,433 | 54,296 | 13,092 |
| 1843 | 75,736 | 9,804 | 65,932 | 40,609 | 34,667 | 10,636 | 9,972 | 55,275 | 10,657 |
| 1844[a] | 76,117 | 9,778 | 66,339 | 40,625 | 41,054 | 13,721 | 11,564 | 66,339 | — |
| 1845[a] | 76,042 | 9,716 | 66,326 | 40,696 | 41,668 | 12,576 | 12,082 | 66,326 | — |
| 1846[a] | 75,339 | 9,578 | 65,761 | 40,583 | 43,173 | 11,450 | 11,138 | 65,761 | — |
| 1847 | 72,859 | 8,210 | 64,649 | 39,798 | 40,429 | 8,815 | 9,098 | 58,342 | 6,307 |

*Sources*: A.N.S.O.M., Martinique, *État de Culture*; Martinique, *État de Population*.

†There are discrepancies between the figures for slave occupations and those for the total slave population. The most likely source of error is in the accounting of agricultural occupations. If this number is increased by 10 in the first instance and 100 in the second, all figures are consistent.

[a]There is apparently a change in the accounting system for these years. All the slaves attached to the estate and not just those actively engaged in production of a crop are counted as being employed in that crop. There also appears to be a similar inconsistency in the classification of occupations for the year 1835.

145

coffee, cacao, and cotton plantations simply to obtain their slaves. In addition, many larger planters of secondary crops abandoned their traditional activity and converted to sugar. Previously the transfer of slaves from secondary crops to sugar had accompanied and complemented the slave trade, but by the 1830s this became the sole source of labor outside natural increase. At best, it was a limited and temporary expedient, and jeopardized the reproduction of the slave population at the very moment that the slave trade came to an end. As early as 1829, sugar planters had been warned that such practices were potentially disruptive of the colonial economy.

> In admitting that the laws against the trade will be strictly upheld as they should be, it would follow from the preceding calculations that the greater development of cultivation would contribute to the acceleration of the reduction of the slave population, that is, quicken the destruction of the very means of production. The incorporation of the blacks from the cotton, coffee, and indigo plantations into the gangs of the sugar estates has furnished the sugar producers with an extremely important resource, but it is only fortuitous. For their own good, the colonists must not forget that this resource cannot be renewed. Perhaps even this operation itself has been detrimental in two respects: first, because of all the colonial crops, sugar cane is the most destructive of the slaves; and second, because by concentrating their purchases above all on the able Negroes of the small plantations, the proprietors of the sugar plantations have contributed to the separation of the sexes and a different distribution of the population.

At the same time that these transfers threatened the stability of the labor force, they increased dependence on sugar and destroyed alternative cultures. The search for more hands for the sugar estates devastated coffee, cotton, and cacao production in Martinique. Nevertheless, this was an inadequate solution to the demand for labor on the sugar plantations. The shortage of labor remained a pressing problem for sugar planters and compelled at least some of them to search for alternatives, while others clung more desperately than ever to slavery.[8]

The demand for land and labor for sugar production virtually destroyed the cultivation of secondary crops. Sugar cane cultivation expanded not just to unoccupied lands, but displaced secondary crops as well (see table 3.5). In 1815, Martinique exported 992 metric tons of coffee, 118 metric tons of cacao, and 39 metric tons of cotton to France. By 1837, these figures had fallen to 295 metric tons of coffee, 92 metric tons of cacao, and only 1 metric ton of cotton. Coffee, cacao, and cotton production fell so sharply that they virtually ceased to be regarded as commercial products. In 1844, Governor Duvaldailly of Martinique wrote in a memorandum to his successor that "the cultivation of sugar can be considered as nearly the sole nourishment of exterior commerce. There are still some communes where cacao, coffee, and cotton are grown, but these products only account for a small propor-

Table 3.5. Distribution of Land and Labor by Crop, 1820–1847

|  | 1820 | 1832 | 1837 | 1842 | 1847 |
|---|---|---|---|---|---|
| Sugar |  |  |  |  |  |
| Plantations | 351 | 466 | 505 | 498 | 498 |
| Land (hectares) | 16,457 | 20,186 | 20,892 | 17,947 | 19,735 |
| Slaves | 30,809 | 32,719 | 32,043 | 37,067 | 40,429 |
| Coffee |  |  |  |  |  |
| Plantations | — | 1,445 | 1,224 | 811 | 628 |
| Land (hectares) | 3,631 | 3,529 | 3,158 | 2,002 | 1,612 |
| Slaves | — | 10,918 | 7,902 | 7,202 | 5,233 |
| Other export crops[a] |  |  |  |  |  |
| Plantations | — | 96 | 7 | — | — |
| Land (hectares) | 957 | 708 | 853 | 523 | 586 |
| Slaves | — | 3,529 | 1,353 | 2,168 | 2,954 |
| Provisions |  |  |  |  |  |
| Plantations | — | 1,014 | 2,274 | 1,852 | 1,586 |
| Land (hectares) | — | 10,197 | 13,181 | 10,333 | 11,979 |
| Slaves | — | 6,250 | 6,720 | 7,433 | 9,098 |

Sources: Sainte Croix, *Statistique de la Martinique*, II, 34, 52, 75, 97; A.N.S.O.M., *État de Culture. Martinique*.

[a]Cacao, cotton, tobacco, indigo.

tion of the revenues of the colony. In giving themselves over almost exclusively to the cultivation of cane, the colonists have yielded to necessity because it is the only commodity which can compensate them for their expenses."[9]

Secondary crops were much less profitable than sugar, and small planters were forced to sell land and slaves to sugar planters or if possible convert to more profitable sugar themselves. The report of the commission of 1829 lamented: "Sugar cultivation appears to invade everything—savannahs, forests, provision grounds, coffee estates, and cotton plantations." Secondary crops were grown only where it was impossible to attempt to grow sugar. Coffee was confined to the crests of the hills or their upper slopes. Cotton was grown only in brushwood on soils where it was impossible to cultivate a more remunerative crop. Sugar, in contrast, was grown on the alluvial plains, in the valley bottoms, and on the gentler slopes, that is, "almost everywhere that cultivation was materially possible."[10]

Coffee was the second leading crop in the colony. At the height of its prosperity in 1789, it covered 6,123 hectares and 4,805 metric tons were exported to France. But between 1802 and 1814, France placed a series of heavy taxes on coffee imports. In addition, the coffee plants in Martinique suffered severe damage from the hurricanes of 1813 and 1817, and planters replaced them with sugar and with provision crops. After 1815, coffee plantations experienced further neglect and deterioration. Coffee planters without capital were forced to sell off their slaves and reduce cultivation or turn to provision crops, while larger planters were cutting down their coffee plants to grow cane. These difficulties were exacerbated around 1830 when an insect (*Elacchysta coffeola*) attacked the plants. Lavollée argued that the sugar boom distracted planters and prevented them from finding a solution to problems of coffee cultivation. Coffee in Martinique was decimated by disease until a resistant species of plant was introduced into the colony in 1888.[11]

Coffee declined precipitously throughout the 1830s and 1840s. In 1832, there were 1,455 coffee plantations covering 3,529 hectares and employing 9,918 slaves. By 1847, the number had fallen to 628 plantations covering 1,612 hectares and employing 5,233 slaves. One official report commented on the "hideous poverty" of the small coffee plantations scattered across the mountains, which stood in contrast with the richness of the natural surroundings. Many of these planters had no slaves. Many of those who did were barely better clothed and housed than their bondsmen and shared a common poverty with them. Another report in 1847 commented that coffee cultivation was declining year by year in fourteen communes as former coffee planters turned to growing sugar or provisions, and concluded that "It is generally believed that in the near future coffee will cease to be grown in the colony."[12]

As in the case of coffee, the planters of Martinique also ignored the potential of the cotton industry and preferred to devote their efforts to sugar cane production. Although natural conditions were favorable for it, cotton was never a major commercial crop in Martinique. Only 2,726 hectares were planted in cotton in 1779, the period of its most extensive cultivation, and, by the time of Lavollée's report, the area in cotton had dwindled to barely two hundred hectares. Poor cotton farmers preferred to sell their slaves to the sugar estates and abandon cotton cultivation in favor of provision crops. By 1847 there were no longer any cotton plantations—properly speaking—in Martinique. What cotton was produced was cultivated where soils were favorable as a second crop by planters growing provisions.[13]

While the cultivation of cacao declined from the 1,184 hectares it covered in 1789, it remained relatively stable at about 500 hectares during the first half of the nineteenth century. Cacao could be cultivated on most soils in almost all of the communes of the colony, but few plantations really specialized in producing it. The 1846 agricultural census indicates only one. According to this document, earthquakes contributed powerfully to decline of cacao plantations, and led to its cultivation on smaller units. Further, Lavollée noted a tendency for small sugar planters to return to the cultivation of secondary crops, especially cacao, as a result of the crisis they suffered in the 1830s.[14]

The decline of secondary commercial crops resulted in the rise of provision crop cultivation (chiefly manioc, yams, and bananas) as small planters who were squeezed out of export crop production turned either to subsistence production or to growing provision crops for markets in the towns or for the sugar estates. These *habitations vivrières* were frequently small and impoverished. Many had only one or two slaves and often none at all. These slaves shared the privations of the master, and their lot was hard. But other provision growers were prosperous small producers selling to local markets. Several *quartiers*, especially in the south and east where conditions were less suitable for sugar, produced not only enough provision crops to feed themselves but also a surplus to sell to neighboring parishes. The produce grown on these plantations made a significant contribution to the food supply of the colony.[15]

## Anatomy of a Sugar Island

The expansion of sugar production in Martinique was conditioned and constrained by the physical environment, and in turn the social and historical significance of the environment was increasingly defined by its relation to sugar. Martinique lies at the center of the chain of islands that make up the Lesser Antilles. Nearly 50 miles long and 22 miles wide at its widest point, its total area is about 425 square miles. Of the other islands of the Lesser Antilles, only Trinidad and Guadeloupe are larger. It is a volcanic island and is dominated by three distinct mountain masses, which extend the length of the island. This chain of peaks ranges from Mount Pelée (1,350 meters) in the north, to the *Pitons du Carbet* (1,270 meters) in the center, and the mountains of Vauclin (505 meters) in south. A secondary chain of high bluffs, or *mornes*, formed from the heavily eroded remains of extinct volcanoes, runs west from Vauclin to Diamant, south of the bay of Fort Royal (Fort-de-France). The relief of the southern part of the island is lower, less steep, and more regular than that of the north. The island enjoys constant northeast trade winds. Rainfall is abundant but irregularly distributed because of the diverse topography. The mountainous terrain creates complex drainage patterns characterized by short watercourses. The highland areas are rugged with narrow plateaus cut by deep gorges and covered with heavy forests. The foothills of the peaks dip down towards the sea and divide the island into a series of narrow valleys, or *fonds*, through which torrential rivers flow. Much of the land is too steep for

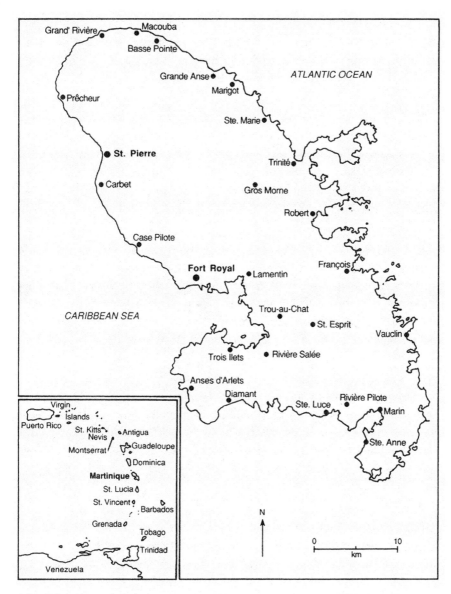

Martinique

Figure 3.1. Map of Martinique.

cultivation, but where the mountain slopes become more gradual and the valleys widen toward the sea, rich agricultural lands are formed from the soils washed down from the highlands. At the foot of the bay of Fort Royal, the broad alluvial plain of Lamentin is the most extensive cultivable area of the island.[16]

Soil, climate, and topography, as well as transportation and access to rivers or steady winds as regular sources of power, conditioned the location of the various types of agricultural activity. Sugar occupied the best lands along the coastal plains, in the valleys, and on the lower slopes of the hills, while coffee was grown in the cooler highlands. Further into the interior, only wastelands, forests, and small farms growing provision crops were to be found. According to Sainte Croix, "Ease of exploitation and embarkation are sought after more than the fertility of the land in Martinique. In general, location much more than the good or bad quality of the soil determines where the establishments must be placed." Overland communications were poor, and, except for a small number of sugar estates located near towns, flat-bottomed barks carried on the coastal trade between the plantations and the port cities of Saint Pierre and Fort Royal. Thus the establishment of new sugar plantations in the interior and far from points of embarkation often caused costs to rise considerably, and the majority of sugar estates were located on the coasts or along the rivers to facilitate transportation.[17]

Martinique offered the planter a variety of climates and soils so wide that one observer wrote, "it seems as if the different quarters do not belong to the same country." In his report on colonial agriculture, Lavollée divided Martinique into two agricultural regions. The north and west of the island were the most fertile parts of the colony, while the south and east enjoyed less favorable conditions and were subject to wider variations of soil and climate.[18]

The first region included the city of Saint Pierre and its environs, and the *quartiers* of Case Pilote, Carbet, Prêcheur, Macouba, Basse Pointe, Grande Anse, Marigot, Sainte Marie, and Trinité. This region extended over 35,341 hectares, of which 8,143 were planted in sugar cane in 1839. From Case Pilote to Basse Pointe, the soils were generally light loams, free from stones and rocks, and easy to cultivate. From Grande Anse to Trinité heavier clay soils predominated. Whichever soil type prevailed, the best agricultural lands in this region were located in the alluvial valleys and plains.[19]

According to Emile Thomas, who inspected agricultural and labor conditions in Martinique in 1848, the fertility of the Antilles was due much more to climate than to soil conditions. The windward side of the island, including the *quartiers* of Macouba, Basse Pointe, Grande Anse, Marigot, Sainte Marie, Trinité, Gros Morne, and Robert, enjoyed abundant rainfall and regular breezes. Cane could be planted and harvested there year round. On the leeward side of the island, however, conditions were much less favorable. In Case Pilote, Carbet, Sainte Pierre, and Prêcheur, planting could only be done during the rainy season beginning in May or June. In Case Pilote and Carbet, lack of rain reduced the harvest. In Case Pilote, cane could only be successfully cultivated in river bottoms, which one observer described as veritable oases in the midst of the parched hills. In Carbet, the land was fertile, and an irrigation canal that drew water from the Carbet River alleviated the lack of water, while Prêcheur was subject to drought, and its soil needed fertilizer.[20]

The series of rich valleys running from Macouba to Trinité provided some of the best land for sugar cultivation in the colony. Soil and weather conditions were exceptional, and the rivers flowing down from the mountains provided power for the sugar mills. Some of the largest and most productive sugar plantations were located there. In this part of the island, cane could be harvested three or four times from a single planting. Although these ratoons (or shoots grown from the root of the old plant) were not as rich as the original planting, Lavollée estimated that an average of 10–12 hogsheads, or between 5,000 and 6,000 kilograms of sugar per carré (1 carré = 1.29 hectares), was produced in the north. There was, of course, considerable local variation in soil productivity. One exceptional example was the Fitz-James plantation in Basse Pointe, perhaps the most fertile *quartier* in the colony. Some of the Fitz-James land was reported to yield as much as 10,000 kilograms per carré. Provision crops were produced in abundance in the highlands of this area. The production of manioc and bananas in Marigot was notable, and the small farms scattered in the hills, particularly in Sainte Marie, grew coffee for export and enough provision crops to market them in Trinité and Lamentin.[21]

Overland transport was difficult in this rugged region. Carbet and Case Pilote lie on the road between Fort Royal and Saint Pierre, the two major cities. However, this was very mountainous terrain and difficult even for a single rider on horseback. Most communication along this route was by sea, a quicker and easier journey. It was impossible to travel by land between Saint Pierre and Macouba, and although overland routes through the mountains connected Basse Pointe and Trinité with Sainte Pierre, the sea was the most efficient way to transport people and goods along the windward coast as well. Trinité was the third-largest town and third-largest port in the colony. It had been a busy commercial center during the eighteenth century, and a small number of commercial ships continued to stop there to purchase goods from the surrounding plantations. Although the anchorage was small and the approaches to it were dangerous, the port of Trinité offered advantages to planters from François to Basse Pointe. They could avoid the commissions charged for purchases and sales in Saint Pierre by exchanging their sugar, syrups, and rum directly for the cod, salt meat, timber, and other plantation stores brought there by American ships. In addition, favorable winds made the voyage from Trinité to Europe several days shorter than sailing from Saint Pierre. Aside from the town of Trinité, the population was concentrated on the sugar plantations. Small villages developed at Basse Pointe, Grande Anse, Marigot, and Macouba, where there were landings suitable for shipping sugar and plantation supplies. A great many plantations had their own landings to ship their goods. However, the strong northeast winds along this coast could make loading and unloading cargoes as well as navigation difficult, if not hazardous.[22]

The southern and eastern region covered 53,370 hectares, of which 11,671 were planted in sugar cane in 1839. It included the *quartiers* of Fort Royal, Lamentin, Trou-au-Chat, Saint Esprit, Rivière Salée, Trois Ilets, Anses d'Arlets, Diamant, Sainte Luce, Rivière Pilote, Marin, Vauclin, François, Sainte Anne, Robert, and Gros Morne. Except for Lamentin and the environs of Fort Royal, the soil was arid and rocky. Long dry spells retarded the growth of the cane, and water for men and animals had to be stored in jars and cisterns. In many areas, including Sainte Anne, Marin, Trois Ilets, Rivière Salée, and Vauclin, the ground was so hard during the dry season that it was difficult to break. On the other hand, parts of several other *quartiers* of this region, including Robert, François, Trou-au-Chat, Anses d'Arlets, and Lamentin, were low and marshy. Their wet soils were good for growing sugar cane, but they were very unhealthy. The broad plain of Lamentin at the foot of the bay of Fort Royal was the largest and most productive *quartier* of the entire colony. Numerous plantations were established along the Lézard River. This river provided power for many sugar mills, but could become a dangerous torrential stream during the rainy season. Even though some drainage projects made the plain of Lamentin less dangerous to health, the residents of this swampy area were subject to many illnesses, especially fevers.[23]

In this part of the island, the agricultural year was divided into two parts. Planting was done during the rainy season or *hivernage*, which lasts from June to November, and the harvest took place in the dry season or *carêmage*, which lasts from December to June. Throughout the colony, planters generally tried to avoid harvesting the sugar cane during the winter season. During this period, the cane plant flowered, the sucrose content of the cane juice declined, and the plant yielded less sugar.[24]

The land in the southern part of the island was less productive than in the north. A carré of land in the south seldom yielded more than four or five hogsheads of sugar, or 2,000 to 3,000 kilograms. Ratoons lasted only a year and yielded one-third less than the original crop. However, in years with good rainfall, soil fertility increased and compared favorably with the richest parts of the north. There was considerable local variation in the south as well. According to Lavollée, a portion of the land on the Hayot plantation in Anses d'Arlets was put under cultivation for the first time in 1839 and yielded more than 13,200 kilograms of sugar per carré.[25]

The variety of soil and weather conditions in this region led to more diversified agriculture, if in places it was less productive. A broad, marshy plain ran along the rugged coastline from Robert to Vauclin. The soil there was excellent for sugar cultivation. The fertility of Vauclin compared favorably with that of Basse Pointe, and numerous large and prosperous sugar plantations were located there. However, this area was subject to drought. If rainfall were adequate, it was among the most productive cane land in the colony, but lack of rain could drastically reduce the crop. In Robert, provision crops, especially manioc, were grown in the hills behind the plain to be sold at Trinité. In François and Vauclin, the mountains rose steeply from the plain, and coffee and provision-crop cultivation predominated at the higher elevations. According to Sainte-Croix, more provision crops were grown in Vauclin than anywhere else in the colony. Roads were poor in this area, and the sea provided the most convenient means of transport.[26]

The extreme south of the island was less prosperous and more diverse. Sugar cane covered the low hills of Sainte Anne. No other crop was grown there, and it was dominated by a small number of large sugar estates, the largest of which had 236 slaves. The predominance of large property led an observer to describe it as "*une sorte de quartier feodale.*" Harvests were excellent if there was adequate rainfall. However, Sainte Anne was extremely susceptible to drought and lacked potable water. In 1843, it was reported that drought so decimated the *quartier* that plantations with over 200 slaves produced only seven to thirty hogsheads of sugar, while other planters did not even bother to harvest the crop.[25]

Marin had nine substantial sugar plantations located along the bay and in the inland valleys. The largest of these had about 125 slaves. Smaller plantations produced coffee and provisions. Rainfall effected agriculture in Marin, but harvests were regular and the problem seems not to have been as severe as in Sainte Anne. The town of Marin, located at the foot of the bay, had a church and rectory and several houses and stores. Because of the safe anchorage, it was the main shipping point for the produce of this part of the island. The port was open to foreign and French ships and a customs house was located there, though only a small amount of commerce was carried on there. Marin also supplied provisions to the surrounding *quartiers*. Planters from several parishes on the leeward side of the island could secure provisions there more cheaply than in Saint Pierre. They could exchange their produce directly for supplies, and thus avoid the commission charged by the merchants in Saint Pierre.[28]

The country to the west of Marin, including Rivière Pilote, Sainte Luce, Diamant, and Anses d'Arlets, was extremely hilly. Overland transport was very difficult. Most communication in this region was by sea, which was always tranquil on the Caribbean side of the island. Rivière Pilote was the most productive of these *quartiers*. Numerous sugar plantations were concentrated in the valleys, and the best coffee plantations in the colony were scattered across the hillsides. Rivière Pilote grew enough provisions to supply Sainte Anne, Anses d'Arlets, and Diamant. The largest of the sugar plantations there had about 170 slaves. There were fewer sugar plantations in Sainte Luce, Diamant, and Anses d'Arlets. The largest and only really significant sugar plantation in Saint Luce had about 185 slaves in 1842. There were also numerous small coffee and provision farms. Anses d'Arlets was the site of the main village in this area. There were few sugar plantations in this *quartier*, but the very productive Hayot estate was among them. Coffee, cotton, and provisions were also grown there.[29]

There were a number of modest sugar plantations scattered along the shore of the bay of Fort Royal from Trois Ilets to Trou-au-Chat. In addition, Trois Ilets produced enough provisions to export the surplus to Fort Royal and Lamentin. It also had a pottery employing over 200 slaves presumably engaged in making clay forms used in draining wet sugar. Further, it was important as a center for shipping the produce of the surrounding area to Fort Royal and Saint Pierre. In addition to sugar, coffee and provisions were grown in the highlands of Rivière Salée and Saint Esprit. Trou-au-Chat was much more suitable for the cultivation of provisions and coffee than sugar. Fruits and provision crops were grown commercially there for sale in Fort Royal and Saint Pierre. The land was very marshy in this part of the island, and the contrast between the dry season and the rainy season was marked. Transportation was difficult, and it was regarded as an unhealthy place to live.[30]

Lamentin was the largest agricultural area in the colony. It had the most slaves and the most sugar plantations. It was linked by road to François, Trinité, Robert, Gros Morne, and Trou-au-Chat. These were excellent in the dry season, though they could become impassable in the rainy season. A canal helped to carry the sugar from the plantations to the bay. Yams, bananas, and manioc were grown in the hills. The town of Lamentin was the fourth-largest population center in the colony. In 1842 it had a free population of 637 and 366 slaves. On Sunday market days an enormous number of buyers and sellers converged on the town. It was a major market for provisions for the surrounding *quartiers*, and the market place was too small for the crowds that gathered there. The land in Lamentin was swampy, unhealthy, and lacked potable water, and various fevers and diseases were common there.[31]

Gros Morne offered a stark contrast to Lamentin. Situated high in the mountainous interior, it had the most numerous population of *petits blancs* in the colony. The free population was 2,000 and the slave population numbered 2,400. Provisions, principally manioc, were grown on smallholdings and sold at Trinité and Lamentin. The soil was not suitable for sugar, although some was grown there along with coffee. According to Soleau, who visited the *quartier* in 1835, some coffee plantations were converted to sugar during the sugar boom. The few small planters who grew sugar cane took it elsewhere to be ground and manufactured into sugar. However, overland transport was difficult and costly.[32]

According to testimony given by planters before the 1829 sugar commission, some privileged lands in Martinique produced up to 7,000 or 8,000 kilograms per carré, but these were rare cases, and the average was 3,000. Yields were slightly lower in Guadeloupe, with one harvest of planted cane and two harvests of ratoons averaging 2,500 kilograms per carré annually. In contrast, the average for Cuba and Puerto Rico was 6,000 to 7,000 kilograms per carré without the use of fertilizer. (Although another source in the same report estimates the average yield in Puerto Rico to be 3,500 kilograms per hectare [1 hectare = .78 carré] at the minimum.) The difference was attributed to the greater fertility and "newer" soil of the Spanish colonies. Lavollée determined that Martinique as a whole produced an average of eight hogsheads of sugar, or between 4,000 and 4,800 kilograms, per carré. He estimated that while yields were much greater in Cuba where much of the soil was still virgin and production techniques were more advanced, the fertility of Martinique was equal to that of Bourbon and superior to that of French Guiana, Antigua, Surinam, and Demarara. Agriculture in Martinique, he concluded, did not suffer from lack of fertility, but from lack of intelligence.[33]

As elsewhere in the Americas, the predominance of the sugar plantation in Martinique stunted the formation of town life. However, these are not the great estates described for Brazil, which substitute for the town—having their own chapels and priests, administration of justice, and so on. Instead, in each *quartier*, small villages grew up around the parish church. Often located at the main shipping point for the produce of the *quartier*, they were generally poor and small—often just a few rude houses occupied by the freedmen of color. Nevertheless, they offered a focal point for social life for the rural population, if only for Sunday services and local markets.

The only real cities in Martinique attest to its colonial character. Fort Royal was the administrative center of the colony, the residence of the governor, and seat of the garrison. It was located on an expanse of flat land between the bay of the same name and the Madame River and was bounded an each side by canals connecting the river with the bay. It had a small but excellent deep-water harbor. Though the city was surrounded by water, the canals were frequently dry, and lack of potable water, both for the city and for provisioning ships, was a constant problem. Fort Royal contained various public buildings, including the arsenal, barracks, and warehouse. La Savanne, the large promenade bordering the sea, was the center of its social life. The predominantly wood construction of the town made it susceptible to earthquakes and fires. Much of the city was destroyed in the 1839 earthquake, which struck the entire island. After that many buildings were rebuilt in stone. (This natural disaster, followed by an epidemic of yellow fever, also jeopardized that year's sugar crop and wiped out many already hard-pressed planters.)[34]

The city of Saint Pierre was the major commercial center of the French Antilles. The *exclusif* granted it a privileged position in the trade between the colonies and France at the expense of Fort Royal, and the other islands were obliged to trade only there. Almost all of the exterior trade of Martinique passed through Saint Pierre. It was also the entrepôt for Guadeloupe and the other French dependencies in the Antilles as well as for trade, authorized and unauthorized, with neighboring foreign colonies. Despite the growth of Saint Domingue in the eighteenth century,

Saint Pierre had remained a port of considerable importance, and it regained its preeminent position after the loss of Haiti. Located at the foot of Mount Pelée, it had a good but unsheltered harbor and handled all long-course and coastal shipping except during the rainy season when the administration ordered all merchant ships to Fort Royal for safer anchorage. This centralization of commerce in Saint Pierre allowed transatlantic ships to return with full cargoes and facilitated further development of sugar cultivation in the more remote parts of the French colonies while control of trade and finance wound up in the hands of its *commissionnaires*.[35]

Saint Pierre was one of the largest cities in the Antilles. The 1819 census counted 1,501 houses, and because many of them were divided, 2,500 hearths in its two parishes. The total population of the town and adjacent rural zones was 17,752. The white population of the town was 2,854. The addition of the garrison and the crews of ships in the harbor raised that number to about 5,000. Except for two rum distilleries and some sugar refineries, there were no manufactures in the city, and a disproportionate number of the populace was engaged in commerce of one type or another. The rural district of the quarter also included sixteen sugar estates, a great number of country houses, and small farms growing food for local consumption. The city boasted sixty-six paved streets in its commercial quarter, numerous fine homes, public and private fountains, and an array of public buildings, including a customs house and treasury, a theater, a government house, a courthouse, a barracks, civil and military prisons, two churches, two convents, a school for young ladies, a maritime hospital, an almshouse, a cemetery, public baths, a market, a promenade along the seashore, and a botanical garden—all of which bore witness to its prosperity and status as the commercial, social, and cultural metropolis of the French Antilles.[36]

The human environment of Martinique was thus profoundly shaped by sugar. It unified the social space of the colony as it created regional differences resulting from soil, climate, transport, and so on, that required diversity of local response and individual initiative. This spatial organization expressed the conditions and limits of the expansion of the colonial sugar industry, but these conditions and limits were not simply natural. Rather, the physical environment was itself socially constructed by slave labor producing for the world market, and it is within the form of social relations of slave production that the specific historical character of these limits is to be found.

## The Limits of Agricultural Expansion

The sugar boom transformed the pattern of agricultural activity in Martinique. More and more resources were devoted to cane production, but the growth of the sugar industry took place without any fundamental alteration of the scale and social-technical organization of the producing units. The majority of sugar lands on the island, and certainly the best of them, had been occupied since the seventeenth and eighteenth centuries. According to Schnakenbourg, the boundaries of almost all the significant sugar plantations had been established in the half-century between 1670 and 1720. It was difficult for these existing estates to respond to the growing demand for sugar during the first half of the nineteenth century. Many of them had vacant lands available within their borders, and the possibility existed for expansion there. However, further expansion on to contiguous lands was often precluded by the proximity of neighboring estates. Further, as will be seen in the following chapters, any increase in the size of individual estates was subject to technical and social constraints that tended to fix the scale of operations and limit the conditions under which changes could be successfully implemented.[37]

The very presence of these already-established plantations limited the resources available for the formation of new production units. In the absence of extensive tracts of unoccupied territory, new plantations had to fit into the interstices of the existing properties. Instead of a significant number of new large estates producing under optimal conditions being created, small and medium-sized plantations proliferated in Martinique. These were frequently in locations with less favorable soil and climate conditions and ones that required higher transportation costs. Further, because of difficulties of transport and the absence of alternatives, the great majority of these new plantations had to process their own sugar. Small in scale and without a great deal of capital to invest, they utilized customary methods of refining rather than adopting the more advanced techniques that were becoming available. These traditional practices were relatively simple, inexpensive, and easily adapted to small-scale operations. However, while they may have seemed well suited to the needs of the individual plantation, they simply reinforced the hold of an increasingly archaic and inefficient technology on the colonial sugar industry.

In their desire to take advantage of the protective duties and high prices, planters in Martinique cleared fields and constructed plantations in locations unfavorable for sugar cultivation either because of climate or soil conditions or because of their distance from refining and shipping facilities. The increased concentration on sugar cane production and the decline of other crops resulted in overplanting and the misuse of resources, which impaired the colony's productivity as sugar monoculture approached the limits of territorial expansion on the island. At the same time, soil exhaustion reduced output per slave. Some planters attempted to offset these conditions by the increased use of fertilizers and the adoption of other innovations, which increased the costs of production. In his report on agricultural conditions in Martinique in 1846, the Director of the Interior wrote that in nine communes sugar production was flourishing because of the use of fertilizer, especially guano, on a wide scale, while in seven other communes production was stationary or declining because of drought or labor shortage.[38]

The unrestrained expansion of sugar cultivation at times upset the delicate ecological balance of the microclimatic zones of the island. Emile Thomas recorded several cases where deforestation accentuated seasonal variations in weather, creating alternate periods of torrential rain and drought. Such expansion not only destroyed rich forest resources but was counterproductive for sugar cultivation as well. Thomas lamented how sugar had deformed West Indian agriculture. "Sugar cane is the only plant really cultivated in our colonies, and the only one which furnishes a commercial and agricultural product. However, not only is it far from being the only crop advantageously cultivable, but it has taken hold of a number of localities where conditions are most unfavorable."[39]

The statistical information available about the distribution of property in Martinique is limited. It is impossible to ascertain the exact size of individual plantations as no survey was made until after the abolition of slavery in 1848. According to Paul Daubrée, the average annual production of a plantation in Martinique and Guadeloupe was 150 hogsheads (75 metric tons), ranging from 40 hogsheads to 500 hogsheads. In 1839, Lavollée reported that there were 495 sugar plantations in Martinique. Of this number, 60 produced between 300 and 600 hogsheads of sugar annually, 100 produced between 150 and 300 hogsheads, and 335 produced fewer than 150 hogsheads. Jean-Baptiste Rouvellat de Cussac also observed in 1842 that 60 large estates dominated the colony, and commented that the others were small estates whose owners were impoverished and indebted. According to Jabrun, a large plantation had 180–200 slaves. Thus, a typical *habitation sucrière* producing 450–500 hogsheads of sugar annually had 200–210 slaves, about half of whom were employed in sugar cultivation, with about 100 carrés in cane. Jabrun classifies estates with 120–150 slaves as medium-sized. His own property in Guadeloupe fit into this category. He had 154 slaves of whom 104 were adults. Sugar was planted on 70 carrés, of which 45 were harvested annually, yielding a product of 225 hogsheads. The number of sugar planters was swollen by small farmers who were either attracted by high prices and the prestige of that crop and cultivated it in small amounts, or kept their slaves in the hope of receiving compensation for them after the declaration of emancipation. Jabrun regarded a plantation with fewer than 120 slaves as small. Perhaps the holding of Cassius Linval can be considered representative of this category. He produced 90 hogsheads of sugar on 20 hectares of land with 56 slaves, of whom 25 were adult workers.[40]

Lavollée stressed the importance of the scale of operations in determining the productivity of the plantation. Refining technology and skill, administrative ability, and to a degree, pure chance, as well as the quality of the soil and other agricultural factors combined in different ways to determine production costs on each plantation. According to Lavollée, production was inefficient at all levels in Martinique, but plantations producing from 300 to 600 hogsheads of sugar annually, because they had more resources at their disposal, had lower costs relative to their output. They were better able to weather the effects of falling prices and increased competition after 1830 than were the medium size plantations (producing 150 to 300 hogsheads). The proprietors of the latter had fewer slaves and work animals at their disposal and could not give the soil the same care as their larger neighbors, while the value of their buildings and materials did not diminish despite the smaller scale of activity. Plantations producing less than 150 hogsheads were established under the most adverse conditions. They were too small to produce sugar efficiently and too weak to withstand the pressure of falling prices. Their existence was marginal and could only by sustained when market conditions were favorable.[41]

The optimal size for a sugar plantation estimated by Higman for Jamaica was between 201 and 300 slaves. According to Higman, this size holding allowed masters to maximize their control over the effective deployment of their slaves and their capital equipment. The large estates in Martinique appear to have been within this range, although it might reasonably be suspected that they were concentrated at its lower end. However, the large plantations in Martinique were considerably smaller than those using the semi-mechanized mill developed in Cuba between 1820 and 1860, and were dwarfed by the mechanized mills introduced into the Spanish colony in the 1840s and 1850s. According to Moreno Fraginals, by 1860 there were in Cuba 889 of the former, with an average capacity of 411 metric tons, and 64 of the latter with an average capacity of 1,176 metric tons. In contrast, the medium-sized mills in Martinique appear to have been comparable to the animal-powered mills in Cuba, which produced an average of 113 metric tons in 1860. However, in Martinique the medium plantations played an extremely important role, and together with the small plantations may have accounted for about half the crop. Also, the distance between the larger of the medium-sized mills and the large mills was not so great as in Cuba, and this may have contributed to greater social cohesion among the planters.[42]

The exceptional number of small plantations was due in large part to the conversion of plantations growing another crop than sugar. In particular many of the larger coffee planters cut down their coffee plants to grow cane instead.

They were generally marginal producers operating on too small a scale and in unfavorable locations. Soleau commented on a number of small *sucreries* of recent origin between Lamentin and Robert. All were former coffee estates with small *ateliers*: "The mountainous terrain on which they are located is not suitable for the cultivation of cane, and the high costs of overland transport raise the price of exploitation. They can never compete with the large plantations of the coastal plain where conditions of cultivation and transport are more suitable. Geography assigns coffee to the center of the island." In Gros Morne he also encountered very small sugar plantations. They too were recently converted coffee plantations, and, in his words, did not amount to very much. According to Schoelcher, the proprietors of Gros Morne generally had more slaves than land and encouraged their slaves to rent themselves out for weeks and months at a time to the sugar estates in Lamentin and Robert, where there was a shortage of hands. Similarly in Case Pilote, the sugar plantations were undermanned, and of some twenty-one estates, only two were considered significant.[43]

The pattern of development that characterized the growth of the sugar industry in Martinique can be seen more clearly by examining the agricultural zones discussed previously. The number of sugar estates, the amount of land planted in cane, and the number of slaves working in sugar increased in all parts of the island between 1820 and 1847, as did the amount of sugar produced (see table 3.6). The number of plantations and amount of land in sugar grew most rapidly between 1820 and 1837, while the number of slaves employed in sugar showed the greatest gain only after 1837. Yet despite the overall growth of the sugar industry, there was no fundamental reorganization of production units. Rather, more land and slaves were concentrated in sugar production through the multiplication of medium- and small-sized plantations. The average amount of land cultivated in sugar per plantation decreased over this same period. The average number of slaves employed in sugar declined until 1837 and then rose sharply, although it never returned to the 1820 level. The average yield per plantation remained fairly stable from 1832 onward, but in this case too, it remained below the figure for 1820 (see table 3.7).

Table 3.6. Regional Distribution of Sugar Production, 1820–1847 (1820=100)

| | 1820 | | 1832 | | 1837 | | 1842 | | 1847 | |
|---|---|---|---|---|---|---|---|---|---|---|
| **SUGAR PLANTATIONS** | | | | | | | | | | |
| West | 49 | 100 | 58 | 118 | 65 | 133 | 66 | 135 | 63 | 129 |
| North | 82 | 100 | 97 | 118 | 101 | 123 | 107 | 130 | 119 | 145 |
| East | 82 | 100 | 120 | 146 | 132 | 161 | 133 | 162 | 134 | 163 |
| South | 138 | 100 | 191 | 138 | 207 | 150 | 192 | 139 | 182 | 132 |
| TOTAL | 351 | 100 | 466 | 133 | 505 | 144 | 498 | 142 | 498 | 142 |
| | | | | | | | | | | |
| **LAND IN SUGAR (HECTARES)** | | | | | | | | | | |
| West | 1,782 | 100 | 2,189 | 123 | 2,064 | 116 | 2,097 | 118 | 2,386 | 134 |
| North | 4,986 | 100 | 5,869 | 118 | 5,982 | 120 | 5,689 | 114 | 6,455 | 129 |
| East | 5,040 | 100 | 6,556 | 130 | 6,354 | 126 | 6,257 | 124 | 6,027 | 120 |
| South | 4,649 | 100 | 5,572 | 120 | 6,492 | 140 | 3,904 | 84 | 4,867 | 105 |
| TOTAL | 16,457 | 100 | 2,0186 | 123 | 2,0892 | 127 | 1,7947 | 109 | 1,9735 | 120 |
| | | | | | | | | | | |
| **SLAVES EMPLOYED IN SUGAR** | | | | | | | | | | |
| West | 4,330 | 100 | 4,252 | 98 | 4,404 | 102 | 7,549 | 174 | 5,687 | 131 |
| North | 8,582 | 100 | 11,801 | 138 | 9,121 | 106 | 10,738 | 125 | 11,448 | 133 |
| East | 9,355 | 100 | 7,055 | 75 | 9,182 | 98 | 9,359 | 100 | 11,082 | 118 |
| South | 8,964 | 100 | 9,611 | 107 | 9,336 | 104 | 9,421 | 105 | 12,212 | 136 |
| TOTAL | 31,231 | 100 | 32,719 | 105 | 32,043 | 103 | 37,067 | 119 | 40,429 | 129 |
| | | | | | | | | | | |
| **SUGAR PRODUCED (METRIC TONS)** | | | | | | | | | | |
| West | 3,051 | 100 | 3,296 | 108 | 2,714 | 89 | 4,244 | 139 | 3,864 | 127 |
| North | 7,911 | 100 | 8,845 | 112 | 11,454 | 145 | 10,353 | 131 | 10,807 | 137 |
| East | 8,186 | 100 | 8,500 | 104 | 7,724 | 94 | 9,108 | 111 | 9,844 | 120 |
| South | 7,381 | 100 | 9,229 | 125 | 8,198 | 111 | 8,610 | 117 | 7,578 | 103 |
| TOTAL | 26,529 | 100 | 29,870 | 113 | 30,090 | 113 | 32,315 | 122 | 32,093 | 121 |

*Sources*: Sainte Croix, *Statistique de la Martinique*, II; ANSOM, *Martinique. État de Culture.*

*West*: Prêcheur, Saint Pierre, Carbet, Case Pilote; *North*: Macouba, Basse Pointe, Grand Anse, Marigot, Sainte Marie, Trinité; *East*: Robert, François, Vauclin, Sainte, Anne, Marin, Rivière Pilote; *South*: Fort Royal, Lamentin, Trou-au-Chat, Saint Esprit, Rivière Salée, Trois Ilets, Anses d'Arlets, Diamant, Sainte Luce, Gros Morne.

Table 3.7. Average Holdings of Sugar Plantations by Region, 1820–1847

| | 1820 | 1832 | 1837 | 1842 | 1847 |
|---|---|---|---|---|---|
| LAND IN SUGAR (HECTARES)/SUGAR PLANTATION | | | | | |
| West | 36.4 | 37.7 | 31.8 | 31.8 | 37.9 |
| North | 60.8 | 60.5 | 59.2 | 53.2 | 54.2 |
| East | 61.5 | 54.6 | 48.1 | 47 | 45 |
| South | 33.7 | 29.2 | 31.4 | 20.3 | 26.7 |
| TOTAL | 46.9 | 43.3 | 41.4 | 36 | 39.6 |
| SLAVES EMPLOYED IN SUGAR/SUGAR PLANTATION | | | | | |
| West | 88.4 | 73.3 | 67.8 | 114.4 | 90.3 |
| North | 104.7 | 121.7 | 90.3 | 100.4 | 96.2 |
| East | 114.1 | 58.8 | 69.6 | 70.4 | 82.7 |
| South | 65 | 50.3 | 45.1 | 49.1 | 67.1 |
| TOTAL | 89 | 70.2 | 63.5 | 74.4 | 81.2 |
| SUGAR PRODUCED (METRIC TONS)/SUGAR PLANTATION | | | | | |
| West | 62.3 | 56.8 | 41.8 | 64.3 | 61.3 |
| North | 96.5 | 91.2 | 113.4 | 96.8 | 90.8 |
| East | 99.8 | 70.8 | 58.5 | 68.5 | 73.5 |
| South | 53.5 | 48.3 | 39.6 | 44.8 | 41.6 |
| TOTAL | 75.6 | 64.1 | 59.6 | 64.9 | 64.4 |

*Sources*: Sainte Croix, *Statistique de la Martinique*, II; A.N.S.O.M., *Martinique. État de Culture*.

*West*: Prêcheur, Saint Pierre, Carbet, Case Pilote; *North*: Macouba, Basse Pointe, Grand Anse, Marigot, Sainte Marie, Trinité; *East*: Robert, François, Vauclin, Sainte, Anne, Marin, Rivière Pilote; *South*: Fort Royal, Lamentin, Trou-au-Chat, Saint Esprit, Rivière Salée, Trois Ilets, Anses d'Arlets, Diamant, Sainte Luce, Gros Morne.

The greatest and most rapid increase in the number of sugar plantations was concentrated in the south and east at the height of the boom from the mid-1820s to the mid-1830s. The largest number of new plantations was established in the south (especially Lamentin, 19; Saint Esprit, 18; Gros Morne, 11; and Trou-au-Chat, 10) during this period. The amount of land planted in sugar also increased in the south between 1820 and 1837, but not at as fast a rate. It reached its highest point for the period in 1837 and fell off sharply thereafter. However, there was no analogous increase in the number of slaves employed in sugar production. The number of slaves increased only slightly until after 1842, when it rose rapidly. Sugar production, on the other hand, reached its peak in 1832, and fluctuated downward thereafter. Despite the inclusion of Lamentin in this region, it had the smallest and most inefficient holdings. The average holding in the south was the smallest in the colony and declined between 1820 and 1837. After 1837, the average number of slaves per sugar estate increased as the total number of estates contracted. Nevertheless, even though average output per plantation recovered somewhat, the average area cultivated in sugar continued to decline. More slaves were working on less land. Thus, in spite of the small averages per productive unit, the south accounted for a substantial portion of the land and slaves devoted to sugar cultivation and the total sugar produced because of the large number of sugar plantations there.[44]

In the east, the number of plantations increased by 50 between 1820 and 1837, with François accounting for 32 of them, and then leveled off. The amount of land planted in sugar increased dramatically between 1820 and 1832, and then contracted very slowly. In contrast, despite the greater number of plantations, the number of slaves employed actually declined until 1837 and only showed a substantial increase between 1842 and 1847, while the total amount of sugar produced in the east showed the greatest growth after 1837. The average size of holdings in the east was the second largest in the colony. Nevertheless, the amount of land cultivated in sugar declined steadily throughout the period. In contrast, the average number of slaves employed in sugar dropped drastically between 1820 and 1832, and then began to recover. Similarly, average production per estate reached a low in 1837 and then began to rise. Despite the recovery, the averages for the east in 1847 did not return to the levels of 1820. Once again, more slaves were working on less land, and there were a greater number of estates that were on average smaller than previously. The east was the second sugar region of the colony, but the average holding and output per plantation remained below that of the north.[45]

By contrast, fewer new sugar plantations were founded in the north and west, and the rate of increase was much more gradual. The plantations in the alluvial valleys of the north had long been among the most prosperous in the colony, and there was less opportunity to create new estates there. Between 1820 and 1847, eighteen new sugar estates were established in Sainte Marie, seven in Trinité, six in Basse Pointe, and five in Grande Anse. The amount of land devoted to cane cultivation increased rapidly between 1820 and 1832, although not so dramatically as the number of slaves employed in sugar. Land under sugar then remained relatively stable until 1842–47, when it showed another significant increase. The number of slaves employed in sugar declined sharply in 1837 and then returned almost to its highest level. The total amount of land and the number of slaves also increased, although the averages per plantation fell. Sugar production reached its peak in the north in 1837, and then declined slightly. By 1847, the north accounted for the most land, the greatest number of slaves devoted to sugar cultivation, and the highest total production. The averages per estate were also the highest in this region. Nevertheless, here too the increased number of estates and greater areas of land and numbers of slaves producing sugar were accompanied by declining averages per plantation.[46]

In the mountainous west, sugar production increased steadily and significantly, but it remained the least important agricultural region and the one least amenable to large-scale expansion. The number of sugar estates increased by only seven in Saint Pierre and by five in Case Pilote between 1820 and 1847. The total amount of land cultivated in sugar remained small in the west, but it expanded rapidly between 1820 and 1832 and then, after a relative decline, reached its greatest extent in 1847. The total number of slaves stagnated until 1837, then jumped sharply before falling off somewhat by 1847. Sugar production coincided with the movement of the slave labor force. It declined until 1837, then expanded markedly. The averages for the west decreased between 1820 and 1837. Afterward, they indicate growing concentration of production. The average amount of land planted in cane per plantation is relatively low, but the average number of slaves employed in sugar is extremely high. This intensive labor appears to have resulted in relatively high average yields despite the small size of holdings.[47]

The increase in sugar production in Martinique after 1815 was due in large measure to the multiplication of inefficient smaller units. Sugar expanded onto marginal lands or displaced other crops. As the number of sugar plantations increased throughout the colony, the average cultivated area contracted. The creation of small sugar estates was common throughout the colony, but was especially concentrated in the south. Up until 1836, an expanding market, exceptionally high sugar prices, and protective tariffs buoyed these small producers and encouraged them to attempt to convert to sugar. After that date, however, their position became less viable as the beet sugar industry in France reemerged as a major competitor, and sugar prices fell. At the same time, the island reached the limits of physical expansion, and the demand for labor resulting from the end of the slave trade began to make itself felt. Under these conditions, the number of marginal small producers declined, and there was a concentration of production on large and medium-sized holdings located in more favorable areas, especially in the north and east. Expansion remained hampered in the south and west, although the large number of small estates in the south continued to account for a major portion of the total production. If in the first period increasing sugar production was due to more extensive cultivation, in the later period it was due to more intensive exploitation of slave labor. After 1837, the total area under cultivation contracted, but the number of slaves engaged in sugar production reached an all-time high. More slaves working on less land increased the total crop.

## Credit, Debt, and Crisis

The restoration of the sugar industry in the French Antilles depended on the extension of credit from the metropolis and dramatically increased the debt of the colonial planters. The planters of Martinique entered the period of expansion with a legacy of debt resulting from the disruption of economic activity by the turmoil of revolution, war, and foreign occupation between 1792 and 1815. The Colonial Council of Martinique drew attention to the misfortunes of the planter class in

1836: "The causes of our debts are found in a series of circumstances that the colonies could neither see nor prevent. We must begin with the revolution of '93 and the emigration of the proprietors, the bad administrations, the sequestration of plantations, the desertions of the slaves, and all the troubles of the period." The report chronicled the events that had such disastrous consequences for the colony: the English occupation from 1793 to 1802; the Napoleonic wars and the extreme difficulty of communicating with France; the long blockade, seige, and seizure of the island; the second English occupation from 1809 to 1814; the exclusion of Martinique's produce from England and the lack of other outlets for it; and finally, the bills of embargo and of nonintercourse passed by the American Congress between 1807 and 1811. During these years, the planters had difficulty marketing their crops, obtaining necessary supplies, and attracting sufficient credit. Revenues dropped below expenditures. Planters were forced to borrow when they could, but often they were unable to repay even the interest on outstanding debts.[48]

Thus, with the return of peace, planters not only had to bear the expenses of putting their properties in order, but also had to pay their outstanding debts and accumulated interest from the entire preceding period. As their financial condition improved during the Restoration and first years of July Monarchy, they were able to repay a significant portion of their old debts. In 1829, de Lavigne reported that the debts of the colonists of Martinique had diminished considerably, although he hastened to add that some planters were still in a wretched condition. However, at the same time that they liquidated their old debts, the planters contracted new debts. The principal cause of this new debt was the reestablishment of the colonial sugar industry and the expansion and amelioration of its operations to take advantage of the favorable market conditions. The planters hoped that by extending their cultivation they could regain their former affluence. According to one observer recorded in the *Enquête sur les sucres*, "As for the new obligations contracted by the colonists, they explain them by the extension of their cultivation for several years, the contracts they had to enter into to augment the size of their work force, ameliorate the condition of their slaves, and increase their herds—in a word, the expansion of their agricultural exploitation and improvement of the quality of their products." Thus, although the old debt diminished appreciably, it remained substantial, and the very process of revitalizing the sugar industry, building sugar works, buying slaves, and improving and extending cultivation incurred new debts that worsened the condition of the planters and tied them ever more closely to sugar monoculture and slave labor. By the mid-1830s, indebtedness rose again as economic and political conditions declined, and the problem became increasingly aggravated until emancipation.[49]

Contemporary sources agree that the slave trade was the principal cause of the new debt up until 1830. Large numbers of new slaves had to be purchased to recover losses suffered during the years when the trade had been cut off and to raise production to a level of commercial prosperity. While the restoration of the slave trade offered great advantages for the colonial sugar industry as a whole, this was not always the case for individual planters. The value of the slave labor force represented an enormous outlay of capital for the planter. According to available records, it was the largest single investment on the plantation. Sainte Croix, writing in 1820, estimates that the slaves represented nearly 42 percent of the value of a plantation producing 450 hogheads of sugar, while in 1839 Lavollée estimated the slaves to be 34.2 percent of the value of a plantation producing 500 hogsheads of sugar annually. Slave prices rose between 1816 and 1828. The price of an able-bodied slave in Martinique in 1816 was between 1,400 and 1,500 francs. In 1828, the average price was 1,800 francs, and planters paid up to 2,400 francs and more for slaves who were good workers. Further, as a result of the impending abolition of the traffic, the price of females became almost equal to that of males.[50]

The size of the debt contracted after 1815 was enormous. However, various business and accounting practices, such as registering the same mortgage twice, once in Saint Pierre and once in Fort Royal, including in the amount of the mortgage not only the principle and interest due but also present and anticipated future interest payments as well as the approximate cost of the eventual foreclosure, and not removing debts already paid from the registers, greatly inflated the official record of the debt and made it difficult to ascertain the actual amount. By 1838, the official recorded value of mortgage debt in Martinique was 228,921,228.57

francs, while the total value of all the capital employed in agricultural production in the colony was officially put at 330,585,450 francs. In 1822, Baron Delamardelle, compensating for the exaggeration of the official figures, estimated the real mortgage debt of rural properties in Martinique at about 65 million francs. Of the 371 sugar estates included in this figure, only 56 had completely or nearly liquidated their debts. There were 120 that owed less than half their value. Another 61 were indebted for more than half their value. Finally, 95 owed more than they were worth. While Delamardelle saw some hope for the other properties, the last-mentioned he regarded as a plague on the colony as a result of their insolvency. In 1838, Lavollée calculated that if these practices were taken into consideration the minimum amount of the debt in Martinique was 60 million francs in mortgages and another 10 million in commercial debts instead of the 250 million francs recorded in the mortgage registers. Further, the proportion of indebted plantations and the degree of their indebtedness appears to have increased as their number grew. In a work published in 1841, Daubrée mentions that three-fourths of the sugar plantations in Martinique were indebted for sums equal to between half and all of the value of their real and chattel property, while Emile Thomas, writing at the time of slave emancipation, estimated that four-fifths of the properties in Martinique and Guadeloupe were encumbered for twice their value.[51]

Between 1830 and 1848, the planters of Martinique found themselves in the grip of a prolonged crisis that reduced the once-flourishing colony to poverty. Throughout the 1830s and 1840s, the planters complained constantly that their expenses exceeded their revenues. In 1829 the value of imports exceeded that of exports for the first time, and after 1837 this trade deficit became permanent (see table 3.8). The organization of production on the basis of slave labor left planters practically helpless as falling prices coincided with rising costs. In 1842 one planter, Charles Dupin, described the condition of the plantations:

They [the colonies] no longer have revenue because the value of their products no longer covers the costs of their production. They no longer have any credit because the credit which is extended to prosperous or protected

Table 3.8. Martinique: Value of Imports and Exports, 1818–1847 (francs)

| Year | Imports | Exports | Year | Imports | Exports |
|------|---------|---------|------|---------|---------|
| 1818 | 23,894,656 | 25,193,060 | 1833 | 12,268,273 | 14,176,044 |
| 1819 | 15,682,807 | 21,746,250 | 1834 | 14,701,026 | 16,189,565 |
| 1820 | 16,095,700 | 20,767,232 | 1835 | 15,310,314 | 14,857,254 |
| 1821 | 16,043,400 | 20,351,768 | 1836 | 15,404,987 | 15,986,324 |
| 1822 | 13,417,179 | 16,908,041 | 1837 | 17,646,696 | 13,942,169 |
| 1823 | 13,627,037 | 16,840,615 | 1838 | 13,877,472 | 13,790,319 |
| 1824 | 13,811,340 | 18,152,853 | 1839 | 16,226,655 | 13,517,546 |
| 1825 | 17,033,339 | 22,418,913 | 1840 | 16,862,244 | 14,445,615 |
| 1826 | 24,621,362 | 26,577,635 | 1841 | 20,696,133 | 15,501,545 |
| 1827 | 23,391,784 | 25,726,196 | 1842 | 17,920,527 | 13,580,977 |
| 1828 | 22,352,587 | 26,171,288 | 1843 | 21,066,338 | 15,054,021 |
| 1829 | 18,625,320 | 17,714,847 | 1844 | 22,679,912 | 19,588,527 |
| 1830 | 13,864,530 | 17,547,862 | 1845 | 20,661,375 | 18,127,978 |
| 1831 | 13,554,477 | 13,746,161 | 1846 | 21,542,939 | 16,185,432 |
| 1832 | 17,381,981 | 13,946,941 | 1847 | 22,841,091 | 18,323,921 |

Source: l'Annuaire de la Martinique (1884), in Liliane Chauleau, Histoire antillaise: la Martinique et la Guadeloupe à la fin du XIXᵉ siècle, 306–7.

industries withdraws from an industry which everything conspires to hurtle toward its ruin. They cannot close down their ateliers and wait because the worker, whether he works or not, is always the charge of the planter. Finally they cannot maintain or repair their estates because the necessities of life, the interest on the debt contracted for the support of their slaves, and the fulfillment of the prescriptions, not only have absorbed what little remains in their treasury, but for a long time has forced them to live off their capital.

As market conditions declined, the slave owner could not reduce his labor force. The costs of maintaining the slave population were independent of the falling sugar prices. The response to falling prices and declining revenues was to produce more sugar. The economic situation of the French West Indian planters was further aggravated by the declining quality of their sugar. Even though the quantity of sugar they produced increased, it was of inferior quality compared to that produced in foreign colonies and, above all, to French beet sugar. Thus, the French West Indian planters were not able to get the best prices, and their financial position was further weakened.[52]

As long as sugar enjoyed high prices, the enormous revenues of the sugar estates could cover the greater part of the advances made to them each year. But when sugar prices fell, the revenues declined and all the partial unpaid advances combined to form a considerable debt. Many plantations fell deeply into arrears and remained there. As we shall see, the property could not be foreclosed, and those that could not free themselves from their charges languished under disrepute. For many planters, these debts were almost equal to the total value of their property, and their only recourse was to fraud. For others, the amount was so considerable that they gave up any hope of repaying it and simply continued their style of life under the weight of their obligations. They could neither pay off the original advances nor build up their own reserves to meet the rising costs of production. The colonists had to continue to borrow to continue to produce.[53]

Property values dropped. In a report to the French government, Jules Lechevalier reported that in Martinique the owner of a sugar plantation of 250 hectares with an excellent gang of 250 creole slaves, all of which was valued at 500,000 francs, had searched in vain for several years for someone to buy it for 200,000 francs. Debt, falling prices, and poor harvest ruined many plantations, especially in the less prosperous southern half of the island. In 1840, 15 large sugar plantations failed in Rivière Salée alone. The surviving plantations displayed only a shadow of their former grandeur and prosperity. They fell into disrepair and took on a neglected appearance. According to Daubrée, those plantations producing about 150 hogsheads a year were especially hard hit. Bertrand, a planter in the *quartier* of Sainte Anne, wrote that the 192 hogsheads of sugar produced on his plantation in 1838 were barely worth what 128 hogsheads were the year before. It was probable that his expenses would exceed his receipts by 3,000 francs. Bertrand further testified that in the previous year only two of twelve plantations in his neighborhood were able to meet their expenses. One, Val d'Or, had a revenue of some 800 francs, and the other, the property of Messrs. Loture and Rivière, with the strongest and most numerous slave gang in the *quartier*, exceeded its expenses by only a bit over 700 francs. The other ten operated at a loss. According to Bertrand, the situation was similar throughout the colony.[54]

While the planter's property in land and equipment languished, his property in slaves was depreciated by the abolition of the slave trade and the prospect of general emancipation. Despite the shortage of labor, planters were reluctant to risk investing in slaves when there was strong likelihood of emancipation without a fixed indemnity. Instead of scarcity driving prices up, the price of slaves dropped sharply, and the number of sales declined (see Appendix 2). "The value of the slaves today cannot be compared to that stated in the inquiry [of 1829]. English emancipation and the uncertainty that prevails regarding the future have led to a great depreciation. Also the sales of slaves are very rare today and, in those few that take place, the price of a negro worker is rarely greater than 1000 francs. For children and the aged the value varies from 200 francs to 600 francs, according to their age or their infirmities," reported Lavollée. This loss had to be made up from the revenues of production, which were themselves shrinking. Furthermore, this drop in the price of slave labor had nothing whatever to do with the costs of slave labor. It neither cheapened the costs of reproducing the laborer nor made him more productive.[55]

The decay of plantation agriculture was both cause and symptom, not only of the decline of the colonial economy in its narrow meaning, but of the distress and exhaustion of the entire planter class and the society they dominated as well. Governor De Moges described the troubled condition of the planters: "With some it is destitution; with others it is the thoughtlessness of a life profoundly agitated by the events of the last half century; almost everywhere, it is the uncertainty of the future. Furthermore, those families that are still well off are in France. Martinique has her absentees as does Ireland and suffers from it as does Ireland. Overseers have neither the outlook, the vitality, the prospects, nor the patriotism of the proprietors." De Moges concluded his report by remarking that the real poverty of the colony was concealed by the extensive cultivation of sugar cane, which gave it the appearance of prosperity.[56]

## Inalienable Property

The problem of the colonial debt was not simply conjunctural, but was rooted in the organization of production itself. Sugar plantations were considered to be indivisible units by their very nature. Land, mill, and slaves were all integral to the process of making sugar. Their separation would have destroyed production and rendered each of them useless. Thus, the property had to remain intact to have any value at all, and it became impractical for creditors to seize sugar estates for debt. This condition resulted in chronic indebtedness throughout the Caribbean sugar colonies. But in the French West Indies it received a legal sanction that effectively prevented land and slaves from being constituted as alienable private property. The creditor was thus left without legal recourse, and the plantation was insulated from the claims of creditors and the influence of the market. Paradoxically, this situation compelled the creditor to continue to make advances or face the loss of his entire capital while it enabled the plantation to continue to operate, even at a "loss." Consequently, the consolidation of rural property was inhibited, and the organization of production became more resistant to change as the debt was exacerbated.

Schoelcher emphasized the speculative nature of the sugar industry in the French Antilles. Plantations were acquired to make money, and according to his sources, there was not a single example of a plantation being sold for cash since the foundation of the colony. Purchases were made on credit, and given the shortage of ready cash in the colony, the seller had no alternative but to accept it. After a down payment of between one-fourth and one-third of the purchase price, the buyer expected to pay the remainder from the proceeds of the estate, usually over a period of ten to fifteen years. He was thus dependent on the maintenance of revenues and the avoidance of catastrophe to pay off the debt.[57]

To protect the planter, the application of metropolitan law (*la coutume de Paris*) was modified in the colonies effectively to prohibit the seizure or division of sugar estates. While recognized in principle, the attachment of sugar plantations for debt (*expropriation forcée*) was virtually impossible in practice. Procedures were long, costly, and difficult, and creditors rarely risked using them for fear of losing their entire claim. However, the Royal Declaration of August 24, 1726, did authorize a procedure known as *déguerpissement*, which allowed those selling plantations to repossess the property for nonpayment. But this partial measure was insufficient. It was still in force as late as the 1840s, and was described by Schoelcher as "so impractical and surrounded with difficulties so insurmountable . . . that its application was unknown." Further, the declaration said nothing about debts other than those resulting from the sale of a plantation, and particularly the commercial debts due merchants whose only recourse was to seize the property.[58]

These restrictions on the seizure of property thus sacrificed the interests of creditors to the sugar industry. Already as the colonial debt began to mount in the eighteenth century, planters increasingly used the inability of creditors to seize property to escape their obligations. By the 1760s there were various efforts by administrators to simplify the procedures to provide effective security for creditors, but nothing was done before the Revolution. Nonexpropriation was reasserted in the colonial civil code of 1805, which declared that compulsory seizure "would be ruinous for the planters because of their longstanding debts. The nature of colonial property, composed principally of slaves and mills, requires a mode of expropriation different from that adopted in France." Not wishing to provoke the disruption of landed property in the midst of war, economic crisis, and slave unrest, the provisions of the code regarding expropriation were to be suspended until one year after the conclusion of a general peace. Yet despite several attempts to formulate a suitable law for the colonies during the Restoration, this suspension remained in force as long as slavery lasted, and for all practical purposes sugar plantations in the French West Indies remained beyond the reach of their creditors.[59]

The problems faced by creditors were compounded by the Code Noir, which declared that the *nègres de jardin*, that is, those slaves engaged in agricultural production, were for certain purposes to be treated as real estate (*immeubles par destination*). They could not be separated from the property to which they were attached. If the property was to be sold, the slaves had to be sold with it. If there was a seizure for debt, the slaves could only be seized with the plantation itself. If the slaves were to be seized separately, production would be threatened. Thus, the creditor lost an important guarantee. To recover the credit the entire property, with all of the expenses and difficulties that it entailed, had to be seized and not just some of the slaves. This alone inhibited the great majority of creditors, who did not have the resources for such an undertaking. This legislation too remained in effect until emancipation.[60]

The laws of inheritance were also organized to maintain the physical integrity of the plantation unit. Its division would destroy manufactures and expose families to ruin. Consequently, the Royal Declaration of August 24, 1726 also modified French practice in this regard and authorized the custom of *partage en valeur des successions* in the colonies. The plantation unit remained undivided among the members of the same family, each of whom profited from his or her portion of the value of the property. The survivor or one of the heirs took possession of the entire property, including land, slaves, and livestock, and was in charge of its exploitation. Each of the others took a mortgage on the property for their share of its estimated value. Then, according to convention, the operator either shared the profits among the co-owners or successively reimbursed the others for the amount of their claim from the profits of the plantation. The latter was the most frequent. The result of this practice was that on each new inheritance the plantation had to reimburse its entire value, and therefore only arrived at solvency after a long time, if ever. If the new proprietor died without dissolving the debt, the situation of the successor could become untenable, especially during a period of low sugar prices such as the July Monarchy.[61]

In the absence of the seizure of real property, the only other means of recovering their loans open to creditors were ineffective. In a country completely deprived of currency, attachment of income (*la saisie-arrêt*) ended up being the substitution of one debtor for another and consequently an illusory solution. As for the sale by court order of the finished product (*saisie-exécution*), the very nature of colonial production rendered it ineffective. The harvest only was carried out successively and by fractions, and the partial value of the objects seized always remained below the expenses advanced. The remaining alternative, the seizure of the standing crop (*saisie-brandon*), was almost impossible to apply as well. The harvest of the cane and its manufacture had to go on simultaneously. If the creditor simply seized the cane when the crop was ready for harvest, the extra hands and facilities necessary for immediate manufacture were not readily available in a slave society. On the other hand, sugar manufacture often required the planter to mix the products of several cane fields together. If the creditor waited until after the cane had been processed, there was no way to distinguish the product of the seized cane from the product of that which had not been seized. Both Schoelcher and Lavollée agree that it was very difficult for the creditor to recover his capital, and some planters unscrupulously took advantage of this situation to defraud their creditors.[62]

Thus the creditor remained completely disarmed under the legislation current in the French Antilles during the first half of the nineteenth century. No legal recourse could effectively reach the debtor, and the good faith of the latter was the only real pledge of security. The law was impotent to prevent debtors of bad faith from fraudulently freeing themselves from the total sum of their credit when it pleased them. The plantation was always encumbered by mortgages held by family members and heirs. Whether these were reimbursed or not, their claims took precedence over those of the real creditors. Thus, the planter always had at hand the bearers of imaginary claims with which to clear the property of its debts by a simulated liquidation and sale. Further, the common practice of the colonists of Martinique, whether by carelessness, good faith, or calculation, was to always discharge their debts by simple contract (*sous seing privé*) without cancelling mortgage registrations. This general usage allowed the debtor of bad faith to rid himself of all the claims against the property. Payment could never be proven by subsequent creditors because it resulted from discharges made directly between the contracting parties while the claims remained registered, and fraudulent liquidations to relatives and bogus creditors left the genuine creditors deprived of their claims without the property having really changed hands. "This is the fraud known in the colonies as *blanchissage*," declared Emile Thomas, "and unfortunately the great majority of the creoles do not consider it an evil." All this from planters of whom Schoelcher ironically commented, "And he does not pardon his slaves when they steal bananas from him!"[63]

These fraudulent practices became so common with the decline of sugar prices during the 1830s that, according to Lavollée, "there were few properties that had not passed through this means of liberation." He described it as a state of complete disorder in the middle of which the solicitors and barristers fattened themselves. Their fees for all services in Martinique amounted to 11,700,000 francs annually, almost the total amount of the colonial budget. The ordinance of June 14, 1829, tried to remedy such abuses by making registrations obligatory and imposing fines on notaries. But the salutary effects of the ordinance were destroyed by allowing the contracting parties to waive this requirement by means of a declaration in the original agreement. This allowed the notaries to escape responsibility and gave the parties more latitude in avoiding their obligations. While some colonial spokesmen defended these practices as the consequence of usury and the only protection colonists had from "truly odious speculation," critics charged that such protection from creditors encouraged profligate behavior and wasteful spending and destroyed public morality. In Lavollée's words: "There where the right of property is not a word, there is no morality, no society."[64]

The absence of guarantees for creditors in the colony raised interest rates and prices. According to Lavollée, the ordinary interest rate in Martinique was 12 percent when the metropolitan lender made the loan directly to the colonial borrower. But because of difficulties in recovering claims in the colonies, loans were customarily made through the intervention of brokers who gave the money to the borrower at 12 percent, but demanded the renewal of the transaction every three months, for which they charged a 1 percent commission. Thus the 12 percent interest really rose to 16 percent per year. This was the lowest rate at which a loan could be contracted in the colonies. At times of commercial crisis it rose to 2.5 to 3 percent or even more per month. In the judgment of Lavollée, the interest rates alone were enough to eventually sink the planters deeply into debt. Bernard, the attorney general of Guadeloupe, blamed the high interest rates in the French West Indies on the lack of an effective mortgage law. According to him, interest rates averaged only 6 percent in the British West Indies because no exceptions were made for sugar estates. The same mortgage law as in England was rigorously applied in the colonies, with the result that British planters had better access to credit and capital when they needed it.[65]

The failure to consolidate property as a social and legal relation was to disrupt plantation agriculture. The measures taken to maintain and protect the integrity of material production had originally been conceived to favor sugar cultivation at the beginning of colonization. Nevertheless, with the accumulation of old and new debt incurred by the restoration of the sugar industry, the prohibitions against the alienation of land and slaves not only occasioned frauds (which became more frequent) but destroyed credit by not providing any effective guarantee for the creditor. Property was often mortgaged beyond its value and the number of nominal creditors inflated, while mortgages only offered illusory security to the real creditors. As the consequence of this insecurity, confidence in the planters declined. Metropolitan capital invested less in colonial property, and West Indian planters practically ceased to have any direct relations with metropolitan merchants. As Schoelcher commented:

> This credit could be reopened formerly because metropolitan commerce gladly opened its coffers to planters who in those times had solvent properties, and who shipped sugar on which considerable profits were made. But the coffers have closed in proportion that the mortgage registers are filled. And today the capitalist is loathe to aid an irresponsible industry. So many desperate efforts to recover old credits make new loans impossible. The interest on money grows from all the risks that it runs, and the proprietor, forced to pay *au poids de l'or* for the funds he needs, sees all his profits devoured by usury. It is notorious that the legal or at least the commercial rate for money is today ten, twelve, and fifteen percent in the colonies! . . . No industry is possible in a country where the instrument of labor known as capital costs so much.

Unable to recover their money when falling sugar prices could no longer keep pace with growing debt and rapidly accumulating interest, metropolitan creditors began to look elsewhere for more profitable fields of investment. Interest rates went up, costs rose, and real debt accumulated. The result was a shortage of credit, which increased the distress of the planter and further impaired production if it did not threaten the existence of individual sugar estates.[66]

The withdrawal of direct metropolitan investment in the colonies resulted in the restructuring of credit relations. In place of long-term loans secured by a mortgage, capital was advanced by colonial merchants for a short term against the next crop. While this "commercial" debt only accounted for a small part of the total debt of the plantations, it was of crucial importance, for these advances alone provided the capital for ongoing operations. This arrangement exerted great pressure on the production and marketing of the crop. The merchants in effect became the intermediaries of metropolitan capital and took the risk that was unacceptable to metropolitan capitalists. They used letters of exchange to obtain credit from the great commercial houses of Havre, Nantes, Bordeaux, and Marseille, which they in turn extended to the planters. Without the benefit of the security afforded by landed property, the merchants' ability to guarantee these loans to their creditors and to obtain new credits from them rested on their control of colonial produce. Similarly, the planter had to continue to borrow to continue to produce and had to continue to produce to continue to borrow. Merchant and planter became locked together in mutual dependency and mutual antagonism. The exclusion of land and slaves from the circulation of capital generated an often-desperate struggle between them over control of the crop and the distribution of the revenue from it that transformed the great majority of planters into tributaries of the merchants. The existing organization of the production units was thereby reinforced, and they were made almost impervious to anything but piecemeal amelioration.[67]

## Merchants and Planters

The commercial and financial activities of Martinique were concentrated in the hands of a small number of merchants in Saint Pierre and to a lesser extent, in

Fort Royal. These merchants were almost always *commissionnaires* or factors, who received the produce of the plantations on consignment and in return furnished the plantations with their supplies. They served as the intermediaries between French commercial houses and West Indian planters and offered several advantages to colonial commerce. Merchants in France depended on the *commissionnaires'* familiarity with the local market. As residents of the colony, they knew the needs of the planters and could more ably ascertain which of them were good credit risks. By centralizing trade in Saint Pierre, they enabled transatlantic vessels to dispose of their goods and obtain full return cargoes quickly. A resident factor could spare French merchant ships a long layover in the Antilles by preparing the outward cargo before the ship arrived and collecting outstanding debts after it left. Turnaround time would thus be reduced, transportation costs lowered, and ship, crew, and cargo spared the consequences of a prolonged stay in tropics.[68]

On the other side of the coin, the centralization of trade in their hands was essential to the exploitation of remote rural estates. It was considered indispensable for each planter or plantation manager to have a *commissionnaire* in Saint Pierre or Fort Royal to handle the affairs of the estate. The *commissionnaire* supplied food, implements, livestock, and whatever else was required for the operation of the plantation throughout the year. The planter was thereby freed from having to leave the supervision of his property and was assured that his stocks would be continually replenished in spite of any temporary shortage of money. Further, the *commissionnaires'* intimate knowledge of market conditions both locally and in France and their direct relations with the shippers and commercial houses of the metropolis were essential in securing advantageous terms of sale for the planter's crop. Finally, the *commissionnaire* provided the planter with the credit necessary to sustain his operations. This was especially important because of the large capital investment required by a sugar estate. Few planters could afford to make purchases in cash, and it took a long time, sometimes as long as two years, for them to realize the profits from the sale of their product.[69]

The *commissionnaires* thus provided a vital commercial and financial link between France and the colonies. Originally, they had been agents for European merchants, but they soon became independent middlemen. They were able to assert control over this strategic point in the circuit of colonial commerce and exploit it to their own advantage. Between eight and ten large-scale *commissionnaires* predominated in Saint Pierre, the most important commercial center of the island. They formed a powerful group, and their position as both buyers and sellers of most of the colony's goods as well as creditors of most of the planters offered them unique opportunities for profit with little risk. In the view of Emile Thomas, it made even the most honorable of them "a plague and leprosy on the planter," and contributed to the indebtedness of the planters and the torpor of colonial agriculture and industry.[70]

The *commissionnaires* used their control of trade and finance to appropriate the surplus of plantation production and force the planters into a position of dependency and indebtedness. The planter paid the factor a commission on all supplies furnished throughout the year and granted him the exclusive right to sell his sugar. The factor charged all purchases to the planter's account and credited the value of the sugar he sold. For his services, the factor also charged a percentage of the gross sale price of the sugar as well as freight and other charges such as hauling, weighing, and storage. The planter was usually allowed to dispose of the molasses and syrups himself, if there were any. These were usually sold to the Americans for cash, which was applied to the planter's domestic expenses. The factors not only received a commission from the planters for selling their sugar, but received an additional 2.5 percent commission from the European commercial houses with whom they had regular relations for buying the same sugar. Accounts were settled on December 31 of each year. If the balance was in favor of the planter, he received payment in money. Only those planters who were free of all obligations and debts to the factor could secure reduced commission charges of 2.5 percent for goods purchased and sold on their behalf. However, these were very few in number. The great majority of planters ended the year indebted to the factors. These were charged commissions fixed at 5 percent as well as 5 percent interest on the outstanding sum, which was carried over to the next year's account. This unpaid balance, carried over year after year, could quickly build up into a burden of debt that was impossible for the planter to remove. In addition, two local decrees in

1817 and 1823 guaranteed the *liaison de habitation*, which obliged the indebted planter to turn over his entire harvest to his factor-creditor.[71]

The commissions and other accessory charges by the factor weighed heavily against the account of the plantation. They represented an exorbitant proportion of the costs of production. When the price of sugar was high and sugar plantations yielded large revenues, the planters paid little attention to them. But as sugar prices began to fall, the maintenance of these charges became ruinous, and planters tried to avoid them if they could. The impact of the charges was unequally distributed. They hit the smaller and less solvent estates the hardest. Some of the larger planters could reduce the costs of transport, weighing, and storage by repacking and weighing the sugar on the plantation and transferring it directly to a transatlantic vessel. If they were also able to establish direct relations with metropolitan shippers, they could free themselves at least partially from the mediation of the factor by making a portion of their purchases directly from France. They could thus pay lower fees to the factors and obtain their provisions much more cheaply. However, only a very few planters could establish such independent relations abroad, and the factor became the intermediary for almost everyone.[72]

The relation between merchant and planter inhibited the rationalization of plantation production and threatened the liquidity of the entire system. The annual balance of accounts invariably favored the merchants. Almost all of the planters were continually in arrears and often owed considerable sums to their factors. Few of them could afford to pay cash to cover their expenses. Instead the great majority of them had to pledge the next year's crop to cover the costs of the current year's production. The position of the plantation was precarious under this arrangement. Negligence, falling sugar prices, or a succession of bad harvests not only meant that the planter was unable to repay the original advance, but also that he had to contract a new one to continue producing. This could quickly drive him into debt or ruin. Sainte Croix writes that a dry season could reduce the harvest by half and force the planter to become deeply indebted to the *commissionnaire*. If there were a second bad year, the *commissionnaire* would not have sold enough produce to be able to make more advances, and the planter would have to sell the sugar he had on hand just to feed his slaves and make the repairs necessary to keep his operations going. According to Sainte Croix, this was not an uncommon state of affairs, and it serves to accentuate the delicate equilibrium of the plantation economy in Martinique.[73]

Dependence on the advances of the *commissionnaire* deprived the planter of the means and incentive to improve agriculture and manufactures and tied him to established routines. The practice of accounting expenditures against the value of the sugar to be sold reduced the amount of cash necessary for the daily operations of the plantation to a minimum. This arrangement made it difficult for the planter to calculate profit and loss on a day-to-day basis, and Thomas suggests that it encouraged the planter to be wasteful, negligent, and dependent on the factor: "Why economize, think of the future, or care for the livestock and the agricultural implements? Why ask the price of goods or fertilizer? All of that is toilsome, and it is so convenient to have recourse to the *commissionnaire* for whom an order suffices."[74]

The credit system forced a self-perpetuating cycle of debt and dependency on the plantation that reinforced sugar monoculture and resulted in the appropriation of the crop by the *commissionnaire*. "Too great a number of planters," wrote Raynal in the 1820s, "are rather the tenants (*fermiers*) of commerce than the proprietors of their plantations." As Buffon has emphasized, the guarantee for the credit advanced was not only the harvest itself, but the planters' dependence on further advances from the factors. Only by continuing to send their sugar to the factors could they maintain a source of credit for the future and not be deprived of the advances and the supplies that were indispensable for the operation of their estates. Thus, the credit system constrained the planters to continue devoting their efforts to sugar cultivation. Not only did they have to continue to borrow to continue to produce, but they had to continue to produce to continue to borrow. The disposition of the crop was already determined before it was planted. The planters had no choice among potential agents or customers. Rather, they were obliged to send their produce to their creditors to continue receiving credit.[75]

During the prolonged crisis that occurred under the July Monarchy this cycle became permanent and irreversible. As planter revenues declined, debt created more debt. The advance of goods in kind against payment in sugar left the planters in a deficit. As the advances continued, the interest was capitalized and the debt rose. The planters were compelled to grow more and more sugar just to keep meeting expenses. However, the increased harvests were not enough to cover the costs of production and the overdue principal and interest. The year's labor only increased the financial burden on the planters. They lost control over their product, and through its continuous appropriation, the merchants in fact became the real masters of the plantation economy.[76]

As the planter was obligated to send his crop to the creditor, so the creditor was the captive of the credit he had already advanced to the planter. In the absence of effective security, a debt-ridden estate was unlikely to face foreclosure. If the creditor were to discontinue making loans to the planter, the possibility of recuperating the capital already advanced was remote and uncertain at best. Repayment was virtually the option of the planter. The only alternative for the merchant was to continue advancing credit to the planters in the hope they could generate enough revenue to pay off a portion of their debt. But this increased the merchant's vulnerability. While the consignment of the crop assured him of a return in a normal year, no juridical mechanism really guaranteed the recovery of the credit. Bad harvests or bad faith on the part of the debtor threatened the creditor's ability to advance future credit. The situation of chronic debt heightened the antagonism between merchant and planter, creditor and debtor. The creditor increasingly resented what he regarded as the planter's waste, mismanagement, and bad faith in meeting his obligations. Under these conditions, the *commissionnaires* clung to the *exclusif* to maintain their control over the colonial economy and assure a return on their capital.[77]

The high rate of interest together with the *exclusif* raised the price of consumer goods in the French colonies and prejudiced plantation production. Merchants, themselves only able to procure funds at high rates and without any means to recover the majority of the advances made to the planters, had to raise the price of their goods to cover their own interest payments and the risks of nonpayment by their debtors. According to de la Cornillère, the scarcity of money created three different prices for the same objects: the money price, the price paid by the cultivator who pays in produce in the course of a year but bypassed a *commissionnaire*, and the price charged by the *commissionnaire*. Sainte Croix estimated that the price of a quintal of cod during the last six months of 1819 and the first six months of 1820 was 40 livres 10 sous in the first case, 63 livres in the second, and between 72 and 76 livres in the third; Lavollée evaluated the difference between purchases made in cash and those made on credit at 30 percent. In their testimony before the 1829 sugar commission, French West Indian sugar planters complained that high interest rates combined with the *exclusif* to undercut their competitive position. In Cuba and Puerto Rico, they argued, credit was much better established at a moderate rate of interest. Those islands received the articles of their consumption freely from ships of all flags and at the best price. They paid less for their supplies than the French colonists and thus had immense advantages to produce cheaply.[78]

As purchasing agents for the plantations, the *commissionnaires* were guaranteed a market for the resale of the supplies they imported. It was, therefore, in their interest to keep the price of imported cod and other essentials high even though it was detrimental to the plantations. High prices and inferior goods provided the merchant with the means to increase his revenues. By buying cheap and selling dear, as well as manipulating the sale of sugar, he not only increased the amount of his commissions but kept the plantations indebted to him. He was always ahead of the planter and continually needed to provoke new purchases to maintain himself there. There were a number of ways that *commissionnaires* could manipulate their strategic position in colonial commerce to increase their profits and maintain the dependency of the planters. The *commissionnaire* who supplied several plantations was responsible for such a large amount of diverse goods that he was obliged to buy on credit. The *commissionnaire* was again able to turn this situation to his advantage at the expense of the planter. The merchant who sold the supplies to the *commissionnaire* knew that he would be paid in eighteen months or two years instead of the customary three months, and that payment would be in sugar, not in money. He surcharged his goods accordingly. The planter, on the other hand, settled his accounts with the *commissionnaire* at the end of each year and found himself burdened with extra interest charges on goods he had already received. The *commissionnaire* did not pay the charges for another eighteen months, gaining six months or a year's interest, which he further increased by paying in sugar.[79]

Other tactics used by *commissionnaires* were even more unscrupulous. Sainte Croix reports that they forced local retail merchants to whom they owed money to accept overpriced inferior grades of sugar in payment of their debts. They were also able to use their power in the market place to force up the charges for freight and storage. Emile Thomas records that when the *commissionnaire* dealt directly with the overseer or plantation manager, the latter almost always received a considerable sum for ignoring the quality of the goods received. Such collusion between the manager and the factor could result in fraudulent practices that were extremely damaging to the estate. Thomas recounted one such case that he believed was far from unique. The administrator of a rich planter financed his brother, a *commissionnaire*, from the operating capital of the estate. Then he bought supplies from a merchant house in Havre on the account of the estate. These goods were delivered to his brother, who retailed them to the plantation at a great profit. Finally, on those occasions when absentee planters left *commissionnaires* in charge of their property, the latter were at once the buyer, the seller, and the cashier. Control of all these operations gave them an excellent opportunity to manipulate the transactions of the plantation for their own gain, especially when goods were damaged or money was scarce.[80]

This commercial system had a debilitating effect on colonial agriculture. It drained the planter of resources and put him tightly in the grip of middlemen. Gueroult describes the planter as the tenant of land that no longer belonged to him, the owner of slaves that were no longer to be his, and devoured by usury. Debt and short-term credit encouraged commercial speculation and dependence on protective legislation rather than systematic improvement of agriculture and manufactures. The planters, according to Lavollée, became by character and by habit the enemies of all foresight and economy: "The majority of plantations are not in the hands of their real owners. Those who use them are the natural enemies of all progress and of all amelioration. For lack of credit they cannot find the means to enter on the right path. They cling to the present state of affairs because any change would be their ruin. Against all things, they raise recriminations or bring up impossibilities which would make one believe that innovations would only make the bad worse." Debt bound the planters more closely to slavery and made them defend it all the more vehemently. They feared that if slavery were abolished and their property in slaves were liquidated, the indemnity would not go to them, but to their creditors. "What indebted planters want," wrote Lavollée, "is to sell their sugar at very high prices as before, and, for the rest, to maintain the status quo, that is, to continue to incur debts and not to pay them." But, Lavollée concluded, debts and credit shortages would ruin the colonial sugar industry, and higher sugar prices would only be a palliative. More fundamental measures were necessary.[81]

The legal constitution of property in the French Antilles reinforced the separation of production from commodity circulation. It resulted in commercial speculation and the stagnation of production that precipitated the crisis of slavery and the sugar industry. The development of the colonial sugar industry was retarded, as Emile Thomas indicates: "Up until now, as a consequence of this troublesome constitution of property, the plantations have never been considered in the Antilles as the means to produce at low cost and as rapidly as possible the values that then go to be consumed in the metropolis. And although the improvement of agriculture and manufacture should be extremely profitable, the perpetually indebted state of the colonists only allows them to do something serious in this regard with great difficulty." This absence of a rigorous mortgage law and effective legal constitution of private property is cited by virtually every contemporary observer as the real cause of the heavy debt and economic distress that weighed on the colonies. While they debated whether the reform of these laws was to accompany emancipation or was a reason to delay it, all agreed that it was a necessary step in the revitalization of the colonial sugar industry. But the legal constitution of property, however damaging its effects, was itself an expression of the social and technical organization of the plantation. Therein lie the deeper reasons for the malaise of sugar and slavery in Martinique. "The links that chain the majority of the planters to the factors," observed Lavollée, "are of such nature that to break them would require nothing less than a regeneration of the social fabric of the colony."[82]

The response of the planters of Martinique to the protected market created by the policies of the French state was the extension of sugar monoculture and a renewed reliance on slave labor. Yet this expansion occurred within the established organization and scale of production. As the growth of the consumer market and the emergence of the beet sugar industry in France, particularly after 1836, increasingly put pressure on colonial planters to improve the quantity and quality of their product and the productive efficiency of their operations, their capacity to respond was limited. The possibilities of territorial expansion were exhausted, and the credit and *commissionnaire* systems subsidized inefficiency as they inhibited innovation. However, at the root of this pattern of expansion, and therefore of the limits of colonial production, was the organization of the plantation itself. Despite considerable experimentation and innovation at the level of individual units, the sugar industry in Martinique as a whole was unable to transcend the limits to production historically established by the proportional relation between land, labor, and manufacture inherent in the self-contained plantation. The absolute increase in sugar production required ever-greater inputs of labor. Costs rose, and productivity fell as more and more was squeezed out of the existing structure. The limited land and labor resources of the colony were cannibalized to sustain the growth of the sugar industry while the existing production units were solidified and made more resistant to change. The expansion of the sugar industry in Martinique is the symptom of its crisis and decline. The failure to alter productivity led to greater dependence on tariffs to secure a market for their product in the short run and ultimately called into question the social and industrial organization of production itself.

# Chapter 4

# Sugar and Slavery

## Forces and Relations of Production

The purpose of this chapter is to conceptualize sugar production and slave labor within the social and historical relations and processes forming the world-economy as a whole, in order to reconstruct the historical development of the sugar plantation in Martinique in the subsequent chapters. The production of sugar as a commodity by means of slave labor is at once a material and a social process. However, material production (the relation of human beings to nature) and the social relations of production (the relations between human beings) cannot be viewed in isolation from one another and treated as though they refer to two different empirical entities. Rather, material production and the social form of its organization are two inseparable aspects of human productive activity. The relation between them is an internal and necessary relation: each aspect exists only in and through the other, and neither is reducible to the other. Thus, the social relations of slavery cannot be treated as relations of property that are external and contingent to categories of economic analysis. Instead, the material production and social relations of production and exchange are conceptually and practically linked to one another through the social form of the commodity. The commodity form shapes not only the conditions in which human beings within given social relations engage in the activity of producing but the conditions of the production and reproduction of these very social relations. It establishes the inner unity of the material conditions of sugar production, the social relations of slavery, and the world market. The concept of the commodity therefore allows the historical reconstruction of the world-economy as a unified, structured, evolving totality.[1]

Thus, production is regarded here as an intrinsically social and historical process. The social relations of slavery and the material conditions of sugar production are two historically interrelated and mutually formative sides of a process of social labor, linked to one another through the commodity form. The social relations of slavery organized sugar production as commodity production and gave to labor its specific social form. Slavery established the social and historical conditions under which labor was brought together with the instruments and materials of labor to engage in social production. In turn, the social relations of slavery were shaped by the material conditions of sugar production. Thus, the social relations of slave production are not an institutional or ideological superstructure impinging on universal and ahistorical economic categories or laws and deflecting their action from their "natural" outcome. Instead, slavery is a specific form of social labor that imposes particular conditions on commodity production and exchange. The "economic sphere" itself—the relations and processes of commodity production and exchange and the categories of economic activity—is constituted by and through the social relations of slave production and derives its specific character from them.[2]

At the same time, the world market and international division of labor remained the historical premise and ongoing condition of slave labor, sugar monoculture, and the reproduction of the plantation as a specific form of social and economic organization. The market was not simply a factor "external" or "secondary" to the organization of the plantation and the immediate process of production. The relation between the world-economy and slave production entails something more than the fact that the product of slave labor is destined for the world market. Rather, the world market, the division of labor, and the level of development of global productive forces enter into the formation of the material and social processes of slave commodity production and shape their social-historical content. Through the world market, the product of slave labor was equated with that of all other forms of commodity production, and the character of the relations of slave production was itself modified. Systematic, large-scale production for the world market transformed slavery into what Marx described as "a calculated and calculating system" of labor, creating pressure for the optimal development of the material conditions of sugar production. At the same time, the imperatives of the market and the demand for surplus labor were imposed on the material conditions of sugar production through the social relations of slavery. The labor process formed from this contradictory unity of market relations, slave relations, and the material processes of sugar production constituted the concrete historical conditions of production and exchange. As a result of their historical development, the scale of production was expanded, and new techniques were adopted. The intensity and duration of work were increased, and workers were subjected to more rigorous labor discipline. Such changes in the material and social conditions of production augmented in complex, uneven, and contradictory ways the cooperative power of social labor.[3]

Thus, slavery cannot be treated in isolation from the ensemble of relations that compose the world-economy. Rather, it is seen in organic interdependence with and changing historical relation to other forms of social labor within a complex of interrelated processes of production and exchange. These material and social processes of commodity production and exchange are interdependent and mutually formative elements of an evolving historical whole. Each element presupposes the others theoretically and historically. None has priority over the others. While fundamental categories of production and exchange, material processes and social relations may be analytically distinguished from one another, they cannot be taken as concrete historical phenomena. Each category by itself remains abstract and one-sided and cannot but yield abstract and one-sided conceptions of historical change. The concrete historical character and content of relations of production and exchange must be established through the theoretical reconstruction of their interrelation and mutual formation in specific historical circumstances. Analytical abstraction serves as a means for grasping and constituting the variability and complexity of historical process, but should not be taken as an adequate representation of that process itself.

From this perspective, the development of the plantation system in Martinique can be understood as the product of the mutual conditioning and the mutual antagonism of the material-social conditions of commercial sugar production, and the social relations of slave commodity production. The slave production of sugar in Martinique both shaped and was shaped by the world sugar market and division of labor, the French national sugar market, and the economic and colonial policy of the French state. It can be neither subsumed under presumably universal economic laws nor conceptualized as a distinct socioeconomic system with its own universal laws. Instead, the specific relations and processes through which sugar production and slave labor in Martinique were constituted and reconstituted in the historical development of the world-economy must be reconstructed. In this way, it is possible to demonstrate the changing historical character and content of slave labor and sugar production and to grasp thereby the crisis of plantation agriculture in Martinique as the product of the transformation of social relations within this specific historical conjuncture of the world-economy. Thus, the purpose of this chapter is to conceptually delineate the material-social conditions of sugar production and the social relations of slave production in order to permit the reconstruction of their historical development and interrelation.

## The Social Requirements of Sugar Production

The sugar plantation provides a precocious development of manufacture that in many respects bears greater resemblance to modern factory production than to the characteristic organization of handicrafts and manufactures in Europe from the sixteenth to the eighteenth centuries. The physical and chemical properties of sugar imparted industrial organization and discipline to plantation production and thereby imposed a pattern of development on slave labor (and through the organization of labor on the general social relations of slavery) different from that of coffee, cotton, tobacco, or other slave-produced commodities. The technical division of labor, combining both the agricultural and manufacturing processes necessary to produce sugar on a commercial scale, allowed and indeed required the development of the productive force of cooperative labor. Further, the coincidence and close interdependence of these technical operations shaped the conditions in which the laborers were combined and their working activities regulated.[4]

Sugar yields a qualitatively uniform product. All saccharoses are the same. They are indistinguishable in taste and chemical composition. In the final product, all traces of origin—whether manufactured from cane or the sugar beet, whether grown in Cuba, Java, or France—are dissolved. The differences between sugars are quantitative. The enormous variety of types and grades of sugar—muscovado, clayed, brown, yellow, white, etc.—are all the same substance, differing only in chemical purity and degree of crystallization. The sucrose content of the plant forms the natural and technical limit of sugar production. The history of sugar technology is the history of the development of means to more completely and perfectly extract and process the given quantity of sucrose contained in the plant. The more technically perfect the process, the more homogeneous and pure the product.[5]

The transformation of sugar from cane to crystals requires a series of agricultural, mechanical, and physical-chemical operations. Each step—planting, cultivating, harvesting, grinding, defecation, evaporation, and crystallization—is necessary in the proper sequence, and none can be omitted if a final product is to be obtained. The spatial concentration of these different aspects of sugar production and their integration within a continuous process are required by the physical properties of sugar. The interdependence of these different phases is most apparent during the harvest season. The cane has to be cut when it is ripe to ensure the maximum quantity and quality of sugar. While the harvest might last from six months to a year because of the amount of cane planted, each individual stalk has to be converted into sugar within hours after it is cut or the juice will ferment and spoil, causing the yield to diminish and product quality to decline. Thus, speed, continuity, and coordination are of vital importance throughout the entire manufacturing process. Implicit in the conduct of these operations is a concern for maximization of yield, technical efficiency, and the quantification and measurement that make possible the increasing standardization of process and product.[6]

For large-scale commercial sugar production, these technical requirements implied the complex combination of many human hands within a developed division of labor. All the sequential phases of the manufacturing process—cutting, hauling, grinding, defecation, evaporation, crystallization—had to be carried out simultaneously, continuously, and as quickly as possible over extended periods of time. To achieve this, each constituent task was permanently assigned to a different group of workers who specialized in it. The division of labor was thus formed by the distinct technical operations involved in sugar manufacture. The activities of each worker or group of workers—field hands, carters, mill hands, refiners—were restricted to a particular exclusive sphere. The final product could only be the result of the combined labor of all of them, and in it all traces of the individual efforts of each disappeared.[7]

The division of labor required by commercial sugar manufacture not only established the qualitative differentiation of tasks, but also created a quantitative relation between these different sectors of production. It was of crucial importance to coordinate the various separate yet interdependent operations throughout the entire crop cycle from planting to harvest. This could only be done by estimating how much could be produced in a given sector in a given amount of time. The capacity of the fields, transport system, mill, refinery, and curing house, along with the activities of each group of workers, had to be assessed and synchronized with one another. The production process formed an organic whole whose constituent parts were related to one another in definite proportions. The allocation of labor and resources was governed by a fixed mathematical ratio that set the parameters of the organization and possible transformation of the labor process.[8]

The integration of the different aspects of sugar manufacture within a continuous process formed the temporal organization of plantation production and established a regularity of activity that was uncommon in preindustrial work rhythms. The specialized labor of each different group of workers provided the raw material for the next phase of the process, and regularity in the performance of each partial task was necessary to maintain the continuity of production. The integration of the labor process could only be achieved on the assumption that a given amount of product could be obtained during a given period of time. The direct interdependence of all workers compelled each individual worker or group of workers to spend no more time than was necessary on the performance of their particular task. This regulation of the amount of labor time necessary to perform a particular task was imposed on the workers as a technical condition of the labor process itself and determined the number of workers in each sector and the intensity and duration of their efforts.[9]

The sugar plantation thus required a labor force that was abundant, cheap, and subject to strict work discipline and social control. Speed, continuity, and cooperation among large numbers of workers, a complex internal division of labor, and the supervision and coordination of the whole process by a hierarchical staff of overseers and managers were imperative for commercial sugar manufacture. These characteristics compelled the organization of labor on the plantation as a mass, collective, and cooperative social force capable of uniform, regular and coordinated action.

## The Cooperative Force of Slave Labor

Historically, the conditions required by commercial sugar production were created through African slavery. The enslavement of Africans and their descendants in the Americas made available a seemingly endless supply of laborers constituted as a legally distinct and subordinate body of labor subject to the most extreme sanctions: this same process established a juridically separate social category defined as alien to the political community and inferior in civil status and legal rights. The superiority of slavery as a form of social labor lies in its capacity to concentrate forcibly large masses of workers and to exact their cooperation. Slavery provided the means by which the combination of laborers into the collective social force necessary for large-scale sugar production was organized on an adequate scale with the necessary degree of complexity and disciplined to the technical and economic requirements of the labor process.

The social form of the organization of slave labor gives rise to the systemic character of slavery. As Marx stresses with examples particularly appropriate for this discussion: "A Negro is a Negro. He only becomes a slave in certain relations.

A cotton-spinning jenny is a machine for spinning cotton. It becomes *capital* only in certain relations. Torn from these relationships it is no more capital than gold itself is money or sugar the price of sugar." Thus, the elements of the labor process—tools, raw materials, labor—are not things in themselves. Rather, the social relations of production determine the social and historical significance of each of the elements of the labor process and of the process as a whole. Within slavery, each element of the production process is related to every other in a manner different from the way they are organized by the capital-wage labor relation. The limitations of slavery as a form of commodity production are thereby established. Taken by itself, each individual element of the labor process, or even the sum of these elements, offers only a partial explanation of the course of historical development of a particular form of social production (slavery, wage labor, etc.). The individual elements themselves become fully comprehensible only when viewed in light of the specific social relations in their totality. The totality of these social relations structures the interrelationship between particular elements and provides a perspective from which their interdependence and mutual conditioning can be grasped and their significance for the course of historical development evaluated.[10]

Thus, for example, it has become almost a commonplace in much historical writing to regard slaves as having no interest in their work. Slaves are viewed as capable only of dull, routine labor performed under constant supervision, and technological innovation is seen to be incompatible with slavery. It is as if slaves were unwilling or unable to perform complex tasks. Not infrequently, the backwardness of slave production is ascribed to these characteristics of slave labor. However, not only can instances of contrary behavior among slaves be found empirically, but, as Antônio Castro has rightly pointed out, indifference to work is what slaves and wage laborers have in common. Moreover, the simplification and routinization of tasks and the extension of control over the activities of the laborer have been the basis for the development of the wage labor process. Thus, to focus simply on the individual aspects of slave labor and wage labor or on the appearance of similarity or difference between individual aspects of slave labor and wage labor would obscure the social historical processes within which these different forms of social production are constituted and, thereby, the qualitative differences between them. Innovation and technical change could and did occur within slavery. But the nature and function of the instruments of production, their relation to labor, the parameters of mechanization, and their implications for social and economic development were shaped by the ensemble of the social relations of slavery.[11]

Although there is no theory of slavery in Marx, the specific social character of slave relations may be seen most clearly by contrasting them to his conception of the wage labor–capital relation. As Marx argues, the constitution of labor-power as a commodity is of decisive importance for the development of the specifically capitalist labor process. The condition of this relation is that the laborer sells to the capitalist neither his person nor the product of his labor, but rather his capacity to labor for a limited amount of time. The capitalist pays for the right to dispose of the worker's living activity during this period. Once purchased by the capitalist, it is his property and becomes one of the constituent elements of capital. Under conditions organized by the capitalist, labor is combined with the instruments and materials of labor to engage in production. The subjective capacity to labor is transformed into the activity of laboring which, in turn, is objectified in the product of labor. But here, each of the elements of the labor process takes the form of a commodity and is thereby related to every other element through its value. The existence of labor-power as a commodity and the relation of value give social form and significance to the categories of labor—labor cost, labor time, productivity of labor—which are fundamental to the capitalist organization of the production process. Labor enters directly into the process of capital as exchange value (the cost of labor-power) and as use value (the activity of creating value). The capitalist must organize the labor process in such a way that the value of the labor objectified in the product exceeds the value expended in the purchase of labor-power (surplus value). The commodity form of labor brings these two values of labor into relation with one another and allows surplus labor or the surplus product to take the form of surplus value.[12]

The apparent exchange of equivalents—money wage for labor-power—between capital and labor mediates the production and appropriation of surplus value.

The power of capital to organize commodity production and exchange is thereby augmented, and the conditions for its renewal on an expanded scale are created within its own processes. Outside of the production process, the worker remains a formally free individual subject only to the quantitative and qualitative restrictions of the wage. Like any other property holder, he is free to act in the marketplace without the direct interference of the capitalist. Having exchanged his commodity for money, he can now purchase the necessities of life. Once these are consumed, he must once again appear on the market as the seller of labor-power to renew the process. Thus, the wage relation not only organizes commodity production, but also constitutes reproduction as a separate and distinct sphere of activity, and regulates the relation between the two through the constant alternation of buying and selling.

With the commodity form of labor-power, the activity of labor has a social existence distinct from the person of the laborer. For the capitalist, the worker is, before anything else, the bearer of living labor, the personification of the commodity labor-power, whose constant appropriation becomes an end in itself and the condition of capitalist production; the laborer, on the other hand, confronts the capitalist organization of work as an objective process and is compelled by economic circumstance to sell his labor over and over again to maintain the conditions of his existence. This separation permits the possibility of restructuring the labor process as the process producing surplus value. Modification of the composition of labor's value is both the means and the end of capitalist development and transformation of the mode of material production. Capital is compelled to maximize the production of surplus value and mimimize the time spent reproducing the value of labor-power. Historically, the social character of labor as a collective force was extended and deepened through cooperation, the division of labor and manufacture, and machine production as the means to increase the mass, intensity, and rate of surplus value production both absolutely and relatively. Labor is expelled from the production process while its higher productivity lowers the value of commodities entering into the value of labor-power. Socially necessary labor time and the time needed to reproduce the value of labor-power are minimized. Work loses its individual character, and the collective, social character of labor is subject to unfettered development as the power of capital separate from and antagonistic to the laborer.[13]

Slavery, in contrast, is a relation of force and direct domination that imposes the commodity form on the person of the laborer and the product of his labor. Economically and legally the slave is treated as property and can be bought and sold. Unlike the employer of wage labor, who purchases the expenditure of the worker's labor-power for a limited length of time, the slaveholder owns the person of the laborer for a period of indefinite duration just as he owns land, seed, livestock, and tools. The slave has no relation to the means of production, but is himself an instrument of production as is an ox or mule. He represents an investment in constant capital no different from that in machinery or livestock. The price of the slave is based on his capacity to produce and is subject to depreciation as the slave is "consumed." But this capital is separate from the capital laid out to exploit him in the production process itself. Legal title to the slave is not identical with the expenditure of his labor but rather is its prior condition. The price of the slave, whether purchased on the market or "produced" on the estate, is a deduction from the capital available for production. Only with the investment of additional capital is the slave owner able to exploit the labor of the slave. If the slave is lost for one reason or another, the capital invested in him is lost and must be replaced with a new outlay of capital.[14]

Within the social relations of slavery, the production and appropriation of a surplus is organized not through the "free exchange of equivalent values" between capital and labor but by the direct and explicit domination of the slaveholder. In principle, the slave, as chattel property, has no voice in determining the conditions of his life and labor. Through the property relation, the slave's control over his person, the labor process, and the whole product of his labor are directly alienated and appropriated by the slaveholder without exchange. The value of labor is subsumed under the value of the slave, and all of the slave's labor appears as surplus labor. The slave owner has to bear the costs of reproducing the laborer, but what is reproduced is the person of the slave, which remains separate from the activity of labor. Even that portion of the slave's labor that reproduces his physical existence, whether through his own efforts or directly or indirectly through the market, does not appear as the reproduction of his labor-power, but as the renewal of the stock of constant capital and is equivalent to the cost of maintenance, fuel, or parts for machines. The cost of labor does not appear directly as the price of labor-power, but rather takes the form of series of investments in constant capital (housing, food, clothing, the purchase of new slaves, etc.). These costs must be paid whether the slave works or not, or else the investment in his person will be lost.[15]

Thus, the activity of laboring is not a cost of production within the social relations of slavery. Because the slave's capacity to labor does not take the form of commodity it cannot thereby be distinguished from his physical being. The category *labor-power* cannot therefore appear as a social relation independent of the person of the laborer. The activity of labor does not possess exchange value. Neither the labor required to reproduce the slave nor surplus labor take the form of value, and the commodity form does not relate the value of labor to the value produced by labor. Value, therefore, cannot measure labor, nor can labor measure value. The labor expended in the production process is thus independent from the value of the slave. The process of material production is not coincident with or absorbed into the social process of producing value but remains separate from it. The property relation and the labor process presuppose one another as given, external conditions, but there is no economic relation mediating between the two. Slave price, the cost of slave maintenance, and the activity of labor remain independent of one another. The slaveholder can compare monetary expenses to the revenue from the sale of the product, but the activity of labor remains outside of this economic calculation and cannot be organized through it.[16]

The absence of the commodity form of labor-power and the assimilation of the slave into the category of constant capital greatly constrained the potential development of the productive capacity of social labor and the expansion of surplus production under slavery. Douglas Hall emphasizes this aspect of the slave relation and implies its significance for the historical development of the Caribbean:

That estate slaves were a form of constant capital investment is beyond argument. Their "labor" was consequently not "labor" in the sense in which we use it in respect of "free laborers," but rather "power" in the sense that it is used for the efforts of livestock or the work of machinery. . . . Emancipation, therefore was of industrial consequence not because it replaced "slave labor" by "wage labor," but because it introduced "labor" as a significant feature of production and accounting, . . . and because it introduced for the first time in the West Indies, significance and real meaning to concepts such as "labor-cost," "labor-productivity," and "labor-saving."

An increase in the output of labor distributes the labor expended over a greater number of commodities, but such a change has no necessary relation to the value of the slave or the value of the product. Labor is not expelled from the production process. Rather, the master retains possession of the laborer and is compelled to provide for the physical renewal of the slave population. Whether this occurs through the purchase of new slaves on the market or the reproduction of the slave population resident on the estate, it takes place outside of the labor process and is a prior condition for it. A rise or fall in these costs—whether the price of slaves, the cost of goods consumed by slaves, or the allocation of human and material resources for the slaves to produce their own subsistence outside of the market—depends on factors external to the labor process itself. Their alteration has no effect on the amount of labor required for the production process or its actual expenditure. Instead, they represent a fixed sum that enters into the determination of the value of the final product as constant capital. They are thus a cost to be deducted from the revenue from the sale of the product, and they present an invariable barrier to the production of a surplus.[17]

The slaves are, in principle, at the disposal of their master twenty-four hours a day, every day, for the duration of their working lives. They became, in the incisive phrase of the eighteenth-century Brazilian Jesuit André João Antonil, "the hands and feet of the master." Consequently, both the production of commodities and the reproduction of the slave labor force are organized through the immediate personal domination of the master within the plantation enterprise. He must provide for the maintenance of the slave population at his own expense. Failure to do so will result in the loss of his property. Thus, in contrast to wage labor, there is no formal distinction between necessary and surplus labor time in the slave relation, as Marx emphasized: "In slave labor, even the part of the working day in which the slave is only replacing the value of his own means of subsistence, in which he therefore actually works for himself alone, appears as unpaid labor for his master. All his labor appears as unpaid labor. In wage-labor, on the contrary, even surplus labor, or unpaid labor, appears as paid. In the one case, the property-relation conceals the slave's labor for himself; in the other case the money-relation conceals the uncompensated labor of the wage-laborer." By means of direct compulsion, the activities and conditions of existence of the slave population are subordinated to the interests of commodity production. Production and reproduction are thereby constituted as separate spheres of activity, and the relation between them is established and maintained by the explicit control of the master. His advantage derives from the organization of both spheres, and the logic of profitability in this system is that by means of force and compulsion the costs of slave maintenance can be reduced to the minimum level and the slaves driven to devote their full energy to staple production. Work is therefore an activity imposed on the slaves and carried out independently of their subsistence, and the division of the working day is the condition and limit of the exploitation of slave labor.[18]

Paradoxically, the extreme objectification of the slave as property and as instrument of production creates its complement in the personalization of social relations that must recognize the individuality of the slave. Labor is never the direct focus of action within slavery but is always mediated through the property relation. Whereas in the wage relation the capitalist controls and organizes human beings through the control of their labor, in slavery the slave owner controls and organizes labor through the possession of human beings. The slave is simultaneously property and instrument of labor; the master is simultaneously owner of property and manager of labor. However, the slave owner can only compel labor insofar as his individual authority as proprietor can be exerted over the person of the slave. Outside of work, the slave remains the master's property, a part of his estate, and dependent on him for his welfare. Even the most hard-driving, calculating, and entrepreneurial of slave owners must be paternalist, not for reasons of ideology or personal predisposition, but because of the social conditions of his own existence. The slave is the master's property to use or abuse, to coerce, cajole, or coopt, but it is only through this property relation that the master has access to the labor of the slave.

Yet however much the master must take the slave's individual characteristics into account, his interest in the slave is not personal. Rather, it is defined by the conditions of commodity production and exchange. The sugar plantation was a commercial enterprise that had to guarantee its reproduction through the market. It was dependent on profit from the sale of its sugar supplemented by credit for its survival, and it had to respond to the demands and criteria of the market economy to operate successfully. The slave was regarded as an instrument of production whose purpose was to produce wealth and bring a return on the capital invested. The efficiency of the plantation as a productive unit and its value as a capital investment was dependent on the well-being of its slave population, both as workers and as a social group. While the slave might be exposed to the caprice, abuse, and violence (or, conversely, benevolence) of the individual slave owner, the conditions of slave life and labor were determined by economic considerations, not personal arbitrariness. The master had to balance his interests as controller of the slave's working capacity against his interests as proprietor of the slave's person. This specific structural relation to labor distinguishes the paternalism of the slave owner from, for example, the paternalism of the employer of free labor.[19]

Like the wage laborer, the slave is dispossessed and has no control over the labor process or the product of labor. The organization of production and reproduction are external to him. They confront him as an objective reality, a fate that befalls him, and, beyond physical survival, offer no systemic incentive to him. His labor is disciplined to the material and social requirements of commodity production and exchange through the immediate supervision of the master and the overseer.

It could thus be molded to the complex internal division of labor of the gang system: workers could be assigned to particular jobs to make the best use of individual capacities, tasks could be subjected to division and simplification, and the interdependence of individual workers, each of whom is assigned to a precise partial task, could be established. But unlike the wage worker, who is in principle ready to adapt to any task that promises higher reward, and who is indifferent to the particular content of his labor, but, as owner of money, learns to discipline himself to the general conditions of commodity production and exchange, the slave must perform every task required of him in the interest of the slaveholder and can only work through the external compulsion of the master who organizes the labor process. The indifference to work shown by the wage worker and by the slave are constituted within diametrically opposed historical processes.[20]

As a form of social production, slavery was a contradictory relation. The slave as collective laborer was negated by the slave as property. The forcible integration of the slaves into the production complex of the sugar plantation and their compulsory collaboration not only enhanced the productive capacity of the individual worker but created a new productive force, that of combined social labor. The productive power of the slave gang was intrinsically social. It was greater than that of the sum of its individual members and increased as a function of the mass of workers employed. The labor of slaves, concentrated, combined, and subject to extreme sanctions, thus created the conditions for the expansion of commodity production and made possible the production of sugar on a commercial scale. However, while the slave owner could constitute labor as a collective social force through the forcible combination of individual workers, he could not directly seize on the social character of their labor as abstract activity. Once the slave labor force was constituted within a given organization of production, the further modification of the division of labor or the introduction of new technology could intensify the activity of labor and increase the total product, but such changes had no necessary relation to the value of the slave or the value of the product. Thus, the superiority of the gang system as a means of organizing cooperative labor was in contradiction with the self-contained plantation and the slave relation. Labor was limited to the reorganization of a predetermined (though historically variable) number of workers and their activities, and it could not be easily pushed to higher levels of socialization.[21]

Paradoxically, while labor-power does not exist as a social relation, the slave owner is constantly surrounded by an abundance of laborers. At some point, technological innovation is suffocated by a superfluity of available laborers. Conversely, the maintenance of the slave population could not be reduced below a physical minimum without endangering the effectiveness of the slave labor force or the investment in the slaves. Thus, the ratio between the cost of maintaining the slave force to its productive capacity moves within very narrow parameters. The expenditure of human muscle-power remains at the center of the slave labor process, and there is a tendency for an equilibrium to form around the predetermined minimal conditions for the physical reproduction of the slaves and the maximum physical capacity of the labor force. Characteristically, slave production expanded by the quantitative extension of more slaves on more land within the given social and technical organization of the labor process than by the qualitative transformation of that process. If labor could have been expelled from the labor process, the alternatives were either that the slaves would became the property of another master within the same organization of production or they would be without masters. The first case represents no change in the rate of surplus production for the system as a whole, and the second represents social chaos in a slave society.[22]

Thus, the material requirements of the mass production of sugar developed the cooperative character of labor within technically determined conditions and formed the content of slave labor as a social relation. Conversely, slavery allowed the development of the material conditions of sugar production and the cooperative character of labor within a specific social form. However, in the absence of the commodification of labor-power, the relation between the technical division of labor and the social organization of the labor force is established through the personal domination of the slave owner. While the material and social conditions of production coincide, there is no necessary inner relation between the two as in the case of wage labor. Instead, they presuppose one another as given external conditions. For the slave labor process to be organized, a fixed number of workers have to be adapted to the technically determined number and type of tasks. If, on the one hand, the productive capacity of a sugar estate was in large measure a function of the number of slaves at its disposition, on the other, the size of a sugar estate's labor force and the complexity of its division of labor were determined by the peak demand for labor during the harvest season and by the various separate but interdependent activities that had to be performed during the crop cycle. The planning and regulation of the labor process, the systematic organization of the division of labor, and the calculation of the mass, intensity, and duration of labor expended derive from the technical requirements of sugar production and the need to maximize the output of a preestablished number of slaves within a fixed period of time rather than from a concern with the rationalization of labor in itself. Once production was established on a given scale and within a given division of labor, the slave relation restricted its further development. The adoption of new production techniques neither saved labor nor reduced the costs of slave maintenance. The social organization of the labor force did not impel the revolutionizing of the technical division of labor, nor did revolutionizing the technical division of labor affect the social organization of the labor force. Rather, the factors of production were fixed in a relatively stable equilibrium tied to the physical capacity of a determinate number of laborers.[23]

The social relations of slavery combined with and reinforced the technical conditions of sugar production to form the plantation as the cell unit of colonial economy and society. The sugar estate in Martinique developed as a self-contained unit combining agriculture and manufacturing operations performed by an appropriated labor force. It was at once an economic enterprise and a human community. The appropriation of the person of the laborer compelled the coincidence of production activity and the social life of the slave population within the same social organization and spatial unit. As the property of the master, the subject population was incorporated into the plantation for life, both as workers and as residents. The production activities of the body of slaves and their reproduction both as labor force and as community was formally organized under the direct domination of the slave owner. Thus, the social and spatial organization of the *habitation sucrière* expressed both the technical imperatives of sugar production and the hierarchical character of social life and labor under slavery. The conditions of their combination gave each estate the appearance of a self-contained and autonomous social, economic, and administrative entity whose relations with the "outside world" were controlled by the master. In the words of one source:

> Thus deprived of all civil rights, of all participation in social existence, the slaves live billeted in their houses, in their plantations. Each plantation, each house is an enclosure which the slave cannot leave without the authorization of the master; each rural workplace [*exploitation*] is an *atelier* where work is performed through coercion. Each plantation forms, in a way, a society apart which cultivates its own provisions, builds, manufactures for itself; a society governed by its own rules, where justice is administered to a certain degree according to the forms that are suitable to it; a miniature state with its private chapel, its prison for delinquents, its nursery for children, its infirmary for the sick, its home for the aged and infirm.

However, the peculiarity of the slave plantation is not simply that it had a resident labor force. Indeed, a resident labor force characterizes many types of nonslave enterprises and is one of the reasons why such labor forces are often regarded as living in a semi-servile state without the advantages of formally free labor. Rather, the point goes deeper with slavery. Without even the formality of exchange to mediate the relation between the direct producers and the owners of the means of production, the distinction between production and social reproduction sustained by it cannot be maintained. There is no sphere of "free activity" within which social reproduction can take place separate from the production unit and the relations of direct production. Instead, the reproduction of the slave population is organized within the confines of the plantation. There is no distinction between the costs of the enterprise and the cost of maintaining the slave population. The development of the slave community is subject to the extreme constraint and coercion of slavery and is directly subordinated to the demands of production. Conversely, the efficiency of the plantation as a production unit is conditioned by broader social relations, processes, and conflicts that are inherent in its form of organization and essential to its operation. The coincidence and mutual interdependence of these various productive and social activities and processes within this single unit conditioned and constrained the course of the evolution of sugar production and of slavery in Martinique.[24]

The expansion of sugar production in the years after 1815 developed this ensemble of technical and social relations to its fullest extent. The mutual interaction of sugar and slavery at once developed and reinforced the plantation as a self-contained unit. This complex of relations and processes shaped the evolution of the sugar plantation in Martinique and determined the limits of its expansion. Within the limits established by the technically determined proportional relations between the various sectors of production, the need to maximize output and "efficiency" integrated the division of labor on each plantation ever more closely and filled in the "empty spaces" in the potentially available labor time. The organization of production became more and more elaborate; at the same time, it became more and more rigid and incapable of adapting to changing conditions. Under this pressure, both the technical organization of production and the slave labor process began to disintegrate, while at the same time they choked off alternative forms of organization. The following two chapters will historically reconstruct the material-technical side of this process, while its social aspects will be treated in the last two chapters.

# Chapter Five

# The *Habitation Sucrière*

## Cell Unit of Colonial Production

The sugar plantation in Martinique integrated within a single productive unit both the agricultural and manufacturing operations necessary to produce sugar. The interdependence of the various sectors of the production process developed the industrial character of sugar production while constraining it within technically determined limits. The plantation formed an integrated mechanism. Each phase of the sequential process of production was dependent on the preceding ones. The distribution of labor and resources within each sector had to be coordinated with the other sectors. The organization of the production process as a whole impelled the maximization of output in each individual sector and of speed and continuity between sectors. At the same time, this tendency was counterbalanced by the need to maintain the technically determined equilibrium among the various sectors of the process. While the ideal limit of production remained the complete extraction and conversion of all the sucrose contained in the cane plant, a wide variety of techniques, all with a significant effect on the quantity and quality of the product, were practiced in every phase of the process. There was no "necessity" for the adoption of any particular technique, hence no "necessity" for progressively improving and developing the productive force of technology. Rather, the selection of particular techniques depended on an enormous variety of political, economic, social, and technical conditions that varied from estate to estate. The transformation of the world and national sugar markets during the first part of the nineteenth century created conditions for improvements in productive technique that developed this integration of agricultural and manufacturing processes to its fullest extent while exposing the self-contained plantation as the limit to technological improvement in the colonial sugar industry.

Within the framework established by the division of labor on the plantation, the techniques of sugar production in Martinique were imprecise. Scientific understanding of the principles of chemistry involved in sugar manufacture remained rudimentary, and instruments to control the processing of the material were unavailable. With traditional methods of fabrication, it was important to take a wide range of individual and local variations into consideration, but these variations often simply reinforced ignorance and prejudice. Sugar refining was regarded as an art acquired only after long individual experience. Knowledge of this craft was the property of the sugar masters and was disseminated through personal contact. The subjective skill and judgment of the planter weighed heavily in the success or failure of the enterprise. Even a small error could have a greatly adverse effect on the outcome. On the other hand, even simple changes and partial amelioration of production techniques could result in significant changes in output. This situation strongly biased the planters against wholesale innovation. Established techniques were preferred over new ones that were potentially risky, and at best of limited effectiveness. This outlook cannot simply be ascribed to the ideology and psychology of "quasi-aristocratic precapitalists" whose concern for social prestige was antithetical to significant technological progress. Rather, it was an economic orientation developed through the material and social conditions of plantation production. Whatever the social values of the planters, their evaluation of the potential benefits and liabilities of technological innovation was shaped by practical economic considerations. Nevertheless, the conservative and particularistic mentality of the planters in Martinique had to be overcome before the methods of sugar production could be transformed and a scientific approach to agriculture could prevail.[1]

# The Cultivation of Sugar Cane

By the 1830s, the conditions of colonial sugar production had pushed the planters of Martinique to reexamine the established methods of cultivation. In the days when sugar prices were high and there was still virgin soil, planters could overcome the effects of soil depletion by simply abandoning their fields and clearing new lands. It was sufficient merely to burn off the forest or brush to prepare a new field. But there was already pressure on the supply of choice sugar lands during the sugar boom of the 1820s. By the following decade, virgin land virtually disappeared, and the effects of soil exhaustion began to be felt. The planters of Martinique were compelled to change their old habits. Some continued to abandon their fields and clear new lands. But increasingly the only alternative available to them was land of inferior quality or far from the mill, which raised the costs of exploitation. Others increased the extent of the area under cultivation to maintain the same yield at a diminished rate. But more and more, planters began to pay attention to the amelioration of agricultural techniques, and slowly and with great difficulty the use of fertilizer and plows entered into the practice of colonial agriculture.[2]

Only a small portion of the land possessed by the plantation was actually planted in cane. Lavollée observed that the large estates that dominated the island often possessed between 300 and 400 carrés of land, but of that amount barely 60 were cultivated in cane. Sainte Croix, who has left one of the most complete accounts of plantation agriculture in Martinique during the first half of the nineteenth century, estimates that a plantation producing 450 hogsheads (225 metric tons) of sugar annually needed at least 130 carrés, including savannahs. However, the cane fields covered only 64 carrés. De Lavigne, the proprietor of an estate producing 450 hogsheads, provides some of the most detailed documentation of a *habitation sucrière* in Martinique. His plantation covered 227 carrés. One hundred carrés were planted in sugar cane, of which 75 were harvested each year. There were 36 carrés for slave provision grounds, 11 carrés planted in manioc, and 40 carrés each in pastures and woodland. The small and medium estates were even less efficient in their use of land. The state-owned plantation, "Châlet," for example, had 118 arable hectares, but just 40 of them were suitable for cane. The plantation of Cassius Linval in the *quartier* of Macouba produced about 90 hogsheads of sugar annually. Of the 146 hectares that he held, 60 hectares were savannah, 50 were woods, and only 20 were planted in sugar cane, while 10 were in cacao and 6 in provisions.[3]

Because the heavy cane stalks were difficult to transport and had to be ground quickly after cutting, it was important that the cane be planted near the mill. On large plantations, there were sometimes several strategically placed mills to facilitate grinding. The cane fields were laid out in rectangular plots with wide lanes between them that served as firebreaks and allowed the carts carrying the cut cane to the mill to get through. They were divided into carefully measured and geometric pieces in an attempt to guarantee the regular application of labor and achieve a standardized and calculable daily output, which could permit the integration of the production process over the course of the agricultural year.[4]

The crop cycle began with planting. This was an arduous task that required a great deal of labor. The fields were cleared by gangs of slaves working under the supervision of overseers or slave drivers. To plant the cane, the slaves of the great gang, each with a hoe and a stake, formed a line across the field. A *commandeur* stood at each end of the line and stretched between them a cord that was knotted or marked at regular intervals. Each slave put his or her stake in the ground at the mark and proceeded to dig a hole two feet square and nine inches deep. After it was completed three cane cuttings prepared in advanced were placed in it. If the planter used fertilizer, a quantity of manure was applied; if not, the plant was re-covered with dirt, leaving a centimeter of the stem exposed. The slaves then moved ahead to dig the next hole. Each slave had to dig about twenty-eight holes an hour, depending on soil conditions. The practice of planting the cane stalks in parallel rows was adopted in the French Antilles during the seventeenth century. Before that the plants were placed indiscriminately across the field. The stalks were planted closely together. According to Guignod, a planter of long experience in Martinique, an average field had 12,000 clusters of cane stalks per carré. This close spacing facilitated planting and spatially concentrated the activities of the plantation. But it resulted in cane of poorer quality and required greater expenditure of effort for weeding, trashing, pruning, and cutting. After fourteen to eighteen months, the plant was mature and ready for harvest. Since the cane was planted over a period of many months, it took a long time for the entire crop to reach maturity. It could be cut gradually and a manageable quantity of ripe cane furnished to the mill each day throughout the harvest season.[5]

After the cane was planted, agricultural work was less rigorous, though this depended on the crop cycle and the schedule of field rotation. The cane plant began to sprout about three weeks after planting, and it was necessary to weed the field for the first time. This was not strenuous work and was ordinarily done by the women and children of the second and weeding gangs. Weeding was very important for sugar cultivation and had a great effect on how well the plants grew and how much sugar they yielded. Grasses that would choke off the plants if left unchecked had to be cleared. Also, if the cane needed it, some fresh soil was put at the foot of the plant for nourishment at this time, and, if necessary, the dried outer leaves were stripped from the stalk to help the plant grow. Weeding usually continued until the cane was between seven and ten months old. The frequency of weedings depended on the quality of the soil and the amount of rain. Nearly everywhere on the island the cane had to be weeded from four to six times.[6]

The same cane planting would continue sending up new shoots, or ratoons, for as many as three to six successive harvests. This ratoon crop represented a great economy for the planter. A field in ratoons would not have to be planted for several years. A toilsome and expensive task could thus be avoided, and men, animals, and money could be spared. A British West Indian source from the 1840s estimated that the cost of cultivating an acre of ratoons was one-fourth that of cultivating an acre of planted cane. In addition, newly planted canes took from sixteen to eighteen months to ripen, whereas ratoons only took from twelve to fourteen months. Further, Reed, writing in the 1860s, suggests that ratoons yielded better-quality sugar and that there was less trouble clarifying and concentrating their juice.[7]

Despite the advantages offered by ratoons, their yield decreased significantly with each successive harvest from the same plant. The rate of diminution varied with the soil and climate, whether or not fertilizer was used, whether the fertilizer was applied to the new canes or to the ratoons, and with the care and frequency of weedings, among other things. In some areas, if well fertilized and cared for, ratoons could yield more than an unfertilized field of new cane. According to Sainte Croix's data from the 1820s, the decline between the yield of the newly planted cane and the first crop from the ratoons could vary from about 30 percent to 50 percent, while de la Cornillère, writing in 1842, describes a decline of about 60 percent. In neighboring Guadeloupe, where agricultural techniques were more advanced and the use of fertilizer more widespread than in Martinique, Lavollée records that the yield diminished between 16 percent and 20 percent from the new crop to the first ratoon crop and from between 40 percent and 50 percent between the first and second ratoon crops. Thus, the cost of planting and fertilizing had to be judged against the diminished yield, and a balance between successive new plantings and ratoons had to be maintained to guarantee the volume and regularity of output. While the sources for the nineteenth century record diverse strategies with which individual planters in Martinique attempted to combine planted canes and ratoons to maximize their yields, the most common pattern appears to have been to harvest three times, the new cane and two crops of ratoons, before replanting. De la Cornillère describes a plantation producing 521 boucauts of sugar (1 boucaut = 489 kilograms) that had 35 carrés planted in new cane and 85 carrés in ratoons. The plantation described by Sainte Croix had 24 carrés in planted cane and 40 carrés in ratoons. He added that at least 24 carrés had to be newly planted each year to insure the same quantity of ratoons the following year, though if the soil did not permit ratoons, more cane had to be planted each year.[8]

It was apparently the customary practice to rotate planting from field to field in successive years (see Figure 5.1). The cane fields were divided into four separate sections. It was preferable that the sections be the same size to standardize the yield, but this depended on local conditions. One field was planted with mature cane ready to be harvested, one was planted with the first crop of ratoons, one with the second crop of ratoons, and one with new cane that would ripen in the following year. After the harvest, the field with the second ratoon crop was dug up

| Year | Season | Field 1 | Field 2 | Field 3 | Field 4 |
|------|--------|---------|---------|---------|---------|
| 1 | Planting | Plant new cane | | | |
| | Harvest | | Harvest 2nd ratoon | Harvest 1st ratoon | Harvest mature cane |
| 2 | Planting | | Plant new cane | | |
| | Harvest | Harvest mature cane | | Harvest 2nd ratoon | Harvest 1st ratoon |
| 3 | Planting | | | Plant new cane | |
| | Harvest | Harvest 1st ratoon | Harvest mature cane | | Harvest 2nd ratoon |
| 4 | Planting | | | | Plant new cane |
| | Harvest | Harvest 2nd ratoon | Harvest 1st ratoon | Harvest mature cane | |
| 5/1 | Planting | Plant new cane | | | |
| | Harvest | | Harvest 2nd ratoon | Harvest 1st ratoon | Harvest mature cane |

Figure 5.1. Field Rotation Scheme without Prolonged Fallow Period.

and planted with new cane, while the field of cut cane and the one with the first ratoon crop were both ratooned to be harvested with the fresh cane planted previously. Basing himself on the report of the 1829 commission on the sugar industry, Schnakenbourg indicates that after the second crop of ratoons was harvested, the field was allowed to lie fallow or planted in manioc for eighteen months before being returned to sugar cultivation. But it is not entirely clear from the evidence whether this was a regular part of the field rotation or an occasional practice used when conditions required. Such a rotation system would, however, require extra reserves of land (see Figure 5.2). Elsa Goveia, describing the field rotation in the British Leeward Islands at the end of the eighteenth century, indicated that the normal fallow period was six months. It overlapped with harvesting and planting and was a natural outcome of the crop cycle. Fields were cropped and harvested not all at once but gradually over six-month periods, and the fallow period formed in the interval between the two operations. In either case, the field rotation system

| Year | Season | Field 1 | Field 2 | Field 3 | Field 4 | Field 6 |
|---|---|---|---|---|---|---|
| 1 | Planting | Plant new cane | | | | Fallow |
| | Harvest | | Harvest 2nd ratoon | Harvest 1st ratoon | Harvest mature cane | |
| 2 | Planting | | Fallow | | | Plant new cane |
| | Harvest | Harvest mature cane | | Harvest 2nd ratoon | Harvest 1st ratoon | |
| 3 | Planting | | Plant new cane | Fallow | | |
| | Harvest | Harvest 1st ratoon | | | Harvest 2nd ratoon | Harvest mature cane |
| 4 | Planting | | | Plant new cane | Fallow | |
| | Harvest | Harvest 2nd ratoon | Harvest mature cane | | | Harvest 1st ratoon |
| 5 | Planting | Fallow | | | Plant new cane | |
| | Harvest | | Harvest 1st ratoon | Harvest mature cane | | Harvest 2nd ratoon |
| 6 | Planting | Plant new cane | | | | Fallow |
| | Harvest | | Harvest 2nd ratoon | Harvest 1st ratoon | Harvest mature cane | |

Figure 5.2. Field Rotation Scheme with Prolonged Fallow Period.

enabled the planters to harvest a crop every year and allowed them to keep the slave labor force fully employed all year round by constantly alternating their activity between planting and harvesting. Yet it was a slow process, and, in consequence of it, the extent of land cultivated and the size of the crop were tied to a cycle that was not readily amenable to rapid changes in the organization of production. The benefits of increased acreage would begin to be felt only after eighteen months and could be fully realized only after at least four years.[9]

If simply increasing the extent of cultivation was not a practical alternative under all circumstances for planters seeking to expand the output of their plantations, the other option was to attempt to increase the yield of the land. Concern for the variety of cane and the effective use of fertilizer, if limited in practice, at least entered the discussions of planters interested in agricultural improvement with greater frequency. Otaheite cane was the type of cane predominantly cultivated in the French Antilles during the nineteenth century. It was introduced into Martinique in the 1790s when Creole cane, the variety originally imported to the colony from the Canary Islands during the seventeenth century, began to degenerate. The diffusion of Otaheite cane to the Atlantic colonies was the product of the rapid expansion of the sugar market at the end of the eighteenth century. Bougainville carried it from its native India to the Ile-de-France between 1766 and 1769. From there, Martin took it to French Guiana, and in the 1790s, Cossigny introduced it to Martinique, Saint Domingue, and the rest of the French Antilles. It was also widespread in the British West Indies during this period. Captain Bligh brought it to Jamaica along with breadfruit, and from there it was diffused throughout the region. Although it arrived in Cuba in the 1780s, it only became popular there in the 1820s. In the opinion of Alexander von Humboldt, it was one of the major acquisitions that colonial agriculture owed to the voyages of the eighteenth-century naturalists and was of greater significance than its more celebrated companion, the breadfruit. It was definitively adopted in Martinique in 1818 when large quantities of it were brought from French Guiana.[10]

Otaheite cane was taller, thicker, and richer in saccharine than the earlier varieties of Creole cane. It matured more rapidly and yielded considerably more sugar, and its thick woody stalk provided abundant bagasse, which helped to resolve the perpetual fuel shortage of the West Indian sugar mills. Its richer sucrose content and higher yield allowed planters to increase their output without having to transform production techniques. According to W. A. Green, in Jamaica Otaheite cane produced two-and-one-half hogsheads of sugar per acre on land that had only produced one-and-one-half hogsheads with an earlier variety. He comments that ironically, the rapid adoption of high-yield Otaheite cane in the British West Indies contributed to the saturation of the British market, falling prices, and planter indebtedness. By the 1830s and 1840s, the structure of the French market relieved colonial planters of any similar preoccupation. The adoption of Otaheite cane in the French Antilles was a great improvement, but by 1839 a decline in its quality was beginning to be noticed. In that year, de Lacharière, a planter from Guadeloupe, warned that unless Otaheite cane was replaced, its degeneration would make agriculture impossible in the colonies. Lavollée wrote that the colonists hoped to import new plants directly from the Pacific to regenerate their stock. Despite this difficulty, Otaheite cane remained virtually the only variety of cane cultivated in the French West Indies throughout the nineteenth century.[11]

Fertilizer could also make an appreciable difference in crop yield. The planters of Martinique began to experiment actively with it, although its use was still hindered by the lingering prejudice that the use of manure as fertilizer harmed the quality of the cane juice. De Lavigne emphasized that fertilizer and, where practical, the use of the plow were important factors in raising the yield of sugar in Martinique. Increased amounts of fertilizer were especially important in compensating for poor soil conditions on some of the new sugar lands. Sainte Croix estimated that a carré of newly planted cane yielded 8,640 livres of sugar if unfertilized and 11,340 livres if fertilized (an increase of 31 percent) while a carré of ratoons yielded 5,940 livres if unfertilized and 8,100 livres if fertilized (an increase of 36 percent). He stressed that it was important to fertilize at least the newly planted fields to insure a good harvest, and this was apparently a common practice. However, he admitted that it was too difficult and expensive to fertilize all the land under cultivation. Guignod estimated that 36,000 baskets of manure weighing twenty livres each were required to fertilize the six carrés he normally planted in new cane each year. This amount of manure had to be carried to the fields in advance of the time it was needed. It was left in heaps along the side of the road where it deteriorated. According to Guignod, to have the required amount of manure on hand during the planting season it was necessary to transport 50,000 baskets or 1,000 cartloads ahead of time. In addition, carrying wet, heavy manure was one of the most exhausting tasks on the plantation and took a physical toll on the slaves.[12]

Planters in Martinique ordinarily used manure produced on the estate, seawater, sea sludge, and seaweed as fertilizer. There were imported fertilizers available, but these were expensive and could add considerably to the costs of production. Spoiled codfish was a powerful fertilizer and esteemed highly by the planters. When it was available, it was very expensive. Fifty kilograms cost between ten and fifteen francs. Guignod estimated that it cost about 500 francs per carré to use codfish or other types of fertilizer that had to be purchased. Paul Daubrée suggested that the heads, bones, and entrails, which were discarded by the North Atlantic fishery, be sold as fertilizer in the Antilles. In the 1840s, guano from Peru became available. Dried cattle blood from the *abattoirs* of Paris cost from ten to fifteen francs per 100 livres and was used with good results, as were some chemical fertilizers. Even though imported fertilizers remained costly, the planters did not effectively utilize the material available to them. Little care was taken to collect and conserve the manure from the livestock on the plantation or to increase the amount the herds produced. Stables were notoriously inadequate. Animals were pastured outdoors at night, frequently on the hilly land on the margin of the estate. Frequent rains washed the dung down the steep slopes, and it was lost to agriculture. Moveable pens that pastured the animals on or near fields about to be planted could yield good results if carefully tended. However, there were no pits to collect and store manure, and while cane leaves were abundant and made excellent litter to be mixed with the dung, Lavollée complained that this source was neglected by the planters. He did note, however, that some planters were beginning to pay attention to these matters and were enjoying notable results.[13]

In spite of the increased emphasis after 1830 on the use of fertilizer, Lavollée records that the use of the various means of fertilization was neither general nor widespread, and Gueroult, another contemporary observer, estimated that the yield of cane on the plantations could have been doubled with the more effective use of fertilizer. Lavollée charged that the majority of planters only used fertilizer as a last resort, and then only on their most depleted lands. In response to Lavollée's criticisms, Guignod admitted that the sugar estates were inadequately fertilized. However, in his view, the problem was not that the planters neglected the production of manure, but that the cane fields devoured such enormous quantities of it that they could not possibly produce an adequate supply. Furthermore, he argued, cane leaves could not be used as litter because they had to be fed to the livestock, and the government restricted the importation of spoiled cod to protect the fisheries. Imported fertilizers were not only expensive, but he reported that French merchants refused to ship them to the colonies, and he complained of fraud as well.[14]

The use of plows was limited in Martinique, and the burdensome task of planting was usually done with hoes. In many localities, rocky soil and steep terrain prohibited the use of plows. Soleau reports that some planters used the plow to break the ground, but that the actual planting was done in trenches dug by slaves using hoes. Many planters also felt that plowing exposed the soil to the elements and decreased its fertility. In the eyes of contemporary observers, the Negro was a *routinier* by nature, and they almost universally commented that it was difficult to break the slaves from their customary patterns of work and train them to use the plow. Further, the use of the plow required an adequate supply of draft animals, a chronic problem in Martinique.[15]

Plows were also expensive and often of poor quality. As with other imported goods, this situation was aggravated by the *exclusif*. According to Guignod, at the time he began planting in 1817 plows of English and American manufacture were common as was a traditional local plow known as a *charrue à fleche*. He also claims that the English plow (*charrue en avant-train*) was produced in the colony. This seems unlikely and may well be a subterfuge to account for the presence of contraband goods. By the end of the 1820s, Belgian-made plows and French-made Dombasle plows were imported in large numbers from France for about 250 francs apiece. However, these were too fragile for the heavier, rockier soils of the Antilles, and their failure helped to convince the planters that plows were unsuitable for plantation agriculture. Some planters were successful with another, sturdier model from Bordeaux. But its price, from 250 to 400 francs, was prohibitive for most, and its use was limited. By way of contrast, Lavollée noted that a plow used in the British colony of Antigua cost only 126 francs, and requested that foreign plows be admitted to the French colonies with only a moderate duty.[16]

Where conditions allowed its use, the plow permitted significant economies in plantation agriculture. Jabrun, a planter from Guadeloupe, whose own land was too rocky and uneven to use a plow, estimated that one slave plowman assisted by two children could do the work of eighteen slaves using hoes. He ascertained that one plow would be sufficient to plant the fifteen hectares of new cane he put in each year. De Lavigne of Martinique, who had two plows valued at 700 francs, reported that he was able to increase the area he had under cultivation from 50 to 100 carrés with the same number of slaves by adopting the plow. Despite obstacles, the use of the plow increased in the colonies, particularly when the end of the slave trade made it difficult to secure new hands. But there were many natural and social restraints to its adoption. The process was slow and failed to transform plantation agriculture, which continued to rest on the back of the slave with the hoe.[17]

A large herd of livestock was essential for the operation of a sugar estate, especially if the plantation had to rely on oxen or mules to power its mill. The number and type of animals needed varied with the size of the plantation, the nature of the terrain, and the capacity and type of mill. In general, a large plantation required thirty-five to fifty oxen and a like number of mules, while smaller plantations needed fewer than twenty-five of each. De Lavigne, whose estate included one wind-powered mill and one animal-powered mill, had forty oxen, twenty cows, and forty mules. Oxen were generally used for plowing and hauling carts of cut cane to the mill where conditions permitted. In more difficult terrain, cut cane was transported to the mill on muleback. Similarly, where refined sugar had to be transported overland from the mill to the point of transshipment, the bad state of roads made the use of ox carts impossible and necessitated the use of mules. Mules were also commonly preferred over oxen as a source of traction for the mill because of their greater speed. The substitution of mules for oxen increased costs. Not only did replacement mules have to be purchased, but they carried a lighter load and required more supervisory personnel. In addition to the work they performed on the sugar estate, the livestock provided fertilizer, and dried ox blood was used in the sugar manufacturing process to clarify the sugar.[18]

The animals were poorly cared for. They were inadequately nourished and exposed to disease in the tropical climate. After performing exhausting tasks during the day, the animals were bedded down for the night in filthy open-air pens that provided no shelter from the elements. To not jeopardize the cane fields, they were pastured on unsuitable land without regard for a safe and sufficient supply of water or for the abundance of noxious plants that grew in the pastures. Normally, Guinea grass was used for cattle fodder, though it was supplemented or replaced by cane syrup mixed with cane tops and straw during the harvest. Maltreatment, epidemics, and epizootic diseases contributed to a high mortality rate among plantation animals, and there was not a single veterinarian in the colony. It is difficult to ascertain the extent to which poisoning by slaves (to sabotage the master's property) may also have contributed to the mortality of the livestock. There is no doubt that poisoning occurred, but it attained such a prominent place in the consciousness of the planters that poison was used to explain animal death due to a variety of other causes. So strong was the belief in poisoning that it resulted in a kind of fatalism among the planters. According to Lavollée, "If . . . an animal falls sick, the belief in poison is so deeply rooted in the minds of the colonists at this point that no remedy is attempted." He charged that if more attention were given to the care and pasturage of livestock with the resources already at hand, the well-being of the animals would improve markedly, and the planters would save considerable expense. But, he lamented, "up to now, they prefer to remain dependent on foreign supplies. . . . they lack the strength to uproot their old habits and the will to force themselves to take the necessary measures. Up until now, self-interest has been incapable of inducing them to follow the example of the few progressive planters."[19]

The replacement of livestock was a constant and considerable expense to the planters. The average life span for a mule was between six and eight years, and for an ox, between four and six years. Epidemics that could carry off whole herds were not infrequent. De Lavigne reported that natural reproduction never offset the losses among his herds and that this situation was the same for the other planters of Martinique. There were no systematic efforts at stock raising, and it was necessary to import animals from abroad to meet the requirements of plantation agriculture. Creole cattle and mules were common in Martinique, and, although small, they were able to endure the rigors of climate and fatigue. Although creole breeds stirred the enthusiasm of the critics of colonial agriculture, the planters preferred to buy animals from abroad rather than try to rear them themselves. The imported breeds were superior in size and strength, although they were expensive. Mules were imported from France as well as the United States and the Rio de la Plata, and their price was variously reported as 600 to 650 and 950 francs per head. There was a thriving trade in oxen and cattle with Puerto Rico. Almost all the cattle came from there and sold for 400–500 francs per head in Martinique. Aside from work animals, animals had to be imported for food. According to Lavollée, an average of 500 sheep and goats and 350 pigs were imported each year for this purpose. Sheep adapted well to the colony, especially in the south. Some planters kept small herds for their own consumption, but no one systematically developed flocks as a source of meat, fertilizer, or wool. In addition, 2,000 cattle were imported annually as replacements for an equal number of work animals that were retired and used to meet the consumption needs of the colony. A small number of beef cattle were also imported from the United States. Lavollée estimated that between food and work animals, the planters of Martinique spent more than a million francs annually to import livestock when they had the potential resources not only to meet their own needs but to produce for export as well.[20]

## The Mill

The harvest (*roulaison*) was the critical phase of sugar production. It was the most demanding and the most exhausting of all operations involved in sugar manufacture, and it mobilized all the human and material resources of the sugar plantation. During the harvest season, production was uninterrupted for six, seven, and, in exceptional cases, twelve months of the year. Work was carried on in shifts laboring at maximum capacity without interruption around the clock. The cane was cut with knives or bills, bundled, and hauled to the mill in ox carts or on muleback. At the mill, the cut cane stalks were crushed between rollers moved by wind, water, animal, or steam power. The juice was squeezed out and carried through a trough to the boiling house to be made into sugar, while the crushed stalks (bagasse) were taken to a drying shed and would later be used as fuel for the boilers.[21]

Commonly, each sugar plantation in Martinique had its own mill and performed all the operations necessary to cultivate and manufacture sugar within the boundaries of the estate. The type of mill predominantly in use in Martinique during the first half of the nineteenth century consisted of three parallel vertically mounted cylinders moved by water, wind, or animal traction. This type of mill provided the technical foundation for the formation of the sugar industry in the French and British Caribbean in the second half of the seventeenth century. It was described then in the classic accounts of Père Jean-Baptiste Labat (*Nouveau Voyage aux Iles de l'Amérique*) and Richard Ligon (*A True and Exact History of the Island of Barbados*). Its use was generalized during this period and continued without modification until the sugar boom in the last decades of the eighteenth century.[22]

Figure 5.3. Seventeenth-century Drawing by Franz Post of a Sugar Mill. [Reproduced by permission of the Royal Museum of Fine Arts, Brussels.]

This type of mill offered a relatively cheap and simple means of grinding sugar cane. It was easily worked by slaves and was readily adaptable to any source of power. Its adoption prevented the big planters from controlling all sugar manufacturing activity through the monopolization of the limited sources of water power on the rivers. Instead, small and medium planters could have their own mills and use other sources of power. They were thus able to play a significant role in the development of the Caribbean sugar industry from its inception, which facilitated the exploitation of all available cane land. Thus, they avoided the Brazilian pattern of powerful *senhores do engenho*, who controlled the sources of water power and monopolized sugar manufacturing, and subordinate *lavradores de cana*, who often grew extensive amounts of cane but did not have their own mills. The self-contained plantation, each with its own mill, became the typical unit of agricultural exploitation in the Caribbean, and the difference between sugar planters was a difference of degree rather than kind.[23]

The mill was the hub of the sugar plantation, and life quite literally revolved around it. After the slaves, it was the planter's major investment and preoccupation. The organization of resources on the plantation was contingent on the mill's capacity and power source. These conditioned the size and location of the fields, the coordination of the tasks, and the number and disposition of slaves and work animals. During the harvest, the cadence of its wheels determined the rhythm and intensity of work and the expenditure of energy of men and beasts. However, sugar manufacture in Martinique was backward and wasteful. The methods of sugar manufacture had remained unchanged since the foundation of the colony, and, according to Daubrée, the grinding mills were almost always poorly constructed and maintained. Wind, water, and animal power provided insufficient and irregular force to propel the mill adequately. The water mill was most productive and produced between 20,800 and 27,000 livres of sugar a week. The winds were less regular than the waterways, and windmills produced less sugar. Animal-driven mills were the least productive, although some exceptional ones rivaled the water mills. Several large plantations had two or three mills of different types to insure that sufficient power would be available for the harvest, but this added enormously to the planter's costs.[24]

The three-cylinder vertical mill, commonly used in Martinique during the first half of the nineteenth century, offered some technical advances over previous types of mills. In the vertical mill, the three rollers were positioned side by side on top of a heavy lead-covered table. They were mounted on bearings, and their weight was evenly distributed. They thus turned easily, and they took cylinders of a smaller diameter than those in the older type of two-cylinder horizontal mill, in use before the seventeenth century. This type of mill integrated the transmission and crushing mechanisms. The center roller was connected to the power source, either directly or by means of a system of gears, and it transmitted the motion directly to the lateral rollers through gears at the top of the rollers. In comparison with the older, two-cylinder mills, the three cylinders made it easier to pass the cane stalks through the mill more than once and thus increased the amount of juice that could be extracted from a given quantity of cane. One slave, usually a woman, fed the cut cane into the mill between the center roller and one of the lateral rollers. Another slave woman stationed on the other side of the mechanism received the crushed cane stalks and fed them back between the center roller and the other lateral roller to be ground a second time. This was the most efficient way to pass the cane stalks through the mill, and the three rollers allowed the cane to be ground twice in a continuous process. (A device called a *doubleuse*, which automatically fed the partially crushed stalks back through the rollers a second time, was also available from the 1760s on.) However, lack of care in grinding the cane could greatly reduce the efficiency of the mill. Sainte Croix complains that some planters in Martinique only passed the cut cane through the mill and neglected to grind the bagasse, while others passed cut cane and bagasse through the mill together. This latter practice was the most common and the most disadvantageous. The pressure of the rollers was uneven because of the resistance of the unground cane stalks. The bagasse also reabsorbed the cane juice and the yield was thereby diminished.[25]

However, even in the best of circumstances, the vertical mill did not efficiently extract the juice from the cane, no matter whether wind, water, or animal power was used. The insufficient pressure applied to the cane stalks left a considerable amount of juice in the bagasse. Lavollée remarked that after grinding, cane juice could still be squeezed from the pulp by hand. Daubrée records that on a large, well-equipped plantation in Guadeloupe, the amount of juice extracted was only 56 percent of the weight of the cane, and he estimates that if the smaller, less-well-equipped plantations were taken into consideration, an average yield of 50 percent of the weight of the cane would be more accurate. The weight of cane was 90 percent juice, but only 50 percent of the juice was extracted; the remaining 40 percent was left in the bagasse. Despite the general inefficiency of the vertical mills, Lavollée observed considerable variation on individual estates. One plantation in Basse Pointe succeeded in extracting juice that was 80 percent of the weight of the cane. In Diamant, his measurements showed a yield of juice that was 67 percent of the total weight of the cane. However, in Anses d'Arlets the juice obtained was only 33 percent the weight of the cane.[26]

The arrangement of the rollers and the inefficient use of power were the two greatest limitations of this type of mill. The distance between the rollers regulated the pressure exerted on the cane. They could be placed closer together or further apart, but once the distance was set, the pressure was fixed. They were generally set as close together as possible to obtain the maximum pressure. However, if the cylinders rubbed against one another, the mill became difficult to turn and at times could even stop. Frequently, grooves were cut either vertically or obliquely into the surface of the center roller, the two lateral rollers, or all three to grip the stalks better. However, these resulted in unequal pressure, which crushed the cane stalks unevenly and prevented them from passing easily through the mill. Unchannelled rollers exerted a more even pressure and were superior. Sainte Croix writes that two configurations of the rollers were in common use in Martinique during the 1820s. In the first, all three rollers were of the same size and turned at the same speed. In the second, known as *rôles tiercés*, the center roller was either the same size or smaller than the two lateral rollers, but the 2:3 gear ratio meant that the lateral rollers turned fewer than three times for every four revolutions of the center roller. The slower speed of the lateral rollers made this arrangement more effective than the first for squeezing the juice from the cane, but the higher relative speed of the center roller shredded the bagasse, making it more difficult to pass through the mill a second time. Whichever arrangement was used, the mills moved by water, wind, or animal power turned the rollers at an uneven speed and generally too quickly to grind the cane stalks effectively.[27]

The vertical placement of the rollers was a still more fundamental source of inefficiency. Instead of spreading across the entire surface of the cylinders, the cane stalks tended to bunch up at the lower part of the roller. According to Sainte Croix, the actual grinding surface covered no more than 33 linear centimeters along the length of the rollers. The major part of the mill's potential capacity was not utilized, and the whole grinding operation went more slowly. More force was required to move the cylinders, and less pressure was exerted on the cane stalks. The resistance of the stalks caused the rollers to wear unevenly and put the whole mechanism out of alignment. This was particularly the case because of the prevalence of wooden parts, which wore down quickly under pressure and aggravated all of the difficulties of this type of mill. For these reasons, a new mill was almost always superior to one that had been in service for some time. These technical limitations of the vertical mill limited its capacity. Because only the lower portion of the grinding surface was utilized, observed Sainte Croix, it yielded a uniform 600 liters of juice per hour no matter what type of power source was used. Moreno Fraginals, basing himself on Cuban sources, estimates that the best-equipped vertical mill could grind only a 170-ton harvest.[28]

The efficacy of the mill increasingly became a preoccupation of planters, agronomists, and engineers from the end of the eighteenth century onward, and especially after 1815. There were a number of innovations in its design and construction during this period, although the extent to which they were adopted is not known. These changes in the mill facilitated the adoption of Otaheite cane, while this variety of cane stimulated the further development of the mill. The all-wood mills used previously could not extract the juice from the thick woody stalk of the Otaheite cane, while the increased pressure needed to grind it frequently broke the wooden shafts and gears. By the 1780s or 1790s, the hardwood cylinders were generally covered with iron shells to increase their durability and the amount of pressure that could be exerted. Dutrône describes rollers made completely of iron in his account of the sugar industry in Saint Domingue published in 1791, but Lavollée indicates that wooden rollers with iron shells were the most common type in Martinique during the 1830s. The wooden gears commonly used were difficult to set and adjust. They broke easily if this were not done properly or if the alignment of the rollers was not exactly vertical. The failure to replace a broken tooth on a gear could result in all the other teeth being broken, too. Such accidents were frequent, and repairs were slow and difficult. The mill could be put out of action during the critical period of the crop cycle. This problem was alleviated somewhat when metal parts became available to replace wooden ones at the end of the eighteenth century. This process culminated with the introduction of all-metal construction in the 1820s.[29]

It was widely recommended that horizontal mills be adopted to resolve the problems presented by the vertical mill. A new type of horizontal grinding mill is first known to have been developed in Jamaica in 1754, and its use appears to have spread to Saint Domingue by 1790, if not before. (As Moreno Fraginals emphasizes, this type of horizontal mill is not to be confused with an earlier type described by Labat whose cylinders were mounted in a straight line and presented some of the same difficulties as the vertical mill.) In this new design, the axles of the three cylinders formed an isosceles triangle with two of the rollers on the bottom. This configuration allowed more cane to be ground in the same amount of time. Cane could be applied over the entire grinding surface. It was easier and safer to feed. The cane could be pushed down a tray into the rollers, thus avoiding accidents to the slaves, who would often get their hands or arms caught in the vertical mills. When properly mounted and maintained, the horizontal mill ground the cane much more efficiently than the vertical mill, and the cane was automatically pressed twice when passed through the rollers. Pressure and wear were distributed evenly over the mechanism, particularly with the development of a spring-and-weight mechanism, which allowed the roller to yield when an irregular piece of cane was fed in. Sainte Croix suggests that it was relatively easy and cheap to convert a vertical mill to a horizontal one, but by the first half of the nineteenth century, all-iron horizontal mills manufactured in England and the United States predominated. During the 1830s, the French firm of Derosne and Cail, a pioneer of sugar technology, developed the first complete sugar-processing system. It featured a three-roller horizontal mill, a cane carrier, defecators, carbon filters, and vacuum evaporators. Further, Daubrée, writing in 1841, singled out the pioneering efforts of the Mazeline brothers of Le Havre in developing a steam-powered horizontal mill in France. Yet in that same year, Lavollée reported that there were only five or six horizontal mills in use in Martinique, all of which were powered by steam.[30]

The majority of sugar mills in Martinique during the first half of the nineteenth century were driven by natural forces. Wind, water, and animal power predominated, and geographical conditions had much to do with the location of various types of mill (table 5.1). Unlike the rest of the Lesser Antilles, where windmills prevailed, animal-powered mills were most common in Martinique. They were in general use in all parts of the island, but were most important in the extreme south (Anses d'Arlets, Trois Ilets, Diamant, Rivière Salée, Sainte Luce, Marin, Sainte Anne, Vauclin, Saint Esprit, François, Robert, and parts of Trou-au-Chat), where the arid climate, absence of waterways, and lack of favorable winds virtually prohibited the use of other sources of power. Windmills were only practical on the east coast, where there were regular winds off the Atlantic, and the majority of them were in Robert, François, and Vauclin. Writing in 1830, after the establishment of many

Table 5.1. Types of Sugar Mills in Martinique, 1820

| Power Source | Number |
|---|---|
| Water | 178 |
| Wind | 20 |
| Animal | 199 |
| Steam | 10 |
| Total | 307 |

Source: Sainte Croix, *Statistique de la Martinique*, II, pp. 34, 52, 74, 96.

new mills in the region, Soleau commented that the plantations he passed on his trip from François to Trinité almost exclusively had wind-driven mills. Watermills were most common in Fort Royal, Lamentin, and Trou-au-Chat, particularly along the Lezard River; in the alluvial valleys along the northeast coast from Macouba to Trinité; and along the short rivers flowing down from the mountains in Prêcheur, Saint Pierre, Carbet, and Case Pilote. Water mills were also important in Rivière Pilote in the extreme south. There were few steam-powered mills in Martinique. Sainte Croix counted ten in 1820, and government statistics listed twelve in 1838. However, several of the more prosperous planters attempted to improve the efficiency of their operations; by 1847, the number rose to thirty-three. It is important to note that the history of the adoption of steam power during these decades is not one of unilinear success and expansion in which steam showed itself demonstrably superior to other sources of power. It was, rather, a faltering process marked by small operations, many false starts, repeated failures, and expensive projects abandoned after a few years of poor or mediocre results, while other men elsewhere, full of hope and optimism, began new experiments under the continuing pressure to increase efficiency.[31]

Alicia Canabrava underscores the importance of the wind-driven mill as the major technical advance of the seventeenth-century Caribbean sugar industry. At first sight, the windmill seemed to offer marvelous advantages to the planter. It was a source of power that cost nothing and spared the enormous expense of animals and fuel. In 1841, Brière de l'Isle, a member of the Société d'agriculture et d'économie rurale, argued that agriculture in Martinique could be improved considerably if windmills were substituted for animal-powered mills, particularly in the region between Pointe du Caravelle and Pointe des Salines, where natural conditions were most favorable and the winds most constant during the harvest season. Windmills would increase the harvest immediately, he contended. They could generate greater force than was possible with animals, and, on the average, they drew 10 percent more juice from the cane. They were not as expensive as was commonly believed, but could be built for 10,000–12,000 francs, and horizontal rollers could be installed as in Guadeloupe. He maintained that the planters of

Martinique were prejudiced against the windmill because they did not understand how to operate it properly. To remedy this situation, Mr. Hendly was brought from Barbados to instruct them in its use. If windmills were adopted, the existing animal-powered mills could be used as a back-up, and the great expense for the maintenance and continual replacement of the large herds of mules required for animal traction mills could be spared. The burdensome mule herds could be replaced by cattle, which were renewable and could be integrated into the plantation economy in a variety of ways.[32]

But the windmill was more costly than it appeared at first sight. Planters complained of the expense of their construction and maintenance, but, more importantly, their operation was irregular. They depended on steady and adequate winds. When the wind was weak, only a small amount of cane could be ground and made into sugar each day. Hands remained idle in all sectors of the production process during the crucial harvest season. When the wind was too strong, it was difficult for workers to keep the mill supplied with cane. At the same time, the speed at which the rollers turned imperfectly crushed the cane, resulting in the loss of more juice than normal. Usually, it was also necessary to have an animal-powered mill for use when the wind was unsuitable. The planter then had to bear the expense of constructing and maintaining two mills and the necessary animals, instead of one. The savings represented by the windmill could disappear rapidly. There were also technical problems with the design and construction of windmills in Martinique. Soleau complained that not only were the blades poorly designed, but the windmills had no brake. Without a brake, it was difficult to quickly bring the mill to a halt. This was a means not only of preventing damage to the equipment, but even more tragic events. When a slave working in the mill got his or her hand or arm caught in the rollers, loss of the limb was almost certain. There was no way to stop the mill.[33]

The watermill was preferred when available. It was potentially the most advantageous source of power, combining force and economy when well constructed. However, according to Daubrée, watercourses in Martinique were, for the most part, insufficient to power the mill. "Good watermills are rare in Martinique," stated a letter to Governor Donzelot in 1820. There were, it continued, many mediocre or poor mills that needed long canals to guarantee an adequate supply of water. These channels were often dug through the heart of the mountains, and their maintenance required considerable expense. The volume of water available varied greatly with the seasons, and many plantations without such canals found themselves without sufficient water during the dry season, which was also harvest time.[34]

Where the water supply was adequate, the mill was often so poorly designed and constructed that it was barely more productive than the other types of mill. Both Soleau and Sainte Croix criticized the efficiency of water mills in Martinique and suggested remedies that would increase their productive capacity without entailing great expense. The principal deficiencies were the design of the mill-race and the paddles and the transmission of the movement from the waterwheel to the mill. The principle of the hydraulic wheel was badly understood in Martinique. Neither the total volume nor the fall of the water was utilized, and the difference between the velocity of the water entering and leaving the wheel gave it an irregular impulsion. When attached to a horizontal mill, the transmission mechanism used with the hydraulic wheel turned the rollers too rapidly to grind the cane effectively. For this reason, planters in Martinique almost universally preferred the vertical mill. But Soleau protested that the transformation of the horizontal movement of the water wheel to the vertical movement of the mill was unnecessary. The mechanism used to do this was overly complicated and only succeeded in reducing the effective power of the mill and making its operation inconvenient. Both Sainte Croix and Soleau argued for the superiority of the properly constructed horizontal mill. But the planters were unwilling to make even simple changes. Innovation was difficult in Martinique, and Soleau criticized the conservatism of the planters: "There is in their minds a strong tendency toward the fixity of principles which not only must have contributed to making their political position more unfortunate, but also to checking the expansion of their production which, we shall see, is very slight."[35]

Animal-powered mills were most common in Martinique. Mules were preferred over oxen because they turned the mill more rapidly and extracted a higher proportion of juice from the cane. A large number of mules were necessary, and ideally their number ought to have been kept proportional to the amount of cane to be processed. The average sugar estate required from fifty to eighty mules for the mill and carts, but Dutrône wrote that this was rarely achieved. For example, de Lavigne, who had both a windmill and an animal-powered mill, used a team of forty mules to operate the latter. The mules were hitched to the arms of the mill in two or three teams of three mules each. A young slave was assigned to guide each team and led it at a fast trot. Teams worked in relays of one to two hours called a *quart*. Two or three other slaves were constantly employed feeding and caring for the mules and preparing new relays. Daubrée complained that mule-driven mills hardly ever provided sufficient power to grind the cane. Planters rarely harnessed more than five or six mules to the mill at once, and that number provided only half the necessary force. In addition, the mules were often imperfectly harnessed. Not only was the power insufficient to grind the cane properly, but the effort of drawing the mill wore out the animals rapidly and resulted in a high rate of mortality among them. Even by the 1820s, mules were scarce and costly in Martinique. They were fragile, and, in addition to overwork, they were exposed to disease and maltreatment. Because mules do not reproduce, the animals constantly had to be replaced. Martinique spent much more for the purchase of mules than the neighboring island of Guadeloupe, where windmills predominated. The need to continually purchase these animals was a significant factor in the colonial debt, and foreign countries demanded payment in hard currency, which drained the colony of money.[36]

The first known attempt to apply steam power to the grinding of sugar cane was made in Jamaica by John Stewart, also known as Robert Rainy, between 1768 and 1770. In the midst of a sugar boom and at the beginning of the Industrial Revolution, Stewart erected and put into operation a steam-powered mill he had shipped to the island from England. Noel Deerr credits this effort with being the first application of steam power to the operation of machinery in a manufacturing process. There were also several other experiments in the application of steam power to sugar manufacture in the Caribbean during these years. These early experiments apparently had no lasting effect, but by the turn of the nineteenth century, a process of continual experimentation with the application of steam power to sugar manufacture was underway. In 1797, Alexander von Humboldt reports, Count Jaruco y Mopex erected a steam mill on his "Seybabo" estate in Cuba. This was the first attempt to use steam power that was of industrial consequence, and although it was not successful, it initiated a sustained effort on the part of Cuban planters to apply the steam engine to their grinding operations. Not surprisingly, English firms were prominent in the development of steam technology in the sugar industry. The order book of Boulton and Watt for cane mill engines begins in 1803. The company built 114 sugar mill engines between that year and 1820, with Jamaica, British Guiana, and Trinidad the major customers. Between 1813 and 1817, Fawcett, Preston, and Company built 79 cane mill engines. Of these, 42 went to British Guiana, 9 to Jamaica, 8 to St. Lucia, 6 to Cuba, 6 to Martinique, 3 to New Orleans, 2 each to Nevis and Bourbon, and 1 to Surinam. The latter firm also sold all-iron horizontal grinding mills as well as steam engines and moved to the forefront in the process of the mechanization of the sugar mill.[37]

Despite these early advances, the reception for the steam engine in Martinique was far from universally enthusiastic or unequivocally successful. The first steam engine was introduced into Martinique during the British occupation in 1813 by M. le Compte de Maupou in Rivière Salée. However, difficulty in obtaining parts and prejudice against "the employment of a dangerous force when it is not managed with art and discernment" impeded its adoption in the colony. Nevertheless, interest in steam power continued after the return of Martinique to France, although the technology remained English. In 1817, Mr. Fawcett, an engineer from Liverpool (and presumably from the firm of Fawcett, Preston, and Company), sent a steam-powered mill to Martinique at the request of the Chamber of Commerce of Nantes. The French consul in Liverpool also went to the Fawcett works to inspect a similar model designed for Bourbon. He praised its construction as far superior to that of the old vertical mill. The six-horsepower engine moved a new-model horizontal mill, and the cane was crushed twice as it passed between the rollers. Its cost was between £300 and £500. The consul concluded his report with the remark that the Fawcett works merited a visit from French mechanics "who doubtlessly could spare us the regret of seeing our colonies remain the tributaries of English industry." On the strength of the successful field test in Martinique and the recommendation of the consul, the Chamber of Commerce of Nantes petitioned the Ministry of the Marine and Colonies to obtain the design of this machine. The adoption of steam power in Martinique appears to have been a rather slow and restricted process, although the documentation may not be entirely reliable. In 1836, government statistics enumerated only twelve steam mills in the entire colony. In 1845, a survey listed twenty, of which eight were described as *ancien*. But the following year, another survey counted ten steam mills out of thirty-five sugar plantations in François alone. Of these only two were designated as *ancien*.[38]

Steam power did not revolutionize sugar manufacture, but rather was adapted to the existing organization of production. The potential improvement in production represented by the steam engine was inhibited by the technical limits of the mill. Up until 1840, sugar mills were designed to be used with any source of power; none was manufactured especially for steam. Instead, steam engines were substituted for other sources of power and adapted to existing mills. The most successful adaptation appears to have been to the new all-metal horizontal mills of the type introduced by Fawcett, Preston, and Company. However, while this combination allowed a greater mass of cane to be ground, it resulted in no improvement in the rate of sugar yielded from a given quantity of cane. In Martinique, the steam engine was frequently used in conjunction with the old vertical mill. Indeed, Soleau expressed his surprise when he encountered this arrangement on his trip from Robert to François in 1835. In 1841, Lavollée reported that there were only five or six horizontal mills in Martinique, all of which were powered by steam. But the government agricultural statistics for that year counted eleven steam mills in the colony. Thus, the evidence suggests that the remainder of the steam engines were attached to vertical mills, which, as Sainte Croix emphasized, had a capacity of 600 liters of cane juice per hour no matter what source of motive power was used.[39]

The great advantage of the steam mill, in the eyes of the planters of Martinique, was not that it produced more sugar than mills powered by other sources of energy, but that it provided a more reliable and regular source of motive power and also spared the enormous expense of mules and oxen. W. Macomb, an engineer who, with the backing of one of the Perrier brothers, proposed to convert the sugar mills of Martinique to steam power, wrote to Governor Donzelot in 1820: "The great interest of the colonists is to adapt the steam engine to the presently existing mills and by that means to replace the incomplete force of water for those who lack it and the costly use of mules whose labor, as I have said, is subject to a number of disadvantages and which is of no use when they are unfit for service." The steam engine, he continued, could replace the second-rate and bad mills, which had a number of disadvantages, by a solid, dependable machine that always generated sufficient power and could be easily and cheaply maintained. Not only would the power necessary for grinding be more reliable, but the continual cost of mules and the slaves to work and care for them could be saved and the loss of foreign exchange to Latin America for their purchase avoided.[40]

The major obstacle to replacing mules and other inadequate sources of power with steam was the great expense involved. Planters were reluctant to purchase steam engines, not only because of the cost of new machinery, but because the considerable amount of capital already invested in existing mills would be lost if these facilities were abandoned in favor of the steam mill. For this reason, Macomb proposed adapting steam power to the existing apparatus of the sugar mill rather than replacing it with all-new equipment and buildings. He argued that the best solution to the problems of the sugar industry in Martinique was to fit the steam engine to the already existing mule-driven mills. A four-horsepower steam engine, he maintained, was most appropriate to this task. Thus, the application of steam power was initially conceived within the framework of the antecedent structure of the sugar plantation. Not only was the potential of steam to transform the production process suppressed by subordinating it to this technical and social organization, but the mill remained underpowered. According to Daubrée, the force necessary to grind sugar cane was commonly underestimated. The new steam mills installed in the colonies were no greater than six or seven horsepower and generated insufficient force. Ten to twelve horsepower was the minimum necessary, and in New Orleans, where admittedly the mills were larger than in the French colonies, twenty horsepower was the smallest steam engine in use.[41]

Governor Donzelot of Martinique organized a committee of planters to study the proposals made by Macomb. This committee recognized that the advantages offered by the steam mill had already led several planters from various parishes successfully to substitute iron mills moved by steam engines for their old animal-powered mills. These efforts were most successful where the planters had been dependent on mules, which were becoming more scarce and expensive. However, the steam engine also presented several disadvantages, which, in the opinion of the committee, discredited this new type of mill among the planters of Martinique. First, the island lacked a sufficient source of fuel. Wood was rare and costly, and coal imported from Europe or wood brought from the neighboring island of Saint Croix was too expensive for planters whose expenses were already excessive and beyond their means. Bagasse was the only possible source of fuel, and, in a work published about the same time as the deliberations of the planters' committee, Sainte Croix remarked that the invention of a device that would allow bagasse to be substituted for coal would represent a great savings to planters and greatly facilitate the adoption of the steam mill. Second, the committee pointed to the lack of water in the southern part of the colony. It was precisely in these *quartiers* that the steam engine would be most useful, but in the dry season, which was also the harvest season, there was not enough water for the boilers. Finally, the committee pointed to the lack of qualified workers in the colony and the impossibility of trusting the complicated steam engine to the care of slaves. The committee concluded that although this proposal had the advantage of adapting the steam engine to existing mills and was less costly than complete replacement of the latter, opinion was too strongly against the introduction of the steam mill, and in general, the planters were little disposed to adopt it, particularly given the difficult financial condition of the colony.[42]

In his report to the Minister of the Marine and Colonies on this matter, Governor Donzelot recommended that in place of the attempt to substitute the steam engine for other sources of energy, effort should be directed toward developing a mechanism that would allow the slower cattle and oxen to turn a sugar mill at the same speed as steam mills. If such a modification were to allow oxen to be substituted for mules, and attention were given to breeding and the development of the cattle herds, the problem of the scarcity and expense of mules would be overcome. The same end as that proposed by the adoption of the steam engine would be accomplished, and the effect on colonial agriculture and plantation life would be salutary. Cattle and oxen would provide not only power, but manure and meat. On the basis of this recommendation, the ministry turned its attention to the development of the cattle mill, and the director of the Conservatoire des arts et métiers was directed to devise a system of levers that would allow oxen to turn a mill at the same speed as mules. While there is no evidence that such a mechanism ever came into use, the episode does illustrate the technical problems presented by the organization of colonial agriculture and the mentality of those attempting to improve it.[43]

The steam engine was not regarded as a universal panacea for the ills of plantation agriculture in Martinique. Although individual planters continued to experiment with steam power and the number of steam mills slowly increased throughout the 1830s and 1840s, for the majority of small and medium planters and even for the large planters who were unable to extend the amount of land under cultivation or the number of slaves at their disposal, the steam engine represented no great advantage over other sources of power and did not justify the expense of its purchase. (Green estimates that the minimum holding required for a steam mill was 350 acres, which probably would exclude most of the sugar estates in Martinique.) Having rejected even the modest application of steam to existing mills, the majority of planters of Martinique devoted their efforts to increasing the efficiency of traditional sources of motive power. Sainte Croix argued that while the steam engine was an excellent source of energy, it was not indispensable. It was necessary to study local conditions for successful innovation, he contended. In some cases, the steam engine could offer great advantages, but, if a water mill were adequate, there was no need to spend the money to invest in an expensive steam engine. For the average-sized mill, he felt that water and even animal power were preferable to steam.[44]

# The Refinery

After the cane juice, or *vésou*, was extracted in the mill, it passed through an open gutter to the *sucrerie* or boiling house to be converted into sugar. There the juice was clarified, evaporated, and progressively concentrated in a sequence of successive boiling and skimming operations. These were carried out in a series of large kettles of varying size commonly called *l'équipage*. The juice was continuously evaporated and passed from one kettle to the next until the sugar was ready to crystallize. It was next ladled first into a cooling vat and then into barrels or clay pots to cool into raw sugar. These barrels or clay pots were then taken to the *purgerie* or cooling house, where the sugar crystals were separated from the viscous part, or molasses that would not crystallize. The molasses was drained off, collected, and either consumed directly, exported, made into a cheap grade of sugar, or distilled into rum. After three or four weeks in the curing house, the sugar was barreled for shipment.[45]

The boiling house was located near the mill to facilitate transporting the juice. The building was made of stone or brick with a tile roof to protect it from fire. It had to be high and well-lighted, and to have good ventilation to carry off the great amount of steam produced in the manufacturing process. After the mid-seventeenth century, the furnaces were enclosed and separated from the interior of the building by a stone or brick wall. While the wall limited access to the kettles and was susceptible to damage from the heat, the refining operations were no longer exposed to the fire, smoke, and dirt of the furnaces, and the slaves engaged in those activities were protected from the danger and discomfort of working over an open flame. Access to the fire and ash boxes was located in the exterior wall of the refinery, preferably on the leeward side of the building, where there was shelter from the trade winds. This area, known as the *galerie*, was covered by a sloping roof but was otherwise open. All the activities of carrying fuel, tending the furnace, and removing the ash took place there.[46]

The productive capability of the refinery varied directly with the boiling surface of the cane juice and was determined by the number of kettles employed. It was integrally related to the other sectors of the plantation, and, in particular, the motor force of the mill. Increased output elsewhere had to be matched in the boiling house. The capacity of the refinery was augmented by simply adding more kettles. Thus, the number of kettles is an index of the size and economic importance of the plantation. The multiplication of kettles has frequently been seen as an example of the backwardness of the colonial sugar industry and of the incompatibility of technological innovation with slave labor. In this view, quantitative increase is substituted for qualitative change. But in his study of the technical evolution of the sugar mill, Brazilian historian Ruy Gama has argued that the multiplication of kettles was an advance of fundamental importance. The use of several kettles in conjunction with one another made it technically possible for sugar production to develop as a manufacturing process. Through the early seventeenth century, engravings of sugar production from the Mediterranean and the Americas show the cane juice being boiled over an open fire in only one or two kettles. This practice persists even today in primitive mills making *rapadura*. Of necessity, this could only be a small-scale operation, and the single kettle determined both the amount of juice that could be treated and the rhythm of the manufacturing process. It took between three and four hours to boil down the syrup and make sugar using a single kettle. During this time, all other operations ceased or were reduced. The entire process of fabrication was discontinuous. Tasks were performed sequentially, and a small group of laborers, at the extreme a single individual, could follow the material through all the phases of manufacture and perform all the operations one after the other. However, the multiplication of the kettles increased the amount of juice that could be treated at one time and made possible the development of the continuity of the process. No one partial task need depend on the completion of the others. All could be performed simultaneously, and the process became continuous. This continuity affected not only the refinery, but also all the other sectors of production. Quantitative increase developed the detail division of labor, specialization of the worker, and the social character of production.[47]

There was no standard arrangement of *l'équipage* in Martinique during the first half of the nineteenth century. Rather, the number, size, and disposition of the kettles varied from plantation to plantation. Commonly four or five, but sometimes as many as six or seven, were used in a single set, or train. Labat, in his classic account of the sugar industry during the early eighteenth century, describes an arrangement of six kettles. However, nineteenth-century sources, including Sainte Croix, Daubrée, Soleau, and Lavollée, indicate that four kettles were most commonly used in Martinique during that period. Nevertheless, large refineries might have more than one "train," and the various kettles or sequences of kettles could be combined in different ways. Moreno Fraginals stresses that there were countless variations of the arrangement of the kettles, and each sugar master prided himself on developing his own individual nuances.[48]

The use of several kettles together in a set was accompanied by the specialization of these utensils. The kettles were divided between those used to purify and concentrate the juice by evaporation and those in which the sugar was cooked or struck. Within each set, they were arranged in order of decreasing size. The diminishing size was proportional to the reduced volume of the raw material as it passed through the refining process. Each kettle was known by an individual name that indicated its size, position, or function. The largest, known as the *grande*, initially received the raw cane juice after it arrived from the mill. There the juice was heated and lime added to remove the impurities it contained. It then passed to the *propre*, so named because the juice in it had been separated from the impurities and reached its greatest clarity (*propreté*). The *flambeau* was next in line. There the juice approached the state of heavy syrup, and the refiner added lime to precipitate a scum that was removed with a wooden paddle. Finally, the sugar was "struck" in the *batterie*. This kettle received its name because at times the syrup had to be beaten forcefully with a paddle as it converted into sugar to prevent the mass of material from puffing up. Sometimes a fifth kettle, known as the *sirop*, was inserted between the *flambeau* and the *batterie*. The juice was supposed to be converted into syrup in it, but, according to Dutrône, this never happened. Sainte Croix describes another variation of a five-kettle set where two *propres* were used instead of one.[49]

From at least the beginning of the eighteenth century, bagasse or cane trash was the only fuel readily available in Martinique. It provided an excellent source of heat for refining the sugar and remained in general use throughout the nineteenth century. After the juice was extracted from the sugar cane in the mill, the crushed stalks were carried to the nearby drying sheds or *cases à bagasse*, where they were kept for five or six weeks until they were ready to be used as fuel. Maintaining an adequate stock of bagasse was a major preoccupation of the colonial planter. As Sainte Croix emphasizes: "The bagasse, as well as the straw, is the wealth of the planter. Great care must be taken to provide it in abundance so that the operations (*la roulage*) never stop." The adoption of Otaheite cane with its thick, woody stalk produced more bagasse than the older Creole variety of cane, but by the first half of the nineteenth century various observers noted that the supply of bagasse was insufficient in Martinique. Its availability was a function of agricultural practices and underscores once again the interdependence of the various sectors of the plantation. The planter's calculations had to balance cane as a source of sugar against cane as a source of energy. Ratoons or cane grown on less fertile soil did not have thick stalks, but the weight of the bagasse was high in proportion to the quantity of juice they contained. They produced an excess of bagasse and rich juice, which needed less combustible. On the other hand, new cane or cane grown on fertile land had thick stalks, but contained a high percentage of liquid relative to the weight of the bagasse. Further, this juice was more aqueous and required more evaporation to be converted into sugar. Thus, the bagasse had to be mixed with cane straw at additional expense to guarantee an adequate supply of fuel.[50]

The need to economize on the use of fuel resulted in the amelioration of the furnace and of the refining process. During the early decades after the establishment of the sugar industry in the French Antilles, each kettle used in sugar manufacture was mounted above its own separate furnace. This arrangement greatly accelerated the process of concentration of the juice and allowed the independent operation of each kettle. However, this configuration consumed a great amount of fuel. This presented no problem while there were still forests available to supply firewood. But as wood became increasingly scarce, fuel conservation became in overriding consideration for sugar manufacturers. Around 1725, the English practice of mounting all the kettles in a line and heating them from a single furnace was adopted. This organization of the furnace and kettles was known as the "English train" in the French colonies. (In Cuba, it was known as the "French train" at the time of its initial introduction there during the late eighteenth century. In the English colonies, it was called the "Jamaica train," the name under which it was reintroduced into Cuba during the nineteenth century.) It both consumed less fuel than its predecessor and allowed bagasse to be used as the sole source of energy. The single fire greatly simplified the activities in the *galerie* and may have reduced the number of laborers required there. However, its use slowed down the process of concentrating the sugar and required the continuous and simultaneous operation of all the kettles in the train. Even though the proper coordination of the kettles with one another was difficult to establish and maintain, the dependency on bagasse as a combustible and the importance of fuel conservation led to its widespread adoption. During the first part of the nineteenth century, Sainte Croix, Payen, Soleau, and other commentators on colonial agriculture complained that the refining process was too slow and the design of the furnace and kettles required too much fuel. Yet their efforts were limited to improving the existing configuration of the furnace and finding more efficient ways to burn bagasse. Despite their criticisms, the English train continued in general use in the French Caribbean until the end of the slavery period.[51]

In the English train, the firebox was built at one end of the furnace, and the heat was transmitted to the kettles by means of a flue. The flue narrowed slightly along the length of its passage to concentrate the heat, and at the end opposite from the firebox, it connected with a chimney whose height was proportional to the length of the furnace. The size of the flue depended on the number and diameter of the kettles that were suspended over it in order of increasing size, with the *batterie* nearest to the firebox and the *grande* nearest to the chimney. The adoption of this arrangement in Martinique was neither completely accurate nor entirely successful. As late as the mid-nineteenth century, both Lavollée and Soleau complained that the design of the English train there suffered by comparison with that of the English colonies. While the details of furnace construction varied with each master mason, the primary structural defects were the placement of the firebox, the shape of the flue, and the length of the furnace and the proportions of its component parts. In principle, the *batterie*, or strike pan, was the only kettle directly exposed to the fire. But in Martinique, the firebox was built immediately under the *batterie*. The flame, instead of rising vertically, was drawn into the flue, where it struck the *flambeau*, causing the latter to boil more rapidly than the *batterie* and disrupting the continuity of the refining process. Further, the level surface of the bottom of the flue gave the hot air a horizontal trajectory as it passed beneath the kettles rather than forcing it to strike against them. Consequently, the surface of the kettles that was heated was too small for the volume of the liquid. The boiling operation was slowed down, and an enormous quantity of bagasse was consumed. In the English colonies, these difficulties were avoided by placing the firebox a bit in front of the train of kettles such that the flame struck the *batterie* directly, while the masonry surface of the flue beneath the kettles, instead of being flat, followed the curve of the bottom of the kettles and forced the hot air to strike each of them in succession. Adapting these modifications in Martinique, according to Lavollée and Soleau, would both speed up the evaporation and concentration process, resulting in more and better sugar, and economize on fuel.[52]

Further, Soleau observed that in Martinique the length of the furnace was usually much shorter than in the British West Indies. As a result of the abbreviated flue, most of the heat escaped up the chimney. It was a common sight in Martinique to see flames coming out of the chimney while the boiling house was in operation. This was generally regarded as a sign that the furnace had a good draw, but, in fact, it indicated inefficient use of heat and a waste of fuel. Sainte Croix estimated that the furnaces in Martinique only used 25 percent of the heat developed by the combustible. Soleau found that even though the planters in Demerara produced relatively less bagasse than their counterparts in Martinique, they burned it much more efficiently and offset their disadvantage. He suggested that the latter lengthen the flue and use six or seven kettles in the train instead of the customary four. If the planters did not want to multiply the number of slaves working in the refinery, he further proposed the adoption of oblong kettles to use the heat more effectively. Sainte Croix emphasized that the firebox, ash box, flue, and chimney all had to be proportional to one another and to the amount of fuel used in order to draw the heat properly. He also recommended that doors be added to the firebox and ash box to regulate the amount of oxygen reaching the fire. Without these doors there was no way to stop the fire, and the furnace remained hot long after production ceased, often damaging the building.[53]

The kettles themselves were made of either copper or cast iron. The distinct physical properties of each of these metals required different construction and installation of the kettles and imposed different conditions on the refining process. Copper was the preferred material because of its resistance to heat, qualities as a conductor, and ease of cleaning. Copper kettles permitted cane juice to be processed more rapidly and effectively than did cast iron ones, and they represented ease of manufacture as well as a saving of both time and fuel. The kettle was constructed with a circular, almost flat bottom made from a single piece of beaten copper that distributed the heat evenly across its entire surface. Great thickness was required to withstand the prolonged exposure to the heat during the harvest. The sides of the kettle sloped outward from the bottom piece and were made of several laminated plates of copper. The whole kettle was held together with copper rivets. When properly constructed, it could withstand the strongest heat without losing its shape and could last up to 100 years. Copper kettles also allowed more solid construction of the furnace and more secure installation than did cast iron ones. Their mounting presented a clean working surface and easy access to the contents of the kettle, which facilitated the transfer of the juice from one kettle to another.[54]

During the seventeenth century, copper kettles were most commonly employed in the Caribbean sugar industry. They remained in general use in the British West Indies. But, by the 1720s, as a consequence of the rising price of copper, cast iron kettles began to be introduced into the French Caribbean, apparently by the Dutch, who had used them in Java for about 100 years. In 1789, Dutrône estimated that the average price of a copper kettle was 3,000 colonial livres compared with only 500 colonial livres for cast iron. Despite this difference, he argued that copper kettles were more durable, technically superior, and more economical over the long run. For these reasons, he indicated that they were preferred by the planters in Saint Domingue. In the less prosperous Lesser Antilles, on the other hand, the low cost of cast iron kettles resulted in their widespread adoption, and contemporary sources agree that they were most prevalent in Martinique during the first half of the nineteenth century.[55]

Cast iron kettles were not only inferior to copper ones, but their inherent limitations were aggravated by the practice of metropolitan merchants who used the *exclusif* to dump substandard manufactured goods in the colonies. Cast iron was a much poorer conductor than copper. It retained the heat in the body of the kettle and did not distribute it evenly through the liquid. This problem was exacerbated by the impure quality of the metal, which contained a great deal of iron oxide. Cast iron was also extremely susceptible to oxidation. The rust could only be removed with great difficulty, and no matter how often the kettles were scrubbed, the water used to clean them always had a black tint that passed to the *vésou* as well. Further, cast iron was very fragile, and no matter how well made, was easily cracked when exposed to sudden changes in temperature or struck by the fire. This was particularly a danger when the kettles were being emptied or filled, since the fire never stopped in the English train. Dutrône estimated that on the majority of plantations at least four cast iron kettles were broken annually, thus leaving another strategic sector of the plantation extremely vulnerable at harvest time and underscoring the precariousness of colonial sugar manufacture.[56]

The design of the cast iron kettles was inefficient as well. It not only resulted in the uneven transfer of heat to the liquid and contributed to greater fuel consumption but also prevented the furnace from being as solidly constructed and the kettles as securely mounted as with copper. The kettles were cast in a single elliptical piece. The capacity of even the largest cast iron kettles was insufficient to treat the requisite amount of cane juice. They were too deep and exposed too small a surface to the heat for the volume of liquid they contained to evaporate it efficiently. Instead, the liquid deteriorated uselessly with prolonged exposure to the high temperature. In addition, because of its hemispheric shape, the heat struck the curved exterior of the kettle obliquely and was reflected off the metal instead of being absorbed by it. The difference in temperature between the upper and lower part of the kettle could cause it to break around its entire circumference and fall into the furnace. When this occurred, not only were the workers endangered and the kettle and its contents lost, but all work had to stop while the furnace wall was partially torn down to remove the broken kettle and then rebuilt to support a new one. Such repairs were costly in time, effort, and money, and offered the planter little guarantee that the same accident would not be repeated once the repairs were completed. [57]

The depth of the cast iron kettles and the bulkiness of the supporting masonry made the work of the refiners more difficult and retarded the sugar-making process. The greater distance between kettles made it harder to transfer the juice from one to another, while the depth of the kettles made it difficult to manipulate the boiling liquid and remove the impurities from it. The refiners could reach only half the surface of the liquid at one time with their paddles. This circumstance compelled them to continue working without rest, and, according to Dutrône, was responsible for the necessity of night work in the refinery. This problem was aggravated by the location of the furnace and kettles against the wall of the refinery. The workers only had access to the kettles from one side and had to lean over them to do their jobs. Besides impeding the process of sugar manufacture, this arrangement made the work more fatiguing and exposed the worker to heat, boiling liquid, and the danger of falling into the kettle.[58]

The *batterie* presented a particular problem when it was made of cast iron. It was most directly exposed to the heat of the firebox. Even though the fire was extinguished while the *batterie* was emptied during the course of the refining process, the hot walls of the furnace caused the residue of syrup in the kettle to caramelize. Burnt cane juice frequently formed a carbonous crust over the entire interior surface of the kettle and gave a dark brown tint to the sugar. This crust could become such a problem that it often had to be burned off several times a day, disrupting the operation of the entire refinery. Even more seriously, fissures developed in the surface of the empty kettle. This could not only cause leaks, but the kettle could even burst when it was refilled. When this happened, the syrup spilled into the incandescent firebox and cruelly burned the fireman. Sainte Croix urged that the *batterie* be made of copper or steel instead of cast iron to avoid these difficulties.[59]

Until the advent of the vacuum pan, the English train remained the technical foundation of West Indian sugar manufacture. It combined the constituent elements of sugar refining—defecation, evaporation, and concentration—in a single uninterrupted process. The operation of the furnace required that these successive steps be carried out simultaneously and continuously. The speed and continuity required by the English train developed and solidified greater specialization both within and between the various sectors of the productive mechanism of the plantation. The capacity of the boiling house and the rate at which it processed sugar were of crucial importance in determining the organization of the entire sequence of production. The cadence and duration of work in the refinery was transmitted to the other sectors of the plantation and regulated activities there. (Indeed, according to several commentators, the technical reason for the necessity of night work during the harvest was the slowness of evaporation in the deep cast iron kettles.) The supply of cane juice from the mill could not exceed the capacity of the kettles or fermentation would result. Conversely, too little juice not only interrupted the process and led to deterioration of the sugar, lost time, and idle hands, but was apt to damage the kettles by exposing them to the heat of the furnace. Thus, grinding the cane was prolonged, slowed down, or stopped in accordance with the work in the refinery. The operation of the mill, in turn, reacted back on the activities of transport and harvesting. In the other direction, the quantity of sugar produced and the rate at which it was treated in the refinery shaped the organization of the *purgerie* and other subsequent steps in the manufacturing process. Thus, the sugar mill developed toward a continuous operation requiring the closest coordination among its constituent sectors in which the sugar moved quickly and without interruption from one stage to the next.[60]

Within limits, small adjustments between sectors did not prejudice the efficacy of the overall production process. But unless the necessary level of integration was achieved, advantages gained in one phase of the process, often at great effort and expense, could be lost elsewhere. The capacity of the boiling house had to remain synchronized with the other sectors of the plantation. Improvements elsewhere had to be matched by improvements in the refinery and vice versa. The mill had to have sufficient capacity to provide a continuous supply of cane juice to the refinery, and the refinery had to convert all of the cane juice it received into sugar efficiently and without delay. Indeed, over the course of the historical evolution of the sugar plantation, the locus of technological transformation and reorganization oscillated between the mill and the refinery in an effort to maintain the necessary equilibrium and prevent the formation of a bottleneck in one or the other sector.[61]

Within the technical constraints of the English train, the refining capability of a plantation could only be significantly increased by increasing the number of kettles, and, given the close inner relation between the kettles of a train, by multiplying the number of trains. Thus, implicitly, certain thresholds of overall production had to be attained or attainable before it became possible to augment the capacity of the boiling house. Already in the 1740s, Oldmixon described large plantations in Barbados with two or three wind-powered mills, each served by a separate train of seven kettles. A considerable improvement over individual trains was the combination of trains in a single boiling house. Ordinarily two trains of kettles were operated simultaneously in the same building. Each was heated by a separate firebox and furnace, but they shared a common chimney located in the center of the structure. This configuration allowed maximum production with minimum fuel consumption under prevailing conditions. Production was centralized, supervision costs were reduced, and economies of scale were realized. The most efficient and technically advanced version of the English train was developed in Saint Domingue by Dutrône during the 1780s. Despite the many advantages it offered, its diffusion appears to have been limited, perhaps because it made its appearance on the eve of the Haitian Revolution. His manual on sugar production was translated into Portuguese in 1800 and into Spanish in 1801. It was influential in Brazil and especially Cuba, but there is no evidence that his design and techniques were adopted in Martinique. However, despite Dutrône's advances, as long as the English train remained the foundation of colonial refining, the response to the problem of large-scale production was the multiplication of kettles. Progress was achieved by the quantitative extension of the existing technology, not its qualitative transformation. By the mid-nineteenth century, it was not uncommon for Cuban *ingenios* to have six, seven, and even ten trains in operation. While the *habitation sucrière* in

Martinique apparently did not reach such extremes, the English train, despite the transformation it had historically worked in sugar manufacture, now presented a quantitative and qualitative limit to the further rationalization of the labor process as the demand for sugar and the need for more efficient production increased.[62]

## Making Sugar

Sugar cane juice or (*vésou*) can be described most simply as a solution of sugar and a small proportion of other substances in water. The refining process consists of clarification or the separation of the impurities from the solution, the evaporation of the water, and the crystallization of the sugar. If the juice were merely composed of sugar and water, refining would be a relatively simple task that could be accomplished by evaporation and crystallization alone. But the presence of the other materials in the juice complicated the process enormously. Though quantitatively only a small percentage of the liquid, these substances inhibited the crystallization of the sugar and coagulated a great bulk of solid matter when the juice was exposed to the heat. While a considerable fraction of these materials could be separated by heat alone, the use of chemical agents was necessary to achieve the degree of purity required for the sugar to crystallize. As a result of the presence of these substances, the refining process became a complex sequence of operations, which, under prevailing technical conditions, demanded great skill and judgment on the part of the refiner, but even under the best circumstances, it was never able even to approximate the ideal of complete separation and crystallization of the sugar.[63]

The quantity and quality of the sugar produced, as well as the timing and coordination of the refining operations, depended in the first instance on the quantity and quality of the sugar in the juice. The latter, in turn, varied with weather and soil conditions, the season, and the age of the plant when it was harvested. Accordingly, the cane juice could be one of four colors when it left the mill. White cane juice was the most highly valued. It was similar to soapy water in appearance and yielded a yellowish-gray sugar that contained little liquid (*d'une cristallisation bien sèche*). Brown cane juice took a long time to purify, but crystallized rapidly. It was rich in sugar and was also highly regarded. Green cane juice was inferior to the other two. It contained a great deal of vegetable albumin that was difficult to separate from the juice, and it had to be struck very carefully to obtain good sugar. Finally, yellow cane juice, which came from burnt cane or cane with fungus, was highly acidic and the least desirable of all. In principle, all of the sugar contained in the cane is crystallizable. According to Soleau, the sugar content of the cane juice from Martinique was superior to that of Demerara and offered the possibility of obtaining a higher yield of crystallized sugar than in the English colony. Lavollée recorded similar readings in Martinique, but was a bit less optimistic and thought that the average for the two colonies as a whole was similar. However, the organization and conduct of the manufacturing process in Martinique prevented complete crystallization from being attained and resulted in a final product that was much inferior to the sugar of its British rival.[64]

Despite the need for speed in treating the juice, it remained exposed to the open air for at least one hour and more often for as long as two or three hours before refining began. After the cane juice was extracted from the stalks in the mill, it passed through an open gutter to the *sucrerie*, where it was collected and held in wooden reservoirs until processing could begin. During this time, the low air temperature and contact with the oxygen in the atmosphere, as well as the presence of bits of bagasse still in the liquid, caused the juice to ferment. To alleviate this problem, Thomas Roughley, a Jamaican planter writing in the 1820s, suggested that a strainer be put between the gutter and the reservoir to remove the pieces of bagasse, leaves, and other solid particles from the liquid before it reached the reservoir. He also advised that no more than one reservoir be used. To reduce the amount of time that the juice was exposed to fermentation during this step, this reservoir should only contain enough liquid to keep the boiling kettles constantly at work and no more. The holding reservoirs were perhaps the most tangible expression of the integration of the mill and the refinery, and it was imperative that the juice not be kept there any longer than necessary or the entire operation could be prejudiced.[65]

The first step in the refining process was to remove the impurities dissolved in the liquid so that the sugar would crystallize. This operation, known as tempering (*défecation* or *enivrage*), required the use of a chemical agent to precipitate the undesirable material. A variety of substances were used as a temper throughout the eighteenth century. These included lye, potash, soda, unslaked lime, ash from certain plants, antimony, alum and certain other salts, ground herbs, and sometimes egg or cattle blood, which were mixed together in various combinations and proportions according to the predilections of the refiner. But by 1815, lime, which was cheap and readily available, had been almost universally adopted for this purpose in Martinique. While lime was successful in precipitating much of the extraneous matter from the solution, its use complicated the manufacturing process and presented a number of difficulties to the refiner. It formed several impurities and uncrystallizable substances, commonly known as *mélasse*, that were a necessary byproduct of the process of tempering the cane juice. Their presence inhibited the separation and crystallization of the remainder of the sugar and discolored the final product. Thus, the goal of the refiner and a measure of his art was to extract the sugar from the juice with the minimum production of *mélasse*.[66]

The preparation and application of the lime was one of the decisive operations in the entire process of refining sugar. As Roughley emphasized, "The event of good or bad sugar being manufactured, greatly depends on tempering the liquor with lime precisely." However, this was one of the most difficult aspects of sugar making and required great skill on the part of the refiner. Just the right amount of temper had to be added to the cane juice at just the right moment. The quantity of lime employed varied with its purity and with the condition of the juice. Critics complained that disregard for purity and careless preparation hindered the effectiveness of the lime. Furthermore, too much lime discolored the sugar, increased the amount of molasses, and resulted in the formation of coarse crystals that cracked and scaled in the cooler, had a light and porous body, and did not pack well. By the end of the eighteenth century, planters, particularly in the British colonies, were becoming increasingly aware of the dangers of using too much lime. But, contrary to the evidence, general opinion in Martinique continued to hold that excessive use of lime was not a serious problem. Rather, a strong dose of temper was seen to be necessary to give the sugar a firm body and to prevent it from decomposing during the sea voyage and arriving in the metropolitan market in the form of paste (*en paté*).[67]

But whatever the beliefs of the planters and refiners, in the absence of scientific knowledge of chemistry, there was no practical way to precisely determine the composition of the juice and to calculate how much lime was necessary to temper the sugar. Rather, the judgment, experience, and craftsmanship of the refiner were of decisive importance in this phase of the operation. The amount of lime required could vary greatly according to the condition of the juice. The latter, in turn, among other things, depended on the season, the age of the cane, and the condition of the cane field where it was harvested. Roughley records that 100 gallons of cane liquor could require as much as three pounds of strong lime or as little as two ounces. The amount of lime necessary varied with soil and weather conditions, whether the juice came from plant cane or ratoons, and whether or not the canes had been trashed and weeded. But in the absence of the means to measure these differences, it was up to the refiner to decide how much lime to use. His judgment was based on the color and texture of the juice as well as his knowledge of the cane. Since it was impossible to come to an exact determination of the quantity of lime that was necessary, the refiner had wide latitude to adjust the amount by trial and error during the subsequent stages of the processing.[68]

In the English train, tempering the cane juice took place in the *grande*. After the liquid was transferred from the reservoirs to the *grande*, the *batterie* was filled with water to protect it from the intense heat of the firebox, and the *grande* was slowly heated. When the temperature of the cane juice reached about 60° centigrade, lime, either in the form of a powder or dissolved in water, was mixed in with it. The lime combined with a portion of the impurities in the liquid to produce a heavy scum that floated to the surface. This residue was carefully skimmed off with a wooden paddle and placed in a gutter that carried it to a special reservoir. It was then taken to the distillery and used in the manufacture of spirits. When the liquid in the *grande* reached the boiling point, it was passed forward to the other kettles in the train, and the *grande* was refilled from the reservoir.[69]

After the cane juice was transferred from the *grande*, it was passed successively to the other kettles in the train, and the processes of evaporation and concentration began. In principle as soon as the liquid in one kettle reached the proper degree of concentration, it was advanced to a kettle closer to the firebox with a higher temperature. As the water evaporated, the juice thickened into syrup and reached progressively greater degrees of concentration until it was ready for crystallization in the *batterie*. The single furnace of the English train conserved fuel but made it difficult to regulate the temperature in accordance with the stage of processing in each kettle. Evaporation of the cane juice depended on the number and size of the kettles, their position in relation to the firebox, the strength of the fire, the richness and quality of the cane juice, and the amount of time the liquid remained over the fire. The larger the surface of the liquid exposed to the air, the greater the difference between the temperature of the air and the temperature of the liquid, and the drier the air, the more rapid was the evaporation. Thus, the hot, humid tropical climate and the steam of the boiling room retarded concentration of the cane juice, as did the deep cast iron kettles, which presented only a small surface for evaporation and distributed the heat unevenly. On the other hand, as the liquid in a kettle evaporated, the temperature of the fire remained the same. The volume of the liquid was no longer proportional to the heat it received. As a result, caramelization and burning, and with them discoloration and loss of sugar as well as rapid deterioration of the kettles, were a constant danger, particularly in the *flambeau* and the *batterie*. But even under the best of circumstances, the destruction of sugar was great in this process. Sugar cannot be boiled even for an instant without a portion of it being decomposed into glucose or grape sugar, which is uncrystallizable. With further boiling, this liquid decomposed in turn into several types of dark, acidic material. The production of these substances was a necessary consequence of the evaporation and concentration of the cane juice, and they formed a portion of the *mélasse*. Their presence reduced the quantity of cane juice that could be converted into crystallized sugar and diminished the quality of the final product.[70]

The great difficulty, if not impossibility, of effectively controlling the heat in the English train resulted in the breakdown of the division between defecation, evaporation, and concentration. Instead of being distinct operations, separate in time and space, they overlapped and interfered with one another, greatly complicating the manufacturing process. The progress of the movement of the juice through the various kettles was determined from two directions. On the one hand, once the liquid in a given kettle reached the proper degree of concentration, its advance to the next kettle could not be postponed. Delay only resulted in unnecessary exposure to the heat and deterioration of the juice. On the other hand, whatever the condition of the liquid in the other kettles, the *batterie* had to be recharged immediately once it was empty, or it would be damaged by the heat of the firebox. The richer the syrup and the stronger the action of the heat on the *batterie*, the more rapid was the concentration. By extension, this requirement also applied to a greater or lesser degree to the other kettles to prevent caramelization of the sugar or damage to the kettles as the train heated up. Thus, it was necessary to advance the juice as soon as it was ready and to keep all of the kettles, and especially the *batterie*, full. But the continuity of this movement and the complementarity of these requirements could by no means be taken for granted. A persistent problem of many individual plantations, for example, was that the kettles farther from the fire received too little heat and evaporation was too slow, while those near the fire received too much heat and evaporation was too rapid. But from whichever direction the impulse came, the English train required that the cane juice be advanced whether it was ready or not.[71]

Furthermore, the English train's inability to keep the cane juice from boiling in the *grande* meant that it was impossible to complete the separation of the impurities from the liquid during this stage of the process. On the one hand, from the moment when the impurities began to precipitate from the juice until the time that it began to boil, at least half of the foreign matter remained dissolved in it and was passed on to the next kettle. On the other hand, once the cane juice began to boil, the action of the liquid made it very difficult to remove the scum. To remedy the deficiencies of clarification in the *grande*, this operation was continued in the other kettles at the same time that evaporation was taking place there. Generally, the tempering was concluded in the *flambeau*, although some authors report the use of lime even in the *batterie*. However, the difficulty with this method was that the syrup often reached such a degree of concentration in the *flambeau* that further precipitation of impurities was no longer possible, and the introduction of more lime at this stage altered the quality of the sugar.[72]

In addition, this procedure was very imprecise and always entailed an element of chance that made the skill and judgment of the refiner more important for the success of the operation while practically reducing the possibility of objective control over it. The signs that guided the actions of the refiner—the scum, the color of the liquid, the nature of the bubbles that formed during boiling—were not always present or did not appear soon enough. These signals were altered or retarded by the action of the heat, which differed in each kettle in the train, by the composition of the juice, and by the quantity and quality of the scum that was precipitated. The refiner, therefore, had no sure way to assess the effect of the lime on the syrup. The more rapid the concentration, the less time there was to judge the action of the temper and skim off the impurities. In each kettle in the train, the liquid was transferred with too much or too little temper, and the refiner continually added more lime by trial and error to complete the removal of the impurities.[73]

The task of clarification became even more difficult because there was no satisfactory means to remove the undesirable material physically from the cane juice. Lavollée complained that the slaves used their wooden paddles badly and skimmed too slowly to be effective. However, Dutrône insisted that the wooden skimming paddles (*écumoires*) were not adequate for this task no matter how carefully they were used. In either case, this difficulty was aggravated by the use of cast iron kettles. They gave the refiners limited access to their contents, while dirt from the kettles and masonry continually contaminated the juice. Beyond this problem, the use of ladles or calabashes to empty and fill the kettles was awkward and inefficient and retarded the entire manufacturing process. The very action of transferring the juice in this manner redivided the impurities that had separated out from the liquid and made their removal even harder. Further, as the amount of cane juice in a kettle was either diminished or increased slowly and bit by bit, it was subject to overconcentration, and there was inevitably caramelization on the surface of the kettle. Finally, since clarification and evaporation were going on simultaneously in the same kettles, the slave refiners had to be engaged in both activities at once. The manipulation of the kettles became particularly cumbersome if the furnace had no gutter to drain off the impurities. The scum then had to be passed back from each kettle to the previous one until it was finally deposited in its own reservoir. This procedure interfered with the sequence of clarification and concentration and intensified one of the most physically exhausting tasks on the plantation.[74]

The problems of defecation and evaporation in the English train became still more difficult as the materials from different kettles became mixed together in the course of manufacturing. Only the *propre* received a single charge from the *grande*. With each other transfer from one kettle to another, the receiving kettle was not entirely empty when new material was added. Juice that was less clarified and less concentrated was constantly being mixed together with juice that was more clarified and more concentrated. Thus, it was difficult to judge the action of the temper or to know the degree of concentration that had been attained, and there was danger of losing control over both processes. The nearer the kettle was to the fire, the more frequent were these transfers, and the more often the contents of the kettle were altered. This problem continued right into the *batterie* and affected not only the quantity but also the quality of the sugar. Every time the *batterie* was ready to be refilled, the more concentrated liquid still remaining in it was diluted by the addition of a portion of the juice that was never entirely skimmed and was often still syrupy. The impurities in the new syrup mixed together with the more-concentrated liquid and were impossible to remove. The failure to properly temper the cane juice and separate out the impurities, on the one hand, and imperfect evaporation of the syrup, on the other, were, Soleau contended, the two major defects of even the most efficient and carefully run plantations in Martinique and were responsible for the poor quality of the sugar produced there.[75]

The process of concentration terminated in the *batterie*. The cane juice was a heavy syrup when it arrived at this stage. It next had to be "struck," or cooked down to the point of crystallization (*la cuite*). However, to prevent caramelization, the sugar could not be allowed to crystallize in the *batterie*, and the water could not be removed completely from the syrup. Nevertheless, all of the sugar contained in the syrup could be dissolved in only a portion of the water, and the more water that was boiled off, the more dense the syrup. Thus, the syrup was heated until it reached the point of optimum concentration. The fire was then extinguished, and the syrup was transferred to another vessel (the *rafraichissoir*) located next to the *batterie*, where it was allowed to cool. As it cooled, it released sugar crystals until, at room temperature, it did not dissolve more than two parts sugar for one part water. This solution formed the drainage syrup (*sirop d'égout*), and the remainder of the material was crystallized sugar. The *batterie* was immediately refilled with the liquid from the *sirop* and the fire rekindled. The whole operation of emptying and refilling the *batterie* took about three minutes to complete. It had to be carried out quickly to prevent the heat of the furnace walls from caramelizing the residue of syrup on the surface of the *batterie* because it would discolor the next batch of syrup.[76]

While striking the sugar depended on the quality of the cane juice and the degree of clarification and concentration attained in previous stages, it was perhaps the single most important step in determining the quality and quantity of the sugar produced. The most effective way to remove the water and increase the density of the syrup was to bring it to the striking point slowly and at a low, even temperature. This was the most delicate operation in the whole manufacturing process. The sugar had to be struck at the optimum moment. However, there was no real way to govern the heat below the *batterie* and to control the regularity and duration of the process. At the very moment that the syrup was most concentrated and most susceptible to caramelization, it was exposed to the highest temperature in the train. If the *cuite* was too weak, crystallization took place on the bottom of the cooling vessel. The syrup then floated to the top and a thin, fragile crust formed on its surface. The sugar that resulted from this process resembled a kind of mush. If, on the other hand, the *cuite* was too strong, the sugar crystals formed a solid mass from top to bottom without any liquid appearing on the surface. In this case, it was slow and difficult to drain the molasses, and the sugar always had a dark color.[77]

Whatever the state and quality of the syrup, it was always given enough heat during the production of muscovado (*sucre brut*) that an aggregated mass of material was obtained afterwards. This practice often led to the destruction of the sugar. It was generally thought that a large quantity of lime would enable the syrup to withstand this high temperature and give the sugar a firm, sparkling grain. But cane juice of inferior quality resists this degree of concentration no matter how much it is tempered. To remedy this lack of concentration, the refiners applied more heat. The worse the juice, the more heat was thought to be necessary despite the deterioration of the juice resulting from the high temperatures. Dutrône records instances where the refiners persisted in augmenting the heat, even though columns of white vapor and a sharp burning odor coming from the syrup indicated its decomposition. At times, this decomposition continued to the point that the material in the *batterie* caught fire.[78]

The success or failure of striking the sugar rested on the craft of the refiner, frequently a slave, who judged whether or not the syrup was ready for this operation. Great experience was necessary on the part of the refiner in order to keep the sugar from remaining over the fire for too long and thus burning. No instruments helped him in his decision. His only guides were the color of the syrup, the way it boiled, and its texture. Several techniques were used to determine the progress of the sugar toward the striking point. When the syrup reached the first stage of concentration, it trickled slowly in separate drops from a paddle dipped into the kettle (*faire la goutte*). At the next stage, it ran off the skimming paddle in a sheet (*faire la toile*). When the sugar got closer to the striking point, the refiner ladled out some syrup, took it between his thumb and forefinger, and drew it out into a thread (*faire le fil*). When, on repeating this last step, the thread broke when it was drawn out (*le fil se rompt*), the sugar had been boiled sufficiently, and it was time to strike it. There were numerous variations and nuances of these categories that were important to know, and the craft knowledge of the refiner consisted of mastery over all these indicators and their possible implications for the manipulation of the syrup during the strike. As early as 1789, Dutrône established the relationship between the temperature of the liquid once it had reached the state of syrup and its degree of concentration during the strike. He urged the adoption of the thermometer, not to supplant the more subjective techniques, but to supplement them and establish more regular control over the process by giving the refiner some fixed points of reference. In his opinion, the old techniques were relatively reliable and too convenient to abandon, while the inability to eliminate impurities from the syrup limited the reliability of the thermometer. Lavollée concurred with the benefits of the thermometer but found only one planter in Martinique using it at the time of his report.[79]

It ordinarily took about six or seven hours from the time that the juice was extracted in the mill until the time it was struck, while it took between three and four hours from the moment the juice entered the *grande* until it left the *batterie*, depending on the number of kettles in the train. The prolonged exposure to the open air and high temperature of the furnace during this period increased fermentation and caramelization of the cane juice and diminished the quantity and quality of the final product. The slow pace was not only detrimental to the sugar, but also dictated the duration of the working day during the harvest season. According to Soleau, a train of four kettles produced 400 livres of sugar every two hours, while Guignod estimated that for a plantation to remain economically viable, it had to produce form fifteen to thirty hogsheads of sugar a week. To attain this level of production it was necessary that work continue day and night without interruption. Lavollée observed that every twenty-four hours, an average sugar estate in Martinique produced from 1,750 to 2,500 kilograms or between 3.5 and 5 hogsheads of sugar. Both Dutrône and Soleau after him argued that by replacing the deep iron kettles with shallower and smaller copper ones, the processing of each batch of sugar could be accelerated. The result would be the production of more and better sugar in the same amount of time, and the diminution of the amount of molasses. Such an innovation would, in Dutrône's view, eliminate the necessity of costly, wasteful, and exhausting night work.[80]

From the striking pan, the liquid sugar (known as the *cuite*, which referred to the degree of concentration it had attained, or as the *batterie*, which referred to the quantity of material processed in a single step) was carried to the cooler or *rafraichissoir*, where cooling and crystallization began. The behavior of the liquid and the size and consistency of the crystals as they formed gave the refiner additional indications of the adequacy of the strike. The cooler itself was either a kettle or a shallow wooden trough, and usually three of them were used. The treatment of the sugar after the strike varied somewhat depending on individual practice and the kind of sugar being manufactured. According to Roughley, who wrote from Jamaica, the sugar was allowed to stand in the cooler for about twenty minutes until a crust was formed on the surface. This crust was then broken and stirred in with the liquid part of the sugar. The operation was repeated until the sugar was cool. In the French colonies by the nineteenth century, the cooler no longer served the function for which it was named, but rather was used only to combine successive *cuites* before they were transferred to other vessels to complete cooling and crystallization. During this stage, the faults of the first *cuite* were corrected by means of the second. The second *cuite* was concentrated a bit more than the first, and the two were mixed together and cooled in the *rafraichissoir* by stirring them carefully. This mixture was called the *empli*. The purpose of mixing the *cuites* together was to give greater uniformity to the product. But, as Sainte Croix complained, the consequence of this practice was that the sugar remained at a high temperature for a longer time, crystallization was inhibited, and the deterioration of the sugar increased. After the *cuites* were mixed together in the cooler, they were transferred to another reservoir to continue cooling and crystallization. This reservoir was filled with four or five *emplis* that crystallized one on top of the other, a practice that further impeded cooling and crystallization. If muscovado was being produced, the sugar was allowed to stand in the reservoir for about twelve hours. During this time it crystallized into a solid mass, which was then broken up with spades and shovels and put directly into barrels with iron scoops. If clayed sugar was being manufactured, the syrup was not concentrated to such a high degree in the *batterie*, and the softer *empli* was put into clay molds to cure.[81]

To make muscovado or raw sugar (*sucre brut*), the *empli* was packed into wooden hogsheads. The barrel had to be filled with care for the sugar to cure properly. The sugar could not be too soft or too hot, and no large lumps could be put into the hogshead. Rather, it had to be broken into small pieces, mixed well, and packed closely, densely, and evenly. The steam and high temperatures of the boiling house were detrimental to crystallization. Consequently, after an hour or two when the sugar was firm enough, the barrels were taken to a separate building called the curing house or *purgerie* to stand and drain. During this time, cooling and crystallization continued inside the barrel while the molasses flowed out through three or four one-inch holes drilled in its bottom and was collected in a reservoir below ground level. This process was slow and imperfect. The molasses never drained completely, and the sugar remained subject to fermentation. On average, a hogshead of 550 kilograms yielded about thirty-two gallons of syrup when it was well drained. Nevertheless, the barrel still contained a great deal of molasses, which tainted the sugar and gave it a dark brown color. The greater or lesser proportion of molasses determined the various grades of raw sugar. If the syrup was of high quality, two-thirds or even as much as three-quarters of the barrel crystallized and drained, but only after two or three months in the *purgerie*. If the syrup was of bad quality, the sugar and the molasses formed a messy paste throughout the barrel, which never crystallized or drained properly. In addition to the molasses, Dutrône estimated that muscovado contained between 10 and 12 percent by weight of dirt and feculent matter. The sugar remained dark, moist, and full of impurities. Usually, the barrels remained in the curing house for three or four weeks. After that time, the sugar was repacked tightly in the barrels and taken to Saint Pierre for shipment to France without any further preparation. It generally required further refining in France before it could be consumed.[82]

Curing the sugar in barrels was less complicated than the use of clay molds and became increasingly predominant in Martinique during the first half of the nineteenth century. Nonetheless, it was an extremely slow and inefficient technique and yielded unsatisfactory results. The molasses in the upper part of the barrel had to pass through a mass of sugar three or four feet deep. The lower layers of sugar did not allow the syrup from above to drain out, while the molasses had a destructive effect on the sugar crystals below. Often the openings at the bottom of the barrel became blocked. In any event, the molasses never drained completely but remained mixed with the sugar crystals and contributed to their discoloration and deterioration. Because of the constant heat of the climate, the molasses began to ferment in the barrel. This fermentation was aggravated by the movement of the ship and the heat of the hold during transport. Since the barrel was not completely drained, the syrup was constantly mixed together with the crystals, and the moisture caused incessant alteration and diminution of the sugar. Fermentation affected the entire mass of sugar and resulted in such decomposition that even a year or two after its arrival in France molasses continued to flow from the barrel. Under these conditions the quantity and quality of the product remained in question during this entire period, and it was difficult to calculate the contents of a barrel. According to Dutrône, between 10 and 30 percent of the contents of the barrel were lost during the voyage from the colonies to France. This waste and deterioration continued in the French warehouses and while the barrels were being transported from the warehouse to overseas markets or elsewhere in France. It only stopped when the barrel was emptied. This loss could not be concealed and always fell to the planter, whether he sent the sugar to France or sold it in the colony. For his part, the merchant either avoided buying sugar in the colony altogether, or, if he did do so, would only evaluate the potential loss at the highest possible rate and charge it to the planter.[83]

The faults of curing the sugar in barrels could in some measure be overcome and better drainage obtained if the sugar was cured in clay molds. Each mold (*forme*) was a conical vase two feet high and thirteen to fourteen inches in diameter. At the bottom of each one was a hole one inch in diameter with a wooden plug. The *empli* was slowly poured into the clay molds and allowed to stand for twelve to fourteen hours while the sugar inside crystallized into one mass. After crystallization was complete, the plug was removed in order to drain the molasses, which had separated from the sugar crystals. The sugar was then taken from the mold, chopped up, and packed into barrels. The remaining molasses was allowed to drain through holes drilled in the bottom of each barrel. While the use of clay molds to produce muscovado yielded about 20 percent more sugar than when curing was done in barrels, it was still far from being a completely satisfactory procedure. Optimally, the molds should be kept in a warm, dry place and the sugar allowed to cool slowly to the ambient temperature before it was removed. The slower the process of crystallization, the better formed were the crystals. However, according to Sainte Croix, no attention was paid to the temperature of the sugar inside the molds. It was usually decanted prematurely, and, because of its high temperature, the syrup that drained off contained as much as two-thirds of its weight in sugar. Further, chopping up the sugar loaf after it was removed from the mold broke the crystals and mixed them together in the barrel in such a way that drainage was blocked. Despite the advantages of clay molds over barrels for curing sugar, Lavollée reports that they were no longer in use in Martinique by 1839. He cites their cost and the constant need to replace molds broken by the slaves as the reason for their abandonment. (In this context, it is interesting to note that by the 1830s the molds used in Cuba were made of metal.) While these factors should not be discounted, it must also be noted that the tariff on the higher grades of sugar, all of which required the use of clay molds, increasingly inhibited their production after 1833.[84]

Some planters produced a grade of semirefined or clayed sugar (*sucre terré* or *cassonade*), which differed from muscovado only by having the molasses removed by the operation of claying (*terrage*). The purpose of *terrage* was to wash away the syrup that clung to the surface of the crystals in the sugar loaf. After draining the clay molds for twenty-four hours after crystallization, the compacted lumps of sugar and bits of dirt and feculent matter still contained in the sugar were first removed as completely as possible. These particles inhibited drainage and attracted syrup, which discolored the loaf. The purity of the various grades of this type of sugar depended on the proportion of these materials present. The exposed surface of sugar at the open end of the cone was then evened out, packed down, and covered with a layer of clay that was mixed with water until it was the consistency of a paste. As the water separated from the clay and percolated through the loaf, it diluted the syrup between the crystals and carried it away. Some sugar crystals were dissolved in this process—as much as from one-fourth to one-third of the sugar in the mold, according to some accounts—but this was far less than if water had been poured over the sugar loaf. This process was repeated two or three times in succession, after which the loaf remained in the mold for twenty days or so to let the remaining molasses drain as completely as possible. The sugar loaves were then removed and exposed to the sun for several hours.[85]

Only at this point did the refiner have an opportunity to see and evaluate the product. Each individual loaf presented a spectrum of several different colors and qualities of sugar. The tip of the loaf was black or dark brown and very moist. This graded into a band of sugar that went from brown to yellow. Finally, there was a layer of dry, white sugar. The tips were removed for further refining, and the loaves were taken to the oven, or *étuve*, where they remained for about two weeks while the heat removed the remaining water. After the loaves were dry, it was the job of the refiner to select the different grades of sugar and divide the loaf precisely. The selection was made by eye and was one of the most difficult and subjective tasks in the manufacturing process. According to some accounts from Martinique, once the tips were removed no attempt was apparently made to further divide the loaves. The loaves were next crushed in large wooden troughs by slaves using pestles, and the sugar was packed into barrels for shipment. A well-made loaf normally yielded two-thirds white sugar and one-third common sugar. The best of the clayed sugars could be consumed directly, while the rest of them, like muscovado, required further purification before being consumed.[86]

While clayed sugar was superior to muscovado, the method of its manufacture was wasteful, and its crystals were dull, soft, and unattractive. It was a less than satisfactory grade of sugar, particularly in comparison with the product of the French beet sugar industry, and, in addition, a prohibitive tariff discouraged its production in the colonies. In 1833, *clairçage*, a new method of purifying sugar, was introduced into the French Antilles as a substitute for *terrage*. This technique was developed in 1804 by Charles Derosne in the French beet sugar factories. Instead of using water to remove the molasses from the sugar crystals, he used saturated and discolored syrup. This process was more rapid than *terrage* and in a single operation produced dryer, firmer, whiter crystals without the loss of sugar entailed in the older method. Its adoption in the colonies resulted in a new classification of white sugar known as *clairçe*, but this too was subject to a surtax of fifteen francs per 100 kilograms on entry into France. Thus, whatever the potential advantages *terrage* and *clairçage* might have offered to colonial planters, discriminatory tariffs impeded their adoption and resulted in muscovado increasingly dominating colonial production, and thus the consumer market, during the 1830s and 1840s. This represented a drastic change from the latter part of the eighteenth century when the production of clayed sugar predominated in the colonies. In 1788, *sucre terré* accounted for 93 percent of the sugar exported from Martinique.[87]

The syrup that drained off and was collected in the reservoir under the curing house (*bassin à mélasse*) still contained a great deal of sugar that could be recovered. The first syrups that came from the clay molds were called *gros-sirops*, while those that were collected during and after *terrage* were referred to as *sirops-fines*. Once a week, the *gros-sirops* were collected and struck in the *équipage à sirop*, two iron kettles located either in the refinery or the curing house. This sugar required a long time for curing and claying. In some cases as much as six months were necessary before it could be put in the drying oven, and, even then, only the base of the loaf could be used because the rest was still full of syrup. The *sirops-fines* were treated about the same way as the *gros-sirops*, although they were less rich and yielded less sugar. The syrups that resulted from this second set of operations (*sirops-amers*) were either sold or taken to the distillery for manufacture into rum. This process for recovering sugar from the syrup was less than satisfactory. The quality of the sugar declined each time the sugar was reboiled. The high temperature required to strike low-quality syrup yielded an inferior product, while prolonged exposure to open air, dirt, and impurities increased the evaporation, fermentation, and deterioration of the juice. It acquired an acidic taste and became uncrystallizable.[88]

On a great many plantations in Martinique, particularly the larger ones, the syrup was converted into rum or tafia. Which was produced depended on the state of the syrup and the conditions of fermentation and distilling. The majority of colonial manufactures concentrated on the production of cheap, low-quality tafia rather than rum. There was a large internal market for it. Low price and long custom encouraged its consumption by all classes of the population, but especially by the slaves. More was consumed in Martinique than was exported abroad, and

Lavollée estimated the annual production at one million liters, which added from one million to 1.5 million francs to the revenues of the sugar plantations. In his view, this amount could be even higher if the planters adopted English distilling techniques and shifted their efforts to the production of rum, which fetched a considerably higher price. But in his opinion, even the manufacture of tafia was an excellent source of revenue for the planter. The expense of the distilling apparatus was compensated for by the sale price of tafia, which was 60 to 80 percent higher per gallon than that of raw molasses. Sainte Croix, on the other hand, emphasized that beyond the cost of the equipment, the manufacture of rum and tafia required between five to nine slaves, depending on the scale of the operation, and consumed a great deal of scarce and expensive wood to heat the still. Not every planter could afford to engage in this activity, and, whether rum or tafia was produced, it was not always remunerative at prevailing prices. Further, he warned against the new methods of distillation using steam power developed by Blumental and Baglioni as being too complicated and dangerous for slaves.[89]

The high percentage of molasses that was produced during the manufacturing process reflected the inefficiency and low technical level of colonial methods of sugar refining. As a result of fermentation, faulty use of lime during tempering, caramelization, and incomplete crystallization, fully 40 to 50 percent of the cane juice that entered the boiling house for conversion into sugar ended up as molasses. This represented the loss and destruction of a considerable amount of sugar. According to Daubrée, molasses ought not to be more than 15 to 20 percent the weight of the *cuite*, while Lavollée, on the basis of chemical experiments, estimated that it should have been possible to produce 95 percent sugar and only 5 percent molasses. In contrast to the results obtained by the colonial sugar industry, metropolitan beet sugar producers, working with juice that was only half as rich as that of cane sugar, had only 12 to 15 percent molasses as a residue. A small portion of the molasses produced on the colonial plantations was fed to the slaves and animals. The great bulk of it was either converted into tafia, or, in the absence of any other alternative, sold to the Americans at 80–90 centimes per gallon. From 1833 to 1837, Martinique annually sold an average of three million liters of molasses to the United States. In exchange, it received planks, barrel staves, and wood for construction. However, while molasses and tafia offered remuneration to the planter and allowed the development of an important supplemental trade that was the exclusive source of essential wood products, they represented waste, extra effort, and a loss of potential revenue for the colonial sugar industry.[90]

The colonial sugar manufacture was extremely wasteful. Lavollée observed that, "in Martinique, the processes of fabrication are so defective that it is astonishing that it is possible to obtain sugar working in such a manner." The sugar cane plant contained by weight 18 to 20 percent sugar. On the average, about 8 percent remained in the bagasse after the cane was ground, while another 5 percent ended up as molasses and was lost to the planter. Thus, only 5 percent, or about one-quarter of the potential product, was successfully converted into crystallized sugar. In exceptional cases, a yield as high as 7 percent was obtained in Martinique. This did not compare unfavorably with other tropical sugar producers. Daubrée estimated that the yield of sugar in Cuba and Puerto Rico was not more than 4 percent the weight of the cane, while in Louisiana 3 percent was achieved only with great difficulty. However, it was far inferior to the average yield of the metropolitan beet sugar industry. While the colonies succeeded in crystallizing only 5/18 of the sugar contained in the plant, their metropolitan rivals obtained 10/18. "There," declared Daubrée, "is the secret of this terrible competition that threatens with ruin even those who ought not to fear it."[91]

Colonial cane sugar was inferior to the product of the beet sugar industry not only in quantity, but in quality. There were no scientifically precise criteria for classifying the quality of sugar. Schnakenbourg lists thirteen general grades of raw sugar recognized in the nineteenth-century French sugar trade. The grade of sugar was determined on the basis of a subjective and empirical evaluation of the color, size, and firmness of the crystals, and the proportion of molasses present. The category *bonne quatrième*, a soft, reddish-brown sugar of intermediate quality, was chosen as the basis for transactions and the standard of what normal colonial sugar ought to be. All other muscovados were judged in relation to it. But according to Lavollée, even in good years barely one-fourth of the sugar produced in Martinique could be classified as *bonne quatrième*, and the remainder was of inferior grades.[92]

The low quality of French West Indian sugar was not in any simple or direct sense the result of the tariff system, but rather was rooted in the imperfections of the manufacturing system itself. It is true that prohibitive duties on clayed or semirefined sugars virtually compelled their abandonment. However, Lavollée argued that while the planters complained with good reason against the surtax that prevented the amelioration of the quality of their product, it could not be held responsible for the inferiority of the sugar they produced. There were, he pointed out, four grades of sugar above *bonne quatrième* before the surtax applied, and the West Indian sugar industry was incapable of manufacturing these on any significant scale. In contrast, Bourbon, which was generally subject to the same restrictions as the French Antilles, produced a much higher grade of sugar than did the other colonies. Indeed, while metropolitan sugar refiners pointedly criticized the poor quality of the sugar produced in the French Antilles during their testimony before the 1829 commission on the sugar industry, Bourbon was explicitly exempted from their remarks. The discriminatory tariff contributed to the low quality of French West Indian sugar production but was not its prime cause. Given the prevailing technique of manufacturing sugar in the French Caribbean, quality was more or less improved, in the case of the clayed or semirefined sugars excluded by the tariff, to the extent that *terrage* or *clairçage* removed the excess molasses. The redress of the protective duties may have given these sugars more favorable access to the French metropolitan market, but it would not necessarily have led to the amelioration of colonial sugar manufacture. In the words of one expert, "to produce brown sugar at all, is evidence of bad manufacture." The fundamental obstacle to the production of better-quality sugar was the enormous amount of molasses produced in the first place, not its effective separation from the sugar.[93]

The other side of the tariff issue is that high protective duties and a virtual monopoly of the French market encouraged colonial planters to produce low-quality sugar. Indeed, metropolitan sugar refiners forced up the surtax on the higher grades of colonial sugar to prevent competition from the colonies and satisfy their own demand for raw sugar. Nevertheless, they complained incessantly that the advantage derived by the West Indian planters from the protective duties led the latter to emphasize quantity over quality and send a great amount of low-grade sugar to France. In testimony before the 1829 sugar commission, the refiners particularly complained that the planters were restriking syrup that they normally would not in order to make what were described as "*des sucres détestables*," which the refiners had no choice but to buy. (Such charges may have been exaggerated. Jabrun claimed that not more than one planter out of one hundred restruck the syrup.) Yet in this case as well, the focus on the tariff, while not incorrect, misses the heart of the issue. Against the colonial prejudice that high-quality sugar could only be obtained at the expense of quantity, Sainte Croix correctly insisted that the better the sugar is, the more will be obtained. Similarly, the manufacture of the four grades above *bonne quatrième* mentioned by Lavollée would have been much more remunerative to the planters, had they been able to produce it, than the inferior types resulting from a second or third strike of the syrup. Whether viewed from the perspective of discouraging the production of the higher grades of colonial sugar or of encouraging the production of poorer grades, the problem of the role of the protective duties resolves itself into the loss and destruction of sugar entailed in open-pan boiling with the English train. In the face of the great amount of molasses produced, the options were either to try to improve the quality of sugar by its effective removal or to reconvert it into sugar, however poor. In the context of the prohibition of the first option by the protective duties, the second is more comprehensible as an attempt to recuperate as much as possible from an enormous potential loss of production and revenue. This loss was more a result of a defective manufacturing process than a direct response to the encouragement given by the duties.[94]

With the emergence of dynamic, new competition from the metropolitan beet sugar industry, French West Indian sugar producers found themselves at a growing disadvantage in terms of both the level of their productivity and the quality of their product. The root of their disability lay in the technical organization of the colonial production process, which was being increasingly outmoded by the rapidly changing conditions of world sugar production and exchange. As Daubrée wrote in 1841: "For about two centuries, sugar has been manufactured in the colonies, and manufactured in the same way. In industry that means that even though it had been manufactured tolerably well two centuries ago, it must be manufactured very badly today. The same system, the same instruments, the same ignorance of the true principles of manufacture." In consequence of this inefficiency and low productivity, only high sugar prices in relation to favorable prices for the factors of production could offer adequate compensation to colonial producers. In the absence of such circumstances, the planters had two alternatives: either fight for more protective duties to maintain their revenues, or reform the technical conditions of colonial production. Charles Derosne, one of the pioneers of the invention and diffusion of the new sugar technology both in Europe and the colonies, stressed the limitations of attempts to resolve the dilemma by legislative means alone: "To always ask the government for the means to establish commercial equilibrium would be bad politics for the colonies and would demonstrate a weakness that would end up by not inspiring confidence in their destiny." Indeed, without the amelioration of the conditions of colonial production, any such equilibrium could only be temporary. Instead Derosne emphasized that it was both necessary and possible to achieve a technical renewal of colonial sugar manufacture: "The art of manufacturing sugar, stationary for such a long time, is finally going to shake the yoke of routine that has oppressed it. The moment has arrived to work a complete revolution in such an important branch of industry and to try to profit from the enormous improvements that the advanced state of chemical and physical sciences in Europe presently provide to it."[95]

# Chapter Six

# Obstacles to Innovation

By the 1830s, the need to reform the organization of sugar production pressed on the plantation system in Martinique. Metropolitan and foreign competition constantly threatened the market position of the colonial product. Further, with the rapid expansion of the previous decades, the effective physical limits of cultivation had been reached, while the abolition of the slave trade prevented the planters from increasing their labor force. Finally, the rapid technological progress of the beet sugar industry made it necessary to reappraise colonial production in the light of scientific principles. Sainte Croix, among others, argued that the advances of beet sugar production should be adapted to colonial sugar manufacture: "The successes of beet sugar manufacture in Europe show how science combined with experience can lead to rapid progress. . . . Let us profit from the efforts of our rivals and use their means in the hope that, in treating a richer and less complex material than theirs, we will arrive at more advantageous results." The colonial planters hoped that by ameliorating their wasteful manufacturing methods the natural superiority of cane over the sugar beet would enable them to overcome the challenge of their metropolitan rivals and restore colonial prosperity. In the words of one such planter: "There is, thus, enormous wealth which perishes each year in the colonies. It is an imposing reserve which cannot but be developed a few years from now and which will change completely the face of the debate."[1]

There were a wide variety of individual responses to these new conditions. The majority of planters lacked the means and often the inclination to apply scientific principles to colonial production and to adopt the methods developed in the beet sugar industry. Traditional routines remained the norm, and the pace of change was slow. But not all of the planters submitted to their fate passively. As Lavollée admonished: "The lack of improvements introduced in sugar manufacture cannot at all be attributed to the carelessness of the colonists. They so little deserve this reproach that, despite the onerous conditions with which the metropolis has surrounded the improvement of their products, they count several plantations on a completely progressive path." The processes and techniques of colonial sugar production underwent systematic scrutiny by agronomists, engineers, political economists, and the planters themselves, and an unprecedented number of technical treatises were published. A growing number of attempts were made to experiment with the new technology, and in 1839, in the face of the hostility of many of their compatriots, a group of leading planters founded the Société d'agriculture et d'économie rurale to study and promote the scientific improvement of agriculture in the colonies.[2]

The debate among the planters was not about whether to accept or reject technological innovation, but under what conditions it could be successfully implemented in the colonies. As a result of long and successful experience, progressive planters such as Guignod, Sainte Croix, and Jabrun were cautious in their approach to reform. Their empirical approach to plantership made them suspicious of abstract formulas and general panaceas and heightened their sensitivity to local variations. They rejected risking wholesale renovation of production techniques, the outcome of which was, in their minds, uncertain. Instead, they chose to emphasize the gradual perfection of the existing organization of production through partial reforms and attempted to adapt each individual plantation to its particular local conditions. Changes were adapted to and elaborated within the prevailing division of labor. During these years, the *habitation sucrière* attained its most complete development and exhausted its technical possibilities. While the processes of sugar production underwent gradual modification, the basic structure of the self-contained plantation remained intact on the scale on which it had been established in the seventeenth century and suppressed alternative paths of development.[3]

Given the social and technical conditions of sugar production in Martinique, this course of action was not illogical. The problem with such a solution, however, was that the planters were guaranteeing their own obsolescence. The changes they introduced were not always insignificant, but their consequences were limited by the effects of the integration and interdependence of the plantation as a whole. By themselves, they were neither sufficient nor widespread enough to rejuvenate the colonial sugar industry. Furthermore, the planters' vision, never realized if not unrealizable, of a perfect equilibrium of the elements of production, where men, implements, land, and animals were combined with complete harmony and maximum efficiency, led them to reject the steam engine and the vacuum pan, the two most revolutionary technical advances in sugar manufacture during the nineteenth century, as being incompatible with the organization of the plantation. Martinique thus continued to lag behind both the French beet sugar industry and other tropical cane sugar producers. In the face of an expanding market, dynamic competitors, and the constant transformation of production processes, the pressure against them could only continue to mount and create the need for more radical solutions.

Precisely such a dramatic alternative was proposed by Daubrée, Derosne, and others. Often not planters themselves, these men realized the inadequacy of piecemeal reforms and maintained that the survival of the colonial sugar industry required the thorough restructuring of the division of labor and plantation system. They advocated the separation of sugar cultivation from manufacturing and the establishment of large central refineries that could take maximum advantage of the potential of the new technology. Alongside of the *habitation sucrière* emerged a new form of organization, the *usine centrale*. It implied the radical transformation not only of the organization of production, but of all economic, social, and political relations in the colony as well. However, the mere presence of several such *usines* was not enough to break down the existing plantation system, and instead, their development was truncated by the persistence of the old forms of organization, which monopolized productive resources within the previous division of labor.[4]

## Sugar, Slavery, and Modern Science

From the first decades of the nineteenth century onward, there were a series of advances in every aspect of sugar refining. This sector was the most defective and the most susceptible to amelioration, and the appearance of these new techniques revolutionized sugar manufacture. For the most part, these advances originated in the French beet sugar industry, which was compelled to seek every possible means to offset the natural disadvantages of the sugar beet. The European beet sugar industry quickly became what Eric Williams has aptly described as "the great school of scientific agriculture." In France, scientific understanding of the process of refining sugar was raised to a new level, and manufacturing techniques were developed that were proven by practical experience. These innovations were directly applicable to the colonial sugar industry; however, the problem of their assimilation into the technical, economic, and social organization of the West Indian plantation remained to be resolved.[5]

Both Lavollée and Soleau agreed that more widespread adoption of the system of clarifiers used in the English colonies would eliminate the difficulties that arose from tempering the cane juice in the *grande* and would improve sugar production in Martinique. First used in Jamaica in 1778, clarifiers were very large kettles, between seventy and eighty inches in diameter, which received the juice directly from the mill or reservoir. They were usually used in groups of two or three, but there were sometimes as many as six or more in the boiling house. Each clarifier had its own source of heat, and the temperature of the liquid could be kept high enough to prevent fermentation but below the boiling point independently of the main furnace. Clarification could be conducted slowly and the impurities removed by a simple process of decantation. After the lime was added and the liquid was heated to the proper temperature, the fire was promptly damped, and the juice allowed to stand. While the scum rose to the top of the liquid, the solid particles formed a sediment on the bottom of the kettle. The clarifier had one or more faucets at various heights from the bottom. These allowed the pure juice to be drained from the upper part of the clarifier into the *grande*, and they could be closed as soon as the first impurities appeared in the liquid. The bottom of the clarifier was slightly concave, with an outlet valve through which the scum and sediment could be drained off into a cistern once the juice had been removed. With this apparatus, tempering of the juice could be completed before it was passed forward to the evaporating pans. Greater purity of the juice simplified the task of sugar making, reduced if not eliminated the fatiguing work of skimming the kettles, and restored a measure of order and proper sequence to the refining process. Although it did not completely eliminate the constraints of individual skill and judgment, the clarifier allowed more reliable measurement of the lime and gave the planter more control over the refining process. Instead of leaving the decision about how much lime to apply to the slave refiner, with his trial-and-error methods, the planter himself could determine the amount necessary to temper the cane juice in a controlled environment and could thus establish the rule for the dosage of lime in the clarifier. Derosne, however, remained critical of this system of clarification. In his view, it required too much time and fuel, and the action of the heat created currents in the liquid that inhibited the precipitation of impurities.[6]

Of even greater potential significance than the clarifier for the colonial sugar industry was animal charcoal (*noir animal, charbon animal*), adapted from the beet sugar refining process. According to Reed: "The employment of animal charcoal in sugar refining marks an era in that manufacture." The principles of its operation were not known, even in the late nineteenth century, but its properties of decoloring and purifying the sugar had a salutary effect on colonial manufacture. Its great advantage was that it permitted the unrestricted use of lime as a clarifier. It not only removed the coloring material from the sugar, but also precipitated lime, calcium salts, and other substances without altering the sugar. The juice could be clarified more thoroughly and a greater mass of scum removed. Its use resulted in pure juice, which simplified the refining process. It yielded up to 20 percent more sugar from the same quantity of juice. Crystallization, color, and taste were improved, and a product the quality of refined sugar could be obtained in a single operation, without claying or *clairçage*. Labor and fuel were saved as a result of its application as well.[7]

Charles Derosne first pioneered the use of animal charcoal in the French beet sugar industry in 1812, and with the active encouragement of the Minister of the Marine and Colonies, turned his attention to cane sugar. In 1819, he successfully adapted the use of animal charcoal and dried animal blood to samples of cane juice brought to Paris from Martinique and Guadeloupe. Initially, it was employed in the form of a fine powder that was thrown into the clarified cane juice. But there was no way to reuse the animal carbon when it was employed in this way, and the resultant high price prohibited its adoption in the colonies. The development of carbon filters by Julien Dumont changed the method of application of the carbon and resolved this difficulty. Coarse grains of animal charcoal were packed in thick layers in large boxes, and the clarified cane juice was passed through it. Also in common use in the French Antilles were bag or stocking filters, known as Taylor filters. As a result of this filtration, the juice had a clear color and purity that had been unattainable by any other means. The great advantage of the filter was that when it was used this way, the animal carbon could be washed with plain water and reused indefinitely. This greatly reduced its cost and made it accessible to colonial planters.[8]

Six or seven planters in Martinique adopted the swing boiler (*chaudière à bascule*) to avoid the problems of exposure to high temperature, caramelization, the high degree of concentration, and lack of control over the strike in the *batterie*. The swing boiler was a flat-bottomed copper kettle with its own furnace that could be emptied quickly in a single movement. It offered the advantage of dividing the strike into two operations and of making the process more regular and controlled. First, the syrup in the *batterie* was heated to a lower temperature and degree of concentration than in the old method. It was then removed to an intermediate reservoir, where it was allowed to cool and make a deposit of sugar before being transferred to the swing boiler, where the strike was completed. With this method, the sugar was not exposed to such high temperatures while it was highly concentrated, and the loss and discoloration of sugar due to caramelization and burning was prevented. The quality of sugar obtained as a result of slower crystallization and more regular boiling was much superior to that produced by the old process. Before its adoption, one proprietor in Martinique produced only sugar of such low quality that it could not be classified. With the swing boiler, he obtained *bonne quatrième*. Two other planters passed the syrup through Dumont and Taylor filters after it left the *batterie* and before it entered the swing boiler. By means of this technique and *terrage*, they produced superior-quality sugar classified as *brut blanc*.

Besides saving a great deal of sugar, this method was more rapid than the traditional process. It also saved labor. Two men could swing in a moment what four to six men could not have done with ladles. Finally, it was more durable than the old system. Neither the swing boiler nor the *batterie* was as subject to the destructive effects of high temperatures. The cost of this apparatus was 4,000–5,000 francs, and Lavollée regarded its adoption as indispensable. (Although once again, it must be noted that metropolitan refiners succeeded in obtaining a discriminatory tariff against *brut blanc* in 1834.)[9]

A still more radical innovation was the substitution of steam heat for the furnace of the English train. Compressed steam, even though used at high pressure, emitted less intense heat than an open fire and could be applied advantageously to the defecation, evaporation, and boiling of the cane juice. The large wrought-iron boilers used as steam generators presented a larger surface to the action of the fire and burned bagasse more effectively than the English train. They were also safer. They could be located in an isolated place, and there was no danger of fire, which was frequent in the old system where there were high temperatures and an accumulation of combustible material. The heat was easy to regulate by means of valves. It did not decompose the sugar, and there was no danger of carmelization. The manufacturing process was thereby simplified. Steam heat provided the most rapid evaporation yet attained, and resulted in a saving of labor, fuel, and time.[10]

Compressed steam was generally adopted for evaporating and boiling beet sugar by the 1830s. Almost no beet sugar manufacturer used an open flame for these operations, especially the latter. Yet Jabrun of Guadeloupe, one of the most technically advanced planters in the French West Indies, thought that the advantages of a complete steam evaporating system were not worth the expense. In his opinion, evaporation with an open fire was acceptable because, before the cane juice reached the *batterie*, it was not sufficiently concentrated to suffer much alteration. However, he felt that the use of steam heat was advantageous for the *cuite*. The steam boiler could be perfectly adapted to the existing system of kettles in use in the colonies. The first steps of the process could be carried out as before and in the same kettles. Once the juice was sufficiently concentrated, it was filtered and struck in a steam boiler. In this way, there was no need to change the existing installation, and the harvest would not be compromised. If there were any difficulties with the new apparatus, the planter could revert to the former method of refining. In addition, the cost of a steam boiler alone was not more than 7,000–8,000 francs and spared the expense that inhibited the adoption of steam heat in the West Indies.[11]

A variety of steam boilers available were similarly designed. The simplest, most solid and reliable of these was that developed by Pecqueurs and introduced about 1828. It consisted of an open, oblong copper kettle enclosing a single or double row of tubes through which the steam passed. The heating element could be rotated about its long axis to allow the pan to be cleaned. About 1837, a new steam apparatus invented by Péan appeared in the colonies and was used with considerable success. It was simpler and easier to maintain and repair than the Pecqueurs pan. This device was a double-bottomed kettle that was inclined and open toward one end. A continuous stream of juice entered the upper end of the kettle. It evaporated while flowing over the undulating surface of the kettle bottom and flowed out of the open end. Depending on the amount of liquid introduced, the process took about three to four minutes to complete. This operation was generally repeated twice for the syrup to reach the striking point. The advantage of this system was that the syrup was in contact with the heat for only a few minutes, and the rapid rate of evaporation reduced the effects of the temperature. The nuance and grain of the sugar crystals could be controlled by regulating the rate of flow of the syrup, though in practice this could be difficult to manage.[12]

The steam boiler allowed more control over the heat than did the open fire, and its use resulted in higher-quality sugar. Jabrun's experiments in Guadeloupe suggested that although on average colonial sugar was quoted at two francs below *bonne quatrième*, on the first strike steam boilers would yield almost-white sugar that was quoted at least five francs above *bonne quatrième*. In addition, the purity of the syrup allowed the sugar to be struck a second time and reduced the amount of molasses left as a residue by at least 25 percent. The steam boiler was used on several plantations in Guadeloupe, but according to Lavollée was completely unknown in Martinique.[13]

The vacuum pan represented a major improvement over the open steam boiler and was destined to revolutionize sugar manufacture. The syrup was introduced into a hermetically sealed chamber from which the air was evacuated by one of several mechanisms. By reducing the air pressure on the juice, the vacuum pan allowed evaporation to take place at a much lower temperature. All the problems arising from the exposure of the syrup to excessive heat and open air inherent in the English train were thereby overcome. The sugar suffered much less decomposition and retained its crystallizable properties, and there was more control over the process. The vacuum pan was also especially effective in recovering the sugar from low-quality syrup or from molasses on the second or third strike. With its adoption, yields in the colonies approximately doubled, and new grades of sugar such as "Demerara crystals" and "Derosne train white" commanded the highest prices on the world's sugar markets.[14]

The vacuum pan was invented in 1812 by Edward Howard, an English chemist, but because of his excessive demands for licensing as well as the high cost of installation, it was not until 1833 that the first one was erected in the West Indies on the Vreeden Hoop estate in British Guiana. It was only in 1828 that Roth succeeded in having a modified model of Howard's vacuum pan adopted in a French sugar refinery. Evaporation in Roth's apparatus took place at a lower temperature than in Howard's vacuum pan, but it was criticized for lack of continuity. The process had to be interrupted after the completion of each batch of sugar. While each of these models produced more and better sugar than previous methods, they still required as much steam and fuel as did open air evaporation. However, the primary technical obstacle to the adoption of both these devices in the colonies was their use of water injection to condense the steam. This method, in Derosne's words, "required a river of water."[15]

The major defects of the Howard and Roth vacuum pans were corrected with a new system of condensation invented by Degrand of Marseille in 1833. This method represented a great advance over its predecessors and was important as an early attempt at the multiple utilization of the latent heat of steam. Instead of injecting water into a condenser, the steam ran through a serpentine over whose surface a sprinkle of water continuously fell. The water evaporated as it came into contact with the serpentine, causing the steam inside it to condense. The quantity of water necessary to condense the steam was thereby greatly diminished, and the adoption of the system in places where there was not an abundance of water became possible. This technique was further improved by the substitution of syrup for water as the cooling fluid. With this change there was no longer any need for water to condense the steam, and the vacuum pan could be used anywhere. In addition, as much water was evaporated from the syrup in the condenser as from the syrup in the evaporating pan. The same quantity of heat thus did twice the amount of work, and as a result, there was a 50 percent saving in fuel. Finally, the syrup evaporated in the vacuum pan provided enough distilled water to supply the steam generators and the other needs of the refinery. Although Degrand and Derosne referred to this process as "double-effect evaporation," it is not to be confused with the system of multiple-effect evaporation developed through the respective efforts of Pecqueur, Derosne, and Rillieux between 1832 and 1844. (Indeed, Derosne's version of the latter incorporated Degrand's system.) Multiple-effect evaporation perfected the vacuum pan. The system utilized the transfer of the same quantity of heat to a sequence of vacuum pans, each of which was maintained at a lower pressure than the one preceding it. The steam produced from the evaporation of the syrup in the first kettle was then used to evaporate the syrup in the following kettle, and so on down the line. This system totally transformed sugar manufacture, and, in the opinion of Deerr, "must have a place among the world's great inventions."[16]

Despite the obvious advantages of the vacuum pan, critics such as Sainte Croix and Jabrun argued that it was unsuitable for use in the colonies and instead recommended the adoption of open steam boilers. In their view, the vacuum pan was a delicate and complicated device. It was very susceptible to damage and was difficult to operate and maintain. The smallest leak and operations had to be suspended. Furthermore, it was prohibitively expensive for most planters. According to Jabrun's figures, a single effect vacuum pan cost at least 40,000 francs, while Derosne's double-effect apparatus cost between 50,000–60,000 francs including transport and installation. In addition, yearly expenses for repairs and interest were estimated at a minimum of 8,000 francs. This latter figure probably ought to be evaluated higher in the colonies, where things deteriorated more rapidly, repairs were more expensive, and interest rates were higher. Only large-scale production could compensate for the high cost of purchasing and maintaining the vacuum pan. Jabrun estimated that it was necessary to produce at least 15,000 kilograms of sugar a day every day of the year to justify the expense of the vacuum pan. This was beyond the range of all but a handful of plantations in the French West Indies. By 1846, Martinique counted only eight and perhaps nine such devices.[17]

These new techniques of sugar manufacture were adopted either individually or in various combinations by a number of planters in the French West Indies. However, their utilization was confined to a minority of large, well-off estates whose owners were in a position to experiment with them, and they failed to resolve the malaise of the colonial sugar industry. The most immediate obstacle to the adoption of the new technology was the lack of money and credit in the colonies. Three-quarters of the planters in the French West Indies were indebted for sums equivalent to half, and sometimes the entirety, of the value of their real and moveable property, and uncertainty over the resolution of the colonial question had sharply restricted commercial credit. In Daubrée's view, some of the richest planters who operated on a large scale were in a position to successfully renovate their entire production facility, but for the great majority who produced on a more modest scale and only made enough to maintain their operations, it was out of the question. Without even considering the vacuum pan, he estimated that there were not 10 out of 100 who were able to bear the expense of even a steam engine or a horizontal grinding mill and not 5 out of 100 who could afford to renew their entire milling and refining system.[18]

Yet the shortage of capital was not at the root of the problem. Rather, the self-contained plantation as it had been historically constituted in Martinique and the organization of labor as slave labor had become the chief obstacles to transforming the production process. The physical requirements of sugar production fixed the relation between the agricultural and manufacturing operations within definite proportions on the *habitation sucrière*, while the appropriation of workers as slaves fixed labor in relation to this technical division of labor. An equilibrium was formed that effectively immobilized the factors of production. A determinate number of workers were adapted to the preestablished organization of the labor process. Once production was established on a given scale, it could be expanded only if all the sectors were increased proportionally and labor was appropriately redistributed. Within limits determined by the quantitative relation between sectors, small economies or inefficiencies in a particular sector would only have a limited impact on overall productivity. But any significant attempt to increase the capacity of one sector without corresponding changes in the other sectors could simply create disequilibrium and waste the intended economy. The changes either became superfluous or increased the burden on the other elements of the process, requiring longer and harder use of slaves, land, animals, or equipment. For example, the adoption of the plow might allow more land to be cultivated and increase the size of the harvest, but such an innovation might upset the balance between arable land and pasture. Valuable pasturage could be reduced just when more animals were needed to draw the plow, or conversely, the potential advantages of the plow could be offset by maintaining or increasing pastureland at the expense of land for sugar. Beyond this problem, increasing the amount of land cultivated and the size of the harvest, even if it were possible, could intensify the pressure on the slaves, the transport system, the fuel supply, the mill, and the refinery, yet have only limited effect on final production unless the capacity of each of these sectors was increased commensurately. Finally, the capital investment entailed in restructuring the labor process might become prohibitive if, for example, in addition to buying new implements, more slaves had to be purchased.[19]

Within the framework of the self-contained plantation, the technical division of labor (the division of tasks) and the social division of labor (the division of laborers) reciprocally develop and constrain one another. The interdependence of agricultural and manufacturing operations develops the elaboration of specialized tasks performed by different workers or groups of workers and their integration within a unified and continuous process. Thus, it develops the cooperative character of labor as a collective force, but only within technically determined qualitative and quantitative limits, beyond which the socialization of labor is blocked. Conversely, within these technical limits, the social relations of slavery historically allowed the development of the social character of labor, the increase of the scale of production, and the expansion of the division of labor. But the physical appropriation of the labor force and its assimilation into the constant capital of the estate impeded the adoption of new technologies, the further development of the division of labor, and the transformation of the labor process. Within the slave form, labor remains invariable. Technological innovation does not save labor or increase its productivity. Thus, the specific form of production relations itself restricts technological innovation and the development of the cooperative force of collective labor. Rather than rationalizing of the labor process, the result of such efforts is to intensify the activity of labor and to rigidify technical and social conditions of production. The relation of slave labor to technological change has been the subject of controversy and requires further discussion.

The limited impact of the new technology on West Indian sugar manufacture has frequently been attributed to the unsuitability of slaves for any but the simplest routine tasks. Indeed, the incompatibility of slave labor with mechanized production processes has virtually become a commonplace in much historical writing. While the slave labor process will be treated in detail in the following chapter, this hypothesis needs to be qualified here. To interpret the failure of these new technological advances to rejuvenate colonial production as due to the inability of slaves to perform specific concrete tasks is a one-sided view that risks misperceiving the relation of slavery and technological change. Among other evidence, the observations of Victor Schoelcher cast doubt on the accuracy of such a formulation of the problem. In the face of claims by some planters, such as Sainte Croix, that slaves were incapable of operating steam engines, Schoelcher noted: "There are some steam engines in the French colonies. There are many of them in the English colonies. Everywhere it is the blacks who run them." The antagonism between slavery and the technological transformation of the labor process is not reducible to the incapacity of individual laborers, whether attributed to their biological or their social characteristics, but derives from the social form of the organization of labor itself.[20]

In opposing the prejudices of colonial planters against innovation and against the capability of slave labor to utilize it, the proponents of the new technology emphasized its simplicity and its role in imposing a new discipline on the activities of the laborer. The purpose of the new machinery was to do away with the complicated manual labor entailed in sugar manufacture and simplify the activities of the worker. The devices described in the preceding pages required no specialized knowledge or skill to run. Derosne, describing an early version of his refining system that combined clarifiers, carbon filters, and flat-bottomed copper swing kettles, contended that, "Any Negro boiler, in one operation, may be taught to use it, without fear or possibility of anything going wrong." Similarly, the routine operation and maintenance of the steam boiling pan was so simple that, according to Jabrun, there was not a worker in the colony who was incapable of learning to run it in a day.[21]

The relationship between technological innovation and slave labor was posed most sharply by the vacuum pan. With each historical development of the instruments of production, the manufacturing process appeared less and less as simply the combination of the subjective activity of various specialized workers; rather, it progressively assumed an objective organization, which confronted the workers as an external, preexisting material condition of production toward which their activity must be oriented. The vacuum pan carried this process to its extreme consequence. It substituted mechanical power and the conscious and systematic application of scientific principles for the skill, dexterity, and strength of the worker. It was the most complex and sophisticated apparatus introduced into the colonies and the one most responsible for revolutionizing the methods of sugar manufacture. An examination of its impact on the labor process can thus illuminate the general process, common to one degree or another to the adoption of all the other technological advances.

Describing their system of vacuum pan evaporation, Derosne and Cail wrote: "Combining the machines with care, the operations have been facilitated and made independent of the workers' lack of attention in such a way that today the worker is subject to the machine itself and is unable to incur the faults that bore witness to his incapacity in the old system. And for the very reason that with the new processes the worker is relieved of every laborious operation, more sustained attention can be demanded of him." This system may have been more complex than the implements previously used in its place, but the work performed by the individual slaves became simpler. The purpose of this new machine was the suppression of manual labor, in terms of the difficulty and complexity of the tasks and of the number of workers required to perform them. As manual labor was reduced or eliminated, the craft skills and subjective judgment of the workers were appropriated as the property of the machine. While particular workers lost their skills and control over their working activity, the vacuum pan recombined and recreated individual skills as the collective social skills of the group and redistributed them among its members. The nature of work was transformed by extending and deepening of the division of labor within a new complex of hierarchically defined, antagonistic relations that reconstituted the difference and division between skilled and unskilled labor. While the skilled workers stepped back from the immediate labor process and became the superintendents of the machine, the unskilled workers were more directly and thoroughly subordinated to its rhythms. Work became the cooperative activity of this collectivity. The machine represented the unity of the workers and the integration of their activity, on the one hand, and the domination of the planter over them, on the other. The vacuum pan fused the technical supervision of the process of material production and social control over the activity of the workers, whose previous separation had been expressed in the coexistence of the black sugar master and the white sugar master. The instrument of labor, freed from control by the worker and transformed into a self-activating mechanism, became the repository of control over both the material process of production and the social process of production and redefined the relation between the two of them. The regulation of material production by the machine was at the same time the imposition of labor discipline. Management was simplified and aspects of it put in the hands of technicians while the workers' activity was subjected to a new sphere of control. The gain in the collective power of social labor was at the expense of the individual worker.[22]

In the colonies, as in France, the complexity of the vacuum pan required a small group of specialized workers for its operation. These generally included an engineer and one or two mechanics or boilermakers. The selection of these workers had less to do with their civil status than with their technical competence. Persons with necessary qualifications were generally not to be found among the colonial population, slave or free, but rather they had to be brought from the metropolis. To focus on the failure of slaves to occupy these positions misses the larger point of the transformation of the labor process and the shifting locus of control over it. Beyond the technical staff, "the main part of the manufacture is only composed of very ordinary labor, as much within the scope of the Negroes as the present manufacture." Far from exerting pressure to transform the social relations of production throughout the other sectors of the labor process, this isolated nucleus of free workers was dependent on slave labor and constrained by its presence. The slaves adapted themselves to this new work regime so successfully that the extent to which the technical staff entered into its routine operation beyond the most general supervision may also be questioned. On the plantation of A. Vincent of Bourbon, where pioneering efforts were made with the vacuum pan beginning in 1838, "All the workers . . . are Negroes, and, nevertheless, they have not had the least difficulty in habituating themselves to the management of the machines." On the estate of Vila-Urrutia in Cuba, where Derosne's vacuum pan was producing 12,000 kilograms of crystallized sugar a day in 1843: "The factory had no other white worker than the sugar master. All the rest of the personnel was composed of Negroes, who have mastered their work very quickly."[23]

For the critics of colonial agriculture, it was not the ability of slave laborers to operate the new equipment that was the impediment to reform, but the lack of qualified mechanics who could make essential repairs on it. The vulnerability of fragile and sophisticated equipment without the development of a technological infrastructure to support it is illustrated by an incident recorded by Governor Mathieu in 1847. While he was visiting the *usine centrale* of the Sinson brothers in François, the iron grinding mill broke down. There was no way to make repairs or replace the broken parts, and the Sinson brothers had no auxiliary mill. The neighboring plantations either had their own sugar to refine or were dependent on the *usine centrale* themselves and could not offer any assistance. The Sinson brothers were faced with the failure of their harvest, the loss of their credit, and ultimately their own ruin and the ruin of the properties dependent on them. However, Mathieu, believing in the importance of their project as an example for the entire colony, acted promptly. He offered the services of a naval engineer and two blacksmiths from a naval vessel. The principal parts, which would have required four or five months to obtain from France, were replaced with hardwood. A new drive shaft was fashioned in the arsenal and various other broken parts repaired. The mill was back in operation in a month. A foundry was established in Trinité by M. Gastel to serve the needs of the modernized plantations, but it had been unable to supply the necessary parts either in this case or in a similar breakdown on a nearby plantation four months previously. Lavollée reported that there was only one qualified mechanic in Sainte Pierre, and his services were very expensive. To resolve such difficulties, Derosne offered to send and subsidize a selected group of experienced machinists to each colony that purchased his equipment to install, maintain, and propagate his system.[24]

The contradiction between slave labor and technological innovation does not reside in the capacity or incapacity of individual workers to perform specific concrete tasks; rather, the specific character of slavery as a social relation determined the conditions under which such changes could be implemented and their consequences for social and economic development. In the slave relation, the instruments of labor did not function as capital. The reorganization of production did not save labor or reduce its cost either relatively or absolutely. Labor was not expelled from the production process, and the costs of slave maintenance remained independent of changes in production. De Lavigne, for example, testified before the commission on the sugar industry that he had used a plow on his plantation for ten or twelve years. Before its adoption, he had 200 slaves and cultivated 50 carrés of sugar. Afterward, he cultivated 100 carrés of which 75 were harvested in an average year, but he still had the same number of slaves. Thus, the cost of slave maintenance remained unchanged, and their labor was distributed over a larger product. Significantly, De Lavigne attributes the adoption of the plow in Martinique to the shortage of labor caused by the abolition of the slave trade, an event outside of the rationalization of the labor process.[25]

Such reorganization of the labor process simultaneously intensified labor and created redundant laborers. The expanded production demanded greater effort of the slaves and shortened their working lives. At the same time, the greater output per slave created a superfluity of laborers whose presence not only drained the slaveholder's resources, but could smother the changes made in the labor process, as the experience of a planter in the British Caribbean suggests: "The plough is certainly coming into more general use than formerly. . . . I was, in fact, compelled to adopt this system, by the small number of slaves which I possessed in proportion to the quantity of cultivable land; and I . . . only discontinued it in consequence of having purchased about fifty additional negroes, whose labour, although of the greatest importance at certain periods of the year, could not have been fully available but by this filling up the intervals of diminished exertion." The transformation of the labor process was blocked. Either machines or men were underutilized. Since labor remained at the disposal of the slave owner and had to be maintained whether there was work or not, the slave owner's concern was that it be usefully employed. On the other side, the intensification of work called forth slave resistance. Even if, for example, the use of the plow reduced the back-breaking toil of planting with a hoe, for the slave the larger crop simply meant more work during the harvest without any positive effect on his consumption. Thus, slave labor could be adapted to a given division of labor, but technological innovation and the alteration of the labor process did not save labor. Rather, the immobility of the division of labor was reinforced. The rigidity of the organization of production and its resistance to structural transformation were strengthened. The result was that labor was more intensively exploited within fixed technical conditions, and the contradictory character of the slave form was heightened.[26]

The closely integrated technical organization of sugar production and the need to maintain the balance between its various elements, including labor, gave internal solidity to the sugar plantation and made it resistant to change. The importance of this technical limitation of sugar production becomes more evident in an old plantation colony like Martinique. There, the primary sugar lands were occupied and the majority of estates in existence during the July Monarchy, including all the principal ones, were established by 1714. The scale and level of productivity of these plantations were constituted by the historically formed relation between agricultural and manufacturing operations prevailing during that epoch. The capacity of the mill and the need for the cane to be planted near it, especially given the bad state of transportation, determined the extent of land that could be profitably cultivated and the size of the labor force. Once most agricultural land on the island had been occupied through the multiplication of these productive units, the relation between agriculture, manufacturing, and labor was stabilized. An equilibrium was formed around the amount of land that could be cultivated on a given estate. The pressure from either sector, field or mill, to increase the efficiency of the other was reduced. Under these circumstances, the structure of the plantation as a whole, rather than the particular conditions in any individual sector, was the major obstacle to the technological transformation of the labor process. The entire organization of production became fixed and rigid. As one nineteenth-century critic of the sugar industry in Martinique complained: "There everything is custom and old habits. The simplest improvements with the most evident outcomes are neglected because to undertake them would require some activity. . . . In general, the processes of fabrication in common use in Martinique today remain what they were 150 years ago. With few exceptions, the machines have preserved all their crude imperfections. Thus the colonists, although working on admirably rich material, only produce sugar of inferior quality." In contrast, through most of the nineteenth century Cuba was still a frontier as far as sugar cane was concerned. The availability of fresh land and labor, whether slave or free, especially in the context of a rapidly expanding world market, made the mill a bottleneck and stimulated its technological transformation. At the same time, the remarkable evolution of the Cuban sugar mill from *trapiche* to mechanized mill, as documented by Moreno Fraginals, could occur as it did because land and labor could be combined with the mill in new proportions as the capacity of the latter developed. The sugar mill in the Caribbean did not have a "normal" course of development, but rather was formed by a variety of historical conditions. Sugar and slavery in Cuba possessed a dynamism that was not possible in Martinique.[27]

The resistance of the *habitation sucrière* to change was the chief obstacle to the technological transformation of the colonial sugar industry in Martinique. The rigid structure of the self-contained sugar plantation restricted technical innovation. To the extent that the adoption of new refining techniques simply extracted more and better sugar from the same amount of juice, it did not upset the internal equilibrium among the various sectors of the production process. But such reforms integrated the division of labor on each individual plantation ever more tightly. The reorganization of production processes within the established form of organization became increasingly elaborate. The changes in production technique resulted in smaller and smaller marginal increases in output, while the internal structure of the plantation as a whole became ever more solidly congealed. Moreover, as Daubrée argued, even presuming that the planters had sufficient finances and were able to adapt simple reforms such as steam-powered horizontal grinding mills, clarifiers, and copper swing boilers to their manufacturing operation, the increased yield would be insufficient to offset the rapidly advancing beet sugar industry. Despite the gains in colonial production, its position relative to beet sugar in the French market would continue to decline.[28]

Daubrée maintained that only the total reorganization of colonial sugar manufacturing would enable the planters to resolve in their favor the concurrence with the metropolitan beet sugar industry. In his view, if the methods of sugar refining used in France, including steam boilers and vacuum pans, were adopted in their entirety in the colonies, production would double, and the richer sugar content of the cane plant would secure the advantage for the colonial planters. The more the perfection of these techniques permitted the extraction of all the sugar contained in the cane plant, the more the balance would swing in their favor. However, as Daubrée demonstrated, even if the average planter in the French Antilles doubled his individual output, he would still operate at a loss because of the enormous investment required by the new machinery. The plantation units in Martinique had become too small to be productive. To make effective use of the new refining technology, Daubrée estimated that a plantation had to produce at least 400,000–500,000 kilograms of sugar annually. This went far beyond the scope of even the largest plantations in Martinique, which, at most, produced no more than half that quantity of sugar each year. Furthermore, the immense amount of raw material necessary to attain such a result required that the area under cultivation be drastically expanded. Unlike some of the British Caribbean colonies, Louisiana, or parts of Cuba, this alternative was no longer possible for individual plantations in the French colony. Instead, the necessary relationship between the various sectors of the production process prevailing on each plantation unit in Martinique formed the historical limit to technological innovation. The alternatives before the planters were clear: either reject the radical implications of the new technology and attempt to amend the existing structure of production through partial reforms, or radically transform the division of labor and integrate the new methods of production into a new form of plantation organization.[29]

## The Usine Centrale: A Blocked Transition

The inability of the *habitation sucrière* to respond to the unusual conditions of the French national sugar market called the form of plantation organization itself into question. A model of plantation organization that was destined to revolutionize the tropical sugar industry made its precocious appearance in the French colonies in the late 1830s, the *usine centrale*. While the new refining techniques were by no means the cause of the breakdown of the self-contained sugar plantation, they did make its supersession a practical possibility. A new pattern of industrial organization began to emerge in Bourbon, where the first attempt was made to apply the vacuum pan to the production of cane sugar. The well-known French firm of Derosne and Cail, pioneers in the manufacture of sugar-refining equipment, sought to demonstrate the applicability of their "double effect" apparatus to cane sugar production to extend the market for the device, which until then had been confined to the European beet sugar industry. In 1838, they supplied A. Vincent, a wealthy planter from Bourbon, with "a complete system of machines made on the model of the most perfect factory in the north of France." To take full advantage of the new techniques, Vincent contracted with his neighbors for the purchase of their cane. His output climbed from 550 metric tons in 1838–39 to 1,000 metric tons in 1840–41. The sugar produced was of superior quality and sold for a remarkable 100 francs per 100 kilograms. After the success of this initial experiment, Vincent ordered a second vacuum pan with twice the capacity of the first model. Inspired by Vincent's example, many other proprietors in Bourbon, whose holdings were too small to take advantage of the new processes individually, sought to overcome their lack of capital by joining together to establish a large factory to collectively process their cane. On the basis of these experiences, Derosne and Cail, in a brief notice published in the journal *L'Outre-Mer* (August 9, 1840), suggested that the establishment of large central refineries which utilized the most advanced techniques and purchased sugar cane from planters who specialized only in its cultivation, was the solution to the malaise of the colonial sugar industry. This was the first mention of the *usine centrale*.[30]

The idea of the *usine centrale* was systematically elaborated by Paul Daubrée in his brochure *Question coloniale sous le rapport industriel*, published in Paris in 1841. Although Daubrée's work appeared at about the same time as the article by Derosne and Cail, he reached his conclusions independently on the basis of his experiences in Guadeloupe. Daubrée advocated the complete separation of agriculture from manufacturing activities. The plantations would specialize in the cultivation of sugar cane, while all refining was to be concentrated in large *usines centrales*, each of which would serve several plantations. On the one hand, such specialization would allow agriculture to develop beyond its existing limits. Planters would be spared the expense entailed in the purchase and maintenance of refining equipment, and in principle, the slaves who had been employed in manufacturing could be returned to agricultural occupations. Using this additional manpower, the planters could augment the size of their crop without having to worry about the efficacy of the refinery. They would realize directly the benefits of agricultural innovation, while the high cash return on their cane would permit them to purchase fertilize, animals, feed, and other essentials and still come out ahead. On the other hand, the centralization of sugar manufacturing in the *usine* would allow an increase in the scale of production and the strict application of scientific principles to the refining process. The vast amount of cane that could be treated would make the investment in new refining equipment economical, while the improved technical efficiency of the new procedures would result in a product whose quality was far superior to that which could be obtained using the old methods. This, in turn, would enable the refiner to purchase cane at prices remunerative for the cultivators yet still realize an additional profit from the higher price this sugar commanded in the French market. Daubrée argued that only such reorganization would allow the colonial sugar producers to compete with their metropolitan rivals and avoid certain ruin.[31]

Daubrée's study was widely read in France and was the point of departure for various projects for restructuring the colonial sugar industry. In 1843, the Minister of the Marine and Colonies purchased 100 copies of it to distribute among members of the two legislative chambers and other influential people concerned with the colonial question. Despite Daubrée's personal equivocation with regard to slavery, the proposal for the establishment of *usines centrales* came to be seen by some as the means to achieve the government's stated intention of eventual slave emancipation. It thus found support among such resolute opponents of slavery as Victor Schoelcher. Schoelcher believed that the future economic survival of the colonies was indissolubly linked to the cultivation of sugar cane, but he hoped that the separation of industry from agriculture would provide the basis for the creation from the ranks of the freed slaves of a class of prosperous smallholders who would specialize in growing cane for the *centrales*. Members of the colonial administration shared a similar perspective. In the opinion of Governor Mathieu of Martinique, such an arrangement provided an incentive to industriousness for freedmen who otherwise would be only marginal producers.

> In general, the freedmen who do not possess any land avoid work, especially work on the plantations. Those who do have a little land lack the means to exploit it and only plant a few provision crops for their own consumption. If they are not impoverished, they live on the border of poverty. Given the opportunity to plant sugar cane on their own account, they will undoubtedly devote themselves to agricultural labor with great eagerness not only because their vanity is flattered, but also because they will receive the fruit of their labor. This outcome must be attained, and it can only be expected from the *usines centrales*.

Thus, the *usine centrale* represented not only the road to economic recovery for the colonies, but the means for their social regeneration as well. In a single stroke, all of their problems could be resolved. Economic viability could be restored, social stability preserved, and the labor force guaranteed without the necessity of slavery.[32]

In contrast to the enthusiasm for *usines centrales* generated in the metropolis, the colonial planters initially reacted to them with caution. They were suspicious for a variety of reasons. The scale of production and investment necessary for the successful operation of a *usine centrale* were simply beyond the capacity of the great majority of planters in Martinique. Few of them were in a position to undertake such an initiative by themselves. Guignod recorded that in the estimation of MM. Barbier and de Fleury, associates of Daubrée, no more than forty of the existing estates in the colony could be converted to *usines centrales*, while he himself thought that the number was closer to eight. Many of the planters doubted the applicability of the new refining technology to the conditions of West Indian agriculture and feared that the creation of *usines* would either deliver them into the hands of their creditors or push them into a position subordinate to the *usine* while promising doubtful results. Sainte Croix warned that the *usines* would benefit only metropolitan bankers and speculators who wanted to monopolize control of the refining process and the sale of machinery. They would restrict the development of the *usines* and use them contrary to the general interests of the colonial proprietors. Finally, for a substantial number of planters, the experiments with free labor that accompanied the proposals for the development of *usines centrales* and in some cases were actually attempted made the *usines* appear as simply another wedge in the attack on slavery.[33]

However, after 1845, with the passage of the *loi Mackau* and successful examples before them in Guadeloupe, the opinion of at least a portion of the planters in Martinique began to shift in favor of the establishment of *usines centrales*. By 1847, the Colonial Council of Martinique, recognizing that *usines centrales* represented the sole means of maintaining the sugar industry with a free labor force, requested a loan of 5 million francs from the French government for their creation. This request represented a complete reversal of policy. Until this point, the majority of council members had believed that *usines* could never succeed in the colonies and had opposed their creation. At the same time, the municipal council of Marin petitioned the governor for a *usine* to serve the littoral from Sainte Luce to Pointe des Nègres, while the municipal council of Rivière Pilote requested funds for two *usines*, each with an annual average capacity of 1,200–1,500 hogsheads.[34]

However, despite this growing interest, few *usines centrales* were actually constructed in Martinique before 1848. In 1845, there were only two in operation. Charles Alexis de la Guignerie, after much expense and difficulty, built a *usine* with an annual capacity of 1,500 hogsheads of sugar in Robert, while John Thorp, an Englishman, built a factory in the city of Fort Royal. The following year, the *centrale* of the Sinson brothers on the "Bellegarde" estate in François, with an annual capacity of 2,000 hogsheads of sugar, was completed; and in 1847, the *centrale* on the "la Frégate" plantation of M. Brière de l'Ile, also of François, commenced operation and began processing cane from three neighboring plantations. All of these were constructed through the efforts of private individuals, rather than with public support.[35]

Few details are available about the *usines* of Laguignerie and Brière de l'Ile. John Thorp's factory at Pointe-Simon in the city of Fort Royal was equipped with two forty- to fifty-horsepower steam engines, a three-cylinder horizontal mill, and a vacuum pan. It was capable of producing ten hogsheads of sugar a day. The equipment and apparently the credit were supplied by the firm of Derosne and Cail. The *usine* employed forty persons and contracted to purchase cane from ten plantations located around the bay of Fort Royal and along the coast between Fort Royal and Sainte Pierre. For every 100 pounds of cane supplied, the planters were paid for five pounds of sugar at the current market price of *bonne quatrième.* Thus, they were compensated for the average quantity of sugar obtained by traditional means, but it was evaluated at a quality that normally could be achieved only with great difficulty. This appears to have been advantageous for many planters, and, according to one report, several of them wanted to enter into a similar arrangement with Thorp after his first year of operations. Thorp's *usine* had a salutary effect on the plantations that contracted to sell him cane: "For many years the excellent fields of the former plantation of M. Sinson Sainville which borders the city of Fort Royal had been left uncultivated due to the absence of manufacturing buildings whose installation would have been very expensive. But the land is already covered with magnificent cane fields. Through the creation of the *usine,* M. Félix Lacale, the present proprietor, found the means and elements of his fortune assured." Despite initial difficulties, the *usine* produced 600 hogsheads of sugar in the first three-and-one-half months of operation. These sold for 350 francs apiece in France. Thorp purchased a steamboat and three iron barges, and by thus improving the facilities for transporting the cane, he hoped to double his output for the following harvest. However, the *usine* faced mounting deficits, and Thorp's financial backers, dissatisfied with the immediate return on their investment, withdrew their credit. Thorp was forced to file for bankruptcy in October 1847. Cail repossessed the property, and in January 1848, on the eve of emancipation, it was still up for sale.[36]

The most detailed documentation available exists for the *usine centrale* of the Sinson brothers in François, which began operation in 1846. The mill was equipped with a vacuum pan built by the firm of the Mazeline brothers of Le Havre. It produced sixty-four hogsheads of sugar during a six-day week without working at night, and they hoped to augment its capacity by importing another vacuum pan from France. The mill employed fifty-five slaves and fifteen to twenty free wage workers. It processed the cane from four neighboring plantations. This was hardly enough to meet the demands of the mill. But instead of simply buying cane from other plantations without regard to the way that it was produced, they organized a system of share-cropping, or *colonage partiaire*, on their estate and sought to increase the efficiency and productivity of agricultural production as well as manufacturing. This attempt to reorganize the social conditions of production made their operation an important experiment, and its lessons were not lost on administrators or other planters on the eve of emancipation.[37]

Although the Sinson brothers owned a large amount of land, they had few slaves and by themselves could not hope to produce enough cane to keep their mill in operation. Instead, anyone who was willing to abide by the conditions they established under the system of *colonage partiaire* was granted a concession of land. In addition, during the first year, the Sinson brothers furnished each *colon* with the cane plants necessary to begin cultivation. They also provided fertilizer whenever it was required. The *colons* had to reimburse them for only half the value of the fertilizer. This amount was deducted from the net product of the cane ground at the *usine* at the end of each harvest season. In return for these concessions, the *colons* were required to grow nothing but sugar cane on the land. They were even forbidden to raise animals on the property. The crop had to be well cared for to retain the concession of land. All the cane grown by the *colon* had to be turned over to the *usine*, which promised to manufacture it into sugar during each harvest season without damage or loss to the planter. The *usine* would accept only cane of good quality cut no more than twenty-four hours before it was brought to the mill. The planter had to bear the expenses of transporting and unloading the cane, while the *usine* reserved the right to regulate the amount of cane brought to the mill and when it could be delivered. The *colons* were paid according to the density of their cane juice measured with a Beaumé hydrometer ten minutes after it was ground. Thus, juice that measured 12° on the Beaumé scale was reimbursed at 6 percent the weight of the cane, 11° at 5.5 percent, 10° at 5 percent, 9° at 4.5

percent, and 8° at 4 percent. Juice below 4° was not accepted. It was paid for at the current price of *bonne quatrième* in Saint Pierre. A deduction was made for the colonial duty, which was charged to the *colon*. In addition, one-fifth of the price of the cane was deducted by the *usine* for the use of the land, and an additional one-fifth if the *usine* provided transport to the mill. (The latter was very likely since the *colons* were not allowed to keep animals on their concessions.)[38]

The organization of the system of *colonage partiaire* was designed not only to guarantee a supply of cane for the mill, but also to create and discipline a new labor force. The *colons* were all drawn from the class of free men of color (*gens de couleur libres*). Some of them owned a few slaves, but the *usine* required that each *colon* work in the fields himself, beside his slaves, to demonstrate that work was an honorable activity worthy of free men. Similarly, the regulation requiring the exclusive cultivation of sugar cane was designed "especially to summon the freedmen to sugar cane cultivation, not only because it is the sole wealth of the colonies, but also to rehabilitate this cultivation in the eyes of all and particularly in the eyes of the slaves. By seeing the freedmen devote themselves to sugar cultivation and draw from it a prosperity superior to their former existence, the slaves will not experience the repulsion formerly felt by the freedmen toward sugar cane cultivation. They [the slaves] must necessarily follow the example set before them." There were thirty *colons* on the estate of the Sinson brothers. These thirty freedmen employed fifty slaves and day laborers, and together they cultivated sixty-three hectares. The success of the Sinson brothers attracted many would-be *colons*, and, according to Governor Mathieu, the Sinson brothers sought to buy neighboring properties to accommodate the growing requests for concessions. "I have no doubt," wrote Mathieu, "that if this mode is propagated it would contribute powerfully to bring back to cultivation many freedmen for whom agricultural labor is repugnant today. In this I believe that MM. Sinson have, above all, rendered a service to the country." He recommended that the Sinson brothers be awarded the Legion of Honor. Many of the Sinson's fellow planters were less enthusiastic about the project, however, and accused them of being agents of M. de Mackau who were paid to bring emancipation to the country.[39]

Despite the promise represented by the *usines centrales*, they had only a limited impact on colonial agriculture and remained isolated enclaves within the interstices of the preexisting system of *habitations sucrières*. The importance of these pioneering efforts lies less in their actual accomplishments than in the indications they gave of the future course of development. While the *usines centrales* might have offered a long-term solution to the problems of the colony as a whole, they did not necessarily meet the immediate interests of the individual planters, and few of the latter were willing to give up the manufacture of sugar to devote themselves exclusively to the production of raw material for the *usine*. Land and labor on the *habitation sucrière* were organized on the basis of the former means of production and were not necessarily optimal for the new conditions of cane cultivation. There was no guarantee that the slaves formerly employed in the mill and refinery were proportional in number to the available arable land or that they could be coerced or persuaded to become efficient agricultural laborers. In addition, the benefits to be gained from entering into a relation with the *usine* had to be calculated against the value of the capital invested in the physical plant of the mill and refinery as well as in the skilled slaves employed there. This entire sum would have to be written off as a loss if the *habitation sucrière* were to convert to simply the cultivation of cane. This transition was further complicated if the planter was in debt to a merchant who had advanced loans against the crop and might not want it committed to the *usine*.[40]

Furthermore, the planters surrendered control over the processing of their crop and placed their fate in the hands of the *usine*. This could entail some risks. Charles Alexis de la Guignerie, for example, grew his own cane in addition to operating a *usine centrale*. Delayed by his own harvest, he was forced to concentrate on grinding his own crop and had to turn down his neighbors' cane. As a result, he suffered an enormous loss, which increased his already large debt. His neighbors had to find an alternative means of manufacturing their sugar during the height of the harvest season or face the loss of their entire year's crop.[41]

Even under the best of circumstances, the contracts offered by the *usines* did not substantially ameliorate the condition of the planter. The cane supplied by the latter was evaluated as containing 4–6 percent of its weight in sugar. This amount was paid for at the price quoted for *bonne quatrième* in the *mercuriale* of Saint Pierre at the time it was ground. Thus, the planter automatically received compensation for what was regarded as the average yield and standard grade of sugar. This arrangement undoubtedly appeared attractive to the considerable number of planters whose production was substandard, yet it was an unequal relation that could be disadvantageous to the planter. The *usines* made deductions for duties, transport, and other costs that diminished the revenues of the planters. Moreover, the rigid formula for determining the ratio of cane to sugar and fixing the price of the latter meant that if the price of the final product fell, the cost of the raw material to the *usine* dropped proportionally. All the dangers of price fluctuations were passed on to the planters, while the *usines* were insulated from their effects. Conversely, the *usine* gained the extra revenue resulting from the production of sugar above the quality of *bonne quatrième* by its modern equipment. [42]

Under such conditions, a traditional sugar planter may well have been attracted by the promise of the immediate gains that could result from the amelioration of his manufacturing methods (however insufficient they may have been in the long run), rather than abandoning this activity to enter into a relation with the *usine*. This reluctance of the old sugar planters to transform their operations was reinforced by the great prestige attached to sugar manufacture. A qualitative gulf separated those who fabricated their own sugar, even if on a modest scale, from those who merely planted "secondary" crops such as coffee, cotton, or provisions. Sugar manufacture was the basis of a claim, however exaggerated and tenuous, to membership in the colonial elite and distinguished the *habitant sucrière* from the *petit habitant*. The *usine centrale* threatened the position of the *habitant sucrière* from two directions. On the one hand, it required him to abandon sugar manufacture and concentrate on the production of the raw material. On the other hand, the promoters of the *usines centrales* sought to induce middle and small producers, including freedmen of color, to abandon their other crops and concentrate on sugar cultivation. Thus, the *usine* represented a real loss of status for the old sugar men, and the distinction between them and other agrarian producers would become one of degree rather than kind.[43]

As a result of these conditions, the usines failed to establish a monopoly of refining activities and transform the *habitations sucrières* into dependent satellites specializing in the cultivation of sugar cane. Instead, land and labor remained bound up in the relations and activities of the *habitations sucrierès*, and the owners of the *usines* had to adapt to the established configuration of production. The *usines* took cane from a variety of cultivators, including *colons*, freedmen who grew a bit of cane on their holdings, small sugar planters, and coffee growers who converted their estates to cane cultivation. Most *usine* owners were concerned only with their supply of sugar cane and were indifferent to the conditions of agricultural production. There was no way to assure that cane cultivation was organized optimally for the colony as a whole and that the *usines* had a regular and adequate supply. All of the *usines* in Martinique were faced with a chronic shortage of raw material and operated below their capacity. The advantages of centralization and mechanization were thus lost. Their expensive equipment was underutilized, and production costs increased. The problem of an insufficient supply of cane was aggravated by the absence of an adequate transportation infrastructure to carry the enormous mass of cane from the plantations to the *centrales*. Land transport was enormously costly and difficult. The badly maintained dirt roads were inadequate, and there were insufficient livestock and carts to carry the cane the distances required. It was probably no accident that the *usine* that was most successful in obtaining cane, Thorp's factory at Pointe Simon, was able to use water transport to collect the cane from the growers. The development of an adequate source of supply for the *usines* had to await the establishment of a railway system. In this context, the attempts of the *usine* owners to establish *colonage partiaire*; to employ jobbing gangs, slaves who could hire themselves out, or wage laborers, and their inconsequential efforts to promote European migration may be viewed as attempts to secure an adequate supply of sugar cane by attracting a labor force from the economically marginal population. Such measures were a manifestation of the weakness of the *usines centrales*. They became necessary because the great mass of slave labor, land, and social product remained firmly under the control of the *habitation sucrière*.[44]

If the *usine centrale* envisaged a solution for the technical, economic, and social problems of the colonial sugar industry, the persistence of the *habitation sucrière* stunted its development and suppressed the alternative path of evolution it represented. The self-contained sugar plantation blocked the attempt to increase the scale of sugar production by changing the division of labor between agriculture and manufacturing, and instead fixed firmly the prevailing social and technical division of labor. Faced with continuing shortages of land, labor, and capital, the usines were unable to modify the organization of colonial production as a whole. They could not fulfill their promise and provide a general solution to the problems of the colony. Only when the old plantation system was broken up and the obstacles it presented removed was the renewal of the colonial sugar industry possible. However, the crisis of the sugar industry in Martinique was not simply the consequence of its technical organization but was rooted more deeply in the social relations of slave production. Renewal was only possible with the abolition of slavery.

# Chapter 7

# A Calculated and Calculating System

## The Dialectic of Slave Labor

Through the social relations of slavery, the demand for surplus labor was imposed on production. The technical-material conditions of sugar production were developed and extended as commodity production, and pressure was exerted for the optimal utilization of available laborers and labor time. Thus, neither "technical necessity" nor the master's domination over the slave alone determined the actual work relations—the mode of cooperation, division of labor, division of laborers. Within the technical framework established by the *habitation sucrière*, the slave relation permitted the increase of the mass of workers, the prolongation of labor time, and the intensification of effort. Concern for regularity, efficiency, quantification, and standardization increasingly came to dominate the organization of the labor process to secure its integration and expand the surplus product. Capital here appears not as the so-called external reality of the market, but enters into the inner constitution of the slave labor process itself.

However, the very processes that increased surplus production revealed the ever-greater inadequacy of the slave relation both as the means of securing the necessary combination of workers and of disciplining their activity to the technical and social requirements of the large-scale commercial production of sugar. Although the adoption of new techniques and efforts to maximize output integrated the division of labor on each plantation ever more closely and filled in the "empty spaces" in the potentially available labor time, the slave form limited the kind and amount of labor at the disposition of the planter, and hence the potential surplus product. Within the limits and conditions of the slave relation, the planter could increase the surplus product only by adapting the activity of a given body of workers to the technically determined conditions of production for a period of fixed duration that was itself subject to natural, technical, and social constraints. As the result of these structural limitations, planters were led to attempt to intensify the exploitation of labor and to discipline more effectively the productive activity of the slaves within the prevailing social and technical conditions. The integration of the slave laborers into the productive mechanism of the plantation was both the condition and the limit of the expansion of surplus production. In this context, labor discipline consisted of the attempt to bind the slaves to the social and technical conditions of production more effectively and to secure the maximum effort possible in conformity with the technical requirements of production.

Thus, the social relations of slave production were not only categories of political economy and value production. They were at the same time processes of social action through which work was imposed on the subject population. For the African bondsman, slave labor in the New World required a radical restructuring of the social relations of work under the most brutal conditions. In the plantation societies of the Americas, the goals and organization of work, as well as the role of work in daily life, were very different from what they had been in Africa. A complex system of political and legal sanctions established the domination of the master over the person of the slave and allowed him to control the labor of the latter. The master regarded the slave as a mere instrument of production, and the pattern of labor he imposed on the slave population formed the matrix of plantation life. Work was separated from ritual and community. Its organization and purposes were no longer defined by mutual obligation, kinship ties, or social duty. It was carried out independently of the subsistence needs of the laborers, and they had no personal interest in it. Instead, work was separated from all other human activities and subordinated to the alien claims of production embodied in the master, while all other aspects of life on the plantation were subordinated to work.[1]

Work assumed new forms and took on new social meanings for the African slave. Systematic production for the abstract market, not direct or indirect consumption, required that the enslaved adapt to a new organization and new purposes of production, appropriation, and distribution that were imposed and structured through the slave relation. The slaves were forced to adopt new work habits, adjust to new work discipline, and learn new values and incentives to work. They had to become accustomed to different motor habits and physiological rhythms, as well as a new range of social conduct. They had to learn to accept the authority of the master and his supervisors, to become proficient at new skills, and to work together in large gangs continuously and regularly at repetitive tasks within a developed division of labor for a period of fixed duration, day after day. The burden of this transition lay heavily on the minds and bodies of the enslaved, and it required a painful cultural adaptation on a vast scale—if not as the personal experience of each individual bondsman, then as the historical experience of the slave population as a whole.[2]

The socialization of African slaves and their descendants into the labor regime of the sugar plantation entailed subtle and complex historical processes of cultural change, accommodation, and resistance that were central both to their adaptation to the New World environment and to the formation of Afro-Caribbean identity and culture. Indeed, the adaptability and creativity of the enslaved made the plantation system possible. But more than this, the irreducible autonomy of the slaves' response to the conditions that confronted them not only presented a barrier to surplus production, but transformed the character of slave relations and the organization of production itself.[3]

With the assimilation of the slave population into the regime of plantation labor, the social relationships of work became increasingly important in shaping their lives. Yet, the slaves were not simply reducible to factors of production, nor was work a sphere of activity completely dominated by the master. Instead, the slave labor process was an arena where the cultural definitions of work and its relation to the larger matrix of plantation life were formed and contested. Europeans and

Africans encountered one another through the unequal relations of slavery and engaged in a day-to-day struggle, sometimes implicit, sometimes overt, over the organization of work and the norms and values it entailed. The master sought to discipline the slaves to the technical and social conditions of plantation production and to inculcate in them appropriate skills, attitudes, and values. But if the enslaved successfully adapted to the exigencies of the new labor regime, their behavior and values did not imitate those of their masters, nor were their motives, meanings, and goals identical to those of their masters. For their part, the slaves, in a complex mixture of accommodation and resistance, struggled both within and against the framework dictated to them, and in the course of their struggle, developed other values, ideas, and cultural forms that enabled them to assert their own purposes, needs, and rhythms in work and social life and to resist the definitions imposed by the masters.

The ability of the slaves to adapt to the routine of the plantation, to organize their own capacity for collective activity, and to physically carry out the tasks assigned to them even under the most adverse circumstances, discloses the contradictory process at the heart of New World slave systems. The labor process is not the one-dimensional creation of the master. Rather, on the one side, the master sought continually to appropriate this slave initiative and turn it to his purpose, while on the other side, this slave self-organization thrust itself against his domination. Within the context formed by antagonistic needs and purposes and by the asymmetrical relations of power, norms of behavior as well as workloads and routines to which both master and slave must acquiesce were established as "customary" and "normal" through this confrontation. The slave relation was simultaneously strengthened and weakened, while the ground of confrontation between master and slave shifted.

However, while the social relationships of work more and more became the focal point of slave resistance, their actions are not simply reducible to economic struggle in its narrow meaning. Rather, they also entailed more generalized and complex cultural resistance to the imposition of a whole way of life on a subject population. At issue in this conflict were not only the specific conditions of labor, but the broader question of the place of work in social life. For the slaves, the plantation was the locus of a network of solidarities and institutions, beliefs, and values that formed a distinctive and autonomous community and culture. Historically these were created and sustained by the slaves themselves, and slave resistance sought to protect and maintain them and to enforce their claims against the economic rationality of the plantation. In this context, specific struggles over work could shape and reinforce broader patterns of community solidarity and cultural resistance and vice versa, while the result of both was to establish and maintain a community and way of life not completely subordinated to the relations of work, property, and the social hierarchy of the plantation system. While the integration of the slave population into the relations and processes of the plantation enterprise was one pole of development, the other was the creation of the slave community and the formation and transformation of new solidarities among the slave group. The slave plantation embodied both enterprise and community and evolved through their mutual dependence and antagonism.[4]

Thus, the relation between master and slave was not static but underwent a continual process of evolution. The very ability of the masters to compel the slaves' participation in the new conditions of life and labor and the complexity and originality of the slaves' response altered the master-slave relation itself. New forms, meanings, and goals of social action emerged alongside older ones and became the focal points of a new constellation of conditions, needs, and capacities on both sides, which moved the struggle between them onto new terrain. This process of "creolization" expressed the historical limits of the master-slave relation and of slave production.


## The Hands and Feet of the Planter

Under slavery, as Max Weber pointed out, workers could not be selected according to technical abilities and needs. In the face of this structural constraint, planters were compelled to adapt the particular workers at hand to the specific requirements of the production process. The goal of the master was to use the slave labor force optimally within the given technical division of labor by making the best use of individual capacities over the course of the slaves' working lives. "It is your business . . . ," Dr. Collins enjoined the planters in his important *Practical Rules for the Management and Medical Treatment of Negro Slaves in the Sugar Colonies*, published anonymously in 1811, "to adapt their stations to their qualities and talents." The division of labor on the plantation was organized as a social process on the basis of the personal attributes of individual slaves. Factors such as age, gender, size, strength, dexterity, aptitude, and reliability entered into determining the distribution of slaves among the various occupations and activities of the sugar estate.[5]

However, even these efforts to rationalize the labor force were mitigated by incorporating the master's residence and the slave community into the plantation. A variety of tasks essential to the operation of the estate but not directly concerned with sugar production—ranging from domestic service to child care—emerged "naturally" in the course of plantation life and were performed by slaves. The division of labor thus became more complex, and a large number of slaves were absorbed in activities whose contribution to the plantation as a productive enterprise was minimal. The difficulties these activities presented for the rationalization of the labor force were exacerbated by the decline of the slave trade to the French Lesser Antilles during the second half of the eighteenth century and its abolition in the 1830s. Without the opportunity to appropriate new slaves, providing for the daily and generational reproduction of the labor force assumed greater importance in the social and economic organization of the plantation, while the demographic composition of the slave population raised on the estate did not coincide with the demand for labor.[6]

Only a portion of the slaves attached to the estate were actually engaged in agricultural production. According to Sainte Croix, 210 slaves were required to produce 450 hogsheads of sugar. But of these, fewer than half were actually engaged in sugar manufacture. The remainder consisted of the aged and infirm, caretakers, wet nurses, children unable to work, and so forth. Though not complete in detail, the report by the planter de Lavigne showed a larger proportion of active workers among his 200 slaves. He recorded that 63 were younger than fourteen years of age; 102 were workers between 14 and 60 years old employed in agriculture; 14 were artisans, drivers, or domestics; and 21 were over 60 years of age and too old to work. Jabrun, in the neighboring colony of Guadeloupe, had 154 slaves more or less evenly divided between men and women. Of these, 104 were between the ages of 14 and 60 and formed the active working population of the plantation. Counted among these were 65 slaves engaged in agriculture, 2 drivers, 3 masons, 2 carpenters, 2 coopers, 2 cart drivers, 2 refiners, 3 herdsmen, 6 domestics, 2 nurses (*gardes-malades*), 4 sick in the hospital, and 8 women pregnant or lying in. The remaining slaves included 35 children under 14 years of age and 15 slaves over 60 years old. In another account, de la Cornillère describes a plantation in Martinique that cultivated 120 carrés of land and produced 521 boucauts of sugar annually (1 boucaut = 489.5 kilograms). There were 255 slaves living on this plantation, but only 54 men and 56 women worked in the fields. There were also 9 skilled workers. The remainder included 18 boys, 18 girls, 6 domestics, 1 midwife, 2 nurses (*hospitalières*), 7 herdsmen, 18 infirm and aged, and 28 small boys and 28 small girls too young to leave the quarters. The smaller plantations were similarly handicapped by the high proportion of unproductive labor. Cassius Linval owned 56 slaves, but only 25 of them were adult workers between the ages of 14 and 60 years, and it is not known how many of these were suited for heavy labor.[7]

The productive force of the slaves resident on the estate was organized and coordinated by the gang system, and the gangs or *ateliers* provided the means through which work was imposed on the slaves from childhood to old age. The number, size, and composition of the gangs varied from plantation to plantation, depending particularly on the size of the estate. On the majority of plantations, the field slaves were typically divided into two gangs. The adults formed the great gang (*grand atelier*), while adolescents and older children formed the second gang (*petit atelier*). However, many planters felt that this arrangement was insufficient. Strength and ability could not be inferred from age. Collins wrote that the consequence of this division is that "either the weaker negroes must retard the progress of the stronger ones, or your drivers, insensible of the cause of their backwardness, or not weighing it properly, will incessantly urge them, either with stripes or threats, to keep up with the others; by which means they are overwrought, and compelled to resort to the sick-house." He concluded that the solution to this problem was to divide the slaves into a greater number of gangs according to their physical capacity. "In order that the weak may not work too much nor the strong too little, it is advisable to divide your force into a greater number of sections or gangs." Such an arrangement created more homogeneity within each gang and allowed for more effective supervision, though it also complicated the task of management. There were thus a variety of arrangements and combinations in use as each planter sought to maximize the force of the laborers at his disposal and make the most effective use of his supervisory staff, and, of course, gangs could be combined or divided or individuals shifted from one gang to another according to particular circumstances.[8]

The *grand atelier* was the pride of the plantation, and its physical strength was the motive force of the production process. Ideally, this gang was made up of adult slaves of both sexes and was selected on the basis of strength and ability. The *grand atelier* ordinarily comprised a bit more than one-third of the total number of slaves on the plantation. On very large estates, these slaves could be divided into two separate gangs to permit separate tasks to be performed simultaneously and for administrative and supervisory purposes. Women generally outnumbered men in the *grand atelier*. This reflected, in part, the greater proportion of females than males in the slave population in Martinique, and, in part, the demand for other types of labor for slaves of each gender on the plantation. The need for refiners, coopers, carpenters, masons, blacksmiths, and other skilled workers as well as slave drivers reduced the number of men available for work in the fields, whereas domestic service provided female slaves with their sole major alternative to the field gang. When a slave became too old or too weak to continue to work in the fields, he or she was given less demanding work such as watching over buildings, cornfields, and provision grounds, or else was retired completely from labor, though that individual was often still regarded as part of the *grand atelier* from an administrative point of view.[9]

The most difficult jobs on the plantation, those requiring strength and skill, were assigned to the *grand atelier*. These included digging the cane holes, planting cane and provisions, trashing heavy canes, woodcutting, feeding the mill, and carrying green bagasse from the mill to the drying shed. Beyond this, road construction and repair as well as building stone walls were counted among their duties. Sainte Croix also included stoking the furnace of the boiling house and skimming the evaporating pans among the jobs assigned to the great gang. These were two of the most physically exhausting jobs on the plantation, and females were exempt from them. The great gang always performed the agricultural tasks on the plantation collectively under the supervision of the overseers and drivers. On large plantations, a gang of between thirty and fifty slaves, each equipped with a hoe or a cane knife, formed a single line across the field with a driver at each end and the overseer in the middle. The line advanced step by step as each slave completed the required task and then moved ahead to repeat it. The overseer and the drivers followed behind, inspecting the work, shouting and threatening, exhorting the slaves on, and, if necessary, reprimanding or whipping the lazy and insubordinate to prevent delays in completing the day's assignment or to punish some serious mistake.[10]

The second gang or *petit atelier* was composed of slaves who were not physically capable of working in the great gang. These included the aged and other adults who were not strong enough for strenuous field work, nursing mothers, those convalescing from childbirth or illness, and most importantly, older children and adolescents between the ages of ten and sixteen. If not working in conjunction with the great gang, as happened during planting, the second gang worked under the supervision of a driver, often a woman, and was charged with the lighter tasks on the plantation, including planting "seed," cleaning and banking young cane, weeding, bundling the cut cane stalks, helping to transport the cane to the mill, and carrying dried bagasse to the furnace in the boiling house. On larger plantations, this gang may have been subdivided into two groups on the basis of strength and assigned to lighter or heavier tasks respectively. Children too big for the grass gang, but not strong enough for the second gang, and convalescents were often employed in jobs such as light weeding and spreading manure over the cane pieces under the supervision of an older woman slave. After two or three years in the *petit atelier*, the young slave was sent to the *grand atelier*, usually between the ages of fourteen and sixteen, when he or she was capable of working with the adults.[11]

Finally, the grass, or weeding, gang, included the children of the estate from the time they left the nursery at the age of five or six years until they graduated to one of the adult gangs. They were gathered under the supervision of an old woman and assigned a number of light tasks to perform, chief among which were cutting grass to feed the livestock and weeding the cane pieces. Beyond these jobs, the grass gang was expected to assist the great gang during planting by throwing manure into the cane holes. The children were supervised, instructed, and encouraged in their efforts by a negro woman experienced in all manner of fieldwork and "armed with a pliant twig, more to create dread, than inflict chastisement." Aside from the practical advantages to be drawn from the employment of the "supple hand of the negro child" in the grass gang, its other purpose was to initiate these children into the discipline of collective labor and to acquaint them with the skills and practices of the plantation routine. Planters feared that if the slave children were neglected and left to their own devices even at a young age, they might acquire habits prejudicial to their future reliability as laborers. Instead, industry, order, and discipline must be carefully cultivated among them. Collins was explicit about the evils inherent in an idle childhood and their remedy. Such small slaves, he cautioned, "for want of other employment, would escape from their nurses, and employ themselves in mischief, such as in breaking canes, or pilfering from absent negroes, or in setting fire to their houses, and in many such amusements, by the practice of which, they are initiated into early roguery and become adepts in the science in time. To prevent this, let them be employed; for employment is the parent of honesty as idleness is of vice." The idiom of this Jamaica planter may have differed from that of his French compatriots, but the sentiment grew from the soil of slavery itself and was common to those who had appropriated their labor force from birth to old age and death. After the children were indoctrinated into collective labor, obedience to authority, and the routines of the plantation they were graduated into the adolescent and adult gangs according to their age, gender, strength, and dexterity. Thus, the grass gang provided a continual supply of creole slaves formed from infancy to the regimen of plantation labor. In it were shaped the field hands, drivers, cattlemen, mule men, carpenters, coopers, masons, and refiners on whose toil the planter would depend in years to come.[12]

Not all of the work on the plantation was done by gang labor. Slaves also performed a variety of more specialized and skilled jobs that were required by the processes of sugar manufacture. The integration of manufacturing operations into the sugar plantation created complexity and diversity in its division of labor and established a hierarchy among the laborers. The skilled slaves and those with specialized jobs had greater personal responsibility in their work and enjoyed greater autonomy in its execution than did field slaves. Many were exempt from direct supervision and had only minimal contact with those in authority. While it was necessary that such slaves function within—and, to some degree, accept—the norms and routines of the plantation, the master was in large measure dependent on their knowledge, initiative, and judgment for the successful operation of the estate. The acquisition of skills allowed these slaves to appropriate aspects of the work routine. Instead of being simply the instruments of the planter's will, their command of essential techniques and the master's dependence on their abilities provided them with a voice in determining their conditions of work as well as the means to contest what they considered to be the excessive demands of the planter. In addition, slave artisans received greater material rewards and had more opportunity to engage in what Sidney Mintz has termed "economic self-defense" than did the slaves in the *ateliers*. The acquisition of skills enhanced individuals' chances of acquiring cash and acquiring property within slavery and gave them an advantage on the market for their services or their product should they become free. No less importantly, the acquisition of such skills also opened an avenue for the exercise of individual capabilities and an assertion of individual worth and self-respect in a system that attempted to deny them.[13]

The mill and the refinery together employed between ten and twenty slaves at a time, depending on the size of the estate. The mill was supervised by the *maître du moulin*, a post to which great prestige was attached. This slave was responsible for the arrival and unloading of the carts, preventing the mules and oxen from being overworked, maintaining of mill and the other equipment, and the care of the stables. The other slaves in the mill were under his supervision. These were generally females aided by slaves who "lacked intelligence and strength." One woman fed the cane into the mill, while another took out the bagasse. One or two young boys were charged with keeping the table of the mill and the gutter carrying the juice to the boiling house free from debris. Two or three women carried the bagasse from the mill to the drying shed and the dried bagasse to the boiling house to be used as fuel.[14]

Work in the boiling house was difficult and hazardous. It demanded long hours of constant attention without rest and involved prolonged exposure to heat, humidity, and the stench of boiling cane juice, yet it had its rewards and was prized by the slaves. According to one author: "The business of a boiler, during the crop, I consider as the most unhealthy of any to which a negro can be applied, and yet so fond they are of heat, and of the privileges of the boiling-house, which comprise unlimited use of hot liquor and sugar, that it is pretty generally coveted." The number of slaves employed in the boiling house depended, of course, on the size of the operation and the organization of the shifts. Ordinarily, two stokers were necessary to keep the fires under the boilers going. This was an extremely fatiguing job. Only the strongest slaves were assigned to it, and it had to be rotated every few hours. Inside the boiling house, four male slaves, including the refiner, worked at the kettles. Skimming the cane juice was also physically demanding work, and only the most robust slaves were given this job. In addition, there were perhaps two or three slaves charged with taking care of the sugar after it was struck.[15]

The head refiner, or "boiler" as he was called in the English colonies, was the most important slave on the plantation. The fate of the entire crop, and thus profit or loss for the estate, was in his hands. The entire operation of manufacturing the sugar took place under his guidance and demanded his constant attention around the clock during the harvest season. He supervised his assistants in the refinery, and the furnace, mill, *cases à bagasses*, and *purgerie* were under his overall command.

The job required intimate knowledge of the processes of sugar making and the particularities of the cane juice, furnace, and kettles. The head refiner had to judge the quality of the cane juice and, therefore, be familiar with "the way the cane has been raised and treated; the kind of soil it grows on; if that soil has been high or low manured; the age of the cane; the species it is of; whether it has been topped short or long in the cutting; if it has been arrowed, bored, or rat-eaten." He had to prepare and apply the temper according to the quality of the cane juice. He determined how long the juice boiled in each of the kettles, supervised its transfer from one to another, and, most importantly, decided when the sugar was ready to strike. He also had to see to the proper crystallization, packing, and draining of the sugar. In the absence of scientific instruments and methods of sugar refining, control over these processes depended on individual skill, judgment, and a wide range of empirical knowledge. The refiner's job was difficult and entailed great responsibility. If he failed to demonstrate the requisite skill or trustworthiness, the consequences for the estate could be severe. "The fairest fruits of a cane field have been destroyed, perverted, and rendered a mass of thick, slimy, dark, sour, cloddy, unprofitable, unmarketable substance (disappointing the expectations of the overseer), by an improper choice of such a member, or having a villain for conducting such a business. The labor of the negroes and stock have often been lost by this means; the trash-house consumed or emptied, shipments disappointed, and adulterated juices sent to the distilling-house, where it will scarcely pay for its boiling," lamented Roughley.[16]

Despite growing scientific interest and inquiry, for all practical purposes knowledge of the techniques of sugar refining remained a craft secret and could only be acquired by long practice and experience. This knowledge was the property of the slaves whose permanence on the estate was assured, and in a society organized by the most extreme social and racial hierarchy, the exercise of the refiner's art came to be seen as their special province. Wrote one observer, "the negro boilers must be more perfect in their business than any white can pretend to be." Although the white sugar master nominally oversaw the boiling house, the slave refiner was in practical control of its activities.

It often occurs, that this man has a very general knowledge of the method of making good sugar, from almost every cane-piece on the estate, is conversant with the soils, the management the canes have received, and when the overseer may be in a dilemma, knows how to correct some perverseness in the cane liquor. The useful slave may by his ready experience, explain the cause, and apply a remedy to prevent its bad consequences. The head boiler and the boatswain of the mill are the leading, ostensible, and confidential persons about the works in crop time, while sugar is manufacturing.

His technical qualification made the slave refiner indispensable to the operation of the estate, and the master was obliged to concede control over the most strategic aspect of the labor process to this craftsman.[17]

The highly subjective judgment and skills of his craft were the source of the slave refiner's power and prestige. The slave's domination of his craft placed the master in a dependent position. The refiner was thereby able to compel an exceptional degree of autonomy and control over work, and despite his servile status, delimit if not challenge the master's authority. As Roughley expressed the generally held opinion: "It will be well for overseers not to chide or check the head boiler much, except a glaring fault occurs in him; he may become despirited, diffident, and careless by so doing." To prevent such friction, an elaborate etiquette marked the interaction between the slave refiner and the white sugar master that expressed the several inequalities in their relationship and the ways in which each was constrained to defer to the other, as Reed illustrates with an example from a Cuban refinery.

The diplomacy that takes place between Sambo and the master is edifying. Some old negro, who may have worked on the estate for twenty years, and who knows all about this particular battery, goes to the teache [the last boiling pan in the train, where the juice reaches its highest concentration before being crystallized], when—taking a little of the syrup between his finger and thumb—he draws it out in a thread, and infers from the appearance of the latter that the juice has been boiled enough. Meantime the sugar master is away though accessible; smoking his cigarette. Sambo tells him the skip is ready; but it would never do for the sugar master to seem to be taught by Sambo. He knows that a few moments will make no practical difference, so he pulls out his watch, and affects to look with much edifying mystery at the dial. At length he lets Pancho, or Pedro, adjust the gutters leading from the teache to the cooler ten feet away, and the skip of emptying the teache is effected.

This ritualized behavior delineates the spheres of authority of the slave refiner and the white sugar master. The sugar master defers to the superior practical knowledge of the slave and does not interfere with his activity. The abstract homogeneous time of the watch cannot be abstracted from and imposed back on a material production process regulated by "natural" time. On the other hand, the illusion of scientific measurement in a totally empirical process upholds the pretense that the slave's expertise is secondary if not inessential. It masks the social domination that the slave in turn acknowledges by going through the ceremony of the sugar master's making the final decision.[18]

The slaves were not powerless in this game. They carefully prevented the whites from learning the secrets of their trade and protected their position in the production process. If the conventions and usages of the boiling house were violated, the slave refiner had the ultimate sanction at his disposal. "Even in the old times of slavery," recollected Reed, "the master or estate proprietor was obliged to humour his slaves whilst the boiling season lasted. . . . should [the boiler] have been spited in any way, he had the means at command for taking revenge out of his owner's sugar. A few tablespoonsful of lemon-juice squeezed into the clarifier, or the grand copper, or the striking teache, and the ruin was accomplished. By this simple process the crystallization of the sugar would be almost completely destroyed."[19]

The strategic position of the slave refiner calls for a reexamination of the prejudice in favor of the brute character of slave labor that has become almost axiomatic in much historical writing. Moreno Fraginals, for example, suggests that the clarifier was too complicated for slaves to use. However, opening a spigot does not seem to be an overly difficult operation, and deciding when to turn it off also seems rather straightforward, given the more difficult and subtle judgments made regularly by the slaves in the boiling house. Yet when it is recognized that with the perfect clarification of the juice, the rest of the refining process would be reduced to the extremely simple operation of evaporation, the argument that the ignorance and awkwardness of the slave made him an obstacle to technological innovation must be seriously questioned. Rather, it becomes at least plausible that the slave's desire to protect established customs and norms in production provided the motive for him to resist such change. To claim that individuals were incapable of performing certain tasks because they were slaves both misreads the historical evidence and misunderstands the nature of social relations, that they really are *relations* and not attributes of individuals. (Still less convincing are attempts to continue this line of argument by ascribing the systemic features of slavery to the characteristics of the slaves: slavery was backward and inefficient because the slaves were backward and inefficient. If one persists in this methodological approach, it is but a short step to the alternative theoretical formulation: the problem was not that the subject population was enslaved but that it was African. While the substantive character of this latter formulation this may be disquieting, from a logical point of view it at least has the virtue of avoiding the tautological character of the first proposition).[20]

In addition to the specialized workers in the mill and refinery, the sugar estate required the services of carpenters, coopers, smiths, masons, and wheelwrights. The large estates tended to become self-sufficient productive units. It was cheaper for the master to train slaves whose labor was always at his disposal than to hire outsiders to do it. While this practice may have degraded manual labor in society generally, the acquisition of special skills was an important economic and social resource for the slaves. As a consequence of the skilled nature of their work, artisans tended to form a more stable and closed group than the domestics or the field slaves. Apprenticeships were often long and represented a great expenditure that would be lost if the slave were sent back to the fields. Craftsmen whose work was seasonal, such as refiners or coopers, ordinarily assisted the other artisans during periods when their particular skills were not needed. However, they could also find themselves working in the fields, either temporarily, for some special task, or permanently if they failed to perform their duties to their master's satisfaction. The permanence and stability of the group of artisans depended, among other things, on the size of the estate, the planting and manufacturing routine, and the patterns of recruitment and formation of the labor force.[21]

The livestock of the estate represented a large portion of the proprietor's capital and were crucial to the operation of the plantation. Tending them was a full-time job. Roughley stressed that the herdsmen should specialize in caring for the cattle and mules in and out of crop and not be drafted into other labor. The head cattle and mule men were charged not only with the care of the animals, but their integration into the work process as well. It was their duty to organize the transport of a constant supply of cane from the fields to the mill and to carry the barrels of sugar to the wharf. They had to select the animals most suited to the fields, mill, or roadwork; see to it that proper harnesses and other equipment were ready for them; spell tired animals and have others ready to replace them; keep them fed and rested; and treat their injuries. They were assisted in these duties by cattle and mule boys. These were preferably creole youth who knew how to lead and yoke cattle and ride and tackle mules. Each boy was charged with the care, harnessing, and working of a number of individual animals assigned to him. The head cattle and mule men had to keep close check not only on the animals but on the men in their charge. Carters were noted for pilfering the sugar and rum they carried down to the wharf or the supplies, especially salt, they carried back up to the estate. Similarly, mule drivers were notorious for taking mules off the property or using them for private purposes. It was the responsibility of the head mule and cattle men to exercise vigilance and prevent these practices.[22]

Finally, the planters' love of luxury and desire for prestige could swell the ranks of domestic servants. The duties of the house slaves included cleaning, cooking, sewing, laundering, and other domestic chores, such as making clothes for slaves without wives. On a large plantation, the master and each member of his family ordinarily had a personal servant. The rest of the household staff typically included a cook, two washerwomen, two or three seamstresses, and two or three women to run errands. The domestics were generally creoles born on the property, and mulatto girls were favored for household chores. These slaves had opportunities for better-quality food, clothing, and shelter for themselves and their families as well as having less arduous work to do than did the field slaves. Household slaves had closer personal contact with the master and his family and were thereby both in a position to win rewards by gaining their favor and more exposed to their caprice. For many, household service was a road to freedom. Perhaps because of closer personal relations with the master and the greater opportunity to amass savings, domestics were often given their freedom or were able to save enough to purchase it. However, Gabriel Debien, in his study of the plantation "l'Anse-à-l'Ane" in the eighteenth century, suggests that more typical were household slaves who served faithfully without attempting to gain their freedom, knowing that they would be treated as freed on reaching their sixtieth birthday.[23]

The craftsmen, mechanics, and domestic servants formed what were in many respects privileged groups among the slaves, and their presence increased the internal differentiation within the slave population. They commonly lived apart from the other slaves and enjoyed better food, housing, and clothing. There were considerable avenues for mobility between groups of slaves on the plantation. Slaves could pass from the fields into domestic service, a path particularly open to females, or if one were particularly talented or intelligent, to apprenticeship in a trade. Jamaican planter Monk Lewis suggests that mulatto children were always employed as craftsmen if male or as domestics if female, but never as field hands. On the other hand, Orlando Patterson, basing himself on several Jamaican sources, cautions that field hands preferred the independence and stability of their position to the constant daily contact with the master and insecurity of domestic service. Craft labor, however, appears to have been universally aspired to. The advantages that these groups of slaves enjoyed may have created an ambivalent but not necessarily conservative response to the slave system on their part. For if they had privileges to protect, intimate contact with the master and his family gave them insights into the nature and limits of power, while it also exposed them to the arbitrariness and eccentricity of those in authority. Indeed, the contradiction between individual dignity and self-worth on the one hand and slave status on the other may have been experienced more palpably by these slaves than others as numerous and varied acts of poisoning, arson, and revolt committed by them throughout the Americas attest.[24]

## Rhythms of Work: Economy of Time

The sugar plantation engaged the slaves in a year-round cycle of work that followed the rhythm of the crop. Planting and harvesting dominated the agricultural year and defined its division. However, the agrarian rhythm formed by this alternation was not simply natural but rather was manipulated to make full use of the productive capacity of the slave gang over the entire course of the planting and harvest seasons. As has been discussed previously, the slaves had to be supported by the estate whether they were working or not, but they contributed to its revenue only while they were producing commodities. In addition, idle hands were the enemy of every slave owner, and maintaining discipline and regular work habits among the slaves was their constant concern. Consequently, an agricultural routine was adopted that minimized the effects of the natural seasonal break while the crop matured and kept the slaves continuously engaged in sugar production throughout the year. The rotation of the fields was carefully planned so that over the fifteen- to eighteen-month maturation period of the sugar cane, the planting of one crop could be constantly alternated with the harvesting of a previous crop (see chapter 5). It took several months to plant and several months to harvest the crop, and one followed on the other as quickly as possible. In this way, the planter could make greater use of the productive potential of the slave labor force and obtain an annual crop while increasing the yield within the natural limits of the planting and harvest seasons.[25]

The demand for labor was most intensive during the harvest season, but even in the so-called "dead season" between harvests the slaves were kept continually busy with a variety of tasks essential to the operation of the plantation. These included not only planting and caring for the cane, but auxiliary tasks (*petits travaux*) such as clearing new fields; planting provisions; carrying manure to the fields; ditching; building and maintaining roads, buildings, and animal pens; cleaning canals; building and repairing carts; and other types of repairs and maintenance. If these jobs were not enough to keep the slaves occupied, new work was created for them to do. Such a routine encouraged the generalization rather than the specialization of slave labor. Individual slaves were constantly shifted from one task to another and thus acquired a broad range of general skills, but at the same time this retarded the development of the division of labor on the plantation and therefore the collective level of skill and the productive capacity of the slave gang as a group. Furthermore, although the dead season was in principle less demanding than the harvest season, this regime harnessed the slaves to a pattern of year-round drudgery that dulled their incentive and efficiency and exposed them to the burdens of prolonged fatigue and overwork. This situation was aggravated when heavy rains or extended periods of drought impeded work during the off-season. There then followed a push to make up for lost time and to complete these tasks before the harvest season renewed its claims on the full energy of the labor force.[26]

The unit of labor time in the Caribbean sugar colonies was the day. This was a variable, natural unit of measurement lasting from sunrise to sunset. Marking the length of the parts of the working day depended on the judgment of the overseer. Beyond the technical problem of measurement, this could lead to conflict between the overseer, who was under pressure to produce as much sugar as possible, and the master, who, particularly after the abolition of the slave trade, desired to protect the well-being of his slaves. The divisions of the day were signaled by the crack of the overseer's whip, the blowing of a whistle or conch shell, or, more rarely on large plantations, the ringing of a bell. Mechanical timekeeping was conspicuous by its absence in the French Antilles. Indeed, even bells were scarce, and the elaborate system utilizing the clerical hours of the church bells to mark the working day, described by Moreno Fraginals for Cuba, appears to have been unknown in Martinique. According to Schoelcher's description: "The whip is the bell of the plantations. It announces the moment of awakening and that of retirement.

The whip marks the hour of work, and also it marks the hour of rest. It is to the sound of the whip that punishes the guilty that the people of the plantation are assembled morning and evening for prayer. The day of death is the only one where the slave enjoys respite without being awakened by the whip." Domination and time, symbol and act, are joined and woven into the texture of everyday life. Through the whip, emblem of the planter's authority and the physical subjugation of the slave, the temporal organization of the plantation is imposed on the lives of the enslaved as an external and alien demand.[27]

In the French colonies, work in the fields before sunrise and after sunset, as well as from noon until two in the afternoon, for whatever reason was forbidden by law. Although it was sometimes attempted during the harvest season, fieldwork done in the dark was both dangerous and difficult to supervise, and this legislation more or less coincided with common practice in the colonies, according to Baron Mackau, a former governor of Martinique. To take maximum advantage of the daylight hours, the slaves were awakened before dawn. After assembly for communal prayers, roll call, and the assignment of the day's tasks, they went off to the fields, accompanied by the overseers (*économe*) and the drivers (*commandeurs*). The slaves' workday began between 5:00 and 6:00 AM with the rising of the sun. At eight or nine o'clock, they stopped work for between thirty and forty-five minutes while breakfast was brought to them in the fields. Work was then resumed and lasted until midday. Work in the fields was avoided during the hottest part of the day, and the slaves had the time from noon until two o'clock to themselves to eat and rest. The slaves were free to return to their cabins, and many of them devoted this time to the cultivation of their private garden plots or provision grounds if these were located near enough to the fields. At two o'clock, they were summoned back for the afternoon work session, which lasted until five o'clock in the summer and sunset in the winter. At the end of the workday, and sometimes during the midday break as well, each slave was required to pick up a bundle of guinea grass for fodder for the animals and carry it back to the animal pens. There was a final assembly and an evening prayer, though this was not as regular or as formal as the morning assembly. The remaining time belonged to the slaves. Each household prepared its own evening meal. The slaves were then relatively free, and all that was required for the remainder of the evening was that general order and tranquility be maintained.[28]

Thus, the effective working day spent in the fields normally lasted between nine and ten hours, depending on the amount of daylight. Further, the technical division of labor left gaps in the working day, and Schoelcher reported that there was much more give and take in the time discipline of the sugar plantations in Martinique than in a European factory. Not infrequently he witnessed the afternoon work session begin at 2:15 or 2:20 rather than at 2:00 PM. In addition, many planters, especially after the end of the slave trade, were very attentive to rest periods and meals and thought them to be essential for the efficiency and well-being of their *ateliers*. However, to the time spent in fieldwork must be added the time spent going to and from the work site and carrying fodder. At the time of the passage of the Law of July 18, 1845, Mackau argued that, contrary to common usage, this time should not be taken out of the slaves' rest periods, while a growing number of planters thought that carrying fodder merely added to the fatigue of the slaves after a long day's work and ought to be given over to a special gang. Nevertheless, both pro- and anti-slavery commentators agreed that this regime did not make excessive demands on the strength and health of the slaves even in the tropical climate. In Schoelcher's words, "the slaves do what they must, and today the masters demand no more of them than they can do."[29]

The "natural" agrarian rhythm of the daily plantation routine was interrupted during the harvest season when the industrial character of sugar manufacture emerged and revealed its dominion over the organization of the entire crop cycle. The harvest season (*roulaison*) was the busiest time of the year and mobilized the entire labor force of the plantation. "The work of making sugar from cane juice is most anxious," warns Reed. "It admits of no irregularity, no laziness. The crop being ripe will not wait long without deterioration, and the juice once expressed will not keep twenty minutes without fermenting if proper treatment not be followed." During this period, the legal restrictions on the working day were suspended, and the slaves were harnessed to the continuous mechanical movement of the mill and the flow of the boiling house where work went on ceaselessly around the clock.[30]

Both the Royal Ordinance of October 15, 1786, which regulated the length of the working day, and the Law of July 18, 1845, which supplemented it, explicitly distinguished between ordinary work and the extraordinary circumstances of the sugar harvest, which absolutely demanded continuity of work, and specifically excluded the latter from the normal prohibitions. The Law of July 18, 1845, or Mackau Law, as it was known, attempted to limit the working day to the period between six in the morning and six in the evening under ordinary circumstances and required rest periods totaling two-and-one-half hours during this time. During the harvest season, when continuous labor was necessary, the maximum amount of labor time could be prolonged by two hours and the hours of work could be transferred from the day to the night, so long as the legal maximum was not exceeded during each twenty-four-hour period and the obligatory rest periods were observed. If work was required during days or hours when it was not obligatory, this legislation prescribed a minimum salary of ten centimes per hour or five francs per month for both male and female slaves.[31]

In some parts of Martinique, attention had to be devoted entirely to sugar production to the exclusion of other activities during the harvest season. Sainte Croix has left an account of the division of labor and number of slaves involved in the harvest on a plantation producing 450 hogsheads of sugar annually. Twenty slaves, supervised by the *économe* and the *commandeurs*, cut the cane. In half a day, twenty cutters could cut about ten *grandes* of cane. (A *grande* was the quantity of cane necessary to provide enough juice to fill the *grande*, the largest kettle in the boiling train. Thus, the *grande* served as the measure both of the amount of cane and the volume of juice. One *grande* yielded enough syrup for seven or eight *formes* of raw sugar weighing between fifty-two and fifty-four livres.) The twenty cane-cutters required ten other slaves to handle the cut stalks and load them on the mules or oxcarts to be transported to the mill. Eight or ten mule drivers or two or three men driving oxcarts were necessary to keep the cane flowing quickly and steadily to the mill. During this period, the maximum effort was demanded of the slave gang, and work in the fields was often prolonged until total darkness made it impossible to continue.[32]

While the available daylight limited work in the fields, this was not the case in the mill and the refinery. During the harvest, night and Sunday work were a necessity, placing an enormous strain on the work force, especially on large plantations. Although night work seems to have been exceptional on small and medium plantations, on large estates work in the refinery continued around the clock without interruption. To maintain this effort, the *atelier* was divided into three groups called *quarts*. According to Sainte Croix, on successive days each of these was rotated from the fields to the mill and refinery, where work went on around the clock in seven-and-a-half-hour shifts. Ideally, the slaves worked one night every five to eight days, depending on the size of the gang. Sainte Croix suggests that 150 slaves were necessary to organize a complete system of shifts and to make sure that no slave worked more than seven-and-a-half hours a day in the mill. Planters with fewer slaves had to restrict themselves to manufacturing sugar only during the day. However, this was an exceptionally large number of active workers for Martinique, and other sources indicate that around-the-clock shifts were carried on with smaller complements of slaves.[33]

This schedule placed an enormous physical burden on the slaves. Depending on the size of the gang and the schedule of rotation, a full day's work in the fields during the most demanding period of the year could be followed by a shift in the mill or refinery at night as well. During the harvest season, eighteen to twenty hours of intensive effort without a break was not uncommon. The refiners in particular were subjected to long and exhausting hours to guarantee the continuity of the manufacturing process. The need to supervise the preparation and application of the temper, the continual skimming of the kettles, and striking the sugar required their constant attention day and night. This unrelenting pace could continue for weeks on end. The exhausting *veillées*, as the night shifts were known, led to fatigue, and negligence and mistakes that threatened both sugar and men were inevitable. The result was often horrible accidents as tired and overworked slaves got a hand or arm caught in the cylinders of the mill or fell into the cauldrons of boiling cane juice.[34]

Despite the enormous and prolonged effort demanded of the slaves, crop time also had its rewards and was the high point of the agricultural year. "Even in the days of slavery," writes Reed, it "has been described as a period of mingled hard work and hilarity, during which man and beast—animals even to swine—grow fat." This was particularly true on small and medium plantations where there was no night work. As compensation for their extra efforts during this season, the slaves were given a ration of sugar and syrup, and the harvest afforded ample opportunity for the slaves to supplement this ration on their own initiative as well. The end of the harvest was an occasion for feasting and dancing. Money was given to the slaves according to their ability to work. Sheep were slaughtered and divided among the slaves, as were vegetables, syrup, and other rewards. The celebration culminated with two days of dancing.[35]

Superimposed on the agricultural calendar was the religious calendar. The Edict of 1685 (the Code Noir) and the Royal Ordinance of 1786 exempted the slaves from labor on Sundays and holidays, and according to all available accounts, these provisions were generally observed. There were, however, fewer religious holidays in the colonies than in France. In prerevolutionary Saint-Domingue, Dutrône calculated that 52 Sundays and 16 feast days, in addition to about 17 rainy days, left the planter with 280 work days a year. (This compares with Kuczynski's figure of 250 days for ancien régime France and 300 days for Protestant Britain.) After the French Revolution, divine virtues gave way to secular ones, and the number of religious holidays was reduced to four: Christmas, Ascension Day, Assumption, and All Saints' Day. In addition, the slaves were customarily given all or part of Saturday off to work in their own gardens and grow their own food. These regulations were suspended during the harvest season, when the demands of production were continuous. The days remaining after the deduction of these exemptions were available for the work of the plantation.[36]

The temporal requirements of sugar production coincided imperfectly with the social relations of slavery. The intensive overwork of the harvest combined with other periods when there was little to do and the work routines were much more flexible. There was careful time discipline, but time was not an abstract and homogeneous standard external to the processes of material production. Instead, time was determined by the physical requirements of sugar making. Indeed, the measurement of tasks by the *grande*—a necessarily imprecise measure depending on the relation between the amount of cane cut, ground, and boiled—suggests the domination of physical processes over the temporal organization of the labor process. Under these conditions, economy of time could only mean that the "natural" temporal limits of these processes were extended and more juice was processed more quickly. However, the rationalization of labor time was not possible. There was no economy of labor time. Instead the laborers had to be regimented to perform the given tasks at hand.

Because the labor force was appropriated as slaves, the number of workers and the quantity of labor time available over the crop cycle was fixed, and the potential output was limited. Under these circumstances, and particularly as changing market conditions put a greater premium on efficiency, there was pressure on planters to manage the time at their disposal effectively. According to Dutrône: "This sum of the working days and the force of the Negroes being determined, their product is also necessarily determined. From this it is easy to see that the time which is lost by not seizing what could be done in the day is lost forever. The Master who governs must handle [*ménager*] time and the force of his Negroes with the greatest care and make the best use of them." Already in the second half of the eighteenth century, the planters in the French Caribbean demonstrated a concern with the systematic measurement and regulation of the activities of the slaves and the rationalization of sugar production. Dutrône pioneered the attempt to establish precise technical control over the labor process (see Figure 7.1). In monthly and annual tables, he kept a careful daily inventory of the number of slaves and their ages, sex, occupations, and condition. He then followed each step in the process of sugar production and recorded the number of slaves employed in each department of the plantation, the amount of work done each day in each sector, and information on temperature and rainfall as well as on the final product and its price. The master

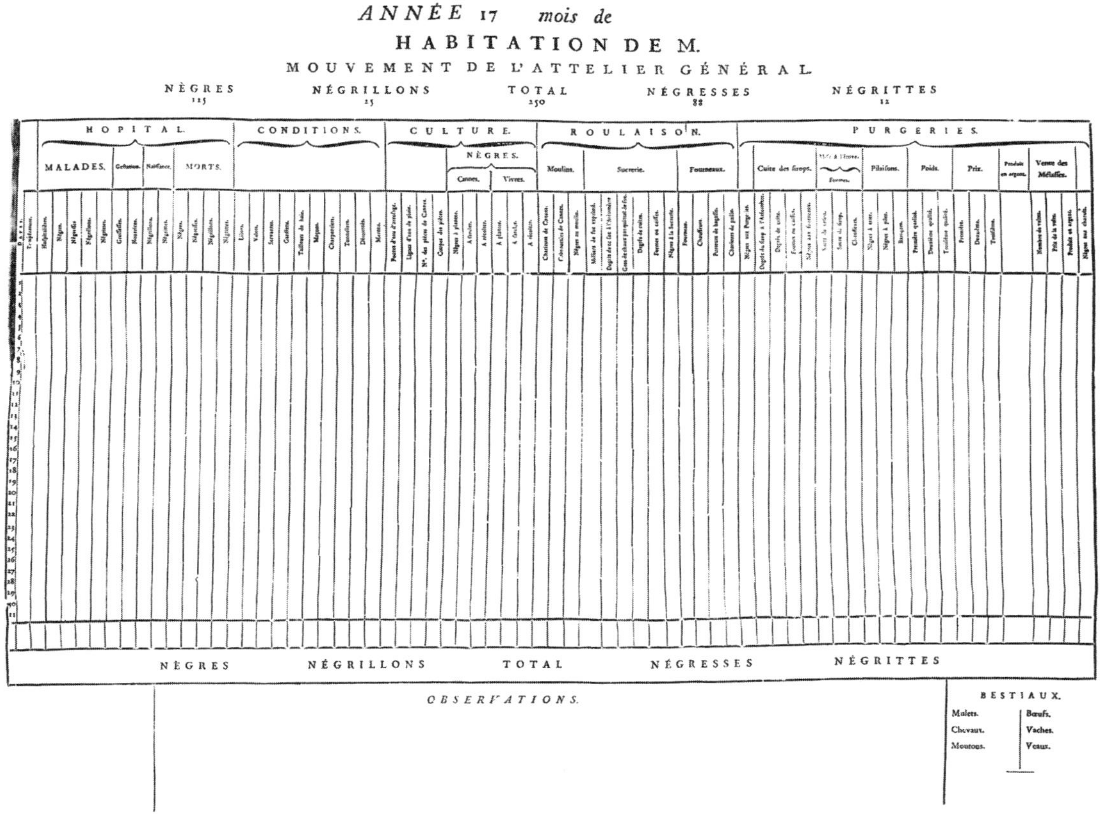

Figure 7.1. *The Dutrône Table*: Distribution of the Slave Labor Force throughout the Agricultural Year.

*Source:* J.-F. Dutrône, *Précis sur la canne et les moyens d'en extraire le sel essentiel, suivi de plusieurs Mémoires sur le Sucre, sur le Vin de Canne, sur l'Indigo, sur les Habitations & sur l'état actuel de Saint-Domingue* (Paris, 1791).

could then follow in detail the particular and the general movement of the labor force and compare one year with another, while absentee owners could have an exact account of their operations. Dutrône's method of organization was influential not only in the French sugar colonies, but also in Cuba, Brazil, and elsewhere, and it served as a model for the elaboration of more refined and precise systems of management that were developed during the nineteenth century.[37]

Various authors have interpreted this concern for the rationalization of the slave labor process, particularly on the sugar plantation, as an anticipation of the purposes and techniques of modern management, and especially Taylorism. Aufhauser, for example, stresses that contrary to conventional belief, the slave plantation and the modern factory offer similar conditions for the application of management techniques, and he enthusiastically identifies task work on the slave plantation, which establishes daily quotas for each worker, with time-motion studies in the modern factory.

> The efforts to keep up the accustomed routine were facilitated by the existence of work that could be divided into distinct tasks. Instructions to overseers read like Taylor's directions in the Midvale Steel Company. First, reduce everything to system; second, introduce daily accountability in every department. Work teams were designed and made responsible for the completion of specific tasks; if the job was not satisfactory, the team would be punished the next day with more arduous labors. . . . The slave plantation shared with the modern industry the technological prerequisites for systematic task work: a large number of very simple operations amenable to time-motion studies. This circumstance both explains why the routine of the plantation seemed anomalous to contemporary observers and why it so closely resembles modern management techniques.

According to Aufhauser, the slave owners, like Taylor, had to rely on a "strict system of rules, laws, and formulae" to guarantee strict labor control. For both, constant supervision was necessary because individual initiative could not be relied on to increase productivity. The common denominator of both systems is that the workers, whether slave or free, are lazy and inefficient.[38]

However, while these two types of labor management share many apparent similarities, and there is arguably an important historical connection between them, their resemblance is superficial and can be misleading. They are constituted within extremely different processes and relations, and they lead to opposite results. Leaving aside its general applicability on the slave plantation, which will be discussed in more detail below, task work, far from establishing the similarity between slave and wage labor, illustrates their difference.

The techniques of modern management have radically restructured the organization of the labor process and transformed the nature of work. They have seized on the individual actions of workers and reduced them to abstract activity. The labor process has been fragmented, and the activity of the worker engaged in production has been broken down into its constituent elements. The division of labor is altered, and the activities of work are recomposed under the control of the manager to increase the productivity of the socialized laborer. In this context, time-motion studies have attempted to subordinate the activity of the wage worker to an objective standard of productivity. With the development of the detail division of labor, the knowledge, skill, and subjective capacities of each worker have come to count for less and less. Space for individual initiative in production is sharply delimited, and every laborer must adapt his action to the objective organization of the production process. Abstract social labor appears to each worker as an external standard, and the individual characteristics of each laborer are subordinated to it, while the wage secures the continuity of effort for the duration of the entire working day.

Slave owners, on the contrary, regiment a preestablished number of individual workers to perform within a technically predetermined structure of production. The technical organization that appeared as something given, immutable, and external, and labor was adapted to it. Thus, an examination of eighteenth- and nineteenth-century sugar manuals reveals that characteristically the planters were considerably more preoccupied with the technical problems of sugar production than with questions of slave management. The purpose of task work on the slave plantation was to create some interest for the slave in executing the labor of the estate and subjectively to bind him to the performance of his work. Task-work quotas were assigned to each individual in the *atelier* on the basis of the amount of work customarily performed by the average adult slave in a day. The slaves could do the job when they pleased and were free to enjoy the time remaining after its completion for their own use. The organization of the division of labor on the estate thus remained intact, and the planter surrendered control over the actual execution of the work to obtain the regular application of a fixed amount of labor during a given period of time. But without the wage relation both to bind the worker to his job for the entire duration of the working day and to offer him the promise of a higher monetary reward for his efforts, the only inducement slavery could offer was a reduction in the hours of compulsory labor. With the task system, an industrious slave could get some free time each day to work in his garden or at some other job for his own benefit, while for his part, the planter guaranteed the performance of a minimal amount of work during this period. But the productive force of labor was not modified at all.[39]

## Domination, Hierarchy, and Labor Discipline

Slavery remained a crude and coercive form of labor extraction. The property relation was the necessary condition for the slave labor process, but it by no means guaranteed that the slaves would work. The actual expenditure of slave labor was dependent on and organized through the explicit domination of the slave owner. Although the slave owner could appropriate the capacity of the slave gang to work collectively, the slave relation provided no systemic incentive for the individual workers to prolong the duration or increase the intensity of their activity. For the slaves, labor was perpetual drudgery without reward. Their needs were reduced to a minimum, and meeting them was independent of their labor in the cane fields. As Schoelcher observed,

If he [the slave] puts one or two more arpents of land under cultivation, I clearly see the increase of his effort, but I search in vain for the increase in his well-being. Let us admit it, to bend down each day to a job without pay, to remain a stranger to a greater abundance that one has created, is a situation that must lead to indifference. . . . In compensation for the five full days of labor given by him to his master, the slave, on the whole . . . really only has the right to work the sixth in order to gain his nourishment for the entire week!

The activity of work could only be an alien imposition under slavery. The slave could be compensated for production, but he could not be made self-interested in production itself. There could be trade-offs in exchange for work (consistent with the maintenance of domination and the property relation), but there is nothing in work itself that could ever reward the slave.[40]

Slavery created indifference to work among the slaves, and they gave their labor reluctantly. "The Negro in the Antilles," writes Schoelcher:

shows no ardor for work. It is repugnant to him precisely because he is forced to do it. He does not hurry because he gains nothing by hurrying. Forced to give all of his time, he gives the least effort possible. It is completely straightforward. . . . It necessarily sets up a struggle between the master and the slave. The latter seeks to give little because as much as he withholds effort is he spared from fatigue. The former seeks to get a great deal because as much extra as the other does is gained for his benefit. Is it surprising that the Negro does not at all like steady, perpetual work for the profit and at the will of others? How could this work have the least attraction in his eyes since the whole harvest is for another? The feeling of no personal advantage being attached to the results of the task that is imposed on him, it is completely natural that this task is odious to him or at least indifferent.

There were, of course, a variety of individual adaptations to slave labor, but, if the Afro-Caribbean slave was integrated into the productive mechanism of the sugar plantation and adjusted his behavior to its routines, this by no means implied that the slave had internalized the norms and values of a European "work ethic," or that the slave was merely imitating planter desires, beliefs, or behavior. The slave was too often an apathetic and untrustworthy worker. Even "good" slaves could not be trusted by their masters, and practices such as malingering and feigning illness were common among them. However, the slave was not simply a lazy, inept, or unproductive worker. Rather, such behavior, where it existed, was engendered by the social relations of slavery. The productive force of slave labor (and thus the relative efficiency of the plantation system) rested on its collective and cooperative character, while the motivation of individual slaves was retarded. The same process that created the image of paternalism and conspicuous consumption on the side of the master created the image of the lazy Negro on the side of the slave.[41]

Under these conditions, constant surveillance and at least the threat of punishment were required to secure the minimal performance of the slaves' duties. Collins stresses this necessity:

> To one point you ought particularly to attend, and never let it escape from your memory, that a negro is an instrument, which requires to be incessantly acted upon to the performance of its duty. Whenever work is to be done, your white servants ought to see that it is done, and not to satisfy themselves with giving orders to the negroes, and trusting to their memories for the execution; for it is ten to one but that they forget it, and by that means incur your displeasure; and it is certainly, in all cases, more pleasant to prevent an offence than to punish the commission of it. The neglect of this rule is the occasion of many severities, which, with a little attention, might easily be avoided.

A hierarchical staff of supervisors was required to organize the work process on the sugar plantation and discipline the workers. Through them the master's antagonistic demand for surplus production was imposed on the slave labor force. Their job was to coordinate the activity of the slave gang and to see to it that the energies of the slaves were put to the master's best advantage. The presupposition and the goal of their activity was not a responsible and self-acting worker, but an automaton integrated into a collective mechanism. "You cannot resign him to the guidance of his own discretion," continued Collins, "but like a soldier in the ranks, he must be a mere machine, without will or motion, other than you impress on him."[42]

The planter, of course, was at the top of the plantation hierarchy. He was the personification of power on the estate. All of its activities were subordinated to his control, and he was the source of all authority. But he in turn had to conform to the requirements of the market and the technical conditions of sugar production. The sugar plantation as a commercial enterprise was an impersonal productive apparatus that translated the planter's personal dominion over the slaves into a concern for the effort to extract the necessary quantity, type, and intensity of labor as he sought to obtain the optimal effort of the collectivity within the prevailing technical conditions. The result was the objectification and instrumentalization of the laborers, which was secured by direct domination and force. "That the population in his power adopts regular habits is the last concern of a planter," lamented Schoelcher. "He only sees, he is only able to see, instruments of labor in the negroes, and provided that they make a lot of sugar, he is happy. The rest does not concern him. On the contrary, the less the slaves pass from the crude state of nature, the less they are to be feared and the less they appear worthy of liberty. Everything that the slaves have acquired in servitude, they owe only to themselves. The masters have never done anything in this respect. What use would it have had for them?"[43]

If the planter was an absentee, the *géreur* or administrator was responsible for the overall operation of the estate. If there was an administrator, he lived on the plantation, either in the big house or in a separate house with his family, if the family were in the colony. Unlike the subordinate whites, who came and went, he often remained in his position for a long time. He maintained a regular correspondence with the owner to whom he was responsible. "His task," according to Debien, "is to squeeze the agricultural and industrial machine by every means possible in order to increase the yield. His activity is translated abroad by numbers. He thus can be pitiless if he decides that the principal goal of his position is to ship the most hogsheads of sugar that he can."[44]

Next in rank were the *économes*, or overseers, who were in charge of the practical day-to-day work of the plantation. The head overseer was responsible for keeping a record of births, deaths, accidents, and the condition of the animals, equipment, and provisions, as well as of the work performed each day. He had to keep an eye on the animals, the fields, the provision grounds, the slave cabins, and the condition of the mill, refinery, and the storehouses. But above all he was entrusted with supervising the slaves. With the exception of the domestics, the overseers were in charge of all the slaves of the estate, including the artisans and the sick as well as the agricultural workers. Beyond directing their work, the overseers administered rations and were generally responsible for the good order of the slaves.[45]

This was an extremely important position. The overseer could make or break the estate. The master or *géreur* were often far removed from the direct management of slaves, and the overseer was the one directly responsible for them. He had to be familiar with the individual characteristics and condition of every slave in the gang. He had to know their character, the state of their health, and their physical capacity in order to coordinate their efforts and utilize their labor most effectively. The job was demanding and required constant activity day and night, especially during the harvest season. Early each morning, he had to tour the plantation to survey the progress of the work and plan the disposition of his forces with the care and precision of a military commander, while his nights were often spent watching over the sugar making and the activities of the slaves in the refinery. The life was hard and the pay low. According to Hilliard d'Auberteuil of Saint Domingue, talent and good conduct were not enough. The job required physical and mental toughness and preferably a sufficiently imposing physique to command the respect of the slaves.[46]

The overseers were at the point of confrontation between the master's drive for surplus production and demand for the maintenance of social control, on the one side, and the recalcitrance of the slaves on the other. The difficulty of their situation could affect the way that they handled the slaves. They were callous and unrelenting toward the slaves. They often believed themselves capable of accomplishing any task, and, if the master or administrator did not watch over them, they were capable of pushing the slaves without regard for fatigue. A few weeks of this treatment could disrupt the slave gang, upsetting their habitual routine, and harassing them without any effect. The slave gang then responded with bad will, working slowly and under the force of the whip, when that had not been necessary before. The overseer could then be recalled and a new one brought in. The process then began all over again.[47]

Beneath the *économes* in authority were the slave *commandeurs* or drivers. Laborie, a planter from Saint Domingue, described the driver as the "soul of the plantation." Slaves themselves, the drivers were responsible for the immediate control of the field hands, but not for the workers in the mill or the refinery or the carters, who had their own supervisors. The drivers directed the execution of the tasks performed by the slave gang and regulated the pace of the work. Each morning it was the responsibility of the head driver to assemble the slaves, report the missing and sick to the overseer, and then accompany the gang to the fields. The drivers carried to the fields the two great emblems of their rank, the whip and an iron-tipped staff on which to lean while supervising the day's tasks. These symbolized both their authority and their exemption from physical labor and clearly differentiated them from the body of the slaves. On large estates, it was frequently the head driver who calculated the amount of work to be done during each morning and afternoon session and designated which slaves were to be assigned to which jobs. If inclement weather retarded the work, the driver had the power to decide whether to try to wait out the storm or to simply suspend work for the day. However, if, under certain circumstances, the driver could reduce the assigned task, he could not increase it or substitute one job for another once the overseer had made his decision. Each evening the drivers reported the progress of the day's work to the *économe* to be recorded in the plantation log. The information included such details as the weather, the number of slaves present for the various tasks in the morning and the afternoon, those slaves who were sick, those assigned to extraordinary work outside of the fields, the number or the name of the cane pieces where the *atelier* had worked, as well as runaways, serious quarrels, punishments, accidents, and unmanageable slaves. In the evening and on Sundays, when there was no work to be done, they were charged with maintaining order and tranquility in the slave quarters and with keeping an eye on the comings and goings and general behavior of the slaves. The driver was of crucial importance for the smooth operation of the *atelier* and economic success of the estate, and the planters had to exercise great care in their selection and training. "Good order in the *atelier*," wrote one planter, "depends absolutely on the intelligence, good conduct, activity and firmness of the *commandeurs*. A good *commandeur* is a rare man and of inestimable value."[48]

Physical coercion remained an integral part of the organization of the slave labor process. Ultimately, the exploitation of slave labor rested on the threat of compulsion, and the slave was exposed to the daily possibility of violence. Force created and sustained the slave as property and as the instrument of labor and was in turn shaped and sustained by the slave relation. But the use of this force was not arbitrary or capricious. On the one hand, it was the means of organizing and animating labor and establishing industrial discipline; on the other hand, it was embedded within and constrained by the purposes, organization, and requirements of production itself. Thus, as many authors have indicated, the treatment of the slaves was restrained by the economic self-interest of the master. But the apparent and carefully constructed rationality of the slaveholder as self-interested economic man could quickly show its other face, irrational violence. If the economic self-interest of the master provided the motive to care for the material well-being of the slave, it by no means guaranteed it. This self-interest was inscribed within and operated through an explicit system of domination that had its own logic. The planter had to maintain control over a broad range of activities of social life to guarantee production, and at any point the fabric that held together domination and material production could rupture. If domination failed to function as an effective means of labor discipline, it could easily become an end in itself and disrupt both production and property.[49]

Slave discipline in the French Antilles underwent considerable amelioration during the July Monarchy, and some of the more brutal aspects of the slave regime were removed. Reports from magistrates sent to inspect the plantations commented almost universally on the moderation of discipline and the mildness of punishments, at least in comparison with earlier conditions. Yet it remained a harsh system, and the whip played a central and perhaps expanding role in the organization of colonial production and the maintenance of order throughout the last decades of the slave period. While a handful of planters experimented with various other means of securing the cooperation of their laborers and enforcing discipline without corporal punishment, the great majority of the planter class defended the whip as the only means of compelling labor from the slaves. It was the most common means of punishing laziness, insubordination, or any serious breach of discipline. The whip was particularly suited to the conditions prevailing after the abolition of the slave trade, as it could be used to inflict punishment without necessarily causing permanent injury. According to one source: "Previously, during the period when the health and the life of the slaves had less pecuniary value, anything went to punish those miserable creatures. Since the abolition [of the slave trade] the creoles have been given this problem to solve: How to make a guilty Negro suffer without making him seriously ill or killing him. They believe that they have found the answer to it in the whip. Today it is the punishment inflicted on the slaves for every type of fault." The whip was regarded as an essential element of labor discipline, and the threat of its use and abuse was always present. In Schoelcher's words: "The whip is an integral part of the colonial regime. It is its principal agent. It is its soul. . . . The whip, in a word, is the expression of work in the Antilles. If one wanted to symbolize the colonies such as they still are, it would be necessary to stack a sugar cane stalk together with the driver's whip."[50]

The Code Noir gave masters the power to beat their slaves with a rod or cord if they thought that they deserved it. But from 1783 onward in Martinique, the number of lashes a master could give a slave was fixed at twenty-nine except for a brief period when fifty were allowed. While some planters protested this legal restriction as an infringement on their absolute authority and right to property as well as a threat to public safety, this number allowed the infliction of an ample amount of pain. As Schoelcher testified: "The force of the executioner depends on the humanity of the master. If he so wishes, twenty-nine blows of the whip will not produce any effect, but, if it is desired, the most robust man can be disabled for six months with only fifteen." Indeed, the case of Braffin, a planter who severely injured four of his slaves without exceeding the legal maximum number of lashes, is evidence of the potential for violence and physical harm that might be inflicted on the enslaved within the limit of the law. Further, even if punishments were normally "mild," the slaves had little formal protection and few recourses from abuses by the master or his staff. Yet while the colonial court records more than enough examples of excessive brutality (and paltry success in prosecuting them), such cases were the exception.[51]

The magistrates who inspected the plantations in Martinique during the 1840s reported that the use of the whip was "moderate" and becoming increasingly mild throughout the colony. In general, the slaves were only whipped enough to maintain good discipline. Punishments did not ordinarily go beyond ten or fifteen lashes, and only for the most serious offenses did they reach the legal maximum of twenty-nine lashes. Excessive punishment might create more problems among the *atelier* than it solved, and the master ran the risk of injuring his property. Further, as Gutman has argued, the significance of whipping as an instrument of labor discipline is not only its effect on the recipient of the blows but also its social visibility among the other slaves. According to Schoelcher, half of the slaves in the rural gangs in the French Antilles had never felt the lash. Intimidation was sufficient to ensure adequate behavior.[52]

Discipline was generally milder on small plantations than on large ones. The master usually lived in close proximity with the slaves, and frequently there was no driver. According to contemporary sources, corporal punishment was unknown on a great many small estates. They did not use prisons, irons, or even the whip.

Instead, the master carried a sort of heavy riding crop (*rigoise*) and used it to administer punishment. Self-interest, proximity to the slaves and familiarity with them, and relatively mild demands on labor served to check brutality and excessive punishment. It was frequently reported that often reprimands alone sufficed to discipline the slaves, and the number of lashes only rarely attained the legal maximum. However, routines and duties were less clearly defined on small estates, and the slaves were more directly exposed to the personal eccentricities of the master. One official warned that the very informality prevailing on many small plantations could cause discipline to become capricious and irregular. The master might tolerate misbehavior for a long time without reproach, and suddenly explode in anger for a frivolous cause. Punishments could then become severe without any motive, and give way to unrestrained brutality on the part of the master.[53]

In contrast, discipline on large plantations was both more severe and more regular. Whipping could be authorized by the master, the administrator, or the overseer, and the number of blows varied with the offense. Serious offenses were always punished some time after they were committed. These cases were decided by the master or the administrator. On well-run estates, great effort was made to ensure that duties were clearly delineated and punishments were regular, calculable, impersonal, and in proportion to the offense. According to one report: "On a large plantation, an offense almost never goes unpunished. But before inflicting the punishment, the master reflects. He thinks. It is a guarantee that the punishment be just and measured. Furthermore, on each large plantation there is a code based on custom which sanctions certain penalties for habitual offenses." Another report elaborates this point. The slave "knows his duties. He is subject to an invariable rule and knows in advance the punishment that will result from his error. The contact not being immediate, the punishment is administered without passion or anger." Indeed, on some estates punishment was sufficiently rationalized that there was a formal set of written rules and punishments.[54]

The drivers on large estates were also given a considerable amount of discretionary power in administering punishment. In the fields, the *commandeurs* were normally authorized to give between four and seven lashes without the master's permission in cases that demanded immediate attention. The planters and overseers realized that these slaves bore direct responsibility for the regular performance of the most difficult tasks and needed this authority to maintain the continuity of the production process. Thus, it was the drivers who most frequently used the whip to enforce labor discipline. However, the planters' ability to regulate the actions of these subordinates, who were subject to pressures to produce and a relation to property and production very different from those of the planter, was an important problem. Their power to punish could easily escape the planter's control. Necessary autonomy could become misuse and at worst degenerate into private vendettas with the slaves.[55]

Yet physical coercion alone provided insufficient motivation for the slaves. It produced sullen and recalcitrant slaves who only worked because of threat of punishment and only did enough work to avoid punishment. According to Schoelcher: "The whip, or rather the threat of the whip is almost the sole stimulus of a slave. It is very conceivable that he only does exactly what is necessary to escape the whip." Some sign of encouragement or favor or small rewards of food or clothing from the plantation's stores for obedience or good work were necessary to temper fear of the lash and obtain some degree of goodwill and cooperation from the slaves. By themselves, such "positive incentives" were at best of limited effectiveness and needed to be backed up by the threat of coercion. If individuals or groups of slaves responded favorably to such rewards, the degree of voluntary cooperation thus obtained was circumscribed and uncertain. Nevertheless, by the 1830s a growing number of planters were attempting to move beyond overt physical coercion and develop more effective means of labor discipline and social control. On many estates, the use of the whip was reduced or abolished. Instead, for ordinary offenses, slaves were confined in the plantation hospital or a special detention cell during the night, assigned extra work during their free time, or not allowed to go to town on the weekend. Similarly, one planter testified that fines were a more effective means of discipline than the whip, the chain, or detention, and the latter were to be used sparingly. "When . . . one of my Negroes [acquires] some savings, he is in my control from then on. Pride and self-love dominate him, and the desire to protect what is his makes him more careful and rarely at fault. If one of my slaves steals a day or more of work from me or commits some injury to one of his comrades, he owes a reparation and [must] repay the damage. His savings diminish, and that is the most severe punishment of all for him." The slaves feared such penalties more than corporal punishment. One magistrate expressed the general opinion: "These means of correction, which are less shocking to humanity, are also more effective. There are few Negroes who would not prefer to receive a considerable number of strokes of the whip than pass the night confined."[56]

Measures such as these suggest the limits of pure coercion as a means of enforcing labor discipline. Their success depended on the integration of the enslaved population into the productive and social system. For them to work, both master and slave had to recognize the existence of certain privileges and at least a limited degree of independence for the slave. Their manipulation became a means of modifying work habits and disciplining slave labor. Paradoxically, however, both the master and slave became more closely tied to the maintenance of these privileges. The possible range of action of each was restricted, and the character if not the content of industrial relations was altered decisively. However, while such measures may have been more effective punishments for breaches of labor discipline, they still failed to provide a positive incentive to work.

The lack of incentive for slave labor constrained the productive capacity of the *atelier* and made it resistant to the modification or intensification of work routines. "The Negro, addicted to routine by nature," commented Lavollée,

becomes by position the enemy of all amelioration. As no personal interest attaches him to the land, as an increase in its products must result in no benefit for him, the change displeases him, and he resists it from the first without another thought. Often, the planter seeks in vain to demonstrate to him that by the adoption of a new process his task will become less long and less difficult. Whether his intelligence cannot grasp the import of such an explanation or rather whether a change that could eventually prove to be of advantage to him does not appear to him to be worth the present disruption of his habits, it is only after a long time and with the greatest difficulties that the planters have introduced some changes among them.

Confronted with the inertia of the slaves, the planters could only resign themselves to utilizing productive forces already at hand as effectively as possible and maintaining the discipline and morale of the slave gang.[57]

The system of task work was implemented to remedy this lack of incentive and animate the slave gang. Its purpose was to create an inducement for the slave to work and thus guarantee the performance of a given amount of labor during the day. According to Soleau, "Currently the black in the Antilles, having no interest in working quickly since he must remain in the master's field the entire day whether he works a lot or a little, does not hurry." However, Soleau continued, "if the quantity of work were fixed he would go more quickly in order to have time to himself." Task work, according to Collins, was the best way of rewarding the slaves: "Wherever there is the least prospect of its being done, it should certainly be attempted; for nothing is so encouraging to your negroes, as the idea of a holiday at the end of their work; nor can anything depress them more, than a tiresome routine of duty, which presents no prospect of end, relief or recompense. In such cases, they labor with incessant regret; rather seeming to work than to work, and anxious only to consume the time, not to dispatch the business."[58]

Through experience, the planter was able to calculate for each of the different types of work to be done on the plantation how much the average slave could do in a day without being overworked. Every morning, each slave in the gang was assigned his daily task based on this customary amount of labor. The slaves could do their daily quota of work as they liked, and were free to dispose of the time remaining after its completion as they wished. "This will encourage every negro to make his utmost exertion, in consequence of which, the work of twelve hours will be dispatched in ten, and with much more satisfaction to themselves," declared Collins.[59]

Under the task system, an industrious slave could gain several hours each day that could be employed in the cultivation of his own garden or some other employment. The slave thus had the opportunity to improve his condition, while the master obtained the required amount of labor. Soleau commented, undoubtedly with some exaggeration, "In the Antilles the organization of work by tasks, with all the opportunity that the blacks have to take advantage of the hours at their disposal, would make the great majority of them rich in a few years without diminishing the revenue of the master." On the other hand, a slave who did not use the time well had to spend the whole day working in the masters' fields to complete the required task. The punishment was proportional to the lack of effort, and if the failure to meet the assignment was too great, the free day given to the slaves could be jeopardized.[60]

Despite the advantages presented by the task system, it was not universally applicable to all the types of work on the sugar plantation. Both Soleau and Collins record that this method could only be employed with the *grand atelier*. Only the slaves in this gang commanded sufficient force to perform a definite and quantifiable amount of labor on a regular basis. In the case of illness or other absence, its numbers could be maintained by occasional or temporary drafts from the second gang, which always contained some slaves sufficiently strong to provide such a substitution. Such manipulation, however, was not possible in the case of the second gang. The weaker slaves of the *petit atelier* performed tasks that were not susceptible to such evaluation. They always worked under the supervision of a driver, and in Soleau's description, performed indifferently the entire day. In addition, certain jobs on the plantation, such as cane cutting, weeding, and carrying manure, were subject to great variation, depending respectively on the type and quality of the cane, the quantity of weeds, and the distance the dung had to be carried, that they were not, as a rule, amenable to a standard evaluation.[61]

Task work could only function when the slave population had sufficiently assimilated the routine of plantation labor to respond to its incentives. For self-regulation to replace external domination, it was necessary for the slaves to understand and accept the rhythm of work, organization of time, and system of rewards and punishments that characterized the plantation regime. Only then could the notion of free time appear as a reward to the slave. Only if the slave formed a concept of his self-interest and appropriated time for himself within this framework could the task system operate and the larger appropriation of the slave's activity by the master take place. This change itself contributed to the mutation of the relations of work. Soleau, writing from the point of view of a defender of slavery, described the task system as a form of contractual agreement: "It is easy to see all the advantages of this system of labor which represents a type of contract between master and slave. The former pledges to feed, dress, lodge, and care for the slave in sickness, in childhood, in old age. The slave, who, for his part, must give a certain determined quantity of labor each day of good health, is thus sheltered from the caprice and arbitrariness of the driver or overseer who directs the work." In Soleau's view, if master and slave fulfilled their obligations to each other, the mutual self-interest expressed by this contract could guarantee social peace in the colonies. The contractual character of task work was a mystification, since the slave could not bargain among employers and enter freely into the agreement. Yet Soleau does catch something of the changing relation between master and slave. Once the slave has a recognized interest, the system can no longer rest on absolute domination and authority, but instead must give way to bargaining and negotiation between interested parties, however unequal and antagonistic their relationship might have been. Thus, task work marks a further transformation of the master-slave relation and the adaptation of the African slave to the American environment, which was both cause and effect of this change.[62]

However, the integration of the slave into the system of task work is itself an expression of the social limit of the slave relation and an element of its crisis. While planters might influence individual behavior and set the parameters of the action of the group through the systematic manipulation of rewards and punishments, such measures merely adapted the slaves to the existing organization of production with a greater or lesser degree of enthusiasm. While the task system guaranteed the completion of a minimum amount of work, and perhaps somewhat reduced the costs of supervision, it did not alter the composition of the working day or increase surplus production. The self-interest created by this system was not a reward earned through commodity-producing activity; instead, it was formed outside of this work and through a release from it. After the slaves completed their predetermined task, they were free to look after their own affairs—literally, they were free to tend their own gardens. Such a system might provide the slaves with an incentive to give a bit more of themselves, but it demonstrates slavery's incapacity to create individual self-interest in production itself. Rather, individual self-interest and identification with the job and the plantation were created, not in commodity production, but in social reproduction. Garden plot cultivation did not lower the value of labor, but rather represented a deduction from the total potential surplus without changing the conditions of surplus production.

## Integration, Autonomy, and Resistance

The pattern of labor imposed by the master structured the social relationships of the plantation and was a focal point of slave experience. The social organization of labor on the sugar estate required that the enslaved acquire new skills; internalize values and attitudes conducive to steady daily work on a cooperative basis; and respond to new patterns of authority, incentives, and discipline. However, work was not a sphere of total domination by the master but an arena where meaning and motivation were contested. Within this perspective, it can be seen that the slaves not only adapted to the organization of plantation production but also contributed to its constitution. Daily encounters between slaves and masters led to mutual accommodation that shaped and continually readjusted "customary" work routines.[63]

The slave gang was the animating force of the sugar plantation. Its work was an occasion for the collective social activity of the group. Antislavery leader Victor Schoelcher wrote of the *atelier*, "Association has such powerful virtues that even slave labor performed thus in common presents an aspect less sad that the solitary and dismal labor of our peasants." This combination of workers stimulated what Marx called their "animal spirits" and heightened the activity of each individual worker. The *ateliers* could perform an enormous amount of labor in a day. The best way to appreciate this force, according to Schoelcher, was to place oneself on a high point from which the whole group of laborers could be observed. "One sees them advance insensibly with the imperceptible rapidity of the flux of the sea, leaving behind them the long traces of their passage."[64]

However, the slave gang did not work by compulsion alone. Anthropologists have compared African institutions for organizing work in complex social settings, such as the Dahomean *dokpwe*, with modern means of mobilizing labor, such as the Haitian *combite* and the Brazilian *mutirão*, emphasizing the ostensibly voluntary and cooperative character of each. But rather than compare precolonial Africa with present-day rural life in the Americas, it may be more revealing to compare it with the contemporaneous slave plantation. While here the continuity of the voluntary, cooperative, and festive aspects of work come into question, at the level of its physical organization and execution the similarities are striking. Herskovits writes of Dahomey: "If a field is to be hoed, each worker takes responsibility for a row and the line of men moves down the acreage to be prepared for planting to the rhythm of drums and gongs, and to the accompaniment of songs which are at once the most characteristic and the most joyous aspect of this communal labor." Of course, not all enslaved Africans and their descendants were Dahomean; and the purposes of work, the structure of its organization and supervision, its rewards and punishments, and even its regularity and duration were very different on the Caribbean sugar estates from what they were in Africa. But while the work of the plantation remained difficult, tedious, and coercive, the resemblance is strong enough to at least suggest that Afro-American bondsmen played a significant role in forming themselves into a collective labor force and shaping the agricultural work routine.[65]

Whatever the phase of the crop cycle, the work of the slave gangs in the fields was very tedious and boring. The slaves had to act mechanically at the signal of the *commandeur* or overseer, repeating the same movements over and over from dawn to dusk, day after day. The best results were obtained, wrote Governor De Moges, when the *atelier* acquired the taste and the habit for such activity. Music often broke the monotony of the work. This practice was encouraged by the masters. Roughley recommended that "An animating inoffensive song, struck up by one of them should be encouraged and chorused while at work; for they are thought to be good composers in their own way." Behind each *atelier* stood a singer who sang a rhythmic tune to which the *atelier* repeated the refrain. De Cassagnac records that drums as well as songs were used to encourage a steady, regular pace while planting cane. A slave placed himself astride a drum a little distance from the *atelier* and beat out a vigorous cadence similar to those of the slave dances (*bamboulas*). At the same time, a female slave improvised a song. The rest of the slaves dug together in time to the music. He commented that the furious rhythm that the music communicated to the slaves as they joined together to sing out the refrain was unimaginable.[66]

This type of singing with soloist and group chorus, and at times even including drums, had its origins in Africa. Melville Herskovits, in his account of peasant life in Haiti, cites a description of such music animating the movement of a slave gang and suggests that it represents an African counterpoint to European domination: "While the material facts of the life of the slaves was at once subordinated to European patterns . . . yet in other matters they could live as they had lived in Africa. Thus one account of the time, quoted by de Vassière, tells how the slaves carried on communal hoeing, timing their strokes to the rhythms of songs that begged some favor from their visitor, or to songs of praise (and, when the white observer was not present, undoubtedly also singing songs of derision), in the characteristic African fashion that . . . has survived in Haitian peasant life to this day." Herskovits's emphasis on the "African" nature and the integrity of these songs and practices appears overstated in the light of subsequent scholarship. The diversity of African cultures and the processes of their diffusion and transformation in the context of slavery and colonialism were more complex than Herskovits's formulation admits. The occasion and context of the music were much different in the New World from what they had been in Africa.[67]

While it may be reasonably presumed that the tradition of satirical singing presented a continuing challenge to the boundaries of "inoffensive song" in the Americas, as Herskovits suggests, the cultural references and the content of the lyrics of the songs undoubtedly changed substantially, if not completely. Schoelcher, for example, reports that such singing could serve as an outlet for the expression of slave grievances and the means for a kind of collective bargaining with the master. If a planter found his animals poisoned or similar anonymous acts of sabotage committed on the estate, he could often learn, not the author of the crime, but the cause of the slaves' discontent—an overseer who was too harsh or an unwanted change in the work routine—by attending to the improvised lyrics of the work songs. If the situation were then redressed, the depredations would cease. At another level of symbolic meaning and action, the slaves were able to interject their own rhythms and forms of sociability into the labor process to establish norms of work and the behavior around work through these songs. If, from the point of view of the master, the songs habituated the slaves to field work and kept its pace steady, for the slaves they broke the monotony of the workday and tempered the absolute separation of work and social life. They provided the means of self-expression and the opportunity for individual slaves to demonstrate virtuosity as singers, drummers, or improvisers of lyrics, while they reinforced the collective solidarity of the slave group.[68]

Resistance to work was a part of the collective experience of the slaves' adaptation to New World conditions. With the integration of the slaves into the plantation regime, the social relations of work increasingly moved to the center of their life experience. As the slaves became socialized into the system of plantation production, the conditions of labor became both the cause and the objective of their resistance. It is of course difficult to isolate industrial conflict from other arenas of struggle because the slave's position as worker necessarily overlapped with social relations more broadly defined. Yet such modes of action as malingering, feigning illness or pregnancy, tool breaking, arson, the destruction of property, deliberate slowdowns, strikes, running away, and even attacks on persons were endemic to slave production. They shaped the social organization of the labor process and presented the slaveholder with a barrier to the expansion of surplus production.[69]

To resist successfully, the slaves had to acquire the necessary skills and knowledge and learn what forms of activity were adequate and appropriate in a given situation. As Mintz has succinctly put the matter. "The house slave who poisoned her master's family by putting ground glass in the food had first to become the family cook." Such resistance—whether the act of an individual or a group—was seldom a random or indiscriminate outburst. Rather, it emerged from the social context created by the slave community and in turn helped to define that community. In the course of adapting to the plantation, the slaves developed expectations about the standard of treatment to which they were entitled, and much day-to-day resistance can be seen as the result of the slave owner's violating these standards. If a master punished his slaves too severely or overworked them, he might well find that they retaliated by running off, poisoning his cattle, or committing arson. Similarly, the breakup of the slave community through the removal of individuals or transferring the group as a whole from one plantation to another and the accompanying separation from family and fellows, burial grounds, garden plots, and familiar work routines could provide the occasion for flight or other acts of resistance. In this framework, individual and collective resistance were legitimated by the slave community, and the community asserted itself against the demands of the master class.[70]

The use of poison was especially prominent among the means of resistance used by the slaves of Martinique and deserves special comment. "This terror of poison seems to prevail most extensively in Martinique," stated the de Tocqueville Commission report in 1839. Schoelcher describes the use of poison by the slaves as a counterpoint to the arbitrary power of the master. "Poison is to the slave what the whip is to the master, a moral force. The black works for fear of the whip. The white is less abusive from the fear of poison." By means of it, the slaves were able to establish an equilibrium between themselves and the master—up to a certain point at least. According to one magistrate, incidents of mistreatment inevitably brought poisoning in their train: "The only action that cruel or unjust punishments can bring about is poisoning." While another magistrate from Gros Morne wrote: "To prevent the master from being tormenting or severe towards their slaves there is a terror that grips this commune more than elsewhere—poison."[71]

Yet the extent to which poisoning actually occurred in Martinique is difficult to assess. The state of medical knowledge in the colony was poor, and there was a lack of qualified personnel and adequate facilities to diagnose suspicious deaths. Perhaps more importantly, poison was commonly regarded as a widespread and almost natural occurrence in the colonies, and the European population of the colony was predisposed to believe that crime rather than natural causes was behind the unexpected death of man or beast. The colonists accepted poison with a fatality that paralyzed any efforts to understand or combat it, and death by disease was frequently attributed to poison. Indeed, the state of collective fear, if not panic, that gripped the planter class with regard to poison underlines the chronic insecurity of slave society and may perhaps be fruitful for studying the planter *mentalité*. Nevertheless, despite exaggerated claims that underestimated the effects of disease on overworked and poorly treated livestock, on the one hand, and the reservations made by doctors, on the other, both Schoelcher and Lavollée agreed that while perhaps poison was not so widespread as popularly believed, it was impossible to dismiss it as a significant aspect of colonial life. "Incidents that were unfortunately too numerous did not permit the existence of poison as a means of vengeance employed by the blacks to be put in doubt," concluded Lavollée.[72]

The attacks were usually directed at the livestock, although occasionally slaves, and even the master or his family, were the objects. The oxen, mules, and horses necessary for operation of the sugar works were the most frequent targets. Their loss disrupted the work routine and created chaos on the estate. These attacks reached such an extent that, in a report to the de Tocqueville Commission in 1839, the governor of Martinique remarked that efforts at raising cattle were discouraged by poison and the planters of the colony took little interest in it.[73]

While poison was used for a variety of motives, it was an important weapon in the slaves' efforts to exert a degree of control over the labor process. "His work is an easy routine," wrote Lavollée. "If the master demands something more or different from what he is accustomed to doing, he combats it by the force of inertia. If the master insists, he responds with poison. The terror of poison is great in the country. By means of it, the slave dominates the master." Through the use of poison the slaves attempted to establish quotas on production, control the duration and intensity of work, define a standard of acceptable treatment by overseers and drivers, and have some say in the processes by which tasks were determined. "A plantation can only make a certain number of hogsheads of sugar or keep a certain number of animals," wrote one observer. "Beyond this number, as though fixed by some kind of mysterious fatality, poison makes an immediate correction." If these rights, duties, and customary routines, at least tacitly understood by both master and slave, were transgressed, the result could be the employment of this deadly sanction against the master. M. Latuillerie, for example, had his *atelier* harvest a cane piece that some free Negroes had planted on shares with him. The slaves did the work without complaint, but immediately afterward, he lost some oxen and mules and was forced to renounce using his slaves for such jobs.[74]

Perhaps more important than the physical effects of poison was the climate of fear that it created, as is illustrated by the case of Levassor Delatouche. He owned two plantations. One, at Lamentin, had more than half again the number of slaves required for its operation, while the other in nearby Petit Morne had only half the number of slaves that it needed. When asked by Schoelcher why he did not move the slaves from one to the other, he replied that such a move would be impossible. There would be an outbreak of poisoning if it were attempted. Thus, the slaves resisted not only the work routine but also the breakup of community bonds formed with other slaves on the plantation and dissolution of group solidarities. The threat of poison protected the slave community and enforced its general claims against the economic rationality of the plantation.[75]

While the great majority of these acts of resistance, whether individual or collective, did not threaten the existence of the slave regime per se, it is important to keep them in their proper perspective and not underestimate their practical importance. These actions are best understood not in the context of the struggle for an abstract concept of freedom, constructed as a universal motive infusing all action or serving to order a hierarchy of forms of resistance. The slave is not an existential rebel who only struggles on the day-to-day level because he cannot overthrow or escape the system as a whole, and the importance and efficacy of these modes of action are not determined by whether or not they culminate in the destruction of the slave regime. Rather, the slave was an historical being struggling over conditions within the slave relation. By such means slaves were able to impose their own sanctions on the organization of work and daily life and to form work routines in accordance with their own values and conceptions of need. For their part, planters expected and tolerated much of this behavior as an unavoidable part of life in a slave society. Except in cases of overt violence, it was often not seen as a threat to public order but rather was treated as a misdemeanor. Indeed, in most cases totally conventionalized means were available to resolve the conflicts entailed in such incidents, and the rules of the game were recognized by both sides. Resistance and accommodation are not either/or alternatives. Instead, the dialectic between them is the moving contradiction that fashions the historical transformation of the social relations of slavery.[76]

The role of slave resistance and its significance for the transformation of the labor process and the social relations of slavery can be seen in the historical development of the practice of the free Saturday given to slaves so that they could tend their gardens and work on their own account. While the free Saturday never ceased to be functional from the master's point of view, it formed a nodal point within the social relations of slavery that allowed slave practices, values, and interests to emerge and develop and to assume autonomous forms of organization and expression. As the slaves became socialized into the routine of plantation labor, they were able to lay claim to the free Saturday and use it for their own ends. They felt that they had a right to such "free" time and resisted any encroachment on it. According to one official, "It would be almost impossible for a planter to take even a little bit of time belonging to his slave, even if the authorities ignored the situation. There is a spirit of resistance among the slaves that prevents anyone from threatening what they consider to be their rights." Another document emphasizes: "There would be discontent if the proprietors took away the free Saturday to give the provisions prescribed by the edict. . . . The Negroes prefer this method, which assures them of an extra day each week. Everywhere that it has not been adopted the blacks desire it and beg for it. To try to abolish it where it was once been established would be to provoke disorder and revolt."[77]

The slaves effectively appropriated a part of the disposable labor time as their own, and, in practice, time on the plantation became divided between time belonging to the master and time belonging to the slaves. The time available for export commodity production was restricted, and the master now had to bargain with the slaves. Time became a kind of currency, and a complex system of time accounting emerged. If the master found that he needed the slaves on a Saturday or at another time when they were exempted from labor, such work was voluntary, and it was rare that the slaves were not compensated for their services. Often, the master indemnified the slaves with an equivalent amount of time rather than money. In Martinique, it was reported that the slaves on one plantation were made to work on Sunday during the harvest but were given the following Monday off. (This report added that the planter would be warned that this change was not in accord with religious rites and the regular habits of the slaves.) On the infrequent occasions when the master of another plantation needed the labor of his slaves on a free Saturday or a Sunday for some pressing work that could not be postponed, they were given an equivalent amount of time on a weekday. A government official reported that this latter planter kept a precise account of the extra time that the slaves put in and indemnified them scrupulously.[78]

Thus, the time belonging to the slaves not only became distinguished from that belonging to the masters, but opposed to it. At the extreme, the former encroached on the latter. For the slaves, the time separate from work became a sphere of autonomous activity—"free" time where they could dispose of their energies as they saw fit and within which they created a community organized around their beliefs, values, and collective action. Their use of this free time could become subversive of plantation discipline. (According to Monk Lewis, a planter in Jamaica, the slaves on his plantation referred to their free Saturday as "playday.") This was especially apparent in the case of the nocturnal activities of the slaves. Although prohibited by law (and in earlier times the Code Noir prescribed whipping and branding and for repeated offenses even death), the slaves in fact enjoyed considerable freedom of movement at night. As one observer in Martinique indicated:

During the week, when work is finished, the slaves leave the plantation and run to those where they have women. . . . The liberty of the night, that is, the right to use their nights as they wish, is a veritable plague. With this type of liberty, the Negroes have every means to indulge in their debauchery, to commit thefts, to smuggle, to repair to their secret meetings, and to prepare and take their revenge. And what good work can be expected during the day from people who stay out and revel the whole night? When the masters are asked why the slaves are allowed such a fatal liberty, they reply that they cannot take it away from them.

"For the blacks," wrote de Cassagnac, "the night is a moment of supreme and incomparable sweetness that the whites will never understand." The night provided an opportunity for the exercise of individual freedom and collective self-expression away from the watchful eye of the authorities. It became the occasion for dancing, music, and religious rites—activities that expressed values antithetical to subordinating one's life to work and that rejected the role of sober, industrious, and self-regulated labor desired by the planters. If the slaves had learned to adapt to the exigencies of plantation labor, they nonetheless refused to reduce themselves to mere instruments of production.[79]

Thus, the free Saturday was important, not only as the appropriation of a quantity of time and the restriction of the labor time of the estate, but also as the qualitative transformation of the meaning of that time. Through this action, the slaves were able, in some limited way, to define the nature of freedom for themselves. "Free" time became free for the slave and not merely a period when sugar was not being produced. Its appropriation provided a base for the assertion of the slaves' purposes, needs, and cultural forms in other aspects of plantation life, including the organization of work and the composition of the working day. Thus, the free Saturday, with its appropriation of free time, became significant both because of its consequences for the material reproduction of the enslaved population and as an arena in which the slaves were able to contest the conditions of domination and exploitation and the conceptions of social life imposed by the plantation regime. For the slaves, their "free" time represented a social space to be protected and, if possible, expanded, while the master had to contain the slaves' demands within the limits of economic efficiency and social order. In the development of this process, the historical trajectory and limits of slave production and the master-slave relation can be traced.

The struggle over labor time, often implicit and submerged in everyday life, could under certain circumstances burst forth as collective action that overtly challenged the organization of labor and threatened public order. In the 1840s, for example, there were persistent attempts by the slaves in Martinique and Guadeloupe to refuse to do night work during the harvest season, and the correspondence of colonial officials records several instances where the authorities had to be summoned to restore order.

The promulgation of the Mackau Law in Martinique, on September 23, 1845, provided both the occasion and pretext for the outbreak of unrest among several *ateliers*. On October 25 of that year, the governor attributed these disturbances to the activities of agitators who had misled the slaves into believing that the government was concealing the true purpose and terms of the law, the immediate abolition of slavery. Despite the suppression of these initial incidents, the agitation continued, and the hated *veillée* became the focal point of the slaves' demands.[80]

On December 14, 1845, Leyritz estate in Basse-Pointe, administered by the mayor of the commune, was the site of a demonstration. The *atelier* of 250 slaves simultaneously refused all night work. Their action practically brought manufacturing on the plantation to a halt and had potentially serious consequences for the state of order elsewhere. The slaves based their refusal on the claim that the Mackau Law had abolished extraordinary work and night work. After several days of useless representations by the magistrates sent to the scene, a show of armed force was judged necessary to end the disorder that threatened to spread to the surrounding plantations. A detachment of infantry was dispatched and quelled the disturbance without bloodshed. After having been dispersed, the slaves gradually returned in small bands and peaceably resumed work.[81]

Two weeks later, on January 10, 1846, Governor Mathieu wrote that the incident had no further consequences. "Tranquility reigns in all parts of the colony. The *ateliers* are working well, and all of the reports that come to me are satisfactory." Yet a later document suggests that sporadic and isolated incidents of such unrest continued throughout much of 1846. In October of that year Governor Mathieu wrote in a letter to the Minister of Colonies: "The state of the *ateliers* continues to offer nothing alarming. It even seems to have calmed down. Demonstrations are becoming more and more rare since the measures taken against the *atelier* of the Acajou plantation in Lamentin. However, there were refusals to work on the estate of M. de Villarson of Sainte Anne and on the plantation of Robert Quantin of Saint Esprit. Order was restored without difficulty by the Justice of the Peace in Sainte Anne and by the mayor of the commune with the assistance of the gendarmerie in Saint Esprit."[82]

In his October 1846 letter, Mathieu commented that it was fortunate that cane was still being harvested in only a few parts of the island and that the work there was well advanced when the new law was promulgated in Martinique. The relative inactivity meant that there were few occasions to resist night work, and the work stoppages were sporadic and localized. Thus, he declared, "the refusal to work (which is always applied to night work) only resulted in isolated demonstrations that from that moment were easier to repress." He expressed the hope that by the next harvest masters and slaves would be better prepared for the new regime and a breakdown could be avoided. He concluded with the warning: "United action among the *ateliers* has not yet presented itself. There are no signs of it, but if it were to take place, the situation would be difficult and serious. The force of inertia, which certainly appears to be the counsel kept by the slaves, is a powerful element of disorder. It is all the more to be feared because it offers little leverage for government action. It is that which I fear the most."[83]

By 1847, the refusal to work, if it did not take the form of concerted action, nevertheless appears to have become much more widespread and generalized and to have had a noticeable effect on the colonial economy. The second of Mathieu's fears was being realized. In March of that year, he wrote to the Minister of Colonies: "There is a fact which is general everywhere, and which I must bring to the attention of Your Excellency. It is the slow down of work. Some estimate it at one-tenth, others at one-fifth, but it is very difficult to assess the figure exactly. Another observation is striking. Everywhere that the masters are resident on the estate the slow down is less, and it is more prominent where there are overseers in charge. The diminution of work is serious. The interests of the master are prejudiced, and there is a perceptible loss in his revenues." Mathieu now viewed this state of affairs as the inevitable consequence of the changes made in the disciplinary system of the *ateliers* instead of being simply the work of agitators. In his view, the prompt formation of disciplinary labor gangs (*ateliers de discipline*) was imperative in order to return things to their normal state. "A great deal of time, patience and encouraging words mixed with a just severity will be necessary to restore to the slaves the full energy they should show in their work."[84]

However not everyone was as sanguine as Mathieu about the possibility of a return to "normalcy." Schoelcher cites a growing body of informed colonial opinion that thought that the slave system in the French colonies had become untenable and that regarded this agitation as the prelude to general insurrection.

[The authorities] no longer feel themselves obliged to conceal [the grave disorders on the plantations] because they now have the possibility of blaming them on the new laws. But in spite of the inexplicable denials of the governors, it is certain that the *ateliers* show themselves to be less submissive, and that must be so. The truth penetrates the depths of the slave huts a little more. The most advanced slaves finally realize the abominable violence that is done to them. They have suffered misfortune for a long time, but now they know that their misfortune is a great inequity. They are beginning to no longer believe that they were created for the pleasure of the colonists, put on the earth to cultivate the cane fields of the planters under the threat of the whip. They are waiting for liberty but only obtain insignificant palliatives, and they act. What could be more natural and easier to explain rationally? We only fear one thing. That the pathetic laws being challenged here cannot prevent a general insurrection like the one that broke out in 1832 in Jamaica. The ground of slavery has been mined for a long time. A spark can make it explode.

The immediate goal of these work stoppages and struggles over night work was not the overthrow of slavery as such but to force the recognition of some limit on labor time and to establish a principle for its regulation. In themselves they were in no way the immediate cause of either the crisis of the sugar economy or the servile insurrection of 1848 that compelled local authorities to declare emancipation. Nevertheless, they were symptomatic of broader processes that by restricting the exploitability of slave labor and challenging the absolute authority of the master threatened to undermine the entire system. These processes did not necessarily feed into larger political struggles, but were at work within the slave relation, transforming its content and dissolving its form. Slowly, at times almost imperceptibly, they prepared the ground for the confrontation of 1848 and shaped

# Chapter Eight

# The Other Face of Slave Labor

## Provision Grounds and Internal Marketing

The slaves' working activity was not confined to the production of export commodities. The planters of Martinique were under constant pressure to reduce the costs of their operations. The easiest and most readily available means to do this was simply to squeeze more out of the slaves. The latter were obliged to produce for their own subsistence in their "free" time, that is, outside of the time devoted to producing the plantation's commercial crop. Instead of receiving the legally required amounts of food and clothing, the slaves were commonly given plots of marginal land and a free day on Saturday to produce at least a portion of their own consumption needs on their own account. (Some planters only gave half a day on Saturday and continued to supply a part of the slaves' rations themselves.) By encouraging the slave to work for himself, the master could avoid the effort and expense of the large-scale cultivation of provisions. Instead, he only had to furnish some clothing, a fixed weekly ration of salt meat or fish and perhaps rum, and occasional medical care.[1]

This arrangement directly benefitted the master, because the expense of maintaining the slave population placed a heavy economic burden on him. Goods imported for consumption were always expensive and their supply was often irregular, while both the land and time for provision cultivation emerged almost naturally from the conditions of sugar production itself. The planters perceived it in their interest to spend as little money, time, or energy as possible on slave maintenance. This perception did not change appreciably, at least as long as the slave trade lasted, and for many it went beyond the end of the slave trade and even of slavery itself. Allowing the slaves to produce for their own subsistence from resources already at hand instead of purchasing the necessary items on the market represented a saving to the master and a reduction of the cash expenses of the estate. The burden of reproduction costs was shifted directly to the slaves themselves, and they were kept usefully employed even during periods when there was no work to be done on the sugar crop. Although it meant that after long hours of toil in the cane fields, the slaves had to work still more just to secure the basic necessities of life, many planters hoped that it would give them a stake in the plantation and instill in them regular habits and the virtues of work and property.[2]

The possibility of self-organized subsistence production emerges from the contradictory nature of the slave relation itself. The same social relation that shaped labor as a mass, disciplined, cooperative force also created the possibility for autonomous individual subsistence production and marketing by the slaves. The commodification of the person of the laborer compressed these two kinds of labor—commodity production and the reproduction of the labor force—into the same social space and defined the relation between them. Slavery thus made possible, and in some respects even required, the development of provision crop cultivation by the slaves as a means of reducing or avoiding market expenditures for their maintenance. But this labor of reproduction developed within the antagonistic relation between master and slave. For the master, the provision ground was the means to guarantee cheap labor. For slaves, it was the means to elaborate an autonomous style of life. From these conflicting perspectives evolved a struggle over the conditions of material and social reproduction in which the slaves were able to appropriate aspects of these activities and develop them around their own interests and needs.

These simultaneously complementary and antagonistic processes crystallized in the practices and embryonic property relations that Sidney Mintz has described as the formation of a "proto-peasantry." He uses this term to characterize those activities that allowed the subsequent adaptation to a peasant way of life by people while they were still enslaved. As Mintz emphasizes, the formation of this proto-peasantry is both a mode of response and a mode of resistance by the enslaved to the conditions imposed on them by the plantation system. Thus, it was not a traditional peasantry attacked from the outside by commodity production, the market economy, and the colonial state; rather, it was formed from within the processes of the historical development of slavery and the plantation system. The cultivation and marketing of provision crops and the acquisition of the necessary agricultural and craft skills emerged seemingly as a matter of course from the interstices of the slave plantation. They were interstitial, not just in the sense that final authority over the use of the land and the disposition of labor resided with the master, but also that the time and space for such activities arose out of the rhythm of plantation life and labor. These were not activities and relations separate from the plantation system, but were intertwined in its logic; they developed within, and were dependent on, its temporal and spatial constraints. Slave provision-ground cultivation is thus intimately linked to the organization of export commodity production and develops in close association with it.[3]

Mintz has been primarily concerned to demonstrate the originality of the proto-peasant and subsequent peasant adaptations that were precipitated out of Caribbean slavery. I would like to extend and qualify this concept by examining the historical interrelation between the various types of laboring activities performed by the slave population. Rather than looking toward the formation of an independent peasantry as some readers of Mintz have done (though not Mintz himself), I would suggest that the focal point of the development of these autonomous cultivation and marketing activities is the struggle between master and slave over the conditions of labor and of social and material life within slavery. Beyond the formal juridical distinction between free and unfree labor, these activities indicate the substantive complexity of slave labor, which combined both "proletarian" labor in the cane fields, mill, and boiling house, and the "peasant labor" of the provision ground. This "peasant" dimension of slave labor emerges within its "proletarian" dimension and forms a counterpoint to it. While provision-ground cultivation arose from the planter's attempts to reduce costs and create an interest for the slave in the well-being of the estate, its further elaboration depended on the assertion by the slaves of their own individual and collective needs within and against the predominant slave relation. As has been seen in chapter 7, the condition of the development of autonomous provision-ground cultivation and marketing was the appropriation of a portion of the estate's labor time by the slaves. This struggle for "free" time entailed, and was reinforced and conditioned by, struggles to appropriate physical space and to establish the right to property and disposition over their own activity. In turn, the consolidation of slave autonomy in provision-ground cultivation provided leverage for more struggles over the conditions of staple crop production. These interrelated practices transformed and subverted the organization of labor within slavery as they reinforced it.[4]

This process reveals both the contradictoriness and historically developing character of the master-slave relation. As the assertion of slave autonomy had a continual tendency to push "beyond" the limits of the slave relation, the master was compelled to try to recapture and rationalize labor under these changing conditions. Thus, for example, task work may be seen as an attempt to create a new, more effective form of labor discipline whose premise is autonomous slave self-interest. Industrial discipline depended on the existence of provision grounds and adequate material incentives recognized by both parties, though meaning something different to each. Slave struggles for autonomy and planter efforts to contain them within the bounds of the prevailing relations of production developed the slave relation to its fullest extent and created both the embryo of postemancipation class structure within slavery, and the conditions for the transition to "free labor." Seen from this perspective, the reconstruction of the post-emancipation plantation system was not simply a unilateral and functional shift to a more adequate and rational "capitalist" form of organization. Rather, it was a process whose outcome was problematic, requiring violence and compulsion to recapture labor in the face of material and social resources acquired by the laboring population while still enslaved. The struggle over conditions of labor and of social and material life was continued in a new historical context.

# Slavery and Subsistence

While the slaves had been given small gardens to supplement their rations since the beginning of slavery in the French colonies, the practice of giving the slaves gardens and a free day each week to grow their own food was brought by Dutch refugees from Pernambuco, who introduced sugar cane into the French Antilles during the first half of the seventeenth century. The origins of this practice can be traced back to São Tomé in the sixteenth century. Thus, the diffusion of sugar cane entailed not merely the movement of a commodity, but the spread of a whole way of life. With the appearance of sugar cultivation in the French Caribbean, subsistence crops for the slaves were neglected in favor of planting cane, and the "Brazilian custom" was rapidly adopted by planters eager to reduce their expenses. Masters no longer distributed rations to their slaves. Instead, the latter were expected to provide their own food, shelter, clothing, and other material needs from the labor of their "free" day.[5]

But this practice had negative consequences. Food production was chaotic, and the slaves were often poorly nourished. Indeed, frequent food shortages prevented the masters from dispensing altogether with the distribution of rations. Critics of the custom of free Saturdays claimed that it gave the slaves too much freedom and encouraged theft and disorder. The metropolitan authorities were in agreement with the critics and sought both to stop what they perceived to be the excesses resulting from the free Saturday and to ensure adequate treatment for the slave population. The proclamation of the Royal Edict of 1685 (the Code Noir) by the metropolitan government was the first attempt to establish a uniform dietary standard for slaves in all the French colonies and to put an end to the prevailing disorder. It sought to make the master totally responsible for the maintenance of his slaves and to prescribe standards for food, shelter, and clothing to be provided to the slaves. The practice of individual slave gardens and free Saturdays in lieu of rations was to be suppressed, and regular weekly food allowances of determined composition and quantity (the *ordinaire*) were mandated.[6]

This edict remained the fundamental legislation governing slavery in the French colonies throughout the ancien régime. The distribution of slave rations seems to have been more widely practiced in Martinique than elsewhere in the French Antilles, and the slaves there had the reputation of being better fed than elsewhere in the French colonies during the ancien régime. Even so, the writings of administrators in Martinique throughout the course of the eighteenth century complain continuously that the slave owners were concerned only with sugar, and, if they provided a part of the slaves' nourishment, they obliged them to secure the rest on their own account. The persistent failure to regulate slave diet and treatment and especially to prohibit the practice of slave provision grounds is evidenced by the succession of declarations, edicts, ordinances, regulations, and decrees, too numerous to recount, promulgated on these matters by both metropolitan and colonial authorities during the seventeenth and eighteenth centuries. The colonial authorities lacked the means to enforce the regulations in a society dominated by slaveholders who were usually hostile to any tinkering with their "property rights," particularly if it cost them time or money. Planters expressed their preference for slave self-subsistence, and the reluctance to spend money on slave maintenance, especially food, persisted throughout the ancien régime and into the nineteenth century. Far from dying out, the practice of free Saturdays and private provision grounds expanded and increasingly became an established part of colonial life during those years.[7]

Ordinances enacted in 1784 and 1786 revised the Code Noir and represent an important attempt to ameliorate the lot of slaves and reconcile the law with the growing importance of provision grounds in the colonies. The practice of the free Saturday was still forbidden, but instead of prohibiting slave provision grounds, this legislation recognized their existence and attempted to regulate their use. It decreed that each adult slave was to receive a small plot of land to cultivate on his or her own account. However, the produce of these plots was to supplement the *ordinaire*, not to replace it. The distribution of rations was still required by the law. This prohibition against substituting the free Saturday for the legal ration was restated by the Royal Ordinance of October 29, 1828, which reformed the colonial penal code. However, the custom was stronger than the law, and ministerial instructions advised colonial authorities to tolerate this arrangement when it was voluntary on the part of the slave.[8]

This legislation was a step toward recognizing the realities of colonial life, but provision-ground cultivation was still regarded as only a supplemental activity, and the slave codes continued to insist on the distribution of the *ordinaire* as the primary means of providing for slave maintenance. However, postwar economic conditions made complete dependence on the ration impractical, and scarcities caused planters to increase their reliance on provision-ground cultivation. According to evidence presented before the commission of inquiry into the sugar industry, before 1823 the majority of plantations could only rarely provide their slaves with the *ordinaire* and had to abandon them to the necessity of providing for their own subsistence, thus depriving themselves of the labor of their slaves. In his testimony before the commission, Jabrun stated that the slaves were better fed, better, better dressed, and better housed than they had been some years previously. However, de Lavigne testified that the lack of affluence and shortage of credit—and consequently, the difficulty in obtaining provisions opportunely—still caused some planters to substitute the free Saturday for the ration. But he added that in general this practice had ceased in Martinique. Almost all the Negroes now received the quantity of codfish and other food prescribed by the regulations, and provision grounds supplemented the ration. While this claim seems exaggerated, de Lavigne also suggests a cyclical aspect of provision-ground cultivation. In contrast to periods of low sugar prices, when land and labor could be given over to provision grounds, with the high prices of the sugar boom of the 1820s, many planters may have preferred to devote their attention entirely to sugar cultivation and purchase necessary provisions. Undoubtedly, a variety of individual strategies were possible, and while the historical continuity of provision-ground cultivation may be demonstrated for the colony as a whole, it may not necessarily have been practiced on individual estates.[9]

Despite the shortcomings and abuses of the practice of free Saturdays and slave provision grounds and the repeated attempts to suppress or regulate them, the scale of these activities increased steadily, and by the nineteenth century they had become more and more central to the functioning of the colonial economy. By the 1830s, the masters, with few exceptions, were encouraging their slaves to grow their own foodstuffs, and the substitution of free Saturdays for rations had become widespread. The slaves were given as much land as they could cultivate. They not only produced but also marketed their crops without supervision, and the colony became dependent on their produce for a substantial portion of its food. As one observer stated, "the plantations which produce foodstuffs [*habitations vivrières*] and the slaves who cultivate gardens more than guarantee that the colony is supplied with local produce." Measures prohibiting these activities were disregarded with the common consent of both masters and slaves. Enforcement not only would have inhibited the efforts of the independent slave cultivators, but also could have reduced the island's food supply.[10]

By the 1840s, colonial authorities no longer regarded these practices as threats to order, but rather felt that they contributed to social harmony. The reports of local officials particularly stressed the social benefits of independent cultivation by slaves. One of them expressed the opinion that the free Saturday was an "effective means of giving [the slave] the taste for property and well-being, and consequently, to make them useful craftsmen and agriculturalists desirous of family ties." For another, writing in 1842, it meant nothing less than bringing the slaves up to the standards of the civilized world: "But the slaves, for whom the custom of free Saturdays is established, prefer it to the ration because they work on their own account and find some profit from that state of affairs. It is clear evidence that man, even though a slave, has an interest in money and likes to enjoy the fruits of his labors while freely disposing of that which belongs to him. The black is forced to enter into types of social transactions that can only serve as a means of civilizing him." This latter aspect was seen to be especially important because of the imminent prospect of emancipation. The report continued: "In this regard, the custom of the free Saturday must be preferred to the legally sanctioned ration because, beyond everything else, it is a road toward free labor."[11]

Thus, slavery, instead of separating the direct producers from the means of subsistence, provided them with the means of producing a livelihood. While the slaves acquired access to the use of property and the possibility of improving the material conditions of life, for them the price of subsistence was work beyond that required for sugar production. With these developments, the time devoted to the slaves' reproduction became separate from commodity production, and a de facto distinction between time belonging to the master and time belonging to the slave was created. However, instead of permitting the rationalization of the labor process, this distinction blocked it. The relation between time devoted to commodity production and the time devoted to the reproduction of the labor force became fixed and rigid. The prevailing conditions of production were thereby reinforced. The economy of time and labor was dissolved into the maintenance and reproduction of a given body of laborers and the regular performance of a predetermined quantity of labor; it thus resolved itself into a social-political question as the master-slave relation was challenged from within.

## The Self-Appropriation of the Appropriated

The successful development of autonomous provision-ground cultivation and marketing in Martinique depended on the response of the enslaved. It was the result of the slaves adapting to New World conditions and acquiring the skills and habits necessary to produce and market these crops. One contemporary document stresses the importance of cultural adaptation on the part of the slaves in developing subsistence agriculture and also suggests that slave provision grounds became more prevalent after the slave trade was abolished.

> Thus, previously, the progress of the population did not take place in accordance with the laws of nature. Each year, the irregular introduction of considerable numbers of blacks increased the possibility of a scarce food supply in the country. These new arrivals in the colonies, knowing neither the soil, the climate, nor the special agriculture of the Antilles, could not count on themselves for their support. It was necessary to provide sufficient and regular nourishment for them, but they had no skills to contribute. Thus, the proprietors were quite properly compelled to plant a certain amount

of provisions since their slaves did not know how or were unable to plant enough. . . . The slaves required more prompt and rigorous discipline [than today] because of the savage stage in which almost all of them had been taken, their ignorance of the work of a sugar plantation, the tiring labor to which they had perhaps not been accustomed, and their sorrow for their country which could lead some of them to commit crimes. . . . The slaves of today have less need of constant tutelage than previously. They are able to supply themselves without depending on the generosity of their masters. The latter hardly plant provisions at all any more because the slaves plant well beyond the amount that is necessary for consumption.

Indeed, nineteenth-century accounts indicate that the slaves by and large preferred to have an extra day to themselves and to raise their own provisions rather than receive an allowance of food from the master. "This practice," observed one government official, "is completely to the advantage of the slave who wants to work. A day spent by him cultivating his garden, or in some other manner, will bring him more than the value of the nourishment the law prescribes for him. I will add that there is no *atelier* that does not prefer this arrangement to the execution of the edict [Code Noir]. Once it has been set, it would be dangerous for the master to renounce it."[12]

The provision grounds and "proto-peasant" activities were not merely functional for the reproduction of the social and material relations of the slave plantation. They also offered a space for slave initiative and self-assertion that cannot simply be deduced from their economic form. Through them the slaves themselves organized and controlled a secondary economic network that originated within the social and spatial boundaries of the plantation, but that allowed them to begin to construct an alternative way of life that went beyond it. In this process, the bonds of dependence of the slave on the master slowly began to dissolve, and the activities of the slaves gradually transformed the foundations of slave society itself. The changing role and meaning of these activities was both cause and response to the increased pressure on the plantation system during the first half of the nineteenth century. While these practices had existed virtually since the beginning of slavery in the colony, they assumed new importance with the changing economic and political conditions of those decades and the imminent prospect of emancipation.

The reforms of the July Monarchy were a decisive step in the recognition of existing practices in the colonies and prepared the way for emancipation. The law of July 18 and 19, 1845, known as the Mackau Law, allowed the substitution of provision grounds for the *ordinaire*. While the land itself remained the property of the master, its produce belonged to the slave, and the law recognized the latter's legal personality and right to chattel property. The slaves could not represent themselves in civil action, but they had the right to administer their personal property and dispose of it as they saw fit in accordance with the civil code. This legislation confirmed and regularized what was already a customary practice and gave it the sanction of law. It thus extended the scope of previous legislation and further legitimized the existing custom. In the words of its authors, "The law only recognizes a state that has long existed in practice and makes it a right to the great advantage of the black and without detriment to the master." These legally enforceable rights were less precarious and dependent on the proprietor's whim than was the previous custom. The slaves could now assert their purposes with the backing of the colonial state. The authorities saw in these practices not the source of disorder but the means to regulate slavery and provide a transition to free labor. The purpose of the legislation was to ease the transition to freedom by giving slaves skills, property, and therefore a stake in society. "On the eve of complete emancipation, it is the interest of the masters to see the taste for labor and the spirit of economy develop in the slaves. Now, without property there is no industrious activity. It is only for oneself that one has the heart to work. Without property there is no economy. One does not economize for another."[13]

The Royal Ordinance of June 5, 1846, allowed the slaves to choose between the Saturday and the *ordinaire*. On request, each adult slave over fourteen years of age could have the disposition of one free day per week to provide his or her own nourishment in place of the weekly ration. The minimum size of the plot to be allotted to each individual slave was set at six ares for slaves on a sugar estate, four ares for a coffee plantation, and three ares for other types of estates, and the master was not to make deductions for plots claimed by other members of the same family. The plot was to be located no more than one kilometer from the center of the plantation unless approved by the authorities. In addition, the master was also to supply the seeds and tools necessary to begin cultivation for the first year, but he was not obliged to renew the supply of these items. The extent of these plots could be reduced by half if the master could justify to colonial authorities that the total arable land at his disposal compared to the number of slaves made it necessary. The slave could only be made to leave the assigned plot when (1) it had been at his disposition for at least a full year; (2) his harvest was completed, and he had been advised not to plant again; and (3) a plot equivalent in size and as far as possible in quality was put at his disposal. Further, on the day reserved to him, the slave had the right to rent himself out, either to his master or to another proprietor in the commune on the condition that he demonstrated that his provision grounds were well maintained.[14]

The slave who claimed a free day had to provide only for his or her own personal nourishment from the provision ground. The husband, wife, children, or other family members to whom the disposition of a free day did not apply were to continue receiving the *ordinaire*, which this new legislation set at six liters of manioc flour, six kilograms of rice or seven kilograms of corn, and one-and-a-half kilograms of cod or salt beef per week for an adult slave over fourteen years. (Although there were some complaints about the lack of meat, all observers, including abolitionists such as Schoelcher, reported that the diet of the slaves who received the *ordinaire* was adequate if plain, and that planters supplemented the legal requirements with salt and rice.) However, an arrangement could be made between the master and the slave mother or father to replace the ration due to the children with additional free time. In this case, the size of plot allotted was to be increased by one-sixth for each child over six years of age. But the right to this supplemental land ended when the child for whom it was claimed reached fourteen years of age. Such arrangements also had to be submitted to the local authorities for approval.[15]

To prevent abuses of this system and to ensure adequate maintenance of the slaves, the request for the free day was to be made verbally in the presence of four adult slaves of the *atelier*, and each planter was to present a list of the slaves on his estate to the justice of the peace with an indication of those who requested the free day. The judge, on his own office or at the planter's request, could void the arrangement when the slave was recognized as incapable of providing his nourishment by his own labor, when he neglected the cultivation of his plot, or when he abused the time at his disposal. This arrangement could also be suspended or annulled at the slave's request, but in this case he could not claim the right to a provision ground again for at least six months without showing sufficient motive to the justice of the peace.[16]

Table 8.1 indicates the extent of provision-ground cultivation and the practice of free Saturdays in Martinique in the 1840s. However, it must be noted that these figures refer to the number of visits made by the inspecting magistrates, not to the number of plantations or slaves in the colony. Many estates were visited several times. Between May 1841 and May 1843, the colonial magistrates charged under the law with inspecting slave conditions made 968 visits to plantations (of these 514 were to sugar plantations, 214 to coffee plantations, and 240 to other types of plantation).[17]

With few exceptions, masters encouraged their slaves to grow their own foodstuffs wherever possible. Among the estates included in this sample, the practice of giving free Saturdays to the slaves appears to have been far more common than the distribution of the legally prescribed *ordinaire* as the means of providing for slave subsistence. The substitution of free Saturdays for the legal ration was almost general throughout the colony, while garden plots were almost universal and appear to have existed even where the *ordinaire* was distributed. For example, according to one report, in Lamentin, where free Saturdays were denied on almost all the plantations and slaves received the legal allotments, the slaves nevertheless kept well-tended gardens and profited from the local markets to draw considerable revenues from them. Alternatively, many planters, especially if they were well-to-do, like the owners of the large plantations in Sainte Marie, preferred to give rations

Table 8.1. Summary of Magistrates' Inspection Reports on Slave Conditions, 1841–1843

| | Arrondissement | | |
| | St. Pierre | Fort Royal | Total |
|---|---|---|---|
| Number of plantations visited | | | |
| Sugar | 205 | 309 | 514 |
| Coffee | 38 | 176 | 214 |
| Provisions and minor crops | 112 | 100 | 212 |
| Mixed crops | 16 | 12 | 28 |
| Total | 371 | 597 | 968 |
| Number of slaves | | | |
| Below 14 years old | 6,556 | 9,670 | 16,226 |
| 14–60 years old | 14,491 | 21,548 | 36,039 |
| Over 60 years old | 1,520 | 2,173 | 3,693 |
| Total | 22,567 | 33,391 | 55,958 |
| Food distribution by plantation | | | |
| Legally prescribed ration | 67 | 129 | 196 |
| Partial ration | 252 | 400 | 652 |
| Mixed regime | 33 | 60 | 93 |
| No information | 19 | 8 | 27 |
| Clothing distribution (by plantations) | | | |
| Legally prescribed ration | 244 | 256 | 500 |
| Partial ration | 54 | 52 | 106 |
| No distribution | 60 | 287 | 347 |
| No information | 13 | 2 | 15 |
| Gardens (by plantation) | | | |
| Well or adequately cultivated | 304 | 384 | 688 |
| Poorly cultivated | 49 | 159 | 208[a] |
| No gardens | 14 | 48 | 62 |
| No information | 12 | 6 | 18 |

Source: Ministère de la Marine et des Colonies, Exposé générale des résultats du patronage des esclaves dans les Colonies françaises, pp. 89–90.

[a]Table gives figure as 200. Presumed addition error.

to their slaves rather than to allow them to cultivate gardens independently. Not surprisingly, the distribution of clothing allowances was more widely practiced than food rations, although the plantation inspection reports reveal that many planters expected their slaves to provide their own clothing as well as their food from the income of their gardens. This practice was especially widespread among the less prosperous planters, particularly in the poorer southern *arrondissement* of Fort Royal. Only planters who were well-off could afford to buy clothing to give to their slaves. Others could do so only when the harvest was good, if at all. Several public prosecutors objected to making the slaves provide their own clothing and admonished the planters to stop the practice. Thus, while there were diverse combinations and possibilities of conditions of subsistence, the slaves appear to have provided a substantial amount of their maintenance through their independent labors beyond their toil in the cane fields, and the gardens and free Saturdays were a widespread experience for the majority of the slaves.[18]

However, not all parts of the island nor all planters were amenable to the cultivation of provision grounds. The instances where there were no gardens or where they were reported as poorly cultivated appear to be overrepresented in the arid and poorer southern part of the island (the *arrondissement* of Fort Royal). In Vauclin, Marin, Sainte Anne, Diamant, Anses d'Arlets, Trois Ilets, and parts of Carbet, dry weather and poor soil prevented the slaves from producing enough to feed themselves and contributed to the malaise of the plantations as well. In 1843, a public prosecutor inspecting plantations in Vauclin wrote: "In the *quartier*, the masters could not substitute the free Saturday for allowances of food without compromising the existence of their *ateliers*. The drought and the quality of the soil would prevent the slaves from satisfying their needs by their own labor. For several years, the products of some very important plantations have not covered their expenses."[19]

For even the most industrious slave, the paternalism of the planter was inescapable. As Schoelcher remarked, "the greater or lesser wealth of the slaves depends a great deal on the benevolence of the master." Whichever mode of providing for the slaves was adopted, one inspection report noted, "their nourishment is assured everywhere, and the master is always ready . . . to come to the aid of the slave when the latter has need of him." Indeed, seasonal fluctuations could require the master to come to the assistance of his slaves. "In years of great drought," de Cassagnac writes, "subsistence crops do not grow. Then planters who previously gave the free Saturday once again give the *ordinaire*. Those are disastrous years."[20]

Although the actual cultivation of the crops was not subject to the direct discipline of the planter, this labor could be compulsory. According to the inspection report of one public prosecutor, "The good or bad state of his provisions is the doing of the slave. However, the master can be accused of negligence if he does not use all the means of encouragement or of correction in his power to compel the slave to work for himself and thus improve his lot. Also, I have given my approval to those planters who have told me that they are just as severe or even more so with the slave who will not cultivate his garden than with the one who will not work with them." But compulsion was not usually necessary, and individual planters often went to great lengths to support the efforts of their slaves. Sieur Telliam-Maillet, who managed the "Ceron" plantation in Diamant, had the land that his slaves were going to use for their provision grounds plowed. Even though he supplied his slaves with the *ordinaire*, M. de Delite-Loture, who owned nearly 300 slaves in the *quartier* of Sainte Anne, bought or rented land in the highlands of Rivière Pilote, which he cleared so his slaves could work it for themselves. Each week, he had them taken nearly two leagues from the plantation to these gardens, and he paid for the transport of their produce as well. Schoelcher reports that in some *quartiers*, the masters provided the slaves who worked such gardens with tools, carts, mules, and a *corvée* of workers, and the masters and the slave cultivators divided the harvest in half. Other masters considered such an arrangement beneath their dignity and simply abandoned the land to the slaves.[21]

According to Schoelcher, the garden was the principal source of well-being available to the slaves in Martinique. Customarily, slaves who were given half a free day a week were only given half a ration, while those who received a full day were to provide their food by themselves. In addition, Sundays belonged to the slaves and could also be devoted to subsistence activities, as could rest periods and evenings during the week. Schoelcher records that on a great number of plantations in Martinique, this arrangement had become a sort of exchange between the master and his slaves. "This transaction," he writes, "is very favorable for the master who no longer has capital to lay out to ensure the supply of provisions. And it is accepted with good will by the black who in working Saturday and Sunday in his garden derives great benefits."[22]

The slaves who wanted to plant gardens were given as much land as they could cultivate. The provision grounds were usually on the uncultivated lands on the margins of the estate, often scattered in the hills above the cane fields. However, both de Cassagnac and Schoelcher write that some planters in the 1840s used the gardens to practice crop rotation. When the sugar cane had exhausted the soil in a field, the slaves were permitted to plant provisions there until the land was again fit for cane. The gardens were then shifted to other fields. (According to historian Gabriel Debien, larger gardens located away from the slave quarters appeared only after 1770, but these were still intended to supplement the rations provided by the master rather than furnish the main items of the slave diet. The staples of the slave diet, manioc, potatoes, and yams, were grown by the master in the gardens belonging to the plantation.) The plots were frequently quite extensive, as much as one or two *arpents*, according to Schoelcher (1 *arpent* = 0.85 acre). All the available sources agree that the slave provision grounds were very well kept. The produce of the gardens was abundant, and the land was not allowed to stand idle. Manioc, the principal source of nourishment of the slave population, was harvested as often as four times a year. Besides manioc, the slaves raised bananas, potatoes, yams, and other vegetables on these provision grounds.[23]

In addition to the provision grounds, there were also small gardens in the yards surrounding the slave cabins. They were intended to supplement the weekly ration, not replace it, and all the slaves, including those who received the *ordinaire*, had them. There the slaves grew sorrel (*oiselle de Guinée*), a type of squash (*giraumon*), cucumbers from France and Guinea (*concombres de France et de Guinée*), green peppers (*poivrons*), hot peppers (*piment z'oiseau*), calabash vines (*liane à calebasse*), okra (*petites racines gombo*), and perhaps some tobacco. They also planted fruit trees and, if the master permitted, kept a few chickens there as well.[24]

The "little Guineas," as the provision grounds have been called, allowed collective self-expression by the slaves and form what Roger Bastide describes as a "niche" within slavery where Afro-Caribbean culture could develop. The slaves had complete responsibility for the provision grounds and were able to organize their own activity there without supervision. The use of these parcels and their product was not simply a narrow economic activity, but was integrated into broader cultural patterns. The work of preparing the soil, planting, cultivating, and harvesting, and the disposition of the product were organized through ritual, kinship, and community, and were important for aspects of slave life as diverse as kinship, cuisine, and healing practices. These activities provided an avenue for the slaves to exercise decision making and demonstrate self-worth otherwise closed off by slavery. But except for Schoelcher's vague comment that the slaves cultivated them "communally," there is little detailed information on how the slaves organized their activities. This lack of documentation is perhaps mute testimony to the genuine autonomy that the slaves enjoyed in the conduct of these activities.[25]

Even at best, the slaves who produced their own provisions were exposed to risk and uncertainty. They were generally given land of inferior quality that was incapable of supporting sugar or coffee. At times, the planters deprived them of their free day under various pretexts. If for some reason they fell ill and could not work, their food supply was jeopardized. Drought or bad weather might make cultivation impossible. The prospect of theft and disorder was then increased, and at the extreme the physical well-being of the labor force was threatened.[26]

Nevertheless, this arrangement could be advantageous for an industrious slave. Access to this property meant that the slaves' consumption was no longer entirely dependent on the economic condition of the master. Rather, they could use their free time and the produce of their gardens to improve their standard of living. They demonstrated exceptional initiative and skill and used the opportunities presented to them to secure at least relative control over their subsistence and a degree of independence from the master. According to one contemporary estimate, the incentive provided by the gardens doubled slave output, while Higman's data suggest an inverse relation between provision ground cultivation and mortality on

Jamaican sugar estates. With the free day and the other free time that could be husbanded during the week during rest periods and after tasks were finished, the slave could produce beyond his or her immediate subsistence needs. The slaves sold this produce in the towns and cities and developed a network of markets that was an important feature of the economic and social life of the colony. The sale of this surplus in the town market allowed the slaves to improve both the quantity and quality of goods available to them and satisfy tastes and desires that the master could not supply. Thus improvement in the slaves' well-being was due to their own effort, not any amelioration of the regime.[27]

Of course, not all slaves were willing or able to endure the burden of extra work that the provision grounds represented. Infants, the aged, the infirm, expectant mothers or those nursing children—all those who could not provide for themselves—received a food allowance from the master even on the plantations where the slaves grew their own foodstuffs. Also included among this number were those slaves who refused to raise a garden. In Fort Royal, a public prosecutor wrote: "Only the lazy receive a ration and they are almost ashamed of it." Of these "lazy" slaves, Schoelcher commented: "We do not want to deny, however, that there are many Negroes who show a great indifference to the benefit of free Saturdays. It is necessary to force them to work for themselves on that day. It does not surprise us that beings, saturated with disgust and struck by malediction, are little concerned to improve their lot during the moments of respite that are given to them. Instead, they prefer to surrender to idleness or become intoxicated to the point of delirium from the melancholy agitation of their African dances." The free Saturday, while generally received enthusiastically by the slaves, was not universally accepted. For many slaves, it simply meant more work, and they refused. They withdrew their voluntary cooperation and threw the burden of maintenance back on the master. De Cassagnac expressed surprise that on many plantations, if the slaves were given the free Saturday, they would not work. They had, in his view, to be treated like children and be forced to work for themselves. It was necessary to have a driver lead them to the gardens and watch them as carefully as when they were working for the estate.[28]

Long before the promulgation of the Mackau Laws the slaves established rights and prerogatives with regard not only to the produce of the land but to the provision grounds and gardens themselves that the masters were compelled to recognize. "The masters no longer acknowledge any rights over the gardens of the *atelier*. The slave is the sovereign master over the terrain that is conceded to him," admitted the Colonial Council of Martinique. "This practice has become a custom for the slaves who regard it as a right which cannot be taken from them without the possibility of disrupting the discipline and good order of the *ateliers*," reported one official. The slaves regarded the provision grounds as their own. When they died, the garden and its produce was passed on to their relatives. "They pass them on from father to son, from mother to daughter, and, if they do not have any children, they bequeath them to their nearest kin or even their friends," wrote Schoelcher. Often, if no relatives remained on the estate, it was reported that kinsmen came from other plantations to receive their inheritance with the consent of the master. Here as elsewhere the autonomous kinship organization of the slave community served as a counterpoint to the economic rationality of the plantation, and the master was obliged to respect its claims.[29]

The slaves defended their rights even at the expense of the master, and there was often a subtle game of give-and-take between the two parties. While travelling through the *quartier* of Robert, Schoelcher was surprised to find two small patches of manioc in the midst of a large, well-tended cane field. M. Tiberge, the proprietor, explained that the slaves planted the manioc when the field had been abandoned. When he wanted to cultivate the field he offered to buy the crop, but they demanded an exorbitant price. The master then called on the other slaves to set what they considered to be a fair price, but this too was rejected by the slaves who had planted the manioc. "I'll have to wait six or seven months until that damned manioc is ripe," Tiberge continued. Another planter, M. Latuillerie of Lamentin, on returning from a long trip, found that his slaves had abandoned the plots allotted to them in favor of his cane fields. He could not simply reclaim his land, but instead he first had to agree to give the occupants another field. Schoelcher also observed large mango trees in the middle of cane fields that stunted the cane plants in their shadow. The masters would have cut them down, but they remained standing because they were bequeathed to some yet-unborn slave. He continued, "There are some planters who do not have fruit trees on their plantations because tradition establishes that such and such a tree belongs to such and such a Negro, and they [the planters] have little hope of ever enjoying them because the slave bequeaths his tree just like the rest of his property."[30]

## The Fruits of Their Labor

Beyond supplying the personal consumption needs of the slaves, the provision grounds produced a marketable surplus of food that was sold to the plantations and in the towns and cities. The main source of revenue for the slaves was the sale of manioc flour and other agricultural products, and among the main customers were the plantations themselves. Almost all of the manioc consumed on the majority of medium and large estates was purchased from the slaves. The planters bought these provisions to replace or supplement provisions cultivated as an estate crop and to distribute as rations to those slaves who were unable to provide their own food. The abundance of slave produce, especially in the years when agricultural conditions were favorable, caused the price of provisions on the local markets to fall sharply. When this happened, the more prosperous planters bought manioc flour from their slaves at a constant price above that of the market and, according to de Moges, gave it right back to them as a ration. One official observed that "every time that manioc flour is cheap, the master buys it from them, usually at a price above the market price. Sometimes he pays double the market price." The report of a deputy public prosecutor in 1843 describes the difficulties caused by low provision prices:

The worthless price to which provisions, especially manioc flour . . . sometimes fall causes even the most industrious slave to become disgusted with labor. In these circumstances, many masters, I believe one could say the majority of them, come to the aid of their slaves, buying from them the quantity of flour which is necessary for the needs of their plantations at a price well above the market price. But sometimes the discouragement of men whose hopes for a better price for their labor have been betrayed is such that they do not plant at all in the following year. Thus dearth often follows abundance.

By subsidizing their slaves' production in hard times, the planters hoped to encourage them to continue growing provisions and thereby avoid a scarcity which would drive prices up, increase the colony's reliance on food imports, and disrupt general economic activity. Instead, they could keep prices low and guarantee a stable supply of essential provisions by supporting the market.[31]

The slaves also developed a network of markets beyond the plantation that were an important feature of the economic and social life in Martinique, and the colony came to rely on the produce of the slave gardens for a substantial portion of its food. Important market towns such as the ones at Lamentin, François, Trinité, and Robert attracted slaves from all parts of the island and brought them into contact with the world beyond the plantation. Soleau describes the Lamentin market: "This town is one of the most frequently visited by the slaves of the colony. It has a fairly large market where they come to sell their produce on Sunday. I have been told that the number of slaves that gather there is often as high as five or six thousand. I passed through there that day while going to the *quartier* of Robert, and encountered many blacks on the road who were going to the town. All were carrying something that they were doubtlessly going to sell—manioc flour, potatoes, yams, poultry, etc." Sunday was the major market day in the towns, but smaller markets were held on other days. These markets allowed the masters to have their slaves acquire goods that were not available on the plantation and would otherwise have to be purchased. An astonishing variety of goods were exchanged at the town markets. These of course included manioc, fruits, vegetables, yams, fresh or salted fish, animals, and slave handicrafts, but also manufactured goods such as shoes, dry goods, porcelain, crystal, perfume, jewelry, and furniture. Undoubtedly, barter played a large part in these exchanges, especially in local markets, but the money economy was significant, and prices were set in major towns for the main articles of trade. The scale of exchanges at these town markets was so great that they caused the urban merchants to complain, but in the words of Sainte Croix, they were nevertheless a great resource for the interior of the island.[32]

The Sunday market was as much a social event as an occasion for exchanging goods. Slaves went to town to attend mass, to meet friends from other parts of the island, drink tafia, smoke, eat roast corn, exchange news and gossip, and perhaps dance, sing, or gamble. It was an opportunity for display, and the slaves wore their best. One observer paints a striking picture of the appearance made by the slaves at the Lamentin market: "These slaves are almost always very well dressed and present the exterior signs of material well-being. The men have trousers, shirts, vests, and hats of oilskin or straw. The women have skirts of Indian cotton, white blouses, and scarves, some of which are luxurious, as well as earrings, pins and even some chains of gold." According to Soleau, the signs of prosperity presented by the slaves of Martinique on market day were unusual in the Caribbean and even in rural France: "One thing struck me that I have never seen in Cayenne, Surinam, or Demerara. It is the cleanliness and the luxury of the clothing of the slaves that I encountered. The lazy, having nothing to sell, remained on the plantations, but in France, generally, the peasants, except for their shoes, were not better dressed on Sunday and did not wear such fine material."[33]

The colorful and bustling markets punctuated the drudgery and isolation of plantation life. Slaves from town and country, young and old, male and female, as well as freedmen, sailors, merchants, planters—anyone who wanted to buy or sell—mingled in the crowds. Such gatherings were potentially dangerous and posed a threat to order and security in a slave society, as Governor Mathieu recognized: "I have posted thirty men and an officer at St. Esprit. This measure was welcomed by the entire commune. St. Esprit is a center of commerce. A great number of people, including many strangers, gather there for the markets that are held each week, especially on Sundays. Thus, police measures are necessary and are linked to those that have been established to prevent bad subjects from stirring up the *ateliers* and inciting unrest."[34]

These markets offered incentives to the slaves and enabled them to improve the material conditions of life as well as to acquire skills, knowledge, and social contacts that increased their independence and allowed them to assert their individuality and vary the texture of their lives. Their initiative led to the development of new economic and social patterns and the mobilization of productive forces that otherwise would have remained dormant.

They were able to obtain money and to purchase a range of goods that would otherwise be unavailable to them. Particularly important were items of clothing, and the more industrious slaves were able to forego the ration and provide for themselves. According to one inspection report: "In general, the slaves are well-dressed. The most industrious of them renounce the distribution of clothing and are well enough off to consider it a disgrace to ask the master for a shirt or a pair of trousers. On the other hand, the laziest of them sometimes oblige the masters to give them more than the regulations prescribe." With the ability to acquire their own clothing, dress became an important expression of independence and status during their free time. While they were working, the slaves dressed poorly. Schoelcher marveled at the tatters they wore. But on "their" time the slaves' appearance could undergo a drastic transformation. On Sundays or special occasions, the slaves wore frock coats and well-made outfits with satin vests, ruffled shirts, boots, and the ever-present umbrella. A public prosecutor described the appearance of the slaves at a New Year's celebration on one plantation: "The costumes of some dancers were luxurious so to speak. For the women, there were skirts of fine material, cambric shirts, coral or jet necklaces, and gold earrings. For the men, costumes of linen or broadcloth. Shoes had been abandoned as unnecessary encumbrances." Another prosecutor reported a runaway slave who wore a black frock coat, boots, and a new silk hat, and who passed for a freedman for several days. "Meeting them like this," wrote Schoelcher, "one does not suspect that they are the same men that were seen the day before working in rags." Boots or shoes were an especially important status symbol among the slaves. In the early days of the colony, they were forbidden to wear shoes. Although these ordinances were no longer enforced, most slaves went barefoot. Schoelcher wrote that it was not uncommon to meet a well-dressed slave on the road to town carrying his shoes and putting them on only after his arrival.[35]

Household goods also figured prominently among the items sought by the slaves. The more prosperous of them often furnished their cabins elaborately. Commentators on slave conditions, both official and unofficial, in favor of slavery and opposed to it, noted such articles as chairs, tables, chests of drawers, mirror wardrobes, and even four-poster beds with pillows, sheets, and mattresses. However, as Schoelcher emphasized, such relative luxury could be found only among a privileged few, such as artisans and *commandeurs*. The less prosperous only had a broken-down bedstead, a chair or bench, some crockery, a cooking pot, a storage box or two, and an earthen floor, while the poorest possessed only a cooking pot, a board or mat to sleep on, a bamboo stalk to store water, and a few pieces of tattered clothing hanging from a string stretched across the room.[36]

The slaves often made great efforts to increase their property during their free time, and in the process they developed a variety of skills. Many slaves raised chickens, rabbits, pigs, sheep, cows, and even horses. Slave-owned herds could be surprisingly large. In addition to their provision grounds, the slaves on the Lacouet plantation had twenty-five hectares to graze their animals. The slaves on the Fabrique plantation in Rivière Salée owned fifteen cattle. The head carpenter on the plantation of Peter Maillet in Saint Esprit personally owned seven cows in addition to pigs, chickens, and rabbits, while the *commandeur* on the same plantation had two horses. Schoelcher reports a herd of 100 sheep belonging to the slaves of M. Douville on the neighboring island of Guadeloupe. Slaves also found other means of augmenting their income or acquiring property if circumstances did not permit them to have provision grounds. Where the soil was poor and little garden produce could be grown, slaves cut wood and made charcoal for sale. Fishing was an important resource for slaves near the coast, although their activities were curtailed after 1837 by an ordinance, designed to prevent slaves from escaping to freedom in the neighboring British islands, which forbade slaves to use boats. Slaves on plantations near towns cut guinea grass during their mid-day break and carried bundles of it into the town to sell as fodder after work in the evening. A young lawyer from Martinique remarked to Schoelcher that the slaves sometimes walked as far as a league with bundles of fodder weighing up to seventy-five livres merely to earn twenty francs a month. Other slaves earned money by hiring themselves out during their free time, either on or off the plantation. In the context of such opportunities to earn money, any skills a slave could acquire were an extremely important resource. A notable example of this was a cook in Vauclin who acquired considerable wealth by preparing most of the banquets in the *quartier*. He was given his freedom when his master died, and he bought his wife's freedom for 1,500 francs.[37]

The provision grounds could be very profitable for industrious slaves. Lavollée estimated that the revenue from one-and-one-half hectares near the Pitons du Carbet, which was worked by three male and three female slaves, was no less than 10 francs per day. Schoelcher wrote that a slave could earn between 200 and 400 francs yearly with free Saturdays—men a little more and women a little less. An official source puts the figure at 700 to 800 francs per year. One public prosecutor reported that many slaves on one exemplary plantation had savings amounting to more than three times their purchase price but had not thought of buying their freedom. According to another public prosecutor, the slaves at the "Grand-Ceron" plantation had 18,000 francs in doubloons and quadruples, while a third prosecutor claimed that the slaves of another plantation had more than 5,000 doubloons worth 432,000 francs. Such estimates must be judged with caution, since we do not know the basis on which they were made or the number of slaves involved. Neither is it very likely that the slaves made a habit of showing their money to visiting public officials. Nevertheless, it is certain that slaves in Martinique were able to accumulate substantial sums of cash as well as other property.[38]

Perhaps the most surprising and extraordinary aspect of the independent economic life of the slaves in Martinique is that some slaves used their earnings to hire other slaves or freedmen to work in their gardens, and a few even owned slaves themselves. One public prosecutor commented on the practice of slaves hiring other slaves and on the source of their labor force: "The Negroes have as much land as they can cultivate. It has reached the point that several of them hire

Negroes from outside or belonging to the plantation to work in their gardens. This supposes that the latter do not cultivate the land on their own account. In fact, on almost all the plantations there are lazy slaves who do not have gardens. But these men, who cannot be motivated to work by the hope of a harvest for which one must wait several months, can be drawn by the lure of an immediate gain, at least to satisfy the needs of their moment." Not only did slaves hire other laborers, including free men, to work for them, but there are also recorded instances of slaves owning other slaves. On the "Perpigna" plantation in Vauclin, the *commandeur* owned a slave, but this *commandeur*, like so many other slave owners, finds that his slave "is never as industrious as he could be." There were several slaves on the plantation of Sieur Telliam-Maillet who owned slaves. "It is a reward from a master who is very happy with his slave," wrote a public prosecutor. "He permits him to buy slaves to replace him when he does not want to work, even in the master's fields." This is probably the ultimate expression of the slave's access to property in a slave society. With it the gap between slave and master, bondsman and free man, was narrowed considerably. But at the same time, such conditions cannot be exaggerated either. The slave's access to property and the opportunity for independent activity are extremely important for understanding the contradictions of the slave system, as well as the role of the slaves in shaping their New World environment. However, only a small minority ever acquired even moderate property, and independence was always limited and conditional on the benevolence of the master. The social distance between the most prosperous and industrious slave and the most impoverished and recalcitrant slave was always much less than between the former and the most destitute master.[39]

This process of the slaves' appropriating the free Saturday and the elaboration of these "proto-peasant" activities had far-reaching consequences for the development of slavery in the French West Indies and was itself an aspect of the crisis of the slave system. It was an initiative by a population that, over the course of its historical experience, had learned to adapt to the labor routine, discipline, and organization of time of the slave plantation and confronted slavery within its own relations and processes. The result was to simultaneously strengthen and weaken the slave system. On the one hand, the slaves became more effectively integrated into slavery and responsive to its rewards and punishments. The operating expenses of the plantation were reduced, and a greater surplus was available to the planter. On the other hand, the slaves were able to appropriate aspects of these processes and establish a degree of control over their own subsistence and reproduction. They claimed rights to property and disposition over time and labor that the masters were forced to recognize, and they were able to resist infringements on them. While it meant more work for the slaves, they were able to improve their material well-being substantially and increase their independence from the master. They restricted his capacity to exploit labor and presented a fixed obstacle to surplus production. The amount of labor time at the disposition of the planter was frozen, and the slaves acquired a means of resisting the intensification of work at the very moment that the transformation of the world sugar market demanded higher levels of productivity and greater exploitation of labor from French West Indian planters.

In this process, the character of the slave relation itself was altered. The assertion of these rights and the exercise of autonomy by the slaves reduced their dependence on the master and undermined his authority. Custom, consent, and accommodation assumed greater weight in the conduct of daily life where coercion had prevailed. The acquisition of skills and property and the establishment of economic and social networks enabled the enslaved to realize important material and psychological gains. The slaves thus began to fashion an alternative way of life that played an important role not only in eroding the slave regime but in forming a transition to a new society. In it can be seen nuclei of the post-emancipation social structure. Significantly, after emancipation the system of petty production and marketing organized by the slaves was to play an important part in helping them to resist the new encroachments of plantation agriculture and shape a new relation between labor and capital.[40]

The ability to elaborate autonomous provision-ground cultivation and marketing within slavery provided the slaves with an alternative to plantation labor after emancipation and allowed them to resist its reimposition. The very activities that the planters had encouraged during slavery now incurred their wrath. Carlyle scorned Quashee and his pumpkin; but far from representing the "lazy Negro," it is a testimony to the capacity of the Afro-Caribbean population to learn, adapt, create, and articulate an alternative conception of their needs despite the harshness of slavery. Probably few could escape the plantation entirely after emancipation, but for the great majority of the freed slaves the existence of provision-ground cultivation and marketing networks enabled them to struggle effectively over the conditions of their labor. Jamaican historian Douglas Hall suggests that on emancipation the freed slaves sought to separate their place of residence from their place of work. Where planters tried to compel a resident labor force, the workers left to establish free villages on lands off the plantations. In either case, the skills, resources, and associations formed through "proto-peasant" activities during slavery were of decisive importance in enabling the free population to secure control over their own conditions of reproduction and establish an independent bargaining position vis-á-vis the planters.[41]

The immediate consequence of emancipation throughout the French and British Caribbean was the withdrawal of labor, particularly the labor of women and children, from the plantation sector, and the onset of struggles with the planters over time, wages, and conditions of work in which the laboring population was able to assert a great deal of independence and initiative. It represented, in Walter Rodney's expression, an attempt to impose the rhythm of the village on the plantation. The successful separation of work and residence forced a new relation of production and reproduction on the plantation system itself as the planters attempted to recapture the labor of the emancipated population or find a substitute for it under conditions that guaranteed profitability. This resulted in the formation of new coercive forms of labor extraction in which the laboring population maintained control over subsistence activities and petty commodity production to one degree or another. This transformation of the plantation system and the transition from one form of coerced labor to another was not the inevitable result of unfolding capitalist rationality; rather, it is best understood as the product of the contradictory relation between production and social reproduction within the relations of slavery and of the struggle between masters and slaves over alternative purposes, conceptions of needs, and modes of organization of social and material life.[42]

# Conclusion

## The Global in the Local:
## World-Economy, Sugar, and the
## Crisis of Plantation Slavery in Martinique

This study has attempted to reconstruct the crises of slave labor and sugar plantation agriculture in Martinique as part of the historical transformation of the nineteenth century capitalist world-economy. It treats plantation slavery in Martinique as a specific historical-geographical complex that is *constituted through* the world sugar market, the world division of labor, the colonial state and French national sugar market, the material and technical conditions of sugar production, and the master-slave relation. Their interaction, with its tensions, conflicts, ambiguities, and contingencies, specifies the historical particularity of Martinique as a site of production within the capitalist world-economy. The character, role, meaning, and course of development of plantation slavery in Martinique are contingent on definite conjunctures of the wider world-economy.

This conceptual strategy discloses firmly linked spatial-temporal differences shaping the nexus of market and production and recovers the temporal and spatial dimensions of political economic processes as themselves products of historical development. Instead of privileging a single cause of the crisis of the slave regime in Martinique—for example, profitability, industrialization, abolitionism, or slave resistance that initiates a linear sequence of events across homogeneous and empty space—this approach reconstructs the specific confluence of political economic relations, historical sequences, and spatial configurations shaping the slave/sugar complex in Martinique. By tracing the interaction of multiple historical sequences through spatially and temporally complex fields of relations, this procedure permits us to explicate the forces, conditions, and constraints shaping the crises of the sugar plantation and slave labor in Martinique as aspects of ongoing processes of social production and reproduction on a world scale. Thus, this approach discloses the world historical origins and consequences of the crises of sugar and slavery in Martinique. At the same time, such a reconstruction of the specificity of historical developments in Martinique contributes to our understanding of the broader transformations of the nineteenth-century world-economy.

The origins of the crisis of slave plantation agriculture in Martinique reside in the world-economic and political conjuncture of the first half of the nineteenth century. The secular expansion of material production, the mobilization of new laboring populations and new forms of social labor, technological innovation, and the reorganization and integration of markets and trade during this period transformed the conditions of sugar production and slave labor throughout the European world-economy. Sugar production and consumption increased dramatically even as it was supplanted by cotton as the leading commodity in world trade. The map of world sugar production was redrawn. New sugar zones emerged both inside and outside of the Caribbean, while old zones increased their output. New forms of social labor developed alongside slave labor. New production and transport technologies and new varieties of cane were adopted. Significantly, beet sugar made its appearance as an alternative to cane sugar. As world sugar production was transformed, markets were reorganized and new patterns of consumption emerged. New relations were established between tropical producers and metropolitan states, merchants, refiners, and consumers. These transformations of the world sugar market were shaped by conflicts between states, among groups within national states, between metropolis and colony, among colonies, among groups within colonies, and between master and slave. They redefined in new and complex ways the nature, role, and significance of sugar, slavery, and empire throughout the world-economy.

The economic and political contours of this conjuncture of world sugar production were in large measure formed by both the Haitian Revolution and the reintegration of world markets under the hegemony of British capital. The consequences of the successful revolution in Saint Domingue resonated throughout the European world-economy. The Haitian uprising at once destroyed slavery in Europe's most prosperous colony and resulted in the dramatic withdrawal of the world's largest sugar producer from the world market in the midst of a cycle of economic expansion. Defeat in Haiti crippled the French colonial system, ended French imperial ambitions in the Americas, and contributed to the elimination of France from contention with Britain for hegemony over the world-economy. Haiti also marked a turning point for the politics of slavery and antislavery throughout the hemisphere. It stirred hopes, fears, and passions among groups throughout the Atlantic world and inspired diverse forms and combinations of resistance, reform, and repression that over time eroded the social and political conditions of slavery throughout the hemisphere.

On the other side of the coin, British hegemony provided the means of reintegrating the world-economy under new conditions. The reorganization of trade, production, and power around the preeminence of British capital extended and accelerated economic activity throughout the world-economy. The Pax Britannica, in combination with financial, commercial, and productive superiority, increasingly allowed Britain to redirect patterns of world trade and reorganize the division of labor that sustained it. Britain's emergence as the entrepôt of world trade and center of distribution of world credit enabled it to control flows of commodities and capital and encouraged integration of markets. In conjunction with Britain's superior industrial plant, they provided the means to assault rival national economies with cheap goods and cheap credit. Together, they propelled Britain toward a policy of free trade. At the same time, British antislavery not only developed as a response to domestic movements for reform and to conditions in Britain's West Indian colonies, but it was interwoven in complex ways with Britain's efforts to restructure the international economic and political order and gained effectiveness through its association with the power of the British state.

These tandem economic and political movements subjected the slave systems of the Americas to contradictory pressures during the first half of the nineteenth century. The expansion and increasing integration of world markets for sugar and other tropical and subtropical products altered the character and conditions of slave labor in the Caribbean and elsewhere. Slavery had to both coexist and compete with a variety of forms of social production. Growing demand, falling prices, and increased competition created pressure for the extension and intensification of slave labor as producers were compelled directly or indirectly to expand output and improve productive efficiency. At the same time, in consequence of the Haitian Revolution, slave resistance, and British antislavery, social and political pressure mounted on the international slave trade and on slavery as an institution.

Of course, these global economic and political forces were not experienced in the same way or to the same degree everywhere throughout the world-economy. British economic and political preeminence enlarged Britain's sphere of activity as it foreclosed opportunities for others and kept them from following a similar path. At the same time, the very operation of British efforts to restructure the world-economy set in motion responses and counterpressures. These too contributed to shaping the course of historical development. Thus, as Britain gained control over the flow of commodities and access to alternative sources of supply (and hence to diverse forms of labor) within and outside of its empire, its dependence on the West Indian sugar colonies and slave labor diminished.

In contrast, the effects of the Haitian Revolution and Britain's ascendency over the world-economy directly circumscribed the possibilities for French economic and political advance. Deprived of its wealthiest colony and unable to compete in foreign markets, France increasingly had to rely on the intensive exploitation of the limited resources of its remaining sugar colonies and on slave labor to rehabilitate not only the colonies but the commerce of its port cities, its merchant marine, and its navy. A policy of economic protectionism, national monopoly, and colonial control created an enclave of privileged economic activity that was the condition for the recovery of this maritime-colonial sector and its key component, the colonial sugar industry.

Yet it would be misleading to see these developments as the result of a simple relation of cause and effect. Rather, the distinct trajectories of Britain and France were shaped through their interrelation and mutual conditioning. On the one hand, the formation of the protected French colonial sugar enclave was inextricably linked to the transformations of the world market and its integration through the hegemony of British capital. On the other hand, the exclusion of foreign producers from the French national market and the privileges granted to French colonial planters influenced the volume, extent, intensity, and direction of commodity flows. The colonial monopoly compelled sugar producers (including French beet sugar producers), refiners, and merchants in France and elsewhere to promote increased output and efficiency in order to compete in the markets that remained open to them. This tension between the closed national economy and competitive markets structured the development of world sugar production and consumption and determined its specific rhythms, sequences, and periods.

From this perspective, the contrasting trajectories of the British and French colonial sugar economies represent not parallel and autonomous historical developments but outcomes of world processes that are formed and reformed through their relation with one another. Each derives its distinctive features from its relational position within the emergent world-scale network of political economic relations and is subject to specific conditions and constraints. Here, economic protectionism, the revival of the colonial sugar industry, and slave labor in the French West Indian sugar colonies are understood not as the persistence of an old pattern of historical relations but as forms of production, exchange, and political domination that are actively redeployed in opposition to British economic expansion and that develop as a counterpoint to British free trade. The zone of protected economic activity created by the French state developed according to its own rhythms and sequences. Historically formed relations and processes peculiar to this spatial-temporal configuration constitute its singular and irreducible "local face." At the same time, however, the scope and internal organization of this zone, and the character of the relations composing it (even as they contributed, in uneven and asymmetric ways, to the development of the world-economy as a whole), were determined within the broader field of world-economic processes, and in particular, against the pressure of British economic and political hegemony.

This general framework provides the theoretical ground within which to reconstruct the French colonial sugar complex as an integral part of the historical conjuncture of the nineteenth century world-economy. It treats the political relations constituting the colonial sugar complex as a provisional methodological boundary that is used to order concepts and observations. Here, the French protected economy delineates a distinct analytical "field within a field." It demarcates a zone of convergence of relations of diverse spatial and temporal extension that are not coterminous with its political boundaries. This construct permits us to trace the interaction of causal sequences across plural yet comprehensive spatial-temporal fields of social action in order to specify and concretize the particular historical development of this complex as a constituent element of the world-economy. In this way, we may contextualize the political relations constituting the colonial enclave rather than treating them as if they defined a priori the absolute boundary between a distinct and fully integrated social entity (metropolis-colony) and its external context. This procedure enables us to reconstitute the specific nexus of global-local relations that creates the tensions, conflicts, possibilities and limits of the French West Indian sugar colonies.

Like a bubble floating in a stream, the French colonial enclave could provisionally maintain its internal stability. However, the movement of the current determined its course. Just as the pressure of the water alters the alignment of forces creating the bubble and ultimately bursts it, so the pressure of increased world production, the restructuring of national and world markets, and falling sugar prices altered the conditions of the protected economy and undermined the alignment of forces that supported it. Over the course of the first half of the century, the very efforts to preserve a monopoly of the French domestic sugar market and promote the development of the maritime-colonial sector transformed the conditions of production and exchange that sustained the protected economy. It provoked conflicts of interest between colonial producers, metropolitan merchants and refiners, beet sugar producers, and the French state.

The establishment of a protected market in France promoted the revitalization of sugar production and a renewed reliance on slave labor in the colonies. In this process, sugar monoculture and the slave plantation in Martinique were pushed to their fullest development as the existing social and material organization of production was reinforced and exploited more intensively. However, this process was a contradictory one. The expansion of the colonial sugar industry was constrained by the very forms and conditions of production and exchange that organized and fostered its growth. At the same time, the progress of colonial cane sugar was challenged by the reemergence of the metropolitan beet sugar industry. The growth and reintegration of the world and national sugar markets provoked a crisis of the colonial sugar industry in Martinique that was inseparable from the crisis of slavery. This double-edged crisis was not simply due to declining profits or the failure to mechanize production in a universally competitive market. Rather, it was a crisis of social relations that was rooted in the social and political organization of the entire circuit of colonial sugar production and exchange itself.

During the economic and political conjuncture following the Napoleonic Wars, French policy tied the recovery of the maritime sector of the French economy and the metropolitan sugar market to the rejuvenation of the West Indian colonies and slave labor. Reestablishment of the *exclusif* was intended to promote the commercial interests of shippers, merchants, metropolitan sugar refiners, and colonial planters as well as the political and naval interests of the French state. A virtual monopoly over colonial trade provided metropolitan merchants and shippers with overseas markets in the face of British commercial and maritime superiority. Conversely, colonial planters, unable to compete with foreign sugar even in France, were granted high protective tariffs to secure a predominant position in the domestic market. In addition, export subsidies gave French refiners a big advantage over their rivals in reexporting colonial sugar to foreign markets. The colonial sugar industry was to animate this circuit of production and trade. However, the protective system was unable either to provide satisfactory conditions for colonial producers or to adequately develop the metropolitan market. Despite the unprecedented increase in colonial sugar production, the inability of planters to lower costs or expand output beyond a certain point prevented them from supplying enough sugar first for the reexport market and then for the domestic market itself. The tariff barriers required to protect colonial sugar from foreign competition kept prices high, limited domestic consumption, and opened the way for the recovery of the beet sugar industry in France.

Preferential duties, expanding French consumption, and high and stable prices promoted the rapid development of the colonial sugar industry until the late 1820s, when world sugar prices dropped. Faced with competition from cheap foreign sugar, colonial planters required still more protection to keep sugar prices above production costs. The sugar legislation of 1826 secured colonial domination of both the French domestic market and the reexport market, and touched off another sugar boom in the French West Indies. However, the colonies were approaching the physical limits of expansion. They could neither lower costs nor increase output. High prices and limited supply blocked the development of the French market. Tensions in the protective system became manifest. Colonial preference inhibited the further development of French foreign trade. Refiners were unable to increase the supply of sugar available to them in order to take advantage of new opportunities in Switzerland, Germany, Italy, and the Levant, while the reexport bounty placed a heavy burden on the state treasury. At the same time, metropolitan merchants, manufacturers, and shippers wanted to sell goods to the emerging markets in newly independent Latin America and to buy their sugar in return, but they were blocked by the sugar tariffs.

The reemergence of beet sugar broke down the relation between production, consumption, and price that the sugar duties sought to maintain. Beet producers were not subject to import duties, and they could take advantage of the export bounty to sell their sugar below cost in foreign markets. (Consequently, government revenues fell.) Technological advances allowed beet manufacturers to drive down the price of sugar and to make a superior product. Attempts to establish equal taxation on the two sugars failed because the continual increase in productivity of beets always upset the balance between them. The protected market, so necessary for colonial producers, could not be sustained. The colonies were compelled to compete under increasingly unfavorable conditions in the only outlet available to them. The colonial sugar industry's only recourse was either to call for free trade or for strict adherence to *exclusif* and the abolition of the beet sugar industry. (Many beet growers supported suppression of their industry if they could receive an indemnity.) However, the colonies could no longer supply the French sugar market. To abolish beet sugar would have been to open France to the domination of foreign sugar over the long run. Unable either to displace beet sugar or to survive competition on the open market, the colonies transformed the *exclusif* into the *pacte colonial*, a defense of their interests that emphasized the obligation of the French state to guarantee them their place in the metropolitan sugar market. The economic relation between metropolis and colonies was inverted. Instead of providing France with a supply of cheap tropical products and stimulating French shipping and overseas commerce, the *exclusif* became a means of guaranteeing remunerative conditions for French colonial sugar in the only market open to it.

The very growth of the colonial sugar industry and its reliance on preferential duties undermined the purposes of the protective system. It not only exposed planters to the ongoing threat from beet sugar but also brought them into conflict with the interests that had fostered their development. As the colonies became increasingly tied to sugar monoculture and protective duties, metropolitan commercial and manufacturing interests became antiprotectionist and wanted to dismantle the system of colonial preferences. Yet like the sugar colonies, they were unable to withstand the competition of overseas markets or to contend with British economic superiority. If the colonies together with French shipping and maritime commerce could not live with the *exclusif,* neither could they live without it.

While attempts to regulate the relations between metropolitan beet and colonial cane sugar kept the French domestic sugar market a political battleground, the intensification of sugar monoculture redefined the economic and social space of Martinique and eliminated alternative activities. Protective duties and high prices created conditions for a speculative sugar boom in the French West Indian colonies. Sugar was virtually the only remunerative crop. The influx of slaves and credit reinforced the hold of sugar monoculture and dependence on slave labor in Martinique. Virtually all available land and labor was devoted to sugar cultivation. New plantations were formed and old ones increased their output. Estates that had grown coffee, cacao, and cotton were converted to sugar or sold to sugar planters who bought them to obtain their land or slaves. Martiniquan planters attained unprecedented levels of production, yet the growth of the sugar industry was circumscribed by geographical, social-historical, and technical constraints that shaped the crisis of sugar and slavery in Martinique and throughout the French colonial sugar complex.

The historical conditions under which land, labor and capital could be combined in Martinique restricted the scope and form of expansion of sugar production and imposed a distinctive pattern of development that reinforced the existing organization of plantation agriculture. The very effort to produce more sugar strengthened forms of productive activity that were becoming increasingly outmoded, as new conditions for world sugar production emerged. Beyond the sheer physical limitations of the small island, the expansion of the sugar industry in Martinique was inhibited by the existing pattern of land tenure and sugar cultivation. Prime cane lands had already been densely occupied since at least the beginning of the eighteenth century. While there existed some possibility for increasing cultivation within the boundaries of existing estates, the presence of neighboring properties meant that contiguous land was not readily available for expansion. Further, there were few tracts of suitable land available for the establishment of new plantations. Consequently, the colony achieved higher levels of output either by intensifying production on existing estates or by the proliferation of relatively inefficient small- and medium-sized plantations that were often located in areas where soil, climate, and transportation were unfavorable. The initial increase in the total sugar production of Martinique was the result of bringing more land under cultivation. After 1836, when competition from beet sugar began to eliminate marginal producers, increased output was due to more slaves working on less land. In both instances, the colony attained higher levels of production without changing the scale or technical organization of plantation units. The growing inefficiency of sugar plantations in Martinique, all the more apparent in relation to the world's advanced producers, was underwritten by the protective duties.

In addition, planters were confronted with an inflexible labor supply. After the initial surge in slave imports between 1815 and 1830, France succumbed to British economic and diplomatic pressure to abolish the slave trade. Planters could no longer expand or replace their labor force through the importation of Africans. They were forced to meet the demand for labor either through natural increase or by shifting slaves from the cultivation of secondary crops to sugar. Although the total slave population gradually declined between 1830 and 1848, its demographic structure remained remarkably stable. There were more women than men in the slave population, and births exceeded deaths in most years. (Manumissions must be included to account for the overall decline of the slave population.) Indeed, the apparent slight increase of the portion of the rural slave population under fourteen years of age may even suggest the possibility of reproducing the labor force through natural increase over the long run. However, the demographic structure of the slave population did not coincide with the demand for labor. Although the general slave population declined slowly after abolition of the slave trade, the number of slaves employed in sugar production increased sharply. The sugar work force grew at the expense of coffee, cacao, cotton, and other secondary crops. Such a strategy was, at best, a limited and temporary expedient. Compelled to rely on the resident slave population as the sole source of their labor, planters could not easily adjust the size and composition of the labor force to the changing requirements of sugar production. Further, such transfers exposed slaves to the brutal regime of sugar production and threatened the reproduction of the slave population by redistributing it and separating male and female slaves.

Finally, the restoration of the sugar industry and especially slave imports between 1815 and 1830 contributed substantially to colonial debt. The further expansion of the sugar production, encouraged by the favorable tariffs of 1826, initiated a second cycle of debt by the mid-1830s. Debt was substantial, and plantations were heavily mortgaged. Declining economic conditions during the 1830s and 1840s aggravated the debt and created a prolonged crisis. Falling sugar prices together with the high cost of imports under the monopoly conditions of the *exclusif* impoverished the colony. Expenses were greater than revenues, and planters could not cut costs.

Maintenance of the slave labor force required a constant outlay that was independent of the price of sugar, necessary imports remained expensive, and credit became more difficult to obtain. At the same time, unpaid advances augmented planter debt. The value of landed property dropped, while the prospect of general emancipation depreciated the value of property in slaves. Faced with debt, declining revenues, and unalterable costs, the planters' only response was to produce more sugar to increase their total revenue. Chronic debt and dependence on credit created a vicious circle that increased sugar production even as the return to planters diminished. Planters had to borrow to produce and produce to borrow. Creditors were compelled to continue lending to recover even a portion of their advances. Local restrictions against foreclosing on sugar plantations or separating slaves from sugar estates for debt removed any effective security for creditors. This resulted in the withdrawal of French capital from the colony and promoted a shift toward short-term credit against the crop by local *commissionnaires* or factors instead of long-term loans against real property. The pervasiveness of such short-term credit reinforced the existing structure of plantation agriculture. It deprived planters of both the incentive and the means to innovate. Inefficient plantations could continue to operate even at an apparent loss to their owners. Factors continually advanced to planters the supplies required to operate the estate throughout the year while the standing crop was encumbered even before it was harvested. This practice resulted in exorbitant interest rates and prices. Specie was drained from the colony, planters were plagued by debt, and the surplus produced on their properties was appropriated by the merchants.

The transformations of the world and French national sugar markets, increasing demand for sugar, and price competition among producers during the first half of the nineteenth century put pressure on planters in Martinique to improve the material processes of sugar production and to increase the output and efficiency of their estates. The abolition of the slave trade, the reemergence of the French beet sugar industry, and the absence of new land for sugar cultivation accentuated these pressures. With quantitative expansion of the colonial sugar industry foreclosed, its qualitative restructuring both at the level of the plantation and of the colony as a whole assumed greater importance. Planters in Martinique experimented with new cane varieties, fertilizer, and plows, and they altered field rotations. They worked to improve mills and refineries. Some adopted steam power and tried new kettle designs and new ways of arranging trains. They succeeded remarkably in increasing the total amount of sugar produced, though at the expense of quality. Yet they were unable to lower costs or improve productive efficiency, especially the productivity of labor. There were particular obstacles to the adoption of individual techniques. Lack of capital and a reluctance to make drastic innovations also played their part. However, the failure to successfully innovate and adapt to new conditions cannot be attributed to any single factor viewed in isolation. Rather, the overall material and social organization of the plantation itself impeded amelioration of sugar production.

While the availability of land, labor, and capital limited the growth of the sugar industry for the colony as a whole, the integrated structure of the *habitation sucrière* together with the appropriation of the labor force as slaves set parameters for the organization and possible transformation of the labor process. The sugar plantation in Martinique combined within a single productive unit the agricultural and manufacturing operations required for sugar making. The need to maintain a definite proportional relation between sugar cultivation, milling and refining inhibited the adoption of new technology and blocked the socialization of labor. To increase the amount of land cultivated, the size of the slave gang, or the capacity of the mill or refinery would not, by itself, increase overall output or productivity. Changes had to be made proportionally throughout all sectors to effectively transform production processes.

Thus, the material and social integration of plantation production created an organizational structure that impeded wholesale innovation and instead encouraged planters to think of piecemeal amelioration. Simple modifications in existing practices could have significant results, but there was little incentive for radical restructuring. Planters clung to the idea that they could substantially improve the efficiency of their operations and the quantity and quality of their product by perfecting operations in each sector and establishing a more adequate balance between them. They rejected steam power and the vacuum pan, the two most revolutionary advances of the beet sugar industry, as not suitable to local conditions. From the perspective of the existing plantation system, the planters were right. Prevailing social and material production relations could not incorporate these advances. They were too expensive and offered no great advantage given the prevailing scale of production. However, in opting to adapt improvements to local circumstances, the planters underwrote their own obsolescence and exposed the self-contained plantation as the limit to technical improvement.

The *habitation sucrière* in Martinique had been consolidated around the size of land holdings, labor force, and milling and refining technologies prevailing in the eighteenth century. Improvements were adapted to and elaborated within the existing division of labor on the sugar estate. However, such partial amelioration integrated the various sectors of sugar production ever more thoroughly and congealed the relation between them. The internal organization of the sugar estate became increasingly rigid and impervious to change. Operations were fixed on a scale that was rapidly becoming outmoded during the first half of the nineteenth century. Sugar plantations in Martinique were too small to take advantage of the technological advances that the beet sugar industry made available. Even when technology was applicable and capital was available, the gains were not sufficient to justify the cost of new machinery and the devaluation of investment in existing equipment.

The appearance of the *usine centrale* represented both recognition of the inadequacy of the organization and scale of sugar production in Martinique and the possibility of overcoming its limits. The radical separation of milling and refining from sugar cultivation would break the stranglehold of the *habitation sucrière* and redefine the division of labor between agriculture and industry in sugar production. The most advanced new technologies, especially the vacuum pan, could be adopted, and Martiniquans would enjoy both higher yields and better-quality sugar. However, experiments with the *usine* failed to transform the sugar industry. Land, labor, and transport were not readily adaptable to their requirements. More importantly, planters (or their merchant creditors) were not prepared to write off the investment in existing mills and refineries. Financial arrangements offered by *usines* to those who supplied them with cane did not appear advantageous to many planters. Few of them were willing to give up control over processing their crop and the prestige that went with having their own mill in order to specialize in cane cultivation. The tenacity of the *habitation sucrière* choked off the development of the *usine central*. While the advent of the beet sugar industry put sugar making on a scientific foundation, sugar making in Martinique remained artisanal. Despite partial improvements, there was little standardization. Techniques were imprecise and subject to a wide range of variation. The craft skills of refiners (often slaves) and their knowledge of particular local conditions were decisive in determining the outcome of the production process. Established routines remained the norm. Despite greater total output, the colonial sugar industry continued to be wasteful and inefficient, and the quality of its product declined. It could not compete with the beet sugar industry. Unable to reform itself, it became increasingly dependent on the sugar duties to subsidize its inefficiency.

The labor of slaves and their capacity to respond to the requirements of sugar production anchored the entire circuit of sugar. However, technological innovation and the alteration of the labor process did not save labor or increase its productivity. Rather, innovation created redundant laborers. Because the person of the laborer was appropriated as property, modification of the labor process and technological innovation function differently in the slave relation than in the wage relation. Labor could not be expelled from the production process, and the costs of slave maintenance were independent of changes in production. Laborers remained in the possession of the master who had to provide for their maintenance whether they worked or not. The presence of such unemployed or underemployed slaves on the estate and the need to maintain social control over them discouraged innovation and instead prompted planters to utilize the resources already at hand. Thus, the slave relation restricted technological innovation and the development of the cooperative force of collective labor not because of the incapacities of the slaves, but because of the characteristics of the relation.

Yet it would be misleading to construe slave relations as if they delineated a unified and independent economy or mode of production. Rather, the character and content of slave labor was itself determined through its relation to the contradictory demands of the market and of the material conditions of sugar production. The transformations of the world and national markets compelled planters in Martinique to increase their output and to improve the efficiency of their operations. At the same time, the integration of material processes of sugar production on the *habitation sucrière* impeded changes in scale or fundamental technological innovation and alteration of the division of labor. Consequently, planters could neither increase the scale of their operations nor modify the division of labor on their estates. Technological innovations did not affect the productivity of labor. Instead, planters were compelled to adapt the social division of labor (the distribution of persons and skills) among the slave labor force to the technical division of labor (the division of tasks) of sugar production. The capacities of individual slaves had to be fit to the technical requirements of the tasks.

Under these conditions, planters attempted to increase their output by intensifying the productive activity of slaves within the prevailing social and material integration of the sugar plantation. Mounting pressure to expand surplus production developed the cooperative character of slave labor and infused it with a new social historical content. It resulted in the increase of the number of workers employed in sugar production, the intensification of work, the prolongation of labor time, and the elaboration of tasks within the technical division of labor. Intensification of labor promoted standardization of tasks and regularity in their execution. The gaps in the existing technical division of labor were filled in, creating more thorough integration of the *habitation sucrière*. The very processes that increased surplus production revealed the ever-greater inadequacy of the slave relation as the means of both securing the necessary combination of workers and disciplining their activity to the technical and social requirements of the large-scale commercial production of sugar. Such efforts to increase output and extract more from the laboring population simultaneously reinforced the immobility of the division of labor and revealed the historical limits of slave labor in Martinique.

Predictably, planter efforts to extract more work from their slaves and secure greater regularity in the execution of tasks made labor discipline and the working day key terrains of contestation and resistance. As slaves adapted to the routines and rhythms of plantation labor, they acquired skills, knowledge, and resources that enabled them to contest plantation slavery from within. In adjusting to the requirements of gang labor, learning the skills necessary for the mill and refinery, and accommodating the hierarchical authority of the plantation and its systems of rewards and punishments, they developed modes of resistance that were appropriate to the particular conditions that confronted them. The organization and rhythms of sugar production together with provision-ground cultivation and independent marketing emerged as key sites of contention. At the same time, as slaves asserted themselves within each sphere, they manipulated the relation between the two spheres to resist economic exploitation and social domination and to expand spaces of individual and collective autonomy and self-expression. Such resistance—sometimes hidden, sometimes overt—aimed at establishing customary standards of treatment, work, and labor discipline. Slaves sought to set quotas on production, control the duration and intensity of work, define a standard of acceptable treatment by drivers and overseers, and have some say in the processes by which tasks were determined. They further sought to expand free time, improve their material well-being and participate in social, economic, and cultural networks beyond the confines of the plantation.

The practices of slave provision ground cultivation and free Saturdays developed as strategic points in struggles against the regime of plantation labor in Martinique. These "proto-peasant" activities were intimately bound up with the organization of work in staple crop production. Taken together, they demonstrate the complex and contradictory unity of diverse activities within the slave relation. Provision-ground cultivation and internal marketing were not simply functionally integrated into the logic of the plantation, nor did they constitute an independent "peasant breach" with a logic of its own. Rather, they were grounded in the slave relation itself and defined an ambiguous intermediate zone that was formed through negotiation and contestation between master and slave.

The slave relation required the master to provide for the maintenance of the slaves. By granting to slaves marginal lands and free time that developed within the routines of sugar production, planters in Martinique sought to reduce costs and to bind slaves more effectively to the estate. For their part, slaves took advantage of the spaces available to them to develop these practices as means to assert their own individual and collective needs. Through the subtle play of initiative and bargaining, they subverted the master-slave relation even as they appeared to conform to its rules. By the nineteenth century, they successfully established customary property rights not merely to the produce of the provision grounds, but to the land itself, at times even against the claims of sugar production. Slave efforts to appropriate provision grounds and develop internal markets were combined with initiatives to secure disposition over their own activity during "free time." Both masters and state came to recognize their claims to free Saturdays for work on their grounds and to Sunday as market day. Through their control of provision-ground cultivation and marketing of their produce, slaves were able not only to diversify their consumption, improve their standard of living, and acquire property, but to establish independent social networks and spaces of autonomous cultural expression within the social relations of slavery.

Slave contestation over provision grounds and free time were intertwined with and reinforced struggles within the processes of sugar production. The interrelation of their resistance in these separate activities established limits to their exploitation and widened the sphere of their collective and individual autonomy. For slaves, resistance in one sphere strengthened that in the other. Consolidation of slave initiatives in provision ground cultivation gave slaves greater leverage to contest the organization, meaning, and motivation of plantation work. Reductions of labor time and changes in labor discipline enlarged the opportunities to elaborate "proto-peasant" activity. The master's domination was more and more tempered by negotiation. At issue were not narrow issues of the quantity of sugar produced or the cost of maintenance, but the disposition of labor time itself and the conditions of Martinique's integration in the capitalist world-economy.

Slave struggles for free days and against night work limited exploitable labor time at the disposition of planters and transformed the social organization of work. Slaves asserted the distinction between "work" time and "free" time against their masters' unrestricted authority to determine the duration and rhythm of their toil. The division between time belonging to the master and time belonging to the slaves hardened, and masters were obliged to compensate slaves for encroachments on their time. For their part, planters attempted to incorporate these initiatives into new work routines and new forms of labor discipline that tempered the domination of the slaveholder even as they made it more effective. Task work represented an attempt to substitute individual interest for the discipline of gang labor to insure regular performance of the daily quota of labor. While it had little effect on overall output, it entailed formal recognition of slaves' appropriation of free time and provision grounds. It required slaves' assimilation into the work routines of the plantation and their capacity to respond to new incentives. Such developments indicate the tension beneath the surface of daily plantation life. The ongoing negotiation of standards of work and treatment established customary rights, duties, and routines that were at least tacitly acknowledged by both master and slave.

Resistance to work was as old as slavery itself, but it assumed new inflections and acquired new significance in the decades of the 1830s and 1840s. Changing world economic and political conditions, planter efforts to extract more labor, abolitionism, and state-sponsored reforms developed the systematic character of the various forms of resistance to the labor regime and altered their context. Slave efforts to restrict labor time and to establish customary rights to property and access to local markets pushed beyond the slave relation even as masters struggled to contain these actions within forms of valorization and social control. Slave initiative and planter response developed the possibilities of slave labor in Martinique to their fullest extent. In so doing, they revealed its inadequacy as a form of labor organization and provoked a crisis of social relations.

The integration of the slave population into the routines and processes of plantation production opened new spaces of contestation and autonomous cultural expression. This terrain sustained individual and collective action that could go beyond immediate issues of labor and social reproduction to sustain more overt resistance to the institutional manifestations of slavery and distribution of social power. Such practices transformed the master-slave relation from within and allowed slaves to redefine their lives and community while still in bondage. In combination, they deepened the crisis of plantation agriculture and created the conditions for the organization of work, property, and social life beyond slavery.

Thus, the forces shaping the crisis of the sugar industry and slave labor in Martinique encompass the simultaneous, complex, and mutually interdependent interplay of relations across global, national, and local fields. The world market, French colonialism, and the material and social conditions of sugar production in Martinique represent not external variables acting on an invariant (essential) slavery, but specific relations through which slave labor in Martinique is historically formed. From this perspective, the crisis of slave labor in Martinique appears not as the secular decline of an archaic institution generated by an "industrial revolution," the development of market forces, and a political and social modernity external to it. The argument of this book emphasizes, instead, the ways slave labor and the sugar industry are transformed by new conditions of production and exchange in the historical conjuncture of world-economy. The growing and increasingly integrated world market, the specific characteristics of the French colonial economy, and the material and social conditions of sugar production in Martinique exacerbated tensions and conflicts specific to the slave form and propelled slavery to its full development even as they undermined its social-political foundations. By this I mean not simply that the intensification of labor deepened the experience of exploitation among slaves, but that the slave form itself was pushed to its limits and generated diverse struggles—economic, political, social, and cultural—throughout the circuit of sugar. These conflicts created the breakdown of slave labor in Martinique and the emergence of possible alternative material processes and social relations of production that exposed its limits. At issue in this crisis were not only the reproduction of slave relations in Martinique, but the reproduction of relations anchored in them. The fate of slavery in Martinique was tied to the organization of the entire circuit of sugar.

Under these circumstances, the colonial planters became increasingly dependent on protective legislation to secure a market for their product even as the level of colonial production increased. However, the very growth of the colonial sugar industry eroded the purposes of the protective system. Despite the greater amount of sugar produced in the colonies, the colonial monopoly restricted the development of the French domestic market and of French foreign trade. The colonies were unable to supply sugar adequate in either quantity or quality, or to provide it at competitive prices. At the same time, with the growth of domestic consumption and the reemergence of the beet sugar industry in France, the tariff system was increasingly unable to guarantee adequate conditions to colonial sugar within the national market. The colonies were trapped in a vicious circle of dependency. The more they were tied to sugar monoculture, the more they required protective tariffs; the more they relied on tariffs, the more they reinforced the hold of outmoded and inadequate forms of productive organization. The sugar colonies' position in the French economy weakened. These colonies became an expensive special interest.

The political and economic forces of the world-economy thus transformed the character of the French colonial system and protected market, the *habitation sucrière*, and slave relations of production and exhausted the social forms of their organization during the first half of the nineteenth century. From the early 1830s onward, a structural crisis gripped the slave plantation in Martinique as productive enterprise and as a form of social organization of labor; this crisis exacerbated the already precarious condition of the entire circuit of French colonial sugar. There was, nonetheless, a degree of flexibility of response within the slave system. Under certain conditions, the limitations of the slave plantation could be at least temporarily overcome by the addition of more slaves and new lands, by the adoption of technological innovations, and by securing political control over the market. These would allow the intensification and multiplication of slave production and the maintenance of market and price levels. However, the very expansion of sugar production progressively eliminated these "compensations" as practical considerations. The sphere of economic initiative of the slaveholders became increasingly circumscribed. Their inability to transform the material conditions of sugar manufacture and increase the productivity of labor led to greater dependence on protective tariffs in the short run and ultimately called into question the social and industrial organization of production itself. Slave relations of production blocked the further development of the sugar industry, and the decline of French West Indian sugar production sealed the fate of slavery. A crisis of sugar and a crisis of slavery were engendered that could only be resolved by the breakup of the plantation system as it had been historically constituted and by the reestablishment of production within a new constellation of land and labor. The condition of this resolution was the abolition of slavery. Only when emancipation brought about the destruction of the slave system were the conditions created for restructuring of the French sugar market and rebuilding the colonial sugar industry in a new political and economic context.

At this point, the limits of an economic analysis of slavery become apparent. The processes described in this book did not, in any immediate sense, "cause" slave emancipation in Martinique. Indeed, the simple facts concerning the end of French colonial slavery warn against any attempt to correlate emancipation with economic processes. Slavery was first abolished in 1794 and restored in 1802. In 1830, the July Monarchy expressly committed itself to the abolition of slavery. Yet despite deepening economic and social crises in the colonies and numerous proposals for abolition presented in the legislative chambers, the slave regime persisted for eighteen more years. Only in the midst of the revolutionary upheavals of 1848 was emancipation finally secured. Thus, the abolition of slavery in the French colonial empire, viewed as a political event, cannot be reduced to an economic "cause." As a political process and as a political movement, abolition has a long and complex history that deserves to be treated in its own right.

Rather than attempting to isolate politics and economics in search of a causal explanation, it is perhaps more useful to see the political event of emancipation in relation to the social and economic conjuncture that transformed the nature of slave relations in Martinique between 1830 and 1848. By focusing on slave commodity production and exchange as social relations, this study has stressed the changing historical character of sugar production and slave labor in Martinique. Slavery in 1848 was not what it had been in 1794, nor even what it had been in 1830. The historical evolution and transformation of the social relations of slavery reveal both the limits of slave production and the economic conditions and consequences of political action. The historical development of the relations of production and exchange formed a field of constraint and possibility within which political interests and actions took shape. It permitted a wide range of perception, motive, and choice and a sphere of action that was properly political. Political action and ideology were neither simply contingent nor the expression of idealized "material interests," but resulted from the active response of historical actors to these complex and evolving processes. In this context, slave emancipation appears as the result of the historical interplay of these political and economic processes.

By locating the political event of emancipation within the broader processes transforming the social relations of production and exchange it is possible to understand the end of slavery in Martinique *as a process of transition* to a new form of social organization. Within the processes that generated the crisis of the *habitation sucrière* and dissolution of the social relations of slave production, the elements of a new organization of labor and property emerged. The *usine centrale* and the formation of a slave population adapted to the relations and processes of plantation labor and autonomous provision-ground cultivation and marketing represented the conditions for the potential reconstruction of the colonial sugar industry. Yet these alternative modes of the material and social organization of production were suppressed by the slave relation itself. The social and material relations of sugar production and slave labor as historically constituted in Martinique were thus incompatible with the changing conditions of commodity production and exchange in the nineteenth-century world-economy.

However, rather than the secular decline of slavery and the transition to a more "rational" and "efficient" form of labor organization, the problem of the crisis of slavery and the transition to free labor is the problem of the political reintegration of capital and labor and the reconstitution of a new plantation system under emerging world and local conditions. This process was historically uneven. If the effective reorganization of production under the conditions prevailing in Martinique required the abolition of slavery, emancipation did not necessarily guarantee the effective reorganization of the colonial sugar industry. Once the constraints of slavery were removed, capital and labor confronted one another on a new terrain. The dramatic expansion of world sugar production and the French beet sugar industry after 1850 made the establishment of *usines centrales* and technological innovation imperative for the survival of the sugar industry in Martinique, even as they made the position of the latter more precarious. However, abolition also provided the opportunity for the laboring population to expand the space of negotiation and contestation and to resist the imposition of a new industrial organization and discipline when freed. The experience acquired while still enslaved by newly emancipated Martiniquans in industrial conflict, autonomous provision-ground cultivation, and internal marketing enabled them to assert their own conceptions of the relation of land, labor, and community. Their ability to establish a degree of control over the conditions of labor and social life on the plantations and in the villages, as workers and as citizens, called forth the efforts the colonial state and the planter class to socially and politically contain such initiatives within new requirements of labor and conditions of social subordination.[1] This continuing confrontation shaped the contours of postemancipation Martinique.

# Appendix 1

# Estimated Volume of the Slave Trade to Martinique, 1814–1831

There are, of course, no exact numbers for the volume of the illicit slave trade. Of all the countries engaged in the illegal slave trade during the nineteenth century, information on the French trade and the trade to the French Caribbean is most difficult to reconstruct. The major source on this trade, the 1845 British Parliamentary paper, underreports the illegal French trade. Philip D. Curtin, in his study of the Atlantic slave trade, attempts to compensate for the lack of data on the French West Indies by drawing inferences from census data and birth and death rates. He estimates that 77,400 slaves were carried to the French Antilles between 1811 and 1830. Of this number, 31,400 arrived between 1811 and 1820. Martinique received 15,200 (48 percent); Guadeloupe, 12,200 (39 percent); and French Guiana, 4,000 (13 percent). According to Curtin, the illegal trade to the French Antilles accelerated during the 1821–30 decade. Of 46,000 African slaves carried to the French West Indian colonies during this period, Martinique received 15,200 (33 percent), Guadeloupe 20,800 (45 percent), and French Guiana 10,000 (22 percent). The majority of voyages were made to Martinique and Guadeloupe rather than chronically weak and impoverished French Guiana. The increase in slave imports to Guadeloupe after 1821, both absolutely and relative to the other colonies, coincides with a similar increase in sugar production. After 1831, the slave trade fell off sharply. Curtin estimates only 3,600 arrivals from 1831–40, of which 1,500 went to Martinique and 2,100 went to Guadeloupe; there were no arrivals at all in the decade from 1841 to 1850.[1]

David Eltis has attempted to revise Curtin's estimate through the imaginative use of the 1845 list and the research of Serge Daget, which indicates that 763 French ships may reasonably be suspected of being slavers. Of these, 193 sailed in the period 1814–20, 552 between 1821 and 1831, and only 17 after 1832. These ships are known at their port of origin, but their destinations are not clear. Slave captains often concealed their destinations for obvious reasons, as well as complicating the whole matter with false papers and other deceptions. Working with the 1845 list, Eltis eliminates the ships for which destinations are known. He estimates that between 1821 and 1833, 338 French slave ships (61 percent of the suspected vessels) arrived in the French West Indies. Multiplying the number of ships by the average cargo landed in Cuba between 1821 and 1830, he estimates that 105,000 slaves were carried to the French West Indies between 1821 and 1833, or a bit more than twice Curtin's estimate. Elsewhere, Daget is more cautious about the average cargo carried by French slave ships and proposes 200 slaves as a reasonable estimate for a ship of 145 tons. This compares with the figure of 311 derived by Eltis from the Cuban data. Though Daget is cautious if not dubious about projecting a total figure from this average, his estimate would yield 67,600 slaves carried to the French West Indies between 1821 and 1833, and 152,600 for the entire French slave trade after 1814. Both figures are still considerably higher than Curtin's estimates.[2]

On the assumption that, as in the 1821–33 period, 61 percent of the 193 French ships probably involved in the slave trade between 1814 and 1820 were also bound for the French West Indies, an estimate, however crude, may be made of slave imports during this earlier period as well. Following Daget's average cargo of 200 slaves, these 118 voyages yield a total of 23,600 slaves imported, while Eltis's estimate of 311 slaves per ship yields a total of 36,614 slaves. Finally, assuming that the geographical distribution of destinations within the French West Indies approximates the percentage indicated by Curtin's data, Martinique accounted for 48 percent of the arrivals for 1814–20 and 33 percent from 1821 to 1830. In this case, it would have received from 11,328 to 17,578 slaves during the first period and from 22,308 to 34,650 during the second. For the first period, the figures for the French West Indies as a whole and for Martinique are close to Curtin's. However, for the second period, these figures are more than twice Curtin's estimates. Daget's data suggest that the volume of French slave trading increased markedly during the decade of the 1820s, despite increased repression during that period. It seems unlikely that the French West Indies received significant shipments from non-French slave traders, although no attempt has been made to estimate the foreign slave trade to the French West Indies. Bernard David, in his work on the history of the population of Martinique, counts only two arrivals of non-French slavers during this period. One is Portuguese and the other Spanish. The statistical base for these figures is extremely fragile and can yield no more than a crude estimate of the illegal slave trade to the French Caribbean. A more adequate approximation will have to await the publication of Serge Daget's *La France et l'abolition de la traite des Noirs, de 1814 à 1831. Introduction a l'étude de la répression française de la traite*, based on French archival sources.[3]

Using Eltis's procedure, the estimated volume of slaves carried in French ships from 1814 to 1833 ranges between 152,600 and 237,293. Aside from the French Caribbean and Bourbon, French slave traders were active in the slave trade to Cuba. Daget has identified 109 ships involved in the trade to Cuba, and contemporary French and British sources agree that the French dominated the trade to Santiago de Cuba and other outports. Aside from Cuba, French slave traders were active in Puerto Rico and perhaps Pernambuco and other ports in northeastern Brazil. Nearly all the French ports were active in the slave trade. Daget lists voyages from Le Havre, Honfleur, Nantes, Bordeaux, Bayonne, and Marseilles as well as ships originating in the colonies. Ports in the French Antilles, Senegal, and Bourbon all participated on their own account. Nantes, the traditional center of the French slave trade, was particularly active and accounted for 47 percent of the trade during this period.[4]

French slave ships drew their human cargoes primarily from Guinea, the Bight of Benin, the Bight of Biafra, and, to a lesser extent the Congo, Angola, and the coast of East Africa. The predominant ethnic groups carried to the French Caribbean included: Bambara (Niger), Aracha (Dahomey), Mina (Togo), Ibo (Niger delta),

Moko or Moco (Calabar, Eastern Nigeria), Cap Vert (Guinea), and Caplou (Ivory Coast), as well as what are described as Congos and Angolas. Not surprisingly, given the immediate demand for labor, the cargoes seem to have been composed of male adults in the majority. David, in his analysis of parish records in Martinique, shows 346 Africans baptized in Rivière Pilote between 1814 and 1824. Of these, 225 (65 percent) were male and 121 (35 percent) were female. Between the beginning of 1825 and April 1829, 297 Africans were baptized in this same parish. Of this number, 199 (67 percent) were male, and 98 (33 percent) were female. He also documents 121 Africans baptized in Case Pilote from 1814 to 1824 and 72 baptisms between 1825 and 1829. The former group was composed entirely of children and adolescents under 20 years of age and included 73 boys and 48 girls. In 1838, the government of Martinique manumitted 239 slaves who had been seized on ships involved in the illegal slave trade and became the property of the state. No mention is made of when these slaves were seized and how long they had been in the possession of the state. The list includes children born after seizure. Men still outnumbered women, but not to the same extent as in the earlier examples. There were 23 boys and 41 girls under 14 and 103 men and 72 women listed.[5]

Between 1814 and 1831, the French slave trade, both legal and illegal, replenished the supply of African laborers to the West Indian colonies and permitted the revitalization of the sugar industry there. While the suppression of this traffic had serious consequences, it did not automatically signal the end of slavery in the colonies. Rather, it altered the rationality of the plantation system. To borrow from the imagery of the slave trade, the days of "tight-packing" were over. Without a continued supply of fresh laborers, planters were obliged to pay more attention to the maintenance and reproduction of their slave populations than previously. The abolition of the slave trade exerted pressure for the amelioration of such diverse aspects of slave life as diet, clothing, housing, health care, work routines, discipline, and family life. While such measures were needed to guarantee the necessary labor force and prolong its efficacy, they also modified the character of the master-slave relation.

# Appendix 2

# Slave Prices by Age and Occupation, 1825–1839 (francs)

## Period 1: 1825–1829

| Occupation | Age | No. Slaves Sold | Total Price of Sale | Avg Price of Sale | Avg Price/ Occupation |
|---|---|---|---|---|---|
| Carpenters, cartwrights, | 1–13 | — | — | — | |
| cabinetmakers, shoemakers | 14–20 | 4 | 8,213.00 | 2,030.75 | |
| bricklayers, harnessmakers | 21–40 | 9 | 20,415.00 | 2,268.33 | 1,973.59 |
| | 41–50 | 9 | 14,881.00 | 1,653.44 | |
| | 51–60 | — | — | — | |
| | | | | | |
| Cooks, bakers | 1–13 | — | | | |
| | 14–20 | — | | | |
| | 21–40 | — | | | 515.00 |
| | 41–50 | 1 | 530.00 | 530.00 | |
| | 51–60 | 1 | 500.00 | 500.00 | |
| | | | | | |
| Male domestics and | 1–13 | 82 | 47,096.00 | 574.34 | |
| workers of various | 14–20 | 22 | 28,346.00 | 1,288.45 | |
| occupations | 21–40 | 24 | 37,325.00 | 1,555.20 | 929.19 |
| | 41–50 | 16 | 21,458.00 | 1,341.12 | |
| | 51–60 | 8 | 7,012.00 | 876.50 | |
| | | | | | |
| Female domestics | 1–13 | 132 | 95,713.00 | 725.09 | |
| and workers of | 14–20 | 109 | 157,263.00 | 1,442.78 | |
| various occupations | 21–40 | 128 | 190,452.00 | 1,487.92 | 1,198.87 |
| | 41–50 | 65 | 91,284.00 | 1,404.36 | |
| | 51–60 | 41 | 34,753.00 | 847.63 | |

*continued on next 5 pages*

| Occupation | Age | No. Slaves Sold | Total Price of Sale | Avg Price of Sale | Avg Price/ Occupation |
|---|---|---|---|---|---|
| Boatmen, fishermen, | 1–13 | — | — | | |
| sailors, etc. | 14–20 | — | — | | |
| | 21–40 | 11 | 23,102.00 | 2,100.18 | 1,943.68 |
| | 41–50 | 5 | 7,997.00 | 1,599.40 | |
| | 51–60 | — | — | | |
| Drivers, sugar-refiners | 1–13 | — | — | | |
| | 14–20 | — | — | | |
| | 21–40 | 8 | 20,445.00 | 2,555.62 | 2,125.71 |
| | 41–50 | 2 | 2,972.00 | 1,486.00 | |
| | 51–60 | 4 | 6,343.00 | 1,585.75 | |
| Agricultural laborers, | 1–13 | 65 | 72,966.00 | 1,122.50 | |
| cart drivers | 14–20 | 70 | 90,334.00 | 1,290.78 | |
| | 21–40 | 133 | 235,879.00 | 1,773.52 | 1,556.95 |
| | 41–50 | 22 | 62,504.00 | 2,841.09 | |
| | 51–60 | 30 | 36,540.00 | 1,218.00 | |
| Women of various ages | | | | | |
| and occupations sold | (male | 27) | | | |
| with their young | (female | 46) | | | |
| children of both sexes | | 73 | 75,608.00 | 1,035.72 | 1,035.72 |
| Individuals—age, sex, | | | | | |
| or occupation not indicated | | | | | |
| on sales records | | 3 | 4,839.00 | 1,613.00 | 1,613.00 |
| Individuals of various | (male) | — | — | | |
| ages and occupations | (female) | — | — | | |
| sold together | | | | | |
| TOTAL | | 1,077 | 1,397,680.00 | | |

## Period 2: 1830–1834

| Occupation | Age | No. Slaves Sold | Total Price of Sale | Avg Price of Sale | Avg Price/ Occupation |
|---|---|---|---|---|---|
| Carpenters, cartwrights, | 1–13 | — | — | — | |
| cabinetmakers, shoemakers | 14–20 | 1 | 1,500.00 | 1,500.00 | |
| bricklayers, harnessmakers | 21–40 | 8 | 14,299.00 | 1,787.38 | 1,755.40 |
| | 41–50 | — | — | — | |
| | 51–60 | 6 | 10,532.00 | 1,755.33 | |
| Cooks, bakers | 1–13 | — | — | | |
| | 14–20 | 3 | 4,600.00 | 1,533.33 | |
| | 21–40 | 6 | 17,000.00 | 3,833.33 | 2,227.27 |
| | 41–50 | 1 | 2,000.00 | 2,000.00 | |
| | 51–60 | 1 | 900.00 | 900.00 | |
| Male domestics and | 1–13 | 70 | 34,597.00 | 494.24 | |
| workers of various | 14–20 | 13 | 16,189.00 | 1,245.30 | |
| occupations | 21–40 | 12 | 14,790.00 | 1,232.50 | 708.82 |
| | 41–50 | 5 | 5,533.00 | 1,106.60 | |
| | 51–60 | 3 | 1,900.00 | 623.33 | |
| Female domestics | 1–13 | 78 | 52,152.00 | 668.62 | |
| and workers of | 14–20 | 45 | 57,932.00 | 1,128.38 | |
| various occupations | 21–40 | 54 | 78,602.00 | 1,455.59 | 1,049.39 |
| | 41–50 | 23 | 26,906.00 | 1,169.83 | |
| | 51–60 | 22 | 17,372.00 | 789.64 | |
| Boatmen, fishermen, | 1–13 | — | — | | |
| sailors, etc. | 14–20 | 2 | 2,000.00 | 1,000.00 | |
| | 21–40 | 3 | 4,372.00 | 1,577.33 | 1,346.40 |
| | 41–50 | — | — | | |
| | 51–60 | — | — | | |
| Drivers, sugar-refiners | 1–13 | 2 | 2,388.00 | 1,194.00 | |
| | 14–20 | 2 | 3,500.00 | 1,750.00 | |
| | 21–40 | 3 | 6,456.00 | 2,152.00 | 1,838.83 |
| | 41–50 | 3 | 6,322.00 | 2,107.33 | |
| | 51–60 | 2 | 3,400.00 | 1,700.00 | |

| Occupation | Age | No. Slaves Sold | Total Price of Sale | Avg Price of Sale | Avg Price/ Occupation |
|---|---|---|---|---|---|
| Agricultural laborers, | 1–13 | 12 | 13,300.00 | 1,194.00 | |
| cart drivers | 14–20 | 32 | 42,368.00 | 1,324.00 | |
| | 21–40 | 56 | 76,681.00 | 1,369.31 | 1,302.50 |
| | 41–50 | 21 | 27,222.00 | 1,296.28 | |
| | 51–60 | 15 | 17,669.00 | 1,177.93 | |
| Women of various ages and occupations sold with their young children of both sexes | (male & female) | 61 | 40,429.00 | 662.77 | 662.77 |
| Individuals—age, sex, or occupation not indicated on sales records | | 53 | 78,053.00 | 1,472.70 | 1,472.70 |
| Individuals of various ages and occupations sold together | (male & female) | 509 | 489,095.00 | 960.89 | 960.89 |
| TOTAL | | 11,127[a] | 1,170,319.00 | | |

## Period 3: 1835–1839

| Occupation | Age | No. Slaves Sold | Total Price of Sale | Avg Price of Sale | Avg Price/ Occupation |
|---|---|---|---|---|---|
| Carpenters, cartwrights, | 1–13 | — | — | | |
| cabinetmakers, shoemakers | 14–20 | — | — | | |
| bricklayers, harnessmakers | 21–40 | 1 | 2,223.00 | 2,223.00 | 2,223.00 |
| | 41–50 | — | — | | |
| | 51–60 | — | — | | |

| Occupation | Age | No. Slaves Sold | Total Price of Sale | Avg Price of Sale | Avg Price/ Occupation |
|---|---|---|---|---|---|
| Cooks, bakers | 1–13 | — | — | | |
| | 14–20 | — | — | | |
| | 21–40 | — | — | | 600.00 |
| | 41–50 | — | — | | |
| | 51–60 | 1 | 600.00 | 600.00 | |
| Male domestics and | 1–13 | 50 | 15,420.00 | 308.40 | |
| workers of various | 14–20 | 26 | 17,164.00 | 660.15 | |
| occupations | 21–40 | 46 | 37,403.00 | 813.10 | 604.10 |
| | 41–50 | 15 | 13,400.00 | 893.33 | |
| | 51–60 | 6 | 3,000.00 | 500.00 | |
| Female domestics | 1–13 | 52 | 23,270.00 | 447.50 | |
| and workers of | 14–20 | 29 | 21,531.00 | 742.45 | |
| various occupations | 21–40 | 46 | 21,190.00 | 460.65 | 506.45 |
| | 41–50 | 22 | 12,584.00 | 572.00 | |
| | 51–60 | 10 | 1,950.00 | 195.00 | |
| Boatmen, fishermen, | 1–13 | — | — | | |
| sailors, etc. | 14–20 | — | — | | |
| | 21–40 | — | — | | |
| | 41–50 | — | — | | |
| | 51–60 | — | — | | |
| Drivers, sugar-refiners | 1–13 | — | — | | |
| | 14–20 | — | — | | |
| | 21–40 | 2 | 3,250.00 | 1,625.00 | 1,237.50 |
| | 41–50 | — | — | | |
| | 51–60 | 2 | 1,700.00 | 850.00 | |
| Agricultural laborers, | 1–13 | 2 | 1,200.00 | 600.00 | |
| cart drivers | 14–20 | 5 | 4,400.00 | 880.00 | |
| | 21–40 | 9 | 11,350.00 | 1,261.11 | 1,032.60 |
| | 41–50 | 6 | 5,900.00 | 983.33 | |
| | 51–60 | 1 | 900.00 | 900.00 | |

| Occupation | Age | No. Slaves Sold | Total Price of Sale | Avg Price of Sale | Avg Price/ Occupation |
|---|---|---|---|---|---|
| Women of various ages and occupations sold with their young children of both sexes | (male (female | 16) 28) 44 | 14,866.00 | 337.86 | 337.86 |
| Individuals—age, sex, or occupation not indicated on sales records | | 48 | 33,563.00 | 699.23 | 699.23 |
| Individuals of various ages and occupations sold together | (male (female | 148) 116) 264 | 205,378.00 | 777.94 | 777.94 |
| TOTAL | | 687 | 452,242.00 | | |

*Source*: Ministère de la Marine et des Colonies, Questions relatives à l'abolition de l'esclavage. Instructions addressées à MM. les Gouverneurs des Colonies. (Circulaires du 18 juillet 1840). Délibérations et avis des Conseils Spéciaux, (Paris, 1843).

[a]Apparent recording error. The sum of numbers in this column is 1,127.

# Notes

## Introduction to the First Edition

1. Jean-François Robert, "Mémoire de l'état présent de la Martinique," p. 261.

2. Sidney W. Mintz, *Sweetness and Power*.

3. Marian Malowist, "Les débuts du système de plantations"; Celso Furtado, *The Economic Growth of Brazil*; Philip D. Curtin, *The Atlantic Slave Trade*; Richard Sheridan, "The Wealth of Jamaica in the Eighteenth Century."

4. Sidney W. Mintz, "Was the Plantation Slave a Proletarian?"

5. In the first edition I intentionally used the term "world economy" because I wished to convey a more open, fluid, and historical sense of relationship than that implied by "world-economy" or "world-system." However, the subsequent appearance of "world history" as a definite historiographical tendency has persuaded me to change. I understand "world history" is an undifferentiated and unstructured concept characterized by the inclusion of non-Western histories as integral to historical inquiry. The object of my concern is a definite and structured set of historical relationships that I designate as the capitalist "world-economy" or "world-system." For this edition I have adopted "world-economy" throughout the text, pace Wallerstein.

6. See Karel Kosík, *Dialectics of the Concrete*; Karl Marx, *Grundrisse*; Derek Sayer, *The Violence of Abstraction*.

7. Although there are significant differences in approach between the various authors in each group, Immanuel Wallerstein and Andre Gunder Frank may be taken as representative of scholars who emphasize production for the market; Eugene Genovese, Manuel Moreno Fraginals, and Jacob Gorender stress the primacy of the social relations of production; and Lloyd Best, George Beckford, and Jay Mandle privilege the plantation. See Immanuel Wallerstein, *The Modern World System*; Wallerstein, *The Capitalist World Economy*; Andre Gunder Frank, *Dependent Accumulation and Underdevelopment*; Frank, *World Accumulation, 1492–1789*; Eugene D. Genovese, *The Political Economy of Slavery*; Manuel Moreno Fraginals, *El ingenio*; Jacob Gorender, *O escravismo colonial*; Lloyd Best, "Outlines of a Model of

a Pure Plantation Economy"; George L. Beckford, *Persistent Poverty*; Jay R. Mandle, "The Plantation Economy."

8. William Roseberry, *Coffee and Capitalism in the Venezuelan Andes*; Sidney W. Mintz, "The So-called World-System"; Georg Lukács, *History and Class Consciousness*.

## Introduction to the Second Edition

1. I have borrowed the concept of the slave/sugar complex from Barbara Solow (2014, esp. pp. 2–3). This concept usefully calls attention to the historical interdependence of the material processes of sugar production and slave labor. As Solow and many others have argued, the slave/sugar complex was of central importance in the historical formation of capitalist world-economy. Reconstruction of the successive transformations through time and space of the relation between sugar production and slave labor provides a privileged vantage point from which to comprehend the processes and relations making and remaking the world-economy itself.

2. Criticism of these perspectives was central to *Slavery in the Circuit of Sugar*. I subsequently developed my arguments more systematically in *Through the Prism of Slavery*, esp. pp. 3–55.

3. Karel Kosík, *Dialectics of the Concrete*, p. 14. I have relied heavily on Kosík, especially the first chapter, in preparing this introduction. *Slavery in the Circuit of Sugar* was intended as a critique both of this functionalist interpretation of the world-systems perspective and Marxist conceptions of mode of production. I have elaborated these critiques in *Through the Prism of Slavery*, pp. 32–55.

4. See for example Charles Tilly, *Big Structures, Large Processes, Huge Comparisons*. I present an alternative comparative approach in *Through the Prism of Slavery*, pp. 120–36. Also see Philip McMichael, "Incorporating Comparison within a World-Historical Perspective."

5. See Derek Sayer, *The Violence of Abstraction*.

6. Hopkins, "World-Systems Analysis," pp. 146–47.

7. Kosík, *Dialectics of the Concrete*, esp. p. 28; Terence K. Hopkins, "World-Systems Analysis: Methodological Issues," 146–52; Karl Marx, *Grundrisse*, pp. 100–8; Jean-Paul Sartre, *Search for Method*, pp. 133–50.

8. Tomich, *Through the Prism of Slavery*, pp. 120–36; Terence K. Hopkins, "The Study of the Capitalist World-Economy," pp. 29–32; Hopkins, "World-Systems Analysis," pp. 146–58.

9. Kosík, *Dialectics of the Concrete*, p. 25.

10. Ibid., p. 15.

11. Ibid., p. 25.

12. Ibid., p. 29.

13. Marx, *Grundrisse*, pp. 83–111; Maria Sylvia de Carvalho Franco, *Homens Livres na Ordem Escravocrata*, p. 11.

14. I have discussed these approaches in greater detail in *Through the Prism of Slavery*, esp. pp. 3–55 and "Rethinking the Plantation," pp. 15–39.

15. Tomich, *Through the Prism of Slavery*, pp. 3–31.

16. Karl Korsch's classic *Karl Marx* remains perhaps the most lucid and straightforward presentation of Marx's concept of historical specification.

17. As Marx famously stated, "Human anatomy contains a key to the anatomy of the ape. The intimations of higher development, however, can be understood only after the higher development is already known." *Grundrisse*, p. 105.

18. As Marx argues, "the simple categories are the expression of relations within which the less developed concrete may have already realized itself before having posited the more many-sided connection or relation is mentally expressed in the more concrete category; while the more developed concrete preserves the same category as a subordinate relation. . . . As a rule, the most general abstractions arise in the midst of the richest possible concrete development, where one thing appears common to many, to all." Marx, *Grundrisse*, pp. 102, 104.

19. Friedrich Engels, cited in Rosdolsky, "Comments on Marx's Method," p. 65.

20. Kosík, *Dialectics of the Concrete*, pp. 23–32.

21. Rosdolsky, "Comments on Marx's Method," p. 65.

22. "This dialectical process of its becoming is only the ideal expression of the real movement through which capital comes into being. The later relations are to be regarded as developments coming out of this germ. But it is necessary to establish the specific form in which it is posited at a *certain* point. Otherwise confusion arises." Marx, *Grundrisse*, p. 310.

23. Georg Lukács long ago emphasized the importance of method for Marx's thought: "Orthodox Marxism, therefore, does not imply the uncritical acceptance of the results of Marx's investigations. It is not the 'belief' in this or that thesis, nor the exegesis of a 'sacred' book. On the contrary, orthodoxy refers exclusively to *method*" (*History and Class Consciousness*, p. 1). This focus on method also led me to look to *Capital* rather than to works such as *The Eighteenth Brumaire* or *The Class Struggles in France* that are generally taken to be Marx's historical writings.

24. Of the many works that have emphasized the dialectical structure of Marx's concept of capital, I have relied most heavily on *The Grundrisse*, Roman Rosdolsky's *The Making of Marx's 'Capital,'* and I. I. Rubin, *Essays on Marx's Theory of Value*.

25. Kosík, *Dialectics of the Concrete*, pp. 1–32.

26. In the sense that only with the commodification of labor-power can the instruments, materials, and activity of labor be related to one another through the concept "value." The

commodification of these three elements of the labor process allows Marx to conceptualize capital as the expanded production of value relations *through its own processes*—accumulation.

27. Even in *Capital* the concept of wage labor is not static, but is subject to new determinations from within its own relations and processes. Simple forms are subsumed into more complex ones and the conceptualization of wage labor and capital is continually deepened, extended, and transformed as Marx theoretically elaborates the totality of value relations.

28. See Tomich, *Through the Prism of Slavery*, pp. 9–13, 39–46.

29. Marx, *Capital*, I, p. 247.

30. The position of the chapters on "So-Called Primitive Accumulation" at the end of volume one is the clearest indication that the structure of *Capital* is not historical, but rather logical and conceptual. Volume one presents the process of production of capital as the analytical core of the totality of relations of capital. It provides the point of departure thatallows Marx to trace the transformations of the capital relation as it reproduces itself on an expanding scale through its own relations and processes (self-expanding value-capitalist accumulation), and on the other hand, to extend his analysis to incorporate other aspects of the capital relation that lie outside of the sphere of production—for example, landed property and rent, credit and finance, trade and markets. Since capital is presented as a historically specific totality of relations, the question of its origins arises. The theoretical sketches of the origins of capital refer to a historical process that lies outside the concept of capital—the movement from not-capital to capital. The German term used by Marx, *ürsprungliche Akkumulation*, refers to origins and is more properly translated as "original accumulation" rather than "primitive accumulation." They designate historic presuppositions of capital, the processes through which capital becomes a totality, but they are not part of the totality. Therefore, these chapters come after the theoretical presentation of the concept of capital in volume one. According to Marx: "The conditions and presuppositions of the *becoming*, of the *arising*, of capital presuppose precisely that it is not yet in being but merely in *becoming*; they therefore disappear as real capital arises, capital which itself, on the basis of its own reality, posits the conditions for its realization. The distinction between historical theory and theoretical history is implicit in this formulation of "original accumulation." Marx continues: "These presuppositions, which originally appeared as conditions of its becoming—and hence could not spring from its *action as capital*—now appear as results of its own realization, reality as posited by it—not as conditions of its arising, but as results of its presence" (Marx, *Grundrisse*, pp. 459–60).

31. "But reality produces a wealth of the most bizarre combinations. It is up to the theoretician to unravel these in order to discover fresh proof of his theory, to 'translate' into theoretical language the elements of historical life. It is not reality which should be expected to conform to the abstract schema," Antonio Gramsci, *Prison Notebooks*, p. 200.

Here I found myself turning in a different direction from E. P. Thompson. For me, Marx's *Grundrisse* provided the means to open up received understandings of his political economy and make its categories useful tools for historical inquiry, whereas for Thompson it provided the occasion for separating Marx's political economy from historical inquiry in favor of the latter (Thompson, *The Poverty of Theory*, esp. pp. 60–69). Precisely because I was concerned with slave formations rather than the waged working class in the *locus classicus* of industrial capitalism, empirically grounded historical narrative was insufficient. Some conceptual framework was necessary to establish the specificity of slave formations in the historical development of capital.

32. I have only recently become aware of the affinity between the way that I conceptualized Martinique in *Slavery in the Circuit of Sugar* and Vitorino Magalhães Godinho's concept of "historical-geographical complex" (Godinho, "Complexo histórico-geográfico," pp. 130–31).

33. In practical terms, this strategy meant that I could not treat some topics and themes that conventionally appear in works on slavery and sugar. As I hope has become clear in the course of this exposition, the methodological perspective that I am presenting requires that politics, race, and culture need to be studied in their own right, through their interrelation within the framework of the world-system.

34. Hopkins, "World-Systems Analysis," p. 147; Sartre, *A Search for Method*, pp. 13–150.

35. I used political events—the end of the Napoleonic Wars and slave emancipation in Martinique—to establish the temporal boundaries of the study. I did not analyze the entire cycle of sugar. This was in part the result of the research that I had done before I reorganized the book from a world-systems perspective and in part it was because my interest was in slavery and slave labor. Nonetheless, even though I only analyze a segment of the cycle, it forms the temporal ground of the analysis (see Hopkins, "World-Systems Analysis," pp. 146–53, on ground-figure). Further, because the assumption of this approach is that particular phenomena derive their meaning form the totality of relations, I trace the individual history of various particulars—for example, the sugar mill or the slave provision ground—before or after the conjuncture under consideration to establish its specific role and meaning within the conjuncture of relations.

36. Hopkins, "World-Systems Analysis," pp. 148–49.

37. Tomba, *Marx's Temporalities*, p. 164.

38. For the importance of the concept of social form for Marx's critique of political economy see Roman Rosdolsky, "Comments on the Method of Marx's *Capital*," pp. 62–72. Also Rosdolsky, *The Making of Marx's 'Capital.'*

39. For a comprehensive account of forms of labor in the historical development of the capitalist world-economy, see Yann Moulier Boutang, *De l'esclavage au salariat: Économie historique du salariat bridé.*

40. Thus, while Marxist accounts place the theoretical presentation of the slave mode of production at the beginning of the book, here, somewhat disconcertingly perhaps, discussion of the slave form appears in the middle.

41. Manuel Moreno Fraginals's *The Sugarmill* was a constant reference while writing *Slavery in the Circuit of Sugar*. It quickly became apparent to me that the combination of factors that inhibited the restructuring of sugar production and the reproduction of slave relations in Martinique did not operate in the same way or have the same consequences in Cuba. This is the origin of the concept that I have come to call "the second slavery" (see Tomich, *Through the Prism of Slavery*, esp. pp. 56–71). In *The Sugarmill*, Moreno's superb reconstruction of the material processes of sugar production in nineteenth century Cuba are imprisoned in an orthodox Marxist conception of slave labor. He regards slavery as incompatible with technological innovation even as he documents the technological transformation of the sugar mill. Critics of Moreno have pointed out that advanced technology and a slave labor force coexisted in Cuban sugar mills, and that slavery persisted despite technological change (Scott, *Slave Emancipation in Cuba*, pp. 26–29; Bergad, "Economic Viability," pp. 95–113). *Slavery in the Circuit of Sugar* raises a different question concerning Moreno Fraginals's argument, and thereby takes some distance from his critics as well. In my view, the important issue is the mutual determination of slave labor, land, and technology and the reconstitution of slave labor under new world-economic conditions.

42. Given the prevalence of studies that emphasize the resistance and agency of subaltern groups, it is worth remembering that if we do not regard actors as formed through social relations and that these social relations provide the conditions, possibilities, and limits of action, we risk treating agency as the attribute of the actors themselves rather than as the relation between actors and relations. To treat agency and resistance as attributes of actors outside of social relations and history is what Sayer calls a "violent abstraction." It creates a suprahistorical conception of agency that ultimately undervalues the capacity of subaltern groups to respond to their conditions, learn from their experiences, and act politically. Here I emphasize that apparently local agencies are formed within the densely mediated historical totality of social relations of the world-economy that produces local difference. Actors are not first local and then become global. I have developed this argument more fully in "Thinking the Unthinkable: Victory Schoelcher and the Haitian Revolution," pp. 401–31.

43. Mintz, *Caribbean Transformations*, pp. 146–250.

44. Tomich, *Though the Prism of Slavery*, pp. 173–91.

45. Tomba, *Marx's Temporalities*, 152.

# 1. Sugar and Slavery in an Age of Global Transformation

1. David Brion Davis, *The Problem of Slavery in an Age of Revolution*, 1770–1823, p. 440.

2. C. L. R. James, *The Black Jacobins*, pp. 25–26.

3. Moreno Fraginals, *El ingenio*, I: 39–47; Curtin, *Atlantic Slave Trade*, pp. 59, 78–79.

4. Moreno Fraginals, *El ingenio*, I: 39–47; Michel Devèze, "Le commerce du sucre à la fin du XXVIIIe siècle," pp. 35–48; Seymour M. Drescher, *Econocide*, pp. 46–54, 79; Curtin, *Atlantic Slave Trade*, pp. 59, 78–79.

5. François Crouzet, "England and France in the Eighteenth Century," pp. 64–67; Devèze, "Le commerce du sucre," pp. 37–47; Moreno Fraginals, *El ingenio*, 1:41–43, 2:98; Sidney W. Mintz, "Time, Sugar, and Sweetness"; Drescher, *Econocide*, pp. 52–53; Alan H. Adamson, *Sugar without Slaves*, pp. 7–8; Walter Minchinton, "Patterns of Demand, 1750–1914," p. 138; William Woodruff, "The Emergence of an International Economy, 1700–1914," pp. 656–63; T. S. Ashton, "The Standard of Life of the Workers in England, 1790–1830," p. 142; Robert Stein, "The French Sugar Business in the Eighteenth Century," p. 16n.

6. Jean Tarrade, *La commerce coloniale de la France à la fin de l'ancien régime*, 2:749; Herbert I. Priestly, *France Overseas through the Old Regime in the Eighteenth Century*, pp. 148, 153–54; Eric Williams, *From Columbus to Castro*, pp. 153, 240; Pierre Boulle, "Slave Trade, Commercial Organization, and Industrial Growth in Eighteenth Century Nantes," p. 71; Anthony G. Hopkins, *An Economic History of West Africa*, pp. 90–91; Moreno Fraginals, *El ingenio*, 1:43–45; Devèze, "Le commerce du sucre," p. 45; Crouzet, "England and France," pp. 64–66.

7. Francois Crouzet, "Wars, Blockade, and Economic Change in Europe, 1792–1815," pp. 568–569; C. A. Banbuck, *Histoire politique, économique, et sociale de la Martinique sous l'ancien régime*, pp. 151–52; Gaston Martin, *Nantes au XVIIIe siècle*, p. 424; Boulle, "Slave Trade, Commercial Organization, and Industrial Growth," pp. 70–112; Crouzet, "England and France," pp. 59–86; W. O. Henderson, "The Anglo-French Commercial Treaty of 1786."

8. James, *Black Jacobins*, p. 41.

9. Ibid., pp. 269–378.

10. Henry Lémery, *La révolution française à la Martinique*.

11. Henry Lémery, *Martinique terre française*, pp. 32–33; Moreno Fraginals, *El ingenio*, 2:98; Guy Josa, *Les industries du sucre et du rhum à la Martinique*, pp. 116–17; Felix Renouard, Marquis de Sainte Croix, *Statistique de la Martinique*, 1:214–25; Ministère du Commerce et des Manufactures, *Commission formée avec l'approbation du Roi. . . . Enquête sur les sucres*, p. 64.

12. Moreno Fraginals, *El ingenio*, 2:98–130; Eric Williams, *Capitalism and Slavery*, pp. 145–53; Georges Lefebvre, *The French Revolution*, 2:347–54; Drescher, *Econocide*, pp. 80–81, 126–33, 143–45, 175; E. O. Von Lippmann, *Historia do açúcar desde a epoca mais remota até o começo da fabricação do açúcar de beterraba*, 2:126; John Bauer, "International Repercussions of the Haitian Revolution," p. 407; Patrick Richardson, *Slavery and Empire*, p. 73; Lowell Ragatz, *The Fall of the Planter Class in the British Caribbean*, pp. 204–15; Crouzet, "Wars, Blockades, and Economic Change," pp. 567–88; William Reed, *A History of Sugar and Sugar Yielding Plants*, pp. 145–49; Francois Crouzet, *L'économie britannique et le blocus continental*, 1:72; Shepherd B. Clough, *France*, p. 92; [Charles] Forbin Janson, *Examen impartial et solution de toutes les questions qui rattachent à la loi des sucres*, pp. 50–51.

13. Karl Polanyi, *The Great Transformation*; E. J. Hobsbawm, *Industry and Empire*, pp. 13–109, 134–53; Philip McMichael, *Settlers and the Agrarian Question*, pp. 1–31; Paul Bairoch, *Commerce extérieur et développement économique de l'Europe au XIXe siècle*, pp. 64–66, 78–87.

14. McMichael, *Settlers and the Agrarian Question*, pp. 12–27.

15. Hobsbawm, *Industry and Empire*, pp. 13–109, 134–53; Woodruff, "Emergence of an International Economy," pp. 65, 8–63; Bairoch, Commerce extérieur et développement économique, pp. 64–66, 78–87; Minchinton, "Patterns of Demand," p. 138.

16. Mintz, *Sweetness and Power*; Reed, *History of Sugar*, pp. 151–52, 185; Richardson, *Slavery and Empire*, p. 73; Woodruff, "Emergence of an International Economy," pp. 658–63; Minchinton, "Patterns of Demand," p. 138.

17. Davis, *Slavery in an Age of Revolution*, p. 55n; Drescher, *Econocide*, pp. 78–83; Tadeusz Lepkowski, *Haiti*, 1:128; Ragatz, *Fall of the Planter Class*; Noel Deerr, *The History of Sugar*, 1:193–202; Williams, *Capitalism and Slavery*, pp. 150–51; Moreno Fraginals, *El ingenio*, 2:107–30; Bauer, "International Repercussions of the Haitian Revolution," p. 407.

18. Drescher, *Econocide*, p. 93; Deerr, *History of Sugar*, 1:198; Ragatz, *Fall of the Planter Class*, pp. 286–456; Moreno Fraginals, *El ingenio*, 2:107–30.

19. Moreno Fraginals, *El ingenio*, 2:106, 156–65; Drescher, *Econocide*, pp. 94–103; Adamson, *Sugar without Slaves*, pp. 22–28; Walter Rodney, *A History of the Guyanese Working People, 1881–1905*, pp. 1–59; Deerr, *History of Sugar*, 1:193–201.

20. E. Labrousse, Aspects de l'évolution économique et sociale de la France et du Royaume-Uni de 1815–1880, pp. 4–44; Polanyi, *Great Transformation*, pp. 3–30, 56–75; McMichael, *Settlers and the Agrarian Question*, esp. pp. 21–27; Karl Marx, *Capital*, 1:643–76; Richardson, *Slavery and Empire*, pp. 98–100.

21. Labrousse, *Aspects*, p. 40.

22. Paula Beiguelman, Pequenos estudos de ciência política, pp. 3–8; Beiguelman, "The Destruction of Modern Slavery: A Theoretical Issue," esp. pp. 71–72, 77–78.)

23. Beiguelman, "Destruction of Modern Slavery," p. 72.

24. Moreno Fraginals, *El ingenio*, 2:157; Drescher, *Econocide*, pp. 155–57; Williams, *Capitalism and Slavery*, p. 152.

25. Williams, *Capitalism and Slavery*, pp. 133–54; Ragatz, *Fall of the Planter Class*, pp. 434–35; Moreno Fraginals, *El ingenio*, 2:157–61.

26. Williams, *Capitalism and Slavery*, pp. 133–54; Ragatz, *Fall of the Planter Class*, pp. 434–35; Moreno Fraginals, *El ingenio*, 2:157–61.

27. Moreno Fraginals, *El ingenio*, 2:147, 173; Caio Prado Junior, *Historia económica do Brasil*, pp. 84–89; Maria Theresa Schorer Petrone, *Lavoura canaveira em São Paulo*; Fernando A. Novais, *Portugal e Brasil na crise do Antigo sistema colonial*.

28. Moreno Fraginals, *El ingenio*, 1:46–47, 67–71, 95–102; Moreno Fraginals,*El ingenio*, 2:96–97; Moreno Fraginals, *The Sugarmill*, pp. 26–28; Curtin, *Atlantic Slave Trade*, p. 34; John Bauer, "International Repercussions of the Haitian Revolution," pp. 403–405.

29. Moreno Fraginals, *El ingenio*, 1:167–255, 2:93–97, 106–74, 3:35–36; Curtin, *Atlantic Slave Trade*, p. 34.

## 2. The Contradictions of Protectionism

1. Arthur Girault, *The Colonial Tariff Policy of France*, p. 51; Henri Blet, *Histoire de la colonisation française*, 2:44; Gaston Martin, *Histoire de l'esclavage dans les colonies françaises*, 253; Drescher, *Econocide*, p. 152; Clough, *France*, p. 92.

2. Blet, *Histoire de la colonisation*, 2:44; Roger Price, *The Economic Modernization of France*; Clough, *France*, pp. 92–101; Crouzet, "Wars, Blockade, and Economic Change," pp. 570–73.

3. Andre-Jean Tudesq, "La Restauration," pp. 45–52; Andre Broder, "Le commerce extérieur," pp. 310, 326–32; Henri Sée, "La vie économique et politique de Nantes, 1831–1848," pp. 309–10; Crouzet, "Wars, Blockade, and Economic Change," pp. 570–73; René Achéen, "Les problèmes antillais devant l'opinion bordelaise," pp. 20–21; Arthur Louis Dunham, *The Industrial Revolution in France, 1815–1848*, pp. 370–72.

4. Tudesq, "Restauration," pp. 45–46, 52–53; Clough, *France*, p. 101; Vincent Marie Vienot, comte de Vaublanc, *Du commerce maritime, considéré sous le rapport de la liberté entière de la commerce*, p. 32; Girault, *Colonial Tariff Policy*, p. 56.

5. Blet, *Histoire de la colonisation*, 2:50–52; Clough, *France*, p. 101; Christian Schnakenbourg, *Histoire de l'industrie sucrière en Guadeloupe*, vol. 1. La crise du système esclavagiste, pp. 76–77.

6. Blet, *Histoire de la colonisation*, 2:50–52, 61; Clough, *France*, p. 101; Arthur Girault, *Principes de la colonisation et de législation coloniale*, 3:363–64; Girault, *Colonial Tariff Policy*, pp. 53–54; Schnakenbourg, *Crise*, pp. 65–68.

7. Girault, *Colonial Tariff Policy*, pp. 24–25; Blet, *Histoire de la colonization française*, 1:310; Louis-Philippe May, *Histoire économique de la Martinique*, pp. 114–17; Priestly, *France Overseas*, pp. 262–65; Martin, *Histoire de l'esclavage*, pp. 148–49; Banbuck, *Histoire politique de la Martinique*, pp. 271–82; Lémery, *La révolution française*, pp. 7–8; Schnakenbourg, *Crise*, pp. 68–73.

8. Girault, *Colonial Tariff Policy*, pp. 26–27; Blet, *Histoire de la colonisation*, 1:310–11; Schnakenbourg, *Crise*, pp. 73–75.

9. Priestly, *France Overseas*, p. 5; Girault, *Principes de la colonisation*, 3:363–364; Girault, *Colonial Tariff Policy*, pp. 51–57; Blet, *Histoire de la colonisation*, 2:13.

10. Jean-Marie Pardon, *La Martinique depuis sa découverte jusqu'à nos jours*, p. 176; Louis-Philippe May, *Le Mercier de la Rivière*, 2:63; Girault, *Principes de la colonisation*, 3:363–64; Girault, *Colonial Tariff Policy*, pp. 53–54; Schnakenbourg, *Crise*, pp. 77–78.

11. Pardon, *La Martinique*, p. 176; May, *Le Mercier de la Rivière*, 1:118–19; Blet, *Histoire de la colonisation*, 2:63; Girault, *Principes de la colonisation*, 3:363–64; Girault, *Colonial Tariff Policy*, pp. 53–54; Schnakenbourg, *Crise*, pp. 77–78.

12. Girault, *Colonial Tariff Policy*, pp. 59–61; Schnakenbourg, *Crise*, pp. 76–79.

13. Schnakenbourg, *Crise*, pp. 78–82; Ministère, *Enquête sur les sucres*, pp. 160–61, 219–21, 254–57; Hyppolite de Frasons, *Considérations sur les causes . . .* , pp. 15–25; Victor Schoelcher, *Des colonies françaises: Abolition immediate*, pp. xxviii–xix.

14. Ministère, *Enquête sur les sucres*, pp. 224–25, 231.

15. Ibid., pp. 2, 225, 231; Amédée Hamon, *Des colonies et de la législation des sucres*, p. 4; Girault, *Colonial Tariff Policy*, p. 51; E. Boizard and H. Tardieu, *Histoire de la législation des sucres . . .* , pp. 9, 17.

16. Ministère, *Enquête sur les sucres*, pp. 2, 225–26; Girault, *Colonial Tariff Policy*, p. 57; Boizard and Tardieu, *Histoire de la législation des sucres*, pp. 9–10.

17. Ministère, *Enquête sur les sucres*, pp. 2–3, 226–28; Boizard and Tardieu, *Histoire de la législation des sucres*, pp. 10–14.

18. Ministère, *Enquête sur les sucres*, pp. 226–29; Reed, *History of Sugar*, p. 150.

19. Ministère, *Enquête sur les sucres*, pp. x, 3, 9–10; Louis Napoleon Bonaparte, *Analyse de la question des sucres*, pp. 11–12; Boizard and Tardieu, *Histoire de la législation des sucres*, pp. 15–17; Hamon, *Des colonies et de la législation des sucres*, p. 6.

20. In 1822, France spent about 33 million francs to purchase 52,300 metric tons of colonial sugar. The following year, in part as a consequence of the war with Spain, the

sale price rose from 63 francs 87 centimes to 83 francs 87 centimes, and France spent 32 million francs for only 38,500 metric tons. In 1824, the average sale price fell to 73 francs 25 centimes, and nearly 57,000 metric tons of colonial sugar were purchased. In 1825, the price of sugar climbed to 83 francs 50 centimes, and consumption fell by about 4,000 metric tons. The following year, the price dropped to 74 francs, and consumption reached a new high of 69,000 metric tons. Ministère, *Enquête sur les sucres*, pp. 230–31; Reed, *History of Sugar*, p. 150.

21. Ministère, *Enquête sur les sucres*, pp. 3, 231; Boizard and Tardieu, *Histoire de la législation des sucres*, pp. 17–18; Forbin Janson, *Examen impartial*, pp. 11–12; Bonaparte, *Analyse*, pp. 11–12.

22. P. Molroguier, *Examen de la question des sucres*, pp. 15–18; Moreno Fraginals, *El ingenio*, 2:167.

23. Ministère, *Enquête sur les sucres*, pp. 83, 230–31; Boizard and Tardieu, *Histoire de la législation des sucres*, p. 21; Bonaparte, *Analyse*, pp. 11–12.

2.4. Ministère, *Enquête sur les sucres*, pp. 83, 263–64; Boizard and Tardieu, *Histoire de la législation des sucres*, p. 21; Girault, *Colonial Tariff Policy*, pp. 57–58; Bonaparte, *Analyse*, pp. 11–12.

25. Schnakenbourg, *Crise*, pp. 83–89.

26. Ministère, *Enquête sur les sucres*, pp. 12, 60–63, 74–75, 80, 88, 97–98, 101, 109, 113, 149–52, 158–59, 162–63, 265.

27. Ibid., pp. 101, 159.

28. Boizard and Tardieu, *Histoire de la législation des sucres*, p. 19; Ministère, *Enquête sur les sucres*, pp. 88, 93, 101–102, 146–47, 151–52, 159, 162–63, 262.

29. Ministère, *Enquête sur les sucres*, pp. 87–88, 93–94, 103, 159, 163.

30. Ibid., pp. 83, 93, 103, 258; Blet, *Histoire de la colonisation*, 2:62; Clough, *France*, pp. 118–19; Tudesq, "Bordeaux sous la Restauration," pp. 52–54.

31. Ministère, *Enquête sur les sucres*, pp. 63, 79, 84–88, 94–96, 102, 104, 136, 162–63, 260.

32. David Landes, "French Entrepreneurship and Industrial Growth in the Nineteenth Century," pp. 45–61; Blet, *Histoire de la colonisation*, 2:62.

33. Dunham, *Industrial Revolution in France*, p. 374; de Chazelles, *Étude sur le système colonial*, pp. 139–40; Blet, *Histoire de la colonisation*, 2:62.

34. Serge Daget, "British Repression of the Illegal French Slave Trade," pp. 423–25; Daget, "L'abolition de la traite des noirs en France de 1814 à 1831," p. 17.

35. Daget, "British Repression," pp. 423–25; Daget, "Abolition de la traite," p. 17.

36. Jean Vidalenc, "La traite négrière en France sous la Restauration, 1814–1830," pp. 198, 200; Daget, "Abolition de la traite," pp. 17–22.

37. Blet, *Histoire de la colonisation*, 2:58–60; Vidalenc, "La traite négrière," pp. 200–203.

38. Vidalenc, "La traite négrière," pp. 201–203; Daget, "Abolition de la traite," pp. 22–24.

39. Vidalenc, "La traite négrière," pp. 201–203; Daget, "Abolition de la traite," pp. 22–30; Martin, *Histoire de l'esclavage*, p. 252.

40. Daget has attempted to reevaluate the role of Portal. He concludes that although Portal was ineffective in policing the trade and defended the government and the Ministry of the Marine against abolitionist attacks, he was not unambiguously a partisan of the trade and made some contribution toward its suppression. Daget, "British Repression," p. 428; Vidalenc, "La traite négrière," pp. 203–07; Daget, "Abolition de la traite," pp. 30–42; Martin, *Histoire de l'esclavage*, pp. 253, 256.

41. Vidalenc, "La traite négrière," p. 202; Blet, *Histoire de la colonisation*, 1:58–60; Daget, "British Repression," pp. 422, 427–29; Daget, "Long cours et negriers nantais du trafic illegal, 1814–1833," p. 108; Daget, "Abolition de la traite," pp. 32–45.

42. Martin, *Histoire de l'esclavage*, p. 262; Daget, "l'Abolition de la traite," pp. 45–53; Daget, "British Repression," p. 421; Vidalenc, "La traite négrière," pp. 207–8.

43. Daget, "British Repression," pp. 428–40; Daget, "L'abolition de la traite," pp. 53–58; Martin, *Histoire de l'esclavage*, pp. 253–79; Suzanne Miers, *Britain and the Ending of the Slave Trade*, pp. 17–19.

44. Martin, *Histoire de l'esclavage*, pp. 280–81; Antoine Gisler, *L'esclavage aux Antilles françaises*, pp. 128–29; Williams, *From Columbus to Castro*, p. 299; Augustin Cochin, *L'abolition de l'esclavage*, 1:40–42; Andre-Jean Tudesq, *Les grands notables en France*, 2:835–38.

45. Martin, *Histoire de l'esclavage*, pp. 281–87; Williams, *Columbus to Castro*, pp. 299–300; Henry Lémery, *Martinique terre française*, pp. 61, 63–65; Tudesq, *Les grands notables en France*, 2:836.

46. Gisler, *L'esclavage aux Antilles françaises*, pp. 131–42.

47. Schnakenbourg, *Crise*, pp. 185–92; Martin, *Histoire de l'esclavage*, pp. 286–91; Yvan Debbasch, "Le marronage," p. 185n; Gisler, *L'esclavage aux Antilles françaises*, pp. 142–47; Williams, *Columbus to Castro*, p. 300; Cochin, *L'abolition de l'esclavage*, 1:50–59; Tudesq, *Les grands notables en France*, 2:838–51.

48. Gisler, *L'esclavage aux Antilles françaises*, pp. 129–31; Martin, *Histoire de l'esclavage*, pp. 287–90.

49. Hamon, *Des colonies et de la législation des sucres*, p. 124; Boizard and Tardieu, *Histoire de la législation des sucres*, pp. 25–26; Deerr, *History of Sugar*, 2:479; Jules Helot, *Le sucre en France, 1800–1900*, p. 41.

50. Clough, *France*, p. 418n; Ministère, *Enquête sur les sucres*, p. 6; Forbin Janson, *Examen impartial*, pp. 4, 10–15, 44; Boizard and Tardieu, *Histoire de la législation des sucres*, p. 26; Hamon, *Des colonies et de la législation des sucres*, p. 125.

51. Deerr, *History of Sugar*, 2:478–80; Timothée Dehay, *Les colonies et le metropole* . . . , p. 18; Chambre des Députés, Session 1837: Rapport Dumon, pp. 2, 9, 54–55; Théophile Malvezin, *Histoire du commerce de Bordeaux*, 4:58–59; Clough, *France*, pp. 93, 103, 117; Boizard and Tardieu, *Histoire de la législation des sucres*, pp. 30–31; Moreno Fraginals, *El ingenio*, 1:168.

52. Ministère, *Enquête sur les sucres*, p. 6; Forbin Janson, *Examen impartial*, pp. 4, 10–15, 44; Boizard and Tardieu, *Histoire de la législation des sucres*, pp. 26, 30–31, 35–36; Hamon, *Des colonies et de la législation des sucres*, p. 125.

53. T. Lestiboudois, *Des colonies sucrières et des sucreries indigènes*, p. 3; Deerr, *History of Sugar*, 2:479–80; Williams, *Columbus to Castro*, p. 383; Cochin, *L'abolition de l'esclavage*, 1:190–91, 200; de Chazelles, Etude sur le système coloniale, pp. 142–45, 156–59, 164–66n; Clough, *France*, pp. 130–31; Moreno Fraginals, *El ingenio*, 3:35–36; Le Baron (François Pierre) Charles Dupin, *Mémoire adressé par le Conseil des Délégués des Colonies, aux Ministres du Roi sur la question des sucres*, pp. 14–15; *Délégués des Colonies, Mémoire sur le travail des affranchis dans les colonies françaises*, pp. 6–9; General Bertrand, *Sur la détresse des colonies françaises en général, de l'île Martinique en particulier*, pp. 25–28; Chambre des Députés, *Rapport Dumon*, p. 15.

54. Forbin Janson, *Examen impartial*, pp. 10, 13–14; Boizard and Tardieu, *Histoire de la législation des sucres*, pp. 26–28.

55. Boizard and Tardieu, *Histoire de la législation des sucres*, pp. 21–23; Jacques Fierain, *Les raffineries du sucre des ports en France*, pp. 197–98; Chambre des Députés, *Rapport Dumon*, table H; Hamon, *Des colonies et de la législation des sucres*, p. 35; de Chazelles, *Etude sur le système colonial*, pp. 147–49.

56. E. Levasseur, *Histoire du commerce de la France*, 4:234–35; Clough, *France*, pp. 130–32; Boizard and Tardieu, *Histoire de la législation des sucres*, pp. 35–36; Dehay, *Les colonies et le métropole*, p. 21.

57. Dehay, *Les colonies et le métropole*, pp. 6–33; Chambre des Députés, *Rapport Dumon*, pp. 12–13; Boizard and Tardieu, *Histoire de la législation des sucre*, pp. 30–36.

58. Forbin Janson, *Examen impartial*, p. 29; Dehay, *Les colonies et le métropole*, pp. 30–35; de Chazelles, *Etude sur le systeme colonial*, pp. 168–71; Boizard and Tardieu, *Histoire de la législation des sucre*, pp. 30–48.

59. De Chazelles, *Etude sur le système colonial*, pp. 174–80, 197–200; Dehay, *Les colonies et le métropole*, p. 65; Hamon, *Des colonies et de la législation des sucres*, pp. 36–38; Molrogieur, *Examen de la question des sucres*, pp. 18–31; Forbin Janson, *Examen impartial*, pp. 84–87; Boizard and Tardieu, *Histoire de la législation des sucres*, pp. 49–51, 55–56.

60. Boizard and Tardieu, *Histoire de la législation des sucres*, p. 54.

61. Ibid., pp. 51–52, 58–59; Molroguier, *Examen de la question des sucres*, pp. 90–91.

62. De Chazelles, *Etude sur le système colonial*, pp. 139–53; Dehay, *Les colonies et le métropole*, pp. 53–56, 256–257, 285–288; Lestiboudois, *Des colonies sucrières*, pp. 6–7, 40–42, 52–54, 104, 125.

63. J. Burat, "Courte réponse à la brochure publiée par M. T. Lestiboudois," passim; Bertrand, *Sur la détresse des colonies*, pp. 29–30; Dupin, *Mémoire*, pp. 4–7.

64. Boizard and Tardieu, *Histoire de la législation des sucres*, pp. 59–62; de Chazelles, *Etude sur le système colonial*, pp. 200–201, 209–14.

65. Molroguier, *Examen de la question des sucres*, 177–87; de Chazelles, *Etude sur le système colonial*, pp. 214–17; Boizard and Tardieu, *Histoire de la législation des sucres*, pp. 62–67.

66. Boizard and Tardieu, *Histoire de la législation des sucres*, pp. 66–71; de Chazelles, *Etude sur le système colonial*, pp. 218–19.

67. Adolphe Gueroult, *De la question coloniale en 1842*, pp. 103–105; cf. Bertrand, *Sur la détresse des colonies*, pp. 31–32; Emile Thomas, *Rapport à M. le Ministre de la Marine et des Colonies sur l'organisation du travail libre aux Antilles françaises*, p. 89; Dupin, *Mémoire adressé par le Conseil des Délégués*, pp. 4–7; de Chazelles, *Etude sur le système colonial*, pp. 160–61, 164–66n, 165–67, 207–208; A.N.S.O.M., Martinique 9 (99), de Moges, "Mémoire à son successeur" (1840).

68. Bertrand, *Sur la détresse des colonies*, p. 32; Général Lafond de Lurcy, *Un mot sur l'emancipation de l'esclavage*, p. 12; Dupin, *Mémoire adressé par le Conseil des Délegués*, pp. 9–13; Gueroult, *De la question coloniale*, pp. 103–105.

69. De Chazelles, *Etude sur le système colonial*, pp. 225–41; Boizard and Tardieu, *Histoire de la législation des sucres*, pp. 68–73.

70. Bonaparte, *Analyse de la question des sucres*; Boizard and Tardieu, *Histoire de la législation des sucres*, pp. 72–92; de Chazelles, *Etude sur le système colonial*, pp. 225–54.

71. Boizard and Tardieu, *Histoire de la législation des sucres*, pp. 87–88.

72. Ibid., p. 92.

## 3. The Local Face of World Process

1. P. Lavollée, *Notes sur les cultures et la production de la Martinique et de la Guadeloupe*, pp. 17–18, 20–23; A.N.S.O.M., Martinique: Etat de cultures (1841); Josa, *Les industries du sucre*, p. 124; A. Moreau de Jonnes, *Recherches statistiques sur l'esclavage colonial et sur les moyens de la supprimer*, p. 57.

2. Christian Schnakenbourg, "Statistiques pour l'histoire de l'économie de plantation en Guadeloupe et Martinique," pp. 57–58, 87–88, 97, 119–20; Lavollée, *Notes sur les cultures*,

pp. iv–v, 5, 20–23, 35; Sainte Croix, *Statistique*, 2:34, 52, 75, 97; A.N.S.O.M., Martinique; Etat de cultures; Hamon, *Des colonies et de la législation des sucres*, pp. 98–100.

3. Lavollée, *Notes sur les cultures*, pp. iv–v, 5, 23, 35; Sainte Croix, *Statistique*, 2:34, 52, 75, 97; Ministère, *Enquête sur les sucres*, pp. 21, 26, 59, 64–65, 237–38.

4. Lavollée, *Notes sur les cultures*, pp. iv–v, 5, 23, 35; Sainte Croix, *Statistique*, 2:34, 52, 75, 97; A.N.S.O.M., Martinique: Etat de Cultures; Hamon, *Des colonies et de la législation des sucres*, pp. 98–100; Ministère, *Enquête sur les sucres*, pp. 21, 26, 59, 64–65, 237–38.

5. Ministère, *Enquête sur les sucres*, pp. 64–65; Lavollée, *Notes sur les cultures*, pp. iv–v, 5, 23, 35; Sainte Croix, *Statistique*, 2:34, 52, 75, 97; A.N.S.O.M., Martinique: Etat de cultures; Hamon, *Des colonies et de la législation des sucres*, pp. 98–100.

6. B. W. Higman, *Slave Population and Economy in Jamaica, 1807–1834*, p. 187; Lavollée, *Notes sur les cultures*, pp. 5–7, 45–46, 125–26.

7. Schnakenbourg, *Crise*, p. 50; A.N.S.O.M., Martinique: Etat de population (1831–50); Sainte Croix, *Statistique*, 1:167; Ministère, *Enquête sur les sucres*, pp. 66, 250–54.

8. Ministère, *Enquête sur les sucres*, pp. 250–54; Schnakenbourg, *Crise*, p. 49.

9. Hamon, *Des colonies et de la législation des sucres*, pp. 97–98, 100; Lavollée, *Notes sur les cultures*, pp. iv–v, 23–25, 35–40; A.N.S.O.M., Martinique: Etat de cultures; A.N.S.O.M., Martinique 10 (100), Duvaldailly, "Mémoire à la successor" (1844), pp. 123–25.

10. Sainte Croix, *Statistique*, 2:19–71; Ministère, *Enquête sur les sucres*, pp. 62, 256; Lavollée, *Notes sur les cultures*, pp. iv–v, 23–25, 35–40.

11. P. Bernissant, *Etude sur le régime agricole des colonies françaises*, pp. 104–105; Lavollée, *Notes sur les cultures*, pp. 23–24, 36–37; John Bauer, "International Repercussions," p. 405; Sainte Croix, *Statistique*, 2:63; Liliane Chauleau, *Histoire Antillaise*, p. 297; Ministère de la Marine et des Colonies, Exposé général des résultats du patronage des esclaves dans les colonies françaises, pp. 93–94.

12. A.N.S.O.M., Martinique: Etat de cultures (1847), note; Bernissant, *Etude sur le régime agricole*, pp. 104–105; Lavollée, *Notes sur les cultures*, pp. 23–24, 36–37; John Bauer, "International Repercussions," p. 405; Sainte Croix, *Statistique*, 2:63; Chauleau, *Histoire Antillaise*, p. 297; Ministère de la Marine et des Colonies, *Exposé général des résultats du patronage*, pp. 93–94, 106–107.

13. A.N.S.O.M., Martinique: Etat de cultures (1847), note; Lavollée, *Notes sur les cultures*, pp. 24–25, 37–38; Ministère, *Enquête sur les sucres*, p. 201.

14. A.N.S.O.M., Martinique: Etat de cultures, esp. (1847), note; Lavollée, *Notes sur les cultures*, pp. iv–v, 23–25, 35–40; Sainte Croix, *Statistique*, 2:19–71; A.N.S.O.M., Martinique 10 (100), Duvaldailly, "Mémoire" (1844), pp. 123–25.

15. Ministère, *Enquête sur les sucres*, pp. 200–201; Schoelcher, *Abolition immediate*, p. 16; Ministère de la Marine et des Colonies, *Exposé général des résultats du patronage*, p. 103; Lavollée, *Notes sur les cultures*, pp. iv–v, 23–25, 35–40; A.N.S.O.M., Martinique: Etat de cultures; Sainte Croix, *Statistique*, 2:19–71; Thomas, *Rapport*, p. 12; A.N.S.O.M., Martinique 10 (100), Duvaldailly, "Memoire" (1844), pp. 123–25.

16. Lavollée, *Notes sur les cultures*, pp. 5–6; P. Chemin Dupontès, *Les Petites Antilles*, pp. 164–65; Thomas, *Rapport*, pp. 9–10; Ministère de la Marine et des Colonies, *Exposé général des résultats du patronage*, pp. 92–99.

17. Lavollée, *Notes sur les cultures*, pp. 35, 86, 99; Sainte Croix, *Statistique*, 2:9–94, 100.

18. Lavollée, *Notes sur les cultures*, pp. 5–7.

19. A.N.S.O.M., Martinique: Etat de cultures; Lavollée, *Notes sur les cultures*, pp. 5–6; Sainte Croix, *Statistique*, 2:9–11, 84–90. Lavollée reports the total area of this region as 32,370 hectares, of which 7,820 were planted in sugar in 1839.

20. Thomas, *Rapport*, pp. 9–11; Sainte Croix, *Statistique*, 2:9–11, 84–90; Ministère, *Exposé général des résultats du patronage*, pp. 97–98.

21. Lavollée, *Notes sur les cultures*, pp. 9–10; Sainte Croix, *Statistique*, 2:68–74, 90–97.

22. Sainte Croix, *Statistique*, 2:12–65, 67, 72, 90–97; Ministère, *Exposé général des résultats du patronage*, p. 99; Lavollée, *Notes sur les cultures*, pp. 6–10; Thomas, Rapport, pp. 9–10. Lavollée gives the area of the south as 50,534 hectares, of which 16,514 hectares were planted in sugar in 1839.

23. Sainte Croix, *Statistique*, 2; 12–65; Lavollée, *Notes sur les cultures*, pp. 6–10; Thomas, *Rapport*, pp. 9–10.

24. Lavollée, *Notes sur les cultures*, p. 44; Sainte Croix, *Statistique*, 2:12–65, 103, 158.

25. Lavollée, *Notes sur les cultures*, pp. 6–10.

26. Sainte Croix, *Statistique*, 2:43–63; Ministère, *Exposé général des résultats du patronage*, pp. 25–96.

27. Ministère, *Exposé général des résultats du patronage*, pp. 97–98; Sainte Croix, *Statistique*, 2:38–41.

28. Ministère, *Exposé général des résultats du patronage*, pp. 94–95; Sainte Croix, *Statistique*, 2:35–38.

29. A.N.S.O.M., Martinique: Etat de cultures (1846), note, Directeur de l'Interieur; Ministère, *Exposé général des résultats du patronage*, pp. 93–94; Sainte Croix, Statistique, 2:29, 49–52.

30. Ministère, *Exposé général des résultats du patronage*, pp. 91–93; Sainte Croix, *Statistique*, 2:20–35.

31. Ministère, *Exposé général des résultats du patronage*, p. 92; Sainte Croix, *Statistique*, 2:12–19.

32. Ministère, *Exposé général des résultats du patronage*, pp. 91–94; Sainte Croix, *Statistique*, 2:63–66; A. Soleau, *Notes sur les Guyanes française, hollandaise, anglaise, et sur les Antilles françaises*, pp. 69–70.

33. Lavollée, *Notes sur les cultures*, pp. 6–10; Ministère, *Enquête sur les sucres*, pp. 47, 63, 212, 234–35. Schnakenbourg regards Lavollée's figures as too high and suggests two tons per hectare as a more accurate estimate (Schnakenbourg, *Crise*, p. 44).

34. Sainte Croix, *Statistique*, 2:9–94, 100; Lavollée, *Notes sur les cultures*, pp. 35, 86, 99; Jean-Baptiste Rouvellat de Cussac, *Situation des esclaves dans les colonies françaises*, p. 24; Pardon, *La Martinique*, pp. 230–38; Soleau, *Notes sur les Guyanes*, pp. 70–71; A.N.S.O.M., Martinique 9 (99), de Moges, "Memoire" (1840).

35. Lavollée, *Notes sur les cultures*, pp. iv–v, 23–25, 35–40; A.N.S.O.M., Martinique: Etat de cultures; A.N.S.O.M., Martinique 10 (100), Duvaldailly, "Memoire" (1844), pp. 123–25; Sainte Croix, *Statistique*, 2:19–71; Liliane Chaulieu, "Sainte-Pierre au XIXe siecle," pp. 25–26.

36. Thomas, *Rapport*, p. 12; Sainte Croix, *Statistique*, 2:75–84.

37. Schnakenbourg, *Crise*, p. 30.

38. Sainte Croix, *Statistique*, 2:75–84; Lavollée, *Notes sur les cultures*, pp. 5–7, 45–46, 125–26; A.N.S.O.M., Martinique: Etat de cultures (1847), note.

39. Thomas, *Rapport*, pp. 11–12; Ministère, *Enquête sur les sucres*, p. 239.

40. Paul Daubrée, *Question coloniale sous le rapport industriel*, pp. 28–29; Lavollée, *Notes sur les cultures*, pp. 35, 85–87, 90, 99, 125–29; Sainte Croix, *Statistique*, 2:9–94, 156–59; Rouvellat de Cussac, *Situation des esclaves*, p. 24; Ministère, *Enquête sur les sucres*, pp. 45–48, 62, 71–73; A.N.S.O.M., Généralités 147 (1238), Mathieu à Ministre de la Marine et des Colonies, 1 Sept. 1846.

41. Lavollée, *Notes sur les cultures*, pp. 5–6, 85–91; Sainte Croix, *Statistique*, 2:9–11, 84–90.

42. Moreno Fraginals, *The Sugarmill*, pp. 83–83; *El ingenio*, 1:170–73; Higman, *Slave Population and Economy*, p. 128.

43. Soleau, *Notes sur les Guyanes*, pp. 60–61; A.N.S.O.M., Martinique: Etat de cultures (1831); Schoelcher, *Abolition immediate*, p. 275; Ministère, *Exposé général des résultats du patronage*, p. 103.

44. A.N.S.O.M., Martinique: Etat de cultures.

45. Ibid.

46. Ibid.

47. Ibid.

48. "Proces-verbaux du Conseil Colonial de la Martinique, Session de 1836," quoted in A. de Chazelles, *Etude sur le système colonial*, pp. 130–31n; Lavollée, *Notes sur les cultures*, pp. 110–11.

49. Ministère, *Enquête sur les sucres*, pp. 25, 60, 69; Lavollée, *Notes sur les cultures*, p. 111; Schnakenbourg, *Crise*, p. 123.

50. De Chazelles, *Etude sur le système colonial*, pp. 134–35n; Sainte Croix, *Statistique*, 2:155–57; Lavollée, *Notes sur les cultures*, pp. 126–29; Ministère, *Enquête sur les sucres*, pp. 52–53, 66, 250.

51. A.N.S.O.M., Martinique 95 (819), Delamardelle, "Etat approxamatif des dettes hypothecates de la Martinique" [1822]; Lavollée, *Notes sur les cultures*, pp. 106–10; Daubrée, *Question coloniale*, pp. 28–29; Thomas, *Rapport*, pp. 23–24. See also Schnakenbourg, *Crise*, pp. 120–21.

52. Dupin, *Mémoire addressé par le Conseil des Délégués*, pp. 3–4; de Chazelles, *Etude sur le système colonial*, pp. 130–35, 165–67; Lavollée, *Notes sur les cultures*, pp. 110–11.

53. De Chazelles, *Etude sur le système colonial*, pp. 130–35, 165–67; Lavollée, *Notes sur les cultures*, pp. 110–11, 116.

54. Jules Lechevalier, *Rapport sur les questions coloniales*, 1:22; A.N.S.O.M., Martinique 9 (99), de Moges, "Mémoire" (1840); A.N.S.O.M., Martinique 7 (83), de Moges à M. le Ministre de la Marine et des Colonies, Saint Jacques, Martinique, 15 Mar. 1839, no. 98; A.N.S.O.M., Martinique 9 (99), de Moges à M. le Ministre de la Marine et des Colonies, Macouba, Martinique, 13 Mar. 1840; Daubrée, *Question coloniale*, pp. 28–29; Bertrand, *Sur la détresse des colonies*, pp. 10–12, 1618; Dupin, *Mémoire addressé par le Conseil des Délégués*, pp. 3–4.

55. Sainte Croix, *Statistique*, 2:155–57; Lavollée, *Notes sur les cultures*, pp. 126–29.

56. Lechevalier, *Rapport sur les questions coloniales*, 1:22; A.N.S.O.M., Martinique 9 (99), de Moges, "Memoire" (1840); A.N.S.O.M., Martinique 7 (83), de Moges à M. le Ministre de la Marine et des Colonies, Saint Jacques, Martinique, 15 Mar. 1839, no. 98; A.N.S.O.M., Martinique 9 (99), de Moges à M. le Ministre de la Marine et des Colonies, Macouba, Martinique, 13 Mar. 1840.

57. Schoelcher, *Abolition immédiate*, p. 297; de Chazelles, *Etude sur le système colonial*, pp. 133–34; Schnakenbourg, *Crise*, p. 124; Alain Buffon, *Monnaie et crédit en économic coloniale*, pp. 111–12.

58. Schoelcher, *Abolition immédiate*, pp. 296–98; Buffon, *Monnaie et crédit*, pp. 112–13; May, *Histoire économique*, pp. 251–52; Schnakenbourg, *Crise*, pp. 133–34.

59. Schoelcher, *Abolition immédiate*, pp. 296–98; May, *Le Mercier de la Rivière*, 1:52–53; de Chazelles, *Etude sur le système colonial*, pp. 132–33n; Buffon, *Monnaie et crédit*, pp. 112–13; May, *Histoire économique*, pp. 251–52; Schnakenbourg, *Crise*, pp. 133–34.

60. Schoelcher, *Abolition immédiate*, p. 297; Lucien Peytraud, *L'esclavage aux Antilles françaises avant 1789 d'après des documents inédits des Archives Coloniales*, pp. 246–64; May, *Histoire économique*, pp. 252–54; Buffon, *Monnaie et crédit*, pp. 112–13; Schnakenbourg, *Crise*, p. 132.

61. Thomas, *Rapport*, p. 43; de Chazelles, *Etude sur le système colonial*, pp. 132–33n; May, *Histoire économique*, pp. 254–56; Buffon, *Monnaie et crédit*, pp. 112–14; Schnakenbourg, *Crise*, pp. 124–25.

62. Lavollée, *Notes sur les cultures*, pp. 111–14; Schoelcher, *Abolition immédiate*, pp. 296–99; Gueroult, *De la question coloniale*, p. 73; Thomas, *Rapport*, pp. 42–45.

63. Thomas, *Rapport*, p. 43; Lavollée, *Notes sur les cultures*, pp. 108–109, 112–15; Schoelcher, *Abolition immédiate*, pp. 299–300.

64. Ministère de la Marine et des Colonies, *Commission instituée par décision royale du 26 mai 1840*, (transcript), pt. 1, pp. 89–92; Lavollée, *Notes sur les cultures*, pp. 108–109, 111–17.

65. Ministère de la Marine et des Colonies, *Commission instituée par décision royale du 26 mai 1840*, pt. 1, pp. 89–92; Lavollée, *Notes sur les cultures*, pp. 2–3, 115–16.

66. Schoelcher, *Abolition immédiate*, p. 300; Schnakenbourg, *Crise*, pp. 131–32.

67. A.N.S.O.M., Martinique 95 (819), Delamardelle, "Etat approximatif des dettes hypothècaires de la Martinique" (1822); Ministère de la Marine et des Colonies, *Commission instituée par décision royale du 26 mai 1840*, pt. 1, pp. 89–92; Lavollée, *Notes sur les cultures*, pp. 101, 111, 117; Ministère, *Enquête sur les sucres*, p. 60; de Chazelles, *Etude sur le système colonial*, pp. 136–37n; Buffon, *Monnaie et crédit*, pp. 101–104, 119–20; Schnakenbourg, *Crise*, pp. 125–26, 132–33.

68. Richard Pares, *Merchants and Planters*, pp. 30–31; May, *Histoire économique*, pp. 208–11, 217–20, 286; Lémery, *La révolution française*, pp. 6–7.

69. Lavollée, *Notes sur les cultures*, pp. 98 et seq.

70. Sainte Croix, *Statistique*, 2:193–97; Pares, *Merchants and Planters*, pp. 30–33; Thomas, *Rapport*, pp. 22–24.

71. Sainte Croix, *Statistique*, 2:161–62, 193–203; Lavollée, *Notes sur les cultures*, pp. 98–101; Thomas, *Rapport*, pp. 23–24; de la Cornillere, *La Martinique en 1842*, pp. 102–3; Schnakenbourg, *Crise*, p. 126; Buffon, *Monnaie et crédit*, pp. 115–16.

72. Lavollée, *Notes sur les cultures*, pp. 99–101; Ministère, *Enquête sur les sucres*, p. 160.

73. Lavollée, *Notes sur les cultures*, pp. 98–100; Sainte Croix, *Statistique*, 2:161–62, 193–97; Buffon, *Monnaie et crédit*, p. 120; Schnakenbourg, *Crise*, pp. 125–26, 130.

74. Sainte Croix, *Statistique*, 2:161–62, 193–97; Thomas, *Rapport*, pp. 23–24.

75. Lavollée, *Notes sur les cultures*, pp. 98–101; de Chazelles, *Etude sur le système colonial*, pp. 133–34; Raynal, cited in Buffon, *Monnaie et crédit*, p. 120; Schnakenbourg, *Crise*, pp. 126, 130–31.

76. Lavollée, *Notes sur les cultures*, pp. 98–101; de Chazelles, *Etude sur le système colonial*, pp. 133–34; Schnakenbourg, *Crise*, pp. 126, 130–31.

77. Lavollée, *Notes sur les cultures*, p. 115; Schoelcher, *Abolition immédiate*, pp. 296–300; de Chazelles, *Etude sur le système colonial*, pp. 132–34; de la Cornillère, *La Martinique en 1842*, pp. 102–103; Buffon, *Monnaie et crédit*, p. 120; Schnakenbourg, *Crise*, pp. 126, 130–31.

78. Sainte Croix, *Statistique*, 2:197–203; de la Cornillère, *La Martinique en 1842*, pp. 102–103; Lavollée, *Notes sur les cultures*, pp. 115–16; Ministère, *Enquête sur les sucres*, pp. 244–45.

79. Sainte Croix, *Statistique*, 2:161–62, 193–97; Lavollée, *Notes sur les cultures*, pp. 98–101; de la Cornillère, *La Martinique en 1842*, pp. 102–3; Buffon, *Monnaie et crédit*, pp. 115–16; Thomas, *Rapport*, pp. 23–24.

80. Sainte Croix, *Statistique*, 2:197–203; Thomas, *Rapport*, pp. 23–24.

81. Gucroult, *De la question coloniale*, pp. 70–73; Lavollée, *Notes sur les cultures*, pp. 116–25; Schoelcher, *Abolition immédiate*, pp. 296–300; Victor Schoelcher, *Histoire de l'esclavage pendant les deux dernières années*, 1:11–12; Ministère, *Enquête sur les sucres*, p. 256.

82. Thomas, *Rapport*, p. 44; Lavollée, *Notes sur les cultures*, pp. 2–3, 99–101, 117; de la Cornillère, *La Martinique en 1842*, pp. 102–3.

# 4. Sugar and Slavery

1. In contrast to neoclassical economic theory as well as some interpretations of Marxism, social relations are not regarded here as external and contingent to categories of economic analysis, but rather are taken to be constitutive of specific historical conditions of production. Neoclassical economic theory presents itself as a purely technical instrument for determining the optimal allocation of scarce resources independent of any particular social or historical context. Taking price formation as its central object and point of departure, modern capital theory abstracts from social relations and constructs categories of economic analysis that are presumed to have universal validity. Hence, slavery presents no special analytical problems for economic science. In the words of Conrad and Meyer, who pioneered this approach, "From

the standpoint of the entrepreneur making an investment in slaves, the basic problems in determining profitability are analytically the same as those met in determining the returns from any other kind of capital investment" (Alfred H. Conrad and John R. Meyer, *The Economics of Slavery and Other Studies in Economic History* [Chicago: Aldine, 1964], p. 47).

From the point of view of economic theory, slaves are treated simply as "capital." They are regarded as a "production function" to be understood in terms of "inputs of slaves and materials required to maintain slaves into staple crop production and production of slave labor." In accordance with these premises, slavery itself is conceived simply as a juridical relation of property. It is treated as a category that is related to the categories of economic analysis only in a contingent and external manner. The origins of slavery are noneconomic— "the outcome of force and compulsion practiced by one group against others and not the outcome of a set of voluntarily exchanged property rights"—and it is economically important only insofar as it affects "the allocation and distribution of economic resources," and therefore the "level and pattern of output in the economy, as well as the distribution of income and utility." In this theoretical framework, the relation of slavery and slave emancipation to the development of the capitalist economy has been posed in terms of the technical evaluation of the "efficiency" and "profitability" of slave systems. Significantly, the major studies based on this approach have emphasized the positive performance of slavery according to these criteria and have attributed the decline of slavery to the success of contingent "extra-economic factors," most notably politics and ideology, in undercutting the viability of the economic system (Stanley Engerman, "Some Considerations Relating to Property Rights in Man," pp. 43–45; Conrad and Meyer, *Economics of Slavery*, pp. 45, 47, 83–84).

Within the neoclassical model, social relations, and more particularly social relations of production, are excluded from consideration. Production itself is treated only from a purely technical point of view. Economic science is concerned only with the technical determination of the proportions in which factors of production are employed to produce goods; otherwise, it regards production as beyond its scope. As a result, slaves are regarded only as inputs and outputs to the general economic process described by the scientist, and social relations are presented as no more than juridical and conjunctural elements. By thus separating the slaves as factors of production from the institution of slavery and assigning a different theoretical status to each, neoclassical economics separates the products from the process—material and social—of their production, and the producers from the social relations to one another and to nature, through which they act. The economy and production are thereby abstracted from history and social relations and are viewed in isolation as technical processes. By means of this logical operation, history and social relations, rather than being formative of economic processes, are transformed into "contexts" whose relation to the universally valid economic categories is conjunctural. The specificity of production relations is thereby eliminated. See Derek Sayer, *The Violence of Abstraction*, esp. pp. 15–82. For examples of the neoclassical view, see Conrad and Meyer, *Economics of Slavery*, pp. 43–84; Engerman, "Some Considerations Relating to Property Rights in Man," pp. 43–65; and Robert William Fogel and Stanley L. Engerman, *Time on the Cross*. G. A. Cohen, *Karl Marx's Theory of History*, provides a contrasting Marxist interpretation.

2. Sayer, *Violence of Abstraction*, pp. 15–82.

3. Marx, *Capital*, 1:345.

4. Antonio Castro, "A economia política, o capitalismo e a escravidão."

5. Fernando Ortiz, *Cuban Counterpoint*, pp. 11–36; Castro, "A Economia política, o capitalismo e a escravidão," p. 92. J.-F. Dutrône, *Précis sur la canne et les moyens d'en extraire le set essentiel*, pp. 261–63.

6. Ortiz, *Cuban Counterpoint*, pp. 21–36; Ruy Gama, *Engenho e tecnologia*, p. 73; Marx, *Capital*, 1:461–67.

7. Ortiz, *Cuban Counterpoint*, pp. 33, 41; Marx, *Capital*, 1:464–66.

8. Marx, *Capital*, 1:461–70; Gama, *Engenho e tecnologia*, pp. 73–82.

9. Ortiz, *Cuban Counterpoint*, pp. 21–36; Marx, *Capital*, 1:464–65.

10. Karl Marx, "Wage Labor and Capital," 1:89; Marx, "Results of the Immédiate Process of Production," p. 1,065.

11. Castro, "A economia política, o capitalismo e a escravidão," pp. 74–79.

12. Marx, *Capital*, 1:270–73, 300–3; Marx, *Grundrisse*, pp. 288–89.

13. Marx, "Results of the Immédiate Process of Production," pp. 1024, 1035, 1037–38; Marx, *Grundrisse*, pp. 341, 585.

14. Karl Marx, *Capital*, 3:809; Marx, "Wage Labor and Capital," p. 83; Marx, *Grundrisse*, pp. 489, 500–501.

15. Karl Marx, *Capital*, 2:554–55; Marx, "Results of the Immediate Process of Production," pp. 1031–34.

16. Marx, *Grundrisse*, p. 489; Marx, "Wage Labor and Capital," p. 83; Marx, *Capital*, 1:680; Max Weber, *Economy and Society*, 1:87–166. Contrast this view to Stanley Engerman's attempt to measure slave exploitation on the basis of slave price ("Some Economic and Demographic Comparisons of Slavery in the United States and the British West Indies," pp. 258–75). Depreciation of slave price is the transfer of value invested in the purchase price of the slave to the product produced. It has nothing to do with the creation of new value and, thus, the exploitation of the slave.

17. Douglas Hall, "Incalculability as a Feature of Sugar Production during the Eighteenth Century," pp. 348–49; Moreno Fraginals, *El ingenio*, 2:11–13, 25; Marx, *Capital*,

1:431–33; Marx, "Results of the Immediate Process of Production," pp. 1031–34; Marx, *Capital*, 2:554–55; Marx, *Capital*, 3:809.

18. Andre João Antonil, *Cultura e opulência do Brasil*, p. 120; Marx, *Capital*, 1:680; Marx, "Results of the Immediate Process of Production," pp. 1031–34; Ida C. Greaves, *Modern Production among Backward Peoples*, pp. 122–23.

19. Castro, "A economia política, o capitalismo e a escravidão," pp. 87–88, 92; Moreno Fraginals, *The Sugarmill*, p. 25; Schnakenbourg, *Crise*, p. 52. Cf. Manuel Moreno Fraginals, "Aportes culturales y deculturacion," pp. 14–15. For a contrasting view, see Genovese, *Political Economy of Slavery*.

20. Marx, "Results of the Immediate Process of Production," pp. 1031–34; Marx, *Grundrisse*, pp. 325–26; Castro, "A economia política, o capitalismo e a escravidão," pp. 92–94.

21. Marx, *Grundrisse*, p. 529n; Marx. *Capital*, 1:443. Cf. Moreno Fraginals, *The Sugarmill*, p. 18.

22. Cf. Moreno Fraginals, *The Sugarmill*, p. 18.

23. Cf. Castro, "A economia política, o capitalismo e a escravidão," pp. 67–107, esp. p. 94.

24. Ministère de la Marine et des Colonies, *Commission instituée par décision royale du 26 mai 1840*, pp. 72–73; Schoelcher, *Abolition immédiate*, pp. 23–24; Castro, "A economia política, o capitalismo e a escravidão," p. 87; Schnakenbourg, *Crise*, p. 27. Cf. Witold Kula, *An Economic Theory of the Feudal System*, pp. 38–40.

## 5. The Habitation Sucrière

1. Felix Renouard, Marquis de Sainte Croix, *De la fabrication du sucre aux colonies françaises et des améliorations à y apporter*, pp. 3–5; Dutrône, *Précis sur la canne*, pp. 261–65; Lavollée, *Notes sur les cultures*, pp. 10–11, 66, 123; A. de Lacharière, "Une lettre de M. A. de Lacharière," *Annales de la société d'agriculture et d'économic rurale de la Martinique, 1839–1840* (Saint Pierre, Martinique, n.d.), 1:91; Sainte Croix, *Statistique*, 2:101–5, 126–28, 157–58; de Chazelles, *Etude sur le système colonial*, pp. 131n, 156; Genovese, *Political Economy of Slavery*, pp. 23–28; Andre Guignod, "Théorie de la fabrication du sucre des cannes," *Annales de la société d'agriculture et d'économic rurale de la Martinique* (Saint Pierre, Martinique, 1841), 2:217–18.

2. Lavollée, *Notes sur les cultures*, pp. 45–46; A.N.S.O.M., Martinique: Etat de cultures (1841).

3. Lavollée, *Notes sur les cultures*, pp. 125–26; A.N.S.O.M., Généralités 147 (1238), Mathieu à M. le Ministre de la Marine et des Colonies, Fort Royal, 26 Nov. 1845, no.

25; A.N.S.O.M., Généralités 147 (1,238), Mathieu à M. le Ministre de la Marine et des Colonies, Fort Royal, 1 Sept. 1846, no. 46; Sainte Croix, *Statistique*, 2:158–59; Ministère, *Enquête sur les sucres*, p. 71.

4. A.N.S.O.M., Martinique 9 (99), de Moges, "Memoire" (1840); Sainte Croix, *Statistique*, 2:111, 122; Adolphe Granier de Cassagnac, *Voyage aux Antilles*, pp. 106–7; Leonard Wray, *The Practical Sugar Planter*, p. 285; Alicia P. Canabrava, *O açúcar nas Antilhas*, p. 134; Lavollée, *Notes sur les cultures*, p. 68; Sainte Croix, *De la fabrication du sucre*, pp. 21, 41–42; Thomas Roughley, *Jamaica Planter's Guide*, pp. 341–43.

5. A.N.S.O.M., Généralités 52 (449), A. Guignod, Fort Royal, 26 Sept. 1843; Elsa V. Goveia, *Slave Society in the British Leeward Islands at the End of the Eighteenth Century*, p. 127; Douglas Hall, *Free Jamaica, 1838–1865*, pp. 49, 60–67; Jean-Baptiste Labat, *Nouveau voyage aux îles de l'Amérique* (The Hague, 1724), 2:233, cited in Alicia P. Canabrava, "João Antonio Andreoni e sua obra," p. 66; Soleau, *Notes sur les Guyanes*, pp. 62–63; Dutrône, *Précis sur la canne*, pp. 265–66; Moreno Fraginals, *The Sugarmill*, p. 39; Roughley, *Jamaica Planter's Guide*, pp. 349–50; Lavollée, *Notes sur les cultures*, pp. 69–72.

6. Gama, *Engenho e tecnologia*, p. 165; A.N.S.O.M., Généralités 52 (449), A. Guignod, Fort Royal, 26 Sept. 1843; Sainte Croix, *De la fabrication du sucre*, p. 72; Reed, *History of Sugar*, pp. 88–89; Lavollée, *Notes sur les cultures*, p. 73; Dutrône, *Précis sur la canne*, pp. 129, 137; Schnakenbourg, *Crise*, p. 42.

7. Lavollée, *Notes sur les cultures*, pp. 5–13; Reed, *History of Sugar*, pp. 75–78; Hall, *Free Jamaica*, pp. 65–66.

8. De Cassagnac, *Voyage aux Antilles*, pp. 310–11; Lavollée, *Notes sur les cultures*, pp. 5–13, 43–44, 53; Reed, *History of Sugar*, pp. 75–78; Sainte Croix, *Statistique*, 2:103, 158–59; de la Cornillère, *La Martinique en 1842*, p. 98; Soleau, *Notes sur les Guyanes*, p. 62.

9. De Cassagnac, *Voyage aux Antilles*, pp. 310–11; Lavollée, *Notes sur les cultures*, pp. 5–13, 43–44, 53; Reed, *History of Sugar*, pp. 75–78; Sainte Croix, *Statistique*, 2:158–59; Schnakenbourg, *Crise*, p. 38; Ministère, *Enquête sur les sucres*, pp. 46, 48; de la Cornillère, *La Martinique*, p. 98; Goveia, *Leeward Islands*, pp. 127–29; Hall, *Free Jamaica* p. 65.

10. Von Lippmann, *Historia do açúcar*, 2:128; Moreno Fraginals, *The Sugarmill*, pp. 84–86; Moreno Fraginals, *El ingenio*, 1:80; Schnakenbourg, *Crise*, p. 38; Lavollée, *Notes sur les cultures*, p. 43.

11. Von Lippmann, *Historia do açúcar*, 2:128; Moreno Fraginals, *The Sugarmill*, pp. 84–86; Moreno Fraginals, *El ingenio*, 1:80; W. A. Green, "Planter Class and British West Indian Sugar Production," p. 454; de Lacharière, "Une lettre de M. A. de Lacharière," p. 96; Goveia, *Leeward Islands*, pp. 127–28.

12. A.N.S.O.M., Martinique: Etat de cultures (1846); Sainte Croix, *Statistique*, 2:157–59; A.N.S.O.M., Généralités 52 (449), A. Guignod, Fort Royal, 26 Sept. 1843; Ministère, *Enquête sur les sucres*, pp. 64–65.

13. Lavollée, *Notes sur les cultures*, pp. 46–47; Daubrée, *Question coloniale*, p. 46n; A.N.S.O.M., Généralités 52 (449), A. Guignod, Fort Royal, 28 Sept. 1843; Ragatz, *Fall of the Planter Class*, p. 60; Hall, *Free Jamaica*, pp. 62–65.

14. Lavollée, *Notes sur les cultures*, pp. 46–47; Gueroult, *De la question coloniale*, pp. 64–67; Généralités 52 (449), A. Guignod, Fort Royal, 28 Sept. 1843; de Cassagnac, *Voyage aux Antilles*, pp. 312–13.

15. W. A. Green, "Planter Class and British West Indian Sugar Production," pp. 449–51; Roughley, *Jamaica Planter's Guide*, pp. 63–64; Lavollée, *Notes sur les cultures*, pp. 47–48; Ragatz, *Fall of the Planter Class*, pp. 58–59; Soleau, *Notes sur les Guyanes*, p. 62; A.N.S.O.M., Généralités 52. (449), A. Guignod, Fort Royal, 28 Sept. 1843.

16. Lavollée, *Notes sur les cultures*, pp. 47–50; Sainte Croix, *Statistique*, 2:101; B. D., "De l'emploie de la charrue à la Martinique," *Annales de la société d'agriculture* (Saint Pierre, Martinique, 1841), 2:161–65; A.N.S.O.M., Généralités 52 (449), A. Guignod, Fort Royal, 28 Sept. 1843.

17. Ministère, *Enquête sur les sucres*, pp. 57–58, 64, 71, 240–41.

18. Lavollée, *Notes sur les cultures*, p. 49; Sainte Croix, *Statistique*, 2:152; Ministère, *Enquête sur les sucres*, pp. 53, 71–72.

19. Ministère, *Enquête sur les sucres*, p. 50; Lavollée, *Notes sur les cultures*, pp. 49–52; de Cassagnac, *Voyage aux Antilles*, pp. 300–2; Sainte Croix, *Statistique*, 2:153–54.

20. Lavollée, *Notes sur les cultures*, p. 68; Lavollée, *Notes sur les cultures*, pp. 49–53; Sainte Croix, *Statistique*, 2:153–54.

21. Lavollée, *Notes sur les cultures*, pp. 43–44; Sainte Croix, *Statistique*, 2:129–30; Ortiz, *Cuban Counterpoint*, pp. 21–26; Richard Pares, *A West-India Fortune*, pp. 15–16; Moreno Fraginals, *The Sugarmill*, pp. 87–91; Schnakenbourg, *Crise*, pp. 36–38.

22. Canabrava, *O açúcar nas Antilhas*, pp. 115–17; Schnakenbourg, *Crise*, pp. 36–41; Ragatz, *Fall of the Planter Class*, pp. 62–63.

23. Antonio Castro, "Brasil, 1610," pp. 679–712; Sainte Croix, *Statistique*, 2:95; Alicia P. Canabrava, "A força motriz"; Canabrava, *O açúcar nas Antilhas*, pp. 115–33; Stuart Schwartz, "Free Labor in a Slave Economy"; Schnakenbourg, *Crise*, p. 21; Sainte Croix, *Statistique*, 2:98; Mervyn Ratekin, "The Early Sugar Industry in Española."

24. Canabrava, "A força motriz," pp. 337–49; Canabrava, *O açúcar nas Antilhas*, pp. 120–33.

25. Lavollée, *Notes sur les cultures*, p. 67; Dutrône, *Précis sur la canne*, pp. 101–104; Castro, "Brasil, 1610," pp. 693–701; Canabrava, *O açúcar nas Antilhas*, p. 117; Moreno Fraginals, *The Sugarmill*, p. 101; Anselme Payen, *Traité de la fabrication et du raffinage des sucres*, p. 67; Sainte Croix, *De la fabrication du sucre*, p. 35.

26. Castro, "Brasil, 1610," pp. 679–712; Canabrava, *O açúcar nas Antilhas*, pp. 119–20; Daubrée, *Question coloniale*, pp. 18–20; Moreno Fraginals, *The Sugarmill*, p. 101; Gueroult, *De la question coloniale*, pp. 64–67.

27. Sainte Croix, *De la fabrication du sucre*, pp. 27–33; Lavollée, *Notes sur les cultures*, p. 67; Canabrava, *O açúcar nas Antilhas*, pp. 117–19; Ragatz, *Fall of the Planter Class*, p. 62; Moreno Fraginals, *The Sugarmill*, p. 101.

28. Lavollée, *Notes sur les cultures*, p. 67; Canabrava, *O açúcar nas Antilhas*, pp. 117–19; Ragatz, *Fall of the Planter Class*, p. 62; Moreno Fraginals, *The Sugarmill*, p. 101.

29. Dutrône, *Précis sur la canne*, pp. 101–102; Lavollée, *Notes sur les cultures*, p. 67; Canabrava, *O açúcar nas Antilhas*, p. 119; Moreno Fraginals, *The Sugarmill*, pp. 86, 101–104.

30. Sainte Croix, *De la fabrication du sucre*, pp. 26–28; Payen, *Traité de la fabrication*, pp. 67–68; Lavollée, *Notes sur les cultures*, p. 67; Daubrée, *Question coloniale*, p. 26; Moreno Fraginals, *The Sugarmill*, pp. 101–102, 111.

31. Sainte Croix, *Statistique*, 2:34, 52, 74, 96; A.N.S.O.M., Martinique: Etat de cultures; Lavollée, *Notes sur les cultures*, p. 49; Soleau, *Notes sur les Guyanes*, pp. 61–62, 68.

32. Canabrava, *O açúcar nas Antilhas*, pp. 128–33; Brière de l'Ile, "Un mot sur les moulins à vent à la Martinique," *Annales de la société d'agriculture* (Saint Pierre, Martinique, 1841), 2:273–78.

33. Daubrée, *Question coloniale*, p. 20; Sainte Croix, *De la fabrication du sucre*, pp. 8–26; Soleau, *Notes sur les Guyanes*, p. 68; A.N.S.O.M., Martinique 20 (169), Macomb à Donzelot, 21 Sept. 1820.

34. Soleau, *Notes sur les Guyanes*, pp. 59–61; A.N.S.O.M., Martinique 20 (169), Macomb à Donzelot, 21 Sept. 1820; Daubrée, *Question coloniale*, p. 20.

35. Soleau, *Notes sur les Guyanes*, pp. 59–61; Sainte Croix, *De la fabrication du sucre*, pp. 9–35.

36. Daubrée, *Question coloniale*, p. 21; Dutrône, *Précis sur la canne*, pp. 105–6; Lavollée, *Notes sur les cultures*, p. 49; Ministère, *Enquête sur les sucres*, p. 63; Brière de l'Ile, "Un mot sur les moulins à vent," p. 275; Payen, *Traité de la fabrication*, p. 70; A.N.S.O.M., Martinique 20 (169), Macomb à Donzelot, 21 Sept. 1820; Noel Deerr and Alexander Brooks, "The Early Use of Steam Power in the Cane Sugar Industry," p. 13.

37. Deerr and Brooks, "Early Use of Steam Power," pp. 12–21; Moreno Fraginals, *El ingenio*, 1:74, 84, 207–14; Moreno Fraginals, *The Sugarmill*, pp. 102–103; Adamson, *Sugar without Slaves*, p. 171.

38. Deerr and Brooks, "Early Use of Steam Power," pp. 16–17; Sainte Croix, *Statistique*, 1:23–24; A.N.S.O.M., Martinique 20 (169), letters of 25 Apr. 1817 and 30 July 1817; A.N.S.O.M., Martinique: Etat de cultures (1836); A.N.S.O.M., Martinique 20 (170), "Tableau des usines à vapeur à la colonie, 1845," and "Extrait d'un rapport de tournée addressé à M. B. Chevalier, Substitut du Procureur du Roi à Saint Pierre, 10 août 1846."

39. Moreno Fraginals, *The Sugarmill*, pp. 102–3, 106; Soleau, *Notes sur les Guyanes*, pp. 61–62; Lavollée, *Notes sur les cultures*, p. 67; A.N.S.O.M., Martinique: Etat de cultures (1841); Sainte Croix, *De la fabrication du sucre*, p. 28.

40. A.N.S.O.M., Martinique 20 (169), Macomb à Donzelot, 21 Sept. 1820.

41. A.N.S.O.M., Martinique 20 (169), Macomb à Donzelot, 21 Sept. 1820; Daubrée, *Question coloniale*, pp. 25–28.

42. A.N.S.O.M, Martinique 20 (169), Donzelot à Ministre de la Marine et des Colonies, Fort Royal, 1 Mar. 1821; de la Cornillère, *La Martinique en 1842*, pp. 98–99.

43. A.N.S.O.M., Martinique 20 (169), Donzelot à Ministre de la Marine et des Colonies, Fort Royal, 1 Mar. 1821; M. le Ministre de la Marine et des Colonies à S. E. le Ministre de l'Intérieur et à M. W. Macomb, "Rapport," 29 July 1821.

44. Green, "Planter Class and British West Indian Sugar Production," p. 461; Sainte Croix, *De la fabrication du sucre*, pp. 8–11.

45. Dutrône, *Précis sur la canne*, pp. 108–109; Pares, *West-India Fortune*, pp. 15–16; de la Cornillère, *La Martinique en 1842*, pp. 99–101; Sainte Croix, *Statistique*, 2:110–18; Gueroult, *De la question coloniale*, pp. 64–67; Daubrée, *Question coloniale*, pp. 18, 21.

46. Dutrône, *Précis sur la canne*, pp. 108–109, 226–27, 245–52; Sainte Croix, *De la fabrication du sucre*, pp. 64, 68, 72, 75; Sainte Croix, *Statistique*, 2:111–12; Payen, *Traité de la fabrication*, p. 70; Richard Sheridan, *Sugar and Slavery*, pp. 114–15; Canabrava, *O açúcar nas Antilhas*, pp. 138–40; Schnakenbourg, *Crise*, p. 39.

47. Moreno Fraginals, *The Sugarmill*, pp. 33–41; Ruy Gama, *Engenho e tecnologia*, pp. 78–79, 91, 103–107, 164–65; Canabrava, *O açúcar nas Antilhas*, pp. 134–35, 141; Soleau, *Notes sur les Guyanes*, p. 64; Green, "Planter Class and British West Indian Sugar Production," p. 461.

48. Daubrée, *Question coloniale*, p. 21; Sainte Croix, *Statistique*, 2:111–14; Lavollée, *Notes sur les cultures*, p. 68; Soleau, *Notes sur les Guyanes*, p. 64; Josa, *Industrie sucrière à la Martinique*, p. 49; Moreno Fraginals, *The Sugarmill*, pp. 38, 106–109; Schnakenbourg, *Crise*, p. 39; Sheridan, *Sugar and Slavery*, pp. 114–15.

49. Canabrava, *O açúcar nas Antilhas*, pp. 135, 141; Moreno Fraginals, *El ingenio*, 3:118, 148, 156; Ruy Gama, *Engenho e tecnologia*, p. 165; Dutrône, *Précis sur la canne*, pp. 110–11; Sainte Croix, *Statistique*, 2:112–13.

50. Sainte Croix, *Statistique*, 2:110–12, 115–16; Ministère, *Enquête sur les sucres*, p. 51; Sainte Croix, *De la fabrication du sucre*, pp. 62–63, 76; Payen, *Traité de la fabrication*, p. 70; Soleau, *Notes sur les Guyanes*, pp. 64–65; Canabrava, *O açúcar nas Antilhas*, pp. 136–37; Moreno Fraginals, *El ingenio*, 1:92.

51. Sainte Croix, *De la fabrication du sucre*, pp. 37, 61–63; Payen, *Traité de la fabrication*, p. 70; Ministère, *Enquête sur les sucres*, p. 51; Sainte Croix, *Statistique*, 2:111–12; Dutrône, *Précis sur la canne*, pp. 108–109, 127–29, 226–27, 245–53; Canabrava, *O açúcar nas Antilhas*, pp. 136–41; Moreno Fraginals, *The Sugarmill*, pp. 38–39, 106–9.

52. Dutrône, *Précis sur la canne*, pp. 225–27; Sainte Croix, *De la fabrication du sucre*, pp. 64–66; Soleau, *Notes sur les Guyanes*, pp. 64–67; Lavollée, *Notes sur les cultures*, pp. 67–68; Canabrava, *O açúcar nas Antilhas*, p. 141; Moreno Fraginals. *The Sugarmill*, pp. 38–39, 106–9; Schnakenbourg, *Crise*, p. 39; Gama, *Engenho e tecnologia*, p. 164.

53. Sainte Croix, *De la fabrication du sucre*, pp. 64–68; Soleau, *Notes sur les Guyanes*, pp. 65–66.

54. Dutrône, *Précis sur la canne*, pp. 107, 204, 206, 209–12; Canabrava, *O açúcar nas Antilhas*, pp. 135–36; Payen, *Traité de la fabrication*, p. 70; Daubrée, Question coloniale, p. 21; Moreno Fraginals, *The Sugarmill*, p. 106; Sainte Croix, *De la fabrication du sucre*, pp. 73–74; Sainte Croix, *Statistique*, 2:111–12; Gama, *Engenho e tecnologia*, p. 164.

55. Dutrône, *Précis sur la canne*, pp. 107, 203–4, 210–12; Canabrava, *O açúcar nas Antilhas*, pp. 135–36; Payen, *Traité de la fabrication*, p. 70; Daubrée, *Question coloniale*, p. 21; Lavollée, *Notes sur les cultures*, p. 68.

56. Dutrône, *Précis sur la canne*, pp. 135–36, 203–7, 212; Lavollée, *Notes sur les cultures*, p. 68; Payen, *Traité de la fabrication*, p. 70; Canabrava, *O açúcar nas Antilhas*, pp. 135–36.

57. Sainte Croix, *De la fabrication du sucre*, pp. 74–76; Dutrône, *Précis sur la canne*, pp. 135–36, 205–209; Canabrava, *O açúcar nas Antilhas*, pp. 135–36; Soleau, *Notes sur les Guyanes*, p. 64; Payen, *Traité de la fabrication*, p. 70.

58. Dutrône, *Précis sur la canne*, pp. 136–37.

59. Ibid., pp. 135–36, 205–9; Sainte Croix, *De la fabrication du sucre*, pp. 58–68; Derosne, *Mémoire*, pp. 40–41.

60. Roughley, *Jamaica Planter's Guide*, p. 345; Moreno Fraginals, *The Sugarmill*, p. 118; Gama, *Engenho e tecnologia*, pp. 74–78; Dutrône, *Précis sur la canne*, pp. 175, 213; Wray, *Practical Planter*, p. 291.

61. Gama, *Engenho e tecnologia*, pp. 73–78.

62. Dutrône, *Précis sur la canne*, esp. pp. 158–74; Payen, *Traité de la fabrication*, p. 70; Gama, *Engenho e tecnologia*, p. 164; Canabrava, *O açúcar nas Antilhas*, pp. 134–35, 141, 176; Moreno Fraginals, *El ingenio*, 3:209–10; Moreno Fraginals, *The Sugarmill*, p. 109; J. G. Cantero and E. Laplante, *Los ingenios de Cuba*.

63. Daubrée, *Question coloniale*, pp. 12, 15; Sainte Croix, *De la fabrication du sucre*, pp. 38–39; Reed, *History of Sugar*, pp. 85–86; Gama, *Engenho e tecnologia*, p. 163; Moreno Fraginals, *El ingenio*, 3:247.

64. Soleau, *Notes sur les Guyanes*, pp. 62–64; Lavollée, *Notes sur les cultures*, pp. 67–68; Dutrône, *Précis sur la canne*, pp. 112, 137; Sainte Croix, *De la fabrication du sucre*, pp. 38–39; Canabrava, "João Antonio Andreoni," pp. 72–73.

65. Lavollée, *Notes sur les cultures*, p. 68; Sainte Croix, *De la fabrication du sucre*, pp. 41–42; Sainte Croix, *Statistique*, 2:111; Soleau, *Notes sur les Guyanes*, pp. 62–64; Roughley, *Jamaica Planter's Guide*, pp. 341–43.

66. Sainte Croix, *De la fabrication du sucre*, pp. 39–43; Sainte Croix, *Statistique*, 2:112–13; Lavollée, *Notes sur les cultures*, pp. 69–72; Canabrava, *O açúcar nas Antilhas*, pp. 140, 157; Moreno Fraginals, *El ingenio*, 3:132; Schnakenbourg, *Crise*, p. 40; Soleau, *Notes sur les Guyanes*, pp. 62–63; Reed, *History of Sugar*, pp. 88–89; Dutróne, *Précis sur la canne*, pp. 131, 265.

67. Canabrava, "João Antonio Andreoni," pp. 72–73; Canabrava, *O açúcar nas Antilhas*, pp. 157–59; Roughley, *Jamaica Planter's Guide*, pp. 344–46; Sainte Croix, *De la fabrication du sucre*, pp. 41–42; Soleau, *Notes sur les Guyanes*, pp. 62–63; Reed, *History of Sugar*, p. 86; Lavollée, *Notes sur les cultures*, pp. 69–70; Dutrône, *Précis sur la canne*, p. 112; Charles Derosne, *Mémoire sur la fabrication du sucre dans les colonies par de nouveaux procédés*, p. 21; Moreno Fraginals, *The Sugarmill*, p. 115.

68. Roughley, *Jamaica Planter's Guide*, pp. 344–45; Dutrône, *Précis sur la canne*, pp. 112, 265–69; Lavollée, *Notes sur les cultures*, pp. 69–70; Soleau, *Notes sur les Guyanes*, p. 63; Reed, *History of Sugar*, p. 86; Sainte Croix, *De la fabrication du sucre*, p. 42; Canabrava, *O açúcar nas Antilhas*, pp. 157–59; Sainte Croix, *Statistique*, 2:135.

69. Soleau, *Notes sur les Guyanes*, pp. 62–63; Dutrône, *Précis sur la canne*, pp. 265–66; Moreno Fraginals, *The Sugarmill*, p. 39; Roughley, *Jamaica Planter's Guide*, pp. 349–50; Lavollée, *Notes sur les cultures*, pp. 69–72.

70. Gama, *Engenho e tecnologia*, p. 165; A.N.S.O.M., Généralités 52 (449), A. Guignod, Fort Royal, 26 Sept. 1843; Sainte Croix, *De la fabrication du sucre*, p. 72; Reed, *History of Sugar*, pp. 88–89; Lavollée, *Notes sur les cultures*, p. 73; Dutrône, *Précis sur la canne*, pp. 129, 137; Schnakenbourg, *Crise*, p. 42.

71. Dutrône, *Précis sur la canne*, p. 137; Roughley, *Jamaica Planter's Guide*, p. 357.

72. Lavollée, *Notes sur les cultures*, pp. 70–73; Dutrône, *Précis sur la canne*, pp. 138–40; Soleau, *Notes sur les Guyanes*, p. 63; Sainte Croix, *De la fabrication du sucre*, pp. 43–45; Roughley, *Jamaica Planter's Guide*, pp. 343, 346–47.

73. Dutrône, *Précis sur la canne*, pp. 138–40; Lavollée, *Notes sur les cultures*, pp. 70–73; Sainte Croix, *De la fabrication du sucre*, pp. 43–45.

74. Lavollée, *Notes sur les cultures*, pp. 70–73; Soleau, *Notes sur les Guyanes*, p. 63; Dutrône, *Précis sur la canne*, pp. 137, 139–40; Sainte Croix, *De la fabrication du sucre*, pp. 43–45; Roughley, *Jamaica Planter's Guide*, pp. 356–60; Daubrée, *Question coloniale*, p. 22.

75. Sainte Croix, *Statistique*, 2:113–14; Lavollée, *Notes sur les cultures*, pp. 68, 73; Sainte Croix, *De la fabrication du sucre*, pp. 43–45; Dutrône, *Précis sur la canne*, pp. 138–39; Soleau, *Notes sur les Guyanes*, pp. 62–63.

76. Sainte Croix, *De la fabrication du sucre*, pp. 44–46; Dutrône, *Précis sur la canne*, pp. 111, 271, 274–76; Goveia, *Leeward Islands*, p. 132; Lavollée, *Notes sur les cultures*, p. 76.

77. Lavollée, *Notes sur les cultures*, pp. 73–74; Sainte Croix, *De la fabrication du sucre*, pp. 44–46; Dutrône, *Précis sur la canne*, pp. 141–43, 274–76.

78. Dutrône, *Précis sur la canne*, pp. 111, 142–43; Canabrava, *O açúcar nas Antilhas*, pp. 158–59.

79. Lavollée, *Notes sur les cultures*, p. 74; Dutrône, *Précis sur la canne*, pp. 175–82, 271, 274–76; Roughley, *Jamaica Planter's Guide*, pp. 85–87, 346–48; Reed, *History of Sugar*, p. 87; Von Lippmann, *Historia do açúcar*, 2:142–43.

80. Daubrée, *Question coloniale*, p. 22; Lavollée, *Notes sur les cultures*, p. 73; Sainte Croix, *Statistique*, 2:114; Soleau, *Notes sur les Guyanes*, p. 64; A. Guignod, "Sucre: Observations presentées à la société d'agriculture," *Annales de la société d'agriculture et d'économie rurale de la Martinique, 1839–1840* (Saint Pierre, Martinique, n.d.), 1:287; Canabrava, *O açúcar nas Antilhas*, p. 160; Moreno Fraginals, *The Sugarmill*, p. 109; Dutrône, *Précis sur la canne*, pp. 175, 213; Sainte Croix, *De la fabrication du sucre*, p. 45.

81. Sainte Croix, *De la fabrication du sucre*, pp. 44, 47; Lavollée, *Notes sur les cultures*, pp. 74, 76; Dutrône, *Précis sur la canne*, pp. 111, 115–18, 142–43, 271; Roughley, *Jamaica Planter's Guide*, p. 361; Sheridan, *Sugar and Slavery*, p. 117; Sainte Croix, *Statistique*, 2:136; Daubrée, *Question coloniale*, p. 22.

82. Dutrône, *Précis sur la canne*, pp. 115–20, 143–45, 264; Roughley, *Jamaica Planter's Guide*, pp. 361–64; Lavollée, *Notes sur les cultures*, pp. 76–77; Sainte Croix, *Statistique*, 2:118, 136, 160–61; Sainte Croix, *De la fabrication du sucre*, pp. 48–49; Canabrava, *O açúcar nas Antilhas*, p. 161; Reed, *History of Sugar*, p. 88; Canabrava, "Joao Antonio Andreoni," pp. 72–73; Moreno Fraginals, *The Sugarmill*, p. 118.

83. Dutrône, *Précis sur la canne*, pp. 118–19, 143–45; Lavollée, *Notes sur les cultures*, pp. 76–77; Sainte Croix, *De la fabrication du sucre*, pp. 48–49; Daubrée, *Question coloniale*, pp. 22–23.

84. Dutrône, *Précis sur la canne*, pp. 117–18, 271–72; Lavollée, *Notes sur les cultures*, pp. 76–77; Sainte Croix, *De la fabrication du sucre*, pp. 47–49; Sainte Croix, *Statistique*,

2:114, 136–38; Sheridan, *Sugar and Slavery*, p. 117; Moreno Fraginals, *The Sugarmill*, p. 116; Boizard and Tardieu, *Histoire de la législation des sucres*, p. 50n.

85. Dutrône, *Précis sur la canne*, pp. 120, 264–65, 272–73; Reed, *History of Sugar*, pp. 50–91; Sheridan, *Sugar and Slavery*, p. 117; Sainte Croix, *Statistique*, 2:136–38; Sainte Croix, *De la fabrication du sucre*, pp. 48–49; Gama, *Engenho e tecnologia*, pp. 170–73; Moreno Fraginals, *The Sugarmill*, p. 118; Derosne and Cail, *De la elaboracién del azúcar*, p. 40.

86. Sainte Croix, *Statistique*, 2:137–38; Dutrône, *Précis sur la canne*, pp. 264–65, 120–23, 264–65, 272–73; Moreno Fraginals, *The Sugarmill*, p. 118; Canabrava, *O açúcar nas Antilhas*, p. 162; Sheridan, *Sugar and Slavery*, pp. 117–18; Gama, *Engenho e tecnologia*, pp. 170–73.

87. Charles Derosne, *Notice on the New Process for Making Sugar, Lately Introduced in the French and English Colonies*, p. 1; Charles Derosne and Jean-Francois Cail, *De la elaboración del azúcar*, pp. 40–41; Chambre des Députés, *Rapport Dumon*, p. 27; Boizard and Tardieu, *Histoire de la législation des sucres*, p. 50n; Reed, *History of Sugar*, pp. 90–91; Schnakenbourg, *Crise*, pp. 40–41; A.N.S.O.M., Martinique 10 (100), Duvaldailly, "Memoire" (1844).

88. Dutrône, *Précis sur la canne*, pp. 122–24, 272–76; Sainte Croix, *Statistique*, 2:137; Sainte Croix, *De la fabrication du sucre*, pp. 48–54; Daubrée, *Question coloniale*, pp. 22–23; Canabrava, *O açúcar nas Antilhas*, pp. 164–65.

89. Lavollée, *Notes sur les cultures*, pp. 146–48; Sainte Croix, *Statistique*, 2:140–42; Dutrône, *Précis sur la canne*, pp. 125–26.

90. Lavollée, *Notes sur les cultures*, p. 146; Daubrée, *Question coloniale*, pp. 12–13, 22–23; Canabrava, *O açúcar nas Antilhas*, p. 163.

91. Gueroult, *De la question coloniale*, pp. 64–67; Daubrée, *Question coloniale*, pp. 23–24; Lavollée, *Notes sur les cultures*, pp. 76–78, 146; Moreno Fraginals, *The Sugarmill*, p. 125; A.N.S.O.M., Généralités 56 (543), "Rapport de Jabrun sur les améliorations à introduire dans la fabrication du sucre aux colonies" (1838), p. 15.

92. Lavollée, *Notes sur les cultures*, p. 66; Schnakenbourg, *Crise*, p. 45; Moreno Fraginals, *The Sugarmill*, p. 119; Fierain, *Les raffineries du sucre*, p. 16.

93. Lavollée, *Notes sur les cultures*, p. 66; Ministère, *Enquête sur les sucres*, pp. 140, 203, 241–42; Evans, *The Sugar Planter's Manual*, pp. 192ff., 214, cited in Hall, *Free Jamaica*, p. 74; Schnakenbourg, *Crise*, pp. 40–41. Cf. Green, "Planter Class and British West Indian Sugar Production," p. 453, for an example of a contrary position.

94. Ministère, *Enquête sur les sucres*, pp. 140, 203, 241–42; Lavollée, *Notes sur les cultures*, p. 66; Sainte Croix, *De la fabrication du sucre*, p. 45; Schnakenbourg, *Crise*, p. 45.

95. Daubrée, *Question coloniale*, pp. 1–8; Derosne and Cail, *De la elaboración del azúcar*, pp. 5, 7.

# 6. Obstacles to Innovation

1. Dutrône, *Précis sur la canne*, pp. 261–64; Sainte Croix, *De la fabrication du sucre*, pp. 3–5; Gueroult, *De la question coloniale*, pp. 64–67.

2. A.N.S.O.M., Martinique 9 (99), de Moges, "Memoire" (1840); *Annales de la société d'agriculture et d'économie rurale de la Martinique*, 1839–1840, 2:45; Lavollée, *Notes sur les cultures*, p. 83; Derosne and Cail, *De la elaboración del azúcar*, p. 6; Moreno Fraginals, *The Sugarmill*, p. 111; Schnakenbourg, *Crise*, pp. 175, 177–78.

3. A.N.S.O.M., Généralités 52 (449), A. Guignod, Fort Royal, 26 Sept. 1843; Sainte Croix, *De la fabrication du sucre*; A.N.S.O.M., Généralités 56 (543), "Rapport de Jabrun sur les améliorations à introduire dans la fabrication du sucre aux colonies" (1838).

4. Daubrée, *Question coloniale*, esp. pp. 39–91; Derosne and Cail, *De la elaboración del azúcar*, pp. 5–26.

5. Derosne and Cail, *De la elaboración del azúcar*, pp. 6, 15; Williams, *Columbus to Castro*, p. 380; Daubrée, *Question coloniale*, pp. 23–24, 29–31; Moreno Fraginals, *The Sugarmill*, p. 111; Schnakenbourg, *Crise*, pp. 175, 177–78.

6. Daubrée, *Question coloniale*, p. 13; Soleau, *Notes sur les Guyanes*, p. 63; Lavollée, *Notes sur les cultures*, p. 71; Dutrône, *Précis sur la canne*, pp. 109–10; Moreno Fraginals, *The Sugarmill*, pp. 39, 108–109; Goveia, *Leeward Islands*, p. 132; Schnakenbourg, *Crise*, p. 178; Derosne, *Mémoire sur la fabrication du sucre*, pp. 22–23.

7. Reed, *History of Sugar*, p. 138; Payen, *Traité de la fabrication*, pp. 73–76; Derosne, *Mémoire sur la fabrication du sucre*, pp. 2, 13, 15, 89; Sainte Croix, *De la fabrication du sucre*, p. 43.

8. Reed, *History of Sugar*, pp. 138–41; Wray, *Practical Planter*, pp. 313–18; Derosne and Cail, *De la elaboración del azúcar*, pp. 36–38; Deerr, *History of Sugar*, 2:572.

9. A.N.S.O.M., Généralités 56 (543), "Rapport Jabrun," p. 3; Sainte Croix, *De la fabrication du sucre*, p. 45; Lavollée, *Notes sur les cultures*, pp. 74–75, 83; Derosne, *Notice on the New Process*, p. 17; Daubrée, *Question coloniale*, p. 27; Schnakenbourg, *Crise*, p. 179.

10. Derosne and Cail, *De la elaboración del azúcar*, pp. 34–35; Wray, *Practical Planter*, pp. 306–307.

11. A.N.S.O.M., Généralités 56 (543), "Rapport Jabrun," pp. 14–17; *Lavollée, Notes sur les cultures*, pp. 75–76.

12. A.N.S.O.M., Généralités 56 (543), "Rapport Jabrun," pp. 3, 18–19; Deerr, *History of Sugar*, 2:556–58; Derosne and Cail, *De la elaboración del azúcar*, pp. 112–19.

13. A.N.S.O.M., Généralités 56 (543), "Rapport Jabrun," pp. 3, 14–15, 18–19; Lavollée, *Notes sur les cultures*, pp. 75–76.

14. Sainte Croix, *De la fabrication du sucre*, p. 58; Derosne and Cail, *De la elaboración del azúcar*, pp. 38–39, 174; A.N.S.O.M., Généralités 56 (543), "Rapport Jabrun," pp. 3–5; Ragatz, *Fall of the Planter Class*, p. 65; Moreno Fraginals, *The Sugarmill*, pp. 111–13; Deerr, *History of Sugar*, 2:561.

15. Derosne and Cail, *De la elaboración del azúcar*, pp. 38–39, 175–76; A.N.S.O.M., Généralités 56 (543), "Rapport Jabrun," pp. 3–5; Moreno Fraginals, *The Sugarmill*, pp. 111–13; Deerr, *History of Sugar*, 2:559–61.

16. Derosne and Cail, *De la elaboración del azúcar*, pp. 38–39, 175–81; Deerr, *History of Sugar*, 2:562–68.

17. Sainte Croix, *De la fabrication du sucre*, p. 58; A.N.S.O.M., Généralités 56 (543), "Rapport Jabrun," pp. 5–7; A.N.S.O.M., Martinique 20 (170), "Tableau des usines à vapeur à la colonie" (1845), and "Extrait d'un rapport de tournée addressé à M. le Procurer Général de la Martinique par M. B. Chevalier, Substitut de Procureur du Roi á Saint Pierre," 10 Aug. 1846.

18. Daubrée, *Question coloniale*, pp. 28–31; Derosne and Cail, *De la elaboración del azúcar*, pp. 16–18; A.N.S.O.M., Généralités 56 (543), "Rapport Jabrun," pp. 5–6.

19. Moreno Fraginals, *The Sugarmill*, p. 26; Ministère, *Enquête sur les sucres*, p. 53; Green, "Planter Class and British West Indian Sugar Production," pp. 448–63.

20. The argument for the incompatibility of slave labor and technological innovation in the sugar industry has been made most forcefully by Manuel Moreno Fraginals. In this interpretation, slaves are viewed as incapable of attaining the minimal technical level required to operate complicated machinery, and the introduction of free wage workers was necessary to modernize production (*The Sugarmill*, esp. pp. 40–41, 112–13, 144). Against this technological determinism, Rebecca Scott has documented for Cuba the high number of skilled slaves performing technically advanced jobs and the dependence of the largest and most mechanized plantations on slave labor (*Slave Emancipation in Cuba*, pp. 3–41, 84–110). See also Ruy Gama, *Engenho e tecnologia*, esp. pp. 79–80; Schoelcher, *Abolition immédiate*, p. 158.

21. Daubrée, *Question coloniale*, p. 17; Derosne, *Notice on the New Process*, p. 12; Derosne and Cail, *De la elaboración del azúcar*, pp. 15–16, 23–24; A.N.S.O.M., Généralités 56 (543), "Rapport Jabrun," pp. 3, 14–15, 18–19.

22. Derosne and Cail, *De la elaboración del azúcar*, pp. 15–16, 21–22.

23. Daubrée, *Question coloniale*, pp. 34, 51–52, 76; Derosne and Cail, *De la elaboración del azúcar*, pp. 8, 15–16, 21–24; Moreno Fraginals, *The Sugarmill*, pp. 11–12.

24. Lavollée, *Notes sur les cultures*, pp. 75–76; Derosne and Cail, *De la elaboración del azúcar*, pp. 15–16; A.N.S.O.M., Martinique 20 (170), Extrait d'un travail de M. Reisser, "Quelques réflexions sur l'instruction élémentaire et réligieux aux colonies" (n.d.);

A.N.S.O.M., Martinique 20 (170), Mathieu à Ministre de la Marine et des Colonies, Fort Royal, 10 Apr. 1847; A.N.S.O.M., Martinique 7 (83), Mathieu à Ministre de la Marine et des Colonies, Fort Royal, 10 Mar. 1847.

25. Lavollée, *Notes sur les cultures*, pp. 5–13; Reed, *History of Sugar*, pp. 75–78; Hall, *Free Jamaica*, pp. 65–66.

26. Sainte Croix, *Statistique*, 2:105; Hall, *Free Jamaica*, pp. 49, 60.

27. May, *Histoire économique*, pp. 57–74, 84–102; Martin, *Histoire de l'esclavage*, p. 32; Canabrava, *O açúcar nas Antilhas*, pp. 133–34, 155; Moreno Fraginals, *The Sugarmill*, pp. 65–73, 82–85; Schnakenbourg, *Crise*, p. 30; Lavollée, *Notes sur les cultures*, pp. 10–11, 66; Dutrone, *Précis sur la canne*, pp. 261–64; Sainte Croix, *De la fabrication du sucre*, pp. 3–5; Von Lippmann, Historia do açúcar, pp. 140–44.

28. Daubrée, *Question coloniale*, pp. 29–30.

29. Ibid., pp. 31–35; A.N.S.O.M., Généralités 56 (543), "Rapport Jabrun," pp. 5–7, 14–19; Sainte Croix, *De la fabrication du sucre*, p. 58.

30. Sidney W. Mintz, "Cañamelar," pp. 337–40; Derosne and Cail, *De la elaboración del azúcar*, pp. 7–9, 26; Schnakenbourg, *Crise*, pp. 200–201, 202–206.

31. Daubrée, *Question coloniale*, pp. 36–48, cf. 80–88; Schnakenbourg, *Crise*, pp. 200–201, 202–206.

32. A.N.S.O.M., Martinique 7 (83), Mathieu à Ministre de la Marine et des Colonies, Fort Royal, 24 Apr. 1847, no. 260; Derosne and Cail, *De la elaboración del azúcar*, pp. 21–22; Schoelcher, *Histoire de l'esclavage*, 2:373–80; Schoelcher, *Abolition immédiate*, pp. xvi–xxii; Schnakenbourg, *Crise*, pp. 201, 206–7.

33. Sainte Croix, *De la fabrication du sucre*, pp. 77–94; A.N.S.O.M., Généralites 52 (449), A. Guignod, Fort Royal, 26 Sept. 1843, pp. 7–8; A.N.S.O.M., Martinique 7 (83), Mathieu à Ministre de la Marine et des Colonies, Fort Royal, 24 Apr. 1847, no. 260; Schnakenbourg, *Crise*, pp. 206–7, 209–20.

34. A.N.S.O.M., Généralités 147 (1328), St. Ange de Sinson à Ministre de la Marine et des Colonies, François, 6 Aug. 1847; A.N.S.O.M., Martinique 7 (83), Mathieu à Ministre de la Marine et des Colonies, Fort Royal, 24 Apr. 1847, no. 260; Schnakenbourg, *Crise*, pp. 206–7, 209–20.

35. A.N.S.O.M., Martinique 20 (170), Mathieu à Ministre de la Marine et des Colonies, "Etablissement d'usines à vapeur à la colonie," Fort Royal, 26 July 1845; A.N.S.O.M., Généralités 147 (1328), St. Ange de Sinson à Ministre de la Marine et des Colonies, François, 6 Aug. 1847; A.N.S.O.M., Martinique 10 (100), Duvaldailly, "Mémoire" (1844), p. 122; A.N.S.O.M., Martinique 20 (170), Mathieu à Ministre de la Marine et des Colonies, Fort Royal, 26 July 1845, no. 453; A.N.S.O.M., Martinique 20 (170), Extrait d'un travail de M. Reisser, "Quelques réflections sur l'instruction élémentaire et réligieux aux colonies";

Ministère de la Marine et des Colonies, Compte rendu au Roi de l'éxécution des lois des 18 et 19 juillet 1845 sur le régime des esclaves, la création des établissments agricoles par le travail libre, etc., pp. 37–39, 50–51; Schnakenbourg, *Crise*, p. 220.

36. A.N.S.O.M., Martinique 20 (170), Extrait d'un travail de M. Reisser, "Quelques réflections sur l'instruction élémentaire et réligieux aux colonies"; *Courrier de la Martinique*, 22 Jan. 1848; Schnakenbourg, *Crise*, pp. 220–25, 234–41.

37. A.N.S.O.M., Martinique 20 (170), Mathieu à Ministre de la Marine et des Colonies, 10 Apr. 1847; A.N.S.O.M., Martinique 7 (83), Mathieu à Ministre de la Marine et des Colonies, Fort Royal, 10 Mar. 1847; Schnakenbourg, *Crise*, pp. 49, 220.

38. A.N.S.O.M., Martinique 20 (170), Mathieu à Ministre de la Marine et des Colonies, 10 Apr. 1847; A.N.S.O.M., Martinique 20 (170), "Réglement de l'usine de Messieurs Sinson frères"; Schnakenbourg, *Crise*, pp. 223–24.

39. A.N.S.O.M., Martinique 7 (83), Mathieu à Ministre de la Marine et des Colonies, Fort Royal, 10 Mar, 1847, no. 210; A.N.S.O.M., Martinique 20 (170), "Extrait d'un rapport de tournée addressé à M. le Procurer General de la Martinique par M. B. Chevalier, Subsitut de Procureur du Roi à Saint Pierre," 10 Aug. 1846; A.N.S.O.M., Martinique 20 (170), Mathieu à Ministre de la Marine et des Colonies, 27 Apr. 1847; A.N.S.O.M., Martinique 20 (170), Mathieu à Ministre de la Marine et des Colonies, 10 Apr. 1847, no. 214; A.N.S.O.M., Martinique 20 (170), "Réglement de l'usine de Messieurs Sinson frères"; A.N.S.O.M., Martinique 20 (170), "Notes interpretatives de l'esprit du réglement d'usine de Messieurs Sinson frères"; Schnakenbourg, *Crise*, pp. 49, 226n.

40. Green, "Planter Class and British West Indian Sugar Production," pp. 461–62.

41. A.N.S.O.M., Martinique 7 (83), Mathieu à Ministre de la Marine et des Colonies, Fort Royal, 10 Apr. 1847.

42. Daubrée, *Question coloniale*, pp. 39–42; A.N.S.O.M., Martinique 20 (170), "Reglement de l'usine de Messieurs Sinson frères"; Schnakenbourg, *Crise*, pp. 222–24.

43. Daubree, *Question coloniale*, pp. 44, 47, 82; Schnakenbourg, *Crise*, pp. 226.

44. A.N.S.O.M., Généralités 147 (1328), Mathieu à Ministre de la Marine et des Colonies, Fort Royal, 26 Nov. 1846; Daubrée, *Question coloniale*, pp. 51–52; Schnakenbourg, *Crise*, pp. 21, 225, 227–82; Green, "Planter Class and British West Indian Sugar Production," p. 462.

## 7. A Calculated and Calculating System

1. Dutrône, *Précis sur la canne*, pp. 334–40; Moreno Fraginals, *El ingenio*, 2:15–29.

2. George P. Rawick, *From Sundown to Sunup*, pp. 27–28; Sidney W. Mintz, "Toward an Afro-American History"; Eric Wolf, "Specific Aspects of Plantation Systems in the New

World," pp. 136–37. See also A. Norman Klein, "West African Unfree Labor Before and After the Rise of the Atlantic Slave Trade"; Moses I. Finley, "Slavery"; Roger Bastide, *African Civilizations in the View World*, pp. 89–90.

3. Gerald W. Mullin, *Flight and Rebellion*, pp. 37–38; Gutman, *Slavery and the Numbers Game*, p. 171; Rawick, *From Sundown to Sunup*, pp. 27, 30–31; Mintz, "Toward an Afro-American History."

4. Sidney W. Mintz and Richard Price, *An Anthropological Approach to the Afro-American Past*, esp. pp. 7, 9–10, 20–21; Rawick, *From Sundown to Sunup*, pp. 31–32; Bastide, *African Civilizations in the New World*, pp. 154–56; Roger Bastide, *The African Religions of Brazil*, p. 96; Yvan Debbasch, "Marronage," p. 85.

5. Weber, *Economy and Society*, 1:129, 162–64; Anon. [Collins], *Practical Rules*, pp. 168–69.

6. Fernando Ortiz, *Los negros esclavos*, p. 182; Mintz and Price, *Anthropological Approach to the Afro-American Past*, p. 14.

7. Sainte Croix, *Statistique*, 2:156; Ministère, *Enquête sur les sucres*, pp. 48–49, 72; de la Cornillère, *La Martinique en 1842*, p. 98; A.N.S.O.M., Généralités 147 (1238), Mathieu à Ministre de la Marine et des Colonies, Fort Royal, 1 Sept. 1846, no. 46; *Martin, Histoire de l'esclavage*, pp. 122–23; Green, "Planter Class and British West Indian Sugar Production," p. 449; Mintz and Price, *Anthropological Approach to the Afro-American Past*, p. 14.

8. Anon. [Collins], *Practical Rules*, pp. 150–51, 157–58; Sainte Croix, *Statistique*, 2:125; Orlando Patterson, *The Sociology of Slavery*, pp. 59–61.

9. Anon. [Collins], *Practical Rules*, pp. 151–52; Roughley, *Jamaica Planter's Guide*, pp. 99–100, 113–18; Schoelcher, *Abolition immédiate*, pp. 23–24; Patterson, *Sociology of Slavery*, pp. 59–61.

10. Roughley, *Jamaica Planter's Guide*, pp. 99–102; Anon. [Collins], *Practical Rules*, pp. 151–52; Sainte Croix, *Statistique*, 2:125; Derosne, *Mémoire sur la fabrication du sucre*, pp. 23, 44–45; Schoelcher, *Abolition immédiate*, pp. 22–23; de la Cornillère, *La Martinique en 1842*, pp. 124–26; Lavollée, *Notes sur les cultures*, p. 123; Ministère de la Marine et des Colonies, *Exposé général des résultats du patronage*, pp. 380–97; Gabriel Debien, *Les esclaves aux Antilles françaises*, p. 125; Richard Thurnwald, *Economics in Primitive Societies*, pp. 213–14; Marx, *Capital*, 1:443.

11. Sainte Croix, *Statistique*, 2:125–26; Roughley, *Jamaica Planter's Guide*, pp. 102–103; Anon. [Collins], *Practical Rules*, pp. 154–55; Ministère, *Enquête sur les sucres*, pp. 48–49.

12. Roughley, *Jamaica Planter's Guide*, pp. 103–109, 121–22; Anon. [Collins], *Practical Rules*, pp. 155–57.

13. Mintz and Price, *Anthropological Approach to the Afro-American Past*, p. 13; Mintz, "Toward an Afro-American History," esp. pp. 327–30; Marx, *Capital*, 1:468–70.

14. Dutrône, *Précis sur la canne*, p. 109; Derosne, Mémoire sur la fabrication du sucre, pp. 23, 44–45; Payen, *Traité*, p. 70; Lavollée, *Notes sur les cultures*, pp. 122–23; Moreau de Saint-Mery, cited in Martin, *Histoire de l'esclavage*, p. 123.

15. Dutrône, *Précis sur la canne*, p. 109; Derosne, *Mémoire sur la fabrication du sucre*, pp. 23, 44–45; Payen, *Traité*, p. 70; Lavollée, *Notes sur les cultures*, pp. 122–23; Anon. [Collins], *Practical Rules*, p. 159; Moreau de Saint–Mery, cited in Martin, *Histoire de l'esclavage*, p. 123.

16. Dutrône, *Précis sur la canne*, pp. 111–12, 140–41, 225; Lavollée, *Notes sur les cultures*, p. 74; Roughley, *Jamaica Planter's Guide*, pp. 85–87; Sheridan, *Sugar and Slavery*, pp. 115–17.

17. Von Lippmann, *Historia do açúcar*, 2:241; A. de Lacharière, "Une lettre de M. A. de Lacharière," p. 91; Dutrône, *Précis sur la canne*, p. 175; Roughley, *Jamaica Planter's Guide*, pp. 339–41; Clement Caines, *Letters on the Cultivation of Otaiti Cane . . .* (London, 1801), p. 98, cited in Goveia, *Leeward Islands*, p. 133.

18. William Reed, *History of Sugar*, pp. 32–33; Roughley, *Jamaica Planter's Guide*, pp. 339–41.

19. William Reed, *History of Sugar*, p. 54; Roughley, *Jamaica Planter's Guide*, p. 364; Goveia, *Leeward Islands*, p. 133; Deerr, *History of Sugar*, 2:582.

20. Moreno Fraginals, *The Sugarmill*, p. 39.

21. Lavollée, *Notes sur les cultures*, pp. 97–98; Sainte Croix, *Statistique*, 2:114–15; Schoelcher, *Abolition immédiate*, pp. 23–24; M. G. Lewis, *Journal of a West India Proprietor, 1815–1817*, p. 70; Roughley, *Jamaica Planter's Guide*, p. 87; Martin, *Histoire de l'esclavage*, pp. 116–27; Gabriel Debien, "Destinées d'esclaves à la Martinique (1776–1778)," pp. 32–35; Patterson, *Sociology of Slavery*, pp. 57–64.

22. Roughley, *Jamaica Planter's Guide*, pp. 83–85, 110–13.

23. Schoelcher, *Abolition immédiate*, pp. 2, 23–24; de Cassagnac, *Voyage aux Antilles*, pp. 116–19; Roughley, *Jamaica Planter's Guide*, pp. 97–98; Debien, "Destinees d'esclaves," pp. 22–31; A.N.S.O.M., Généralités 167 (1,348).

24. Lewis, *Journal of a West India Proprietor*, p. 70; Patterson, *Sociology of Slavery*, pp. 57–64; Roughley, *Jamaica Planter's Guide*, p. 87; Schoelcher, *Abolition immédiate*, pp. 23–24; Martin, *Histoire de l'esclavage*, pp. 126–27; Debien, "Destinées d'esdaves," pp. 32–35; Ministère de la Marine et des Colonies, *Exposé général des résultats du patronage*, pp. 345–46.

25. Goveia, *Leeward Islands*, pp. 127–29.

26. Goveia, *Leeward Islands*, pp. 127–29; Gwendolyn M. Hall, *Social Control in Slave Plantation Societies*, pp. 15–19; Green, "Planter Class and British West Indian Sugar Production," p. 449; Moreno Fraginals, "Aportes culturales y deculturación," pp. 28–29.

27. Anon. [Collins], *Practical Rules*, pp. 162–63; Moreno Fraginals, *El ingenio*, 2:32; Lavollée, *Notes sur les cultures*, pp. 122–123; Schoelcher, *Abolition immédiate*, pp. 22, 84; Jacques Le Goff, *Time, Work, and Culture in the Middle Ages*, pp. 44–49.

28. Ministère de la Marine et des Colonies, *Exposé général des résultats du patronage*, pp. 301–305; Lavollée, *Notes sur les cultures*, pp. 122–23; de la Cornillère, *La Martinique en 1842*, pp. 124–26; Sainte Croix, *Statistique*, 2:125–26; Schoelcher, *Abolition immédiate*, p. 22; A.N.S.O.M., Martinique 9 (99), de Moges, "Memoire" (1840); Debien, *Les esclaves aux Antilles françaises*, pp. 147–49; Schnakenbourg, *Crise*, pp. 53–54; Goveia, Leeward Islands, p. 130; Ortiz, *Abolition immédiate*, pp. 182–91; Patterson, *Sociology of Slavery*, pp. 67–69.

29. Schoelcher, *Abolition immédiate*, p. 22; A.N.S.O.M., Martinique 9 (99), de Moges, "Mémoire" (1840); Ministère de la Marine et des Colonies, *Exposé général des résultats du patronage*, p. 207; Lavollée, *Notes sur les cultures*, pp. 122–23.

30. Reed, *History of Sugar*, pp. 53–54.

31. Ministère de la Marine et des Colonies, *Exposé général des résultats du patronage*, pp. 213, 223, 301–303; Ministère de la Marine et des Colonies, *Compte rendu au Roi de l'emploi des fonds allouées depuis 1839*, pp. 99–105.

32. Sainte Croix, *Statistique*, 2:110–11, 128–29, 131–35; Lavollée, *Notes sur les cultures*, pp. 73–74, 122; Gueroult, *La question coloniale*, 64–67; Debien, *Les esclaves aux Antilles françaises*, p. 149. Cf. Pares, *A West-India Fortune*, pp. 15–16.

33. Ministère de la Marine et des Colonies, *Exposé général des résultats du patronage*, p. 108; Sainte Croix, *Statistique*, 2:139; Lavollée, *Notes sur les cultures*, pp. 73, 122–23, 132; A.N.S.O.M., Martinique 9 (99), de Moges, "Mémoire" (1840); Dutrône, *Précis sur la canne*, pp. 140–41; Debien, *Les esclaves aux Antilles françaises*, pp. 149–52; Schnakenbourg, *Crise*, pp. 53–54; Ortiz, *Los negros esclavos*, p. 186; Goveia, *Leeward Islands*, pp. 129–31; Moreno Fraginals, *El ingenio*, 2:32–34.

34. Lavollée, *Notes sur les cultures*, pp. 73, 122–23, 132; Sainte Croix, *Statistique*, 2:139; Dutrône, *Précis sur la canne*, pp 140–41; A.N.S.O.M., Martinique 9 (99), de Moges, "Mémoire" (1840); Debien, *Les esclaves aux Antilles françaises*, pp. 149–52; Schnakenbourg, *Crise*, pp. 53–54; Ortiz, *Los negros esclavos*, p. 186; Goveia, *Leeward Islands*, pp. 129–31; Moreno Fraginals, *El ingenio*, 2:32–34.

35. Reed, *History of Sugar*, pp. 53–54; A.N.S.O.M., Martinique 9 (99), de Moges, "Mémoire" (1840); Ministère de la Marine et des Colonies, *Exposé général des résultats du patronage*, pp. 108, 303–305, 392; Ministère de la Marine et des Colonies, *Compte rendu au Roi de l'exécution des lois des 18 et 19 juillet*, pp. 657–59.

36. Debien, *Les esclaves aux Antilles françaises*, p. 154; Dutrone, *Précis sur la canne*, pp. 335–36; Jürgen Kuczynski, *A Short History of Labor Conditions under Industrial Capitalism*,

pp. 44–45; A.N.S.O.M., Martinique 9 (99), de Moges, "Mémoire" (1840); Ministère de la Marine et des Colonies, *Exposé général des résultats du patronage*, pp. 301–302; Sainte Croix, *Statistique*, 2:128–29; Moreno Fraginals, *The Sugarmill*, p. 56.

37. Dutrône, *Précis sur la canne*, pp. 334–40; Moreno Fraginals, *El ingenio*, 2:15–29.

38. Aufhauser, "Slavery and Modern Management," esp. pp. 812–18; Fogel and Engerman, *Time on the Cross*, 1:208; Herbert Gutman, *Slavery and the Numbers Game*, pp. 82–83.

39. Soleau, *Notes sur les Guyanes*, pp. 8–10; Anon. [Collins], *Practical Rules*, pp. 152–54.

40. Anon. [Collins], *Practical Rules*, pp. 169–70; Schoelcher, *Abolition immédiate*, p. 274.

41. Schoelcher, *Abolition immédiate*, pp. 273–74; Roughley, *Jamaica Planter's Guide*, p. 94; Anon. [Collins], *Practical Rules*, pp. 165, 170–71. Cf. Gutman, *Slavery and the Numbers Game*, esp. pp. 14, 171; Fogel and Engerman, *Time on the Cross*, 1:146–53.

42. Anon. [Collins], *Practical Rules*, pp. 165, 171–72.

43. Schoelcher, *Abolition immédiate*, pp. 5–6; Sainte Croix, *Statistique*, 2:101–5, 126–28, 157–58; Lavollée, *Notes sur les cultures*, pp. 66, 123; de Chazelles, *Etude sur le système colonial*, pp. 131n, 156.

44. Debien, *Les esclaves aux Antilles françaises*, p. 108.

45. Ibid., pp. 114–15.

46. Ibid., pp. 112–15; Hilliard d'Auberteuil, 1:165, in ibid., p. 115; Roughley, *Jamaica Planter's Guide*, pp. 40–41.

47. Debien, *Les esclaves aux Antilles françaises*, pp. 116–17.

48. Ibid., pp. 119, 124–25, 128; Marquis de Casaux, *Essai sur l'art de cultiver la canne et d'en extraire le sucre*, p. 267, in de Casaux, *Essai*, p. 124; Roughley, *Jamaica Planter's Guide*, pp. 79–80.

49. Anon. [Collins], *Practical Rules*, pp. 169–70.

50. Schoelcher, *Abolition immédiate*, pp. 84, 90–93; Ministère de la Marine et des Colonies, *Exposé général des résultats du patronage*, p. 130. See also Davis, *Problem of Slavery in an Age of Revolution*, p. 464.

51. Schoelcher, *Abolition immédiate*, pp. 89–90; Ministère de la Marine et des Colonies, *Exposé général des résultats du patronage*, p. 359.

52. Ministère de la Marine et des Colonies, *Exposé général des résultats du patronage*, pp. 380–82, 384–85; Schoelcher, *Abolition immédiate*, pp. 89–90; Gutman, *Slavery and the Numbers Game*, pp. 19, 32.

53. Ministère de la Marine et des Colonies, *Exposé général des résultats du patronage*, pp. 380, 382–85, 392, 394–95.

54. Ibid., pp. 380–85, 394–95; Debien, *Les esclaves aux Antilles françaises*, pp. 125–26; Schoelcher, *Abolition immédiate*, p. 85.

55. Schoelcher, *Abolition immédiate*, p. 85; Ministère de la Marine et des Colonies, *Exposé général des résultats du patronage*, pp. 380–85. See also Debien, *Les esclaves aux Antilles françaises*, p. 126.

56. Anon. [Collins], *Practical Rules*, pp. 170–71; Schoelcher, *Abolition immediate*, pp. 90–94, 273–74; Ministère de la Marine et des Colonies, *Exposé général des résultats du patronage*, pp. 384–95.

57. Lavollée, *Notes sur les cultures*, pp. 45–46.

58. Soleau, *Notes sur les Guyanes*, pp. 8–9; Anon. [Collins], *Practical Rules*, pp. 152–54.

59. Soleau, *Notes sur les Guyanes*, pp. 8–10; Anon. [Collins], *Practical Rules*, pp. 152–54.

60. Soleau, *Notes sur les Guyanes*, pp. 8–10.

61. Anon. [Collins], *Practical Rules*, pp. 152–54; Soleau, *Notes sur les Guyanes*, pp. 8–9.

62. Soleau, *Notes sur les Guyanes*, pp. 8–9; Edward Brathwaite, *The Development of Creole Society in Jamaica*, pp. 198–99.

63. Mullin, *Flight and Rebellion*, pp. 37–38; Gutman, *Slavery and the Numbers Game*, p. 171; Rawick, *From Sundown to Sunup*, pp. 27, 30–31; Mintz, "Toward an Afro-American History," pp. 317–31.

64. Schoelcher, *Abolition immédiate*, pp. 22–23; Marx, *Capital*, 1:443; Sainte Croix, *Statistique*, 2:123–27; Lavollée, *Notes sur les cultures*, p. 123; de la Cornillère, *La Martinique en 1842*, pp. 124–26; Ministère de la Marine et des Colonies, *Exposé général des résultats du patronage*, pp. 380–97.

65. Melville J. Herskovits, *Life in a Haitian Valley*, pp. 2, 3–24; Bastide, *African Civilizations in the New World*, pp. 18–30; Rawick, *From Sundown to Sunup*, p. 31; Karl Polanyi, *Dahomey and the Slave Trade*, pp. 60–80. See James Leyburn, *The Haitian People*, pp. 199–201, for a criticism of Herskovits's contention that the Haitian *combite* has its origins in Dahomey; and see esp. Maria Sylvia de Carvalho Franco, *Homens livres na ordem escravocrata*, pp. 29–40, for a discussion of the institutionalized violence entailed in the Brazilian *mutirão*.

66. A.N.S.O.M., Martinique 9 (99), de Moges, "Mémoire" (1840); Schoelcher, *Abolition immédiate*, pp. 22–23; de Cassagnac, *Voyage aux Antilles*, pp. 308–309; Roughley, *Jamaica Planter's Guide*, pp. 100–101.

67. Herskovits, *Life in a Haitian Valley*, p. 57. See Mintz and Price, *Anthropological Approach to the Afro-American Past*, for a more sophisticated view of the cultural change entailed in the historical process of African slavery.

68. Herskovits, *Life in a Haitian Valley*, p. 57; Leroi Jones, *Blues People*, esp. pp. 17–31; Schoelcher, *Abolition immédiate*, p. 128.

69. See esp. Raymond Bauer and Alice Bauer, "Day to Day Resistance to Slavery," pp. 40–57; Debbasch, "Marronage" (1962), pp. 195–96; Roger Bastide, "Nègres marrons et nègres libres," p. 173; Mullin, *Flight and Rebellion*, pp. 35–38.

70. Rawick, *From Sundown to Sunup*, p. 107; Mintz, "Toward an Afro-American History," pp. 321–22; Debien, *Les esclaves aux Antilles françaises*, pp. 461, 463; Debbasch, "Marronage" (1961), pp. 17–19; Schoelcher, *Abolition immédiate*, pp. 128, 131.

71. Ministère de la Marine et des Colonies, *Exposé général des résultats du patronage*, pp. 115, 383; Alexis de Tocqueville, "Rapport fait au nom de la commission chargée d'examiner la proposition de M. Tracy relative aux esclaves aux colonies," pp. 12–13; Schoelcher, *Abolition immédiate*, pp. 121–22.

72. Lavollée, *Notes sur les cultures*, pp. 51, 60; Schoelcher, *Abolition immédiate*, pp. 121, 127; A.N.S.O.M., Martinique 1 (6), Commandant de la Gendarmerie de la Martinique (1814), "Aperçu sur l'utilité de la Gendarmerie dans les colonies suivies de quelques réflexions sur le régime observer dans les habitations"; A.N.S.O.M., Martinique 9 (99), de Moges, "Mémoire" (1840); Yvan Debbasch, "Le crime d'empoisonnement aux îles pendant la période esclavagiste," pp. 143–53; Debien, *Les esclaves aux Antilles françaises*, p. 402.

73. Schoelcher, *Abolition immédiate*, p. 128; Tocqueville, "Rapport," pp. 12–13; Debien, *Les esclaves aux Antilles françaises*, pp. 401–402.

74. Lavollée, *Notes sur les cultures*, p. 124; A.N.S.O.M., Martinique 9 (99), de Moges, "Mémoire" (1840); Schoelcher, *Abolition immédiate*, p. 128.

75. Schoelcher, *Abolition immédiate*, pp. 121–22; Debien, *Les esclaves aux Antilles françaises*, p. 461.

76. A.N.S.O.M., Martinique 9 (99), Governeur de Moges à Ministre de la Marine et des Colonies, Macouba, 13 Mar. 1840; Bastide, "Negres marrons et negres libres," p. 173; Mullin, *Flight and Rebellion*, pp. 35–36. Cf. Melville J. Herskovits, *The Myth of the Negro Past*, pp. 99–105.

77. Sidney W. Mintz, *Caribbean Transformations*; Ministère de la Marine et des Colonies, *Exposé général des résultats du patronage*, pp. 180–88, 290, 303–305.

78. Mintz, *Caribbean Transformations*; Ministère de la Marine et des Colonies, *Exposé général des résultats du patronage*, pp. 303–305.

79. Debien, *Les esclaves aux Antilles françaises*, p. 209; Lavollée, *Notes sur les cultures*, pp. 123–24; Lewis, *Journal of a West India Proprietor*, p. 81; Peytraud, *L'esclavage aux Antilles*

*francaises avant 1789*, p. 156; de Cassagnac, *Voyage aux Antilles*, pp. 168, 211. Cf. Schoelcher, *Abolition immédiate*, p. 53n; Debbasch, "Marronage" (1962), pp. 131–38.

80. Ministère de la Marine et des Colonies, *Compte rendu au Roi de l'emploi des fonds allouées depuis 1839*, pp. 104–105; Ministère de la Marine et des Colonies, *Exposé général des résultats du patronage*, p. 392.

81. Ministère de la Marine et des Colonies, *Compte rendu au Roi de l'emploi des fonds allouees depuis 1839*, pp. 104–105.

82. Ibid.; A.N.S.O.M., Martinique 11 (106), Mathieu à Ministre de la Marine et des Colonies, Fort Royal, 10 Oct. 1846.

83. A.N.S.O.M., Martinique 11 (106), Mathieu à Ministre de la Marine et des Colonies, Fort Royal, 10 Oct. 1846.

84. A.N.S.O.M., Martinique 7 (83), Mathieu à Ministre de la Marine et des Colonies, Fort Royal, 10 Mar. 1847.

85. Schoelcher, *Histoire de l'esclavage*, 1:477–91.

# 8. The Other Face of Slave Labor

1. Soleau, *Notes sur les Guyanes*, pp. 9–10; Ministère de la Marine et des Colonies, *Commission 16 mai 1840*, p. 205.

2. Sainte Croix, *Statistique*, 2:105.

3. Mintz, *Caribbean Transformations*, pp. 132–33; Ministère de la Marine et des Colonies, *Exposé général des résultats du patronage*, pp. 303–5. See also Sidney W. Mintz, "Slavery and the Rise of Peasantries," pp. 213–42; Mintz, "Currency Problems in Eighteenth Century Jamaica and Gresham's Law," pp. 248–65; Sidney W. Mintz and Douglas Hall, *The Origins of the Jamaican Internal Marketing System*.

4. Walter Rodney, "Plantation Society in Guyana," pp. 643–66; Sidney W. Mintz, "Descrying the Peasantry," pp. 209–25.

5. Debien, *Les esclaves aux Antilles francaises*, pp. 178–86; Peytraud, *L'esclavage aux Antilles françaises avant 1789*, p. 217.

6. Debien, *Les esclaves aux Antilles françaises*, pp. 176–86; Ministère de la Marine et des Colonies, Exposé général des résultats du patronage, pp. 177, 219–25; A.N.S.O.M., Généralités 167 (1,348); Gisler, *L'esclavage aux Antilles françaises (XVIIe–XIXe siecle)*, pp. 23–25, 35–38; Peytraud, *L'esclavage aux Antilles françaises avant 1789*, pp. 216–24.

7. Debien, *Les esclaves aux Antilles françaises*, pp. 176–77, 181, 183–86, 115; Gisler, *L'esclavage aux Antilles françaises*, pp. 23–25, 35–38; Peytraud, *L'esclavage aux Antilles fran-*

*caises avant 1789*, pp. 216–24; Ministère de la Marine et des Colonies, *Commission 16 mai 1840*, p. 205.

8. Schoelcher, *Abolition immédiate*, pp. 8–9; Ministère de la Marine et des Colonies, *Exposé général des résultats du patronage*, pp. 177, 267; May, *Le Mercier de la Rivière*, 1:119–21.

9. Ministère, *Enquête sur les sucres*, pp. 23, 52, 67, 156, 248.

10. Sainte Croix, *Statistique*, 2:105; Lavollée, *Notes sur les cultures*, p. 10; Ministère de la Marine et des Colonies, *Exposé général des résultats du patronage*, pp. 182–87; Ministère de la Marine et des Colonies, *Commission 26 mai 1840*, p. 205.

11. Ministère de la Marine et des Colonies, *Exposé général des résultats du patronage*, pp. 183–84, 290.

12. Ibid., pp. 104–105, 180–88, 290; A.N.S.O.M., Généralités 144 (1221), "Exécution de l'ordonnance royale," 2:40, 51.

13. Ministère de la Marine et des Colonies, *Exposé général des résultats du patronage*, pp. 177–88, 288–91, 332–33; Ministère de la Marine et des Colonies, *Commission 26 mai 1840*, pp. 205–206, 208–209.

14. A.N.S.O.M., Généralités 167 (1350); Ministère de la Marine et des Colonies, *Exposé général des résultats du patronage*, pp. 195–96.

15. A.N.S.O.M., Généralités 167 (1350); Ministère de la Marine et des Colonies, *Exposé général des résultats du patronage*, pp. 195–96.

16. A.N.S.O.M., Généralités 167 (1350).

17. Ministère de la Marine et des Colonies, *Exposé général des résultats du patronage*, pp. 89–90.

18. Ibid., pp. 89–90, 182–85, 177, 219–25, 288–91, 332–33; A.N.S.O.M., Martinique 9 (99), de Moges, "Mémoire" (1840).

19. Ministère de la Marine et des Colonies, *Exposé général des résultats du patronage*, pp. 183–85; Gisler, *L'esclavage aux Antilles françaises*, p. 48; de Cassagnac, *Voyage aux Antilles*, p. 175; Schoelcher, *Abolition immédiate*, p. 7.

20. Ministère de la Marine et des Colonies, *Exposé général des résultats du patronage*, pp. 180–88, 290; Schoelcher, *Abolition immédiate*, pp. 12–13; de Cassagnac, *Voyage aux Antilles*, pp. 174–75; A.N.S.O.M., Martinique 7 (83), Dupotêt à Ministre de la Marine et des Colonies, Fort Royal, 5 Apr. 1832.

21. De Cassagnac, *Voyage aux Antilles*, pp. 174–75; Schoelcher, *Abolition immédiate*, p. 12; Ministère de la Marine et des Colonies, *Exposé général des résultats du patronage*, pp. 182–85, 288–91, 332–33; A.N.S.O.M., Martinique 9 (99), de Moges, "Mémoire" (1840).

22. Schoelcher, *Abolition immédiate*, p. 11; Lavollée, *Notes sur les cultures*, p. 123.

23. Debien, *Les esclaves aux Antilles françaises*, pp. 178–91, 205–207; Ministère de la Marine et des Colonies, *Exposé général des résultats du patronage*, pp. 182–87, 290; Ministère de la Marine et des Colonies, *Commission 16 mai 1840*, p. 206; de Cassagnac, *Voyage aux Antilles*, pp. 174–75; Schoelcher, *Abolition immédiate*, pp. 9–12; Lavollée, *Notes sur les cultures*, p. 10; Sainte Croix, *Statistique*, 2:105.

24. Ministère de la Marine et des Colonies, *Exposé général des résultats du patronage*, pp. 180–88, 290; Schoelcher, Abolition immédiate, pp. 9–13; A.N.S.O.M., Généralités 144 (1221), "Exécution de l'ordonnance royale," 2:40, 51; Debien, *Les esclaves aux Antilles françaises*, pp. 178–91; Mintz, *Caribbean Transformations*, pp. 225–50.

25. Herskovits, *Life in a Haitian Valley*, pp. 67–68, 76–81; Schoelcher, *Abolition immédiate*, p. 9; Lewis, *Journal of a West India Proprietor*, p. 88; Bastide, *African Religions of Brazil*, p. 58.

26. Soleau, *Notes sur les Guyanes*, pp. 9–10; Lavollée, *Notes sur les cultures*, p. 123; Debien, *Les esclaves aux Antilles françaises*, pp. 178–80; Peytraud, *L'esclavage aux Antilles françaises avant 1789*, p. 117; Gisler, *L'esclavage aux Antilles françaises*, p. 48.

27. Mintz, *Caribbean Transformations*; A.N.S.O.M., Généralités 144 (1221), "Exécution de l'ordonnance royale," 2:40, 51; Higman, *Slave Population and Economy*, p. 129; Soleau, *Notes sur les Guyanes*, pp. 9–10; A.N.S.O.M., Martinique 7 (83), Dupotêt à Ministre de la Marine et des Colonies, Fort Royal, 5 Apr. 1832.

28. De Cassagnac, *Voyage aux Antilles*, p. 176; Schoelcher, *Abolition immédiate*, p. 12; Anon. [Collins], *Practical Rules*, pp. 87–94.

29. Schoelcher, *Abolition immédiate*, pp. 9–13; Ministère de la Marine et des Colonies, *Exposé général des résultats du patronage*, pp. 180–88, 290; Ministère de la Marine et des Colonies, *Commission 26 mai 1840*, pp. 208–209; A.N.S.O.M., Généralités 144 (1221), "Exécution de l'ordonnance royale," 2:40, 51.

30. Ministère de la Marine et des Colonies, *Exposé général des résultats du patronage*, pp. 180–88, 290; Schoelcher, *Abolition immédiate*, pp. 9–13; A.N.S.O.M., Généralités 144 (1221), "Exécution de l'ordonnance royale," pp. 40, 51.

31. Schoelcher, *Abolition immédiate*, p. 11; A.N.S.O.M., Martinique 9 (99), de Moges, "Memoire" (1840); Ministère de la Marine et des Colonies, *Exposé général des résultats du patronage*, p. 186; Ministère de la Marine et des Colonies, *Commission 26 mai 1840*, p. 206.

32. Soleau, *Notes sur les Guyanes*, p. 59; Herskovits, *Life in a Haitian Valley*, pp. 81–85; A.N.S.O.M., Généralités 144 (1221), "Exécution de l'ordonnance royale," p. 51; A.N.S.O.M., Martinique 7 (83), Mathieu à Ministre de la Marine et des Colonies, 10 Mar. 1847, no. 1508; Sainte Croix, *Statistique*, 1:13–15; de la Cornillère, *La Martinique en 1842*, pp. 123–24.

33. De la Cornillère, *La Martinique en 1842*, pp. 123–24; Soleau, *Notes sur les Guyanes*, p. 59; Ministère de la Marine et des Colonies, *Exposé général des résultats du patronage*, p. 102.

34. A.N.S.O.M., Martinique 7 (83), Mathieu à Ministre de la Marine et des Colonies, 10 Mar. 1847, no. 1508.

35. Ministère de la Marine et des Colonies, *Exposé général des résultats du patronage*, pp. 119–25, 332; A.N.S.O.M., Martinique 7 (83), de Moges à M. le Ministre de la Marine et des Colonies, Saint Jacques, 15 Mar. 1839, no. 98; Benoît Duschene-Duvernay, *Mémoire sur la Martinique avec des notes explicatives*, pp. 22–27; Schoelcher, *Abolition immédiate*, pp. 4–7, 14–15.

36. Schoelcher, *Abolition immédiate*, pp. 1–3; Ministère de la Marine et des Colonies, *Exposé général des résultats du patronage*, pp. 111, 268–77, 288–91, 332–33.

37. Schoelcher, *Abolition immédiate*, pp. 12–13; Ministère de la Marine et des Colonies, *Exposé général des résultats du patronage*, pp. 288–89, 332–33; A.N.S.O.M., Martinique 7 (83), Dupotêt to Ministre de la Marine et des Colonies, Fort Royal, 5 Apr. 1832; Duschene-Duvernay, *Mémoire sur la Martinique*, pp. 17–19.

38. Ministère de la Marine et des Colonies, *Exposé général des résultats du patronage*, p. 100, 111, 332–33; Schoelcher, *Abolition immédiate*, p. 11; Lavollée, *Notes sur les cultures*, p. 10.

39. Ministère de la Marine et des Colonies, *Exposé général des résultats du patronage*, pp. 289–90, 331–33; Mintz, "Was the Plantation Slave a Proletarian?"

40. Mintz, *Caribbean Transformations*.

41. Ibid.; Douglas Hall, "The Flight from the Plantations Reconsidered."

42. Rodney, "Plantation Society in Guyana."

## Conclusion

1. I have discussed the initiatives of the emancipated population in Martinique to define and extend the gains that they had achieved while still enslaved after the abolition of slavery in 1848 and the efforts of the colonial state to contain their efforts in *Through the Prism of Slavery*, pp. 173–91.

## Appendix 1. Estimated Volume of the Slave Trade to Martinique

1. "Return of the Number of Slave Vessels Arrived in the Trans-Atlantic States since 1814," Great Britain, Parliamentary Papers 49 (1845): 593–633; David Eltis, "The Direction and Fluctuation of the Transatlantic Slave Trade, 1821–1843," pp. 274–75; Daget,

"British Repression," pp. 419–42; Curtin, *Atlantic Slave Trade*, pp. 234–35; Martin, *Histoire de l'esclavage*, pp. 253–56, 263–68; de Chazelles, *Etude sur le système colonial*, pp. 134–35n; Cochin, *L'abolition de l'esclavage*, 1:38.

2. Eltis, "Direction and Fluctuation," pp. 282, 287–88; Daget, "British Repression," p. 434.

3. Daget, "British Repression," pp. 426–30; Daget, "Long cours et nègriers nantais," pp. 112–14; Curtin, *Atlantic Slave Trade*, p. 216; Tarrade, *Commerce colonial de la France*, 2:/59–60 (table 11); Bernard David, *Les origines de la population martiniquaise au fil des ans*, pp. 95–100.

4. Daget, "British Repression," pp. 421–22; Eltis, "Direction and Fluctuation," pp. 287–88, 299–301.

5. Debien, *Les esclaves aux Antilles francaises*, pp. 39–68; David, *Origines de la population martiniquaise*, pp. 94–97, 100; David Eltis, "The Export of Slaves from Africa, 1821–1843," pp. 422–26; Eltis, "Direction and Fluctuation," pp. 291–96; Daget, "Long cours et nègriers nantais," p. 112; *Bulletin official de la Martinique* (1838), pp. 113–20, 148–50, 155–57.

# Works Cited

## Primary Sources

*Manuscript Sources. Archives Nationales-Section Outre-Mer (A.N.S.O.M.)*

*FONDS GÉNÉRALITÉS. CARTON (DOSSIER)*

52 (449) La situation économique des Antilles. 1843.

56 (543) Rapport de Jabrun sur les améliorations à introduire dans la fabrication du sucre aux colonies. 1838.

117 (995) Minutes de Rapports concernant la condition des esclaves, la traite, l'affranchissement. Sans dates, début du XIXème siècle.

143 (1214) Exécution de la loi du 18 juillet 1845. Correspondance générale. Dossier commun aux 4 colonies. 1844–1847.

144 (1221) Condition des esclaves. Publication d'un exposé sommaire des mesures prises dans les differentes colonies pour l'éxécution de l'ordonnance royale du 4 janvier 1840. 1841–1843.

147 (1236) Demande de passages et propositions diverses pour l'immigration de travailleurs dans les colonies. 1845.

147 (1328) Organisation du travail libre. Combinaisons et propositions diverses. 1845–1847.

151 (1265) Décrets coloniaux pour l'éxécution de la loi du 18 juillet 1845.

167 (1348) Conditions des esclaves. Rapports, correspondance, coupures de journaux concernant le sort fait aux esclaves dans les differentes colonies. 1818–1845.

167 (1349) Amélioration du sort des esclaves.

167 (1350) Régime des esclaves. 1803–1846.

167 (1351) Correspondance général relative à l'ordonnance royale du 5 juin 1846 sur la nourriture et l'entretien des esclaves.

176 (1415) Rapport de Lechevalier sur l'esclavage. 1844–1846.

179 (1427) Ateliers de discipline. 1839–1848.

186 (1447) Sévices exercés à l'encontre des esclaves. 1819–1848.

187 (1448) Dossier commun. Ordonnance du 5 janvier 1840 et les instructions générales. 1840–1848.

192 (1479) Régime disciplinaire des esclaves. Projet d'ordonnance. 1841–1846.

207 (1514) Régime disciplinaire. Atelier de discipline. 1846–1848.

207 (1517) Atelier de discipline. 1842–1847.

221 (1598) Rapports entre les administrations des diverses colonies d'Amérique dans l'intérêt du politique du gouvernement. 1845.

235 (1675) Rapport de M. Emile Thomas.

262 (1816) Fragment d'un rapport d'un commission d'étudier la sort des esclaves. 1840.

630 (2736) Dossiers divers traitant du travail et des conditions de vie des esclaves. 1819 à 1847.

*FONDS MARTINIQUE. CARTON (DOSSIER)*

1 (6) Esclavage. Gens de couleur. 1814–1816.

6 (70) Lettres du Gouverneur au Ministre de la Marine. 1830 à 1851.

7 (83) Tournées du gouverneur. 1829–1851. 1870.

9 (99) Correspondance générale. Rapports. 1840. C. A. de Moges, Gouverneur.

10 (100) Esclavage. Gens de couleur. Mémoire à la successor. 1845.

11 (106) Correspondance générale du 1846 au 1848. M. C. A. Mathieu.

13 (127) Police de travail.

20 (169) Machines et moulins à sucre. 1817–1834.

20 (170) Fabrication du sucre. Usines centrales.

95 (819) Dettes hypothécaires. 1822–1823.

*Martinique, État de Cultures, 1831 à 1850*

*Martinique, État de Population, 1831 à 1850*

## Newpapers and Periodicals

Bulletin Official de la Martinique

Courrier de la Martinique

Revue Maritime et Coloniale

# Official Publications

*Avis des Conseils Coloniaux de la Martinique, de la Guadeloupe, et de la Guyane française, sur diverses propositions concernant l'esclavage.* Paris, 1839.

Chambre des Députés. *Session 1837. Rapport fait au nom de la Commission chargée d'examiner le projet de loi sur les sucres par M. Dumon.* Séance de 8 mai 1837 (no. 200).

Délégués des Colonies, *Mémoire sur le travail des affranchis dans les colonies françaises, exigés par la loi de 18 juillet 1845.* Paris, 1847.

*Exécution de l'ordonnance royal du 5 janvier 1840 relative à l'instruction primaire, et au patronage des esclaves. Exposé sommaire.* 2 parties. Paris, 1841, 1842.

Lavollée, P. *Notes sur les cultures et la production de la Martinique et de la Guadeloupe.* Paris, 1841.

Lechevalier, Jules. *Rapport sur les questions coloniales adressé à M. le duc de Broglie président de la commission coloniale à la suite d'un voyage fait aux Antilles et aux Guyanes pendant les années 1838 et 1839.* 2 vols. Paris, 1843.

―――. *Réorganisation des colonies à esclaves. Emancipation des noirs, combinée avec le propriété foncière, l'organisation du travail libre et la colonisation des terres vacantes.* Paris, 1845.

Ministère de la Marine et des Colonies. *Commission instituée par décision royale du 26 mai 1840, pour l'examen des questions relatives à l'esclavage et à la constitution politique des colonies.* 2 vols. Paris, 1840, 1841, 1842, 1843.

―――. *Exposé général des résultats du patronage des esclaves dans les colonies françaises.* Paris, 1844.

―――. *Questions relatives à l'abolition de l'esclavage. Instructions adressées à MM. les Gouverneurs des Colonies. (Circulaire du 18 juillet 1840) Déliberations et avis des Conseils Spéciaux.* Paris, 1843.

Ministère du Commerce et des Manufactures. *Commission formée avec l'approbation du Roi . . . pour l'examen de certaines questions de législation commerciale. Enquête sur les sucres.* Paris, 1829.

Ministre de la Marine et des Colonies. *Compte rendu au Roi de l'emploi des fonds allouées depuis 1839, pour l'enseignement religieux et élémentaire des noirs, et de l'exécution des lois des 18 et 19 juillet 1845 relatives au régime des esclaves, à l'introduction des travailleurs libres aux colonies, etc.* Paris, 1846.

―――. *Compte rendu au Roi de l'éxécution des lois des 18 et 19 juillet 1845 sur le régime des esclaves, la création des établissments agricoles par le travail libre, etc.* Paris, 1847.

Thomas, Emile. *Rapport à M. le Ministre de la Marine et des Colonies sur l'organisation du travail libre aux Antilles françaises et sur les améliorations à apporter aux institutions coloniales.* Paris, 1849.

United Kingdom. "Return of the Number of Slave Vessels Arrived in the Trans-Atlantic States since 1814." *Parliamentary Papers* 49 (1845): 593–633.

## Books, Pamphlets, and Articles

*Annales de la société d'agriculture et d'économie rurale de la Martinique, 1839–1840.* 2 vols. Saint Pierre, Martinique, n.d.

*Annales de la société d'agriculture et d'économie rurale de la Martinique.* 2 vols. Saint Pierre, Martinique, 1841.

Anon. [Collins], *Practical Rules for the Management and Medical Treatment of Negro Slaves in the Sugar Colonies.* London, 1811.

Antonil, André João. *Cultura e Opulência do Brasil.* Lisbon, 1711; repr. Paris: Institut des Hautes Études de l'Amérique Latine, 1965.

Bella, F.-L. *Réflexions sur la question des sucres.* Paris, 1840.

Bertrand, Général. *Sur la détresse des colonies françaises en général, de l'île Martinique en particulier; et de la nécessité de diminuer la taxe exorbitante établie sur le sucre exotique.* Paris, 1838.

Bonaparte, Louis Napoleon. *Analyse de la question des sucres.* Paris, 1843.

Bouchet-Saint-Arnoult. *Mémoire adressé à Monsieur le Ministre des Finances sur la fabrication des sucres indigènes et exotiques et sur la question d'impôt de l'un et de l'autre.* Paris, 1837.

Burat, J. "Courte réponse à la brochure publiée par M. T. Lestiboudois sous le titre des colonies sucrières et des sucreries indigènes," *Le Commerce,* n.d.

Cassagnac, Adolphe Granier de. *Voyage aux Antilles.* Paris, 1842.

Cantero, J. G., and E. Laplante. *Los Ingenios de Cuba.* Repr. Barcelona, 1984.

Chaudron Junot. *De régime colonial et de son influence sur le commerce, l'industrie et la marine de la France, suivi d'une lettre publiée avant la présentation du projet de loi sur les primes à l'exportation des sucres.* Paris, 1833.

Chazelles, A. de. *Étude sur le système colonial.* Paris, 1860.

Cochin, Augustin. *L'Abolition de l'esclavage.* 2 vols. Paris. 1861.

Cornillère, M. Le Comte E. de la. *La Martinique en 1842. Intérêts coloniaux, souvenirs du voyage.* Paris, 1843.

Cussac, Jean-Baptiste Rouvellat de. *Situation des esclaves dans les colonies françaises. Urgence de leur emancipation.* Paris, 1845.

Daney, Sidney. *Histoire de la Martinique depuis la colonisation jusqu'en 1815*. 6 vols. Fort Royal, 1846.

Daubrée, Paul. *Question coloniale sous le rapport industriel*. Paris, 1841.

Dehay, Timothée. *Les colonies et le métropole, le sucre exotique et le sucre indigène, trésor, marine, commerce, agriculture. Emancipation commerciale de nos colonies, et abolition de l'esclavage*. Paris, 1839.

Derosne, Charles. *Mémoire sur la fabrication du sucre dans les colonies par de nouveaux procédés*. Paris, 1824.

———. *Notice on the New Process for Making Sugar, Lately Introduced in the French and English Colonies*. 1833.

Derosne, Charles and Jean François Cail. *De la elaboración del azúcar en las colonias y de los nuevos aparatos destinados a mejorarla*, trans. D. Jose Luis Casaseca. Havana, 1844.

Dupin, le Baron (François Pierre) Charles. *Mémoire adressé par le Conseil des Délégués à Messieurs les Membres du Conseil des Ministres*. Paris, 1842.

———. *Mémoire adressé par le Conseil des Délégués des Colonies aux Ministres du Roi sur la question des sucres et sur la crise imminent dont elle menace les ports et les colonies*. Paris, 1842.

Duschene-Duvernay, Benoît. *Mémoire sur la Martinique avec des notes explicatives*. Paris, 1832.

Dutrône, J.-F. *Précis sur la canne et les moyens d'en extraire le sel essentiel, suivi de plusieurs Mémoires sur le Sucre, sur le Vin de Canne, sur l'Indigo, sur les Habitations & sur l'état actuel de Saint-Domingue*. Paris, 1791.

Forbin-Janson, [Charles-Théodore-Antoine-Palamède-Félix]. *Examen impartial et solution de toutes les questions qui ratachent à la loi des sucres*. Paris, 1840.

Fournier, L. *Le sucre colonial et le sucre indigène*. Paris, 1839.

Frasons, Hyppolite de. *Considérations sur les causes auxquelles il faut attribuer l'état de déperissement ou se trouvent nos colonies des Antilles, et sur les moyens d'y remédier*. Paris, 1822.

Gueroult, Adolphe. *De la question coloniale en 1842. Les colonies françaises et le sucre de betterave*. Paris, 1842.

Hamon, Amédée. *Des colonies et de la législation des sucres*. Paris, 1839.

Jonnes, A. Moreau de. *Recherches statistiques sur l'esclavage colonial et sur les moyens de la supprimer*. Paris, 1842.

Labat, Jean-Baptiste. *Voyages aux îles de l'Amérique (Antilles), 1693–1705*. 2 vols. Paris, 1931.

Lestiboudois, T. *Des colonies sucrières et des sucreries indigènes. Mémoire lu à la société royale des sciences, de l'agriculture et des arts de Lille, et inseré dans le recueil des travaux de cette société*. Lille, 1839.

*Lettre d'un ancien négociant de Nantes sur le système colonial, et réflexiones sur le même sujet remises par ce négociant au Ministre du Commerce en janvier 1825 et 1831*. Nantes, 1831.

Lewis, M. G. *Journal of a West India Proprietor, 1815–1817*. Boston, 1929.

Lurcy, Général Lafond de. *Un mot sur l'emancipation de l'escavage, et sur le commerce maritime de la France, en réponse à M. le Duc de Broglie, au projet du gouvernement et aux rapport de M. Merilhou à la Chambre des Pairs*. Paris, 1844.

Mathieu de Dombasle, C[harles] J[oseph] A[lexandre]. *Du sucre indigène, de la situation actuelle de cette industrie en France, de son avenir, et du droit on propose de la charger*. Nancy, 1836.

———. *De l'impôt sur le sucre indigène. Nouvelles considérations*. Paris, Nancy, 1837.

———. *Question des sucres. Lettre à un Député*. n.p., n.d.

Molroguier, P. *Examen de la question des sucres*. Paris, 1840.

Pardon, Jean-Marie. *La Martinique depuis sa découverte jusqu'à nos jours*. Paris, 1877.

Payen, Anselme. *Traité de la fabrication et du raffinage des sucres*. Paris: Thomine Libraire, 1832.

Reed, William. *A History of Sugar and Sugar Yielding Plants Together with an Epitome of Every Notable Process of Sugar Extraction and Manufacture from the Earliest Times to the Present*. London: Longmans, Green, & Co., 1866.

Rey, Dr. H. *Étude sur la colonie de la Martinique, topographie, metéorologie, pathologie, anthropologie, démographie*. Paris, 1881.

Robert, Jean-François. "Mémoire de l'état présent de la Martinique, 21 avril 1696." In *Rélations et mémoires pour servir à l'histoire de la France dans les pays d'outre-mer*. Ed. Pierre Margery. Paris, 1867, pp. 230–80.

Rodet, D. L. "Les colonies à sucre et la production indigène," *Revue des deux mondes* VI (15 avril 1836), 177–201.

Roughley, Thomas. *The Jamaica Planter's Guide; or, A System for Planting and Managing a Sugar Estate, or other Plantations in the Island, and Throughout the British West Indies in General*. London, 1823.

Sainte Croix, Félix Renouard, Marquis de. *Statistique de la Martinique*. 2 vols. Paris, 1822.

———. *De la fabrication du sucre aux Colonies françaises et des améliorations à y apporter*. Paris, 1843.

———. "Principes fondamentaux d'agriculture applicables au travail de la canne à sucre dans les colonies," *Annales Maritimes et Coloniales*, 3 ser. (April, 1846), 417–60.

Schoelcher, Victor. *Des Colonies françaises. Abolition immédiate de l'esclavage*. Paris, 1842.

———. *Histoire de l'esclavage pendant les deux dernières années*. 2 vols. Paris, 1847.

Soleau, A. *Notes sur les Guyanes française, hollandaise, anglaise, et sur les Antilles françaises (Cayenne, Surinam, Demerary, la Martinique, la Guadeloupe)*. Paris, 1835.

Tocqueville, Alexis de. "Rapport fait au nom de la commission chargée d'examiner la proposition de M. Tracy relative aux esclaves aux colonies," *Société français pour l'abolition de l'esclavage*. No. 14 (1839). Paris, 1839.

Vaublanc, Vincent Marie Vienot, comte de. *Du commerce maritime, considéré sous le rapport de la liberté entière de la commerce*. Paris, 1828.

Wray, Leonard. *The Practical Sugar Planter, A Complete Account of the Cultivation and Manufacture of the Sugar-Cane, According to the Latest and Most Improved Processes*. London, 1848.

## Selected Secondary Sources

Achéen, René. "Les Problèmes Antillais devant l'Opinion Bordelaise (1830–1838)," *Cahiers du CERAG. Centre D'Études Régionales Antilles-Guyane* 22 (1971), 1–113.

Adamson, Alan H. *Sugar Without Slaves. The Political Economy of British Guiana, 1838–1904*. New Haven, CT: Yale University Press, 1972.

Amselle, Jean-Loup. *Les négociants de la savane*. Paris: Anthropos, 1977.

Anstey, Roger. *The Atlantic Slave Trade and British Abolition, 1760–1810*. Atlantic Highlands, NJ: Humanities Press, 1975.

Ashton, T. S. "The Standard of Life of the Workers in England, 1790–1830." In *Capitalism and the Historians*, Ed. F. A. Hayek. Chicago: University of Chicago Press, 1954, pp. 123–55.

Aufhauser, R. Keith. "The Profitability of Slavery in the British Caribbean." *The Journal of Interdisciplinary History* 5, no. 1 (1974), 45–67.

———. "Slavery and Technological Change." *Journal of Economic History* XXXIV (1974), 36–50.

———. "Slavery and Scientific Management," *Journal of Economic History* 33, no. 4 (December 1977), 811–24.

Bairoch, Paul. *Commerce extérieur et développement économique de l'Europe au XIXe siècle*. Paris: Mouton, 1976.

Balandier, Georges. *Daily Life in the Kingdom of the Kongo from the Sixteenth to the Eighteenth Century*. Trans. Helen Weaver. New York: Meridian Books, 1969.

Banbuck, C. A. *Histoire politique, économique et sociale de la Martinique sous l'Ancien Régime*. Paris: Marcel Rivière, 1935.

Barrett, Ward. "Caribbean Sugar-Production Standards in the Seventeenth and Eighteenth Centuries." In *Merchants and Scholars. Essays in the History of Exploration and Trade*. Ed. John Parker. Minneapolis: University of Minnesota Press, 1965, pp. 147–70.

Bastide, Roger. "Nègres Marrons et Nègres Libres." *Annales, E.S.C.* 20, no. 1 (Jan.–Fev., 1965), 169–74.

————. *African Civilizations in the New World*. Trans. Peter Green. New York: Harper and Row, 1971.

————. *The African Religions of Brazil: Toward a Sociology of the Interpenetration of Civilizations*. Trans. Helen Sebba. Baltimore: Johns Hopkins University Press, 1878.

Bauer, John. "International Repercussions of the Haitian Revolution." *The Americas* XXVI, no. 4 (April 1970), 394–418.

Bauer, Raymond, and Alice Bauer. "Day to Day Resistance to Slavery." In *American Slavery: The Question of Resistance*. Eds. John H. Bracey, August Meier, and Elliot Rudwick. Belmont, CA: Wadsworth, 1971, pp. 38–60.

Beckford, George L. *Persistent Poverty: Underdevelopment in Plantation Economies in the Third World*. New York: Oxford University Press, 1972.

Beiguelman, Paula. *Pequenos Estudos de Ciência Política*. São Paulo: Biblioteca de Ciências Sociais, 1973.

————. "The Destruction of Modern Slavery: A Theoretical Issue." *Review* II, no. 1 (Summer 1978), 71–80.

Bernissant, P. *Etude sur le régime agricole des colonies françaises*. Paris: Université de Paris—Faculté de Droit, 1916.

Best, Lloyd. "Outlines of a Model of a Pure Plantation Economy." *Social and Economic Studies* 17, no. 3 (September, 1968), 283–324.

Blackburn, Robin. *The Overthrow of Colonial Slavery, 1776–1848*. London: Verso, 1988.

Blet, Henri. *Histoire de la colonisation française*. 3 vols. Grenoble and Paris: B. Arthaud, 1946.

Boizard, E. and H. Tardieu. *Histoire de la législation des sucres (1664–1891) suivie d'un résumé général des lois et règlements en vigueur, d'annexes, de tableaux statistiques et d'une table chronologique et analytique des lois, règlements et decrets depuis l'origine*. Paris: B.S.I.C., 1891.

Boulle, Pierre. "Slave Trade, Commercial Organization and Industrial Growth in Eighteenth Century Nantes." *Revue française d'histoire d'outre-mer* LIX, no. 214 (1972), 70–112.

Brathwaite, Edward. *The Development of Creole Society in Jamaica, 1770–1820*. Oxford: Oxford Univ. Press, 1971.

Broder, André. "Le commerce extérieur: l'échec de la conquête d'une position internationale." In *Histoire économique et sociale de la France*, III, 1. Ed. Fernand Braudel and E. Labrousse. Paris: Presses universitaires de France, 1976, pp. 305–46.

Buffon, Alain. *Monnaie et crédit en économie coloniale. Contribution à l'histoire de la Guadeloupe. 1635–1919*. Basse-Terre: Société de l'histoire de la Guadeloupe, 1979.

Canabrava, Alicia P. "A Força Motriz: um problema da técnica industria do açucar colonial (A Solução Antilhana e a Brasiliera)." *Anais do Primero Congresso de Historia da Bahia* IV (Salvador, 1950), 337–49.

————. "A Lavoura Canaveira nas Antilhas e no Brasil (Primeira Metade de Século XVIII)." *Anais do Primero Congresso de Historia da Bahia* IV, (Salvador, 1954), 351–79.

————. "João Antônio Andreoni e sua Obra." Introduction to *Cultura e Opulência do Brasil*, Joào Antônio Andreoni André João Antonil. São Paulo: Companhia Editora Nacional, 1966.

————. *O Açúcar nas Antilhas (1697–1755)*. São Paulo: Instituto de Pesquisas Econômicas—Universidade de São Paulo, 1981.

Castro, Antônio. "A Economia Politica, O Capitalismo e a Escravidão." In *Modos de Produção e Realidade Brasiliera*. Ed. José Roberto do Amaral Lapa. Petropolis: Vozes, 1980, pp. 67–107.

————. "Brasil, 1610: Mudanças técnicas e conflitos sociais." *Pesquisa e Planejamento Econômico* (Rio de Janeiro), 10, 3 (Dezembro, 1980), 679–712.

Chauleau, Liliane. *Histoire Antillaise. La Martinique et la Guadeloupe du XVIIe siècle à la fin du XIXe siècle*. Pointe-à-Pitre: Désormeaux, 1973.

————. "Sainte-Pierre au XIXᵉ siècle." In *Compte-rendu des travaux du colloque de Saint-Pierre*, 14–16 (Decembre 1973). Centre Universitaire Antilles Guyane, 1975, pp. 23–33.

Chemin Dupontès, P. *Les petites antilles*. Paris: Désormeaux, l'Harmattan [1979].

Clough, Shepherd B. *France. A History of National Economics, 1789–1939*. New York: Scribner, 1939.

Cohen, G. A. *Karl Marx's Theory of History. A Defense*. Princeton, NJ: Princeton University Press, 1980.

Conrad, John H., and John R. Meyer. *The Economics of Slavery and Other Studies in Economic History*. Chicago: Aldine, 1964.

Crouzet, François. *L'Economie britannique et le blocus continental*. 2 vols. Paris: Presses universitaires de France, 1958.

————. "Wars, Blockade, and Economic Change in Europe, 1792–1815." *Journal of Economic History* XXIV, no. 4 (1964), 567–90.

————. "England and France in the Eighteenth Century: A Comparative Analysis of Two Economic Growths." In *Social Historians in Contemporary France. Essays from the Annales*. Ed. Marc Ferro. New York: Harper and Row, 1972, pp. 59–86.

Curtin, Philip D. *The Atlantic Slave Trade. A Census*. Madison: University of Wisconsin Press, 1969.

Daget, Serge. "L'abolition de la traite des noirs en France de 1814 à 1831." *Cahiers d'Etudes Africaines* XI, no. 1 (1971), 14–58.

———. "Long cours et négriers nantais du trafic illégal, 1814–1833." In *La traite des noirs par l'Atlantique. Nouvelles approches.* Paris: Société Française D'Histoire D'Outre-Mer, 1976, pp. 90–134.

———. "British Repression of the Illegal French Slave Trade: Some Considerations." In *The Uncommon Market. Essays in the Economic History of the Atlantic Slave Trade.* Eds. Henry A. Gemery and Jan S. Hogendorn. New York: Academic Press, 1979, pp. 419–42.

David, Bernard. *Les origines de la population Martiniquaise au fil des ans (1635–1902).* Fort-de-France: Société d'Histoire de la Martinique, 1973.

———. "La population d'un quartier de la Martinique au début du XIXᵉ siècle, d'après les registres paroissiaux: Rivière Pilote, 1802–1829." *Revue française d'histoire d'outre-mer* LX, no. 220 (1973), 330–63.

Davis, David Brion. *The Problem of Slavery in the Age of Revolution, 1770–1823.* Ithaca, NY: Cornell University Press, 1975.

Debbasch, Yvan. "Le marronage. Essai sur la désertion de l'esclave antillais." *Année Sociologique* (1961), 1–112; *Année Sociologique* (1962), 117–95.

———. "Le crime d'empoisonnement aux îles pendant la période esclavagiste." *Revue française d'histoire d'outre-mer* L, no. 179 (1963), 137–88.

Debien, Gabriel. "Destinées d'esclaves à la Martinique (1776–1778)." *Bulletin de l'institute français d'Afrique Noire*, Série B, Sciences Humaines, XXII, nos. 1–2 (janvier–avril, 1960), 1–91.

———. *Les esclaves aux Antilles françaises (XVIIe–XVIIIe siècles).* Basse-Terre: Société d'histoire de la Guadeloupe; Fort-de-France: Société d'histoire de la Martinique, 1974.

Deerr, Noel. *The History of Sugar.* 2 vols. London: Chapman and Hall, 1945.

Deerr, Noel, and Alexander Brooks. "The Early Use of Steam Power in the Cane Sugar Industry." Newcomen Society for the Study of the History of Engineering and Technology. *Transactions* 21 (London, 1941), 11–21.

Devèze, Michel. "Le Commerce du sucre à la fin du XXVIIIᵉ siècle: la concurrance franco-anglaise." *Congrès National des Sociétés Savantes: Actes. Section d'Histoire Moderne et Contemporaine* 93 (1968), 35–47.

Drescher, Seymour M. *Econocide. British Slavery in the Era of Abolition.* Pittsburgh: University of Pittsburgh Press, 1977.

Dunham, Arthur Louis. *The Industrial Revolution in France, 1815–1848.* New York: Exposition Press, 1955.

Eltis, David. "The Export of Slaves from Africa, 1821–1843." *Journal of Economic History* XXXVII, no. 2 (June, 1977), 409–33.

———. "The Direction and Fluctuation of the Transatlantic Slave Trade, 1821–1843: A Revision of the 1845 Parliamentary Paper." In *The Uncommon Market. Essays in the Economic History of the Atlantic Slave Trade*. Eds. Henry A. Gemery and Jan S. Hogendorn. New York: Academic Press, 1979, pp. 273–302.

Engerman, Stanley. "Some Considerations Relating to Property Rights in Man." *Journal of Economic History* XXXIII, no. 1 (March 1973), 43–65.

———. "Some Economic and Demographic Comparisons of Slavery in the United States and the British West Indies." *Economic History Review*, 2nd ser., XXIX, no. 2 (May 1976), 258–75.

Fierain, Jacques. *Les raffineries du sucre des ports en France. XIXe–début du XXe siècles*. New York: Arno Press, 1977.

Finley, Moses I. "Slavery." *International Encyclopedia of the Social Sciences* XIV (1968), pp. 307–14.

Fogel, Robert William, and Stanley L. Engerman. *Time on the Cross. The Economics of American Slavery*. 2 vols. Boston: Little, Brown and Company, 1974.

Franco, Maria Sylvia de Carvalho. *Homens Livres na Ordem Escravocrata*. São Paulo: Editora Atica, 1976.

Frank, Andre Gunder. *World Accumulation, 1492–1789*. New York: Monthly Review Press, 1978.

———. *Dependent Accumulation and Underdevelopment*. New York: Monthly Review Press, 1979.

Furtado, Celso. *The Economic Growth of Brazil. A Survey from Colonial to Modern Times*. Trans. Ricardo W. de Aguiar and Eric Charles Drysdale. Berkeley: University of California Press, 1986.

Gama, Ruy. *Engenho e tecnologia*. São Paulo: Livraria Duas Cidades, 1983.

Gemery, Henry A., and Jan S. Hogendorn. *The Uncommon Market. Essays in the Economic History of the Atlantic Slave Trade*. New York: Academic Press, 1979.

Genovese, Eugene D. *The Political Economy of Slavery*. New York: Vintage Books, 1967.

Girault, Arthur. *Principes de la colonisation et de législation coloniale*. 3 vols. Paris: Larose, 1904.

———. *The Colonial Tariff Policy of France*. Oxford, UK: Clarendon Press, 1916.

Gisler, Antoine. *L'Esclavage aux Antilles françaises (XVIIe–XIXe siècle). Contribution au problème de l'esclavage*. Fribourg: Éditions Universitaires Fribourg Suisse, 1965.

Gorender, Jacob. *O Escravismo Colonial*. São Paulo: Editora Atica, 1988.

Goveia, Elsa V. *Slave Society in the British Leeward Islands at the End of the Eighteenth Century*. New Haven, CT: Yale University Press, 1965.

Gutman, Herbert G. *Slavery and the Numbers Game: A Critique of Time on the Cross*. Urbana: University of Illinois Press, 1975.

Greaves, Ida C. *Modern Production among Backward Peoples*. London: Allen & Unwin, 1935.

Green, W. A. "The Planter Class and British West Indian Sugar Production, Before and After Emancipation." *Economic History Review* XXVI (1973), 448–63.

Hall, Douglas. "Incalculability as a Feature of Sugar Production during the Eighteenth Century." *Social and Economic Studies* X, no. 3 (September, 1961), 305–18.

———. "Slaves and Slavery in the British West Indies." *Social and Economic Studies* XI, no. 4 (December, 1962), 305–18.

———. *Free Jamaica, 1838–1865. An Economic History*. New Haven, CT: Yale University Press, 1959; rpt. Caribbean Universities Press, n.d.

———. *Five of the Leewards, 1834–1870*. St. Laurence, Barbados: Caribbean Universities Press, 1971.

———. "The Flight from the Plantations Reconsidered: The British West Indies, 1838–1842." *The Journal of Caribbean History* 10–11 (1978), 7–23.

Hall, Gwendolyn M. *Social Control in Slave Plantation Societies. A Comparison of St. Domingue and Cuba*. Baltimore, MD: Johns Hopkins University Press, 1971.

Hardy, Georges. *Histoire sociale de la colonisation française*. Paris: Larose, 1953.

Helot, Jules. *Le Sucre en France, 1800–1900*. Cambrai, France: Deligne, 1900.

Henderson, W. O. "The Anglo-French Commercial Treaty of 1786." *Economic History Review* 2nd ser., X, no. 1 (1957), 104–12.

Herskovits, Melville J. *The Myth of the Negro Past*. Boston: Beacon Press, 1958.

———. *Life in a Haitian Valley*. New York: Knopf, 1937.

Higman, B. W. *Slave Population and Economy in Jamaica, 1807–1834*. Cambridge, UK: Cambridge University Press, 1976.

Hobsbawm, E. J. *Industry and Empire*. Baltimore, MD: Penguin Books, 1969.

Hopkins, Anthony G. *An Economic History of West Africa*. London: Longmans, 1973.

James, C. L. R. *The Black Jacobins: Toussaint L'Ouverture and the San Domingo Revolution*. New York: Vintage Books, 1963.

Jones, Leroi. *Blues People. The Negro Experience in White America and the Music that Developed from It*. New York: William Morrow and Company, 1963.

Josa, Guy. *Les industries du sucre et du rhum à la Martinique (1639–1931)*. Paris: Les Presses Modernes, 1931.

Klein, A. Norman. "West African Unfree Labor Before and After the Rise of the Atlantic Slave Trade." In *Slavery in the New World. A Reader in Comparative History*. Eds. Laura Foner and Eugene D. Genovese. Englewood Cliffs, NJ: Prentice-Hall, 1969, pp. 87–95.

Kosík, Karel. *Dialectics of the Concrete. A Study of Problems of Man and World*. Trans. Karel Kovanda with James Schmidt. Dordrecht, Holland, and Boston: D. Reidel, 1976.

Kuczynski, Jürgen. *A Short History of Labor Conditions under Industrial Capitalism*. 4 vols. London: F. Muller, 1945.

Kula, Witold. *An Economic Theory of the Feudal System. Towards a Model of the Polish Economy. 1500–1800*. Trans. Lawrence Garner. London: New Left Books, 1976.

Labrousse, C.-E. *Aspects de l'évolution économique et sociale de la France et du Royaume-Uni de 1815–1880*. Paris: Centre de Documentation Universitaire, 1954.

———."Panoramas de la crise." In *Aspects de la crise et de la dépression de l'économie française au milieu du XIXe siècle. 1846–1847. (Bibliothèque de la Révolution de 1848, Tome XIX)*. Ed. C.-E. Labrousse. La Roche-sur-Yon, France: La Société d'Histoire de la Révolution de 1848, 1956, pp. iii–xxiv.

———. "The Crisis in the French Economy at the End of the Old Regime." In *The Economic Origins of the French Revolution. Poverty or Prosperity?* Ed. Ralph W. Greenlaw. Boston: D. C. Heath, 1958, pp. 59–72.

———. "1848–1830–1789: How Revolutions are Born." In *Essays in European Economic History, 1789–1914*. Eds. F. M.-J. Crouzet, W. H. Chaloner, and W. M. Stern. London: Edward Arnold, 1969, pp. 1–114.

Landes, David. "French Entrepreneurship and Industrial Growth in the Nineteenth Century." *Journal of Economic History* IX, 1 (May, 1949), 45–61.

Laserre, Guy. *La Guadeloupe. Étude géographique*. Paris: Union Française D'Impression, 1949.

Lefebvre, Georges. *The French Revolution*, trans. Elizabeth Moss Evanson. 2 vols. New York: Columbia University Press, 1962.

Legier, Emile. *Histoire des origines de la fabrication du sucre en France*. Paris: Bureau de la Sucrerie indigène et coloniale, 1901.

Le Goff, Jacques. *Time, Work, and Culture in the Middle Ages*. Trans. Arthur Goldhammer. Chicago: University of Chicago Press, 1980.

Lémery, Henry. *La révolution française à la Martinique*. Paris: Larose, 1936.

———. *Martinique terre française. Le conflit des races et l'opinion métropolitain. Victor Schoelcher*. Paris: G.-P. Maisonneuve & Larose, 1962.

Lepkowski, Tadeusz. *Haiti*. 2 vol. Havana: Estudios del Centro de Documentación Sobre América Latina Juan F. Noyala, Casa de las Americas, 1968.

Levasseur, E. *Histoire du Commerce de la France*. 4 vols. Paris: A. Rousseau, 1911–1912.

Leyburn, James. *The Haitian People*. New Haven, CT: Yale University Press, 1966.

Lippmann, E. O. Von. *Historia do Açúcar desde a Epoca mais Remota até o Começo da Fabricação do Acucar de Beterraba*. Trans. Rodolfo Coutinho. 2 vols. Rio de Janeiro: Instituto do Açúcar e do Alcool, 1942.

Lukács, Georg. *History and Class Consciousness: Studies in Marxist Dialectics*. Trans. Rodney Livingston. London: Merlin Press, 1971.

Malowist, Marian. "Les débuts du système de plantations dans la période des grandes découvertes." *Africana Bulletin* X (Warsaw,1969), 9–30.

Malvezin, Théophile. *Histoire du commerce de Bordeaux*. 4 vols. Bordeaux: Bellier, 1892.

Mandle, Jay R. "The Plantation Economy: An Essay in Definition." *Science and Society* XXXVI (Spring, 1972), 49–62.

Margery, Pierre, ed. *Rélations et mémoires inedits pour servir à l'histoire de la France dans les pays d'outre-mer*. Paris, 1867.

Martin, Gaston. *Histoire de l'esclavage dans les colonies françaises*. Paris: Presses universitaires de France, 1948.

———. *Nantes au XVIIIe siècle. L'Ere des négriers (1714–1774)*. Paris: Librairie Félix Alcan, 1931.

Martineau, Alfred, and Louis-Philippe May. *Trois siècles d'histoire antillaise: Martinique et Guadeloupe de 1635 à nos jours*. Paris: Société de l'histoire des colonies françaises et Librarie Leroux, 1935.

Marx, Karl. *Grundrisse. Introduction to the Critique of Political Economy*. Trans. Martin Nicolaus. Harmondsworth, UK: Penguin Books, 1973.

———. *Capital*. Vol. I. Harmondsworth, UK: Penguin Books, 1976.

———. "Results of the Immediate Process of Production," Appendix to *Capital*. Vol. I. Harmondsworth, UK: Penguin Books, 1976.

———. *Capital*. Vol. II. Harmondsworth, UK: Penguin Books, 1978.

———. *Capital*. Vol. III. Moscow: Progress Publishers, 1966.

———. "Wage Labor and Capital." *Selected Works*. 2 vols. Moscow: Foreign Languages Publishing House, 1962.

May, Louis-Philippe. *Histoire économique de la Martinique (1635–1763)*. Fort-de-France, Martinique: Société de Distribution et Culture, 1972.

———. *Le Mercier de la Rivière (1719–1801)*. 2 vols. Aix-Marseille, France: Editions du Centre National de la Recherche Scientifique, 1975.

McMichael, Philip. *Settlers and the Agrarian Question, Foundations of Capitalism in Colonial Australia*. Cambridge, UK: Cambridge University Press, 1984.

Meillassoux, Claude, ed. *L'esclavage en Afrique précoloniale*. Paris: Maspero, 1975.

Miers, Suzanne. *Britain and the Ending of the Slave Trade*. New York: Africana Publishing Co., 1975.

Miers, Suzanne, and Igor Kopytoff, eds. *Slavery in Africa. Historical and Anthropological Perspectives*. Madison: University of Wisconsin Press, 1977.

Minchinton, Walter. "Patterns of Demand, 1790–1914." In *Fontana Economic History of Europe*, 3. Ed. Carlo M. Cipolla. London: Fontana Books, 1973, pp. 77–186.

Mintz, Sidney W. "Cañamelar: Rural Sugar Plantation Proletariat." In *The People of Puerto Rico*. Ed. Julian H. Steward. Champaign: University of Illinois Press, 1956, pp. 314–417.

———. "Currency Problems in Eighteenth Century Jamaica and Gresham's Law." In *Process and Pattern in Culture*. Ed. Robert A. Manners. Chicago: Aldine, 1964, pp. 248–65.

———. "Toward an Afro-American History." *Cahiers d'Histoire Mondiale* XIII, no. 2 (1971), 317–31.

———. *Caribbean Transformations*. Chicago: Aldine, 1974.

———. "The So-Called World-System: Local Initiative and Local Response." *Dialectical Anthropology* 2 (1977), 253–70.

———. "Was the Plantation Slave a Proletarian?" *Review* II, no. 1 (Summer, 1978), 81–98.

———. "Time, Sugar, and Sweetness." *Marxist Perspectives* 2, no. 4 (Winter, 1979–80), 56–73.

———. "Slavery and the Rise of Peasantries." *Historical Reflections* VI, no. 1 (Summer, 1979), 213–42.

———. "Descrying the Peasantry." *Review* VI, no. 2 (Fall, 1982), 209–25.

———. *Sweetness and Power. The Place of Sugar in Modern History*. New York: Penguin Books, 1985.

Mintz, Sidney W., and Douglas Hall. *The Origins of the Jamaican Internal Marketing System*. Yale University Publications in Anthropology, Number 57. New Haven, CT: Department of Anthropology, Yale University, 1960.

Mintz, Sidney W., and Richard Price. *An Anthropological Approach to the Afro-American Past: A Caribbean Perspective*. Philadelphia: Institute for the Study of Human Issues, 1976.

Moreno Fraginals, Manuel. *El ingenio. Complexo económico social cubano del azúcar*. 3 vols. Havana: Editorial de Ciencias Sociales, 1978.

———. *The Sugarmill. The Socioeconomic Complex of Sugar in Cuba*. Trans. Cedric Belfrage. New York: Monthly Review, 1976.

———. "Aportes Culturales y Deculturación." In *Africa en América Latina*. Ed. Manuel Moreno Fraginals. Mexico: Siglo XXI and UNESCO, 1977.

Mullin, Gerald W. *Flight and Rebellion. Slave Resistance in Eighteenth Century Virginia*. New York: Oxford University Press, 1974.

Novais, Fernando A. *Portugal e Brasil na Crise do Antigo Sistema Colonial (1777–1808)*. São Paulo: Editora Hucitec, 1981.

Ortiz, Fernando. *Cuban Counterpoint. Tobacco and Sugar*. Trans. Harriet de Onís. New York: Vintage Books, 1970.

———. *Los Negros Esclavos*. Havana: Editorial de Ciencias Sociales, 1975.

Pares, Richard. *A West-India Fortune*. London: Longmans, Green, 1950.

———. *Merchants and Planters*. Cambridge, UK: Economic History Society, 1970.

Patterson, Orlando. *The Sociology of Slavery. An Analysis of the Origins, Development and Structure of Negro Slavery in Jamaica*. Cranbury, NJ: Associated University Presses, 1969.

Petrone, Maria Theresa Schorer. *Lavoura Canaveira em São Paulo*. São Paulo: Difusão Europeu do Livro, 1968.

Peytraud, Lucien. *L'Esclavage aux Antilles françaises avant 1789 d'après des documents inédits des Archives Coloniales*. Pointe-à-Pitre, Guadeloupe: Désormaux, 1973.

Polanyi, Karl. *The Great Transformation. The Political and Economic Origins of our Time*. Boston: Beacon, 1957.

———. *Dahomey and the Slave Trade: An Analysis of an Archaic Economy*. Seattle: University of Washington Press, 1966.

Prado Junior, Caio. *Historia económica do Brasil*. São Paulo: Brasiliense, 1981.

Price, Roger. *The Economic Modernization of France*. New York: Wiley, 1975.

Priestly, Herbert I. *France Overseas through the Old Regime*. New York: Appleton-Century Co., 1939.

Ragatz, Lowell. *The Fall of the Planter Class in the British Caribbean, 1763–1833*. New York: Octagon Books, 1971.

Ratekin, Mervyn. "The Early Sugar Industry in Española." *Hispanic American Historical Review* 34 (February, 1953), 1–19.

Rawick, George P. *From Sundown to Sunup. The Making of the Black Community*. Westport, CT: Greenwood Press, 1972.

Revert, Eugene. *La Martinique. Étude géographique*. Paris: Nouvelles Editions Latines, 1949.

Richardson, Patrick. *Slavery and Empire*. New York: Harper and Row, 1972.

Rodney, Walter. *A History of the Guyanese Working People, 1881–1905*. Baltimore, MD: Johns Hopkins University Press, 1981.

———. "Plantation Society in Guyana." *Review* IV, no. 4 (Spring, 1981), 643–66.

Roseberry, William. *Coffee and Capitalism in the Venezuelan Andes*. Austin: University of Texas Press, 1983.

Sahlins, Marshall. "Tribal Economics." In *Economic Development and Social Change: The Modernization of Village Communities*. Ed. George Dalton. Garden City, NY: Published for the American Museum of Natural History [by] the Natural History Press, 1971, pp. 41–61.

Sayer, Derek. *The Violence of Abstraction: The Analytical Foundations of Historical Materialism.* Oxford, UK: Basil Blackwell, 1987.

Schnakenbourg, Christian. "Note sur les origines de l'industrie sucrière en Guadeloupe au XVIIe siècle (1640–1670)." *Revue française d'histoire d'outre-mer* LV, no. 200 (1968), 267–315.

———. "Statistiques pour l'histoire de l'économie de plantation en Guadeloupe et Martinique (1635–1835)." *Bulletin de la Société d'Histoire de la Guadeloupe* 31 (1977), 3–121.

———. *Histoire de l'industrie sucrière en Guadeloupe (XIXe–XXe siecles). Tome I: La Crise du système esclavagiste. 1835–1847.* Paris: l'Harmattan, 1980.

Schwartz, Stuart. "Free Labor in a Slave Economy: The Lavradores de Cana of Colonial Bahia." In *The Colonial Roots of Modern Brazil.* Ed. Dauril Aulden. Berkeley: University of California Press, 1973, pp. 147–97.

Scott, Rebecca J. *Slave Emancipation in Cuba: The Transition to Free Labor, 1860–1899.* Princeton, NJ: Princeton University Press, 1985.

Sée, Henri. *Economic and Social Conditions in France During the Eighteenth Century.* Trans. E. H. Zeydel. New York: Crofts & Co., 1927.

———. "La vie économique et politique de Nantes, 1831–1848." *Revue Historique* 163 (1930), 297–322.

———. *Histoire économique de la France.* 2 vols. Paris: A. Colin, 1939.

Sheridan, Richard. *Sugar and Slavery.* Eagle Hall, Barbados: Caribbean Universities Press, 1974.

———. "The Wealth of Jamaica in the Eighteenth Century: A Rejoinder." *Economic History Review* 21 (1968), 46–61.

———. "The Plantation Revolution and the Industrial Revolution, 1625–1775," *Caribbean Studies* IX, no. 3 (October, 1969), 5–25.

Stein, Robert L. *The French Slave Trade in the Eighteenth Century. An Old Regime Business.* Madison: University of Wisconsin Press, 1979.

———. "The French Sugar Business in the Eighteenth Century: A Quantitative Study," *Business History* 22, no. 1 (Jan. 1980), 3–17.

Tarrade, Jean. *Le Commerce colonial de la France à la fin de l'Ancien Régime.* 2 vols. Paris: Presses universitaires de France, 1972.

Thomas, Keith. "Work and Leisure in Pre-Industrial Society." *Past and Present* 29 (December, 1964), 50–66.

Thompson, E. P. *The Making of the English Working Class.* Harmondsworth: Penguin Books, 1968.

———. "Time, Work Discipline, and Industrial Capitalism." *Past and Present* 38 (1967), 56–97.

Thurnwald, Richard. *Economics in Primitive Societies.* London: Oxford, 1932.

Tudesq, André-Jean. *Les grands notables en France (1840–1849). Etude historique d'une psychologie sociale.* 2 vols. Paris: Presses universitaires de France, 1964.

———. "La Restauration. Renaissance et déceptions." In *Bordeaux au XIXe siècle.* Eds. Louis Desgraves and Georges Dupeux. Bordeaux, France: Fédération historique du Sud-Ouest, 1969, pp. 35–59.

———. "Les Débuts de la Monarchie de Juillet." In *Bordeaux au XIXe siècle.* Eds. Louis Desgraves and Georges Dupeux. Bordeaux, France: Fédération historique du Sud-Ouest, 1969, pp. 61–82.

Vidalenc, Jean. "La Traite négrière en France sous la Restauration, 1814–1830," Actes du 91e Congrès national des Sociétés savantes, Rennes, 1966, Section d'histoire moderne et contemporaine. Vol. I. Paris: Bibliothèque nationale, 1969, pp. 197–229.

Wallerstein, Immanuel. *The Modern World-System. Capitalist Agriculture and the Origins of the European World-Economy in the Sixteenth Century.* New York: Academic Press, 1974.

———. *The Capitalist World-Economy.* Cambridge, UK: Cambridge University Press; Paris: Maison des Sciences de l'Homme, 1979.

Weber, Max. *Economy and Society.* 2 vols. Berkeley: University of California Press, 1978.

Williams, Eric. *Capitalism and Slavery.* New York: Capricorn Books, 1966.

———. *From Columbus to Castro. The History of the Caribbean, 1492–1969.* New York: Harper and Row, 1970.

Wolf, Eric. "Specific Aspects of Plantation Systems in the New World: Community Sub-Cultures and Social Classes." *Pan-American Union Social Science Monographs* VII (Washington, DC, 1959), 136–47.

Woodruff, William. "The Emergence of an International Economy, 1700–1914." In *Fontana Economic History of Europe* 4, no. 2. Ed. Carlo M. Cipolla. London: Fontana Books, 1973, pp. 656–737.

# INDEX

Abolitionist movement (France), 107, 110–113

Absentee planters, 176

Administrator, 341–342

Animal charcoal, 281–282

Antigua: average yield (sugar), 158; sugar production in, 63

Antonil, André João, 205

Ashton, T. S., 56

Aufhauser, Robert K., 336

Australia, sugar production in, 74

Bagasse, 221–222; and fuel supply, 242, 246–247; Otaheite cane and, 247

Bahia, sugar production in, 71

Barbados: multiplication of English train on plantations in, 254; sugar production in, 63

Barbier, 300

Barrot, Odilon, 110

Bastide, Roger, 384

Bayonne, participation in slave trade, 423

Beckford, George, 431n7

Beet sugar (France): 404–405; abolition of industry, 123–125; and crisis of 1838–39, 122–123; decline after Napoleonic Wars, 90, 113–114; export bounty, 114; and import duties, 91–92; and *pacte colonial*, 127–129; production, 114–115,

121–123, 126, 129–130; resurgence of, 114–115; taxation of, 118–129; and technological innovation in colonies, 277–279, 296–297

Beiguelman, Paula, 69

Berbice, occupation by Britain, 65–66

Best, Lloyd, 431 n7

*Blanchissage* (fraud), 180

Bligh, Captain, and diffusion of Otaheite cane, 221

Blumental and Baglioni, 272

Boiling house. *See* Refinery

Bonaparte, Napoleon, and slave trade, 106

Bordeaux, 57; and credit to colonies, 183; decline of, 80–81, 101; participation in slave trade, 423

Bougainville, and diffusion of Otaheite cane, 221

Boulton and Watt, 239

Bourbon (Réunion), 80; average yield (sugar), 158; French slave trade to, 290; sugar duties, 90–91; sugar production in, 74; and *usine centrale*, 297–298

Brazil: expansion of slavery in, 71–72; *mutirão*, 354; participation in slave trade, 423; sugar production in, 71–72; trade with France, 82

Brière de l'Isle, 235; *usine cent rale* of, 301–302

Conrad, Alfred H., 450–452n1
Constant, Benjamin, 108
Continental blockade, 60, 80, 139, 171
Contraband trade, 87–88
Cornillère, Comte E. de la: on credit and prices, 188–189; on degeneration of Otaheite cane, 221–222; on sugar yielded from cane, 218–220
Cossigny, and diffusion of Otaheite cane, 221
Cotton: displacement by sugar in Martinique, 149; production in Martinique, 147, 149, 157; world production and consumption, 62
Credit: absence of security, 177–179; and commissionnaires, 186–188; comparison with British West Indies, 181–182; and high prices, 188–190; and interest rates, 179–180; shortage of, 179–183; substitution of short-term commercial credit for long-term mortgage credit, 182–183
Creole cane, 221
Crespel-Delisse, 114
Cuba: average yield (sugar), 158; credit and prices, 188–189; and diffusion of Otaheite cane, 221; efficiency of sugar manufacturing process compared with Martinique, 273; expansion of slavery in, 70–71; French slave trade to, 422–423; multiplication of English (Jamaica) train on plantations in, 254–255; size and distribution of sugar estates, 164; slave population, 72–73; slavery and use of vacuum pan in, 292; sugar frontier permits technical innovation, 295–296; sugar production in, 65, 72–73; sugarmill in, 72–73; trade with France, 82
Curing house, 253, 266–271
Currency drain, 87–88, 188–190; and purchase of mules, 238, 240–241
Curtin, Philip D., 2, 421, 422

Daget, Serge, 107, 422–423, 442n40
Dahomey, and dokpwe, 354
D'Auberteuil, Hilliard, 342
Daubrée, Paul: arrangement of boiling kettles, 246; average size of sugar plantation, 162–163; on debt and technical innovation, 287; on decline of property values, 175–176; on efficiency of mill, 229–231, 234; on fertilizer, 223; on inadequacy of animal power for mill, 238; on inadequacy of steam mill, 241; on inadequacy of watermill in Martinique, 236–237; on inefficiency of colonial sugar manufacture, 272–274; on necessity of total reorganization of colonial sugar industry, 296–297; on size of debt, 173; on technical stagnation of colonial sugar industry, 275–276; and usine centrale, 298–300
David, Bernard, 423
Davis, David Brion, 53
Debien, Gabriel: on creation of provision grounds, 383; on domestic servants, 326; on role of administrator, 341–342

Guadeloupe, 80; abolition of slavery in (1794), 59–60; adoption of compressed steam heat in, 283–284; average yield (sugar), 158; estimated volume of illegal French slave trade to, 421–422; occupation by Britain, 59–60, 65–66

Gueroult, Adolphe, 126; on debt, 190; on fertilizer, 223

Guignerie, Charles Alexis de la, *usine centrale* of, 301

Guignod, 216–217; average output of sugar-mill, 265; on fertilizer, 222–224; and partial reform of colonial sugar industry, 278; on types of plows, 224; on *usine centrale*, 300–301

Gutman, Herbert, 346

*Habitation sucrière:* area under cultivation, 215–216; average output, 265; and *commissionnaires*, 185–187; declining value of, 175–176; distribution by size, 161–163; as obstacle to technological innovation, 213–214, 279, 287–290, 293–297, 409–410; as obstacle to *usine centrale*, 308, 410–411; pattern of expansion, 165–170; prohibition of seizure or division of, 111–113; secondary crops converted to sugar estates, 164–165; typical size of estates, 163–164

*Habitation vivrière*, 149–150

Haiti, and *combite*, 354, 355–356

Haitian Revolution, 54–55, 58–59, 399–400

Hall, Douglas, 204–205, 395

Hawaii, sugar production in, 74

Herskovits, Melville, 354, 355–356

Higman, Barry, 384

Honfleur, participation in slave trade, 423

Howard, Edward, and vacuum pan, 285

Hugues, Victor, 59

Humann (Minister of Finance), 118

Humboldt, Alexander von, on Otaheite cane, 221, 239

Indemnity, 124, 126–129, 190–191

India: and diffusion of Otaheite cane, 221; French possessions in, 80; sugar duties, 91–93; sugar production in, 74

Internal markets, 157–158, 388–390; goods exchanged in, 157–158; as incentive to slaves, 39–391; and police, 389; prices in, 388–389; and slave property ownership, 390–391; social aspects of, 389

Isambart, 108

Jabrun: on adoption of compressed steam heat, 283; on number and size of sugar estates in Martinique, 314–315; and partial reform of colonial sugar industry, 278; on slave labor and technological innovation, 290; on slave maintenance, 373; on unsuitability of vacuum pan, 286; on use of plows, 224–225

Jamaica: adoption of clarifiers in, 280–281; adoption of steam power in, 238; and diffusion of Otaheite cane, 221–222; slave emancipation, 65; sugar production in, 55, 65

James, C. L. R., 54

Jaruco y Mopex, Count, 239

Java, sugar production in, 74

Jonnes, A. Moreau de, on accuracy of colonial statistics, 136

July Monarchy: abolition of slave trade, 102–103, 107; amelioration of slavery, 108, 111, 113; and slave emancipation, 377, 418

Kuczynski, Jürgen, 333

Labat, Père Jean-Baptiste: arrangement of boiling kettles, 245–246; description of grinding mill, 228

Labrousse, C. E., 68

Lamartine, Alphonse de, 108, 111

Land, in sugar, 139–141

La Rochelle, 57

Lavollée, P.: on adoption of clarifiers, 280; on agricultural statistics, 135; on arrangement of boiling kettles, 245–246; on average output of sugarmill, 265; on colonial planters and technical innovation, 277–288; on comparative sugar yields, 138–139; on construction of mill, 232–233; on credit and prices, 188–189; on credit shortage, 181–182; on debt and stagnation of colonial agriculture, 177–178; on decline of

slave prices, 175–176; on defects of English train, 248; on efficiency of mill, 230–231; on fertilizer, 223–224; on fraud (*blanchissage*), 181; on inefficiency of colonial sugar manufacture, 272–273; on lack of mechanics in colonies, 163–164; on livestock, 225–227; on merchants and planters, 190–191; on need to restock Otaheite cane, 221–222; on number and size of sugar estates in Martinique 163; on quality of sugar produced in Martinique, 272–273; on quality of sugar and tariff system, 273–274; on scale and efficiency of sugar estates in Martinique, 163–164, 215–216; on size of debt, 172–173; on slaves' resistance to innovation, 349–250; on sugar yielded from cane, 314–315; on use of poison by slaves, 357–358; on use of plows, 224; on use of thermometer in crystallization of sugar, 265; on value of slaves, 172

*Lavradores de cana* (Brazil), 229.

Lechevalier, Jules, on declining property values, 175

Le Havre, 57; and credit to colonies, 183; decline of, 36; and slave trade, 105, 423

Lestiboudois, T., 124

Lewis, Monk, 326, 361

Ligon, Richard, description of grinding mill, 228

Livestock, 225–227; poisoning of, 226 355–356, 357–358